The Wiley Handbook of Sustainability
in Higher Education Learning and Teaching

Wiley Handbooks in Education

The Wiley Handbooks in Education offer a capacious and comprehensive overview of higher education in a global context. These state-of-the-art volumes offer a magisterial overview of every sector, subfield and facet of the discipline-from reform and foundations to K-12 learning and literacy. The Handbooks also engage with topics and themes dominating today's educational agenda-mentoring, technology, adult and continuing education, college access, race and educational attainment. Show casing the very best scholarship that the discipline has to offer, The Wiley Handbooks in Education will set the intellectual agenda for scholars, students, and researchers for years to come.

The Wiley Handbook of Paulo Freire
By Carlos Alberto Torres (Editor)

The Wiley Handbook of Problem-Based Learning
By Mahnaz Moallem (Editor), Woei Hung (Editor), and Nada Dabbagh (Editor)

The Wiley Handbook of Early Childhood Care and Education
By Christopher Brown (Editor), Mary Benson McMullen (Editor), and Nancy File (Editor)

The Wiley Handbook of Teaching and Learning
By Gene E. Hall (Editor), Donna M. Gollnick (Editor), and Linda F. Quinn (Editor)

The Wiley Handbook of Violence in Education: Forms, Factors, and Preventions
By Harvey Shapiro (Editor)

The Wiley Handbook of Global Educational Reform
By Kenneth J. Saltman (Editor) and Alexander Means (Editor)

The Wiley Handbook of Ethnography of Education
By Dennis Beach (Editor), Carl Bagley (Editor), and Sofia Marques da Silva (Editor)

The Wiley International Handbook of History Teaching and Learning
By Scott Alan Metzger (Editor) and Lauren McArthur Harris (Editor)

The Wiley Handbook of Christianity and Education
By William Jeynes (Editor)

The Wiley Handbook of Diversity in Special Education
By Marie Tejero Hughes (Editor) and Elizabeth Talbott (Editor)

The Wiley International Handbook of Educational Leadership
By Duncan Waite (Editor) and Ira Bogotch (Editor)

The Wiley Handbook of Social Studies Research
By Meghan McGlinn Manfra (Editor) and Cheryl Mason Bolick (Editor)

The Wiley Handbook of School Choice
By Robert A. Fox (Editor) and Nina K. Buchanan (Editor)

The Wiley Handbook of Home Education
By Milton Gaither (Editor)

The Wiley Handbook of Cognition and Assessment: Frameworks, Methodologies, and Applications
By Andre A. Rupp (Editor) and Jacqueline P. Leighton (Editor)

The Wiley Handbook of Learning Technology
By Nick Rushby (Editor) and Dan Surry (Editor)

The Wiley Handbook of Adult Literacy
By Dolores Perin

The Wiley Handbook of Gender Equity in Higher Education
By Nancy S. Niemi (Editor) and Marcus B. Weaver-Hightower (Editor)

The Wiley Handbook of Sustainability in Higher Education Learning and Teaching
By Kelum A. A. Gamage (Editor) and Nanda Gunawardhana (Editor)

The Wiley Handbook of Collaborative Online Learning and Global Engagement
By Deirdre Johnston (Editor) and Irene López (Editor)

The Wiley Handbook of Sustainability in Higher Education Learning and Teaching

Edited by Kelum A. A. Gamage and Nanda Gunawardhana

WILEY Blackwell

This edition first published 2022
© 2022 John Wiley & Sons, Inc.

All rights reserved. No part of this publication may be reproduced, stored in a retrieval system, or transmitted, in any form or by any means, electronic, mechanical, photocopying, recording or otherwise, except as permitted by law. Advice on how to obtain permission to reuse material from this title is available at http://www.wiley.com/go/permissions.

The right of Kelum A. A. Gamage and Nanda Gunawardhana to be identified as the authors of the editorial material in this work has been asserted in accordance with law.

Registered Office
John Wiley & Sons, Inc., 111 River Street, Hoboken, NJ 07030, USA

Editorial Office
111 River Street, Hoboken, NJ 07030, USA

For details of our global editorial offices, customer services, and more information about Wiley products visit us at www.wiley.com.

Wiley also publishes its books in a variety of electronic formats and by print-on-demand. Some content that appears in standard print versions of this book may not be available in other formats.

Limit of Liability/Disclaimer of Warranty
While the publisher and authors have used their best efforts in preparing this work, they make no representations or warranties with respect to the accuracy or completeness of the contents of this work and specifically disclaim all warranties, including without limitation any implied warranties of merchantability or fitness for a particular purpose. No warranty may be created or extended by sales representatives, written sales materials or promotional statements for this work. The fact that an organization, website, or product is referred to in this work as a citation and/or potential source of further information does not mean that the publisher and authors endorse the information or services the organization, website, or product may provide or recommendations it may make. This work is sold with the understanding that the publisher is not engaged in rendering professional services. The advice and strategies contained herein may not be suitable for your situation. You should consult with a specialist where appropriate. Further, readers should be aware that websites listed in this work may have changed or disappeared between when this work was written and when it is read. Neither the publisher nor authors shall be liable for any loss of profit or any other commercial damages, including but not limited to special, incidental, consequential, or other damages.

Library of Congress Cataloging-in-Publication Data

Names: Kelum A. A. Gamage, 1983– editor. | Gunawardhana, Nanda, editor.
Title: The Wiley handbook of sustainability in higher education learning
   and teaching / edited by Kelum A. A. Gamage and Nanda Gunawardhana.
Other titles: Handbook of sustainability in higher education learning and
   teaching
Description: Hoboken, NJ : Wiley-Blackwell, 2022. | Series: Wiley handbooks
   in education | Includes bibliographical references.
Identifiers: LCCN 2021048463 (print) | LCCN 2021048464 (ebook) | ISBN
   9781119852827 (cloth) | ISBN 9781119852841 (adobe pdf) | ISBN
   9781119852834 (epub)
Subjects: LCSH: Education, Higher–Social aspects. | Sustainable
   development. | Sustainable Development Goals. | Educational change.
Classification: LCC LC191.9 .W55 2022 (print) | LCC LC191.9 (ebook) | DDC
   378–dc23/eng/20211109
LC record available at https://lccn.loc.gov/2021048463
LC ebook record available at https://lccn.loc.gov/2021048464

Cover Design: Wiley
Cover Image: © arthon meekodong/Getty Images

Set in 10/12pt WarnockPro by Straive, Pondicherry, India

10 9 8 7 6 5 4 3 2 1

Contents

List of Figures and Tables *ix*
List of Contributors *xi*

1 **Sustainable Development: Embedding Sustainability in Higher Education** *1*
   Kelum A. A. Gamage and Erandika K. de Silva

   Part I   Transforming the Curriculum – Pedagogy Focused Initiatives *11*

2 **Activist Learning for Sustainability: A Pedagogy for Change** *13*
   Zoe Robinson, Rebecca Laycock Pedersen, and Sarah Briggs

3 **Outcome-Based Education Toward Achieving Sustainable Goals in Higher Education** *41*
   G. R. Sinha, Nanda Gunawardhana, and Chih-Peng Fan

4 **Transforming Ourselves to Transform Societies: Cultivating Virtue in Higher Education for Sustainability** *59*
   Amparo Merino and Estela Díaz

5 **Factors that Hinder the Implementation of Sustainability Initiatives in Higher Education Institutions** *79*
   David Slim Zepeda Quintana, Javier Esquer, and Nora Munguía

6 **Developing Stakeholder Agency in Higher Education Sustainability Initiatives: Insights from a Change Laboratory Research Intervention** *99*
   John Scahill and Brett Bligh

7 **Technology-Enhanced Education: Improving Students' Learning Experience in the Higher Education Context** *133*
   Mengting Yu

8 **Sustainability Assessment Tools in Higher Education Institutions: Comprehensive Analysis of the Indicators and Outlook** *153*
   M. Mapar, P. Bacelar-Nicolau, and S. Caeiro

9 COVID-19 Disruptions to SDG 4 in Higher Education Institutions *187*
  Luis Velazquez

  Part II Transforming the Curriculum – Discipline-Specific Initiatives *205*

10 Integrating Harmonious Entrepreneurship into the Curriculum: Addressing the Sustainability Grand Challenge *207*
   David A. Kirby, Iman El-Kaffass, and Felicity Healey-Benson

11 Sustaining Place Transformations in Urban Design Education: Learning and Teaching Urban Density, Mix, Access, Public/Private Interface, and Type *221*
   Hesam Kamalipour and Nastaran Peimani

12 Sustainability of Innovations in Health Professions Education *237*
   Gominda Ponnamperuma, Asela Olupeliyawa, Madawa Chandratilake, and Kosala Marambe

13 Sustainability in Energy Systems Analysis and Design *257*
   J. McKellar, H. Gaber, and D. Hoornweg

   Part III Global Trends – Country Specific Initiatives *277*

14 Sustainability Teaching in Higher Education and Universities in Spain *279*
   Sergio Nogales Delgado, Silvia Román Suero, and Beatriz Ledesma Cano

15 Sustainability in Higher Education in Egypt: Perception, Challenges, and Way Forward *297*
   Marwa Biltagy

16 Youth Communicators as an Engine for Sustainable Development: A Case Study for Achieving SDGs in Remote Higher Education Institutions *317*
   Saira Ahmed, Amir Qayyum, Azza Malik, and Hassan Ali

17 Streamlining Higher Education in the Maldives: Issues and Challenges *333*
   Abdul Hannan Waheed

18 Embedding Sustainability into the Education Process in the Faculty of Horticulture and Landscape Engineering, SUA in Nitra, Slovakia *353*
   Tatiana Kaletová, Ivana Mezeyová, Ján Mezey, Mária Bihuňová, Roberta Štěpánková, Andrej Tárník, Ján Horák, and Kristína Candráková

   Part IV Equity and Inclusion within Sustainability Education *377*

19 Inclusive Education and Sustainable Development: Challenges and Opportunities in Higher Education for Students with Disabilities *379*
   Samanmala Dorabawila, Sakunthala Yatigammana, and Anoma Abhayaratne

20 Embedding Sustainability in Learning and Teaching: Communication Barriers to Learners with Special Needs *397*
Leena Seneheweera and Varunadatta Edirisinghe

21 Sustainable Higher Education for Disabled Students: Comprehensive and Quality Support for All Process Participants – University of Zagreb Support Model *421*
Lelia Kiš-Glavaš

22 Barriers, New Developments, and Emerging Trends in Sustainability in HE *453*
Kelum A. A. Gamage and Erandika K. de Silva

Index *461*

List of Figures and Tables

Figure 5.1	Green roof at Warsaw University Library.
Figure 8.1	The methodology of analyzing the sustainability assessment tools in HEIs.
Figure 8.2	The proportion of core elements of sustainability implementation at HEIs within the tools.
Figure 8.3	The profile of the sustainability dimensions within the assessment tools.
Figure 8.4	The top core thematic areas based on subcriteria in the studied sustainability assessment tools.
Figure 13.1	Simplified process flowchart for hydrogen life cycle. Depending on the LCA scope, it can be appropriate to include, for example, the hydrogen-fueled vehicle, as well.
Figure 13.2	A simple representation of energy systems analysis and design from (a) an exaggerated conventional approach and (b) a sustainability-oriented approach. Develop't = Development.
Figure 13.3	Learning outcomes and energy systems engineering education.
Figure 13.4	Main themes of an energy systems engineering program.
Figure 13.5	Proposed sustainability stream within an engineering program, leading to the achievement of the requisite learning outcomes.
Figure 14.1	Significant landmarks on policies and education in the context of sustainability.
Figure 14.2	Most valued skills in Spain according to OECD Skills for Job Report, where skills related to environmental management are missing (OECD 2021).
Figure 14.3	Research publications about sustainability and environment education in Spain. Data from Scopus(2021).
Figure 14.4	Main barriers for sustainability education implementation.
Figure 14.5	Transversality for sustainability education.
Figure 14.6	Main actions taken by universities concerning sustainability.
Figure 15.1	Students enrolled in private universities in 2019/2020.
Figure 16.1	Circular steps for curriculum development by NCRC, HEC.
Figure 18.1	Students taking water quality measurements.
Figure 18.2	Waste analysis in a small municipality.
Figure 18.3	Measurement of water velocity in a stream during the practical course of hydropedology.
Figure 18.4	Presentation of Biotope City, Vienna, as a contribution to sustainable, climate-sensitive urban open spaces.
Figure 18.5	Practical training in fruit tree pruning.

Figure 18.6	An excursion of Horticulture study program students to the most modern hydroponic companies.
Figure 18.7	Interactive experimental garden.
Figure 18.8	International cooperation for the purpose of creating an interactive cultivar collection within an innovative project supported by the Visegrad Fund.
Figure 18.9	Example of the green walls in the interior of the FHLE.
Figure 18.10	Kokedams in the interior of the FHLE.
Figure 18.11	Picnic of the FHLE.
Figure 18.12	Punch of the FHLE.
Figure 21.1	Cooperation of university bodies with the Office for Students with Disabilities.

Table 2.1	Distinguishing characteristics between formal, non-formal, informal, and hidden curricula.
Table 2.2	Summary of advantages and disadvantages of promoting activist learning through formal, non-formal, or informal curricula.
Table 2.3	Recommendations to support activist learning.
Table 3.1	Assessment and mapping of questions and their responses of tests.
Table 3.2	Specific SLOs for the recorded version of response to the assignment.
Table 3.3	Specific SLOs of the recorded version of response to the assignment in CSE 5X08.
Table 3.4	Research impact in OBE (last five years).
Table 3.5	OBE versus old education system.
Table 5.1	Contribution of HEIs via different channels.
Table 5.2	An overview of university contributions to the SDGs.
Table 5.3	Energy saving strategies in the faculty of electrical engineering, Universiti Teknologi Malaysia (UTM).
Table 6.1	Actions of the expansive learning cycle mapped onto the CL research workshops.
Table 6.2	Summary of Change Laboratory session design.
Table 6.3	Timeline and key events in the formation and development of the Campus Sustainability Statement.
Table 6.4	The development of participants' transformative agency mapped against the session timeline in the development of the Campus Sustainability Statement.
Table 8.1	Overview of sustainability assessment tools included in this research.
Table 8.2	A review of 27 sustainability assessment tools at HEIs.
Table 8.3	Distribution of core elements at HEIs on the 27 studied tools.
Table 8.4	Scope of the different sustainability tools analysis.
Table 8.5	The thematic areas applied in the studied sustainability assessment tools at HEIs.
Table 12.1	Commonly used models of program evaluation in medical education.
Table 15.1	Students enrolled in governmental universities in 2019/2020.
Table 15.2	The distribution of public educational expenditure by educational stage in 2019/2020.
Table 16.1	Details of the project.
Table 16.2	Community approaches for the youth leaders and communicators of the project.
Table 18.1	Study programs offered by the FHLE.
Table 18.2	List of supported education projects related to sustainable development.
Table 18.3	List of short-term international CEEPUS excursions organized by SUA.
Table 19.1	Disability prevalence in East Asian and South Asian countries.
Table 19.2	Total disability persons by education level.
Table 20.1	Questionnaire for survey of SNLs and teachers related to the study.
Table 20.2	CSD course schedule for 04 semesters (a total of 12 months).

List of Contributors

Anoma Abhayaratne is a Professor in Economics, at the University of Peradeniya, Sri Lanka. She received her PhD in Economics and MA in Econometrics from the University of Essex, UK, and her MPhil and BA (Hons) from the University of Peradeniya. During her 37 years of teaching career at the university, she served in administrative positions including Head of the Departmen and Dean of the Faculty, and was a member of the Governing Council of the University. She was a Visiting Professor at the University of Essex, UK, Rouen University, France, University of Malaya, Malaysia, and South Asian University, India. Her research interests are in the areas of development-related issues including poverty, FDI, foreign aid, social welfare, and the empowerment of marginalized persons. She has wide experience in coordinating international projects and is currently the coordinator of two international projects.

Saira Ahmed works at the Capital University of Science & Technology (CUST) in Pakistan as the Director of the Directorate of Sustainability and Environment. She is also the founding director for the research group on Solutions to Energy & Environmental Problems (STEEP). She is extensively involved in supervising peer-reviewed research and teaches courses in Microeconomics, Public Finance, and Environmental Impact Assessment. Dr. Ahmed was awarded a PhD in Economics, Markets, and Institutions from the IMT Institute for Advanced Studies, Italy, in 2010. She is the team lead for Pakistan's COVID-19 fiscal response project for the International Development Research Centre (IDRC), Canada, and the Partnerships for Economic Prosperity (PEP) Network. She is also the lead coordinator for the Pakistan–Italy Network (PIN), an emerging initiative of the Agency for Italian Development Cooperation (AICS) for building international technical, vocational, and research collaborations.

Hassan Ali is a Telecoms Relationship Manager with four years' experience working alongside the executive team of Pakistan Telecommunications Mobile Ltd – Ufone. He specializes in project management and is responsible for capacity building and training of other employees on the use of progressive machine-learning systems and applications, including mass communication procedures and organizational applications. He has extensive experience in project coordination and execution. He has served as the Project Associate for the Youth Communicators for Development program of the Luiss Business School, Italy. During the course of the program, he handled multiple teams and field projects across five remote districts of Pakistan. He obtained his MS degree in Project Management from Bahria University, Pakistan, in 2018 and his MSc in Banking and Finance in 2016. He is currently pursuing Project Management Professional (PMP) certification from the Project Management Institute (PMI), in the US.

P. Bacelar-Nicolau holds a degree in Plant and Applied Biology at the University of Lisbon, Portugal, and a PhD in Environmental Microbiology at the University of North Wales, Bangor,

UK. She is Assistant Professor at the Universidade Aberta (UAb), Portugal. She is also a senior researcher at the Centre for Functional Ecology at the Universidade de Coimbra, Portugal, and a collaborator researcher at the E-learning Laboratory of UAb. Her main research areas include e-learning in environmental sciences, education for sustainable development, biology conservation, and environmental microbiology. She has mentored several postgraduate students, published papers in peer-review International Scientific Information (ISI) journals, book chapters, and international conference proceedings, and has participated in several international research and development projects.

Mária Bihuňová is researcher and lecturer at the Institute of Landscape Architecture. She is also a vice dean for international relations of the Faculty of Horticulture and Landscape Engineering SUA in Nitra. She has long-term experience in coordinating international research and educational projects, organizing training schools and workshops. She is currently coordinating a national research project on green infrastructure in urban areas and landscapes, in the context of changing climate. Her research interests include assessment and design of the various types of urban greenery; assessment of the recreational potential of the open spaces and landscapes; new trends and smart solutions in the fields of landscape architecture and presents of the fruit trees and activities of urban gardening in the cities. She is the author and co-author of 15 publications in the WOS and SCOPUS databases, 1 scientific monograph, with 73 citations (in WOS and SCOPUS databases – 49 citations). She is a member of Steering Committee of Slovak Association for Garden Design and Landscaping.

Marwa Biltagy received the prize of Best MSc and PhD thesis at Cairo University in 2005 and 2010, respectively. She was also awarded the Encouragement Prize from Cairo University in the field of Humanities and Educational Sciences in 2016 and has received many awards from Cairo University for Outstanding Scientific Publishing in 2012, 2013, 2014, 2015, 2016, 2017, 2018, 2019, and 2020. In addition, she won the State Incentive Award for Women in the field of Social Sciences in 2020. She is a member in several professional associations, such as American Economic Association (AEA), Middle East Economic Association (MEEA), and International Association for Feminist Economics (IAFE), and her work has been published in many publications in prestigious international journals.

Brett Bligh is a lecturer in the Department of Educational Research, Lancaster University, UK. His research interrogates the nexus of institutional change and technology through an activity theory lens. Much of his research concerns adult learners and, particularly, the higher education sector. Recurring themes include co-design, interventionist methodologies, and the roles of the built environment in educational institutions. He is co-director of the Centre for Technology Enhanced Learning and co-editor of the diamond open-access journal *Studies in Technology Enhanced Learning*. He is currently leading on a project co-producing a new communal garden space with university, further education college, school, and local community stakeholders.

Sarah Briggs is a Sustainability Project Officer at Keele University, UK. She has a BSc in Environment and Sustainability and is currently studying for an MA in Higher Education Practice. In her role, she works across estates and operations, and student and academic spheres, and provides direct support to students who are interested in developing their own sustainability projects. She is a Fellow of the Higher Education Academy.

S. Caeiro holds an undergraduate degree in Environmental Engineering from NOVA University of Lisbon and a master's in Science in Coastal Zones from the University of Aveiro. She also holds a doctorate in Environmental Engineering from NOVA University, and in Habilitation in Sustainability, Environment and Global Changes from the Universidade Aberta (UAb). She is currently an Associate Professor in the Department of Science and Technology at UA and a Senior Researcher at the Centre for Sustainability and Environmental Research (CENSE) at NOVA University. She also collaborates with the e-learning laboratory of UAb. Her main research and teaching areas include environmental management and assessment, education for sustainable development, e-learning, and environmental sciences. She is the coordinator of the PhD in Social Sustainability and Development, and vice-coordinator of the Complementary Program for Environmental Engineering at UAb. She is Associate Editor for the *Journal of Cleaner Production*, Elsevier.

Kristína Candráková is a referent actively working with projects and courses at the Project Grants and Lifelong Learning Center at the Faculty of Horticulture and Landscape Engineering at Slovak University of Agriculture in Nitra. She is currently working within the EU-supported project "Support of information activities focused on flood risk mitigation and on objective information about negative impact of the climate change." She is also responsible for administering accredited courses and for co-organizing scientific conferences and similar events.

Madawa Chandratilake, MBBS (Colombo), MMEd (Dundee), PhD (Dundee), is the Chair and Professor of Medical Education, at the Faculty of Medicine, University of Kelaniya, Sri Lanka, and an external tutor for the Centre for Medical Education, University of Dundee, UK. He has extended his consultancy services in medical education to many countries, including the UK, Malaysia, Indonesia, Pakistan, and Oman. His interests in medical education embrace professionalism, assessment curriculum development, and quality assurance. He has been an invited speaker at many national and international conferences and a resource person for many workshops. He has edited a book, authored many book chapters in medical education, published research papers extensively in well-reputed academic journals, and presented these papers at national and international conferences. He has expanded his research interests to clinical reasoning and the use of augmented reality and virtual reality technologies in supplementing health professions education.

Erandika K. de Silva uses an interdisciplinary approach to voice her concerns for social justice. She is a lecturer in English Literature at the University of Jaffna. Her first degree is a BA (Hons) in English from the University of Peradeniya. She was an APMA scholar funded by the European Commission's European Instrument for Democracy and Human Rights (EIDHR) and holds an MA in Human Rights and Democratization from Mahidol University, Thailand. She is currently pursuing her graduate studies in English.

Estela Díaz is a researcher and lecturer in the Department of Business Management at Pontifical University Comillas-Madrid, and is an activist for human and animal rights, nongovernmental organization (NGO) advisor, and humane educator. She holds a PhD in Economics and Business Administration (Universidad Pontificia Comillas), a master's in Sustainability and CSR (UNED and UJI), a master's in Research in Economics and Business Administration (Universidad Pontificia Comillas), and a degree in Law (University of Granada). Her principal area of research focuses on ethical and transformative consumption, human–animal relations, gender, sustainable transitions, theories of power, and education. She also supervises doctoral students, has presented papers in conferences and seminars, and has published in high-impact journals such as *Human Ecology Review, Psychology & Marketing, Macromarketing, Sustainability, Anthrozoös,* and *Society & Animals*.

Samanmala Dorabawila is a Senior Lecturer in the Department of Economics at the University of Peradeniya, Sri Lanka, and was the Head of the Department of Law at the same University. She was a Visiting Scholar at the American University Washington, DC, and completed the Graduate Certificate on Gender Analysis in Economics. She received her MA. and PhD in Economics from Clark University in the US, and her M Sc in Applied Statistics from the Postgraduate Institute of Science, University of Peradeniya. Her research interest lies in labor, gender, health, and development economics. Currently, she functions as a member of American- and European-funded projects and was the coordinator of a project funded by the World Bank.

Varunadatta Edirisinghe holds a bachelor's degree in Western Classical Culture from the University of Peradeniya, Sri Lanka, a master's in Latin, and a PhD in Greek and Latin from Indiana University in the US. She is a Senior Lecturer attached to the Department of Classical Languages, University of Peradeniya, Sri Lanka, and, among other courses, teaches ancient Greek and Latin, Greek and Latin literature, and literary criticism. Her research interests include Greek and Latin poetry, drama, philosophy, comparisons of Greek, Latin, and Theravada Buddhist literature, and art and disability.

Iman El-Kaffass is an academic and international consultant with proven expertise consulting with international development and donor organizations as well as with government agencies, public and private enterprises, and local non-governmental organizations (NGOs) around the world. Her consultancy work, teaching, and publications focus on education transformation, youth, and women entrepreneurial development, and organizational assessment and development. She has worked and consulted in sub-Saharan Africa, the Near East and North Africa, Central and Southwest Asia, and the Americas. She is a holder of a PhD in Higher Education Administration from Bowling Green State University, Ohio.

Javier Esquer has a BSc in Industrial and Systems Engineering at the University of Sonora (UNISON), and holds a Doctor of Science degree in Cleaner Production from the University of Massachusetts Lowell as well as a Sustainable Development Certificate from UNISON. He is currently working as a full-time Professor in the Department of Industrial Engineering and in the Sustainability Graduate Program at UNISON. Dr. Esquer has been an enthusiastic promoter of sustainable development in his community and has participated in several initiatives on environmental awareness. Additionally, he has authored and co-authored articles in scientific/academic publications with international recognition and has been a speaker and lecturer at international events. His areas of interest include, among others, sustainable development, pollution prevention, occupational health and safety, cleaner production, sustainability management systems, energy efficiency, and education for sustainable development.

Chih-Peng Fan received his BS, MS, and PhD degrees, all in electrical engineering, from the National Cheng Kung University, Taiwan, in 1991, 1993, and 1998, respectively. In 2003, he joined the Department of Electrical Engineering at National Chung Hsing University in Taiwan, becoming an Associate Professor in 2007and a full Professor in 2013. He has more than 110 publications, including technical journals, technical reports, book chapters, and conference papers. His teaching and research interests include deep-learning for digital image processing and pattern recognition, digital video coding and processing, digital baseband transceiver design, very large-scale integration (VLSI) design for digital signal processing (DSP), and fast prototype of DSP systems with FPGA (Field Programmable Gate Array)-based and embedded SOC platforms. He is member of the editorial boards for the *Journal of Image and Graphics* (since 2020) and the *Journal of Real-Time Image Processing* (since July 2021), and has been Supervisor of the Taiwan Consumer Electronics Society since 2020.

H. Gaber is a full Professor in the Faculty of Energy Systems and Nuclear Science at Ontario Tech University, and director of the Smart Energy Systems Lab (SESL). He is the recipient of the Senior Research Excellence Award for 2016 and is recognized among the top 2% of scientists worldwide in the area of energy. He leads national and international research in the areas of smart energy grids, resilient hybrid energy systems, and plasma-based waste to energy. Dr. Gabbar obtained his BSc with first class honors from Alexandria University (Egypt, 1988) and gained his PhD from Okayama University (Japan, 2001). He joined the Tokyo Institute of Technology (Japan, 2001–2004), as a research associate and Okayama University (Japan, 2004–2008) as an Associate Professor, in the Division of Industrial Innovation Sciences. He has more than 230 publications, including patents, books and chapters, journal articles, and conference papers.

Kelum A. A. Gamage received his BSc in Electrical Engineering from the University of Moratuwa, Sri Lanka and his PhD from the University of Lancaster, UK. He is an Associate Professor in the James Watt School of Engineering, a Co-Director of the Centre for Educational Development and Innovation and a winner of the Teaching Excellence Individual Award (2020/21) at the University of Glasgow, UK. He is also the founder and co-lead of the University Sustainability in Learning and Teaching Community of Practice and a member of the University Sustainability Working Group (SWG). He holds the position of Visiting Professor at Sri Lanka Technological Campus (SLTC).

He has authored over 150 peer-reviewed technical articles and book chapters, and also holds a patent. He is the Editor-in-Chief for STEM Education Section of *Education Sciences* (MDPI, Switzerland,), editor of *Humanities & Social Sciences Communications* (Springer Nature), and *Sensors* (MDPI, Switzerland). He is also a Chartered Engineer of the Engineering Council (UK), a Principal Fellow of the Higher Education Academy, a Fellow of the IET, and a Fellow of Royal Society of Arts and a Senior Member of IEEE.

Nanda Gunawardhana works as the Director of Research and International Affairs at Sri Lanka Technological Campus, Sri Lanka. Prior to that, he worked as the Director of the International Research Centre at the University of Peradeniya, Sri Lanka. He received a bachelor's degree specializing in Chemistry from the University of Peradeniya, Sri Lanka, and a PhD from Baylor University in the US. He has worked as a Japan Society for the Promotion of Science (JSPS) postdoctoral fellow at Saga University, Japan, and at the Fukuoka Industry and Science Foundation, Japan.

He has authored over 100 peer-reviewed technical articles and a book chapter, and also holds a patent. He was named the best young scientist in Sri Lanka by the National Science Foundation, and by the Third World Academy of Science, Italy in 2015. In addition, he is a recipient of Presidential awards for his scientific publications. He has received many research and capacity-building grants from the European Union, Pakistan, Japan, and Sri Lanka. Since 2012, he has worked as the Associate Editor of the *International Journal of Chemistry* (The Canadian Center of Science and Education).

Felicity Healey-Benson, founder of EmergentThinkers.com and co-founder, with Professor David A. Kirby, of the Harmonious Entrepreneurship Society, is an academic, Entrepreneurial Learning Champion, and doctoral candidate at the University of Wales Trinity St. David.

Her phenomenological research supporting the facilitation of higher-order thinking focuses on future-proofing educator professional development. She graduated from the London School of Economics and Political Science and Swansea University. Passionate about sustainability, she is committed to promoting entrepreneurship, and specifically a harmonious approach, as key to the transformation of our current learning ecosystem, promoting new literacies and applied creativity and innovation in support of the United Nations' Sustainability Development Goals.

D. Hoornweg, PhD, PEng, is Associate Professor, Associate Dean, and Richard Marceau Chair at Ontario Tech University. For almost 20 years Dan was with the World Bank, including as Lead Advisor overseeing Sustainable Cities and Climate Change programs. He was the Chief Safety and Risk Officer for the Province of Ontario 2012–2020 (Technical Standards and Safety Authority, TSSA). His academic background includes degrees in Earth Sciences, a master's in Environmental Engineering and a PhD in Civil (Sustainability) Engineering (University of Toronto, 2015). He researches energy and material flows of cities and urban systems. He is a Fellow with Canada's Transition Accelerator, the Global Cities Institute at University of Toronto, and Futures Cities at Evergreen Brickworks.

Ján Horák is an Associate Professor at the Faculty of Horticulture and Landscape Engineering, Slovak University of Agriculture in Nitra. He received his PhD in landscaping in 2009. His main teaching area is climatology and his research is focused on studying the application of biochar to soil on greenhouse gas emissions, the physical and chemical properties of soil, and crop yields. He has over 30 peer-reviewed publications in impactful journals related to his research topics, and has coordinated and participated in several national and international educational and scientific projects.

Tatiana Kaletová is an Assistant Professor at the Faculty of Horticulture and Landscape Engineering, Slovak University of Agriculture in Nitra, Slovakia. She is a teacher of Hydraulics, Forest Amelioration, and Agricultural Water Management, and the practical training Monitoring of Environment. Her research focuses on the impact of land use on water quality and quantity in the landscape, especially the agricultural landscapre. She is an author and co-author of several textbooks and scientific articles and cooperates closely with teachers and researchers from Europe and Uzbekistan. She coordinates and participates in several national and international educational and scientific projects.

Hesam Kamalipour is Co-Director of the MA Urban Design Programme and the Co-Founding Director of the Public Space Observatory Research Centre at Cardiff University, UK. His research has focused on the challenge of understanding the dynamics of informal urbanism and the ways in which different forms of informality work in a global context. He has previously served as Research Fellow at Monash University, Research Assistant and Guest Lecturer in Urban Design at the University of Melbourne, and Doctoral Academy Member at the Melbourne Social Equity Institute. He holds a PhD in Urban Design from the University of Melbourne.

David A. Kirby, professor, is a pioneer of entrepreneurship education in the UK and internationally and holder of The Queen's Award for Enterprise Promotion. At the University of Durham (1988–1996), where he held the UK's first Chair in Entrepreneurship, and at the University of Surrey (2000–2017) he taught entrepreneurship to both Business and Engineering students, while at the British University in Egypt (2007–2017) he introduced entrepreneurship not only to the university, but to the country. With Felicity Healey-Benson he co-founded, in

Global Entrepreneurship Week 2020, The Harmonious Entrepreneurship Society based on his research with Dr. Iman El-Kaffass. He is an Honorary Professor of Almaty Management University and the University of Wales Trinity St. David, and a member of the Accreditation Council for Entrepreneurial and Engaged Universities.

Lelia Kiš-Glavaš has full Professor tenure at the University of Zagreb, Faculty of Education and Rehabilitation Sciences, Department for Inclusive Education and Rehabilitation. She is coordinator for students with disabilities at the faculty and a member of the scientific board. From 2004 to 2009 she was Vice Dean for Science and from 2009 to 2011 she was international cooperation leader. From 2012 to 2014 she was a director of study programs Rehabilitation and Educational Rehabilitation. At the University of Zagreb (2007–2016), she was chair of the committee for students with disabilities and was a leader of Tempus project "Education for Equal Opportunities at Croatian Universities – EduQuality." She is a member of number of professional non-governmental organizations (NGOs) and committees and she has participated in creating several legal drafts. She is a member of the Croatian National Board for the improvement the social dimension of higher education and of the Government of the Republic of Croatia Committee for persons with disabilities.

Rebecca Laycock Pedersen is a Postdoctoral Researcher and Assistant Coordinator for Sustainability in Education at Blekinge Institute of Technology (BTH), Sweden. Her interests lie in using sustainability education to shape a better future, especially through the medium of food and food-growing. Her doctoral research focused on understanding how to manage the impacts of students' transience in student-led university food gardens, focusing on the National Union of Students-funded program, "Student Eats." She has also worked with embedding sustainability across disciplinary curricula and in the student experience at an institutional level at both Keele University, UK, and BTH. She has a Postgraduate Certification in Learning and Teaching in Higher Education and, in 2017, she won an Excellence Award in Teaching and Learning for her participatory, inclusive, and student-centered approach to teaching.

Beatriz Ledesma Cano is a researcher at the Applied Physics Department of the University of Extremadura (Spain). Skilled in the use of biomass, hydrocarbonization, gasification, adsorption, and energy, she has published papers, book chapters, and international conference proceedings. Her research work is complemented by teaching tasks through the direction of final degree projects, seminars or laboratory practices, participation in teaching innovation groups, and numerous teacher training courses. She has interests in ethical competencies, project-based learning, development cooperation, and education for sustainable development, and has participated in the publication of book chapters related to these topics.

Azza Malik is a Research Associate and an analyst. She works on interdisciplinary research in different fields, but mostly on business and marketing related themes. She is also a data science professional and provides analysis for companies, and has been a tutor for undergraduate students and has mentored them in their pursuits. She likes to spend time reading and researching on how to build a sustainable environment and making it carbon free. Her aim is to build multisectoral strategies to achieve the United Nations Sustainable Development Goals in her country, Pakistan. Currently she is doing an MS in Marketing at the Faculty of Management and Social Sciences, Capital University of Science & Technology (CUST), Pakistan.

M. Mapar holds an undergraduate degree in industrial engineering from Kar University, Qazvin, Iran, a master's in Environmental Management (Health, Safety, and Environment), and a PhD in Environmental Management, both the latter from Tehran Science and Research Branch, Azad University, Tehran, Iran. Currently, she is a Research Collaborator and Post-Doctoral Researcher at the Centre for Environmental and Sustainability Research (CENSE) at NOVA University Lisbon, Portugal. She also collaborates with the Department of Sciences and Technology at Universidade Aberta (UAb), Portugal. Her research activity is centered on sustainability assessment and management, including public sector and higher education institutions, assessment indicators, and the integration of health, safety, and environmental (HSE) aspects of sustainability.

Kosala Marambe, MBBS (Colombo), PhD (Maastricht), is Professor and Head of the Department Medical Education of the Faculty of Medicine, University of Peradeniya, Sri Lanka, and has contributed to undergraduate teaching and student assessments in the university's Faculties of Medicine and Allied Health Sciences and postgraduate training through the Post Graduate Institute of Medicine, University of Colombo. She also supervises MPhils and PhDs in health professions education and is 2021–2022 President of the College of Medical Educationists, Sri Lanka. She has published her work in national and international peer-reviewed journals, conferences, and seminars and has authored book chapters, edited conference proceedings, and served as a reviewer for national and international conferences and journals. She also has wide experience in coordinating and conducting staff development programs for academic staff of the faculties of health sciences, and in curriculum review and revision work, coordinating the quality assurance activities, and developing innovative teaching learning methods.

J. McKellar is an Associate Professor in the Faculty of Energy Systems and Nuclear Science at Ontario Tech University and is a licensed Professional Engineer in Ontario, Canada. She leads the Energy Systems Analysis research group. The group's goal is to contribute to the development of sustainable energy systems by (i) developing analytical tools in support of decision- and policy-making, and (ii) completing techno-economic and environmental assessments of energy systems. Dr. McKellar has taught courses on Solar Energy Technologies, Fuel Cell Design, and Life Cycle Assessment. Her undergraduate and master's degrees are in Chemical Engineering, and her doctorate is in Civil Engineering, with a focus on Environmental Engineering. Following her PhD, she held a Postdoctoral Fellowship jointly with the Universities of Toronto and Calgary. Prior to pursuing her PhD, she worked in environmental consulting, focusing on air quality.

Amparo Merino is researcher and lecturer in the Department of Business Management at Pontifical University Comillas-Madrid, where she teaches undergraduate and postgraduate courses related to strategic management, social entrepreneurship, and business and sustainability. Her research trajectory is framed by the multidisciplinary research field of Sustainability Transitions, and her current research interests focus on three levels: individual agency (e.g. sustainable behavior and interconnectedness with nature), organizations (e.g. social enterprise and business models for sustainability), and underlying structures (e.g. business logics and institutional entrepreneurship; critical, emancipatory, and transformative approaches to education for sustainability). In these areas she has taken part in several funded research projects and published scientific papers in high-impact journals, such as *Environmental Education Research*, *Environmental Innovation and Societal Transitions*, *Journal of Cleaner Production*, *International Journal of Management Education*, *Journal of Macromarketing*, and *Human Ecology Review*. She also supervises doctoral students and participates in conferences related to sustainability transitions.

Ján Mezey's activity is aimed at optimizing the growing technologies of fruit trees and grapevines in the context of preserving and increasing the content of bioactive substances in fruits. It is also focuses on the selection and analysis of nutritional indicators of individual species and varieties and the subsequent optimization of technological processing of fruits into juices with the aim of preserving bioactive and other substances.

Ivana Mezeyová is an Assistant Professor at the Department of Vegetable Production, Faculty of Horticulture and Landscape Engineering, SUA, Nitra, Slovakia. In addition to activities related to pedagogical activities, her main activities include research and collaboration on several projects. Her scientific and research activities are associated with the management of field experiments with spices, aromatic plants, and lesser-known species of vegetables, selected laboratory analyses, data processing, and statistical analyses. During her doctoral studies she participated on scientific research led by Professor RNDr. Bernard Šiška, PhD, who contributed to the Nobel Peace Prize for 2007 being awarded to the Intergovernmental Panel on Climate Change (IPCC). She led an international project funded by the V4 (Visegrad: Slovakia, Poland, Hungary, and the Czech Republic) Foundation, focusing on lesser-known vegetable species and spice and aromatic plants. She is the author and co-author of four publications in the WOS and SCOPUS databases, and she has 57 citations in these databases.

Nora Munguía is an alumna of the doctoral program at the University of Massachusetts Lowell in Engineering Science with a major in Cleaner Production. She is full time Professor in the Department of Industrial Engineering and also serves as a researcher in the Sustainable Development Graduate Program in the University of Sonora in Mexico. Dr. Munguia is a member of the National System of Researchers and her most recent works are focused on promoting strategies to prevent, eliminate, and reduce occupational hazards in the Mexican industry.

Sergio Nogales Delgado was born in Badajoz (Spain) in 1984. He is researcher at the Department of Chemical Engineering and Physical Chemistry at University of Extremadura (UEX, Spain). His main interests are related to a wide range of fields, such as minimally processed fruits and vegetables, biomass or biodiesel, and biolubricant production, among others. During his career, he has had the opportunity to share this knowledge, being involved in different teaching tasks, mainly at university level (such as scientific exhibitions, seminars, laboratory practices, and especially final degree projects). As a result, he has taken part in different education projects in order to create brief didactic guides or publish the main insights in several research articles.

Asela Olupeliyawa, MBBS (Colombo), PhD (NSWS), is Professor in Medical Education at Faculty of Medicine, University of Colombo. He has over 15 years' experience in curriculum and assessment development in medical education. He was the former Director of Curriculum Implementation of the MBBS program at Colombo and currently leads quality assurance activities at the Faculty of Medicine. He graduated in Medicine in 2005 and obtained his PhD at the University of New South Wales, Australia in 2012. His PhD thesis investigates how workplace-based assessment among medical students facilitates the learning of collaborative competencies for internship. He has over 20 peer-reviewed publications and over 50 international presentations, and is first author in original research publishing in high-impact medical education journals such as *Academic Medicine, Medical Education,* and *Medical Teacher.* He has extensive experience in faculty development of medical teachers, postgraduate clinical educators, and teachers in other health professions.

Nastaran Peimani is the Co-Director of the MA Urban Design Programme and the Co-Founding Director of the Public Space Observatory Research Centre at Cardiff University, UK. Her research focuses on the intersections of urban design, the built environment, and urban transport. Her recent projects have investigated transit urbanism, urban morphology, spatiality of street vending, public space and urbanity, and urban design education and pedagogy. She holds a PhD in Urban Design from the University of Melbourne.

Gominda Ponnamperuma, MBBS (Colombo), Dip. Psychology (Colombo), MMEd (Dundee), PhD (Dundee), is Professor and Head of Department of Medical Education, in the Faculty of Medicine, University of Colombo, Sri Lanka. He has served as an invited speaker and resource person in many international symposia and conferences. Author of several journal articles and books, he sits on the editorial boards of four international medical education journals. He is a postgraduate tutor, examiner, and resource material developer for national and international medical education courses. He has served as an advisor, visiting professor, consultant, and fellow in several academic institutes and educational projects and is a founder co-chair of the Asia Pacific Medical Education Network (APME-Net). His research interests are in assessment (including selection for training), and curriculum development and evaluation.

Amir Qayyum is currently Professor at Capital University of Science and Technology (CUST), Islamabad, Pakistan. He obtained his master's degree and PhD from the University of Paris-Sud, France in 1996 and 2000, respectively, and completed his research work at INRIA, Rocquencourt, France. He did his bachelor's degree in Electrical Engineering at the University of Engineering and Technology, Lahore, in 1991. He is the founding director of the Center of Research in Networks and Telecom (CoReNeT) and has led several funded research projects. He has numerous publications in international conferences and journals. His research interests include wireless networks, software-defined networking, vehicular and mobile ad hoc networks, and sensor networks for healthcare. He is also a founding member of Pakistan France Alumni Network (PFAN). In recognition of his services for research and cultural collaborations with France, he was awarded the medal of "Chevalier dans l'Ordre des Palmes Académiques" by the Government of France.

Zoe Robinson is a Professor of Sustainability in Higher Education, Co-Director of the Institute for Sustainable Futures, and Director of Education for Sustainability at Keele University, UK, with responsibility for embedding sustainability across the curriculum and student experience. She is a researcher, educator, and practitioner in the field of sustainability science with a background in sustainability, climate change, and energy transition education, and community engagement. In recognition of her work in education for sustainability, she was awarded a National Teaching Fellowship in 2012, is a Principal Fellow of the Higher Education Academy (PFHEA), and was shortlisted in the "Most Innovative Teacher of the Year" category of the Times Higher Education Award in 2019. She has worked in an advisory capacity around education for sustainability for the Environmental Association of Universities and Colleges and National Union of Students and was in the Advisory Group of the new QAA and Advance HE (2021) Education for Sustainable Development Guidance.

Silvia Román Suero (Badajoz, 1980) is full time Professor at the Applied Physics Department of the University of Extremadura (UEX, Spain) and is involved in teaching subjects such as physics, thermodynamics, thermal engineering, thermosolar plants, energy from biomass, and energy storage. Her research is mainly focused on the use of biomass waste as fuel or as activated carbon precursor, by means of different thermal processes, as well as the application of carbon porous materials in adsorption processes both in liquid and gas phases. With her teaching duties, Silvia tries to provide additional skills to her students, and she is always open to educational innovation to enhance abilities such as teamwork, challenge-based learning, and resilience. Regarding a more social aspect, she tries to incorporate methodologies in which she covers environmental issues, gender approaches, empathy and respect towards others, and strength of self-esteem. She is currently the coordinator of the UAE (Unidad de Atención al Estudiante, in English, Student Office) of the Industrial Engineering School of the UEX.

John Scahill is a lecturer and researcher in the Department of Building and Civil Engineering in the Galway Mayo Institute of Technology, Ireland. He is a chartered mechanical and electrical building services engineer who specializes in low energy and low impact building technologies. He teaches in undergraduate and postgraduate programs on sustainable construction, climate resilience, and education for sustainable development (ESD). His research interests are focused on sustainability in higher education (SHE) and the use of the Change Laboratory as a methodology to implement change in higher education settings. He has a particular interest in the role of interdisciplinary collaboration in the enhancement of SHE and the promotion of ESD in higher education. He is currently managing a multi-institute collaborative development project focused on sustainability in the built environment and is also leading a multidisciplinary project focused on the United Nations Sustainable Development Goals.

Leena Seneheweera holds a bachelor's degree in Fine Arts and an MSc in Archaeology from the University of Kelaniya, Sri Lanka. She completed her PhD at the Shanghai Conservatory of Music, China. She is currently a Senior Lecturer in the Department of Fine Arts, and Academic Coordinator of the Special Needs Resource Unit of the Faculty of Arts, University of Peradeniya, Sri Lanka. She is also an active member of the ERASMUS+ Capacity Building in the Higher Education Project – Developing Inclusive Education for Students with Disabilities in Sri Lankan Universities (IncEdu). She is a singer of Sri Lankan semi-classical music, and a music therapist who plays Sri Lankan and Chinese musical instruments. Her research and teaching cover, inter alia, musicology, music therapy, Sri Lankan, Indian, and Chinese music, disability studies, Buddhist art, Sri Lankan folk music and drama, intangible cultural heritage, epigraphical poetry, and expressive arts.

G. R. Sinha is Adjunct Professor at the International Institute of Information Technology Bangalore (IIITB) and is currently deputed as Professor at Myanmar Institute of Information Technology (MIIT), Mandalay. He was Visiting Professor (Honorary) in the Sri Lanka Technological Campus Colombo during 2019–2020 and at the University of Sannio, Italy, during September 2020–March 2021. He has published 277 research papers, book chapters, and books at international level and is Associate Editor of five SCI/Scopus indexed journals. He has 23 years' teaching and research experience and has been delivering Association for Computing Machinery (ACM) lectures as ACM Distinguished Speaker in the field of digital signal processing since 2017. He has delivered more than 50 keynote/invited talks and chaired many technical sessions in international conferences. He has also been an Expert Member of the Professor Promotion Committee of the German-Jordanian University in Jordan. His research interestsincludes cognitive science, computer vision, outcome-based education, and information and communications technology tools for developing employability skills.

Roberta Štěpánková is an Assistant Professor at the Department of Landscape Architecture, at the Faculty of Horticulture and Landscape Engineering, SUA in Nitra, Slovakia. In addition to activities related to pedagogical activities for landscape engineering and architecture study programs, her main activities include research and collaboration on several projects focused on architectural and urban development and the renewal of settlement (mainly rural spaces) and public spaces. The main topic of her research is oriented to the historical heritage of SUA in Nitra, and architecturally valuable objects. She is the author and co-author of a scientific monograph, university textbooks, and scientific and professional works, with more than 60 citations in the WOS and SCOPUS databases.

Andrej Tarnik is researcher and lecturer at the Faculty of Horticulture and Landscape Engineering, Slovak University of Agriculture in Nitra. He finished his PhD in 2015 and is a studentss advisor, helpsing students with setting up proper study plans. His topics are related to hydrology and hydropedology. He is responsible for the practical course of Hydropedology for students of the Landscape Engineering study program. His research is focused on the dynamics of soil moisture changes, spatial and temporal variability of soil water storage, and climate change impact on soil moisture. He is author or co-author of several scientific papers published in indexed journals (CC, WoS, SCOPUS).

Luis Velazquez is a senior sustainability researcher with over 30 years' experience as an industrial engineer. He holds a doctoral degree in Engineering Science with a major in Cleaner Production and Pollution Prevention from the University of Massachusetts Lowell. Dr. Velazquez has led curriculum design in bachelor's, master's, and doctoral programs. In addition, he has been a sustainability research intern at several higher education institutions, such as the Center for Health and the Global Environment of the Harvard School of Public Health, Boston, in the US; the Universidade Paulista, Sao Paulo, Brazil; Erasmus University, Rotterdam, the Netherlands; and the University of Applied Sciences in Zittau/Gorlitz, Germany.

Abdul Hannan Waheed was educated in Kuwait, Egypt, UK, India, and Australia, and is currently the Chief Executive Officer of the Maldives Qualifications Authority (MQA). Dr. Hannan is a renowned expert in multiple fields. He has worked in the field of higher education quality assurance since 2004 and holds a PhD in this field from the Queensland University of Technology, and has been instrumental in the development and strengthening of higher education quality assurance in the Maldives. He is a multilingual (Dhivehi, English, Arabic) language expert and is a Chartered Linguist and Member of the Chartered Institute of Linguists, UK. He is a current affairs analyst on a live weekly TV program called *Dhuniye (World)* on VTV. He is also a talented Arabic calligrapher.

Sakunthala Yatigammana is a professor in the Department of Education in the Faculty of Arts at the University of Peradeniya. Sakunthala received her PhD from the Graduate School of Education, The University of Bristol, UK in 2011 and MSc from the Postgraduate Institute of Science, University of Peradeniya. She is involved in a number of European and Canadian funded projects as a co-investigator. Further, she has published more than 30 papers in journals and conferences and has also co-authored five books. Her current research interest focuses on the use of mobile phones for science teaching and learning, Educational Technology, Pedagogy, Inclusive Education and Comparative Education

Mengting Yu is a PhD student in the Department of Educational Research at Lancaster University, UK. She holds a master's degree in Educational Research from the University of Glasgow, UK, and an undergraduate degree in English Literature from Tianjin University of Technology (TJUT), China. She worked as a language teacher and overseas educational consultant in Beijing from 2015 to 2019. Such enriched working experiences have provided her with a broad view of research interests, including higher education, digital learning, language education, interdisciplinary and technological pedagogies, and innovation in education. Her present study focuses on how technology-supported classrooms, together with the trend to move from traditional teaching to student-centered teaching methodologies, impact the learning experiences of international students.

David Slim Zepeda Quintana is a researcher and lecturer in the Department of Industrial Engineering of the University of Sonora, Mexico where he teaches undergraduate and graduate courses in the field of sustainable development and where he is a full-time researcher in the Sustainability Graduate Program. He holds a BSc in Industrial and Systems Engineering from Universidad del Valle de Mexico and a master's degree in Sustainability from the University of Sonora. His major research and teaching interests are sustainable development, sustainable management systems, sustainability in higher education, cleaner production, corporate social responsibility, and sustainable innovation.

1

Sustainable Development: Embedding Sustainability in Higher Education

Kelum A. A. Gamage and Erandika K. de Silva

1.1 Introduction

The concept of "sustainable development" has become far-reaching due to the major breakthrough in efforts toward the 2030 Agenda for Sustainable Development adopted by the United Nations (UN) General Assembly in 2015. Following the UN Conference on Sustainable Development held in Rio de Janeiro in 2012, a global framework was developed to "redirect humanity towards a sustainable path." This global framework is the 2030 Agenda for Sustainable Development that is centered around 17 Sustainable Development Goals (SDGs) that branched out from the previous Millennium Development Goals (MDGs) agenda.

The SDGs describe major development challenges faced by humans universally. Consequently, SDGs are considered "challenges for humanity" giving them a sense of urgency in both international and national agendas. UN SDGs emerged with the aim of securing "a sustainable, peaceful, prosperous and equitable life on earth for everyone now and in the future" (UNESCO 2017). As SDGs cover global challenges that need to be overcome for the survival of humanity, they establish "environmental limits and set critical thresholds for the use of natural resources" (UNESCO 2017).

Poverty and associated challenges such as the lack of access to education, healthcare and sanitation, employment opportunities, and social protection are detrimental to human lives and human dignity. UN SDGs are based on the basic premise, that ending poverty, requires strategies that develop economies. Economic development, therefore, is understood and realized alongside a range of social needs that include education, health, social protection, and employment opportunities simultaneously with climate change and environmental protection. Inequality, unsustainable consumption patterns, weak institutional capacity and environmental degradation are identified as the key systemic barriers to sustainable development.

For the realization of the long-term goals put forward as SDGs, the active involvement of governments, the private sector, civil society, and all of humanity is needed. Governments are expected to establish national frameworks, policies, and measures for the implementation of the 2030 Agenda that focuses on 17 SDGs, where Quality Education (SDG 4) is understood as ensuring "inclusive and equitable quality education and promote lifelong learning opportunities for all."

In 1987, the UN's World Commission for Environment and Development (WCED) published the report "Our Common Future," also known as the "Brundtland Report" in honor of the chair of the Commission, former Norwegian Prime Minister Gro Harlem Brundtland.

The Wiley Handbook of Sustainability in Higher Education Learning and Teaching, First Edition.
Edited by Kelum A. A. Gamage and Nanda Gunawardhana.
© 2022 John Wiley & Sons, Inc. Published 2022 by John Wiley & Sons, Inc.

The publication of the report was a milestone in raising international awareness, calling for action, and creating discourse on the importance of sustainable development and global partnerships. This makes the Brundtland Commission an indispensable forerunner in sustainability discourse. Therefore, this book adopts the Brundtland Commission's definition that sustainable development "meets the needs of the present generation without compromising the ability of future generations to meet their own needs" (Brundtland Report 1987, p. 8). The Commission concludes that two concepts are embedded in this overarching concept of sustainability. The first is the concept of needs, that is the essential needs of the poverty-stricken populations that demand the priority of intervention networks; the second is the idea of limitations imposed on the environment's ability to meet present and future needs due to the state of technology and social organization (Brundtland Report 1987).

Very often, sustainability is understood as having three dimensions: environmental, social, and economic. Kagawa (2007), Dvořáková and Zborková (2014), and Venkataraman (2009) are prominent scholars who contributed to the sustainability discourse by envisioning sustainability as a three-dimensional endeavor. Efforts to achieve sustainability of these three dimensions collectively is understood as sustainability. For instance, environmental sustainability is achieved through efforts to conserve and enhance the natural resource base through sustainable consumption patterns. Social sustainability includes efforts to promote equity, diversity, and social justice. At the same time as environmental and social sustainability, economic sustainability is achieved through efforts to reduce poverty and promote fair trade. Garcia et al. (2017) state that the term "sustainable development" originates from the three dimensions, namely the environmental, economic, and sociocultural. On that ground, they emphasize the importance of "extensive collaboration among diverse partners" to implement a holistic approach to sustainability goals. They maintain that all three pillars of sustainable development need to be served to attain the transition to a sustainable society. Sustainability education, too, must therefore address these three dimensions to equip individuals with the knowledge, skills, and attitudes to make informed decisions in shaping sustainable futures. Earlier policy statements on sustainable transformations through education include environmental education (EE) in 1977, the introduction of education for sustainable development (ESD) during the Earth Summit in Rio in 1992, the announcement of the Decade for ESD in 2002 during the World Summit on Sustainable Development, the launch of the Global Action Programme (GAP) for ESD in 2014, and the Incheon Declaration (Education 2030: Toward Inclusive and Equitable Quality Education and Lifelong Learning for All). EE is the earliest form of ESD that is notable for its emphasis on public environmental concern and finding solutions for environmental issues. EE and ESD approaches to sustainability have certain overlaps as they are founded on the idea of conserving natural resources for the benefit of present and future generations. These overlaps have made them intrinsically connected. Even though EE emerged before ESD, it is understood today as part of ESD. In 2009, a UNESCO analysis identified that EE–ESD relationships can be understood in three ways: EE and ESD as equals; EE as a part of ESD; and ESD and EE as distinct. However, both EE and ESD are identified as crucial approaches to sustainable development (UNESCO 2009; Pavlova 2012).

Sustainable development requires thinkers with the knowledge, skills, values, and attitudes that empower them to contribute to social, environmental, and economic sustainability. This becomes possible only through education. However, ESD does not mean education that focuses on economic growth alone. Economic growth-oriented education also runs the risk of an increase in unsustainable consumption patterns that upset the ecological balance by depleting natural resources. On the contrary, the approach of ESD is believed to enable lifelong learning and empowers learners to make informed decisions and carry out responsible actions for environmental integrity, economic success, and a just society for present and future generations.

Garcia et al. (2017) state that ESD requires participatory teaching and learning methods. They claim that such teaching and learning methods motivate and empower learners to move beyond acquiring knowledge, and change their behavior to take action for sustainable development.

The purpose of ESD is to empower every individual to be responsible and accountable for their actions for the benefit of the present and future generations. Reflecting on their actions and their social, cultural, economic, and environmental implications from a local and a global perspective helps individuals transform their own actions. Addressing learning content and outcomes, pedagogy, and the learning environment, ESD provides holistic and transformational education. UNESCO understands ESD as transformational education through four major pillars: (i) learning content; (ii) pedagogy and learning environment; (iii) learning outcomes; and (iv) social transformations. As transformational learning content, UNESCO understands the integration of pressing issues, such as climate change, poverty, biodiversity, disaster risk reduction (DRR), and sustainable consumption and production (SCP), into the curriculum. Apart from integrating such content into the curriculum, ESD focuses on interactive, learner-centered teaching and settings. This enables a smooth shift from teaching to learning and demands an action-oriented, transformative pedagogy that accommodates self-directed learning, participation and collaboration, problem-orientation, inter- and transdisciplinarity, and the linking of formal and informal learning (UNESCO 2017). Such transformational pedagogy and learning environments are conducive to exploratory, action-oriented transformative learning in a learner and also demand the rethinking of both physical and virtual learning environment to inspire learners to take action for sustainability. The third pillar, learning outcomes, encapsulates stimulating learning and promoting core competencies such as "critical and systemic thinking, collaborative decision-making and taking responsibility for future generations." The final pillar that supports ESD is societal transformation that is expected to "empower learners to transform themselves and society they live in." Enabling a transition to greener economies and societies, equipping learners with skills for greener jobs, and encouraging people to have sustainable lifestyles are some examples of societal transformation (UNESCO 2017).

The SDG on education recognizes ESD as part of Target 4.7 together with global citizenship education (GCED), which UNESCO promotes as a complementary approach. Moreover, realization of the SDG on education is crucial to the realization of the 16 other SDGs. ESD presents its learning objectives as specific cognitive, socioemotional, and behavioral learning outcomes. In short, ESD aims at equipping all individuals with the knowledge and competencies required to bring about transformation and thereby contribute to achieving SDGs. It demands the embedding of non-formal and informal education with key cross-cutting competencies related to sustainability in curricula in all educational institutions ranging from preschool to tertiary education.

Despite the promise with which ESD has been seen, one can also view ESD with skepticism since empirical studies on its effectiveness is scant. McKeown (2002), Scott (2015), and Kioupi and Voulvoulis (2019) point out that few studies that review learning and pedagogical practices in ESD highlight inconsistencies, incongruences, and deficits in curricula. ESD has also drawn skepticism due to the definition education is assigned in different contexts (UNESCO 2014). Similarly, "sustainable society" (Seatter and Ceulemans 2017) and "sustainability in education" are arguably vague concepts that are open to contestation (UNESCO 2012). Nonetheless, this book focuses on exploring ways of embedding sustainability in higher education by tracing current practices, challenges, and novel trends and developments. Section 1.2 of this chapter reviews the existing literature on ESD by tracing its history and evolution. Section 1.3 then explores the need for promoting sustainability in higher education. The book then branches out to explore its subject under four main Parts, the theme of each Part being investigated in several chapters. Drawing insights from current practices and disciplinary and pedagogical challenges, the last chapter of this book summarizes the emerging good practices in promoting sustainability in higher education as well as barriers to embedding sustainability in higher education.

1.2 Background

Higher education for sustainable development (HESD) does not require novel inventions and four long-standing concepts constitute the fundamental philosophy, disciplinary content and pedagogy required for ESD: liberal education, interdisciplinarity, cosmopolitanism, and civics (Sherren 2008). Drawing from existing literature, Sherren reiterates Kohlstedt's view (1997) that "education for sustainable development" is fundamentally connected to nature studies and EE. According to Sherren (2008), literature on EE and ESD for more than 30 years has emphasized "teaching and learning methodologies and the engendering of values or world views, as opposed to imparting specific disciplinary content." She uses the two alternate terms, education for sustainability (EFS) and ESD, as synonyms. Dovers (2005, p. 9) understands sustainability in relation to a range of issues covering "resource depletion and degradation," "pollution and wastes," "fundamental ecological life support services," and "society and the human condition" with a number of constituent issues that are interconnected. As Orr (1992) points out, the key goal of ESD is "ecological literacy," which, according to him, is "a broad understanding of how people and societies relate to each other and to natural systems, and how they might do so sustainably" (p. 92). According to scholars such as Tilbury and Wortman (2004), the ESD movement displays a shift from education about the environment to an education that facilitates better stewardship of it.

Sherren argues that the future of ESD may be found in its history and in the history of EE. The approach to ESD suggested by Sherren is learning through the history of ESD and EE in order to promote the "future environment" perspective. As a solution, what is proposed is an education that enables and develops "critical thinking skills, broad and integrated contextual knowledge and the desire and capacity to apply that knowledge" (Sherren 2008). What is noteworthy is that Sherren identifies key competencies expected through HESD as the same as humanist graduate characteristics such as critical thinking, independent inquiry, problem-solving, creativity, sensitivity, empathy, foresight, self-expression, and broadened perspectives. Sherren further proposes a liberal, interdisciplinary, cosmopolitan, civic model of education, but also notes certain barriers to such a model. Among those barriers, Sherren first identifies the risk of overburdening staff and students with innovative pedagogical methods and relevant curricular structures, compromising on flexibility, equity, and intellectual challenge. Second, there is the impracticality of implementing values education in higher education institutions (HEIs). On a final note, Sherren argues that the popularity of the "market model" in the higher education sector, with its vulnerability to national funding priorities and a culture of competition, makes values education challenging but not impossible.

David Orr also shares a similar perspective about HEIs and their deficiency in values education. In "What is Education For?" Orr (1991) discusses six myths about the foundations of modern education, and six new principles to replace them. In the first part of his essay, he points out how university-educated individuals are the cause of most modern-day issues. According to Orr, the first myth about modern education is the belief that ignorance is solvable. In Orr's perspective, "ignorance is not a solvable problem, but rather an inescapable part of the human condition." The second myth is the belief that with enough knowledge and technology planet Earth can be managed. He debunks this myth by revealing how ignorant humans are about even the top inch of topsoil. Orr's belief is that what can be managed is only *us*, by which he means human desires, economies, politics, and communities. Third, he points out the myth that implies that human goodness increases as knowledge increases. Orr maintains that data is not equal to knowledge and argues that human kindness does not increase as knowledge increases because certain indigenous or vernacular knowledge is lost as certain other knowledge is discovered. The fourth myth is that we can adequately restore what we have dismantled. On this, Orr points out the grievous repercussions of compartmentalized education. He explains how modern economists lack even the most rudimentary knowledge of ecology, which eventually leads to dire consequences for human civilizations. As the fifth myth, Orr cites the notion that education gives upward social mobility, countering this by stating that "successful" people are not the most pressing issue of our times, but rather peacemakers, healers, restorers, storytellers, and lovers of every shape and form. Orr stresses the importance of "people who live well in their places, . . . people of moral courage willing to join the fight to make the world habitable and humane" (Orr 1991, p. 4). Finally, Orr debunks the myth that our culture represents the pinnacle of human achievement – the idea that we alone are modern and developed. Orr argues that "Communism failed because it produced too little at too high a cost," while "capitalism failed because it destroys morality altogether" and therefore culture is not a symbol of the pinnacle of human achievement.

Orr, then, presents his propositions to rethink education. First, he states that all education is EE by which he means that all education, by and large, ought to reflect on how it impacts the environment. Second, Orr presents the principle that the goal of education is not the mastery of the subject, but of one's person. His third proposition is that knowledge carries with it the responsibility to see that it is well used in the world. Fourth, Orr maintains that knowledge is not achieved until we learn the effects of knowledge on real people and their communities. In his fifth proposition, Orr stresses the importance of "minute particulars" and the power of examples over words. On this, Orr points out the importance of exemplary faculty, administrators, and institutions who provide role models of integrity, care, and thoughtfulness. Finally, Orr suggests the use of pragmatic ways of learning and teaching and states that the way learning occurs is as important as the content of particular courses.

Orr then moves on to propose assignments for campuses. His first recommendation is to engage in a campus-wide dialogue on education and the means of education. As guiding questions, Orr presents the following:

> Does four years here make your graduates better planetary citizens or does it make them, in Wendell Berry's words, "itinerant professional vandals"? Does this college contribute to the development of a sustainable regional economy or, in the name of efficiency, to the processes of destruction? (Orr 1991, p. 6)

His second suggestion is to examine resource flows on campus (food, energy, water, materials, and waste) and understand the environmental damages caused by it. He recommends that campuses start education by teaching their faculty and students to seek real-world solutions to real-world issues in their immediate environments. Orr's third recommendation is that campuses reexamine their endowments to find out if they invest in companies that act responsibly to cater to the needs of the world. On a final note, Orr proposes setting a goal of ecological literacy in students and provides a list of guiding themes or topics.

What is noteworthy is that Orr's idea of education resonates with the rationale behind ESD and SDGs. From the UNESCO point of view, HEIs play a key role in ESD-GAP Priority Action Areas. Higher education constitutes the learning environment for all educational professionals and providing ESD literacy to professionals is of utmost importance. Leaders of HEIs hold key positions in contributing to an equitable and ecologically sound future by establishing sustainable development as a central academic and organizational focus. This could be further facilitated by: (i) research initiatives in universities and higher education networks, (ii) providing advice and guidance on strengthening national education systems, and (iii) capacity building for sustainable development across different sectors. UNESCO believes in the contribution of HEIs in providing expertise and support to local ESD initiatives. Universities have the potential to combine the knowledge and experience at the local level with information housed at higher levels. Using evidence-based data, and problem-based scientific research, HEIs can strengthen the interface between research findings and decision-making (Heiss 2021).

During the past 10 years, HEIs have made significant efforts to address sustainability in campus operations. This includes the development and sharing of tools and reporting frameworks. Universities have adopted new sustainable development related and specialized programs and courses. Networks of HEIs have emerged building capacity and promoting sustainable development teaching. Many HEIs have become pioneers in adopting a whole-institution approach to ESD. Heiss (2021) also identifies a number of challenges to ESD, one of them being that implementing commitments to sustainable development requires coordinated change at multiple levels – in governance, planning, academic programs, facility management, and financial systems. Another challenge is the level of innovative thinking and involvement ESD demands in staff development and across institutions in order to transform curricula and pedagogy.

1.3 Promoting Sustainability in Higher Education

The need for a more holistic approach to ESD in the curriculum emerged with Hopkins and McKeown's (2005, p. 13) emphasis on it in the UN Decade of Education for Sustainable Development (DESD) of 2005–2014. Following this, HEIs adopted holistic approaches that were translated into practice with a focus on knowledge, methods, and curriculum change. In terms of a formal ESD curriculum, it takes the form of a new ESD subject and/or the development of ESD as a cross-curriculum topic. However, a more effective holistic approach is that of curriculum and institutional change contributing to the overall reorientation of education toward sustainability (2005, p. 13).

From the recent past, "Rio+20 People's Sustainability Treaty on Higher Education" is a significant international effort that was jointly developed by over 30 HEIs and networks under the special guidance of the International Association of Universities and the UN University – Institute of Advanced Studies of Sustainability. This treaty promotes eight Evolving Principles (Rio+20 People's Sustainability Treaty on Higher Education (n.d.), p. 4), emphasizing a holistic and transformative perspective for sustainable higher education: (i) to be transformative, higher education must transform itself; (ii) efforts across the higher education system must be aligned; (iii) partnership underpins progress; (iv) sustainable development is an institutional and sector-wide learning process; (v) facilitating access to the underprivileged; (vi) inter and trans-disciplinary learning and action; (vii) redefining the notion of quality higher education; (viii) sustainable development as a whole-of-institution commitment (Rio+20 People's Sustainability Treaty on Higher Education (n.d.), pp. 4–5).

HEIs worldwide employ institutional sustainability provisions in the form of "sustainability policy," "sustainability plan," or "sustainability statement." What is observable is their lack of shared understanding of what constitutes ESD and the lack of a shared approach to ESD. This brings us back to the question of institutional provisions and the need to find a common ground in ESD.

Harvard University's 2015–2020 Sustainability Plan is "the roadmap for building and operating a healthier, more sustainable campus community" that centers around five core topics: (i) Emissions and Energy, (ii) Campus Operations, (iii) Nature and Ecosystems, (iv) Health and Well-Being, and (v) Culture and Learning. It is a resolute document that governs key strategic interventions by Harvard in sustainability issues on- and off-campus. What is noteworthy is Harvard's sustainability commitment to employing innovations and solutions developed within the university with the active engagement of its students and staff (Harvard University Sustainability Plan).

Under Emission and Energy, Harvard commits to reduce university-wide greenhouse gas emissions and energy emissions. Campus Operations aim to design and maintain the built environment and develop cutting-edge programs to enhance the health, productivity, and quality of life of students and staff. This includes efforts to maintain Green Building Standards, reduce wastewater, maintaining green-cleaning and sustainable IT standards, reducing campus fleet and shuttle emissions, and developing standards for climate preparedness and resilience. Through landscaping operations, campus design, and conservation and education, Harvard aims to commit to Nature and Ecosystems. By protecting and enhancing the ecosystems and green spaces in the university, Harvard also sets a precedent in enhancing regional biodiversity and personal well-being. Moreover, Harvard's Health and Well-Being commitment aims to conserve resources, reduce pollution and enhance personal well-being through reducing the university community's exposure to toxic chemicals and developing sustainable and healthful food standards. Similarly, under the core topic of Culture and Learning, Harvard employs research and teaching, governance, external partnerships, communications, and community action to combat sustainability challenges (Harvard University Sustainability Plan n.d.). These five core topics show a close affinity with Dover's understanding of sustainability as an intricately connected range of issues covering "resource depletion and degradation," "pollution and wastes," "fundamental ecological life support services," and "society and the human condition" with a number of constituent issues (2005, p. 9). Similarly, the University of Michigan's sustainability plan is centered around six goals that bear a close resemblance to Dover's understanding of sustainability: climate action through greenhouse gas reduction; fuel efficiency; waste reduction; sustainable foods; healthy environments and protecting the Huron river; and community engagement (Sustainability Goals 2021).

The University of Michigan's President, Mary Sue Coleman, emphasizes the crucial role of an environmental focus in adopting sustainability concepts in the university operations and thus acknowledges the urgency of addressing environmental sustainability:

> The pressing challenge of environmental sustainability is a huge global concern... From teaching and research, to hand on engagement, we are going to leverage our many strengths to make significant contributions to an urgent and extraordinarily complex problem. (University of Michigan News, 2009)

A question may arise as to why ESD is urgent. The answer is that the urgency is felt so greatly because of the increasing number of global issues and the incapacity of former and current generations in managing these complex issues. Sustainability is not a destination, rather it is an ever-continuing state of events that needs to be maintained at the pace of social transformation. The reason why ESD, like other sustainability goals, has failed in its implementation is due to a number of barriers that impede this ongoing sustainability journey.

References

Brundtland Report (1987). Report of the world commission on environment and development: our common future. https://sustainabledevelopment.un.org/content/documents/5987our-common-future.pdf (accessed 24 November 2021).

Dovers, S. (2005). *Environment and Sustainability Policy: Creation, Implementation and Evaluation.* Sydney, NSW: Federation Press.

Dvořáková, L. and Zborková, J. (2014). *Integration of Sustainable Development at Enterprise Level.* doi:https://doi.org/10.1016/j.proeng.2014.03.043

Garcia, J., da Silva, S.A., Carvalho, A.S., and de Andrade Guerra, J.B.S.O. (2017). Education for sustainable development and its role in the promotion of the sustainable development goals. In: *Curricula for Sustainability in Higher Education,* 1e (ed. J.P. Davim), 1–18. Cham, Switzerland: Springer.

Harvard University Sustainability Plan (n.d.). Cambridge, MA: Harvard Office for Sustainability. https://green.harvard.edu/sites/green.harvard.edu/files/Harvard%20Sustainability%20Plan-Web.pdf.

Heiss, J. (2021). The role of higher education in sustainability science for implementing the SDGs. UNESCO. https://en.unesco.org/sites/default/files/panel_3_presentation_juliaheiss.pdf (accessed 16 July 2021).

Hopkins, C. and McKeown, R.. (2005). Guidelines and recommendations for reorienting teacher education (Technical Paper No. 2), 13. Paris: UNESCO. http://unesdoc.unesco.org/images/0014/001433/143370e.pdf (accessed 24 November 2021).

Kagawa, F. (2007). Dissonance in students' perceptions of sustainable development and sustainability: implications for curriculum change. *International Journal of Sustainability in Higher Education* 8 (3): 317–338.

Kioupi, V. and Voulvoulis, N. (2019). Education for sustainable development: a systemic framework for connecting the SDGs to educational outcomes. *Sustainability* 11 (21): 6104. https://doi.org/10.3390/su11216104.

Kohlstedt, S.G. (1997). Nature study in North America and Australasia, 1890–1945: International connections and local implementations. *Historical Records of Australian Science* 11 (3): 439–454.

McKeown, R. (2002). ESD toolkit version 2. 1–142. http://www.esdtoolkit.org/esd_toolkit_v2.pdf (accessed 29 October 2019).

Orr, D.W. (1991). What is education for? Six myths about the foundations of modern education, and six new principles to replace them. In: *Earth in Mind: On Education, Environment, and the Human Prospect.* Island Press http://nsdl.library.cornell.edu/websites/comm/uploads/David_Orr.pdf.

Orr, D.W. (1992). *Ecological Literacy: Education and the Transition to a Postmodern World.* Albany, NY: State University of New York Press.

Pavlova, M. (2012). Environmental education and/or education for sustainable development: what role for technology education? https://research-repository.griffith.edu.au/bitstream/handle/10072/46566/74769_1.pdf?sequence=1&isAllowed=y (accessed 23 May 2021).

Rio+20 People's Sustainability Treaty on Higher Education. (n.d.). Copernicus Alliance. https://www.copernicus-alliance.org/images/Documents/treaty_rio.pdf.

Scott, W. (2015). Education for sustainable development (ESD): a critical review of concept, potential and risk. In: *Schooling for Sustainable Development in Europe: Concepts, Policies and Educational Experiences at the End of the UN Decade of Education for Sustainable Development* (ed. R. Jucker and R. Mathar), 47–70. Cham, Switzerland: Springer International Publishing.

Seatter, C.S. and Ceulemans, K. (2017). Teaching sustainability in higher education: Pedagogical styles that make a difference. *The Canadian Journal of Higher Education* 47: 47–70. https://eric.ed.gov/?id=EJ1154160.

Sherren, K. (2008). A history of the future of higher education for sustainable development. *Environmental Education Research* 2008 (14): 238–256.

Sustainability Goals (2021). University of Michigan - Office of Campus Sustainability, University of Michigan, 27 Jan. 2021, Available online: ocs.umich.edu/sustainability-goals/. (Accessed on 10 February 2021).

Tilbury, D. and Wortman, D. (2004). *Engaging people in sustainability*. Gland, Switzerland and Cambridge, UK: Commission on Education and Communication https://portals.iucn.org/library/efiles/documents/2004-055.pdf.

UNESCO (2009). Climate change and environmental education. *A Companion to the* Child-Friendly Schools Manual. https://s25924.pcdn.co/wp-content/uploads/2017/11/CFS_Climate_E_web-1.pdf (accessed 15 October 2021).

UNESCO (2012). *Shaping the Education of Tomorrow: 2012 Report on the UN Decade of Education for Sustainable Development (abridged)*, 89. Paris, France: UNESCO. https://library.wur.nl/WebQuery/wurpubs/fulltext/246667.

UNESCO (2014). *Global Monitoring Report 2013/4: Teaching and Learning: Achieving Quality for All*. Paris, France: UNESCO https://en.unesco.org/gem-report/report/2014/teaching-and-learning-achieving-quality-all.

UNESCO (2017). Education for Sustainable Development Goals: learning objectives. http://unesdoc.unesco.org/images/0024/002474/247444e.pdf (accessed 24 November 2021).

University of Michigan News (2009). President Coleman launches multifaceted sustainability initiative. https://news.umich.edu/president-coleman-launches-multifaceted-sustainability-initiative (accessed 18 February 2021).

Venkataraman, B. (2009). Education for sustainable development. *Environmentalist Magazine* 51 (2): 8–10.

Part I

Transforming the Curriculum – Pedagogy Focused Initiatives

2

Activist Learning for Sustainability: A Pedagogy for Change

Zoe Robinson, Rebecca Laycock Pedersen, and Sarah Briggs

2.1 Introduction

2.1.1 Education for Sustainability in Higher Education

There is increasing acknowledgment of the responsibility of universities in contributing to a more sustainable future, and our role as educators in ensuring our students have the agency to enact change (Robinson 2019). The responsibility of universities goes beyond the traditional estates-based environmental management focus toward a more holistic understanding of the ways in which universities can contribute to sustainability, through their engagement and outreach with local communities, their research activities, as well as their educational mission. Education can be a thread which weaves these areas of responsibility together.

These potential contributions to sustainability by universities cross the breadth of interconnected and interdependent environmental, social and economic issues that embody our understanding of "sustainability" (Gibson 2006; Purvis et al. 2019). The United Nations Sustainable Development Goals (SDGs), ratified in 2015, comprise 17 goals and 169 targets and, although not without criticism (Adelman 2018; Liverman 2018), might represent the best blueprint we have for a more sustainable future. These models of interconnected issues highlight that sustainability challenges are complex "wicked problems" which can be time-consuming and difficult to address due to involving multiple stakeholders, dimensions and conflicting needs (Ackoff 1974; Waddock 2013) and therefore need holistic and systemic approaches.

Quality Education is an SDG in its own right, which alongside targets relating to access to and inclusion within education, includes a specific "education for sustainable development and global citizenship" target with a goal of ensuring that "all learners acquire the knowledge and skills needed to promote sustainable development and sustainable lifestyles, human rights, gender equality, promotion of a culture of peace and non-violence, global citizenship and appreciation of cultural diversity and of culture's contribution to sustainable development" (UNESCO 2021a). Education, however, is not restricted to its own goal, but is an enabler for all other goals through empowering "people with the knowledge, skills and values to live in dignity, build their lives and contribute to their societies' (UNESCO 2021b).

Education for sustainable development (ESD) needs to be widely adopted across higher education to enable a fundamental, transformative shift in thinking and decision-making in all of society's leaders (Cortese 2003) through enabling the development of sustainability literate graduates, whose leadership in society can take many forms throughout their lives (Robinson and Molthan-Hill 2021). Higher education is also a liminal moment in the lives of many students given that many experience independent living and decision-making for the first time, providing an opportunity for the development of new (sustainable) habits (Verplanken and Wood 2006; Haggar et al. 2019).

However, despite the potential of our higher education systems in driving sustainability, "it is the people coming out of the world's best colleges and universities that are leading us down the current unhealthy, inequitable, and unsustainable path" (Cortese 2003, 16). Therefore, it is essential that we consider both what and how we educate, as well as think critically about the educational systems in which we sit.

Many models of education for sustainability have been discussed in the literature (e.g. Scott and Gough 2003; Sterling 2003, 2004; Vare and Scott 2007) with clear distinctions being made between education *about* sustainability, education *for* sustainability, and education *as* sustainability (Sterling 2004) as different levels of educational response and transformation. Vare and Scott (2007) distinguish between two interrelated and complementary approaches that they refer to as ESD1 and ESD2. ESD1 relates to informing specific skills and behaviors to guide positive actions, based around a set of underlying values and behavioral outcomes. Whereas, ESD2 focuses on the development of the capacity to think critically, analyze and question alternatives, make sound choices in the face of complexity, and explore the contradictions of sustainable living (Vare and Scott 2007).

Shephard (2008) argue the importance of considering affective attributes with ESD, such as values, attitudes, and dispositions that underpin knowledge, skills, and competencies, although they acknowledge that affective attributes can be difficult to address in higher education. Increasingly, learning outcome taxonomies incorporate values and attitudes alongside knowledge and skills as desirable personal qualities in the context of professional education (e.g. Carter 1985). However, for others, the role of higher education in engaging with values, behaviors, and attitudes is contestable, and some teaching staff may be uncomfortable with this approach (Ostrow Michel et al. 2020; Shephard 2008).

Alongside the cognitive and affective dimensions of learning, others emphasize the importance of including the practical (or psychomotor) domains of ESD and holistic consideration of the "whole person" across "head, heart and hands" (Sipos et al. 2008; Mahmud 2017). Cognitive learning (head) focuses on understanding information and how it can be applied. Affective learning approaches (heart) engage with attitudes, values, and behaviors and enable students to make emotional connections with the curriculum (Shephard 2008). Learning processes incorporating the hands include practical skills development and physical labor, such as building, painting, and planting (Sipos et al. 2008), and can align particularly with informal curriculum activities, such as involvement in student gardens or conservation activities.

The approach to embed sustainability across formal, non-formal/informal, and hidden curricula became established as a way to incorporate ESD throughout the student experience (Hopkinson et al. 2008). Table 2.1 summarizes the distinction between these different curricula domains. The *formal* curriculum refers to curricula developed for academic credit, guided by formally articulated learning outcomes. *Non-formal* and *informal* curricula are a relatively heterogeneous group that overlap considerably. Non-formal curricula are typically "organised, but . . . could have learning objectives (or not) and be intentional (or not)" (OECD 2007). The informal curriculum is somewhat of a misnomer given that the term "curriculum" implies some degree of intentionality and one of the principal characteristics of informal learning is that it is not intentional (OECD 2007). In the context of sustainability in higher education, the non-formal and informal curricula include the opportunities available for students to become involved with outside of their coursework, such as involvement in societies or volunteering

Table 2.1 Distinguishing characteristics between formal, non-formal, informal, and hidden curricula.

	Organization of learning	Presence of learning objectives	Intentionality of learning	Duration	Leads to a qualification
Formal curriculum	Highly organized	Present	Highly intentional	Rather long and/or full-time	Almost always
Non-formal curriculum	May or may not be organized	Sometimes present	Can be intentional or unintentional	Rather short and/or part-time	Usually not
Informal curriculum	Not organized	Not present	Unintentional	N/A	No
Hidden curriculum	Not organized, but has potential to be	Not present, but has potential to be	Almost always unintentional	N/A	No

Source: Based on Table 2 from OECD (2007), and drawing on material from Cotton et al. (2013).

initiatives, which enable learning but are unlikely to be formally articulated or assessed (other than in the context of non-formal schemes where some submission of work is still required). The hidden curriculum, a term originally coined by Jackson (1968), refers to what students learn through implicit messages of societal, institutional, or lecturers' values (Cotton et al. 2013). In the context of sustainability this has been defined as the "implicit messages a university sends about sustainability through the institutional environment and values" (Winter and Cotton 2012: 783), which includes the implicit messages within the campus environment itself (Cotton et al. 2020). In his 1993 essay "Architecture as Pedagogy," Orr explores the implicit messages embodied within our university buildings including the inconsequence of environmental and energy costs from which we learn "carelessness that accompanies waste and inefficiency, as well as callousness to the degradation of other places where materials and energy originate" (Orr 1993, p. 226). In the context of ESD, it is important to consider how sustainability is integrated into the formal, informal/non-formal, and hidden curricula, and how these different domains of learning intersect and provide opportunities for the "transformational sustainability learning" of integrating the head, heart, and hands (Sipos et al. 2008).

Alongside the developing interest in embedding ESD in higher education, there has been development of other educational agendas, including increasing graduate employability and entrepreneurship skills (Rae 2007). As such, there is an increasing sector-wide emphasis on graduate employability and the attributes that ought to be achieved by graduates during their time at university through curricular and non-formal/informal curricular opportunities. Yet there are potential synergies (although not without their tensions) between the employability agendas and ESD in higher education. For at least a decade, links have been made between the clear demand for graduates to be equipped with sustainability skills, from employers (see BITC 2010), interest in skills for sustainable growth and a green economy (BIS 2010; HMG 2011) as well as clear evidence that students see sustainability skills as being important to their future employers (Bone and Agombar 2011; Drayson et al. 2014).

There have been developments to create a framework for what competencies ESD comprises (e.g. Frisk and Larsen 2011; Wiek et al. 2011; Brundiers et al. 2021) beyond more knowledge-oriented approaches to ESD (Redman 2020), leading to the introduction of a framework of sustainability competencies from the United Nations (UNESCO 2017). This framework incorporates a range of knowledge, understanding, skills, values, and attributes under the following eight competencies: systems-thinking, futures-thinking, values-thinking, strategic-thinking, interpersonal, critical-thinking, self-awareness, and integrated problem-solving (UNESCO 2017).

Traditional learning and teaching contexts limit the possibilities for students to develop this range of competencies (Brundiers et al. 2021); therefore, innovative pedagogical approaches and educators' willingness to question their role and the activities they conduct are required. Despite these emerging frameworks, key questions remain as to what this means to our practice as educators and practitioners in ESD: How do we enable students to gain the kinds of competencies needed to bring about transformative social change toward sustainability in their own universities and wider communities? How can we move beyond preparing students for employment and produce graduates who are genuinely change agents and ready to be the change they want to see in the world?

2.1.2 Activist Learning and Education for Sustainability

The questions in the preceding paragraph require a pedagogical approach suited to empowering and motivating students to drive change. Experiential learning theory is based on a learning cycle incorporating concrete experience, abstract conceptualization, reflective observation, and active experimentation (Kolb and Kolb 2017) and is derived from Kolb's seminal 1984 work on experiential learning that draws on the work of Lewin, Dewey, and Piaget. This approach is seen as involving the whole person and is applicable not just to the formal classroom, but to all areas of life (Kolb and Kolb 2017). Experiential learning is used here as an umbrella term encompassing a range of active pedagogies and approaches that integrate the interconnections of theory and action (Ludlow 2010). It has been suggested that experiential learning can support students to move beyond generic dissatisfaction about the way things are, to feel empowered to drive change through focusing on specific issues, targets, and actions (Ludlow 2010). Such approaches, particularly where there is the goal of driving social change, have connections to other fields of learning design and philosophy including emancipatory learning, social purpose education, critical pedagogy, and radical adult education (Ollis 2008).

Within this chapter we explore the synergies between activism and forms of activist-oriented learning with ESD that cross the formal, informal/non-formal, and hidden curricula. Activism can be defined as a process whereby individuals act to impact social change (Ollis 2008). Here we define activist *learning* (in the context of sustainability), as a strategy for generating sustainability competencies that encapsulate the knowledge, understanding, skills, values, and attributes that allow learners to contribute to a more sustainable future through engagement and leadership in (broadly defined) community activism. In the context of more formal curriculum approaches, the expectation is that they will use their academic learning to inform action in the world with the aim of bringing about positive social, political, and cultural change (Still and Kent 1996), whereas within the non-formal/informal curriculum such connections to academic learning might or m not exist. Clearly, activism or activist learning do not take place in the curriculum alone, with work-placed activism (e.g. Costa et al. 2021b) and community activism, amongst others, important areas of actions and development.

Sustainability requires activism. For some, our current times lack strong and vibrant social movements (Bubriski and Semaan 2009), with the suggestion that beyond the recent trend of climate-related activism (e.g. de Moor et al. 2020) few students participate in movements for social change (Bubriski and Semaan 2009); others argue that activism is an ever-increasing aspect of student life (Eagan et al. 2015). Some educators see embedding activism in the classroom as imperative, merging theory and action to ensure curricula that engage with societal injustices beyond just consciousness-raising, allowing students to implement in practice what they have learned and to drive social and systemic change (Bubriski and Semaan 2009). Buchanan and Griffin (2010: 5) assert that embedding ESD within the curriculum "is hollow and insincere in the absence of practical and social action on site and perhaps beyond." Hence in this chapter we take the perspective that activist learning has an important role to play as part of ESD.

One way in which experiential learning and community action has been embedded in the curriculum, particularly in North America where it has a long tradition, is through service learning, founded on John Dewey's philosophy of the link between practice and theory and the role of education in fostering the common good. Definitions of service learning vary, but the key components include: (i) participation in community service for academic credit; (ii) reflection to enable connection between the action and curriculum content; and (iii) a desire to enhance a sense of civic responsibility (Bringle and Hatcher 1999; England and Marcinkowski 2007). For such experiential learning to be effective, it has been argued that reflection should draw on both cognitive and emotional registers (Ludlow 2010), thus integrating both affective and cognitive learning approaches, while much service may also incorporate practical action; hence engagement of "head, heart, and hands."

The literature on the *impact* of service learning is varied with inconclusive results, thought to be partly due to the range in the quality of service learning (Covitt 2002). However, a long-term study of an environmental service learning course in middle schools in the US highlighted that the greatest impact was directly on students' environmental actions and its long-term empowerment, through helping participants realize that they can make a difference as young people and have the skills and knowledge to drive change (Hobert 2010).

However, the service learning model is critiqued for its encouragement of passive participation and failure to challenge the underpinning, systemic issues which perpetuate social inequalities (Bubriski and Semaan 2009). Another criticism is that the service or experience itself does not necessarily produce learning, without critically reflective thought creating new meaning, leading to growth and the ability to take informed actions (Bringle and Hatcher 1999). Service learning also presents a number of hurdles such as communication and relationship-building within the communities served, students' cultural competency, and challenges of short-term service learning (Tryon and Stoecker 2008). This indicates that there is space to explore other forms of activist learning.

Activist learning can be said to challenge the structural cause of social and environmental injustice unlike the more passive engagement implied by service learning (Bubriski and Semaan 2009; Ludlow 2010). Another key difference lies in service learning tending to respond to a pre-articulated community need, whereas activist learning may be more driven by the students' own interests in driving change. Hence, activist learning can turn students' own potential dissatisfaction and disempowerment into political activism and moral agency (Ludlow 2010). In addition, rather than the more usual focus on wider community *needs* of service learning, many examples of activist learning in higher education involve action on the university and college campuses themselves (e.g. Ludlow 2010). Gruenewald (2003) argues for the value of place-conscious education, arguing that students' localized places of study, work, and recreation are centers of their experience and understanding of how the world works. Our university campuses might, therefore, be one of the most immediate places that connect to a student's own experiences and awareness of unsatisfactory conditions upon which they can act.

With its emphasis on bringing about the kinds of social changes needed to create a more sustainable society, the aspirations of ESD seem to encourage an activist learning approach. Students pursuing activism projects in their communities have powerful potential to generate the transformative education of true ESD. Many students already recognize the need for change on campuses (Barlett and Chase 2004; Drayson et al. 2014) and beyond to enable a more sustainable society, and are motivated to adapt their own behavior (Dagiliūtė et al. 2018; Rodríguez-Barreiro et al. 2013) and influence others (Cotton et al. 2016). Encouraging and supporting students to channel their energies and values – in a way that is determined and driven by them – seems a vital way to generate truly transformative learning, while for students who lack a sense of responsibility for the sustainability of their surroundings, activist learning can also potentially generate a greater sense of agency and empowerment. Wherever a student's starting point as a sustainability activist is, opportunities to engage in activist learning have the potential to empower students to build sustainability competencies through systems thinking, problem-solving and enacting social change, in contrast to more passive learning activities.

While it is generally accepted that university students should be encouraged to take part in volunteering and work experience for the development of employability skills, the idea that they might be *encouraged* to engage in social or political activism as part of their studies is seldom discussed and undoubtedly controversial. Intentionally encouraging activism may seem an unneeded distraction from the core curriculum, or may even be seen to threaten academic objectivity and liberty. Even where such high-level objectives as tackling social justice exist at a university or program level, few courses teach strategies for engaging in social change (Brinkman and Hirsch 2019), highlighting the potential, and we would argue, need, for more development of activist learning opportunities across the formal, non-formal/informal, and hidden curriculum domains.

2.1.3 Aim

This chapter explores the concept of "activist learning for sustainability," drawing on staff reflections and student interviews of a student-led project to explore and promote "sustainable student living." Reflecting on the experiences of this project and related literature, the chapter considers the students' motivations and experiences of the project, the students' learning and development, the role of the formal, informal, and hidden curricula in creating campus-based activist learning opportunities for students, and considerations of staff and student interactions across the public and private spheres of student life and campus-based activism. The chapter concludes with recommendations for ESD practitioners engaging with the development of activist learning opportunities.

2.2 Methodology and Case Description

2.2.1 Case Description: The Sustainable Student House

The Sustainable Student House (SSH) project was conceived by four first-year students of a sustainability-focused undergraduate degree at Keele University, UK in 2010. These students expressed that they wanted the opportunity to live on the university campus in a more sustainable way than they felt was possible in traditional student halls, and they particularly wanted a space to grow food. With encouragement and coaching from their course directors, the students wrote a proposal detailing their vision and presented it to university management. After several months of lobbying and negotiation, they were permitted to rent a 1960s bungalow on the campus for the following academic year.

The designated bungalow had four bedrooms, a living room, a small kitchen, and a large garden. It had no specific eco-efficient features or credentials prior to the project. Transforming it into a genuinely more SSH involved a significant amount of work indoors and out. This included establishing a vegetable garden with raised beds, a polytunnel, and a compost heap, supported by alumni funding and labor from student volunteers organized by the students themselves.

To make changes to the interior of the house, the students gained sponsorship from an energy company who donated energy-saving appliances, and then installed other small energy-saving measures, such as reflective radiator backing. The university also installed new double-glazed windows and a new, more efficient boiler. With a view to making the bungalow a learning space for visitors, the students posted signs and labels around the house explaining different aspects of sustainable living and the environmental (and financial) savings that could be made from different measures.

Beyond making their living space as sustainable as possible, a key objective of the students was to make an impact on the wider student community. They communicated the project via a website, a blog, articles in the student magazine, and social media. Over recent years, housemates have utilized Facebook to reach the student population and created an Instagram account, regularly producing video content and collaborating with university social media teams to do "takeovers" of the main university Instagram account. The house itself has become an important hub and meeting space for student activities, bringing students together to organize new sustainability-related projects. The project has attracted media attention (e.g. Zoo and Steed 2019), and the university uses the project to promote the university's sustainability activities. The project is still active at the time of writing.

In the first few years of the project, only students from the undergraduate sustainability or environmental science program were invited to apply to live in the SSH. However, in later years, to make the opportunity available for a wider range of students, students from other disciplines were invited to apply, although in order to maintain connection with the curriculum, a minimum of one "environmental student" was required. Applications were viewed preferentially if they came from groups of four students rather than individuals to ensure that the students in the house would get along and be willing to collaborate on projects.

Existing literature about sustainable student housing (e.g. Hassanain 2008; Watson et al. 2015) or sustainability within student housing (e.g. Parrott et al. 2011; Li et al. 2015; Botsaris et al. 2021) tends to focus on the implementation and effectiveness of sustainable technologies in student residences and environmental impacts of student behaviors. However, equally important is understanding how the non-formal and informal learning about and for sustainability that inevitably takes place in student housing can shape the extent to which students are and feel competent to enact pro-sustainability changes in their lives and professional work in future.

The SSH differs from the norm in sustainable student housing developments in that the house itself is not inherently sustainable. Many sustainable student housing projects do not principally consider the dwellers as active agents of change within their own living space. Instead, the spaces are designed to be environmentally friendly both architecturally and technologically (e.g. the HSB Living Lab at Chalmers University, University of Victoria's Sustainable Student Housing and Dining). As most graduates will be unlikely to move into the few eco-friendly homes on the market, and do not have access to funds to build such a home even if they would like to, it is much more likely that they will live in rented accommodation (Knight Frank Research and UCAS 2020) with limited opportunity for environmentally friendly retrofitting and minimal eco-friendly features. Living in the SSH, therefore, provides students with opportunities to learn from experiences they will be more likely to encounter in post-university homes following completion of their degree.

2.2.2 Method

We used a single, holistic, descriptive case study (Yin 2003) focusing on the SSH to describe an instance of sustainable student living as a potential example of activist learning. Given that using on-campus housing for activist learning is relatively unique, the case can be considered a revelatory case (Yin 2003). We draw on two main sources of information for our analysis: interviews with students who were residents in the bungalow and reflections from the authors who have been closely involved in the project.

The interviews were carried out in 2012 with five students, two of whom were involved in setting up the project and lived in the house in the first year of the project (2010–2011), and three who lived in the house in the second year of the project (2011–2012).

We (the authors) have relevant reflections, having worked with the SSH in a professional capacity. Robinson was one of the Course Directors that supported students in their interactions with the university when initially securing access to the house, and in working with the early years of the project. She has also led research and dissemination related to the project and advised and supported the Project Officers who became more closely involved in the project. As a result of her role in the project and as teacher to students on the undergraduate sustainability course, she was able to observe both students' learning associated with the SSH and how the project was perceived by academic, operational, and student support staff.

Laycock Pedersen supported managing the SSH as a Sustainability Project Officer between 2013 and 2015. This mainly included supporting students with gardening activities, organizing tours of the house, and helping with the transition between groups of housemates. She conducted her doctoral research about student-led food growing projects that focused on a related project (see Laycock Pedersen 2019), which meant that the SSH came up in some interviews she conducted. While these interviews were not analyzed for this chapter, they provided depth of understanding into the project.

Between 2014 and 2017, Briggs was a student of the sustainability-focused undergraduate program that gave rise to the SSH. She did not live in the SSH during her studies; however, she was engaged in SSH activities, such as gardening and social events. Following her studies, she became a university-employed Sustainability Project Officer (her current role at the time of writing). In this new role, she has supported the SSH through acting as a first point of contact for students living in the house, advising and supporting students on projects they want to lead during their tenancy, facilitating network-building between students and professional services teams, including grounds, the energy manager and university communications teams, and supporting housemate participation in sustainability events. From her time as a student and as a Sustainability Project Officer, she has gained insights into the project as a peer to the housemates and highly involved staff member. This meant she has been privy to aspects of living in the SSH that the housemates would be unlikely to share with academic staff.

As an authorial team, we offer complementary perspectives, having been involved in the project in different capacities and at different times. We interpreted the interviews and our own reflections through the lens of scholarship about service learning (and related areas), adult activist learning, and education for sustainability.

2.3 Student Motivations and Experiences of the SSH Project

2.3.1 Motivations for Initiation and Involvement in the Project

The students interviewed expressed diverse motivations for initiating and taking part in the SSH project, as could be expected for any student activist project. Motivations ranged from (i) wanting to drive long-term social change through providing a legacy for other students to learn about and experience food growing, and giving students the right to grow their own food[1]; to (ii) more individual experiential motivations, including wanting a different, more unusual

---

[1] It should be noted that not long after the start of this project, a campus allotment was established with specific space for a student food growing society.

university learning experience and the opportunity to grow their own food; to (iii) a desire to apply knowledge about sustainability beyond their degree. Two of the students interviewed approached the project seeing themselves as more knowledgeable "advisors" to other students, wanting to share their own knowledge about and passion for sustainability with others. Others saw their involvement as an opportunity for their own learning through active experience. This mirrors findings in other informal activism where there is typically a range of participants from those new to the field and those acting in more informal mentoring capacities (Ollis 2008).

2.3.2 A Sustainability Community: Benefits and Challenges

Students interviewed in both years acknowledged that they had experienced issues with group communication and organization in the SSH. At the same time, particularly in the project's first year, the communal, group nature of the project clearly provided motivation and fun for the students, in comparison to more traditional forms of student living in individual halls rooms:

> It's [living sustainably in the bungalow] more fun as well and if you are doing it in a community actually it's just generally more enjoyable. I think there's a certain feeling of individualism to modern day cooking and modern day student living that actually is not so enjoyable on the whole, whether it's getting expensive take-outs or whether it's kind of going out and getting drunk every night. Actually living in a kind of community where you are growing your own food, you can still have an incredible amount of good fun but a lot cheaper and a lot more enjoyable really. (Student 1, Year 1 of project)

The SSH provides a physical space for social learning (Reed et al. 2010). In the first year of the project, the interviews suggest that social learning took place both within the small group of students living within the house and in the wider network of students who became involved in the house activities through the food growing and outside space, communal cooking, the visual messaging around sustainability and energy, and meetings of a student sustainability society:

> A lot of these students [wider body of students involved in the house] were sort of open to the ideas of sustainability but did not really have any sort of concrete foundations in it, and the project gave them the ability to debate and discuss while working and playing with surrounding issues. You know, getting out in the garden and doing some digging on a sunny day with a beer is as good as lounging around and having a beer on a sunny day, but when that's mixed with people who are interested in debating and discussing things, it's magic. So I'd say it was very effective for some individuals. (Student 2, Year 1 of project)

However, in the second year of the project, one student described experiencing a lack of group cohesion, a lack of direction and support, and a feeling that they were taking on the burden of the project alone:

> I've felt like. . .I've practically been running the house, even though I have not actually been. . .I wasn't in the position formally. . . as well as doing the data, and as well as doing the media stuff on top of doing third year. (Student 3, Year 2 of project)

The interviews highlighted that students had very different starting points in terms of understanding and commitment to the project goals, engagement with and knowledge of sustainable living practices, and motivations for engaging in the project. These differences led to some disillusionment and discontentment, some students feeling that others were not "behaving sustainably enough" or contributing enough, and were not educating others who visited the house about the project:

> Another challenge I suppose would be that they have not really engaged with the actual sustainability aspect as much as I would have hoped. I've actually been told off for turning off too many lights, and it's just been difficult in that aspect. (Student 3, Year 2 of project)

Where these challenges were experienced, students identified that many issues came down to difficulties communicating amongst the group living in the house, and reflected that more regular meetings, setting of objectives, and willingness to engage in possible areas of conflict in order to tackle issues could have helped the project to achieve more by providing a clear direction and regular reminders of required activities.

The process of sharing experiences in a group is an important part of engaging in social action, and the experience of collectively working toward a common cause can be profound (Williford 2015). Informal environmental activist learning occurs through engagement in social movements and social processes situated in our daily interactions with others (Ollis 2008). The SSH clearly has the potential to create a genuine community of practice (Wenger 1999) in which social learning about both sustainable living and activism can occur. However, the degree to which this potential is achieved is dependent on the skills, knowledge, and attributes of those involved, and the ability and motivation to ensure effective communication and participation. As with student group work in other contexts (e.g. Hassanien 2006), interpersonal issues, including communication, scheduling, conflict, and equal participation are seen as key challenges in service learning projects (e.g. Crump 2002; Parece and Aspaas 2007). Even where individuals live in the same house, creating the time, space, and willingness to communicate effectively can be difficult. The academic staff supporting students to initiate the project encouraged the students to take on specific roles and responsibilities, including leadership for the project, although the interviews suggest that this distribution of responsibility was not realized. A reason why more formal leadership and structures of project management (such as regular meetings amongst the housemates) were not taken up might be because students did not want such formal structures within their private spheres.

In any student activism initiative, students involved will have different degrees of readiness to take action (Brinkman and Hirsch 2019), and with this might come different expectations of "success." Two of the students interviewed in the second year of the project were positive about their learning and the experience, while the other student interviewed was disappointed by what had been achieved:

> Well I'm fairly disappointed, to be honest, with this year. The main projects. . .have kind of been set up, that have not really been finished. . .So, in terms of what I'm proud of I suppose it's making the project continue rather than actually adding to the project I suppose. (Student 3, Year 2 of project)

The success of project results can be particularly meaningful to those who view themselves as activists (Bilon 2021). This disappointment in the project could be self-interpreted as "failure" and ultimately lead to a decrease in the perception of their agency (referred to by Bilon 2021, p. 173 as the "non-learning of agency"). As activist learning inevitably carries a risk of failure (Ludlow 2010), support for students in understanding the risks of failure, and managing the impacts of perceived failure are a potential area for staff involved in activist learning projects, to explore.

2.3.3 Students' Transience

University students are inherently transient members of the university community, both through the year (marked by holiday periods and uneven academic workloads) and due to the time-limited nature of their studies (typically three years for non-vocational, undergraduate courses in the UK). In the SSH project, annual turnover of housemates was enforced to allow a new cohort of students each year to live in the SSH. However, many students were informally associated with the project before becoming a resident and stayed involved in the project in some way after they had moved.

Students' transience can pose several challenges for activism projects (Laycock Pedersen et al. 2019). Ensuring ongoing maintenance and continuity can be logistically challenging (especially for the garden) and requires students to plan for maintenance during their absences. Furthermore, maintenance of such a project is so demanding that it can limit the types and amounts of new projects students can take on. One interviewee (Year 2) expressed disappointment with what was achieved in their year, feeling that in that year they had "only continued" rather than added to the project. Creativity and agency are important aspects of both learning and motivation and therefore opportunities for students to exercise these through new project developments are not only desirable (Briggs et al. 2019), but necessary for the project to contribute to activist learning. As such, there is a tension between the need to support students with new projects and encourage students to maintain and continue with existing projects.

A chronic issue within transient projects is knowledge handover (Laycock Pedersen 2019). This issue is particularly acute for the SSH because of students' relatively limited food growing competencies. To mitigate the lack of a handover, students were encouraged to produce a report or other artifact to pass on their project learning (including such prosaic information as crop rotations used) to the following year's students. This was carried out partially and reluctantly and, likely as such activities felt like "work," competed with formal curriculum deadlines and/or there were no consequences for outgoing residents if this information was not completed. Knowledge was likely more effectively transferred where more informal student involvements overlapped between years. Subsequent housemates living in the SSH in 2019–2020 and 2020–2021 set up and developed a shared drive with resources, photos, and guides which help address the knowledge transfer issue.

At the start of each year, the new housemates demonstrated limited understanding about the complexity of driving real change. For example, their insight was limited regarding the need for involvement and negotiations with diverse stakeholders. In particular, there was a lack of understanding about the importance of negotiating with the university in order to carry out activities (such as digging, hedge trimming) in the SSH grounds. Many change projects require development of relationships and trust between diverse stakeholders over long-term periods beyond the timescale of any one student's time at university (Brinkman and Hirsch 2019). This means that if university staff have negative experiences of one group of housemates, it can tarnish the relationship with the next. As a result, long-term stakeholders need to understand that each set of students comes fresh to the project, without the learning and experience acquired by previous students. There also needs to be an understanding that the SSH is intended to be fundamentally pedagogical in nature, and therefore the tangible outcomes of student projects may vary in quality and impact. As such, it is important that there are permanent members of staff who understand the pedagogical nature of the project to support and mediate good quality student–university relationships.

2.3.4 Time Management and Competing Priorities

Time management was a key issue for students living in the SSH, whether juggling competing demands between academic studies, personal issues and the SSH project, or competing demands of a myriad sustainability-related projects. Time pressures were articulated as being particularly severe when SSH residents were in the final year of their degrees.

The initial year of the project involved greater set-up time than in later years. As a result, one interviewee acknowledged that his academic work was negatively affected by his participation. However, he saw that learning through the project could compensate for any negative educational impacts:

> Provided the [garden foundations] were in, I knew future years would have an easier time. They'd still struggle but they'd have an easier time. But you know, that's part of the learning curve, understanding how you have to integrate sustainability with everything else you are doing, even as students. So I think if it does affect people's grades in the future I think it compensates for the skills it gives. The only problem is there's no quantification for those skills that are learnt in a project like this other than references or fitting it in somewhere and talking about the key skills you have developed, but there's no qualification for it. (Student 2, Year 1 of project)

This student acknowledged that the learning that took place was informal, unquantified, and potentially unrecognized. Because there is no formal recognition of this learning, students must rely on their ability to articulate it, first to themselves, and then to others.

It is notable that this student, who appeared willing to sacrifice individual academic achievement for the project, expressed his goals for the project through language clearly aligned with activism. He highlighted students' rights to grow food, and the desire to drive long-lasting change through a project with temporal continuity.

As this project sits purely within the informal curriculum with no real accountability other than to each other for project achievements, it is unsurprising that for many students the SSH took a backseat to other commitments. For many, trying to find a workable balance between the project's goals, their academic studies, and normal student social life seemed elusive.

Although burnout was not mentioned by any students interviewed, the subtext of the interview with Student 3 (Year 2) hinted at symptoms of burnout. We have also observed burnout in students involved in this and other sustainability activist projects in later years, including seeing the negative implications to their academic studies. In the context of activism, burnout can be described as "the end result of a process in which idealistic and highly committed people lose their spirit" (Pines 1994, p. 381). Many studies of youth activism have highlighted the dangers of burnout (e.g. Gagnon 2020). In addition to their activism, student activists are faced with academic pressures, leading to risk of more immediate and intense burnout (Gagnon 2020). Although acknowledging the learning and growth that can occur as a result of engaging in activism, activism takes students' time and energy away from activities that lead to educational benefits and college experiences (Linder et al. 2019) and can result in negative physical, emotional, and mental health consequences (Vaccaro and Mena 2011). Burnout in young activists can mean that, without finding the right support systems, they might fail to meet their potential (Gagnon 2020). Furthermore, activist burnout can lead to the destabilization of activist movements (Gorski and Chen 2015). Although we believe that activist learning is a good thing, without proper support and care it can come with problems, which may be exacerbated by the combination of: deeply rooted passion and motivation; lack of formal structure, support, and accountability; diverse motivations and expectations; and diverse and competing time pressures. Academics supporting student activism need to consider effective mechanisms to support student activists through both the formal and non-formal/informal curriculum.

We have explored some of the challenges of the SSH project and student activism in general, set against some of the learning such projects enable. In Section 2.4, we will explore the implicit and articulated learning and development of students from participation in the SSH project.

2.4 Areas of Student Learning: Embodied vs. Abstract Learning

As staff members interested in ESD and observers of the project, we saw the substantial potential for learning from the project: appreciating that enacting change is not as simple as the desire to see it happen; the level of research and decision-making needed to underpin action; increased awareness of barriers to implementing change and how to overcome them; the range of different stakeholders and perspectives necessary in change processes; and the skills of lobbying, negotiation, persuasion, working with people constructively, public speaking, and grant application writing. All these learnings are in addition to the adoption of more pro-environmental behavior. Our list of possible learning outcomes is long; however, are they achieved, and if not, how can such learning potential be realized?

Unsurprisingly, with such diverse motivations for taking part in the project, the learning students articulated was varied. The most frequently articulated learnings, for those not already viewing themselves as knowledgeable in these areas, were on everyday, visible practices such as recycling, composting, and food growing, and for some, increasing awareness of energy use through use of an in-home energy display. When prompted, students were able to articulate that they had developed generic skills important for change agents, such as interpersonal communication skills and writing for an audience and managing multiple, competing tasks. The transformative learning about driving change that we envisaged, such as developing skills related to interacting and negotiating with different stakeholders toward a desired outcome, were not articulated by students in the interviews, in spite of being something we observed. One student did express learning about the nature of driving change:

> It seems like it's very easy to just say [ideas] out loud and put them up, but when it actually comes to sitting down and planning them, fitting it in, trying to get the communication, the contacts we need, it's quite difficult. (Student 4, Year 2 of project)

It could be somewhat disheartening to see limited articulation of deeper areas of learning, and a focus on learning of everyday practices. However, this could be in part due to the lack of reflection on learning, and the more abstract nature of their learning. As ESD academics and practitioners, we aspire for our students to develop broader sustainability competencies and a deeper understanding of systemic causes of unsustainability.

Yet the interviews highlighted that there *is* a need to develop basic competencies related to sustainable everyday practices. For example, one international student had never experienced waste segregation for recycling and developed new patterns of behavior:

> Now after a year it's kind of now become in our pattern of life and it's the right thing to do, so doing it the other way just would not fit. (Student 4, Year 2 of project)

All students were eager to take their practical learning into their future lives. One interviewee also highlighted that focusing on sustainable living in the home gave them the "first hand experience" of sustainability, which would inevitably lead to more activity outside the home and advocacy with others:

> If you get into doing it at home, learning why it's important and how it can help you and not only you, I think you would start doing it more often outside of the house and speaking about it to more people, because it's first-hand experience. (Student 4, Year 2 of project)

Another student highlighted the importance of universities as places where students could develop sustainable everyday living practices:

> I think that universities are the perfect place for it because people are moving out of their house, you need to develop those kind of skills anyway, whether it's cooking or growing food or being self-sustaining in general. It's the perfect place for it. (Student 1, Year 1 of project)

In addition, this student highlighted that universities are also places where *bad* habits can be developed, for example, through regular consumption of takeaway food. Through the hidden curriculum of the home, projects like the SSH have the potential to counter such bad habits, through provision of communal spaces and access to food growing and promote the development of more sustainable patterns of behavior.

In the academy, the role of the body in learning is often diminished by educators, giving preference to abstract, cerebral types of knowing (Ollis 2008). While the importance of embodied learning is increasingly recognized by ESD practitioners and in ESD scholarship, there still remains a reticence to incorporate it into everyday teaching, possibly due to lingering biases, methodological uncertainties, or impracticalities of trying to do so in educational institutions that have been built for didactic, classroom-based learning. These areas of practical and visible learning, such as recycling and composting, conform to Vare and Scott's (2007, p. 193) ESD1, and as they acknowledge "it's a basic form of learning but it's still learning" which still comes with wider social and environmental benefits. Indeed, research by Chaplin and Wyton (2012, p. 413) highlight how even though students perceive sustainability as important "they demonstrate a lack of understanding of the concept or behavior that accords with these values," and that further action is needed so that actions such as energy saving become normative behavior. The SSH provides a place for social modeling, an important way of learning pro-sustainability behaviors, new routines, and social practices within the fabric of everyday living (Blewitt 2006). It provides a place to develop a community of practice and social learning through daily interactions with others.

Still and Kent (1996:131) describe the activist learner as one who "takes an active, assertive role in supporting measures that affect our common good – first, and continually, seeking to increase her/his level of conscious awareness of personal, social, political, economic, cultural and environmental realities." By choosing to live in the SSH, students demonstrated a commitment to at least some of these areas. Chase (2000, in Ollis 2008) identified five different areas of learning of environmental activists: technical knowledge, political knowledge, personal growth, life skills, and knowledge of organizations. Even if we may find ourselves disappointed with what seems to be a lack of learning about political knowledge and knowledge of organizations, we do see the development of technical knowledge, personal growth and life skills. Our students, like all activists, must start somewhere. As with all communities of practice there are people at different stages of knowledge, newcomers as well as those who can pass on their knowledge, skills, and experience (Ollis 2008).

Student 2 is quoted in Section 2.3.2 referring to the SSH as a space for informal debate and discussion amongst residents and guests, in which we can assume that the deeper and systemic issues contributing to unsustainability may be considered. However, it is clear that students struggle to articulate deeper learnings, or to identify them as valid and legitimate learnings worthy of being mentioned in an interview. However, the questions remain – can this deeper level of learning take place in informal curriculum projects, and how can it be better promoted?

Even within the informal curriculum, staff-facilitated reflection to support learning may be possible through integration into the project's student support. There are also examples of written reflection requirements for awards relating to non-formal curriculum activities. However, opportunities for reflection clearly differ between activities that may be classed as situated in the non-formal curriculum, which are top-down and university/Students' Union initiated, and those which are genuinely student-led (the informal curriculum of Table 2.1). The formal curriculum may also have a role in fostering habits of critical thinking and reflection that enable students to independently make these links between everyday practices and underlying systemic challenges.

2.5 Activist Learning across the Formal, Informal, and Hidden Curriculum

There is growing interest in the role of the informal curriculum, the interrelations between formal and informal sustainability learning (Winter and Cotton 2012; Gramatakos and Lavau 2019), and the links between the formal, informal, and campus (part of the hidden, Cotton et al. 2020) curriculum (Hopkinson et al. 2008). This section explores these connections within the context of the SSH project and how the connections can be used to maximize learning.

The degree of university (or Students' Union) involvement in informal and non-formal curricula can vary widely, as can the different learning communities that students create and engage with (Gramatakos and Lavau 2019). These range from top-down designed and managed, but non-credit bearing, official schemes (non-formal curriculum), to structures, support, training, and recognition for student-led societies, to the range of university-linked activities in which students might be engaged that can be invisible to staff (informal curriculum; Table 2.1). The SSH project on which reflections in this chapter draw has moved in time from the non-formal end of the informal spectrum, where although student-initiated and non-credit bearing, staff were more closely involved and had expectations of student reporting, to a more informal context, with no real external accountability requirements. Staff still take a key role in promoting the SSH project to recruit new students, and hence the project can be viewed still as having non-formal elements.

The project has connections to the formal curriculum, which acted as a source of student inspiration, cohort creation, and recruitment to the project; it takes place across the non-formal-informal curriculum spectrum, and involves the hidden curriculum, through the place in which it is situated. Each of the four project initiators studied the same sustainability-focused degree program. Students choosing this degree, already clearly had an interest in and passion for sustainability, making it easy for students with similar interests and passions to find each other. It is unlikely that such a project would happen with a student working in isolation, and so the opportunity for like-minded students to meet and share ideas is important and can be catalyzed by the curriculum. This degree program also specifically aims to empower students to drive change, and one core module has an explicit aim of providing students "with the knowledge, understanding and skills to improve the environmental performance of their current and future employers" (Keele University 2021), which can be interpreted as the aim of developing change agency skills. This module also provides students with insights into sustainability in the university and the opportunity to think critically about existing university sustainability practices and to make recommendations for change. This provided a fertile backdrop for the development of the SSH project.

Activist learning activities situated in the formal curriculum have the advantage of providing scaffolding of support for students. The student in the second year of the project who expressed dissatisfaction at how much was achieved, referred to a number of challenges that they felt affected what the project achieved. This included the perception of limited commitment of others in the house, difficulties with communication, and resignation that they were unable to come up with ideas:

> I'm not very much of an ideas person, which I think is another issue with me living in the bungalow this year because I am a doer rather than a thinker. (Student 3, Year 2 of project)

In a formal curriculum setting, several of these issues could have been addressed with staff support to help manage group challenges and help provide inspiration for action. However, in the context of the project being entirely student-led and centered around their own private time and living spaces, any communication of difficulties and requests for support needed to be student driven.

The interviews with students demonstrated little reflection on learning beyond surface level knowledge and skill development. A lack of reflection in activism has the danger of being labeled as "naive activism," devoid of reflection and purpose (Costa et al. 2021b). Within the formal curriculum, formal reflective assessment, scaffolded by training in reflective and critical thinking, may have helped students to develop further as true activist learners.

Yet, if activist learning is situated firmly in the formal curriculum, this undoubtedly will have its challenges. Student 2, who expressed the most externally focused activist goals for the project, saw a value to the project in being:

> a place to make mistakes. (Student 2, Year 2 of project)

A project for academic credit does not leave that same space for mistakes and failure or for unplanned and spontaneous experimentation. Requiring activism of students in a course, inherently requires risk for the students (Bubriski and Semaan 2009; Ludlow 2010). One could argue that reflective assessments in the formal curriculum, *could* provide the opportunity for failure where the assessment is based on reflection rather than the project outcome itself, yet failure that takes the form of diminishing interest and motivation and burnout – real challenges in activist projects – would undoubtedly impact on a credit-bearing assessment. Student activist projects clearly come with challenges for the students involved. Activism located in the informal curriculum at least allows students to step away from projects if the pressures become too great, although this could compound pressures on other students still committed to the project.

Another disadvantage of activist learning in the informal curriculum is the potential for cliques to form (Briggs et al. 2019), making it difficult for new students or students with different backgrounds or divergent interests to engage with projects. This is likely specifically heightened for the SSH, because it takes place in a private home. Although the SSH became a hub for student sustainability activism, debate, and discussion, it is likely that this was at the exclusion

Table 2.2 Summary of advantages and disadvantages of promoting activist learning through formal, non-formal, or informal curricula.

	Advantages	Disadvantages
Formal curriculum	• Staff support to help students through a range of issues • Opportunity for formal reflection to enable engagement with deeper systemic issues and enhance articulation of learning • Easier to ensure continuity of project(s) (where this is desirable) • Easier to develop and maintain trusted relationships with external stakeholders • Reduces competing time pressures for students as contributes to academic credit • Can be more inclusive of diverse participants • May be an easier entry point of activism for some students	• Difficult to allow failure in the ways associated with real-world activism • If projects are staff-initiated projects may be less meaningful to students reducing "motive fulfillment" • Creates a greater focus on individual grades, rather than community gains or project outcomes • Students may still not develop agency to drive their own projects if relying on staff support
Non-formal	• Can include requirements for reflection • Inclusive of diverse participants • Includes some staff support • May be an easier entry point of activism for some students • Voluntary nature of opportunities mean students will be motivated by project • Little implication of failure (to student)	• Reduces student agency • Students may still not develop agency to drive their own projects if relying on staff support • Requires opportunities to be developed which are of interest to diverse students • Opt-in and might not interest/impact large numbers of students
Informal curriculum	• Enables creativity and agency of students to act on their own inspiration • Provides a space for failure and experimentation • Allows students to disengage if needed for their own well-being • Reliance on peer support and learning • Potential for more working in a more genuinely collaborative way, in contrast to the sometimes more individualized, competitive ethos of formal education	• Can be cliquey and exclude more diverse participants • Might involve more limited reflection, and more surface level learning • Might lack support systems if students face difficulties • Students might have difficulty navigating systems and • Reliance on peer support and learning

of other individuals and groups, who did not feel comfortable entering this private space. Table 2.2 summarizes some of the advantages and disadvantages of promoting activist learning through the formal, non-formal, and informal curriculum.

Where does this leave us in thinking about whether activist learning belongs in the formal or informal curriculum, and what can we learn about how we as educators and ESD practitioners can support activist learning?

Even within the formal curriculum, activist learning can take place across a spectrum from more staff-led to more student-initiated projects, each of which will have their place depending on the intended learning outcomes, and student level and background. Dewey's four conditions to maximize the educative potential of inquiry-based learning requires activities: (i) to generate interest in the learner, (ii) to be intrinsically worthwhile to the learner; (iii) to present problems that awaken new curiosity and create a demand for information; and (iv) to cover a considerable time span and foster development over time (Bringle and Hatcher 1999:181). These conditions suggest that it is important to ensure student interest, which may help with more student-initiated projects. More staff-led projects run the risk of lower levels of "motive fulfillment," and less alignment between projects and students' ability to achieve their *personal* goals (Covitt 2002), compared to more student-led projects. *Quality* service learning has been described as including choice for students, as well as opportunities for meaningful action, with research suggesting that service learning designed by teachers can have limited impact on students' intentions of motive fulfillment (Covitt 2002). The formal curriculum can also lead to an individual, grade focus, rather than on broader, community, and change-focused aims (Ludlow 2010). Even within the same class, the diversity of students may mean one side of the spectrum between staff or student-initiated projects may be more appropriate for some students than others. Students could be given the option of a self-initiated project *or* a predesigned project *or* a choice of projects. It is conceivable that the SSH project could have been developed within the formal curriculum if the students had been given the freedom within their curriculum to initiate such a project.

The formal curriculum followed by the students involved in the introduction of the SSH project has a strong element of reflective learning as well as critically reflective discussion about sustainability issues, with the hope that this would develop a habit of reflection and criticality in all parts of their lives. Yet, at least in the interviews, there was limited evidence of reflection or critical thinking about broader sustainability issues (although the interviews might not have teased out deeper thinking that might have been occurring). Consideration of different ways in which reflective and critical thinking is developed in the formal curriculum could support this in informal curriculum learning, for example by introducing clear and explicit models of reflective and critical thinking that could be applied to projects, as well as through case studies demonstrating where these approaches are applied in the real world of activism.

One of the areas of challenges faced in the SSH project that was raised by several students related to communication and organization within the group. The formal curriculum can provide the space for explicit exploration of group roles and preferences (e.g. Belbin 2004) and group management and conflict techniques that students could draw on, both directly and indirectly, within informal curriculum projects.

Informal activist learning also takes place where activists learn "on the job" (Ollis 2008) whereby skills and knowledge are developed in the processes and practices of activism. Ollis (2008) describes how activist learning takes place through embodied and holistic practices, using the physical body and emotions to learn. Much traditional activism uses the body as part of protest (e.g. picket lines, locking one's body to objects) (Ollis 2008). It can be argued that the SSH also uses the body as part of this activism of the everyday, in the physical act of gardening or construction. This also forms an explicit part of the learning for some students:

> As far as the students go, some of them had never even done anything outdoors like this. Some of them had never held a saw or a screwdriver or even attempted to knock two bits of wood together, let alone build a raised bed, and there was a lot of doubt and resistance to giving it a go. (Student 2, Year 1 of project)

Engagement of the "head, heart, and hands" is seen as an effective and holistic approach to ESD, through engaging the cognitive, affective and practical dimensions of learning (Sipos et al. 2008; Mahmud 2017). This calls for maybe a greater degree of physical activity and action in the formal curriculum, a greater engagement of cognitive engagement in the informal curriculum, and ensuring the opportunities for students to act on their own affective domains in both formal and informal approaches.

2.6 The Relationships Between Staff and the Activist Learner

Staff involvement in the SSH project came from academic staff, university sustainability practitioners, and professional services staff such as the university grounds team and cleaning and accommodation services. Responsibilities from these teams lay around the upkeep and esthetics of the garden area, regular cleaning of the property, upkeep of the building, and adherence to regulations. Academic staff were involved initially in supporting the students in making the case to the university decision-makers for the establishment of the project, working with the university sustainability practitioners who took over overseeing annual recruitment into the house, and providing a point of support and guidance.

Professional service teams were essential in making the project happen, in agreeing to the idea, finding a suitable property, and adjusting residence recruitment processes, as well as the regular maintenance associated with any university-owned student residence on campus. However, there were also tensions around the roles and responsibilities of the students versus the professional services staff, including: decisions and responsibilities around the upkeep of the grounds; conflicts over the cleanliness of the house, exacerbated by the number of students (often with muddy boots) regularly using the property as a hub for student sustainability activity; the storage of materials students salvaged from waste found elsewhere on the campus, including blocking exit points; storage of bikes indoors; and behavioral complaints. Some of these tensions directly contravened university regulations. Observations over the years of the projects suggested that the student housemates in many ways appeared to believe themselves to be outside of such regulations, while the SSH is also more visible to accommodation staff due to its location close to their offices, further exacerbating tensions.

The students who initiated the project recognized the important role of the academic staff members in helping gain university support for the project. Having an established relationship with the academic staff, heightened by small cohort discussion-based teaching, ensured that students had a staff contact that they felt they could approach. As academic staff, Robinson was able to negotiate the appropriate university decision-making channels on behalf of the students, as well as provide reassurance to decision-makers about the students involved. Without this staff support we feel it is unlikely that the project would have been sanctioned.

However, tensions arose due to the different expectations of academic staff and students and their different perspectives and ambitions for the project. For the staff, this was an exciting, innovative student-led project which provided interesting research potential, and received external funding to support research into the pedagogy surrounding the project, as well as profile and publicity for sustainability initiatives at the university and the degree programs linked to the project. For the students, this was their university living experience and their personal lives. These tensions led rapidly to a more hands-off approach, allowing the project to be entirely student directed, with staff being available for guidance. Academic staff also became an avenue for additional communication, acting as enforcer and mediator, between professional services and students, where the student behavior was deemed unacceptable by professional services. In later years, university sustainability practitioners replaced academic staff in providing support for the students and the connection to the relevant university professional services. They also asked students how they wanted support throughout the year, which varied with each set of housemates from monthly or once-a-semester meetings to ad hoc support through a Facebook group chat when students had specific questions. The role of the sustainability practitioner removed the direct connection between academic staff with official responsibilities toward students through teaching and credit-bearing assessment, and the students' personal time and space. What can we learn from these experiences of relevance to supporting student activism more generally?

Projects that span the formal and informal curriculum can sit in an awkward space where both staff and student identities become blurred, expectations diverge, and the locus of control and self-determination shifts. Such projects span both the public and private spheres of student life. This caused several challenges. For the sustainability practitioner staff, who had a more informal relationship with students, were uncomfortable with how much of their personal lives students disclosed to them. Tensions also arose as a result of staff seeing university benefit for the project, and therefore tried to bring the students' private sphere into the public sphere through more direct control over the project, enforcing traditional staff–student power hierarchies, but within the students' private space. Although as an academic member of staff we may look on and see the lost potential of elements of the project, it should be remembered that this is student-led, that it is in their own private sphere into which we must be invited and onto which we cannot impose. Therefore, we must co-create the project expectations with students rather than impose our expectations, and ultimately be sensitive to their lives as students.

Staff support can clearly be important in a number of ways, including negotiating institutional structures and power dynamics, and advocating on behalf of students where others in the university may be cautious about student-led initiatives. Brinkman and Hirsch (2019) found that successful student advocacy projects involved staff from an early stage, providing continued mentoring and access to resources and social capital that a student might not have. Additionally, permanent staff may make it easier to help keep long-range projects going beyond the length of any individual student's time at university (Brinkman and Hirsch 2019; Laycock Pedersen et al. 2019). Ludlow (2010) describes how staff support can help unpick problematic issues of academic accuracy in student's work before it is more widely disseminated. Ludlow (2010) also highlights the risks that are required of activism, the potential challenge that comes with activism, and hence the need for mechanisms of clear accountability and avenues through which the intended audience can feed back. While in some ways it may be recommended that an academic member of staff takes on this role, particularly where activism is situated as part of formal curriculum activities, Ludlow (2010) discusses the dangers of staff seeing themselves as "protectors" of the students and the reinforcement of hierarchies that activist learning may seek to challenge.

The areas discussed here are all important areas of development of change agency. However, if such functions are carried out on behalf of and in isolation from students, then the opportunity for students to develop these change agency attributes becomes limited. Nor will learning about these processes of change consciously occur without reflection. Therefore, we suggest ensuring that students are included in these processes, treated as partners, and included in communication, and reflective discussions are facilitated, which might incorporate the role of more "academically neutral" university support.

The promotion of activist learning holds potential risk for academic staff (Ludlow 2010; Williford 2015), although this risk will in part be related to their standing and institutional capital (Ludlow 2010). The willingness to take such risks can relate to staff identities as professional activists (Costa et al. 2021a,b), also referred to as scholar-activists (Williford 2015). Although many ESD educators and practitioners might not see themselves as activists, many could be described as such, based on activist characteristics of knowing that they cannot take a neutral position, the desire to change the world (Ollis 2008), and the championing and challenging for systemic change (Costa et al. 2021a). By encouraging activist learning for students, work itself becomes a place of activism for the educator and practitioner. Bubriski and Semaan (2009: 96) encourage the educator to push students to "come out of their comfort zone – to try something new and potentially scary"; maybe we as educators should also be challenging ourselves in the same way.

2.7 Conclusion and Recommendations

The SSH project is student-led, aligned to the formal curriculum, and aims to enact social change through providing opportunities for exploration of sustainable living for future students, inspiring and informing a wider student body about sustainable living, developing change agency skills, and changing habits and behaviors of the students residing in the SSH itself. We therefore feel this project deserves the moniker of "activist learning."

As with most activism-oriented educational projects, the SSH project is limited in its lack of longitudinal evaluation of the impacts of such an approach. Such evaluation across a range of timescales is needed to help us understand what makes quality, not just any, activist learning.

In Table 2.3 we provide a series of recommendations that can be used to support activist learning across the formal, non-formal/informal, and hidden curriculum.

Table 2.3 Recommendations to support activist learning.

Curricula position of activism	Recommendation for educators
Activism projects in the formal curriculum	<ul><li>Create a range of project opportunities to suit different students and stages of activist engagement, from student-initiated projects to choices of prescribed projects</li><li>Be sensitive to different cultural interpretations and associations of activism</li><li>Encourage reflection on links between activist projects and the Sustainable Development Goals and sustainability competencies</li><li>Use sustainability competency frameworks (e.g. UNESCO 2017) to support reflection framing</li><li>Provide support for students particularly with negotiating different avenues of power, governance, and decision-making, but include students as partners in the process</li><li>Build in evaluation of the impact of activism projects on students at different timescales (gaining permission/communication channels for future contact for longer-term longitudinal evaluation)</li><li>Encourage and support more staff to engage students in activism projects throughout their degrees</li></ul>
Using the formal curriculum to support informal and hidden curriculum activism	<ul><li>Include theories of activism and activist learning in the formal curriculum</li><li>Emphasize the importance of inclusion and participant diversity as part of activism and sustainability requirements</li><li>Introduce reflective models and case studies of reflection used in activism</li><li>Emphasize the role of reflective practice in learning and project success</li><li>Encourage students to question what they see and what they want from the campus environment</li><li>Encourage students to understand their power and agency as key stakeholders in the university and wider communities.</li><li>Help students to understand the structures of universities and other organizations that can support change (such as Students' Unions)</li><li>Develop a curriculum which aims to inspire and empower students to take action</li><li>Use the formal curriculum to develop effective group and communication skills, techniques, and understanding.</li><li>Encourage quality relationships with academic and non-academic staff, providing a safe place to seek support to initiate projects</li></ul>

(Continued)

Table 2.3 (Continued)

Curricula position of activism	Recommendation for educators
Informal activism with staff involvement	• Ensure clear boundaries, responsibilities and expectations of staff and students are discussed at the start and reviewed. What support do students want from staff? • Encourage consideration of the impact of activities on inclusion of diverse participants • Involve academically neutral staff (e.g. university sustainability practitioners) as direct contact with students to reduce tensions and conflicts between different staff roles, particularly with projects in the student's more private spheres • Build in facilitated reflective review opportunities, with academically neutral staff where appropriate • Understand that students have different starting points and expectations of activism projects • Provide support for students particularly with negotiating different avenues of power, governance and decision making, but include students as partners in the process throughout • Support student ideas for activism • Support the continuation of projects, maintain relationships with key stakeholders, support the transfer of knowledge between student years • Support students with managing and interpreting failure
Informal activism without staff involvement	• Foster a culture of openness and support for activism within the university • Be available as a critical friend

As an ESD practitioner it is all too easy to uncritically extol the virtues of activist learning projects, and the role of such activist learning projects in the informal curriculum for the potential development of a wide range of sustainability competencies. Yet, our reflections uncover questions about the limitations within the informal curriculum, including whether the informal curriculum alone can deliver the learning potential the projects are capable of, without at least some informal structure for guided reflection and discussion. Yet, imposing a structure for reflection detracts from genuine student-ownership of projects, and might not be possible in genuinely student-led activity.

We might then look to the formal curriculum to deliver the potential of activist learning. The formal curriculum might allow us space for student-initiated activist projects and opportunities to structure assessment around a set of sustainability competencies, allowing deeper reflection and development of these competencies (see Robinson and Molthan-Hill 2021), and space for critical discussion and debate around deeper, systemic issues. Publicly declaring an activist agenda in learning and assessment design is itself controversial, with the risk of accusations of promulgating a particular political agenda or being at odds with other educational priorities and agendas. Yet activist learning projects can deliver to many different educational agendas from employability, student experience, and students as partners. It is also difficult in the formal curriculum to genuinely provide the space for mistakes and failure. Activism projects can also come with serious challenges from burnout to conflict, and the formal curriculum does not allow students to walk away from projects which are no longer working for them.

Working toward a more sustainable future needs action, and a holistic approach, engaging head, heart, and hands. It needs action which is underpinned by understanding, critical thinking, reflection, and inclusion, and allows students to drive change in their own areas of interest.

A traditional knowledge-based education does not give students the experience of taking action and applying their knowledge and thinking skills to driving change in the real world. Therefore, it is imperative that our universities provide spaces for students to take action and to become activist learners and provide the motivation and skills to both drive change, but to also reflect and learn. This requires the development of "activist learning for sustainability" opportunities within the formal, non-formal/informal, and hidden curricula, that can provide an exciting and innovative approach to meeting the aspirations of a range of agendas within higher education and empower our learners to drive the change they want to see in the world.

Acknowledgments

We would like to acknowledge the support and discussions around the project with Dr. Sophie Bessant and Dr. Sherilyn MacGregor, the student interviewees, and all the students involved in the project through the years, and to thank the Higher Education for funding to support the project.

References

Ackoff, R.L. (1974). *Redesigning the Future: A Systems Approach to Societal Problems*. New York: Wiley.

Adelman, S. (2018). The sustainable development goals, anthropocentrism and neoliberalism. In: *Sustainable Development Goals* (ed. D. French and L.J. Kotzé), 15–40. Edward Elgar Publishing.

Barlett, P.F. and Chase, G.W. (2004). Introduction. In: *Sustainability on Campus: Stories and Strategies for Change* (ed. P.F. Barlett and G.W. Chase). Cambridge, Massachusetts: The MIT Press.

Belbin, R.M. (2004). *Management Teams: Why they Succeed or Fail*, 2e. Oxford: Butterworth Heinemann.

Bilon, A.D. (2021). Toward an agentic approach to activist learning: the interplay between agency and learning in the narrative of polish activist. *Adult Education Quarterly* 71 (2): 166–183.

BIS (Business, Innovation and Skills) (2010). Skills for sustainable growth: strategy document. Executive summary. https://www.gov.uk/government/publications/skills-for-sustainable-growth-strategy-document (accessed 26 August 2021).

BITC (Business in the Community) (2010). Leadership skills for sustainable economy. https://sustainability.glos.ac.uk/wp-content/uploads/2017/07/BITC_Leadership_Skills-Report_July10.pdf (accessed 26 August 2021).

Blewitt, J. (2006). *The Ecology of Learning.: Sustainability, Lifelong Learning and Everyday Life*. Earthscan.

Bone E. and Agombar J. (2011) First-year attitudes towards and skills in sustainable development. Higher Education Academy. https://www.advance-he.ac.uk/knowledge-hub/2011-first-year-student-attitudes-towards-and-skills-sustainable-development (accessed 29 August 2021).

Botsaris, P.N., Giourka, P., Papatsounis, A. et al. (2021). Developing a business case for a renewable energy community in a public housing settlement in Greece—the case of a student housing and its challenges, prospects and barriers. *Sustainability* 13 (7): 3792.

Briggs, S.J., Robinson, Z.P., Hadley, R.L., and Laycock Pedersen, R. (2019). The importance of university, students and students' union partnerships in student-led projects: a case study. *International Journal of Sustainability in Higher Education* 20 (8): 1409–1427. https://doi.org/10.1108/IJSHE-01-2019-0050.

Bringle, R.G. and Hatcher, J.A. (1999). Reflection in service learning: making meaning of experience. *Educational Horizons* 77 (4): 179–185.

Brinkman, B.G. and Hirsch, K. (2019). From proposal to action: supporting student advocacy during graduate counseling training. *Journal for Social Action in Counseling & Psychology* 11 (1): 51–66.

Brundiers, K., Barth, M., Cebrián, G. et al. (2021). Key competencies in sustainability in higher education—toward an agreed-upon reference framework. *Sustainability Science* 17: 1–17.

Bubriski, A. and Semaan, I. (2009). Activist learning vs. service learning in a Women's studies classroom. *Human Architecture: Journal of the Sociology of Self-Knowledge* 7: 91–98.

Buchanan, J. and Griffin, J. (2010). Finding a place for environmental studies: tertiary institutions as a locus of practice for education for sustainability. *Journal of Teacher Sustainability* 12 (2): 5–16.

Carter, R. (1985). A taxonomy of objectives for professional education. *Studies in Higher Education* 10 (2): 135–149.

Chaplin, G. and Wyton, P. (2014). Student engagement with sustainability: understanding the value-action gap. *International Journal of Sustainability in Higher Education* 15 (4): 404–417.

Chase, S. (2000). The education and training needs of environmental activists and organizers. Unpublished PhD thesis. University of New England.

Cortese, A.D. (2003). The critical role of higher education in creating a sustainable future. *Planning for Higher Education* 31 (3): 15–22.

Costa, A.L., Vaz, H., and Menezes, I. (2021a). The activist craft: learning processes and outcomes of professional activism. *Adult Education Quarterly* 71 (3): 211–231.

Costa, A.L., Vaz, H., and Menezes, I. (2021b). Exploring the meanings of professional activism. *Community Development* 52 (2): 244–261.

Cotton, D., Winter, J., and Bailey, I. (2013). Researching the hidden curriculum: intentional and unintended messages. *Journal of Geography in Higher Education* 37 (2): 192–203.

Cotton, D., Shiel, C., and Paço, A. (2016). Energy saving on campus: a comparison of students' attitudes and reported behaviours in the UK and Portugal. *Journal of Cleaner Production* 129: 586–595.

Cotton, D., Bailey, J., and Tosdevin, M. (2020). Higher education and the climate emergency: exploring the hidden curriculum of the campus. In: *The Hidden Curriculum of Higher Education* (ed. T. Hinchcliffe), 29–40. AdvanceHE.

Covitt, B. (2002). Motivating environmentally responsible behavior through service-learning. In: *Advances in Service-Learning Research*, vol. 2 (ed. S.H. Billig and A. Furco), 177–197. Age Publishing.

Crump, J.R. (2002). Learning by doing: implementing community service-based learning. *Journal of Geography* 101 (4): 144–152.

Dagiliūtė, R., Liobikienė, G., and Minelgaitė, A. (2018). Sustainability at universities: Students' perceptions from Green and Non-Green universities. *Journal of Cleaner Production* 181: 473–482.

Drayson, R., Bone, E., Agombar, J., and Kemp, S. (2014). Student attitudes towards and skills for sustainable development. www.heacademy.ac.uk/sites/default/files/resources/student_attitudes_towards_and_skills_for_sustainable_development.pdf (accessed 27 August 2021).

Eagan, K., Stolzenberg, E.B., Bates, A.K. et al. (2015). *The American Freshman: National Norms Fall 2015*. Los Angeles: Higher Education Research Institute, UCLA.

England, Y.A. and Marcinkowski, T. (2007). Environmental service-learning programs in Florida high schools and colleges: nature, status and effects as determined by a statewide program census. *The Journal of Environmental Education* 38 (4): 51–60.

Frisk, E. and Larsen, K. (2011). Educating for sustainability: competencies & practices for transformative action. *Journal of Sustainability Education* 2: http://www.jsedimensions.org/wordpress/wp-content/uploads/2011/03/FriskLarson2011.pdf.

Gagnon, J. (2020). Campus activism: understanding engagement, inspiration, and burnout in student experiences. Honors Scholar Theses. 665. https://opencommons.uconn.edu/srhonors_theses/665 (accessed 24 November 2021)

Gibson, R.B. (2006). Beyond the pillars: sustainability assessment as a framework for effective integration of social, economic and ecological considerations in significant decision-making. *Journal of Environmental Assessment Policy and Management* 8 (3): 259–280. https://www.worldscientific.com/doi/abs/10.1142/S1464333206002517.

Gorski, P.C. and Chen, C. (2015). "Frayed all over:" the causes and consequences of activist burnout among social justice education activists. *Educational Studies* 51 (5): 385–405.

Gramatakos, A.L. and Lavau, S. (2019). Informal learning for sustainability in higher education institutions. *International Journal of Sustainability in Higher Education* 20 (2): 378–392.

Gruenewald, D.A. (2003). Foundations of place: a multidisciplinary framework for place-conscious education. *American Educational Research Journal* 40 (3): 619–654.

Haggar, P., Whitmarsh, L., and Skippon, S.M. (2019). Habit discontinuity and student travel mode choice. *Transportation Research Part F: Traffic Psychology and Behaviour* 64: 1–13.

Hassanain, M.A. (2008). On the performance evaluation of sustainable student housing facilities. *Journal of Facilities Management* 6 (3): 212–225.

Hassanien, A. (2006). Student experience of group work and group assessment in higher education. *Journal of Teaching in Travel & Tourism* 6 (1): 17–39.

HM Government (2011). Skills for a green economy: a report on the evidence. https://www.gov.uk/government/uploads/system/uploads/attachment_data/file/32373/11-1315-skills-for-a-green-economy.pdf (accessed 26 August 2021).

Hobert, T.M. (2010). A Follow Up Study of Eco education's environmental service learning program. PhD thesis. University of Minnesota.

Hopkinson, P., Hughes, P., and Layer, G. (2008). Sustainable graduates: linking formal, informal and campus curricula to embed education for sustainable development in the student learning experience. *Environmental Education Research* 14 (4): 435–454.

Jackson, P.W. (1968). *Life in Classrooms*. New York: Holt, Reinhart and Winston.

Keele University (2021). ESC-10043 module specification. www.keele.ac.uk/catalogue/2020-21/esc-10043.htm (accessed 26 August 2021).

Knight Frank Research & UCAS (2020). Student accommodation survey 2020. https://content.knightfrank.com/research/1663/documents/en/knight-frank-ucas-student-accommodation-survey-report-2020-6841.pdf (accessed 24 November 2021)

Kolb, D.A. (1984). *Experiential Learning: Experience as the Source of Learning and Development*. Englewood Cliffs: Prentice-Hall.

Kolb, A.Y. and Kolb, D.A. (2017). Experiential learning theory as a guide for experiential educators in higher education. *Experiential Learning & Teaching in Higher Education* 1 (1): 7.

Laycock Pedersen, R. (2019). Understanding and managing the impacts of transience in student-led university food gardens. Doctoral dissertation. Keele University.

Laycock Pedersen, R., Robinson, Z.P., and Surman, E. (2019). Understanding transience and participation in university student-led food gardens. *Sustainability* 11 (10): 2788.

Li, X., Tan, H., and Rackes, A. (2015). Carbon footprint analysis of student behavior for a sustainable university campus in China. *Journal of Cleaner Production* 106: 97–108.

Linder, C., Quaye, S.J., Lange, A.C. et al. (2019). "A student should have the privilege of just being a student": student activism as labor. *The Review of Higher Education* 42 (5): 37–62.

Liverman, D.M. (2018). Geographic perspectives on development goals: constructive engagements and critical perspectives on the MDGs and the SDGs. *Dialogues in Human Geography* 8 (2): 168–185.

Ludlow, J. (2010). Ecofeminism and experiential learning: taking the risk of activism seriously. *Transformations: The Journal of Inclusive Scholarship and Pedagogy* 21 (1): 42–59.

Mahmud, S.N.D. (2017). Engaging head, heart and hands: holistic learning approach for education for sustainable development. *International Journal of Learning and Teaching* 9 (2): 298–304.

de Moor, J., De Vydt, M., Uba, K., and Wahlström, M. (2020). New kids on the block: taking stock of the recent cycle of climate activism. *Social Movement Studies* 1–7.

OECD (2007) Thematic review on recognition of non-formal and informal learning. Country background report: United Kingdom. https://www.oecd.org/unitedkingdom/41782373.pdf (accessed 24 November 2021)

Ollis, T. (2008). The accidental activist: learning, embodiment and action. *Australian Journal of Adult Learning* 48 (2): 316335.

Orr, D.W. (1993). Architecture as pedagogy. *Conservation Biology* 7 (2): 226–228.

Ostrow Michel, J., Holland, L.M., Brunnquell, C., and Sterling, S. (2020). The ideal outcome of education for sustainability: transformative sustainability learning. *New Directions for Teaching and Learning* 161: 177–188.

Parece, T.E. and Aspaas, H.R. (2007). Reedy Creek clean up: the evolution of a university geography service learning project. *Journal of Geography* 106 (4): 153–161.

Parrott, K.R., Mitchell, K.J., Emmel, J.M., and Beamish, J.O. (2011). If you could be in charge: student ideas for promoting sustainability in housing. *International Journal of Consumer Studies* 35 (2): 265–271.

Pines, A. (1994). Burnout in political activism: an existential perspective. *Journal of Health and Human Resources Administration* 164: 381–394.

Purvis, B., Mao, Y., and Robinson, D. (2019). Three pillars of sustainability: in search of conceptual origins. *Sustainability Science* 14: 681–695. https://link.springer.com/article/10.1007/s11625-018-0627-5.

Rae, D. (2007). Connecting enterprise and graduate employability challenges to the higher education culture and curriculum? *Education and Training* 49 (8/9): 605–619.

Reed, M.S., Evely, A.C., Cundill, G. et al. (2010). What is social learning? *Ecology and Society* 15 (4): 1–10.

Redman, A. (2020). Assessing the development of key competencies in sustainability. PhD thesis. Arizona State University.

Robinson, Z.P. (2019). Geography as responsibility: sustainability through teaching and learning within geography. In: *Handbook for Teaching and Learning in Geography* (ed. H. Walkington, J. Hill and S. Dyer), 256–268. Edward Elgar Publishing.

Robinson, Z.P. and Molthan-Hill, P. (2021). Assessing competencies for future-fit graduates and responsible leaders. In: *Assessment and Feedback in Apost-Pandemic Era: A Time for Learning and Inclusion* (ed. P. Baughan), 196–213. Advance HE.

Rodríguez-Barreiro, L.M., Fernandez-Manzanal, R., Serra, L.M. et al. (2013). Approach to a causal model between attitudes and environmental behaviour: a graduate case study. *Journal of Cleaner Production* 48: 116–125. https://doi.org/10.1016/j.jclepro.2012.09.029.

Scott, W.A.H. and Gough, S.R. (2003). *Sustainable Development and Learning: Framing the Issues*. London: Routledge.

Shephard, K. (2008). Higher education for sustainability: seeking affective learning outcomes. *International Journal of Sustainability in Higher Education* 9 (1): 87–98. https://doi.org/10.1108/14676370810842201.

Sipos, Y., Battisti, B., and Grimm, K. (2008). Achieving transformative sustainability learning: engaging head, hands and heart. *International Journal of Sustainability in Higher Education* 9 (1): 68–86.

Sterling, S. (2003). Whole systems thinking as a basis for paradigm change in education: explorations in the context of sustainability. Doctoral dissertation. University of Bath.

Sterling, S. (2004). Higher education, sustainability and the role of systemic learning. In: *Higher Education and the Challenge of Sustainability: Contestation, Critique, Practice, and Promise* (ed. P.B. Corcoran and A.E.J. Wals). Kluwer Academic.

Still, G. and Kent, E. (1996). Connecting learning and activism: an experiment in adult higher education. In: *Celebrating Excellence: Learning and Teaching in Adult Higher Education. National Conference on Alternative and External Degree Programs for Adults (15th, Columbus, Ohio, October 5–7, 1995)*, 130–135. Washington, DC.: Alliance, an Association for Alternative Degree Programs; American Council on Education, Available at: ED402510.pdf (accessed 21 August 2021).

Tryon, E. and Stoecker, R. (2008). The unheard voices: Community organizations and service-learning. *Journal of Higher Education Outreach and Engagement* 12 (3): 47–60.

UNESCO (2017). Education for Sustainable Development Goals: learning objectives. https://unesdoc.unesco.org/ark:/48223/pf0000247444

UNESCO (2021a). Sustainable development goal 4 and its targets. https://en.unesco.org/education2030-sdg4/targets (accessed 19 August 2021).

UNESCO (2021b). Leading SDG 4 - education 2030. https://en.unesco.org/themes/education2030-sdg4 (accessed 19 August 2021).

United Nations (2015). 17 Goals to transform our world. https://www.un.org/sustainabledevelopment (accessed 24 November 2021)

Vaccaro, A. and Mena, J.A. (2011). It's not burnout, it's more: queer college activists of color and mental health. *Journal of Gay & Lesbian Mental Health* 15 (4): 339–367. https://doi.org/10.1080/19359705.2011.600656.

Vare, P. and Scott, W. (2007). Learning for a change: exploring the relationship between education and sustainable development. *Journal of Education for Sustainable Development* 1 (2): 191–198.

Verplanken, B. and Wood, W. (2006). Interventions to break and create consumer habits. *Journal of Public Policy & Marketing* 25 (1): 90–103.

Waddock, S. (2013). The wicked problems of global sustainability need wicked (good) leaders and wicked (good) collaborative solutions. *Journal of Management for Global Sustainability* 1 (1): 91–111. https://www.ejournals.ph/article.php?id=16147.

Watson, L., Johnson, C., Hegtvedt, K.A., and Parris, C.L. (2015). Living green: examining sustainable dorms and identities. *International Journal of Sustainability in Higher Education* 16 (3): 310–326.

Wenger, E. (1999). *Communities of Practice: Learning, Meaning, and Identity*. Cambridge: Cambridge University Press.

Wiek, A., Withycombe, L., and Redman, C.L. (2011). Key competencies in sustainability: a reference framework for academic program development. *Sustainability Science* 6: 203–218.

Williford, B. (2015). Combining problem based learning and activism in a feminist classroom. *Theory in Action* 8 (1): 23–50.

Winter, J. and Cotton, D. (2012). Making the hidden curriculum visible: sustainability literacy in higher education. *Environmental Education Research* 18 (6): 783–796.

Yin, R.K. (2003). *Applications of Case Study Research*, 2e. Thousand Oaks: Sage.

Zoo, A. and Steed, B. (2019). Bungalow life: The students living sustainably on campus. *BBC News* (24 September). https://www.bbc.com/news/in-pictures-49727821 (accessed 24 November 2021)

3

Outcome-Based Education Toward Achieving Sustainable Goals in Higher Education

G. R. Sinha, Nanda Gunawardhana, and Chih-Peng Fan

3.1 Outcome-Based Education (OBE) and its Significance

Among the 17 Sustainable Development Goals (SDGs) (García Reyes 2013; Swaminathan and Kesavan 2016; Hall and Tandon 2017; Rieckmann et al. 2017; TWI2050 – The World in 2050 2018; UN and Australian Government 2018; Franco et al. 2019; Kioupi and Voulvoulis 2019; Marshall and Oxfam Education 2019; Wright 2014; Nations 2015; Swaminathan and Kesavan 2016; UNESCO 2016; van't Land and Herzog 2017; UN and Australian Government 2018; Kioupi and Voulvoulis 2019; UNESCO 2019; Sinha 2021), sustainable growth in higher education has been placed in the important position of SDG 4 and it has been envisaged that by 2030 equality in access and the right to education will be same for all, including women, across the world. Education is key to resolving a number of problems that lead to socioeconomic challenges everywhere, and thus education and appropriate awareness among people in general can act as solution to most of the problems. A number of reforms, policies, strategies, and transformation measures have been developed from time to time in the field of education. In this chapter, the emphasis is given to higher education in which the OBE framework (Pritchett 2015; Kioupi and Voulvoulis 2019; UNESCO 2019; UNICEF 2019; Sinha 2021) has great significance and suggests that the outcome of education lies in the true assessment of student learning outcomes (SLOs) (Pritchett 2015; Kioupi and Voulvoulis 2019; UNESCO 2019; UNICEF 2019).

OBE-based education does not only empower the students or learners in developing the academic quality but strengthens a set of employability skills (Franco et al. 2019) in them. This set of skills helps develop competence in learners that enables further excellence. The ultimate goal of education is to achieve or to strive toward excellence, leading to an improvement in quality in life. As we know, OBE is envisaged to ensure the actual SLOs and should be reflected in activities, performance, acts, behavior, and attitude of the students when placed in industries or workplace. Generally, SLOs are articulated or formulated by keeping in mind the following important components of higher education organizations:

- Vision and mission of the university or organization.
- Program educational objectives (PEOs).
- Program outcomes (POs) (will be associated with graduate attributes).
- Course outcomes (COs) (will have course objectives as well).

The Wiley Handbook of Sustainability in Higher Education Learning and Teaching, First Edition.
Edited by Kelum A. A. Gamage and Nanda Gunawardhana.
© 2022 John Wiley & Sons, Inc. Published 2022 by John Wiley & Sons, Inc.

Every organization has its specific vision and mission statements (Coughlan 2011; Kioupi and Voulvoulis 2019) along with some short range goals (SRGs) and long range goals (LRGs) (Swaminathan and Kesavan 2016; Hall and Tandon 2017; UN and Australian Government 2018; Kioupi and Voulvoulis 2019). These goals, mission, and vision statements play a most significant role in formulating PEOs and POs; of course, POs (García Reyes 2013; UNESCO 2016; United Nations Development Programme 2017) are just expected outcomes which need to be truly validated at the end of the program if the POs are mapped with set PEOs. This requires an important process used in higher education and its transformation (Sinha 2021) that maps the relevance and the extent to which POs are actually seen in the students. The PEOs are major objective statements of specific programs and thus each program in a university department will have its own PEOs that are written not as simple statements but are formulated taking a number of stakeholders into consideration. The formulation of PEOs and POs involves a strong interaction and network with following stakeholders:

- Relevant industries
- Alumni
- Institutes/universities practicing research par excellence
- Parents
- Employers
- Students and others

This list of stakeholders (Franco et al. 2019; Kioupi and Voulvoulis 2019) plays a large role in articulating PEOs and POs because the expectations and dreams of each of the stakeholders are taken into consideration. Each program offers a number of courses and thus COs will be associated with all the courses offered (Coughlan 2011), and also the course educational objectives (CEOs). Before mapping happens between POs and PEOs, the same process needs to be performed to see whether envisaged COs are in congruence with the CEOs. In addition, the COs will be a subset of the POs and thus achieving or attaining a particular CO means contributing something toward any one of the POs. Vision and mission statements are also devised for departments and can be derived or formulated by keeping in mind the vision and mission statements of the overall organization. The mapping of SLOs with PEOs is explained in Section 3.2 with examples of practices that have been adopted to actually measure the attainment of SLOs in the students.

The CO can be expressed as: CO = {CO1, CO2, CO3, CO4, CO5, CO6, CO7,...} where {CO1, CO2, CO3, CO4, CO5, CO6, CO7,...} are, respectively, COs of course 1, course 2, course 3, and so on. Similarly, we can also write the PO as a sum or union of the POs of various programs. In addition, the PO is attributed to a number of COs. There are multiple COs because of the number of courses offered in the program, each with specific objectives and learning outcomes. The SLO are used to assess the impact of teaching learning and bringing about change in learners or students.

3.1.1 Significance of OBE

In the last decade, competition among the young has become tough in the job market and candidates can perform badly, even if they are employed in a good workplace. This happens because they do not possess a set of appropriate skills. A candidate or graduate can get employed or receive a job offer, that might be based on a strong academic background leading to the first impression of them during the interview as being satisfactory; however, this does not mean that the candidate is competent. This is a gray area to which most academic organizations do not pay attention, concentrating more on strengthening academic performance. The true significance of the OBE framework lies in ensuring a holistic view of studies; it not only requires good academic performance but a set of skills as well. The most important set of graduate skills needed to ensure that the SLOs are measurable, are:

1) **Strong written and verbal communication** (Coughlan 2011; Hall and Tandon 2017; TWI2050 – The World in 2050 2018): This is needed to present the knowledge acquired or product developed. Communication plays a significant role in the overall growth of a candidate and thus must be assessed carefully during a student's study.
2) **Critical and conceptual thinking** (Franco et al. 2019; Kioupi and Voulvoulis 2019): When students are exposed to the teaching learning process (TLP) of observable and assessable systems, then the development of critical thinking is inevitable. The ways students learn and think out of the box in a different manner, determine their ability to think critically.
3) **Fundamental knowledge** (Franco et al. 2019; Kioupi and Voulvoulis 2019; UNICEF 2019): Procedural study with a focus on understanding rather than rote learning, helps develop conceptual or fundamental knowledge of a subject.
4) **Self-initiative for learning and knowledge upgrades** (Coughlan 2011; Franco et al. 2019; UNESCO 2019). This can be developed by engaging students in suitable activities.
5) **Strong motivation, teamwork and integrity** (TWI2050 – The World in 2050 2018):
6) **Problem-/project-based learning approach**: Students should be given the opportunity to handle tasks individually or in a group, with certain objectives to be achieved and, of course, under the supervision of a teacher.
7) **Values in professional and personal life**: The ultimate aim of education is to improve the quality of life of self and others in society, and thus values have the same importance as academic aptitude does. Values can also be developed through a number of societal and technosocietal events aimed at improving the societal life.
8) **Positive attitude** (United Nations Development Programme 2017): Aptitude alone does not work, but aptitude combined with a positive attitude assists someone to attain growth. A greater height in sustainable growth can be achieved with a positive attitude in the workers. A positive attitude can also be learned during studies with the help of a number of co-curricular and extracurricular activities.
9) **Research-based approach** (Coughlan 2011; Wright 2014; UNESCO 2016; Hall and Tandon 2017; TWI2050 – The World in 2050 2018; Franco et al. 2019): Low-level research-centric tasks need to be assigned so that the students can understand the role of research and its importance in improving the quality of life through various advances in science and technology.
10) **Ability to think outside the box, and much more** (UNESCO 2019).

This list is not limited and there might be more skills that would empower the students. The OBE framework can include schemes for direct and indirect assessment, measurable outcomes, observable changes in the students, and positive ripples in the learners. The major salient points related to the importance of OBE are:

- It is a system of education in which student outcomes need to be seriously evaluated.
- The evaluation of the SLOs indicates the competence of the students or learners.
- The outcomes help students as well as employers in choosing the appropriate positions.
- The system requires the active and considerable participation of learners and teachers.

OBE provides a framework where one can truly assess the skill development, growth, and overall progress of students in any academic organization. The role of OBE is pertinent in evaluating the employability of graduates that further ensures that they not only are suitable for jobs but can also achieve sustainable growth in the job place. OBE can therefore be considered as an important tool for measuring the abilities of sustainability in students in the universities or any academic study place (McKeown 2006; Nations 2015; Swaminathan and Kesavan 2016; UNESCO 2016; Rieckmann et al. 2017; van't Land and Herzog 2017; UN and Australian Government 2018; Franco et al. 2019; Kioupi and Voulvoulis 2019; UNESCO 2019).

3.1.2 Sustainable Growth in Higher Education

According to SDG 4 of the SDGs (McKeown 2006; García Reyes 2013; Wright 2014; Nations 2015; UNESCO 2016; van't Land and Herzog 2017; TWI2050 – The World in 2050 2018; UN and Australian Government 2018; Marshall and Oxfam Education 2019; UNESCO 2019), sustainability in education is mainly controlled by curriculum (Franco et al. 2019), teaching methods (Coughlan 2011; García Reyes 2013; Marshall and Oxfam Education 2019), extracurricular activities, and learning assessment rubrics. To attain measurable outcomes in the students, we need to work on each of these categories very carefully. Despite a lot of challenges in achieving SDG 4, UNESCO (McKeown 2006; UNESCO 2016; Rieckmann et al. 2017; UNESCO 2019) has suggested wonderful guidelines and recommendations as to how the outcomes can be truly achieved and sustainability can be practiced. Students also need to be made aware of societal responsibilities (Coughlan 2011; TWI2050 – The World in 2050 2018; Kioupi and Voulvoulis 2019; UNESCO 2019) and responsibilities toward nature and climate change (UNESCO 2019). The following are recommended as major requirements for achieving sustainability in higher education:

- Formulating the achievable, measurable and pragmatic goals.
- Setting the objectives for learning keeping in mind about SDG 4.
- Involving all the stakeholders while writings POs and PEOs, not just getting online. feedback but also having interactions at regular intervals.
- Providing a holistic ambience of problem-based, research-based, and project-based learning.
- Motivating learners about the practical significance of OBE and SLO.s
- Outreaching to institutes of eminence which are actually practicing OBE in a true sense.
- Mapping the POs/SLOs with PEOs using suitable rubrics or mechanisms.
- Participating significantly on the part of policy-makers, revisiting the educational policies and modifying them as and when needed.

3.2 Pragmatic Mapping of Student Learning Outcomes and Learning Objectives

As we have discussed throughout Section 3.1, SLOs play a very significant role in the future prospects of the students and graduates. There are practices in SLOs and in their attainment that can be seen in the accreditation documents of most universities where the record of mapping between the student learning objectives and their learning outcomes is highlighted with the help of several examples from various programs and departments. However, the important thing in all the practices that are reported is the actual impact of mapping and the pragmatic approaches used in developing SLOs in the students. The activities that directly or indirectly impact the SLOs of the students are broadly:

1) **Curricular**: This includes academic activities mainly related to various components of the courses offered in the program, such as tests, assignments, examinations, and other direct assessment.
2) **Co-curricular**: The activities which are associated with various courses as supportive components such as seminars, group discussions, project based events etc.

3) **Extracurricular**: This is completely beyond curriculum and plays very important role in developing a set of skills in students, namely sports, various competitions etc. Case studies and survey on certain relevant topics also enable the students for developing unique qualities through these extra-curricular activities.

These activities are not uncommon and can be seen being practiced everywhere, but the ways in which they are carried out or performed actually determine the SLOs in the students. For the approaches that can be truly assessed through direct or indirect feedback or mechanisms it can be claimed that the outcome in the students through such activities has been truly inculcated. So, mapping that reflects the change in students is of great importance whether this has been part of assessment of the activities, academic, research, co-curricular, etc. Let us look at some pragmatic approaches that were used while assessing the SLO in the students, with the help of the delivery and assessment of two courses – Signals and Systems (ECE 3X20) and Image Processing (CSE 5X08). These two courses are among the many that were delivered by Sinha (one of the authors of this paper), and they are briefly discussed here to show a few of the pragmatics and unique methods of evaluating SLOs.

3.2.1 Specific Outcomes in ECE 3X20

A course, on Signals and Systems (ECE 3X20) was delivered to second year Engineering students in a BE (Hons) program that was offered to two streams Electronics and Communication Engineering (ECE) Students and Computer Science and Engineering (CSE) students. The number of students who registered for this course was 120 and the course was common for both CSE and ECE students. The assessment included the following main components:

1) Tests (Test-1, Test-2, Test-3, mid-term and comprehensive examinations [CEs]): The number of tests was kept to three in the subject being discussed here. However, that number can be changed, depending on the course being assesses. The mid-term examination is conducted in the middle of the semester and the comprehensive one is done at the end of the semester.
2) Group assignment (different approach).
3) Question-answering and a response during the lectures.

In normal tests, listed in (1) above, the practices were not very uncommon. Of course, the questions were set in such a manner to cater for all the objectives stated in the subject's course plan. The response was evaluated in each of the answer book how the answer could fulfill a particular objective which further means what outcome was attained by the student. Table 3.1

Table 3.1 Assessment and mapping of questions and their responses of tests.

Question number	Objectives	Outcomes	Mapping
1	Student Learning Objective (SL)-SL1	SLO1	Excellent attainment (EA)
	SL2		Average attainment (AA)
	SL3	SLO2	AA
2	SL2	SLO1	EA
	SL3		
3	SL1	SLO1	AA
	SL3		

shows a brief outline of the attributes which were seriously observed. This exercise was extensive and done for all the students.

The attainment was seen and evaluated on the basis of the quality of responses and thought process involved while answering the questions by the students. In addition, we also tried to see how the SLOs are contributing to the POs of the program in the department. In the OBE framework, the POs are important components of the vision and mission of any institute. The hierarchy is as follows:

- Vision of the university or department
- Mission of the program
- Program objectives (POBs)
- POs
- COs

The COs are derived from POs and, therefore, can have multiple SLOs. The COs are expressed as CO= {CO1, CO2,....} = {SLO1, SLO2, . . .}, meaning that a CO is a set of many COs and many SLOs. These outcomes are derived from the vision, mission, SRGs and LRGs. The next component is a group assignment that played the most important role among all three evaluation components. The description of the group assignment is briefly as follows:

- Each group (in our case, a pair) of students was assigned a topic to be worked. The group had one student each from CSE and ECE. The topics were problem-based, such as: "Why is a Fourier transform used in signal processing?"; "Give examples of five discrete signals that you see in your university and explain how the signals contribute in the system."
- The group had to study the topic thoroughly and understand the necessary concept and its significance.
- Then, the understanding of the topic had to be demonstrated in the form of a short PowerPoint presentation, preferably with no more than 15 slides.
- The students had to present this and record it as a video. A copy of the presentation and the video had to be submitted.
- Students were also given the option to present the topic directly via Skype.

Next the specific observations made during the evaluation were reported, as listed here:

- The students were apprehensive while the task was being assigned. The students seemed to lack both confidence and teamwork.
- The students were not at all prepared to undertake a Skype presentation. Only two teams of the 55 teams agreed to present this way.
- Generally, inside the classes while the course was being conducted, students were not very confident in responding to the queries or about having active interaction with the faculty.

The next stage was the evaluation of the students for the task just described. For the recorded presentation, the specific outcomes were observed as shown in Table 3.2.

Aa can be seen in Table 3.2, students exhibited a few important outcomes in good number. The students who demonstrated critical thinking were smallest in number and those who performed excellently in demonstrating communication skill and conceptual knowledge are very good in number. The observation required a lot of time and participation by the faculty. An interesting and noteworthy point was that the SLOs were measurable and observable in better ways compared with conventional tests and assessment components. Moreover, a significant

Table 3.2 Specific SLOs for the recorded version of response to the assignment.

SLOs	Number of students performing at different levels			
	Average	Excellent	Outstanding	Not exhibited
Fundamental/conceptual knowledge of the topic	52	32	21	15
Communication/presentation skill	56	41	19	04
Knowledge of mathematical concepts used	41	34	23	22
Critical thinking	23	16	12	69

change was reported in the four students of the two teams who agreed to present the topic via Skype. The important and positive changes that were measurable in the students were:

- The two students who had never been active and responsive inside the class, did very well. The reason for this performance includes encouragement, an opportunity to work something in team, active participation, responsibility for making the topic understandable, etc. The ways the students presented the topic, with a lot of research studies, using their references, and explaining properly, were wonderful.
- One student whose academic performance is generally excellent who is always reluctant to respond and interact during the conduct of the course, performed outstandingly in this assignment.
- The students learned online presentation and communication skills that will greatly help them in their career interviews and growth.

There was another important evaluation component, question-answering, involved during the course. Generally, most of the students do not respond or interact during the delivery of the lectures and course until a constant motivational environment is created inside the class. To overcome this difficulty and to encourage all to participate, the component of question-answering was made compulsory so that everyone could get the opportunity and exposure to be involved inside the classroom. The weighting of this component was made 5% of the maximum marks allotted in the subject for generating grading. This different type of assessment component resulted in the following measurable changes in the students:

- Students who had never tried before started answering, thanks to the constant motivation and weighting of the assessment.
- Students had to respond or even ask queries during the class hours.
- This could help them demonstrate a few important explicitly set skills, such as participation skills, communication skills, the ability to overcome hesitancy while responding, and the conceptual approach of learning.
- The students started asking questions whenever there was any ambiguity or doubt.
- Thus, the level of confidence was seen to be considerably high in the maximum number of students.

3.2.2 Set of Skills Developed in CSE 5X08

A different approach to the assessment and practice of OBE-centric components was followed in several other courses, one such being that of Image Processing (CSE 5X08). The components

Table 3.3 Specific SLOs of the recorded version of response to the assignment in CSE 5X08.

SLOs	Number of students performing at different levels			
	Average	Excellent	Outstanding	Not exhibited
Fundamental/conceptual knowledge of the topic	18	11	07	06
Communication/presentation skill	10	18	09	05
Knowledge of mathematical concepts used	17	12	06	07
Critical thinking	12	07	04	19
Programming skill	17	15	08	02

used in this course were almost similar to those in course ECE 3X20, except one more component was added. The components are:

1) Tests (Test-1, Test-2, Test-3, mid-term and CEs)
2) Group assignment (different approach)
3) Question-answering and a response during the lectures
4) Problem statements for practicing in a MATLAB or PYTHON environment

The assessment of the first three was similar to that for ECE 3X20. The number of students was different; however, the assessment impact of the tools used and observable ripples in the students remained same. The pattern of attainment of various types of skill set and SLOs remained the same as that of ECE 3X20. Table 3.3 shows the exact number of students in a class of 42 students who attended the course. This table presents the SLOs for each assignment component. This course also helped the students to attain programming skills since the theoretical fundamentals were practiced in a MATLAB environment.

The programming skill assessment component was also evaluated with the help of a structured assignment of tasks. The fundamental concepts covered in the class were formulated as major problem statements to be solved using either MATLAB or PYTHON, whichever the students were more comfortable with. This could help the students in developing strong programming skills and this aspect was observed while examining the programs, their concepts, algorithms, and application.

So, the ways in which the courses were conducted and assessed, as discussed, could truly helped in assessing the attainment of SLOs in the students. The attainment of SLOs is being emphasized because they empower students and make them competent so that they can enjoy a sustainable career growth. We know that the OBE framework is of great importance in achieving sustainable goals of higher education; moreover, the SLOs and their mapping with POs and COs play an even more important role in determining if students can actually demonstrate what has been taught or delivered to them.

The SDG 4 agenda highlights objectives of sustainability in education that talk about the specific set of skills to exist in learners in the education system (Tom et al. n.d.; TWI2050 – The World in 2050 2018; Franco et al. 2019; Kioupi and Voulvoulis 2019). Major competencies that were set as learning objectives under SDG 4 are:

- Critical thinking and system thinking competence
- Strategic and collaboration competence
- Anticipatory and strategic competence
- Problem-solving and self-awareness competence

If the above competences are seen in context with the case studies of mapping SLOs and objectives then we find that critical thinking, problem-solving, self-awareness, and collaboration can be seen and measured very clearly using the tool that has been discussed in the two courses. These two were not the only courses using this approach; the same or similar schemes were adopted in many other courses and SLOs were evaluated honestly.

Another initiative, TWI2050 (The World in 2050; 2018), discusses the transformative approaches and measures that can be used to achieve SDG 4 goals for higher education. The key domains of TWI2050 are listed as:

- **Human capacity and demography** (Franco et al. 2019): This is related to the development of human capital and associated demography with elated human resources.
- **Consumption and production** (UNESCO 2019): This is directly associated with the economy and also indirectly impacts the area of education.
- **Decarburization and energy** (Coughlan 2011): The impact of OBE also lies in responsibility toward nature by utilizing energy optimally.
- **Food, biosphere, and water** (Marshall and Oxfam Education 2019).
- **Smart cities** (Carminati et al. 2021) (Ullo and Sinha 2021).
- **Digital revolution** (UNESCO 2016).

All the above domains are correlated with SDG 4 one way or another because education and its transformation affect all the above sectors of growth and sustainability. Human capacity and human resources at the top of the list are the most precious resource that governs all other domains because the enhanced human capital will add to every other domain of the transformation listed in the TWI2050.

3.2.3 Question Level Mapping with CEOs and COs

Mapping becomes very relevant when it is performed at the question level, as each question in the test or in any of a course's examination component will be associated with one of more specific objectives and outcomes, that is CEOs and COs, the latter being expected to be attained on completion of the course. The COs will be subset of POs of the program under which the course is offered. For example, in a course called Signal Processing (ECE 4X09), named as SP, there are number of examination components and CE is one of them. In the CE, there are the following questions:

- Q1, Q2, Q4, Q5, Q7, Q9 are descriptive questions.
- Q3, Q6, Q8 are objective questions.
- Q10 is a numerical question.

The questions are set in such a manner that each question aims at assessing a certain SLO or CO in the student. The questions which are descriptive can have multiple parts, such as (a), (b), etc., or a single conceptual or design question. In either case, each question or part of the question must aim at assessment of a specific outcome of the student, which requires a lot of participation and effort from the teacher concerned with the course. In the course SP, if the COs articulated by the faculty are CO1, CO2, and CO3 and the objectives are CEO1, CEO2, CEO3, and CEO4, it becomes essential that each question be mapped with some CEOs, and attainment of a particular CO or multiple COs should be carefully evaluated while examining the answer book of a candidate. So, in the course SP, the following observations were reported:

- Q10 was associated with CO3 and it was evaluated whether the student has developed this. This indicates the ability of applying a problem statement and the data given, and solving the problem accordingly. The CO3 was mapped with CEO1 and CEO2 and it was found that the extent of the correlation was 77% while mapping the CEO1 and CO3. For mapping between CEO2 and CO3, the situation was found to be somewhat bleak, namely at 54%.

- The objective questions Q3, Q6, and Q8 were mainly associated with CO1 for attaining some fundamental knowledge of signal processing. The objective questions were not direct or rote-learning based but required lot of thinking and analysis. The students could answer these questions only if the course was fundamentally strong for the candidate. In addition, the mapping was estimated between CO1 and the related objectives CEO2. For questions Q3, Q6, and Q8, we observed the percentage of mapping as 34, 67, and 46% respectively for one candidate among 120 students. This indicates that the attainment for this student is satisfactory in Q6 but needs improvement for the other two questions.
- Similarly, we performed the analysis and mapping assessment for Q1, Q2, Q4, Q5, Q7, and Q9 which are descriptive questions.

3.2.4 Topic Level Mapping

As we know, each program has a number of courses and each course has a set of topics that are covered during the conduction of semester. So, when we discuss CEOs and COs, we should also reach up to the topic level for mapping; this would strengthen the mapping outcome and assessment of SLOs in the students. For example, the course ECE 4X09 has the following objectives:

- To understand basics of signals and systems (CEO1).
- To interpret the working of system and its characteristics (CEO2).
- To enumerate the examples of practical systems and their elementary processing (CEO3).

The same course has following learning outcomes to be attained at the completion of the course:

- The students will be able to define and identify various types of signals and systems (CO1).
- Students will be able to explain the real-time applications of various systems (CO2).
- Students will be able to simulate the signals and design typical systems for real-time applications.

The next stage is mapping between objectives and outcomes, and the COs can be realized in all the course topics, especially in the way the topics are handled during delivery of course. The major topics or the course are definition, types, and classification of signals and systems; elementary signals; representation of signals; definition and characteristics of systems; signal processing using ordinary filters; transforms used in signal processing. If these topics are mapped into any of COs, that would be the best possible scenario for attainment of learning outcomes in the students. There might be more ways to evaluate SLOs in addition to those we have discussed in previous sections and used in our case studies. For example, homework, research projects, essays, report writing, case study analysis, independent study, and other verbal quizzes.

3.3 Current Research on OBE

We explored the amount of research contributions in recent years in the area of OBE, SLOs, and sustainable goals in higher education. These contributions include research papers, articles, patents, and others. We have attempted to find out the research impact in these research fields, exploring some important databases, namely Google Scholar, Science Direct, ACM Digital Library, and Wiley Library. Our findings are summarized in Table 3.4, where it is very

Table 3.4 Research impact in OBE (last five years).

Research area	Number of research contributions			
	Google Scholar	Science Direct	ACM Digital Library	Wiley Library
Outcome-based education (OBE)	901 000	191 213	152 932	142 247
Assessment of student learning outcomes	157 000	31 754	145 258	82 003
Sustainable goals in higher education	193 000	47 054	131 806	29 755

clear that the research impact in OBE in general is higher than that of SLOs. While investigating the amount of research, we observed that generalized theories and significance are much researched, in comparison with the actual assessment tools and their impact, especially in the areas of SLOs. Overall, research activities in a focused manner, need to be much strengthened.

When we look at all 17 SDGs, we see that SDG 4 primarily deals with the higher education sector. This does not mean that other goals are to be achieved in complete isolation, rather there should be interrelation with educational goals. The following goals are associated with SDG 4 directly or indirectly:

- Gender equality (SDG 5) and good health (SDG 3) (UNESCO 2019) (TWI2050 – The World in 2050 2018)
- Descent work and economic growth (SDG 8) (UNICEF 2019)
- Reduced inequalities (SDG 10) (Pizarro Milian and Davies 2020)
- Sustainable communities (SDG 11) (UNICEF 2019)
- Climate action (SDG 13) (Franco et al. 2019; Kioupi and Voulvoulis 2019; Leal Filho et al. 2019; UNESCO 2019)
- Peace and justice (SDG 16) (Kioupi and Voulvoulis 2019)

The above SDGs do have a close association with education either directly or indirectly. For example, we aim at gender equality in providing access to education for all and, in reciprocation, the education and awareness among the general populace would also help in eradicating the menace of gender inequality. Thus, the educational goals and other SDGs actually help in transforming society and mankind so that everyone on the planet can lead a happy and healthy life. Good health is not accessible to most underprivileged people for two main reasons: the first is lack of financial ability and the second, which is an even more important factor, is related to education and proper awareness. Sometimes people suffer and die despite the health facilities and cover supported by government because the knowledge about accessing the facilities available does not exist. The economic growth of an individual as well as a country is predominantly affected by the quality of education. Through good quality education, research can be carried out and funds generated, and competent graduates who have passed through the OBE system will be capable of self and the national growth. Education, if truly imparted and evaluated, helps in addressing a number of societal issues that prevail in the society. Those who are properly educated will also be responsible citizens and will be sensible toward climate, nature, environment protection, societal values, and peace and justice for all. When we explored the research activities on major components and goals of sustainable development, we found that very limited research has been done – a situation which needs immediate attention. Research in education pedagogies and delivery is equally important as that which we do in other fields of science, technology, and engineering.

In a UNICEF (United Nations Children's Emergency Fund) report (UNICEF 2019), 1.8 billion children will be in middle- and low-income countries, out of which 420 million of them will not learn basic skills and 825 million will not acquire basic secondary level skills. This is an alarming situation which needed to be tackled by the world community so that every person has an equal opportunity to learn and to develop skills. An even more important factor than the quantity of learning is the quality of learning. The developed nations might step up and help low- and middle-income countries to elevate their education standards and make the basic infrastructure available so that each child can learn, but what is more important is the quality learning that depends on the ways in which teaching learning take place. The TLP has to be steered in a such a manner that the appropriate set of skills is developed in most children. In the UNICEF report, it is mentioned that a nineteenth-century education system cannot fulfill the requirements of twenty-first-century learning and this is why OBE is of the utmost importance; the OBE framework makes sure that learning takes place properly and leaves a unique mark in learners in the form of skills.

OBE also motivates growth in individuals as well as the organizations, which we can understand easily. Suppose student A of an institute I was found taking an interest in all the activities associated with the course, and more importantly the faculty F was sufficiently capable

to motivate student A to participate in teaching learning activities, then Student A could develop a unique set of skills in addition to an excellent academic profile, and gain employment at the end of final semester. The candidate could have tremendous growth in the industry and could now also contribute to a number of social activities and perform corporate social responsibility (CSR) as well. Another student B at another institute $I1$, might be even more intelligent than student A, both academically and in general aptitude, but might never have focused on skills, especially project-based skills and a research-based learning attitude. This candidate, too, might get employed but will have to face a lot of hardships and never progress in their professional career. This example motivates other students as well as institutes to follow the OBE approach.

3.3.1 OBE versus the Traditional Education System

We have had discussions with many subject experts in various courses, who have been imparting technical and science education for the last 40 years or more, and we found very interesting and contradictory responses about OBE. Most of them were of the opinion that there is nothing new in the OBE system but that all educational strategies have been followed for many decades. There were more than 65 participants from different diversities and streams of science, engineering, humanities, and technology in our discussions and we have included the general apprehensions, opinions, and our response defending OBE versus the old education system in Table 3.5.

Based on above discussion and response to the apprehensions raised, the following are the major advantages and disadvantages of the OBE system of education:

1) OBE and its impact are quantifiable and measurable, if suitable rubrics are genuinely used.
2) OBE encourages participation of candidates and all stakeholders in addition to continuous improvement in quality of the graduates.
3) OBE has the potential to contribute toward SDG 4 with the help of the practices used.
4) OBE enables candidates for lifelong learning, making them competent and able to strive toward excellence in their profession.
5) The major challenge is the participation of teachers and students, and this can be overcome by creating awareness about the importance and advantage of OBE to both learners and teachers.

Table 3.5 OBE versus old education system.

Opinion/Apprehension regarding OBE	Our response based on practicing OBE in a number of courses
OBE was already there and no need for mapping or assessing outcomes is felt even today (80% of the participants opined)	In the past, competition was not tough and most of the candidates who performed above average and who had good academic records were absorbed by employers, mostly in public sectors. However, those who had a specific set of skills always saw tremendous growth in their career. Of course, there was no need for mapping learning outcomes with the objectives.
OBE is a customary framework (i.e. documented but not practiced) and nothing new (92% of the participants opined)	We agree that there have been brilliant scholars, scientists, and other academicians in the past who have come through the traditional education system. However, time has changed and competition is cut-throat, and selection committees look for uniqueness in the candidates, not just academic records. This is where the role of outcomes in terms of specific skill set, also known as employability skills, arises. The continuous monitoring of mapping between learning objective and SLOs in all program courses always helps in improve graduates.
OBE and its impact cannot be quantified (67% of the participants opined)	This is not really true because there are number of rubrics and metrics by which the changes in students can be measured either directly or indirectly. The 360° feedback also provides reflection of students' performance in the workplace.
How does OBE improve the system? (74% of the participants opined)	The 360° feedback from all the stakeholders helps in revisiting all the PEOs, POs, SLOs, and even the vision and mission statements of the organization, and then the POs are aligned to see the desirable changes in the students.
The outcome is nothing but employment! (89% of the participants opined)	This statement is not completely correct. Though getting a job or employment is the result of an impactful outcome in the graduates, what is more important is the performance of the candidate after getting employed and achieving sustainability in growth of the self and the organization where the candidate is working.
The OBE framework is practiced in paperwork (98% of the participants opined)	This opinion arises because most of the average performing academic institutes do not like that the OBE details and outcome-attainment are maintained as paperwork, and they do not like doing this rather than actually practicing. This does not apply to good performing universities and organizations. It requires a lot of pragmatic approaches, best practices, and the involvement of learners, teachers, policy-makers, and the management of the universities.

There is great saying by an iconic spiritual monk, Swami Vivekananda, which goes "Education is the manifestation of perfection already in men." This has much relevance to OBE since OBE gives opportunities for every student or candidate to manifest their potential. In another important quote "Each soul is potentially divine," we find that the divinity is the eternal power that needs to be demonstrated, requiring the rubrics and practices to measure the quantum of manifestation in students. The million-dollar question is whether OBE has the capability to bring the infinite potential demonstrable in students. The answer is a big YES because OBE and its hierarchical structure support the manifestation and make it observable.

3.4 Strategies to Enhance Student Learning Outcomes and Concluding Remarks

Based on background studies, current literature, and the research on the impact of OBE for sustainable growth in higher education, discussed in this chapter, we recommend some specific strategies toward true mapping between POs/SLOs and PEOs so that we can achieve sustainability in higher education sector. The strategies are outlined here according to the major factors of the OBE framework:

1) **Formulation of vision and mission statements**: In most mediocre academic organizations, the vision and mission statements are formulated and shared among all stakeholders just as a customary, especially in most of the Asian nations. The statements formulated actually determine the roadmap of the institutes and thus, while being developed, the stakeholders who are accountable and associated with the progress of institute and the students need to be taken into consideration. This requires 360° feedback from all stakeholders, namely employers, industries, students, alumni, parents, etc. The feedback will provide an exact estimate of where the institute stands and what more needs to be achieved. Accordingly, the goals of the institution can be set as LRGs and SRGs. The goals so written should be in sync with SDG 4 in all their components or expectations.
2) **POs and PEOs**: Similar to vision and mission statements, POs and PEOs of the institutes have to be articulated in accordance with those vision and mission statements and must be derived from the organization's SRGs and LRGs. The goals set are to be SMART (specific, measurable, achievable, result-oriented, and timebound) so that the assessment can be made practically and plans made to overcome any gaps that might be present. Accordingly, POs and PEOs can be modified from time to time.
3) **Mapping**: Mapping is the most important step in a true assessment of growth in students if the students are to meet any of the goals under SDG 4 of sustainable goals of development. True mapping requires a lot of participation, time, and effort from learners as well as teachers. If the mapping is performed properly, then the identification of any gaps is ve,ry easy and accordingly the POs, COs, PEOs, CEOs, SLOs, and even the goal statements if required, can be modified. If we still believe that the set POs are achievable, then we will modify our best practices so that we can achieve the goals associated with the POs.
4) **Rubrics**: Mapping in a true sense between PEOs and POs requires a mechanism, metrics, or rubrics as important approaches that can quantify the impact of education in transforming the students into employable graduates. The rubrics play a very important role because scoring is evaluated in terms of suitable rubrics which can have three main components: rating scale, performance criteria, and indicators. The ability of rubrics lies in their determination of actual outcomes in students in the institute or in workplace.
5) **Focus on research and industry interaction**: A research culture and project-based learning have to be essential parts of the curriculum at all levels to help develop competence and a set of skills in students.
6) **Inclusion of independent studies and special projects in the curriculum**: Independent studies (IS) and special projects (SP) of three and four credits respectively can be offered to help develop a specific skill set in students. IS is actually a focused study on a certain topic that exposes students to the complete description, review, analysis, survey, and research about the topic assigned. This is a very important component in developing analytical skills, survey skills, critical thinking, judgment ability, reasoning, and critical review skills; if they study IS seriously, students demonstrate measurable changes in their skill set. Similarly, the SP is also offered, involving some kind of research, which is not very extensive, and other subcomponents of IS, aimed at developing a skill set beyond conventional academic components.

3.4.1 Strategies for Meeting SDG 4

"Every child learns" is the strategic statement of the 2019–2030 UNICEF plan. UNICEF has been trying its best to make sure that every child in the world is literate and formally educated so that they can stand on their own. In a broad statement of sustainable development for the planet, SDG 4 is dedicated to higher education and was set with a very specific 2030 agenda. Important points were included in the agenda, keeping some essential factors in mind. The main aim of the agenda is to provide education and access to it to all equally. So, our recommendation or strategic thoughts toward meeting SDG 4, are as follows:

1) **Primary and secondary education completely free to all**: This is an important agenda in visualizing SDG 4 so that absolute poorest can access education, since primary and secondary education are important ladders to higher education for employment and sustainable growth in personal and professional life. As far as OBE is concerned, it has not much to do with primary and secondary education. However, if the OBE type of pedagogy is adopted right from the start, then that would greatly help in getting goals achieved well in time. In fact, many practices are used in schools and institutes that actually help teachers to assess the changes in their students, but a formal or procedural means assessment can help this sector to ensure that we can meet the agenda in time for 2030.
2) **Equal access to quality education**: Access not only to education but to quality education has to be ensured; only then can we think about achieving this part of the SDG 4 agenda.
3) **Affordable technical, higher, and vocational education**: Access to all levels of education, including technical and vocational, is envisaged in SDG 4. In fact, better assessment of OBE and SLOs can be ensured in vocational and technical education. This chapter has discussed this with the help of some case studies. As far as vocational education is concerned, it involves lot of practical experiences that help students to attain the SLOs efficiently. Moreover, the assessment is visible and measurable in this system of education. So, while aiming at achieving goals articulated under SDG 4, continuous evaluation, mapping, feedback, and remedial measures can be taken adaptively.
4) **Skilled people for financial success**: The focus on skills development in young students and adults has to be relentless, as a skilled workforce is very much required to achieve sustainable goals in education as well as other sectors. The relevant set of skills must be inculcated and developed with practical knowledge, in addition to accessibility to an education system that not only caters for conventional education but also delivers skills enhancement and development. A student's skills play a major role in their career growth and make graduates competent professionals able to work against all odds and hardships and enjoy continuous growth that in the end helps the sustainable growth of the organization where they are working. Universal growth is determined by growth *for* all and growth *of* all. As we know, OBE is mainly based on assessment and it becomes much easier to evaluate if a set of skills is present in graduates; relevant skills are essential factors in the overall growth of students as well as the workforce. Another point to be noted here is that financial gain or freedom is achievable by skilled persons. With formal education, a skilled candidate can always have financial independence and can contribute toward family, organization, and the universe.
5) **No discrimination in education**: Discrimination is the biggest obstacle in education at any level and thus there should be a drive toward appropriate awareness and motivation so that there is no discrimination at all in terms of race, gender, etc. OBE and SDG 4 both aim at holistic growth for all, which demands inclusive education and growth for all through equal access to education and equal opportunities for all.
6) **Universal literacy**: This is another point of the agenda that ensures literacy for all. In fact, there is a philosophy in India for a holistic way of education, growth, health and society. The

vasudhaiv kutumbkam is the philosophy which means that the entire universe is a family. This can be a guiding principle in teaching pedagogy so that everyone in the world becomes literate, as education or proper literacy is the key to all growth and the eradication of all problems.

7) **Global citizenship**: The guiding philosophy also encourages everyone to be a global citizen, which makes candidates globally responsible for all.
8) **Safe schools and scholarships for developing nations**: This is also an important initiative for which the developed nations should come forward and help under-developed and developing countries through scholarship assistance so that their students can also have opportunities for quality and higher education in reputed educational institutions.
9) **Quality teachers in developing countries**: The true impact of education lies in its quality and hence teachers imparting education at all levels need to deliver quality teaching. This again requires assistance and support from elite educational institutes and countries that should come forward and help others in providing appropriate quality education techniques, assessment measures, and a 360° feedback mechanism to check if quality education is being received by all.

3.4.2 Knowledge Economy Through OBE

It is said that the world will be dominated or ruled by a knowledge economy, rather than the traditional economy indicated by gross domestic product (GDP). OBE has all potential to transform the youth of any nation into a competent workforce or knowledge agents that would be responsible for driving the major components of growth and indicators of the world. Therefore, OBE empowers the nation indirectly to become a knowledge economy, which becomes a further major reason for all-round growth in a professional and national sense. The salient characteristics of a knowledge economy nation are:

- Skilled workforce
- Demonstrable learning outcomes in graduates
- Lifelong learning attitude
- Self-awareness and improvement
- Learning from experience and revisiting the goals
- Competency development

If an organization or a nation has the OBE system satisfying all the above attributes, then the knowledge economy will not be very far from the SDG 4. Thus, OBE, through pragmatic examples and best practices shows how an individual or an organization can incorporate sustainability in their growth by gaining the attributes with the help of this outcome-based mechanism.

3.4.3 Concluding Remarks

We have presented the theoretical background, introduction, samples of case studies, and recommendation strategies to meet higher education goals under SDG 4. The concluding remarks of this chapter can be listed as:

- OBE needs to be genuinely practiced by all.
- The formulation of vision, mission, and goal statements should be written very carefully, taking all stakeholders into consideration.
- The mapping between outcome and objectives should be performed continuously.
- The goals of higher education and its sustainability should be tracked and attained in sync with SDG 4 goals.

- The attainment of goals needs to be monitored and necessary feedback has to be applied so that remedial measures can help in addressing any gap.
- Capacity building measures must be taken regularly with proper evaluation and monitoring.
- The feedback system in the education system, especially TLP assessment, must be very strong.
- Policy-makers need to revisit the entire system of devising the policies, strategies, functions, and other operational mechanisms used in education sector.

Acknowledgment

The authors express their sincere thanks to MIIT Mandalay, Myanmar for providing an excellent ambience to practice such an OBE framework and assessment tools for SLOs in students. We also express thanks to the students and faculty members who were involved in such an impactful study, and to the organizations of all the authors for providing great support in realizing the OBE type of educational pedagogy. The experience achieved through such a framework is the main source of encouragement for writing a chapter like this which would be impossible without the participation of students and, therefore, we finally thank our respective students and their involvement in participative learning.

References

Carminati, M., Sinha, G.R., Mohdiwale, S., and Ullo, S.L. (2021). Miniaturized pervasive sensors for indoor health monitoring in Smart cities. *Smart Cities*. Multidisciplinary Digital Publishing Institute 4 (1): 146–155. http://doi.org/10.3390/smartcities4010008.

Coughlan, M. (2011). *National Strategy for Higher Education to 2030*. Dublin: Department of Education and Skills: https://hea.ie/assets/uploads/2017/06/National-Strategy-for-Higher-Education-2030.pdf (accessed 24 November 2021).

Franco, I., Saito, O., Vaughter, P. et al. (2019). Higher education for sustainable development: actioning the global goals in policy, curriculum and practice. *Sustainability Science*. Springer Japan 14 (6): 1621–1642. http://doi.org/10.1007/s11625-018-0628-4.

García Reyes, L.E. (2013). SUSTAINABLE FOUNDATIONS: A guide for teaching the sustainable development goals. *Journal of Chemical Information and Modeling* 53 (9): 1689–1699.

Hall, B. and Tandon, R. (2017). Community Based Participatory Research and Sustainable Development Goals. Ottawa, Canada. https://unescochair-cbrsr.org/pdf/resource/BHALL_Community_Based_Research_ENG_Dec13.pdf (accessed 24 November 2021).

Kioupi, V. and Voulvoulis, N. (2019). Education for sustainable development: a systemic framework for connecting the SDGs to educational outcomes. *Sustainability (Switzerland)* 11 (21): http://doi.org/10.3390/su11216104.

Leal Filho, W., Shiel, C., Whereat, N. et al. (2019). Sustainable Development Goals and sustainability teaching at universities: Falling behind or getting ahead of the pack. *Journal of Cleaner Production* 232: 285–294. https://doi.org/10.1016/j.jclepro.2019.05.309.

Marshall, H. and Oxfam Education (2019). The Sustainable Development Goals: A Guide for Teachers. 32. https://oxfamilibrary.openrepository.com/bitstream/handle/10546/620842/edu-sustainable-development-guide-15072019-en.pdf?sequence=1&isAllowed=y (accessed 24 November 2021).

McKeown, R. (2006). Education for Sustainable Development Toolkit Version 2. UNESCO, (503), 1–142. https://unesdoc.unesco.org/ark:/48223/pf0000152453 (accessed 24 November 2021).

Pizarro Milian, R. and Davies, S. (2020). Inequality in higher education. *The International Encyclopedia of Higher Education Systems and Institutions.* 1699–1705. http://dx.doi.org/10.1007/978-94-017-8905-9_41.

Pritchett, L. (2015). Creating education systems coherent for learning outcomes: Making the i(December). Working paper. Research on Improving Systems of Education (RISE). https://riseprogramme.org/sites/default/files/2020-11/RISE_WP-005_Pritchett.pdf (accessed 24 November 2021).

Rieckmann, M. Mindt, L., and Gardiner, S. (2017). *Education for Sustainable Development Goals Learning Objectives.* UNESCO.

Sinha, G.R. (2021). *Assessment Tools for Mapping Learning Outcomes With Learning Objectives.* IGI Global.

Swaminathan, M.S. and Kesavan, P.C. (2016). Achieving the sustainable development goals. *Current Science* 110 (2): 127–128. http://doi.org/10.2307/j.ctv1gwqmr4.10.

TWI2050 – The World in 2050 (2018). Transformations to achieve the Sustainable Development Goals – Report prepared by The World in 2050 initiative, International Institute for Applied Systems Analysis. http://dx.doi.org/10.22022/TNT/07-2018.15347.

Ullo, S.L. and Sinha, G.R. (2021). Advances in IoT and smart sensors for remote sensing and agriculture applications. *Remote Sensing.* Multidisciplinary Digital Publishing Institute 13 (13): 2585. http://doi.org/10.3390/rs13132585.

UN and Australian Government (2018). Report On The Implementation Of The Sustainable Development Goals 2018. www.dfat.gov.au/sites/default/files/sdg-voluntary-national-review.pdf (accessed 24 November 2021).

UNESCO (2016). Unpacking sustainable development goal 4: education 2030; guide – UNESCO Biblioteca digital. *Environmental Education Research* 4 (7): 1–32. https://www.campaignforeducation.org/docs/post2015/SDG4.pdf.

UNESCO (2019). Discussion on SDG 4 – Quality education. *High-level Political Forum on Sustainable Development.* 14. https://sustainabledevelopment.un.org/content/documents/23669BN_SDG4.pdf (accessed 24 November 2021).

UNICEF (2019). Every Child Learns: UNICEF Education Strategy 2019–2030. *Unicef.* https://www.unicef.org/media/59856/file/UNICEF-education-strategy-2019-2030.pdf (accessed 24 November 2021).

United Nations (2015). *World Trends in Education for Sustainable Development.* http://doi.org/10.3726/978-3-653-04538-3

United Nations Development Programme (2017). SDG accelerator and bottleneck assessment. 1–72. https://www.undp.org/content/dam/undp/library/SDGs/English/SDG_Accelerator_and_Bottleneck_Assessment_Tool.pdf (accessed 24 November 2021).

van't Land, H. and Herzog, F. (2017). Higher education paving the way to sustainable development: Aglobal perspective. 28. Paris: International Association of Universities. https://www.iau-aiu.net/IMG/pdf/higher-education-paving-the-way-to-sd-iau-2017.pdf (accessed 24 November 2021).

Wright, T. (2014). Education for sustainable development. In: *Encyclopedia of Quality of Life and Well-Being Research*, 1814–1816. http://doi.org/10.1007/978-94-007-0753-5_839.

4

Transforming Ourselves to Transform Societies: Cultivating Virtue in Higher Education for Sustainability

Amparo Merino and Estela Díaz

4.1 Introduction

Over the last decades, it has become apparent that prevalent sociotechnical systems pose increasing challenges to social justice and to natural systems that sustain our lives (Kothari et al. 2014; Steffen et al. 2015). Systems such as those of water, energy, food, and mobility are dynamic social structures because they are constantly reproduced, shaping actors' perceptions of problems and guiding their agency (Augenstein and Palzkill 2016). Yet, actors (and their agency) are embedded in interdependent networks, in mutual dependencies, and in collective imaginaries that contribute to the stability of those systems, even though they are not coherent with sustainability principles (Geels 2004; Kallis and Norgaard 2010). Systemic transitions toward sustainable societies imply the coevolution of ecosystems, institutions, and technologies, as well as of the ideation or paradigms behind them (Kemp et al. 2007; Göpel 2016; Köhler et al. 2019).

Given this need to deconstruct imaginaries and paradigms toward sustainability transitions, the role of education to enable people to live together in a sustainable way has been widely recognized. For instance, Agenda 21 (UNCED 1992) referred to education as "critical for achieving environmental and ethical awareness, values and attitudes, skills and behavior consistent with sustainable development and for effective public participation in decision-making" (UNCED 1992, ch. 36.3). In the same vein UNESCO (2005), emphasizes that the fundamental aim of education from sustainability principles is to teach students "how to make decisions that consider the long-term future of the economy, ecology and equity of all communities" (p. 17).

However, education is arguably contributing to unsustainable living. Education is not providing learners with enough opportunities to question their own lifestyles and the structures that allow and promote unsustainable living, since educational institutions form part of those structures (Tilbury 2011; UNECE 2012). In particular, higher education institutions are failing to provide the forum for reflection, discussion, and action that enables learners to handle sustainability challenges (Foster 2001). As Wals and Jickling (2002) argue, higher education institutions hold the "responsibility to continuously challenge and critique value and knowledge claims that have prescriptive tendencies" (p. 221). Nevertheless, the dominant paradigm of education, embedded in a neoliberal ideology, encourages a type of knowledge that allows neoliberal[1] tenets to be internalized into the self-concept of students (Mitchell 2003; Foucault 2008). Therefore, little room is left for more critical, transgressive, and imaginative learning approaches capable of embracing alternative ways to define and organize social reproduction. This is the case of assumptions underlying the prevailing economic paradigm (e.g. the faith in infinite growth; the dominance of market mechanisms; the subservience to private capital) (Kothari et al. 2014; Feola 2020). As Orr (1990, p. 238) claims, more education of the same type, that "emphasizes theories, not values; abstraction rather than consciousness; neat answers instead of questions; and technical efficiency over conscience," will aggravate our socioecological problems.

Thus, shifting educational paradigms is paramount and yet challenging, given the dynamic and complex nature of systemic socioecological problems. These problems are poorly defined and typically involve conflicting framings on their causes and solutions; consequently, there is no innovative and permanent response to solve them (Blok et al. 2016). A clear illustration of such complexity is the controversial meanings associated with the idea of "sustainability." Hopwood et al. (2005) mapped the existing approaches to the sustainability debate, with very different worldviews and perceptions of the changes that are necessary to "achieve the goal" of sustainability. Some (dominant) views consider that a few adjustments within the present structures are sufficient; instead, others assume that those structures are at the very roots of the current socioecological crisis and, therefore, a substantial mind shift is required to deal with them (Göpel 2016).

Ultimately, the variety of worldviews coexisting in societies enlightens the fact that education is neither political nor morally neutral, and that it can serve different purposes, as stressed by critical pedagogists. From their perspective, education is always situated in a cultural context and it should integrate theory, reflection, and action to work toward social change (Gruenewald 2003). In this sense, they consider that a flexible and critical spirit would be a skill especially needed by societies in transition to highlight the contradictions between the ways of being, understanding, and behaving (see a seminal work on critical pedagogy by Freire 1974). Barnett (2004, p. 252) is adamant in this respect: "If there are no stable descriptions of the world, then there are no stable descriptions of 'me'. The 'I' is liable to be destabilized." Therefore, education as learning to live together in a sustainable way would involve questioning the assumed categories to describe our world. This exercise includes our understanding of who we are, how we relate to everything around us, and what we should do about it (Barnett 2004; Ehrenfeld and Hoffman 2013).

In sum, education for sustainability is both a moral and a political or civic endeavor, which implies opening spaces for learning to transform ourselves and to transform our society (i.e. spaces for free participation, consensus and disagreement, pluralism and self-determination [Wals 2010]). It is noteworthy that this transformative approach underlines the educational pillars of "learning for being" and "learning to live together," traditionally less prominent than those of (individually) "learning to know" and "learning to do." These components define the well-known framework of education developed by Delors (1998). An additional one was included afterwards by UNESCO (2008): "learning to transform oneself and society." This pillar integrates and provides direction to the others, as it emphasizes knowledge, values, and skills for self-reflection as well as for imagining futures, responsible lifestyles, adaptability, and active citizenship. In this sense, what Mustakova-Possardt (2004) describes as mature moral consciousness becomes key to addressing the present socioecological challenges: "a way of being, an optimal path of human development, which exhibits a wholesome engagement with meaning and positive change in one's social world" (p. 246).

---

1 A mostly cited definition of neoliberalism is provided by Harvey (2005, p. 2) as "a theory of political economy that proposes that human well-being can best be advanced by liberating individual entrepreneurial freedoms and skills within an institutional framework characterized by strong private property rights, free markets, and free trade."

From this rationale, we argue that we propose virtue ethics, as a fruitful approach to ground the development of moral and political dimensions of socioecological problems from a social transformative paradigm of education. Virtue ethics promotes the acquisition of virtuous ways of thinking, feeling, and acting. Ultimately, it helps to develop a virtuous way of seeing the world in so much as it is not primarily focused on individual duty and utility, but rather on excellence of character for the common good (MacIntyre 2007; De Ruyter and Steutel 2013; Carr et al. 2017). Inspired by the Aristotelian approach to virtues, we contend that virtue tradition provides a particularly appropriate framework to learn to *be in the world* when dealing with the systemic complexity and changing nature of current socioecological challenges.

In what follows, we first provide a brief background for a paradigm shift in (higher) education focused on transforming our beings to live together in a sustainable way. Second, we offer arguments to uphold our view that the Aristotelian approach to virtue ethics may help to nurture both the moral and political dimension of achieving that transformative purpose. Then, we provide some illustrations of how training the virtue of practical wisdom in the classroom might look like. We conclude this chapter with some final remarks on the challenges that we might face when educating from virtues on sustainability.

4.2 A Call for a Different Paradigm of Education: From Reproducing Systems to Transforming Ourselves and Society

Education for sustainability (ES hereafter) aims at bringing innovative responses for a long-term future of the economy, ecology, and equity of all communities, as mentioned in Section 4.1. Nevertheless, how to develop that goal is controversial. The debate can be structured around two main paradigms: the dominant *transmissive and instrumental* view of education; and the *transformative and emancipatory* paradigm (Foster 2001; Wals and Jickling 2002).

The transmissive and instrumental approach of education is focused on changing learners' behaviors; hence it implies a predetermined direction. Oriented to the promotion of certain ways of thinking and acting, it is built over a specific assumption: that learning occurs by mainly accumulating knowledge that is coherent with predetermined behavioral outcomes shaped by the requirements of market economies (Foster 2001; Vare and Scott 2007; Wals 2011). However, the complex, systemic and dynamic nature of sustainability challenges is marked by the diversity of views about the definition of the problems, which are intermingled with the definition of solutions, as clearly illustrated by the case of the climate crisis. Thus, the critical view of this approach resists an articulation of education that depicts sustainability as an "undisputed product" (Wals and Jickling 2002, p. 222), a linear mechanism that can be specified in advance by inducing the appropriate cognitive, conative, and affective skills (Gough and Scott 2003; Sipos et al. 2008). This paradigm ultimately accepts the assumption that we can agree on a desired behavioral outcome of an environmental education, and achieve it through carefully designed interventions (Jickling and Wals 2008).

This paradigm of education may be effective to deal with a type of problem in which the space of solutions, the systems of restrictions, and the performance function are definable, what make them fully solvable (Rittel and Webber 1973). However, the ill-defined socioecological problems are not like that and, as a consequence, demand a different type of education: a transformative and emancipatory education, defined by its processes rather than by its outputs; this implies an open-ended endeavor (Vare and Scott 2007; Barth and Rieckmann 2016). Furthermore, from this approach, education is characterized by enabling learners to think, feel, and act in a way that allows them "to cope with uncertainty, poorly defined situations and conflicting or at least diverging norms, values, interests, and reality constructions" (Wals 2011, p. 179). In sum, transformative and emancipatory education pursues the raising of critical awareness and, eventually, transforming problematic frames of reference (i.e. mindsets, habits of mind, and meaning perspectives, Mezirow 2003), with an aim to enhance citizenship for sustainability (Jickling and Walls 2008). Consequently, this type of education implies not only "doing things better" and "doing better things," but "seeing things differently" (Sterling 2011, p. 25). This approach is transformative and yet emancipatory, given that it may allow learners to raise awareness on how certain worldviews or ideologies pervade education. Neoliberalism is an example of these ideologies: a view that functions as a form of governmentality, as learners may understand that there is no other choice at the systemic levels, hence making it difficult to question it (Davies 2006).

Under transformative and emancipatory education "knowledge is not fixed, cut up in pieces and handed over, but rather (co)created by transacting with prior tacit knowledge, the curriculum, and other learners" (Jickling and Wals 2008, p. 8). Therefore, the focus of education moves from knowledge acquisition to a collaborative creation by a learning community, delving into the depth of human existence in the world, as Jarvis (2005, p. 14) highlights from a holistic approach to human learning:

> The combination of processes whereby the whole person, body (genetic, physical and biological) and mind (knowledge, skills, attitudes, values, emotions, beliefs and senses), is in a social situation and constructs an experience which is then transformed cognitively, emotively or practically (or through any combination) and integrated into the individual's own biography.

Specifically, our moral norms have significant implications on democratic citizenship, on civic action, and, ultimately, on our capacity to address complex socioecological challenges (Mezirow 2003; Sterling 2011; Jordan and Kristjánsson 2017). In fact, cognitive understanding of sustainability challenges and the agreement on the need to reformulate technical, economic, and social structures have not proven to be enough to change paradigms (Maiteny 2005). Mustakova-Posardt (2004) argue for the need to educate not only on critical systemic thinking, but also on critical moral consciousness.

The development of this critical moral consciousness is central for transformative ES, since it implies transforming ourselves to transform our social world. We defend that virtue tradition and character education may facilitate a productive space for such a moral development, allowing for an active dialogue between our inner and our outer world, i.e. between the moral and the political dimension of sustainability. Such space would be defined, as Dobson (2003) suggests, by the source of moral responsibility (i.e. "why are we obliged?") rather than by the object of obligation (i.e. "we have the obligation to do what?") (p. 48).

In short, virtue-oriented approaches to socioecological problems might allow us to acquire new ways of being in the world directed by the ultimate purpose of collective flourishing, as we will develop in Section 4.3.

4.3 A Response from Virtue Tradition

As a first approximation, virtues can be defined as moral dispositions that guide thinking, feelings, and acting (MacIntyre 2007). Although there is not a unitary approach to virtues, three features are shared among the defenders of virtue ethics (Nussbaum 1999): concern with the *agent*, together with choice and action; concern with the agent's *inner moral life* (patterns of reasoning, motives, and emotions); and concern with the *whole course* of the agent's moral life (patterns of commitment, conduct, and passion). From this common ground, cultivating compassion, for instance, would involve not only carrying out specific actions that show compassion, but also (and more importantly) developing compassionate thoughts, emotions, values, and attitudes (Hartman 2006). In other words, a compassionate character includes perceiving the necessity of compassion, experiencing it permanently, and driving one's life from feelings of compassion. Subsequently, concerning the role of good character in addressing ill-defined socioecological problems, virtues might enhance more sustainable ways of life based on inner feelings and dispositions for sustainability, rather than on a list of externally defined practices to be performed.

We specifically follow an Aristotelian approach to virtue (Aristotle 2014, hereafter Nicomachean Ethics, NE), mainly because of its aim at forming souls of excellence for the common good: *eudaimonia*, normally translated as "flourishing," "true happiness," or "a life worth living" (Hartman 2006; Kristjánsson 2015; Roberts 2017). As a non-instrumental goal or an end in itself, *eudaimonia* cannot be achieved without actualizing virtues (Kristjansson 2016; Roberts 2017). In addition, although Aristotle leaves the constituent and preconditions of *eudaimonia* open, he applies a political stance to it and considers it as a *common* good (Kristjansson 2016). In this regard, it is noteworthy that previous work in the field of environmental virtue ethics brought character traits to the field of environmental issues (Cafaro 2015); some examples are virtues of communion with nature, sustainability, respect for nature, stewardship, and environmental activism (Sandler 2018). In the same vein, we should highlight proposals of new virtues oriented to include interconnectedness with nature, such as the virtue of acknowledged dependence (Hannis 2015) and the virtue of harmony with nature (Jordan and Kristjánsson 2017).

Building on this literature we bring out four dimensions of Aristotelian virtue to ground the moral and political dimensions of ES: directional, relational, situational, and learnable.

4.3.1 Virtues Are Directional

As mentioned in Section 4.1, socioecological problems call for innovative responses that involve transforming ourselves to embrace new mindsets and behaviors in accordance with the complex nature of those problems. However, this complexity poses a huge challenge for coordinated social action. We argue that a virtue framework provides a coherent and plausible approach for tackling these problems, since virtues include awareness, thinking, and feeling that provide appropriate motives and disposition for appropriate action (MacIntyre 2007). For Aristotle, virtuous behavior, rather than the rightness of action, refers to the cultivation of virtuous character, which will guide the right actions (Carr et al. 2017). This distinction is very important because it highlights the relevance of acting *from* virtues versus acting in *accordance* with virtues. For instance, a generous person would act *from* generosity, which means that they have the internal disposition and motivation for generosity, rather than just in *accordance* with generosity, which may be due to the expectation of some type of external incentive (e.g. receive a reward or avoid a sanction). When explaining such an agent-centered approach to behavior, Aristotle argues that doing things virtuously is possible only when certain conditions are present inside the agent (NE 1105b):

> First, if he does them knowingly; second, if he deliberately chooses them and deliberately chooses them because of themselves; and third, if he does them from a stable and unchangeable state.

Such a stable character of a virtuous person nurtures their disposition to respond to *the right thing*, for *the right reason*, and in *the right way*, while also having *the right feelings* about it. As this idea shows, the Aristotelian account of virtue involves both rational and non-rational processes, thus reinforcing the internal component of virtue that provides orientation toward the *right* (i.e. societal flourishing). Moreover, emotion, together with reasoned action, is a central product of virtues (Roberts 2017). In this regard, Aristotle believed that virtue of character is "concerned with feelings and actions and it is in these that there is excess, deficiency, and the mean" (NE 1106b). In fact, emotions may be considered as an indicator that reveals the moral quality behind the action chosen by a person with good character (Hartman 2006). In this sense, Aristotle argues that virtuous actions are intrinsically pleasant: "No one would call a person just who did not enjoy doing just actions, or generous if he did not enjoy doing generous ones" (NE 1099b).

Thus, pro-environmental behavior sourced from good character and framed by the pleasure of acting from the internal source of character rather than from an externally imposed obligation and sacrifice might make a difference in terms of efficacy (Treanor 2014). As a result, virtue ethics may contribute to the much-needed societal coordination for sustainability problems inasmuch as it is one of the most agreed upon ethical frameworks, both historically and cross-culturally (Peterson and Seligman 2004; Crossan et al. 2013). The ideas of virtue and vice have been consistently used along history to express stable states of character that reflect praiseworthy or blameworthy behaviors, and that include perception, emotion, desire, deliberation, and action (Kristjánsson 2013). Consequently, this perspective could be easily accepted in a coordinated multistakeholder approach to the management of sustainability problems.

4.3.2 Virtues Are Relational

Virtues and the virtuous person are not self-generated, but are developed in relationship with the agent's communities (see Sanderse 2012). More specifically, virtues are relational because they are created *by* the community, from a specific cultural value and set of frames of reference virtues are learned and displayed *in* the community, through the interactions with our environments; and virtues are intended *for* the community, insomuch as personal flourishing is regarded as a collective task. Aristotle considered that a flourishing life is understood only as a shared life in the *polis* and can be realized only in a well-governed community (NE 1094b). Thus, a good life would be part of the general discipline of politics (Kristjánsson 2013, 2016).

As noted, ill-defined socioecological problems require collective work to map, identify, and reconcile values and goals behind action (Blok et al. 2016). Virtues, as the expression of collective flourishing, can provide a general compass for that collective work. The relational nature of virtues would emphasize agents' *commitment to* and *responsibility toward* the flourishing of the community rather than their *rights* in the community (Dobson 2003). Therefore, virtues would provide an effective moral and political grounding to ES and its focus on cultivating citizenship for sustainability.

4.3.3 Virtues Are Situational

A virtuous character includes values (with social flourishing as a compass) and the disposition to act on them in a stable way. Thus, even though virtue ethics emphasizes the agent's whole moral inner life rather than the rightness of their isolated actions, virtues can also be interpreted as inspiring principles or creating general prescriptions to act, i.e. doing what is honest, generous, just; or not doing what is dishonest, mean, unjust (Hursthouse 1999; Hartman 2006). However, the application of those general prescriptions is dependent on time, place, and culture (Sanderse 2012; Russell 2015), i.e. the agent requires the ability to perceive, sense, and deliberate how to act from virtue in each particular situation (Hartman 2006), as clearly illustrated by Yearley (1990, p. 14): "I do not act benevolently in order to be benevolent (...). I act benevolently because the situation I face fits a description of a situation that elicits my benevolence." Therefore, virtues provide the appropriate reasons and emotions to decide what to do in each situation we face (and why). This is especially convenient for contexts marked by complexity, novelty, rapid change, and uncertainty, as socioecological challenges are. In these situations, a predefined set of rules or a focus on the (unforeseeable) consequences of behaviors may be a doubtful foundation for knowing how to act.

The variety of skills needed to act virtuously across very different situations involves all kinds of virtues at play. However, Aristotle conceives virtues as interrelated and interdependent (Jacobs 2017) through one virtue: the virtue of practical wisdom or *phronesis*. Understood as a meta-virtue, since no other virtue can be exercised without it (Hursthouse 1999), *phronesis* can be defined as "the knowledge of which acts are virtuous in which situations" (Curzer 2012, p. 12). Aristotle highlights that, unlike scientific or theoretical knowledge, practical wisdom "is concerned with human affairs and what can be deliberated about (...). Nor is practical wisdom knowledge of universals only. On the contrary, it must also know particulars. For it is practical, and action is concerned with particulars" (NE 1141b).

Since *phronesis* is so central to virtuous choice, it deserves special attention when it comes to the ES of virtue, as we will develop in Section 4.4.

4.3.4 Virtues Are Learnable (and Teachable)

Aristotle distinguishes natural virtue from full virtue (NE 1144b). While we may have an innate disposition for justice, courage, compassion, or generosity, for instance, we need to develop understanding for those dispositions to be fully just, courageous, compassionate, or generous. In other words, it is because we learn to become fully virtuous that makes the virtuous acts actually virtuous (Curzer 2012, p. 12). For Aristotle, full virtue and practical wisdom are strongly intertwined, since "it is neither possible to be fully good without practical wisdom nor practically wise without virtue of character" (NE 1145a).

This means that we have to learn how to turn our natural receptivity to virtues into full virtues. We grow into virtues through habituation, and virtues require practice, in a similar way to acquiring skills, e.g. we evolve as a generous person by performing generous actions, as we become pianists by playing the piano (NE 1103a). But acquiring both virtues and skills is not a passive process; both need effort, focus, and the right kind of practice (Russell 2015). Nevertheless, there is a difference between acquiring skills and acquiring virtues: unlike skills, virtues are essential for flourishing, and their scope and depth for human life are broader (Kristjánsson 2013). Thus, it is not only the amount of practice that matters, but rather the way the agent understands and carries on that practice. Aristotle is adamant: "It makes a huge [difference], or rather, all the difference" (NE 1103b). So *eudaimonia* as collective human flourishing or true happiness for the common good would be the lodestar guiding the acquisition of virtue, and arguably also guiding ES projects. In this sense, Kristjánsson (2016) concludes from his review on flourishing as an overarching aim of education (p. 18):

> The uniqueness of a flourishing paradigm on human well-being lies in its insistence that education and teaching is woven into the very fabric of flourishing – as work in progress until our dying day – and that any effort deserving of the name "education" must be characterised as education for flourishing.

It follows from the above reasons that the practice of cultivating virtues requires guidance. This guidance goes well beyond mechanically imitating the acts performed by virtuous exemplars, but focusing on the qualities that make a person virtuous, allowing students to choose their particular perspective aimed at developing the right criteria to become so (Athanassoulis 2018). That perspective can only be understood from within (Sherman 1989, p. 418). Again, *phronesis* lies at the heart of the qualities that make a person virtuous, manifested in the ability "to see" what is required in each situation to arrive at a virtuous decision (Waddock 2010; Russell 2015).

4.4 Virtue Education in Practice: Exploring Pathways to Develop *Phronesis* for Sustainability

The arguments presented so far support the focus on cultivating practical wisdom in the goal to ground the moral and political dimensions of ES from virtue ethics. *Phronesis*, as mentioned, is not just another virtue, but the necessary one for moral virtues to be exercised. Reciprocally, one cannot execute practical wisdom without having all the moral virtues – they are interrelated in a kind of unity (Russell 2009) – since *phronesis* involves identifying the right virtues to the right ends of action: "It is evident that it is impossible to be wise in practice without being good," Aristotle states (NE 1144a).

Phronesis, therefore, provides the good judgment to resolve problems of specificity, relevance, and conflict by perceiving the moral aspect of a situation and by deliberating on how to act in the interest of the right end (Schwartz and Sharpe 2006; Russell 2015). Thus, the challenge of enabling people to address the complexity of socioecological problems would benefit from establishing *phronesis* as an explicit learning goal of ES. Cultivating practical wisdom helps us to act from virtue in the multiple situations in which socioecological global challenges unfold (e.g. when a policy-maker participates in discussions about new regulations affecting the climate; when a consumer makes a decision about whether to buy an attractive product or refrain from buying it; when an entrepreneur is faced with a conflict between social and economic benefit).

However, since practical wisdom comes from experience in real situations, theoretical knowledge is not sufficient to teach *phronesis* (Ames and Serafim 2019). This might seemingly make it difficult to include practical wisdom as a learning objective in formal education (Schwartz and Sharpe 2006); nevertheless, to the extent that experiential approaches are common in most educational projects, including a *phronesis* perspective in learning objectives would be worthwhile and feasible to implement.

In the following, we suggest pedagogical approaches that might serve as illustrations on how to bring *phronesis* into the classroom in the context of ES.[2] For that purpose, we draw upon the four-component model of *phronesis* by Kristjánsson et al. (2021), that aims to contribute to the operationalization of practical wisdom and to fill the gap between moral knowledge and action: (i) the ability to perceive the moral components and implications of a situation (*constitutive function*); (ii) the ability to judge and to prioritize virtues in conflicting or dilemmatic situations (*integrative function*); (iii) the ability to reflect on and understand what means flourishing (*blueprint function*); and (iv) the ability to adjust and foster the emotions that would be conducive to that flourishing life (*emotional regulative function*). For the sake of greater clarity, we present specific pedagogies associated with each one of the four components; however, they are by no means exclusive to this component, as is evident throughout the text.

---

2 As we explained in the Introduction, our standpoint is mainly that of higher education. However, the arguments provided and the pedagogies suggested to develop *phronesis* might well be applicable to all educational levels.

Also, it is important to note that, alongside this multifaceted quality of *phronesis*, its processual nature is also part of the emphasis of virtues on how (and why) the agent arrives at the right action, rather than the emphasis on the rightness of the action itself. In this sense, the *phronetic* process involves different stages, as explained by MacIntyre (1999):

> A chain of reasoning whose first premises concern the human good, whose intermediate steps specify what the virtues require, if human good is to be achieved, and whose conclusion is the action that it is good and best to perform here and now. (pp. 158–159)

Recognizing this spiral movement of awareness, deliberation, and choice through which *phronesis* develops according to the particularities of a situation can help guide its formation. As such, it is integrated into our proposals.

4.4.1 Perceiving (Constitutive Function)

The first stage in the chain of reasoning of *phronesis* entails the discriminatory capacity to recognize the moral issues of a given situation and which virtues are required (Kristjánsson et al. 2021). As Russell (2009) highlights, it is about the ability to "sense" and to "read" a situation so as to reflect on what to do.

Moral imagination stands out as a relevant ingredient in this stage in order to train practical wisdom, as it provides awareness and understanding of the consequences of different actions that may derive from a situation (Waddock 2010). In a well-cited work, Werhane (2002) defines moral imagination as "the ability in particular circumstances to discover and evaluate possibilities not merely determined by that circumstance, or limited by its operative mental models, or merely framed by a set of rules or rule-governed concerns" (p. 93). Moreover, Sanderse (2012) conceives moral imagination as a virtue itself, needed to deal with suffering and with the vulnerability of human life since it awakens our sense of commonness with others.

Thus, cultivating moral imagination to develop the *phronetic* capacity to "sense" and "read" the moral dimensions of challenges involves perceiving in a transformative way, as we argued in Section 4.2. In this sense, educators might focus on the awareness of dominant mental models as well as on the envisioning of new ones better aligned with the challenges posed by socioecological crises.

For that purpose, the development in the classroom of pedagogical activities designed from a systems perspective is key. The challenge of tackling most socioecological problems derives from the complex network of systemic relationships between worldviews, institutions, and technologies that define our current sociotechnical systems (Kallis and Norgaard 2010), as mentioned in Section 4.1. Thus, a systems approach has been widely acknowledged as necessary to address the dynamic interdependencies among economic, political, social, and ecological issues across temporal and spatial dimensions (Williams et al. 2017). A systems-thinking and multiple-perspective approach addressing such a complex network of relationships would be required so that moral imagination can be at work to question and reframe mental models (Werhane 2002, 2008; Waddock 2010). Ultimately, pedagogies that train systems thinking will be particularly useful for developing *phronesis* by focusing on the multiplicity of moral issues arising in the sociotechnical systems in which we are embedded.

A tool that might well contribute to achieve that goal is the use of maps in the classroom. If a picture is worth a thousand words, mapping might effectively connect learners with the multiple and interrelated domains, scales, actors, cause–effect relationships, feedback loops, and other systemic features of socioecological problems (see the proposal to operationalize the systems-thinking competence for sustainability by Wiek et al. 2015, and Werhane 2002, 2008 for working with the stakeholder theory). As Corbett and Lydon (2018, p. 113) state, maps "reflect our relationship to ourselves, to one another and to the environment .... Whether conscious or not, our cognitive or mental maps guide the paths and routes that make up our lives." Maps may thus be tools for transformation.

Students can be invited to brainstorm on the components involved in a socioecological problem they have identified. First, they could freely write down on a large piece of paper different words representing these components from as many different perspectives as they can imagine. For instance, words referring to concepts, emotions, principles, beliefs, technologies, causes, effects, institutions, collective actors, individual actors, time, places, geographies, and so on. When participants feel that no other elements come to their minds, they can be asked to think of the resulting word cloud from a systemic view rather than as a set of disconnected elements. As Meadows (2008) suggests, some questions can guide that task: "Do the parts affect each other?... Do the parts together produce an effect that is different from the effect of each part on its own?... Does the effect, the behavior over time, persist in a variety of circumstances?" (p. 13). Participants can then envision and depict connections among elements, again from all possible angles. Interconnections might include issues of power, time, causality, emotions, conflict, cooperation, harm, restoration, ideologies, sectors, levels, among many others. Finally, learners can be invited to deeply connect with the resulting "brainstorm system map" to disentangle the spaces of intervention where moral issues are relevant, so that they can individually and collectively reflect on those moral issues.

This type of activity might eventually contribute to the process of moralization, i.e. "the acquisition of moral qualities by objects or activities that previously were morally neutral" (Rozin et al. 1997, p. 67), of socioecological issues that have been traditionally addressed from technical grounds, such as urban mobility and emissions, or meat consumption. Moralization involves shifting mental models, at both individual and cultural levels, turning preferences into values (Rozin et al. 1997), thus potentially contributing to addressing more effectively the complexity of socioecological problems.

4.4.2 Judging (Integrative Function)

This second component of *phronesis* highly relates with the situational nature of virtues, which are so sensitive to the specific circumstances of the context and the agents in a situation. The integrative function involves the combination of different virtues as required by the situation (Kristjánsson et al. 2021), such as compassion for the suffering of others and the courage to do what might alleviate it. This function highlights the Aristotelian "unity of virtue" thesis (see a discussion on this view in Russell 2009) that arises from the very notion of practical wisdom: just as virtues require *phronesis* to be exercised, *phronesis* requires all virtues to judge what virtues are needed in a situation. Regardless of this unity, dilemmatic situations also can need the ability to arbitrate between different virtues being in conflict and to adjudicate priority (Kristjánsson et al. 2021), for example, between generosity and temperance in a context of resource scarcity.

Moral imagination is also salient here, as it allows us to conceive alternatives about how we could act from different virtues in a given situation and the corresponding consequences that would follow. But along with the use of moral imagination, the development of the integrative function of *phronesis* is deeply associated with the experience of facing complex situations in which the need arises to evaluate and weigh different and possibly conflicting virtues and courses of action.

However, the classroom context poses some limits to the variety of real-life situations in which learners can experience the integrative component of *phronesis*. Therefore, pedagogies involving simulations, role-play exercises, drama, and the like will be particularly useful. In any case, students must master the language and notions of virtues so that their moral imagination is not impoverished and they are able to describe and argue about the moral issues of a situation (Hartman 2006). Thus, educating students in the language of virtues and character would be a precondition for a more effective formation of the integrative function.

A fairly common pedagogical resource in many disciplines – particularly in business ethics and management education – is case study, a technique recognized as valuable for developing good character and bringing it through practical wisdom to complex situations (Hartman 2006; Jarvis and Logue 2016). Students are presented with a case that often involves moral dilemmas and controversies, in situations characterized by multiple variables, perspectives, stakeholders, and possible courses of action. Participants can then decide what actions to take, either by playing a previously assigned role in the case or from a more theoretical and detached perspective.

When role-play exercises and dramatic rehearsal are included in classroom activity, the understanding of morals as lived experience is fostered. The Deweyan proposal of dramatic rehearsal as an instrument for moral imagination and deliberation may provide young – and immature – students with valuable opportunities to make moral judgments and reflections, putting *phronesis* into practice without the risk of hurting others (McVea 2007; Jarvis and Logue 2016). In short, dramatic rehearsals "engage the whole human actor – her reason, emotions, and imagination – through a process of experimentation and reflection" (McVea 2007, pp. 376–377). For example, role-play and dramatic rehearsal could be used to confront students with the complexities of the energy poverty problem, which involves multiple actors, such as people suffering from lack of affordable energy access, energy companies, local, national, and international institutions, communities, non-governmental organizations, and social entrepreneurs – all of them interrelated in a complex network of relationships, implying issues of power and vulnerability, along with established business logics, technological dimensions, resource scarcity, and political dynamics, among others. Playing different characters in a dramatic rehearsal on energy poverty provides students with rich opportunities to feel the experience of a citizen with limited access to energy services and a lack of opportunities to live a fulfilling life, a corporate manager constrained by the pressures of global financial markets, a policy-maker struggling to address many conflicting interests, or an energy community seeking to address the variety of needs of its members. These experiences foster students' ability to understand – from reason and from emotion – the moral dimensions of the problem and to judge what kinds of virtues are most relevant to bring into play.

Finally, as in other activities to develop *phronesis*, individual and collective reflections on the learning experience of dramatic rehearsal help students to improve their awareness of the morals of a situation and, ultimately, to challenge their own assumptions and habits. In this regard, it is important to note that along with modeling and practice, dialogue is central to moral development in the classroom (Sanderse 2012).

4.4.3 Understanding (Blueprinting Function)

Blueprinting is about specifying and individualizing the general idea of how to live well by acquiring a deep understanding about our own moral identity and by making the appropriate decisions for this end (Kristjánsson et al. 2021). Thus, this function of practical wisdom allows learners to reflect on their own lives, to know what is important for themself. In other words, it can be understood as a pursuit of a "unify and integrated life" (Sanderse 2012, p. 147), a quest for living a virtuous life that is coherent and meaningful with the inner self, which would allow progress in the journey toward moral excellence or *eudaimonia*. In the end, realizing this component would mean "taking the formation of one's character into one's own hands"

(Sanderse 2012, p. 140), which constitutes a central message for Aristotle. In this regard, *phronesis* makes it possible to reflect on how to *be in the world*, in the sense of knowing oneself well to act virtuously (see Ames and Serafim 2019).

In blueprinting, the cultivation of virtuous thinking and virtuous motivation stands out. Thus, it would be pertinent to use pedagogical methods that help to identify and reflect on learners' moral judgment and commitment, attitudes, values, capabilities, aspirations, and behavior. We should emphasize here that learners' moral identity is always political, since becoming virtuous can only be understood in relation to others, to the community in a broad sense of the term (human and non-human world). This means that each one builds their moral identity not from solitude or in a vacuum, but from the moral dilemmas that arise from our relations with other beings: "We depend on others for our well-being" (Sanderse 2012, p. 142).

This remark is very important because the pedagogies chosen that aimed to strengthen and nurture those patterns of thoughts and motivation should reinforce this idea of interconnection with other entities by bringing up not only the self of the learner but also the moral identities of those other beings. That said, pedagogies focused on training the ability to discover oneself *in* the relationships with others, can find inspiration in contemplative practices, such as meditation. Let us illustrate.

Meditation has been gaining attention in the educational and academic realm in the last two decades (La Forge 2004; Boellinghaus et al. 2013; Hattam and Baker 2015; Upton 2017). There are many modalities of meditations, such as discursive and non-discursive meditation, mindfulness meditation, transcendental meditation, and mindfulness-based stress reduction (La Forge 2004; Black et al. 2009). Nevertheless, Upton (2017) highlights three features as central to any meditation: (i) employs self-focus skill (e.g. through the use of a mantra, item, process, or object); (ii) involves "logic relaxation," in which the practitioner tries to avoid evaluating or analyzing his/her thoughts and the actual experience; and (iii) brings "mental silence," together with a state of physical relaxation. Sometimes, meditation also involves a self-induced state, in which the participants are involved in "altered state/mode of consciousness, mystic experience, enlightenment, or suspension of logical thought processes" (Bond et al. 2009, p. 132).

In what follows, we propose a loving-kindness and compassion meditation (LKM hereafter) to show how this practice can be brought into the classroom to develop the current moral self and to imagine the self yet to be. LKM meditation is of Buddhist origin and aims to experience wisdom (defined as understanding the true nature of oneself and others) by incorporating cognitive and emotional aspects related to friendship, empathy, generosity, and respect (Salzberg 1995, 2005). LKM is based on a "nonjudging, nongrasping, nonrejecting orientation toward the present moment, an orientation that invites and makes room for calmness, clarity of mind and heart, and understanding" (Salzberg 1995, p. x).

A LKM meditation session lasts approximately 15–20 minutes and is normally divided into four main stages. The practice begins with awareness of the body and the mind, with the aim of turning their attention inward (e.g. body position, external factors, and state of mind). The next phase focuses on directing love and compassion toward themself by bringing to their mind the people who have loved them and wished them well. In the third phase, students will be asked to send love and compassion to people and other beings they know (e.g. friends, acquaintances, living or deceased relatives, non-human animals with which they live). Lastly, learners will send the same positive wishes of love and fulfillment to other people they do not know as well as to all living beings. After the meditation, the professor may encourage students to reflect or even write in a personal diary about their experience (e.g. what thoughts and emotions have arisen during the practice, if they have noticed changes compared to other times, how they feel afterwards).

This habit of writing about themselves leads us to another interesting pedagogy for nurturing blueprinting, that of using narratives for moral development. By narratives we mean any account or story involving real or fictional characters who face situations or have to make decisions that affect themself or others. The use of stories in class can be a fruitful way to encounter learners' thoughts and attitudes about the moral (or immoral) elements expressed in the texts under analysis (Sanderse 2012). Narratives can offer useful insights into the internal struggles, unsettlingly, doubts, conflicts, ambivalences that need to be confronted in order to become virtuous (Carr 2005, 2006a, b; Treanor 2014). Those stories can be based entirely on fiction, created by the professor or by the students (individually or in groups), or based on reality. In the latter case, stories can be narrated or inspired about situations in which the professor had to deal with moral dilemmas; or, even better, the professor has the student write about their moral experience. This last option is particularly interesting, if we take into account the relevant role that one's own experiences have in the development of virtues and the cultivation of *phronesis*.

In relation to sustainability, consumer diaries can be a good example of how to use story-writing in the classroom. The professor, at the beginning of the semester, will instruct students to choose a format (e.g. a notebook or folder) in which to document their experience of dialoguing with themselves regarding their consumption habits. The main objective of this exercise is to take an honest and critical look at their thoughts, motivations, emotions, and intentions that underlie their daily decisions. Little by little, as they observe and talk with themselves, students become aware of parts of themselves that they do not regularly pay attention to, such as what is important to them, what makes them excited, whether they think they consume excessively or not, what they consume for, what needs they try to respond to with consumption, and with whom they share these experiences. As a result of answering these questions, it is normal that they also start projecting themselves into the future, setting challenges for themselves, and reflecting their well-being and that of others. In sum, through these diaries, the students "understand and construct *themselves* through a process of imagining and telling stories about their lives" (Sanderse 2012, p. 148).

4.4.4 Feeling (Emotional Regulative Function)

As we have already pointed out, virtues are internal dispositions that guide thinking, feelings, and behavior (MacIntyre 2007). In other words, acting virtuously is the result not only of virtuous thoughts and motivations but also of virtuous emotions. *Phronesis* also helps in this regard, by overseeing the emotions that are at play in the particular situation and modulating the agent's emotional response most appropriate to the context. This process should be understood as infusing emotion with reason, instead of reason controlling or suppressing emotions (Kristjánsson et al. 2021). Although emotions have been largely neglected in moral education (Carr 2005), moral education is vital for finding "psychosocial equilibrium" (Kristjánsson et al. 2021, p. 11), in the sense of harmoniously aligning the reasons and emotions that lead us to a wise decision.

It is important to note that a wise decision does not mean a perfect decision, as it would always involve some kind of loss, struggle, and even sacrifice in the sense of giving up something or making an effort for the right end. Interestingly, while the other three components of practical wisdom (especially, the constitutive and integrative functions) help the agent to understand how other people see the world, the emotional regulatory function helps us to elucidate the most appropriate way(s) to see the world in a specific situation (Kristjánsson et al. 2021). Here it is also relevant to introduce otherness into the equation, since emotional regulation involves understanding not only one's own emotions, but also those of others. For Upton (2017) the relevance of the emotional regulatory function is evident, for example, in the cultivation of the virtue of helpfulness, in which the subject needs to be aware of their affective state, develop ways to regulate those affective states, and practice mental states that connect the subject to others (e.g. compassion, generosity).

That said, among the different pedagogies that can serve to cultivate this function, meditation seems also to be very appropriate. Upton (2017, p. 469) advocates for the cultivation of virtues through meditation, "which can help us to identify and regulate our emotions and moods. Further, meditation enables us to develop the attentional focus, emotional intelligence, and sense of social connection that ground (many of) the virtues and, thus, our virtuous behavior."

Leaving aside the goodness of meditation practices for the self, which we have also mentioned in the blueprinting function, we suggest that the use of art, such as music, painting, dance, literature, and film, also deserves special attention in terms of transforming emotions into a virtuous disposition (e.g. Cain 2005; Carr 2005, 2006a, b; Winston 2006). As Sanderse (2012, p. 137) notes: "Because music and other arts are believed to have the power to influence people's emotions, Aristotle believed that they can also be used to change those emotions for the better." This reminds us of Plato's connection between the "good," the "beautiful" and the "true," recently rescued by some authors (for instance, Winston 2006; Diessner et al. 2006; Sanderse 2012; Waddock 2010).

The use of art forms in class can be an effective method for students' emotional growth by allowing self-distancing from one's own judgments, providing new space for the moral, political, and spiritual aspects of the self, as well as facilitating reevaluation of one's own emotional responses (Carr 2005; Sanderse 2012). Furthermore, through art, students can gain relevant moral insight into themselves and society by inviting them to identify and reflect on their moral biases and normative perspectives, and by understanding that wrong ends can result not only from serious character flaws, but also from disordered desires and passions (Carr 2005). Finally, art can be a valuable tool to help students develop the virtue of compassion through understanding human diversity and vulnerability, as well as to connect emotionally with other people's aspirations, challenges, and struggles (Sanderse 2012).

As an example of how art can be included in the classroom to address these moral issues, an activity based on documentary pedagogies is suggested. First, the professor can choose a couple of film documentaries that they think students can feel emotionally and rationally engaged with and that are related to current sustainability problems, e.g. "Cowspiracy" or "Seaspiracy" to address issues of human and non-human animals relationships; "Miss Representation" and "The Mask You Live In" to reflect on gender differences in our society; or "Minimalism" to think on the excess of personal consumption. Second, the professor can ask them to write an individual essay in which they reflect on the moral issues raised in the documentaries and the different moral positions of the people involved in them, as well as their moral stances and emotions while performing the whole activity. As a last step, it is recommended to open a collective dialogue on their most relevant impressions about the documentaries; special emphasis should be placed on how they have regulated their emotions, and on their understanding of how their emotions affect their moral self and behavior. During the activity, the teacher should remind students that the classroom is a safe space in which to share experiences or ideas in a climate of trust that allows active and empathetic listening.

4.5 Final Remarks

Educating oneself and others in virtues is an exciting but complicated process and, as such, it is not without challenges. So far, we have presented arguments in favor of using virtues to educate for sustainability; in the following we would like to address some of the difficulties that we, as educators, can face when educating in virtues.

First, virtue education continues to be seen with skepticism; this attitude is sometimes based on a misunderstanding of what virtues are and what the purpose of using this approach is (see Kristjánsson 2013 for a review of myths about virtue education). For example, virtue education has sometimes been accused of being used as a tool for indoctrinating children (Sanderse 2012). This view may be partly influenced by one's own idea of education and the role it plays in society. In this sense, virtues could encounter more resistance if one assumes that education is a neutral activity and that educational communities should be spaces in which knowledge is simply to be transferred to students.

Another common criticism of virtue education is that it is overly individualistic, with the understanding that it is too agent-focused. However, both the concept of the good life and the path toward it only make profound sense as a collective enterprise; a journey influenced by the specific situation of the agent, but also by the idiosyncrasy of their pluralistic community that aspires to collective excellence.

In practical terms, a considerable challenge for educators is how to bring virtues into the classroom and how to integrate them into the curriculum. The literature suggests that it would be optimal to have the support of the whole educational community. In this sense, it would be advisable that professors receive some kind of training on how to use pedagogies aimed at fostering moral growth (Sanderse 2012). Additionally, it would be desirable that the culture of virtues and *eudaimonia* permeate the entire educational community (Kristjansson 2016); otherwise, there is a danger that it will become something exceptional (even freakish), relegated to a single course or understood as a personal project of some group of professors.

Even with institutional support, educators need to face another important issue: the role they play in the process of learners' virtue habituation. In this regard, studies of model education pedagogies could be very revealing (Kristjánsson 2006; Sanderse 2013; Athanassoulis 2018). We agree with Sanderse (2012) that we should not seek to become a person that students admire and want to imitate; instead, we should aspire them to become what we exemplify by inviting them to reflect on what it means for them to be virtuous. To this end, we must keep in mind that it is not enough that we behave in a virtuous manner. Given the relevance that intentions have in virtues, then we must also explain the reason underlying our (virtuous) actions.

Also, at times, it is possible that we, as educators, want to see ourselves as the spark that inspires students to self-change and flourish. However, we must be vigilant, as our ego may come to the fore. Instead, we might think of ourselves as part of a larger system working toward excellence.

Such a responsibility demands a great deal of humility. Becoming virtuous is a life project, an open-ended process; we need to remind ourselves that our relevance comes not because we are realized virtuous persons, but because we recognize the value of becoming virtuous and we strive for virtues (Sanderse 2012). In this sense, our moral interactions with students are micro-moments in our moral, political, and spiritual growth. The meaningfulness of these micro-moments will depend on the stage of moral development of students and our own, and where both meet on the journey.

References

Ames, M.C.F.D.C. and Serafim, M.C. (2019). Teaching-learning practical wisdom (Phronesis) in administration: a systematic review. *Revista de Administração Contemporânea*. 23: 564–586.

Aristotle (2014). *Nicomachean Ethics* (Translated by C.D.C. Reeve. Indianapolis: Hackett Publishing Company.

Athanassoulis, N. (2018). Acquiring Aristotelian virtue. In: *The Oxford Handbook of Virtue* (ed. N.E. Snow), 415–431. Oxford: Oxford University.

Augenstein, K. and Palzkill, A. (2016). The dilemma of incumbents in sustainability transitions: a narrative approach. *Administrative Sciences.* 6 (1): 1–23.

Barnett, R. (2004). Learning for an unknown future. *Higher Education Research and Development* 23 (3): 247–260.

Barth, M. and Rieckmann, M. (2016). State of the art in research on higher education for sustainable development. In: *Routledge Handbook of Higher Education for Sustainable Development* (ed. M. Barth, G. Michelsen, M. Rieckmann and I. Thomas), 100–113. London: Routledge.

Black, D.S., Milam, J., and Sussman, S. (2009). Sitting-meditation interventions among youth: a review of treatment efficacy. *Pediatrics.* 124 (3): e532–e541.

Blok, V., Gremmen, B., and Wesselink, R. (2016). Dealing with the wicked problem of sustainability: the role of individual virtuous competence. *Business and Professional Ethics Journal.* 34 (3): 297–327.

Boellinghaus, I., Jones, F.W., and Hutton, J. (2013). Cultivating self-care and compassion in psychological therapists in training: the experience of practicing loving-kindness meditation. *Training and Education in Professional Psychology.* 7: 267–277.

Bond, K., Ospina, M.B., Hooton, N. et al. (2009). Defining a complex intervention: the development of demarcation criteria for "meditation". *Psychology of Religion and Spirituality.* 1: 129–137.

Cafaro, P. (2015). Environmental virtue ethics. In: *The Routledge Companion to Virtue Ethics* (ed. L. Besser-Jones and M. Slote), 451–468. New York: Routledge.

Cain, A. (2005). Books and becoming good: demonstrating Aristotle's theory of moral development in the act of reading. *Journal of Moral Education.* 34 (2): 171–183.

Carr, D. (2005). On the contribution of literature and the arts to the educational cultivation of moral virtue, feeling and emotion. *Journal of Moral Education.* 34 (2): 137–151.

Carr, D. (2006a). Moral education at the movies: on the cinematic treatment of morally significant story and narrative. *Journal of Moral Education.* 35 (3): 319–333.

Carr, D. (2006b). The significance of music for the moral and spiritual cultivation of virtue. *Philosophy of Music Education Review.* 14 (2): 103–117.

Carr, D., Arthur, J., and Kristjánsson, K. (2017). *Varieties of Virtue Ethics.* London: Springer.

Corbett, J. and Lydon, M. (2018). 5. Community-based mapping: a tool for transformation. In: *Learning and Teaching Community-Based Research* (ed. C. Elmanski and B.L. Hall), 113–134. Toronto: University of Toronto Press.

Crossan, M., Mazutis, D., and Seijts, G. (2013). In search of virtue: the role of virtues, values and character strengths in ethical decision making. *Journal of Business Ethics* 113 (4): 567–581.

Curzer, H.J. (2012). *Aristotle and the Virtues.* Oxford: Oxford University Press.

Davies, B. (2006). Subjectification: The relevance of Butler's analysis for education. *British Journal of Sociology of Education* 27 (4): 425–438.

Delors, J. (1998). *Learning: The Treasure Within.* UNESCO.

Diessner, R., Rust, T., Solom, R.C. et al. (2006). Beauty and hope: a moral beauty intervention. *Journal of Moral Education.* 35 (3): 301–317.

Dobson, A. (2003). *Citizenship and the Environment.* Oxford: Oxford University Press.

Ehrenfeld, J.R. and Hoffman, A.J. (2013). *Flourishing: A Frank Conversation about Sustainability.* Sheffield: Stanford University Press.

Feola, G. (2020). Capitalism in sustainability transitions research: time for a critical turn? *Environmental Innovation and Societal Transitions.* 35: 241–250.

Foster, J. (2001). Education as sustainability. *Environmental Education Research.* 7 (2): 153–165.

Foucault, M. (2008). *Birth of Biopolitics: Lectures at the College de France 1978–79*. New York: Palgrave Macmillan.

Freire, P. (1974). *Education for Critical Consciousness*. New York: Continuum.

Geels, F.W. (2004). From sectoral systems of innovation to socio-technical systems: insights about dynamics and change from sociology and institutional theory. *Research Policy*. 33 (6–7): 897–920.

Göpel, M. (2016). *The Great Mindshift: How a New Economic Paradigm and Sustainability Transformations Go Hand in Hand*. Switzerland: Springer Nature.

Gough, S. and Scott, W. (2003). *Sustainable Development and Learning: Framing the Issues*. New York: Routledge.

Gruenewald, D.A. (2003). The best of both worlds: a critical pedagogy of place. *Educational Researcher*. 32 (4): 3–12.

Hannis, M. (2015). The virtues of acknowledged ecological dependence: sustainability, autonomy and human flourishing. *Environmental Values*. 24 (2): 145–164.

Hartman, E.M. (2006). Can we teach character? An Aristotelian answer. *Academy of Management Learning and Education*. 5 (1): 68–81.

Harvey, D. (2005). *A Brief History of Neoliberalism*. Oxford: Oxford University Press.

Hattam, R. and Baker, B. (2015). Technologies of self and the cultivation of virtues. *Journal of Philosophy of Education* 49 (2): 255–273.

Hopwood, B., Mellor, M., and O'Brien, G. (2005). Sustainable development: mapping different approaches. *Sustainable Development*. 13 (1): 38–52.

Hursthouse, R. (1999). *On Virtue Ethics*. New York: Oxford University Press.

Jacobs, J. (2017). Aristotelian ethical virtue: naturalism without measure. In: *Varieties of Virtue Ethics* (ed. D. Carr, J. Arthur and K. Kristjánsson), 125–142. London: Springer.

Jarvis, M. (2005). Towards a philosophy of human learning: an existentialist perspective. In: *Human Learning. A Holistic Approach* (ed. P. Jarvis and S. Parker). New York: Routledge.

Jarvis, W.P. and Logue, D.M. (2016). Cultivating moral-relational judgement in business education: the merits and practicalities of Aristotle's phronesis. *Journal of Business Ethics Education* 13: 349–372.

Jickling, B. and Wals, A.E. (2008). Globalization and environmental education: Looking beyond sustainable development. *Journal of Curriculum Studies* 40 (1): 1–21.

Jordan, K. and Kristjánsson, K. (2017). Sustainability, virtue ethics, and the virtue of harmony with nature. *Environmental Education Research*. 23 (9): 1205–1229.

Kallis, G. and Norgaard, R.B. (2010). Coevolutionary ecological economics. *Ecological Economics*. 69 (4): 690–699.

Kemp, R., Loorbach, D., and Rotmans, J. (2007). Transition management as a model for managing processes of co-evolution towards sustainable development. *The International Journal of Sustainable Development and World Ecology*. 14 (1): 78–91.

Köhler, J., Geels, F.W., Kern, F. et al. (2019). An agenda for sustainability transitions research: state of the art and future directions. *Environmental Innovation and Societal Transitions*. 31: 1–32.

Kothari, A., Demaria, F., and Acosta, A. (2014). Buen Vivir, degrowth and ecological Swaraj: alternatives to sustainable development and the green economy. *Development* 57 (3): 362–375.

Kristjánsson, K. (2006). Habituated reason: Aristotle and the 'paradox of moral education'. *Theory and Research in Education*. 4 (1): 101–122.

Kristjánsson, K. (2013). Ten myths about character, virtue and virtue education–plus three well-founded misgivings. *British Journal of Educational Studies*. 61 (3): 269–287.

Kristjánsson, K. (2015). *Aristotelian Character Education*. New York: Routledge.

Kristjansson, K. (2016). Flourishing as the aim of education: towards an extended, 'enchanted' Aristotelian account. *Oxford Review of Education*. 42 (6): 707–720.

Kristjánsson, K., Fowers, B., Darnell, C., and Pollard, D. (2021). Phronesis (practical wisdom) as a type of contextual integrative thinking. *Review of General Psychology* 1–9.

La Forge, P.G. (2004). Cultivating moral imagination through meditation. *Journal of Business Ethics.* 51 (1): 15–29.

MacIntyre, A.C. (1999). *Dependent Rational Animals: Why Human Beings Need the Virtues*, vol. 20. Chicago: Open Court Publishing.

MacIntyre, A. (2007 [1981]). *After Virtue: A Study in Moral Theory.* London: Duckworth.

Maiteny, P. (2005). Education for sustainability and development: psycho-emotional blocks and catalysts. *Development Education Journal.* 11 (2): 12.

McVea, J.F. (2007). Constructing good decisions in ethically charged situations: the role of dramatic rehearsal. *Journal of Business Ethics.* 70 (4): 375–390.

Meadows, D.H. (2008). *Thinking in Systems: A Primer.* Chelsea Green.

Mezirow, J. (2003). Transformative learning as discourse. *Journal of Transformative Education.* 1 (1): 58–63.

Mitchell, K. (2003). Educating the national citizen in neoliberal times: from the multicultural self to the strategic cosmopolitan. *Transactions of the Institute of British Geographers.* 28 (4): 387–403.

Mustakova-Possardt, E. (2004). Education for critical moral consciousness. *Journal of Moral Education.* 33 (3): 245–269.

Nussbaum, M.C. (1999). Virtue ethics: a misleading category? *The Journal of Ethics.* 3 (3): 163–201.

Orr, D.W. (1990). What is education for? In: *Hope Is an Imperative. The Essential David Orr* (ed. D.W. Orr), 237–245. Washington DC: Island Press.

Peterson, C. and Seligman, M.E. (2004). *Character Strengths and Virtues: A Handbook and Classification*, vol. 1. New York: Oxford University Press.

Rittel, H.W. and Webber, M.M. (1973). Dilemmas in a general theory of planning. *Policy Sciences.* 4 (2): 155–169.

Roberts, R.C. (2017). Varieties of virtue ethics. In: *Varieties of Virtue Ethics* (ed. D. Carr, J. Arthur and K. Kristjánsson), 17–34. London: Springer.

Rozin, P., Markwith, M., and Stoess, C. (1997). Moralization and becoming a vegetarian: the transformation of preferences into values and the recruitment of disgust. *Psychological Science.* 8 (2): 67–73.

Russell, D.C. (2009). *Practical Intelligence and the Virtues.* New York: Oxford University Press.

Russell, D.C. (2015). Aristotle on cultivating virtue. In: *Cultivating Virtue: Perspectives from Philosophy, Theology, and Psychology* (ed. N.E. Snow), 17–48. New York: Oxford University Press.

de Ruyter, D.J. and Steutel, J.W. (2013). The promotion of moral ideals in schools; what the state may or may not demand. *Journal of Moral Education.* 42 (2): 177–192.

Salzberg, S. (1995). *Loving-Kindness: The Revolutionary Art of Happiness.* Boston, MA: Shambhala.

Salzberg, S. (2005). *The Force of Kindness: Change Your Life with Love and Compassion.* Boulder, CO: Sounds True.

Sanderse, W. (2012). *Character Education: A Neo-Aristotelian Approach to the Philosophy, Psychology and Education of Virtue.* Delft: Eburon Academic Publishers.

Sanderse, W. (2013). The meaning of role modelling in moral and character education. *Journal of Moral Education.* 42 (1): 28–42.

Sandler, R. (2018). *Environmental Ethics.* New York: Oxford University Press.

Schwartz, B. and Sharpe, K.E. (2006). Practical wisdom: Aristotle meets positive psychology. *Journal of Happiness Studies.* 7 (3): 377–395.

Sherman, N. (1989). *The Fabric of Character: Aristotle's Theory of Virtue.* Oxford: Clarendon Press.

Sipos, Y., Battisti, B., and Grimm, K. (2008). Achieving transformative sustainability learning: engaging head, hands and heart. *International Journal of Sustainability in Higher Education.* 9 (1): 68–86.

Steffen, W., Broadgate, W., Deutsch, L. et al. (2015). The trajectory of the Anthropocene: the great acceleration. *The Anthropocene Review.* 2 (1): 81–98.

Sterling, S. (2011). Transformative learning and sustainability: sketching the conceptual ground. *Learning and Teaching in Higher Education.* 5 (11): 17–33.

Tilbury, D. (2011). Higher education for sustainability: a global overview of commitment and progress. *Higher Education in the World.* 4 (1): 18–28.

Treanor, B. (2014). *Emplotting Virtue: A Narrative Approach to Environmental Virtue Ethics.* New York: Suny Press.

UNCED (1992). Report of the United Nations Conference on Environment and Development, Rio de Janeiro. New York: United Nations.

UNECE (2012). Learning for the future. Competences in education for sustainable development. Geneva: UNECE.

UNESCO (2005). UN Decade for Education for Sustainable Development (2005–2014). Paris: UNESCO.

UNESCO (2008). Education and the search for a sustainable future, policy dialogue 1: ESD and development policy. UNESCO. https://archive.erisee.org/sites/default/files/UNESCO-Education%20and%20the%20search%20for%20a%20sustainable%20future%20%282009%29.pdf (accessed 23 July 2021).

Upton, C. (2017). Meditation and the cultivation of virtue. *Philosophical Psychology.* 30 (4): 373–394.

Vare, P. and Scott, W. (2007). Learning for a change: exploring the relationship between education and sustainable development. *Journal of Education for Sustainable Development.* 1 (2): 191–198.

Waddock, S. (2010). Finding wisdom within—the role of seeing and reflective practice in developing moral imagination, aesthetic sensibility, and systems understanding. *Journal of Business Ethics Education.* 7: 177–196.

Wals, A.E. (2010). Mirroring, gestalt switching and transformative social learning: stepping stones for developing sustainability competence. *International Journal of Sustainability in Higher Education.* 4: 380–390.

Wals, A.E. (2011). Learning our way to sustainability. *Journal of Education for Sustainable Development* 5 (2): 177–186.

Wals, A.E. and Jickling, B. (2002). "Sustainability" in higher education: from doublethink and newspeak to critical thinking and meaningful learning. *International Journal of Sustainability in Higher Education.* 3: 221–232.

Werhane, P.H. (2002). Moral imagination and systems thinking. *Journal of Business Ethics.* 38 (1): 33–42.

Werhane, P.H. (2008). Mental models, moral imagination and system thinking in the age of globalization. *Journal of Business Ethics.* 78 (3): 463–474.

Wiek, A., Bernstein, M.J., Foley, R.W. et al. (2015). Operationalising competencies in higher education for sustainable development. In: *Routledge Handbook of Higher Education for Sustainable Development* (ed. M. Barth, G. Michelsen, M. Rieckmann and I. Thomas), 265–284. London: Routledge.

Williams, A., Kennedy, S., Philipp, F., and Whiteman, G. (2017). Systems thinking: a review of sustainability management research. *Journal of Cleaner Production.* 148: 866–881.

Winston, J. (2006). Beauty, goodness and education: the arts beyond utility. *Journal of Moral Education.* 35 (3): 285–300.

Yearley, L.H. (1990). *Mencius and Aquinas: Theories of Virtue and Conceptions of Courage*, vol. 2. Albany: State University of New York Press.

5

Factors that Hinder the Implementation of Sustainability Initiatives in Higher Education Institutions

David Slim Zepeda Quintana, Javier Esquer, and Nora Munguía

5.1 Introduction

More than three decades have passed since the term "sustainable development" became popular through the Brundtland Report. Much has been done in the transition to more sustainable lifestyles; however, there are still many challenges to face. One of the most pressing challenges in recent years has been implementing sustainability initiatives in higher education institutions (HEIs). HEIs play an essential role in achieving sustainable development. Through these institutions, professionals, leaders, and citizens of the future are prepared and trained with a more sustainable conscience. They also serve as a seedbed and field of practice for implementing structural and physical strategies focused on the saving of and efficiency of resources and can serve as motivating and encouraging institutions for more sustainable lifestyles.

Although the implementation of sustainability initiatives on campuses is increasingly popular, there is a lag in policies, guides, and guidelines that ensure a significant positive impact. In this chapter, the factors that hinder the implementation of sustainability initiatives in HEIs will be addressed. This will be done as follows. In Section 5.2, the role of HEIs will be analyzed in more detail in sustainability and its participation in the achievement of the Sustainable Development Goals (SDGs) of the United Nations 2030 Agenda. In Section 5.3, the most popular and relevant strategies carried out in HEIs in different countries will be reviewed and analyzed. For this chapter, these initiatives are divided into strategies that promote sustainability in HEI facilities and those focused on education for sustainable development (ESD). In Section 5.4, the different challenges that exist to implement sustainability initiatives in HEIs will be discussed; an analysis is provided on the policies that HEIs carry out in terms of sustainable development, and, in addition, a series of challenges divided into three categories are analyzed: (i) economic challenges, (ii) sociopolitical challenges, and (iii) technical challenges. Finally, the last section will explore the factors that can contribute to overcoming the challenges previously analyzed in Section 5.3. As a result, this chapter aims to contribute to strengthening the capacities of HEIs around the world to implement sustainability initiatives at all levels and in all areas.

The Wiley Handbook of Sustainability in Higher Education Learning and Teaching, First Edition.
Edited by Kelum A. A. Gamage and Nanda Gunawardhana.
© 2022 John Wiley & Sons, Inc. Published 2022 by John Wiley & Sons, Inc.

5.2 Sustainability in Higher Education

Sustainability has become a central topic in higher education (Figueiró and Raufflet 2015). Over the years, it has become clear that education requires a process of adaptation to face the current challenges of our globalized and highly interconnected world. The Brundtland Report, Agenda 21, and the Earth Summit explicitly mention this challenge that education has faced in recent decades (Lozano et al. 2013). This became even more evident with the Talloires Declaration in 1990, where officially, for the first time, universities recognized this challenge and committed to sustainability through academic activities and also by adopting sustainable practices within institutions (ULSF 1990).

This evolution of education (higher education in particular) toward a more sustainable approach was formalized in December 2002 with the proclamation of the United Nations Decade of Education for Sustainable Development (UNDESD) led by UNESCO. The objective of this collaborative effort was "to integrate the principles, values, and practices of sustainable development into all aspects of education and learning" (UNESCO 2002). This transformation of education requires a holistic view of the modern world's environmental, social, and economic challenges. Therefore, it is about sharing sustainability topics in an academic environment and promoting a change in habits in students and in the entire scholarly community that favors the transition toward more sustainable lifestyles (Velazquez et al. 2005). It is for this reason that sustainability in higher education has garnered significant interest in recent years.

Of course, this transition has not been easy. There is still much to do; however, one of the most significant sustainability achievements in higher education is its wide dissemination worldwide (Blanco-Portela et al. 2017). As mentioned at the beginning of this section, the Talloires Declaration marked the beginning of a more real HEI commitment to sustainability in the 1990s; three decades later, sustainability in higher education is a mature field of study, widely discussed and, practically, the trend in terms of the operation of campuses internationally.

This is proof that HEIs, by conviction and will, have adopted sustainability principles at all levels (Stephens and Graham 2010). They have initiated systematic and significant changes in the way they educate, research, manage, and operate on a day-to-day basis. Additionally, they have involved different sectors of society, which has resulted in a symbiosis between the academic sector and the productive, governmental, and social sectors that potentiates the change of habits (Wals 2014). The HEIs themselves have become spaces that train and educate the professionals of the future in an environment that encourages the adoption of more sustainable lifestyles and, at the same time, they are the primary agents that push sustainability initiatives within and outside their campus (Velázquez et al. 2008).

5.2.1 The Role of HEIs in Sustainability

As mentioned in the Introduction to this chapter, HEIs play a key role in achieving sustainable development, particularly in communicating sustainability and boosting societal awareness; nevertheless, their impact is far broader. In this sense, HEIs' academic performance has changed throughout time from passive knowledge creation to a more proactive and engaged role within their communities (Peer and Penker 2016). In addition, as universities work with industry and government, the economic focus of universities' regional roles has shifted to encompass the triple helix system (Razak and Saad 2007). Furthermore, HEIs have an impact on local communities by serving as role models for sustainability and delivering socioeconomic benefits to their host communities through graduates that are employed in the area, or by developing living laboratories in collaboration with community stakeholders (Disterheft et al. 2012; Evans et al. 2015).

The contribution of HEIs to sustainability has been widely addressed in the literature, as has how they might operationalize their efforts to fulfill this contribution. For example, Lozano et al. (2015) conducted one of the most widely discussed and mentioned studies, establishing seven spheres in which HEIs can engage in sustainability implementation: (i) institutional framework, (ii) campus operations, (iii) education, (iv) research, (v) outreach and collaboration, (vi) on-campus experience, and (vii) assessment and reporting.

Stephens et al. (2008), for their part, broaden the definition of sustainable development by focusing not just on university operations but also on the content of teaching and research activities to characterize four different types of university action that assist long-term transitions toward sustainability:

1) Providing a model of sustainable practices for society.
2) Teaching students how to deal with complex problems and exercise system-thinking.
3) Performing practice-based research activities.
4) Promoting and enhancing engagement between individuals and universities situated as transdisciplinary agents.

In order to discuss in greater detail the role of universities in sustainability, we will address the analysis carried out by Radinger-Peer and Pflitsch (2017), who describe four main channels through which HEIs can contribute to sustainability, as shown in Table 5.1. These channels are teaching, research, outreach, and organizational and field-level influences.

HEIs, without a doubt, have several characteristics that can help us make the transition to a more sustainable future. First, universities have begun the transition to a new paradigm in their substantive functions, even though it is a complex process (Luna-Krauletz et al. 2021). Second, HEIs have a direct and indirect impact on society, which carries an inherent responsibility to contribute to the construction of a more sustainable society (Findler et al. 2019).

5.2.2 Higher Education on the 2030 Agenda

Although HEIs have shown a commitment to sustainable development through disseminating the concept and implementing sustainability strategies in their operations, they had never been formally included in international development agendas until the birth of the 2030 Agenda (Mallow 2020). The Agenda document contains 17 SDGs, which continue the Millennium Declaration's goals (UN 2015). The SDGs address challenges that are important for optimal human growth, gender equality, disparities reduction, climate action, and high-quality education are among the development goals outlined (DESA 2016).

Higher education is an important aspect of the 2030 Agenda; in particular, the terms "university" and "higher education" are mentioned in SDG 4: Quality Education, which was not the case in its two significant predecessors, the Millennium Development Goals and the UNESCO Education for All Framework (Mallow 2020). Although they had not previously been mentioned in international agendas and have not prevented HEIs from adopting sustainability principles, their official acknowledgment in the current agenda demonstrates how critical they are to achieving the SDGs.

The SDGs address a wide variety of difficult social, economic, and environmental issues, and meeting them will necessitate changes in how societies and economies operate, as well as how we interact with our environment. Education, research, innovation, and leadership will be critical in assisting society in dealing with these issues (Avelar et al. 2019). With their broad mandate for knowledge development and dissemination and their unique position within society, HEIs play a key role in achieving the SDGs. Without HEIs, meeting any of the SDGs would be impossible.

According to the Sustainable Development Solutions Network (2017), HEIs can: (i) provide the knowledge and solutions to underpin the implementation of the SDGs; (ii) create current and future SDGs implementers; (iii) embody the principles of the SDGs through organizational governance, operations, and culture; and (iv) provide cross-sectoral leadership in implementation. In addition, universities can directly contribute to the fulfillment of the SDGs through

Table 5.1 Contribution of HEIs via different channels.

Teaching	Teaching activities can be considered a key driver of long-term institutional change in the region, as graduates and their sustainability awareness function as multipliers and can deal with the region's complex challenges.
	While a theoretical understanding of sustainability concerns aids in raising awareness, practical student initiatives in conjunction with regional stakeholders can directly impact the region's transition route.
	Sustainability could be used as a theoretical component in various lectures or a springboard for actual student initiatives. In addition, it is possible to integrate new educational approaches, such as service-learning, or organizational contexts, such as inter- or transdisciplinary seminars.
Research	Sustainability research can be done in individual disciplines or through transdisciplinary research platforms that bring together scholars from many fields as well as practitioners.
	Sustainable transdisciplinary research differs from multi- and interdisciplinary research in that it has a substantial problem focus, evolving methodologies tailored to the specific problem under investigation, and collaborative knowledge generation between researchers and stakeholders – not just during the problem solution phase but also during the problem definition stage.
	It allows for a comprehensive approach to environmental and social problems that are not hampered by disciplinary knowledge limitations. As a result, transdisciplinary projects are significantly more likely to produce immediately helpful practical knowledge for the region.
Outreach	There are three types of outreach activities: passive, active, and proactive. A passive position entails HEIs (re)acting on demand (for example, expertise, external consultation, or presentations). In contrast, an active role encompasses the creation of new platforms and discourses in the region and (voluntary) participation in advisory boards and political engagement.
	Actors may engage in spontaneous or infrequent interactions with their regional environment and more frequent and broad-based interactions. More lasting types of association allow for the establishment of social and cognitive proximity between actors and the building of trust.
	Another contribution could be forming networks and alliances with key actors both inside and outside the region to influence political decision-making processes that affect the transition to sustainable development and obtain resources such as financial support for regional pilot projects.
Organizational and field level influences	Internal rules, strategies, mission statements, and guidelines influence individuals' behavior because they want the associated incentives or wish to avoid sanctions. University and higher education legislation, funding organizations and programs, policy initiatives, and programs in related disciplines such as regional, scientific, and innovation policy are all examples of regulatory mechanisms that can be used to impose coercion or provide incentives.
	Values and norms are both normative drivers. While some values and norms apply to all members of the collective body, others are only applicable to specific types of actors or social positions. As a result, members of the rectorate or department heads may be expected to serve as role models and contribute to sustainability in various ways.

Source: Adapted from Radinger-Peer and Pflitsch (2017).

their substantive functions: research, education, operations and governance, and external leadership. An overview of the key contributions to achieving the SDGs is given in Table 5.2.

In all of their dimensions, the SDGs are a fundamental part of HEIs' social responsibility, which must be addressed and fulfilled. HEIs can contribute to the SDGs in various ways, including through their core operations and other more innovative approaches. Cooperation,

Table 5.2 An overview of university contributions to the SDGs.

Research	Education	Operations and governance	External leadership
Research on the SDGs Interdisciplinary and transdisciplinary research Innovations and solutions National and local implementation Capacity building for research	Education for sustainable development Jobs for implementing the SDGs Capacity building Mobilizing young people	Governance and operations aligned with SDGs Incorporate into university reporting	Public engagement Cross-sectoral dialogue and action Policy development and advocacy Advocacy for sector role Demonstrate sector commitment

Source: Adapted from Australia/Pacific SDSN (2017).

collaboration, and knowledge sharing among diverse state and non-state entities from different parts of the world (different cultures, viewpoints, and working methods) are critical to achieving the 2030 Agenda (Vilalta et al. 2018). To face the challenges of implementing the 2030 Agenda, HEIs have begun a renewal process that includes considerable changes in courses and curriculum, teaching, research programs, campus operations, and partnerships (Paletta and Bonoli 2019).

5.3 Sustainability Initiatives in HEIs

Implementing sustainability initiatives on campuses remains a challenge. Despite having guides, documents, and policies that establish the commitment of HEIs with the objectives of sustainable development, there is a lag between the institutional vision and the academic, administrative, and social activities carried out on campuses. That is why a transformation is required of issues related to the educational context and physical changes of learning spaces that contribute to the complete integration of sustainability initiatives in HEIs.

Two main factors influence sustainable behaviors in HEIs; the first is related to internal factors (e.g. knowledge, values, feelings, and emotions) and the second is the external factors (e.g. infrastructure, cultural factors, and economic situation) (Rodríguez-Barreiro et al. 2013). In this context, to promote sustainability in HEIs, strategies must take a holistic approach that allows the notion of sustainability to be integrated into the institution's values, policies, processes, systems, and methodologies (Ciegis et al. 2009).

Sustainability initiatives in HEIs can boost productivity and efficiency by better utilizing resources like energy, water, and other resources, as well as encouraging sustainable waste management and recycling practices, lowering the institution's ecological footprint, and increasing market visibility (Rauen et al. 2015; Berchin et al. 2017). This section provides an overview of some of the most prominent sustainability initiatives being implemented on university campuses worldwide.

5.3.1 Greening the Campus

University campuses function as the spaces where the professionals of the future are academically trained. They also serve as a seedbed and field of practice for implementing structural and physical strategies focused on the saving of and efficiency of resources. This can be achieved through initiatives focused on the greening of campuses.

The term "greening" is frequently used to refer to any environmentally responsible intervention or strategy to transform spaces, products, or brands into a more environmentally friendly version (Greening4life 2007). However, in university campuses, the concept has expanded to involve structural changes in the curriculum and their operation and has become an essential element in implementing sustainability at the university level (Leal Filho et al. 2015; Rodríguez Lima 2019). According to Creighton (1999), greening the campus is a process targeted toward reducing the multitude of on- and off-site environmental impacts resulting from campus activities and operations and raising environmental awareness within the human communities of a college or university.

Greening the campus goes beyond the creation of new spaces or infrastructure. It addresses the creation of information and efforts to change the lifestyles of each student, teachers, and staff toward more sustainable lifestyles. According to Jiménez-Martínez (2017), greening the campus covers issues such as (i) recording of ecological practices carried out in daily university operations (energy consumption decrease, reuse of water, waste classification, etc.); (ii) the consideration of practices and perceptions of students and professors regarding sustainability; and (iii) incorporating sustainability as an academic discipline and as a study program of higher education.

It is essential to highlight that the physical space does not impede the execution of academic activities. For instance, good academic staff and properly motivated students can perform at a high level. A well-designed physical space that integrates the concept of sustainability in its facilities and fosters an environment suitable for the adoption of sustainable practices and habits throughout its community can be achieved. The physical facilities of the IES should promote this adoption of sustainable practices and habits throughout the community, and to accomplish this, the Collaborative for High-Performance Schools (CHPS 2015) mentions that the physical facilities of the university campuses must be:

- Healthy
- Comfortable
- Energy efficient
- Material efficient
- Easy to maintain and operate
- Commissioned
- An environmentally responsive site
- A building that teaches
- Safe and secure
- A community resource
- Stimulating architecture
- Adaptable to changing needs.

Currently, there are many successful cases in the implementation of greening the campus initiatives. In this regard, the Wageningen University & Research in the Netherlands, the University of Oxford, the University of Nottingham and the Nottingham Trent University in the United Kingdom, and the University of California in the United States stand out, and constituted the top five universities in the overall ranking by the UI GreenMetric World University Rankings in 2020. These universities stood out for obtaining the highest score in the six criteria that the ranking evaluates:

1) **Setting and infrastructure**: More space for greenery and in safeguarding environment, as well as the campus sustainable development budget.
2) **Energy and climate change**: Increase the effort in using energy-efficient appliances and develop renewable energy.

3) **Waste**: Some programs and waste treatments (i.e. recycling program, toxic waste, organic and inorganic waste, etc.).
4) **Water**. Decrease groundwater usage, increase conservation program, and protect the habitat.
5) **Transportation**: Transportation policy to limit the number of private vehicles, pedestrians.
6) **Education and research**: Courses, research, publication, website, report related to green and sustainability (UI GreenMetric World University Rankings 2021).

Greening the campus initiatives have had a significant boom in recent years, and, as Sima et al. (2019) comment, they can become an important indicator that can make a difference in the ranking of HEIs. In addition, the wide dissemination of the concept has led to the creation of organizations and institutions focused on contributing to the implementation of greening the campus strategies, including The Green Institute in Nigeria, The Green Campus Initiative at Institute of Technology Sligo in Ireland, The New England Environmental Assistance Team (NEEATeam) in the United States, among others.

5.3.2 Campus Mobility

The challenges related to mobility inside and outside university campuses remain a problem that lacks an optimal solution. This is because university campuses have complex characteristics and social dynamics that resemble small cities. Den Heijer (2012) performs an analysis of four main attributes that show the similarity between university campuses and cities as it follows:

- **Strategically**: They have become a knowledge marketplace.
- **Financially**: They should have a high level of floor productivity (more users per m^2, more output per m^2, i.e. diplomas, publications, patents).
- **Physically**: There should be less private space and more shared public space.
- **Functionally**: There should be more multifunctional spaces (to increase space use).

In addition, the environmental and social impacts generated by the transportation of students, professors, staff, and visitors are significant and will probably worsen if mobility on campus continues to increase (Platje 2012). For this reason, mobility on university campuses has gained interest in recent years and is an issue that must be dealt with by any university committed to sustainability (Miralles-Guasch and Domene 2010).

Currently, the trend in terms of mobility is toward a reduction in it (Fang et al. 2020). In the context of university campuses, this becomes problematic, as many universities cover a large area of land, and some even have more than one campus. This inevitably causes the university community to have to get around mainly through the use of the car. However, sustainability initiatives focused on attacking the mobility problem on campus have begun to modify the current paradigm, in part also driven by the COVID-19 pandemic (Andersen et al. 2021; Yıldırım et al. 2021).

To contribute to the generation of sustainable mobility initiatives on university campuses, the International Alliance of Research Universities (IARU) established in the Green Guide for Universities (2014) a hierarchy of sustainable transport. This guide serves as a reference for the development of more sustainable campus mobility by placing a preference on minimizing the necessity for transportation or by employing healthier modes of transportation. The hierarchy is as shown as follows:

1) Reduce need for transport
2) Healthy transport (cycling/walking), human-powered mobility, non-motorized mobility, or active transport

3) Shared transport (public, pooling, ride-together)
4) Non-fossil/alternative fuels, efficient driving, small cars
5) Offset

An interesting example of sustainability initiatives that are focused on improving mobility conditions on university campuses is the Australian National University (ANU). Since the 1990s, the ANU has actively pushed and supported more environmentally friendly modes of transportation. The university's carpooling program, an expansion in on-campus housing, the installation of a bicycle infrastructure across campus, and the establishment of Australia's most prominent corporate bicycle fleet have all contributed to this. Furthermore, the ANU Environmental Management Plan (EMP) has achieved substantial advances, such as an increase of green commuting, the minimization of single-occupant vehicles, reduction of the fleet vehicle emissions, and the offset of a share of the carbon dioxide equivalent load from air travel (ANU 2012).

5.3.3 Building Energy Efficiency in HEIs

Efficient energy consumption on university campuses is critical to improving the sustainability of HEIs. This is a challenging task considering that many activities are carried out in their facilities and that a vast infrastructure is required, such as classrooms, laboratories, offices, sports facilities, service facilities, among others. All these activities and facilities need significant energy consumption in order to function correctly; we are talking about lighting, heating, cooling, among others (Leal Filho et al. 2019). At the same time, HEIs are responsible for meeting these energy needs while reducing their environmental and social impacts through sustainability initiatives (Faghihi et al. 2015).

As mentioned in this chapter, college campuses can represent unique seedbeds. In their facilities, innovative technologies and services can be evaluated to achieve energy sustainability. However, this will only be possible with the involvement of the entire university community since energy consumption is defined by several factors such as the climate, special events, building size, number of occupants at the time, equipment to be used. At the same time, the effectiveness of the initiatives to be implemented depends on both the existing technology and, to a great extent, on the habits and patterns of energy consumption by building occupants (Kim et al. 2012; Huebner et al. 2013).

In the first instance, energy efficiency initiatives can seem costly and time-consuming since they can involve changes in buildings' physical facilities and equipment. Nevertheless, most of the successful cases of implementing energy efficiency programs in university campuses are the opposite. For instance, it is proven that changes in consumption patterns and user habits directly impact reducing energy waste, especially in HEIs facilities, since students' activities and behavior significantly contribute to the electricity consumption of a campus (Jafary et al. 2016).

There are many examples of initiatives that involve energy efficiency programs in HEIs. It is worth mentioning the case of the Universiti Teknologi Malaysia (UTM). It designed several strategies focused on modifying consumption patterns and habits through awareness and dissemination campaigns within the campus (Ahmad et al. 2012). The strategies consisted of minor modifications regarding the use of electronic devices and the use of artificial lighting. Table 5.3 gives examples of some of those that were implemented in different electrical engineering faculty areas.

These strategies do not require a significant financial investment or drastic modifications of the facilities. With these small interventions, a 14% reduction in energy consumption in the faculty was achieved in one year. However, in some cases, these interventions are not enough to generate significant energy savings.

Table 5.3 Energy saving strategies in the faculty of electrical engineering, Universiti Teknologi Malaysia (UTM).

Targeted place	Initiative taken
Laboratories	1) Switch off lights and computers when leaving the laboratory. 2) Switch off unnecessary lights during the lunch hour or when there are no laboratory sessions. 3) Light up small area only. 4) Use a network printer.
Lecture hall and lecture room	1) Switch off split-unit air-conditioners, LCD projectors as well as computer when a class finishes. 2) Use lecture rooms with split-unit air-conditioner only for weekend classes. 3) Reallocate classes in the evening so that the class will be conducted inside a lecture room with a split-unit air-conditioner.
Office	1) Switch off lights and computers when leaving the office. 2) Switch off lights and computers during the lunch hour. 3) Switch off the split-unit air-conditioner when leaving the offices. 4) Switch off all unnecessary office lights and equipment during the lunch hour.

Source: Ahmad et al. (2012).

University campuses located in areas with extreme climates have the challenge of generating thermal comfort conditions within their facilities, either through more efficient heating or cooling systems or through energy efficiency technologies (Abidin et al. 2017). Some initiatives rely on bioclimatic construction strategies, which aim to generate comfortable conditions while saving energy consumption since the design of the facilities performs the functions of cooling or heating. Some examples of these initiatives are green roofs in university buildings, such as Warsaw University Library (Figure 5.1) and the School of Art, Design, and Media at Nanyang Technological University in Singapore.

5.3.4 Waste Management in HEIs

Another of the critical challenges faced by HEIs is the management of their waste. In recent years, the implementation of initiatives focused on managing the generation and disposal of waste more sustainably has multiplied. This is because consumerism and convenience are based on a purchase-use-disposal system (linear approach) (Tangwanichagapong et al. 2017). This has generated an increase in the generation of waste and has brought different challenges that threaten the environmental sustainability of university campuses and the communities surrounding them.

Figure 5.1 Green roof at Warsaw University Library. *Source:* Authors' own creation.

One of the most common sustainability initiatives for reducing waste and promoting student participation has been waste management programs on campus (Mason et al. 2003). This kind of program aims to make sure that waste is handled in a way that preserves both human health and the environment (Missouri Department of Natural Resources 2017). In addition, these programs can provide economic and environmental benefits while also contributing to improving current waste management systems.

Waste management operations have often been used as a starting point for campus sustainability initiatives at several HEIs worldwide. In Mexico, for example, the Autonomous University of Baja California (UABC) performed a study to characterize its waste generation to identify its recycling possibilities. It was identified that more than 65% of the waste generated daily could be recycled (Armijo de Vega et al. 2008). In Canada, the University of Northern British Columbia characterized its waste generation as a starting point for sustainability initiatives. It was identified that more than 70% could have been diverted through waste reduction, recycling, and composting activities. Three of the most important material types for targeted waste reduction and recycling initiatives were paper and paper products, throwaway drink containers, and biodegradable organic material (Smyth et al. 2010). This demonstrates the attractiveness of waste management programs at HEIs. Not only environmental benefits are obtained through the reduction of waste, but it also opens a range of possibilities for getting economic benefits through recycling and the creation of by-products, such as compost.

Increasing the efficacy of waste management programs requires people to be engaged. Students are generally motivated to solve waste management issues sustainably; nevertheless, their awareness and disposition vary depending on their sociodemographic factors. For this reason, waste management programs must always be accompanied by awareness and communication campaigns to ensure proper implementation (Desa et al. 2012). In New Zealand, Massey University adopted a source separation and concourse-based recycling program. This program managed to increase awareness about the recycling scheme and, in addition, the concourse reported high levels of participation that demonstrated that the program was relatively well supported by students and staff (Kelly et al. 2006).

Waste management programs can serve as a driving force during the early phases of a broader sustainability initiative at HEIs. The tools and methods that can be used to assess the sustainability of a university waste management system are numerous. They can help HEIs achieve higher waste diversion rates while also identifying the challenges universities and colleges may face in transitioning to sustainable campus waste management (Smyth et al. 2010).

5.3.5 Education for Sustainable Development

Even though the strategies we have mentioned are the most popular, or at least the most mediated, they continue to pose obstacles in terms of their actual contribution to the change of university community lifestyles and the achievement of SDGs. That is why, at least in the long run, strategies that require a shift in present paradigms, a broader view of current challenges, and a critical knowledge of the consequences of human activities on ecosystems are likely to have the most significant influence.

ESD demonstrates a range of approaches and initiatives for incorporating sustainability into various aspects of higher education (Lambrechts et al. 2018). Its goal is to equip learners of all ages with the knowledge, skills, attitudes, and values needed to address the interconnected global challenges we face, such as climate change, environmental degradation, biodiversity loss, poverty, and inequity (UNESCO n.d.). Leal Filho (2015) defines ESD as "an educational process characterized by approaches and methods aimed at fostering awareness about the issues pertaining to sustainable development (e.g. social, political, economic and ecological matters)."

The implementation of ESD in HEIs is vital because it raises awareness of environmental issues, encourages critical thinking, and aids in creating sustainable communities (Nasibulina 2015). As a result, education that focuses on sustainability provides knowledge and experiences while also encouraging environmental awareness and ethical behavior (Teixeira 2013).

The most common strategies to implement ESD at HEIs focus on curriculum, competencies, pedagogies, learning, and instruction (Wals and Blewitt 2010). In the realm of ESD, the conceptualization of competencies for sustainable development has become a popular approach. To apply it, a variety of models and sets have been formulated. Still, the essential qualities of these competencies, namely systems thinking, anticipatory thinking, normative competence, strategic competence, and interpersonal competence, appear to be in agreement (Wiek et al. 2011).

Many HEIs have begun to implement curriculum innovation and change in order to promote the curricular integration of ESD-related generic skills (de la Harpe and Thomas 2009). For example, the University of Sonora in Mexico has integrated various sustainability courses within the engineering faculty's curriculum, resulting in a shift in students' attitudes and perceptions toward sustainable development (Zepeda Quintana et al. 2019). In addition, the Delta Business School in New Zealand researched how its students' perceptions of sustainable development had evolved and identified whether the information they received had helped them improve their sustainable business practices. According to the findings, students' awareness of sustainable business practices were significantly enhanced as a result of their courses (Sharma and Kelly 2014). This means that curriculum innovation and changes toward ESD can potentially create in students the cognitive capabilities necessary to contribute to sustainable development.

5.4 Challenges for the Implementation of Sustainability Initiatives in HEI

The implementation of sustainability initiatives is a very important challenge facing HEIs around the world. In order to achieve an adequate implementation, active participation is required by different social actors, such as governments, non-governmental organizations, civil society, and companies. Also, it is necessary to delve into the discussion on the applicability of the SDGs and the type of initiatives that should be designed and operationalized on the campus of the HEIs to favor their achievement. Although the implementation of sustainability initiatives has been widely discussed in the academic sphere, the results on university campuses are still not ideal. According to Ralph and Stubbs (2014), the barriers to integrating sustainability initiatives in universities are predominantly internal. This does not mean that issues such as the political climate, globalization, or other macroeconomic aspects do not affect the implementation of sustainability initiatives (Supe et al. 2018).

Implementing sustainability in HEIs is fraught with difficulties. HEIs are complex and multifaceted institutions (Lozano 2006). Because of the dynamic nature of economic, environmental, and social systems, a multisystemic understanding is required (Waas et al. 2010). Because of the dynamism, observing communications and interactions between and within HEI stakeholders is difficult (Baker-Shelley et al. 2017). This results in a lack of internal and external stakeholder awareness and involvement (Disterheft et al. 2015), which has a detrimental impact on the implementation of sustainability initiatives as well as on the SDGs.

In this section, the most relevant challenges that HEIs present to implement sustainability initiatives in all their areas will be detailed. For convenience, the discussion will be approached from four different perspectives: HEI policies for sustainable development, economic challenges, sociopolitical challenges, and technical challenges.

5.4.1 HEI Policies for SD

Policies and procedures are an essential part of any organization. They give a road map for day-to-day operations when used together. They also guarantee adherence to rules and regulations, provide decision-making assistance, and streamline internal processes (PowerDMS 2020). It is for this reason that establishing sustainability policies in institutions, particularly HEIs, is critical. Although the adoption of sustainability policies is on the rise in higher education, there are still obstacles to the full implementation of policies that promote the transition to more sustainable lifestyles (Shawe et al. 2019).

One of the most significant hurdles in developing sustainability policy at HEIs is a general lack of understanding and expertise of sustainability issues (Leal Filho 2011). This condition can generate confusion and a lack of staff commitment to implement in an adequate form the sustainability policies and initiatives. Also, it can result in a perceived lack of expertise by policy-makers (Wright 2010).

Furthermore, HEIs share characteristics with public organizations, posing challenges not only in the development of policies and procedures, but also in their execution (Evangelinos and Jones 2009). Unlike private organizations, which have a defined end aim (profit), HEIs lack a publicly acknowledged and comprehensive end goal for their operations, as well as understanding about how each member of a community contributes to that end (Zahariadis 1999).

Another challenge is that when establishing a sustainability policy, the scope is short since the writing focuses on including definitions of sustainability and related concepts, instead of defining strategies and guidelines that allow modifying the organizational culture of the institutions (Wright 2010). Although it is commendable that the definition and principles that contribute to the spread of sustainability are explicitly mentioned, the addition of a sustainability plan or guidelines is required for proper policy implementation.

Among other challenges for the implementation of sustainability policies in HEIs are a marked favoring of the environmental sphere over the economic and social spheres, adjustment to existing internal and external documents or policies. and the existence of a highly operational approach, where the establishment of environmental goals is prioritized (e.g. waste management, energy efficiency, toxic use reduction, greenhouse gas emissions reduction, etc.) (Vaughter et al. 2016).

5.4.2 Economic Challenges

It is very common to find in the literature that the main barriers to the implementation of sustainability initiatives in HEIs are lack of financial resources and funding. According to Lucianelli and Citro (2017) "Central governments are reducing their financial support to universities (as well as local government entities)." This situation substantially limits the opportunities for HEIs to create adequate sustainability initiatives.

Moreover, there is a marked tendency to manage HEIs under a profit-oriented approach. Even though there are significant distinctions between universities and business organizational structures, chancellors tended to operate universities as if they were a private corporation. As institutions have become increasingly bureaucratized, presidents and chancellors have resembled CEOs rather than academic leaders (Aronowitz 2000). For many presidents of HEIs, it appears that fundraising is their ultimate purpose.

University administrators strive to ensure that every operation increases earnings or minimizes expenditure. If an initiative allows people to save money, they are more inclined to support it (Barnes and Jerman 2002). This situation reduces the interest in sustainability initiatives on the part of HEI administrators since these initiatives are unable to accomplish money-oriented goals, at least in the short term. However, they provide intangible academic benefits that are frequently overlooked and do not fit into cost–benefit analyses.

Another economic and financial challenge is the lack of support from university administrators (Velazquez et al. 2005). This is primarily due to the perception that sustainability practices and initiatives are a low-priority expenditure (Aleixo et al. 2018). Furthermore, the financial resources available to the HEIs are frequently tied to the number of registered students and the number of high-quality research projects that are being produced, and this scenario makes it difficult to get financial resources owing to political influence. This condition makes it difficult to obtain financial resources and, therefore, on many occasions, sustainability initiatives are financed by the teachers themselves or by volunteers, which puts at risk not only the fulfillment of the proposed objectives but also the creation of more initiatives (Velazquez et al. 2005).

5.4.3 Sociopolitical Challenges

Pursuing sustainability at universities necessitates fundamental shifts in the community's mentality and lifestyle, as well as transdisciplinary and multidisciplinary activities. Because sustainability is such a big topic that necessitates collaboration at numerous hierarchical levels, solo efforts may have a limited impact (Saleh et al. 2011). Furthermore, the implementation of sustainability initiatives may adversely affect some interest groups (Velazquez et al. 2005). According to Dresner (2012), any attempt to achieve sustainability will be met with fierce opposition from a large number of people. Sustainability is viewed as an intruder in a given academic subject by those impacted, who believe it will disrupt the way education and research are conducted (Perez 2002).

Another challenge is the will, opinion, and perception of sustainability by senior managers. Decision-makers' actions have a direct impact on the long-term viability of sustainability initiatives (Larrán Jorge et al. 2015). Since deans change every four years, a university's environmental and sustainable character can shift as a result of divergent interests or goals (Ávila et al. 2017).

5.4.4 Technical Challenges

Although there is a greater awareness of the fundamental role that HEIs play in the implementation of the SDGs, there is not much material available to put it into practice, as the existing guidelines on the implementation of the SDGs in other sectors do not address the unique needs and opportunities of HEIs (Ramos 2009).

The lack of specific working groups, committees, and sustainability offices is another barrier that reduces the proper implementation of sustainability initiatives. It is critical to have established committees or, preferably, specialized sustainability offices in order to provide guidance (Ávila et al. 2017). They must be cross- and multidisciplinary, as well as hierarchically multi-leveled, in order to avoid potential conflicts of interest.

Because of the lack of performance metrics, claiming the effectiveness of sustainability initiatives is extremely challenging. Serious reports are nearly non-existent and despite the fact that there are a number of sustainability indicators in the literature, their true worth must be determined (Velazquez et al. 2005). However, indicators for long-term sustainability are being debated, notwithstanding that sustainability indicators are typically used to monitor environmental rather than social or economic issues (Lozano 2011).

5.5 Factors that Overcome the Challenges for the Implementation of Sustainability Initiatives in HEIs

The challenges described in Section 5.4 can determine the success or the failure of adequate implementation of sustainability initiatives in HEI. Although it has already been pointed out how difficult it is to integrate these types of initiatives in educational institutions, much progress has been made in strategies and plans that will facilitate their implementation.

The strategic implications of sustainability at universities go beyond specific curricular changes, isolated environmental practices, and environmental policies, necessitating adjustments to academic priorities, organizational structures, and financial systems (Ryan et al. 2010). According to Tilbury and Cooke (2005), there is a need to link campus management to research, curriculum, and administrative practice in such a way that sustainability initiatives can be integrated into all aspects of institutional operations synergistically.

One of the essential factors in successfully implementing sustainability initiatives in HEIs is a leadership focused on sustainability. According to Leal Filho et al. (2020), leaders, politicians, and academics use the techniques to execute sustainable development policies, and other activities within their organizations are referred to as sustainability leadership. It includes techniques, strategies, and systemic solutions for resolving issues and influencing institutional policy toward a more sustainable organization. HEIs require leadership to develop strategies that have a long-term vision and connect critical areas, as well as to engage stakeholders through coaching processes, inspire individuals, and strengthen communities through adaptability (Broman et al. 2017).

When it comes to HEI sustainability management, Adams (2013) identifies six characteristics that can help overcome the challenges of implementing sustainability initiatives: (i) proactive leadership, (ii) clear and consistent communication, (iii) the inclusion of sustainability in the HEI strategy, (iv) multidisciplinarity in research and courses, (v) student and staff engagement, and (vi) other initiatives that promote student and staff engagement in sustainability practices. For Barth (2013), the implementation process of sustainability initiatives is also driven by a flexible organizational structure based on ongoing communication, support systems, and leadership. The involvement of high administration is crucial in this matter since they are in charge of developing the policies and guidelines that will guide the entire operation of the HEIs. By having higher levels of awareness and involvement at the highest levels of the institutions (e.g. rector, chancellor, dean, etc.), the chances of successfully implementing sustainability initiatives will increase significantly (Leal Filho et al. 2020).

University management, academic staff, and leaders must be enabled to utilize a new model that truly reflects sustainable practices related to outcomes for institutions to promote change that leads to sustainability (Lozano et al. 2013). However, the type of organizational changes that HEIs require to achieve full integration of sustainability initiatives is bound to face resistance at the different administrative levels (Blanco-Portela et al. 2017). Lozano (2006) mentions that these adverse effects from resistance to change can be minimized through strategies that include negotiation, participation, change in values, collaboration, among others.

Sustainability indicators and reporting are other factors that can contribute to implementing sustainability initiatives. These provide critical information for decision-making, planning, implementation, and assessment of sustainable development policies and targets and assist stakeholders in overcoming the obstacles posed by sustainability. HEIs are expected to be entirely devoted to these indisputable principles of sustainability, similar to the attitudes and behaviors observed within sophisticated organizational environments already using sustainability indices to evaluate and report their institutional performance (Casarejos et al. 2017).

Despite all the debate over the factors that can overcome the challenges in implementing sustainability initiatives in HEIs, the main driver is the commitment of all participants (Godemann et al. 2014; Too and Bajracharya 2015). Although universities worldwide are making the required changes to integrate sustainability principles at all levels, efforts are still overly centralized, alienating students and other stakeholders from the process (Abubakar et al. 2016). Only with the involvement of HEI leaders (rectors, presidents, and directors), faculty (researchers and professors), students (students and alumni), and external entities can progress be made on the path to sustainability.

References

Abidin, N.I.A., Zakaria, R., Pauzi, N.N.M. et al. (2017). Energy efficiency initiatives in a campus building. *Chemical Engineering Transactions* 56: 1–6.

Abubakar, I.R., Al-Shihri, F.S., and Ahmed, S.M. (2016). Students' assessment of campus sustainability at the University of Dammam, Saudi Arabia. *Sustainability (Switzerland)* 8 (1): 1–14.

Adams, C.A. (2013). Sustainability reporting and performance management in universities: challenges and benefits. *Sustainability Accounting, Management and Policy Journal* 4 (3): 384–392.

Ahmad, A.S., Hassan, M.Y., Abdullah, H., et al. (2012). *PECon 2012: 2012 IEEE International Conference on Power and Energy.* The Magellan Sutera Resort, Kota Kinabalu, Malaysia (2–5 December 2012).

Aleixo, A.M., Leal, S., and Azeiteiro, U.M. (2018). Conceptualization of sustainable higher education institutions, roles, barriers, and challenges for sustainability: An exploratory study in Portugal. *Journal of Cleaner Production* 172: 1664–1673. https://doi.org/10.1016/j.jclepro.2016.11.010.

Andersen, M.S., Bento, A.I., Basu, A. et al. (2021). College openings, mobility, and the incidence of COVID-19. medRxiv. https://www.medrxiv.org/content/10.1101/2020.09.22.20196048v3 (accessed 25 November 2021).

Armijo de Vega, C., Ojeda Benítez, S., and Ramírez Barreto, M.E. (2008). Solid waste characterization and recycling potential for a university campus. *Waste Management* 28 (Suppl. 1): S21–S26.

Aronowitz, S. (2000). *The Knowledge Factory: Dismantling the Corporate University and Creating True Higher Learning.* Beacon Press.

Association of University Leaders for a Sustainable Future (1990). The talloires declaration. http://ulsf.org/talloires-declaration (accessed 25 November 2021).

Australia/Pacific SDSN (2017). Getting started with the SDGS in Universities: A guide for universities, higher education institutions and the academic sector. Australia, New Zealand, and Pacific Edition: Sustainable Development Solutions Network. https://reds-sdsn.es/wp-content/uploads/2017/09/University-SDG-Guide_web.pdf (accessed 25 November 2021).

Australian National University (ANU) (2012). *Environmental Management Plan Implementation Mid-Term Report.* Canberra: The Australian National University Sustainability Office.

Avelar, A.B.A., da Silva-Oliveira, K.D., and Pereira, R.d.S. (2019). Education for advancing the implementation of the sustainable development goals: a systematic approach. *International Journal of Management Education* 17 (3): 100322. https://doi.org/10.1016/j.ijme.2019.100322.

Ávila, L.V., Leal Filho, W., Brandli, L. et al. (2017). Barriers to innovation and sustainability at universities around the world. *Journal of Cleaner Production* 164: 1268–1278.

Baker-Shelley, A., van Zeijl-Rozema, A., and Martens, P. (2017). A conceptual synthesis of organisational transformation: how to diagnose, and navigate, pathways for sustainability at universities? *Journal of Cleaner Production* 145: 262–276.

Barnes, P. and Jerman, P. (2002). Developing an environmental management system for a multiple-university consortium. *Journal of Cleaner Production* 10 (1): 33–39.

Barth, M. (2013). Many roads lead to sustainability: A process-oriented analysis of change in higher education. *International Journal of Sustainability in Higher Education* 14 (2): 160–175.

Berchin, I.I., Grando, V.d.S., Marcon, G.A. et al. (2017). Strategies to promote sustainability in higher education institutions: a case study of a federal institute of higher education in Brazil. *International Journal of Sustainability in Higher Education* 18 (7): 1018–1038.

Blanco-Portela, N., Benayas, J., Pertierra, L.R., and Lozano, R. (2017). Towards the integration of sustainability in higher education institutions: a review of drivers of and barriers to organisational change and their comparison against those found of companies. *Journal of Cleaner Production* 166: 563–578.

Broman, G., Robèrt, K.H., Collins, T.J. et al. (2017). Science in support of systematic leadership towards sustainability. *Journal of Cleaner Production* 140: 1–9.

Casarejos, F., Frota, M.N., and Gustavson, L.M. (2017). Higher education institutions: a strategy towards sustainability. *International Journal of Sustainability in Higher Education* 18 (7): 995–1017.

Ciegis, R., Ramanauskiene, J., and Martinkus, B. (2009). The concept of sustainable development and its use for sustainability scenarios. *Inzinerine Ekonomika-Engineering Economics* 2 (62): 28–37. http://www.ktu.edu/lt/mokslas/zurnalai/inzeko/62/1392-2758-2009-2-62-28.pdf#page=1&zoom=auto,-274,848.

Collaborative for High Performance Schools (CHPS) (2015). Introduction to CHPS: Getting started with CHPS. Sacramento, CA. https://chps.net/getting-started-chps (accessed 25 November 2021).

Creighton, S.H. (1999). *Greening the Ivory Tower. Improving the Environmental Track Record of Universities, Colleges, and Other Institutions*. Cambridge: MIT Press.

DESA (2016). Transforming our World: the 2030 agenda for sustainable development. United Nations.

Desa, A., Abd Kadir, N.B., and Yusooff, F. (2012). Environmental awareness and education: A key approach to solid waste management (SWM) – A case study of a university in Malaysia. In: *Waste Management – An Integrated Vision* (ed. L.F.M. Rebellon). IntechOpen https://doi.org/10.5772/48169.

Disterheft, A., Ferreira Da Silva Caeiro, S.S., Ramos, M.R., and De Miranda Azeiteiro, U.M. (2012). Environmental management systems (EMS) implementation processes and practices in European higher education institutions – top-down versus participatory approaches. *Journal of Cleaner Production* 31: 80–90.

Disterheft, A., Caeiro, S., Azeiteiro, U.M., and Leal Filho, W. (2015). Sustainable universities – a study of critical success factors for participatory approaches. *Journal of Cleaner Production* 106: 11–21.

Dresner, S. (2012). *The Principles of Sustainability*. Routledge.

Evangelinos, K.I. and Jones, N. (2009). An analysis of social capital and environmental management of higher education institutions. *International Journal of Sustainability in Higher Education* 10 (4): 334–342.

Evans, J., Jones, R., Karvonen, A. et al. (2015). Living labs and co-production: university campuses as platforms for sustainability science. *Current Opinion in Environmental Sustainability* 16: 1–6. http://doi.org/10.1016/j.cosust.2015.06.005.

Faghihi, V., Hessami, A.R., and Ford, D.N. (2015). Sustainable campus improvement program design using energy efficiency and conservation. *Journal of Cleaner Production* 107: 400–409.

Fang, H., Wang, L., and Yang, Y. (2020). Human mobility restrictions and the spread of the Novel Coronavirus (2019-nCoV) in China. *Journal of Public Economics* 191: 104272. https://doi.org/10.1016/j.jpubeco.2020.104272.

Figueiró, P.S. and Raufflet, E. (2015). Sustainability in higher education: a systematic review with focus on management education. *Journal of Cleaner Production* 106: 22–33.

Findler, F., Schönherr, N., Lozano, R. et al. (2019). The impacts of higher education institutions on sustainable development: a review and conceptualization. *International Journal of Sustainability in Higher Education* 20 (1): 23–38.

Godemann, J., Bebbington, J., Herzig, C., and Moon, J. (2014). Higher education and sustainable development: Exploring possibilities for organisational change. *Accounting, Auditing, & Accountability Journal* 27 (2): 218–233.

Greening4life (2007). What is greening? [online] Resource for Advancing Green and Sustainable Environment. http://greening4life.org (accessed 25 November 2021).

de la Harpe, B. and Thomas, I. (2009). Curriculum change in universities. *Journal of Education for Sustainable Development* 3 (1): 75–85.

den Heijer, A. (2012). *Managing the University Campus: Exploring Models for the Future and Supporting Today's Decisions*. CELE Exchange. OECD Publishing https://doi.org/10.1787/5k9b950gh2xx-en.

Huebner, G.M., Cooper, J., and Jones, K. (2013). Domestic energy consumption – what role do comfort, habit, and knowledge about the heating system play? *Energy and Buildings* 66: 626–636. http://doi.org/10.1016/j.enbuild.2013.07.043.

International Alliance of Research Universities (IARU) (2014). Green guide for universities [online]. http://www.iaruni.org/images/stories/Sustainability/IARU_Green_Guide_for_Universities_2014.pdf (accessed 25 November 2021).

Jafary, M., Wright, M., Shephard, L. et al. (2016). Understanding campus energy consumption – People, buildings and technology. In: *IEEE Green Technologies Conference* (April 2016), 68–72.

Jiménez-Martínez, N.M. (2017). Educacion ambiental universitaria. Sistematización del Diplomado en gestión medioambiental en el campus morelos de la UNAM. *Debates en Evaluación y Currículum – Congreso Internacional de Educación Currículum 2017* 3 (3): 1–11.

Kelly, T.C., Mason, I.G., Leiss, M.W., and Ganesh, S. (2006). University community responses to on-campus resource recycling. *Resources, Conservation and Recycling* 47 (1): 42–55.

Kim, A., Faghihi, V., and Hessami, A.R., (2012). Designing perpetual sustainability improvement programs for built infrastructures. *Proceedings of the 30th International Conference of the System Dynamics Society* (July). St. Gallen, Switzerland.

Lambrechts, W., Van Liedekerke, L., and Van Petegem, P. (2018). Higher education for sustainable development in Flanders: balancing between normative and transformative approaches. *Environmental Education Research, [online]* 24 (9): 1284–1300.

Larrán Jorge, M., Herrera Madueño, J., Calzado Cejas, M.Y., and Andrades Peña, F.J. (2015). An approach to the implementation of sustainability practices in Spanish universities. *Journal of Cleaner Production* 106: 34–44.

Leal Filho, W. (2011). About the role of universities and their contribution to sustainable development. *Higher Education Policy* 24 (4): 427–438.

Leal Filho, W. (2015). Education for sustainable development in higher education: Reviewing needs. In: *Transformative Approaches to Sustainable Development at Universities*, 3–12. Springer.

Leal Filho, W., Shiel, C., do Paço, A., and Brandli, L. (2015). Putting sustainable development in practice: campus greening as a tool for institutional sustainability efforts. In: *Sustainability in Higher Education* (ed. J. Paulo and C. Davim), 1–19.

Leal Filho, W., Salvia, A.L., Paço, A.d. et al. (2019). A comparative study of approaches towards energy efficiency and renewable energy use at higher education institutions. *Journal of Cleaner Production* 237: 117728.

Leal Filho, W., Eustachio, J.H.P.P., Caldana, A.C.F. et al. (2020). Sustainability leadership in higher education institutions: an overview of challenges. *Sustainability (Switzerland)* 12 (9): 3761.

Lozano, R. (2006). Incorporation and institutionalization of SD into universities: breaking through barriers to change. *Journal of cleaner production* 14 (9–11): 787–796.

Lozano, R. (2011). The state of sustainability reporting in universities. *International Journal of Sustainability in Higher Education* 12 (1): 67–78.

Lozano, R., Lukman, R., Lozano, F.J. et al. (2013). Declarations for sustainability in higher education: becoming better leaders, through addressing the university system. *Journal of Cleaner Production* 48: 10–19.

Lozano, R., Ceulemans, K., Alonso-Almeida, M. et al. (2015). A review of commitment and implementation of sustainable development in higher education: results from a worldwide survey. *Journal of Cleaner Production* 108: 1–18.

Lucianelli, G. and Citro, F. (2017). Financial conditions and financial sustainability in higher education: a literature review. In: *Financial Sustainability in Public Administration: Exploring the Concept of Financial Health* (ed. M.R. Bolívar), 25–53. Cham: Palgrave Macmillan.

Luna-Krauletz, M.D., Juárez-Hernández, L.G., Clark-Tapia, R. et al. (2021). Environmental education for sustainability in higher education institutions: design of an instrument for its evaluation. *Sustainability* 13 (7129).

Mallow, S. (2020). Transforming our world: higher education and the Agenda 2030. *Ambiens* 2 (4): 105–121.

Mason, I.G., Brooking, A.K., Oberender, A. et al. (2003). Implementation of a zero waste program at a university campus. *Resources, Conservation and Recycling* 38 (4): 257–269.

Miralles-Guasch, C. and Domene, E. (2010). Sustainable transport challenges in a suburban university: the case of the Autonomous University of Barcelona. *Transport Policy* 17 (6): 454–463. http://doi.org/10.1016/j.tranpol.2010.04.012.

Missouri Department of Natural Resources (2017). Waste management program [online]. https://dnr.mo.gov/document-search/2016-2017-waste-composition-study (accessed 25 November 2021).

Nasibulina, A. (2015). Education for sustainable development and environmental ethics. *Procedia – Social and Behavioral Sciences* 214: 1077–1082.

Paletta, A. and Bonoli, A. (2019). Governing the university in the perspective of the United Nations 2030 agenda: the case of the University of Bologna. *International Journal of Sustainability in Higher Education* 20 (3): 500–514.

Peer, V. and Penker, M. (2016). Higher education institutions and regional development: a meta-analysis. *International Regional Science Review* 39 (2): 228–253.

Perez, R. (2002). Sustainable development as line of investigation in the division of economic and administrative sciences of the University of Sonora. Paper presented at *Clean Production and Pollution Prevention at Universities: Inside Stories International Conference*. Sonora: University of Sonora in Hermosillo.

Platje, J. (2012). Current challenges in the economics of transport systems – a stakeholder and club good approach. *Logistics and Transport* 2 (15): 37–49.

PowerDMS (2020). Following policies and procedures and why it's important [online]. Policy Management. https://www.powerdms.com/policy-learning-center/following-policies-and-procedures-and-why-its-important (accessed 6 June 2021).

Radinger-Peer, V. and Pflitsch, G. (2017). The role of higher education institutions in regional transition paths towards sustainability: the case of Linz (Austria). *Review of Regional Research* 37 (2): 161–187.

Ralph, M. and Stubbs, W. (2014). Integrating environmental sustainability into universities. *Higher Education* 67 (1): 71–90.

Ramos, T.B. (2009). Development of regional sustainability indicators and the role of academia in this process: the Portuguese practice. *Journal of Cleaner Production* 17 (12): 1101–1115.

Rauen, T.R.S., Lezana, Á.G.R., and da Silva, V. (2015). Environmental management: an overview in higher education institutions. *Procedia Manufacturing* 3 (Ahfe): 3682–3688.

Razak, A.A. and Saad, M. (2007). The role of universities in the evolution of the triple helix culture of innovation network: the case of Malaysia. *International Journal of Technology Management and Sustainable Development* 6 (3): 211–225.

Rodríguez Lima, R.M., 2019. Campus greening and sustainable development. Leal Filho W. (ed) *Encyclopedia of Sustainability in Higher Education*, pp. 1–7 Cham: Springer, https://doi.org/10.1007/978-3-319-63951-2_69-1.

Rodríguez-Barreiro, L.M., Fernández-Manzanal, R., Serra, L.M. et al. (2013). Approach to a causal model between attitudes and environmental behaviour. A graduate case study. *Journal of Cleaner Production* 48: 116–125. http://doi.org/10.1016/j.jclepro.2012.09.029.

Ryan, A., Tilbury, D., Corcoran, P.B. et al. (2010). Sustainability in higher education in the Asia-Pacific: Developments, challenges, and prospects. *International Journal of Sustainability in Higher Education*. Special Issue 11 (2): 105–194.

Saleh, A.A., Kamarulzaman, N., Hashim, H., and Hashim, S.Z. (2011). An approach to facilities management (FM) practices in higher learning institutions to attain a sustainable campus (case study: university technology Mara – UiTM). *Procedia Engineering* 20: 269–278. http://doi.org/10.1016/j.proeng.2011.11.165.

Sharma, U. and Kelly, M. (2014). Students' perceptions of education for sustainable development in the accounting and business curriculum at a business school in New Zealand. *Meditari Accountancy Research* 22 (2): 130–148.

Shawe, R., Horan, W., Moles, R., and O'Regan, B. (2019). Mapping of sustainability policies and initiatives in higher education institutes. *Environmental Science and Policy* 99: 80–88.

Sima, M., Grigorescu, I., and Bălteanu, D. (2019). An overview of campus greening initiatives at universities in Romania. *International Journal of Sustainability in Higher Education* 20 (3): 410–422.

Smyth, D.P., Fredeen, A.L., and Booth, A.L. (2010). Reducing solid waste in higher education: the first step towards 'greening' a university campus. *Resources, Conservation and Recycling* 54 (11): 1007–1016.

Stephens, J.C. and Graham, A.C. (2010). Toward an empirical research agenda for sustainability in higher education: exploring the transition management framework. *Journal of Cleaner Production* 18 (7): 611–618.

Stephens, J.C., Hernandez, M.E., Román, M. et al. (2008). Higher education as a change agent for sustainability in different cultures and contexts. *International Journal of Sustainability in Higher Education* 9 (3): 317–338.

Supe, L., Zeps, A., Jurgelane, I., and Ribickis, L. (2018). Factors affecting the competitiveness of a higher education institution: systematic literature overview. *Research for Rural Development* 2: 245–251.

Tangwanichagapong, S., Nitivattananon, V., Mohanty, B., and Visvanathan, C. (2017). Greening of a campus through waste management initiatives: experience from a higher education institution in Thailand. *International Journal of Sustainability in Higher Education* 18 (2): 203–217.

Teixeira, S.R. (2013). The environmental education as a path for global sustainability. *Procedia – Social and Behavioral Sciences* 106: 2769–2774.

Tilbury, D. and Cooke, K. (2005). A national review of environmental education and its contribution to sustainability in Australia: Frameworks for Sustainability. In: *Canberra:*

Australian Government Department of the Environment and Heritage and Australian. Research Institute in Education for Sustainability.

Too, L. and Bajracharya, B. (2015). Sustainable campus: engaging the community in sustainability. *International Journal of Sustainability in Higher Education* 16 (1): 57–71.

UI GreenMetric World University Rankings (2021). Overall rankings 2020 [online]. Overall Rankings 2020. https://greenmetric.ui.ac.id/rankings/overall-rankings-2020 (accessed 25 November 2021).

UN (2015). List of MDGs English – UN. [online] http://www.un.org/millenniumgoals (accessed 25 November 2021).

UNESCO (2002). UN Decade of ESD. [online] UN Decade of ESD. https://en.unesco.org/themes/education-sustainable-development/what-is-esd/un-decade-of-esd (accessed 25 November 2021).

UNESCO (n.d.) Educación para el desarrollo sostenible. [online] Educación para el desarrollo sostenible. https://es.unesco.org/themes/educacion-desarrollo-sostenible (accessed 25 November 2021).

Vaughter, P., McKenzie, M., Lidstone, L., and Wright, T. (2016). Campus sustainability governance in Canada: a content analysis of post-secondary institutions' sustainability policies. *International Journal of Sustainability in Higher Education* 17 (1): 16–39.

Velazquez, L., Munguia, N., and Sanchez, M. (2005). Deterring sustainability in higher education institutions: an appraisal of the factors which influence sustainability in higher education institutions. *International Journal of Sustainability in Higher Education* 6 (4): 383–391.

Velázquez, L., Munguía, N., Zavala, A., and Navarrete, M.D.L.Á. (2008). Challenges in operating sustainability initiatives in Northwest Mexico. *Sustainable Development* 16 (6): 401–409.

Vilalta, J.M., Betts, A., and Gómez, V. (2018). Higher education's role in the 2030 Agenda: The why and how of GUNi's commitment to the SDGs. In: *Sustainable Development Goals: Actors and Implementation. A Report from the International Conference*, Barcelona (18–19 September 2017), 10–14. Global Universities Network for Innovation.

Waas, T., Verbruggen, A., and Wright, T. (2010). University research for sustainable development: definition and characteristics explored. *Journal of Cleaner Production* 18 (7): 629–636.

Wals, A.E.J. (2014). Sustainability in higher education in the context of the un DESD: a review of learning and institutionalization processes. *Journal of Cleaner Production* 62: 8–15. http://doi.org/10.1016/j.jclepro.2013.06.007.

Wals, A.E.J. and Blewitt, J. (2010). Third-wave sustainability in higher education: some (inter) national trends and developments. In: *Sustainability Education: Perspectives and Practice Across Higher Education* (ed. P. Jones, D. Selby and S. Sterling), 55–74. London: Earthscan.

Wiek, A., Withycombe, L., and Redman, C.L. (2011). Key competencies in sustainability: a reference framework for academic program development. *Sustainability Science* 6 (2): 203–218.

Wright, T. (2010). University presidents' conceptualizations of sustainability in higher education. *International Journal of Sustainability in Higher Education* 11 (1): 61–73.

Yıldırım, S., Bostancı, S.H., Yıldırım, D.Ç., and Erdogan, F. (2021). Rethinking mobility of international university students during COVID-19 pandemic. *Higher Education Evaluation and Development* 15: 1–16.

Zahariadis, N. (1999). Ambiguity, time, and multiple streams. *Theories of the Policy Process* 1999: 73–93.

Zepeda Quintana, D.S., Esquer, J., and Anaya, C. (2019). Teaching and mindsets regarding sustainable development – a Mexican case study. *The Central European Review of Economics and Management* 3 (4): 91–102.

6

Developing Stakeholder Agency in Higher Education Sustainability Initiatives: Insights from a Change Laboratory Research Intervention

John Scahill and Brett Bligh

6.1 Introduction

This chapter positions education for sustainable development (ESD) as a project of ongoing educational change, and explores how such change might take place within higher education institutions (HEIs) in ways that empower stakeholders. Our core objective is to explore the central role of developing participants' collective agency – often conceptualized in prior literature as capacity building – where institutions attempt to build their own bespoke sustainability strategies.

The literature on educational change emphasizes that top-down attempts to impose reform typically fall at the hurdles of ownership, commitment, and clarity. Bottom-up change, on the other hand, is difficult to scale and often fails to endure over time. Where initiatives overcome these different problems, it is usually because they succeed in capacity building – meaning, among other things, developing the social capital and sense of motivation *of* and *within* collaborative groups (Fullan 2016). In this chapter we explore how a particular approach, the Change Laboratory (CL), was used as a vehicle for sustainability-related capacity building in one institution in the Republic of Ireland in 2016 with a particular focus on the development of agency of and within a collaborative group of stakeholders.

In the project that we draw on, a range of institutional stakeholders – varied in seniority, professional role, and disciplinary background – came together in workshops, over several months, and co-designed a range of outcomes. Those include a Campus Sustainability Statement (CSS; the main focus of this chapter), a mechanism for highlighting sustainability linkages with the curricula of existing academic programs, proposals for new academic programs (now offered), and an outline idea for a research Centre for the Study of Community Sustainability (recently funded). Below, rather than celebrating these outcomes, we explore the nature of the capacity building that was achieved in the group. To do so, we draw on a theoretical framework of transformative agency, which foregrounds how the collective agency of people involved in change efforts is produced and maintained over time. We document important aspects of the design of the project; consider how agency was manifested in the change process, with a particular focus on the CSS; and draw lessons for how change initiatives relating to sustainability in HEIs might be conceived in future, in order to maximize the chances of capacity building.

The reason for focusing on these issues relates to the emerging scholarly discussion on the nature of sustainability-related change within HEIs. It has been recognized for several decades that HEIs play a crucial role, throughout wider society and the globalizing economy, in supporting change relating to sustainable development. As early as 1972, for example, the United Nations (UN) Conference on the Human Environment in Stockholm acknowledged the centrality of university involvement in sustainability initiatives (Lozano et al. 2013). Moreover, the importance of engaging higher education partners, if global challenges are to be addressed and strategic actions supported, has been repeatedly reaffirmed over the intervening period (Fischer et al. 2015). Yet HEIs have often been seen as lagging behind in enacting sustainability-related change within their own practices – thereby damaging their credibility with outside stakeholders, undermining their stated educational mission, and perpetuating the direct environmental footprint of their activities (Lozano et al. 2013). Recognition of this problem has grown in recent years. As Omazic and Zunk (2021) put it in relation to the 17 UN Sustainable Development Goals (SDGs), "HEIs are expected to provide guidance for various stakeholders on this matter, but also to implement this agenda and the SDGs in their institutions" (p. 1). Such recognition has provided a strong moral imperative, in recent times, for promoting suitability within institutions.

This increased emphasis on sustainability priorities inside HEIs has led to a wide array of initiatives that address an increasing variety of functions within particular organizations. Lozano et al. (2015), for example, propose that interventions be categorized according to whether their object is institutional frameworks, campus operations, educational provision, research, outreach and collaboration, on-campus experiences, or assessment and reporting. Yet recent reviews have emphasized that most institutional practice, notwithstanding this variety of initiatives, remains inadequate (Lozano et al. 2015; Berchin et al. 2018; Omazic and Zunk 2021). A recent report from the Environmental Association for Universities and Colleges (EAUC), which generated data from 18 institutions across several countries, suggests that typical problems with institutional initiatives arise from two sources: first, the adoption of fragmentary approaches lacking either practical coordination or overall vision and, second, the attempt to import models from elsewhere that prove inappropriate to the local context (Appleton 2017). As the foreword to the report highlights:

> One key thing the EAUC has learnt in its 20 years is that there is no one standard approach to sustainability. Off the peg or tick box approaches can appear attractive on the surface but change can often be just that, on the surface. For the EAUC, the key to success is for a university or college to define sustainability for itself and build a unique strategy and structure which reflects its particular nature, context and geography (Appleton 2017, p. 2).

Our discussion in this chapter of how the CL approach was used in one institution does – inasmuch as it involved defining sustainability before building a bespoke strategy – fit Appleton's template. Our analytical purpose, however, is less to confirm Appleton's observations about successful initiatives than to understand some of the means by which such approaches can be so generative. Recalling our discussion earlier in this section, we suggest that some of the success of such approaches is a function of their capacity building. Drawing on the activity theory tradition that underpins the CL approach, we seek to map how the research-intervention we describe fostered the transformative agency of those who participated. Doing so, we hope, will encourage readers of this volume to understand the importance of associating sustainability in higher education (SHE) with a concept of change and development, rather than (as is more common) one of "implementation" or "promotion."

In this chapter, then, we set out the basic principles that underpin the CL approach and the conception of transformative agency that will underpin our later analysis; describe the concrete design of the approach, which involved tailoring the CL principles to the problems of sustainability and the context of the institution; identify some of the core expressions of stakeholder agency that were evident as the change process unfolded, illustrating, in particular, how that agency was developed throughout the development of the CSS; and discuss the implications for scholarship and future practice in HEIs. Before doing so, we briefly review some pertinent strands of the literature on SHE.

6.2 Literature Review

The body of knowledge on SHE exhibits a near unanimous agreement that universities, and the higher education (HE) sector in general, have a significant role to play in the creation of a sustainable future. Yet universities can, it is argued, only take on such a role if they are willing to grapple with difficult issues of change within their own institutions (UNESCO 2005; Lozano 2006; Sidiropoulos 2010; Leal Filho 2011; Karatzoglou 2013; Sterling et al. 2013). The case for SHE is thus typically presented in moral and ethical terms: that HEIs have responsibilities in relation to sustainability and must engage with internal change if they are to play a role in creating a just and sustainable future for society more widely (Cortese 2003; Baker-Shelley et al. 2017; Findler et al. 2019).

The combination of moral imperative and acknowledged difficulty of change leads to a proliferation of papers highlighting particular issues that must be confronted and overcome. In this review we briefly look at two issues foregrounded in this literature: the challenges presented by sustainability related terminology, and the role of engagement and empowerment in sustainability initiatives.

6.2.1 Sustainability-Related Terminology in Higher Education

Sustainability, both as a term and as a concept, has multiple interpretations; it is context sensitive and can be interpreted to have a wide range of meanings. The range of understandings about what terms like "sustainability" and "sustainable development" mean are often seen as a significant and problematic issue in HE (Mader et al. 2013; Gale et al. 2015; Owens and Legere 2015; Cheeseman et al. 2019). Different understandings can, for example, create communication problems (Djordjevic and Cotton 2011) and contribute to an overall lack of understanding and awareness of about what sustainability is, and more importantly, how it be addressed and dealt with.

Such problems are even identified in scholarship. Sustainability and sustainable development (SD) are often used interchangeably in the HE literature (Mader et al. 2013; Holden et al. 2014; Viegas et al. 2016; Wu and Shen 2016), yet some authors emphasize that they are not the same thing (Lozano 2008). Moreover, both terms are subject to a range of interpretations (Gibson 2000; Leal Filho 2011; Sidiropoulos 2012) and can mean different things to different people (Leal Filho 2011). Johnston et al. (2007) estimate that approximately 300 definitions of sustainability and sustainable development, each subtly different, are being used in the area of environmental management and similar fields.

Much effort has been placed on providing official and/or precise definitions for such terms. Ralph and Stubbs (2014, p. 72), for example, describe sustainability as "a paradigm for thinking about the future in which the economic, environmental and social dimensions are intertwined, not separate, and are balanced in the pursuit of an improved quality of life." Wu and Shen (2016) define sustainability (based on Rhodes 2006) as "the effort to frame social and economic policy so as to preserve, with minimum disturbance, the earth's bounty – its resources, inhabitants and environments – for the benefit of both present and future generations."

These definitions are very similar to the broadly accepted, albeit contentious, definition of sustainable development proposed in the report of the Brundtland Commission of 1987:

> Sustainable development is the development which meets the needs of the present without compromising the ability of future generations to meet their own needs.
> *(World Commission on Environment and Development 1987, p. 42)*

Yet even high-profile attempts at producing official definitions have proven contentious. Sidiropoulos (2010, p. 45), on the other hand, offers a different perspective:

> Sustainable development (SD) is regarded as the vehicle for shifting away from the dominant (growth oriented) model of development towards one that is able to balance needs of people (social development), planet (environmental development) and profit (economic development). However, SD cannot be absolutely defined and there is no "one size fits all."

Both concepts revolve around the convergence of three entities – people (social); planet (environment); and profit (economy) – which are popularly known as either the three pillars of sustainability or the triple bottom line (TBL). In turn, models of sustainability are often considered "weak" or "strong" based on the extent to which these entities are seen as interacting and how their connections are framed.

Weak sustainability (mechanistic/functional approach) assumes that human and natural capital are interchangeable entities and that sustainability is achieved as a coincidence of the three pillars. This form is regarded by many proponents (Barrett 1996; Meadows et al. 2004; Steiner and Posch 2006; Orr 2009; Thogersen and Crompton 2009; Flavin 2010), as unlikely to restore the earth's natural capital for future generations. (Sidiropoulos 2011)

The "strong form" on the other hand, is seen a holistic approach which situates the economy centrally, but depicts it as subordinate to and nested within society, which, in turn is nested within the environment. The fundamental difference in focus between these two views of sustainability (a coincidence of the three pillars, as against an unequivocal hierarchical relationship) reflects a chasm that exists when it comes to perceptions of the concept.

Such debates have led, in some quarters, to an emphasis on conceptual pluralism. Lozano (2018), for example, emphasizes that there are no clear definitions of sustainability in organizations and that the same is true for HE. It is widely acknowledged that terminological issues are problematic in HE (Mader et al. 2013; Figueiró and Raufflet 2015; Gale et al. 2015; Owens and Legere 2015; Cheeseman et al. 2019) and it is clear that this can lead to problems when trying to get groups of people to agree on a set of ideas or a course of action, yet attempts to resolve such issues have proven unsuccessful.

However, competing concepts are not random but a product of wider practices and social structures. With specific references to HE, Gale et al. (2015), for example, suggest that this situation of "conceptual multiplicity" reflects a "disciplinary contestation," which highlights the need for interdisciplinary collaboration but also the problems that multidisciplinarity brings to fields of enquiry and action.

Many authors suggest that sustainability education benefits from a holistic approach where environmental, global, social and cultural issues are explored from an inter-, multi- and/or transdisciplinary perspective (e.g. Green 2015; Dlouhá et al. 2017; Cheeseman et al. 2019).

Gale states that, because concepts, worldviews, and values relating to "sustainability" are variously constituted in different disciplines, they can create confusion over what sustainability is within HEIs. Such confusion brings issues for action in HEI initiatives. According to Ralph and Stubbs (2014), for example, a lack of clarity (on definitions) can lead to a lack of staff commitment to implementing sustainability programs (Evangelinos and Jones 2009; Wright 2010).

One of the most obvious problems related to lack of definitions and lack of clarity are issues with communication. Djordjevic and Cotton (2011) conclude that, if two parties do not share the same understanding about the meaning or value of sustainability, then actions carried out based on the receipt of communication may be at odds with the original intentions.

Such issues are central to the project we report on in this chapter. From the beginning, we were aware of the importance of taking a multidisciplinary approach if change was to be fostered within the institution, but wary (justifiably, as it turned out) of the conceptual contestation that might arise as a consequence of doing so. In the account that follows we emphasize how the CL approach supported stakeholders from a range of backgrounds within one particular HEI to confront and address such terminological issues.

6.2.2 Stakeholder Engagement and Sustainability Initiatives in Higher Education

Stakeholder engagement is typically seen as important because it serves as a driver for SHE. Some writers emphasize the role of particular stakeholders in institutionally senior or strategic positions. In such writing, leadership, consistent and effective communication (Adams 2013; Vargas et al. 2019), and a clear commitment from senior management are considered key drivers for SHE (Hoover and Harder 2015). Other authors (Adams 2013; Mader et al. 2013; Godemann et al. 2014; Too and Bajracharya 2015; Aleixo et al. 2018) place more emphasis on engagement by participants and stakeholders in a more general sense. Within particular institutions, such positions are not mutually exclusive. Indeed, one purpose of clear communication, from management, about commitment and leadership is to foment and encourage stakeholder engagement more generally. Yet most of the literature emphasizes how stakeholder engagement can be promoted at particular levels: as a consequence of strategic approaches, organizational culture, or individual commitment.

A wide range of strategic approaches for promoting and developing staff engagement have been suggested in the literature. The most notable are:

- Including sustainability in the HEI strategy (Adams 2013).
- Signing a sustainability declaration or charter (thereby allowing members of the University to specify its meaning during internal negotiation about its integration at the institute) (Müller-Christ et al. 2014).
- Developing mission statements and sustainability guidelines (potentially derived from the content of declarations that the HEI are signed up to) (Velazquez et al. 2006; Müller-Christ et al. 2014).
- Promoting inter- and multidisciplinarity in research and program design (Adams 2013).
- Providing coordination units or processes to help keep projects alive and distribute responsibility (Ferrer-Balas et al. 2008).

A second strand of scholarship emphasizes that stakeholder engagement is largely a product of organizational culture. Verhulst and Boks (2014), for example, propose that employee empowerment can be a significant change driver or success factor for the implementation of SHE. Other authors call for a culture of connectedness. Müller-Christ et al. (2014) and Wright (2002), for example, cite the need for universities to connect, within actual practice, curriculum, campus, research, and community strategies and action.

Other authors, meanwhile, argue that, while management can employ a range of measures to encourage staff engagement with SHE, it is ultimately down to the level of commitment of each staff member as an individual as to how this is demonstrated or enacted. The role of individual commitment has been identified as a key driver (Verhulst and Lambrechts 2015), with individual leaders and sustainability champions therefore viewed as vital in overcoming the challenges of embedding sustainability within HE (Lozano 2006; UNESCO 2006; Ferrer-Balas et al. 2008; Christensen et al. 2009).

It is still relatively unusual in the literature for authors to consider relationships between these different levels or how those relationships serve to drive SHE, though particular examples can be found. A culture of employee empowerment, for example, is positioned by Akins et al. (2019) as a motivational tool, whereby administrators, faculty, staff, and others become sustainability proponents. It has also been recognized that individuals working collectively (in groups) can be a good vehicle for driving SHE; it has been noted, for example, that "green campus" (or "green flag") initiatives have been a significant contributor to SHE for many years (Dahle and Neumeyer 2001; Leal Filho et al. 2015; Amaral et al. 2020). In our view, such examples are particularly important, and in this chapter, we wish to highlight how such a group worked to develop and nurture individual passions and commitments about sustainability into a vehicle for reimagining organizational culture and suggesting strategic approaches (many of which have since been implemented). Our chapter places a particular emphasis on the process by which this was achieved, which has received scant attention in the existing scholarship.

6.3 Transformative Agency

The theoretical framework we use to frame our analysis in this chapter is *transformative agency* (Haapasaari et al. 2016). That framework has arisen from a long trajectory of research in the activity theory tradition (which we discuss in more detail in Section 6.4.1), by scholars investigating corporations undergoing complex transformation in the wake of radical economic and technological change. We adopt the framework in this chapter because it has long been used to examine how people develop agency within organizational change efforts, and because its framing of agency as a form of joint subjectivity resonates with aspects of the capacity building that the literature argues is so essential for successful change in educational institutions. We are aware that, at the time of writing, the framework has not been much used in the literature on sustainability or SHE, and for that reason we introduce the principles in some detail.

Transformative agency proceeds from the recognition of what Virkkunen (2006) calls "an increasing need for deep qualitative transformation in business activities involving the development and implementation of entirely new concepts" (p. 43). Transformative agency, in short, attempts to address questions concerning the kinds of agency that are required for such qualitative transformation to occur.

6.3.1 Conceptualizing Stakeholder Agency

The general notion of agency has become increasingly central to discussions of change and development across wide swathes of the social sciences. In broad language, the term refers to how people actively strive toward objectives, take initiative, and/or influence their own lives. Yet scholarly attempts to formulate what comprises agency more precisely have been highly contentious, to the extent that Eteläpelto et al.'s (2013) review acknowledges that there is "confusion surrounding the whole concept" (p. 46). Indeed, where comparisons are made even between the best-known conceptions of agency — such as the agency-structure approach of Giddens, the analytical dualism of Archer, the knowledge/power-based framework of Foucault, and the temporality-based conception of Emirbayer and Mische — there are wide divergences on important issues such as autonomy, knowledge, context, and power (Pattison 2020).

The distinctive argument of those scholars who have developed and promoted the notion of transformative agency is that, where change happens within complex cultural social formations, it is because people come together and enact change as a group, with the collective exhibiting a form of agency that cannot be reduced to that of the separate individuals in the group. Scholars of this view, therefore, criticize much existing literature on grounds of individualism and for insufficiently accounting for how change (and especially radical change) is actually accomplished as a process. Work on transformative agency, as a consequence, deliberately foregrounds how individuals come together to form a collective subject, and how, in doing so, they break away from the social situation that confronts them and progressively develop initiative to transform that situation (Virkkunen 2006). The effect, as Haapasaari et al. (2016) underline, is to shift analytical attention toward the transitions that occur as people work toward systemic change:

> Transformative agency differs from conventional notions of agency in that it stems from encounters with and examination of disturbances, conflicts and contradictions in the collective activity. Transformative agency develops the participants' joint activity by explicating and envisioning new possibilities. Transformative agency goes beyond the individual as it seeks possibilities for collective change efforts. [. . .] Transformative agency is not limited to the relations of an individual expert in that it underlines the crucial importance of expansive transitions from individual initiatives toward collective actions to accomplish systemic change. Transformative agency also goes beyond situational here-and-now actions as it emerges and evolves over time, often through complex debates and stepwise crystallisations of a vision to be implemented (p. 233).

Transformative agency has been used in scholarly work for some time and has proven its value as an analytical approach in understanding radical transformation (Engeström 2011). It has also been used to study relationships between change and empowerment in HEIs more specifically (Moffitt 2019). Common points of emphasis in studies of transformative agency include how interprofessional working, social accountability, and multivocal challenge are developed and nurtured, and – reflecting the rejection of one-size-fits-all approaches in the sustainability literature – the acknowledgment of diversity between activities and organizations.

Studies of transformative agency have long emphasized that developing such agency is a process. The development of transformative agency, where successful, will involve a movement, over time, from rudimentary expressions of opinion to commissive speech (publicly committing to action), and from individual initiative to better coordinated forms of joint action. Yet the process is certainly not smooth, with attempts to develop joint agency encountering a range of false starts, changes in direction and, in some cases, outright failure. Recent scholarship on the topic has sought to understand these processes in more detail via detailed examinations of the dynamics of change processes (Haapasaari et al. 2016).

Two notions arising from this scholarship are crucial for our subsequent narrative in this chapter: first, that it is important to understand how agency is being expressed by participants as change efforts unfold and, second, that the development of the agency of the group is heavily shaped by influential moments – turning points – which change their perspective.

6.3.2 Expressions of Transformative Agency

Studying how transformative agency is being expressed by participants in change initiatives typically involves recording meetings within the initiative and examining speaking turns made by the various participants. Haapasaari et al. (2016) propose the following typology for understanding how transformative agency is expressed in such meetings:

- **Resisting** suggestions, initiatives, or the direction of the overall change effort, in ways that might be directed at managers, co-participants or other colleagues, or the researchers present.
- **Criticizing** existing ways of working in the organization.
- **Explicating** new potential in the activity being discussed, typically by recounting positive experiences.
- **Envisioning** new ways of working, by making suggestions for new models or patterns.
- **Committing** to taking action to change the activity, in ways that are concrete and time-bound.
- **Reporting taking actions** to change the activity, typically in-between meetings of the change initiative.

In what follows, we will use this typology to structure the analysis of the CL project – drawing attention to examples of each expression of transformative agency and considering how the design of the research-intervention supported participants in developing the agency underpinning those expressions.

6.3.3 Turning Points in the Development of Agency

Understanding the development of transformative agency as a process should not be taken to mean that the process is gradual, linear, or smooth. The concept of turning points has been used in the literature on transformative agency, as Haapasaari et al. (2016) summarize, to draw attention to events that result in abrupt transitions in how participants engage with a change initiative. Turning points have been variously discussed as events that:

- Change the focus of the initiative,
- Lead to a widening or narrowing of perspective about the existing point of focus, or
- Mark a distinct change in the quantity and/or category of discursive expressions of agency (p. 243).

In our analysis, we shall discuss how the different discursive expressions of agency we encountered were associated with turning points in the change initiative. The purpose is to underline that nurturing and developing participant agency is important across the length of sustainability-related change initiatives in HEIs, and that doing so can have a range of impacts throughout.

6.4 The Change Laboratory

The design of the institutional initiative we document in this chapter is based on the CL, an established methodology for conducting research-interventions in which the purpose is to generate research knowledge within genuine change efforts (Virkkunen and Newnham 2013). In this section, we explain some of the relevant tenets of the approach so that the reader may understand the rationale behind the project design we discuss subsequently.

Compared with work in other interventionist traditions, such as design-based research and action research, the CL approach places greater emphasis on how participants identify (and successively reformulate) the nature of the problem being confronted as the initiative proceeds (Virkkunen and Newnham 2013, p. 9). Participants in such projects generate their own concepts, refine them as they are explored and implemented and, in the process, come together to develop both new systems and their own agency. The focus of the CL approach, then, strongly resonates with what Appleton's (2017) report recommends as a successful approach to sustainability-related change (discussed in this chapter's Introduction). Though the approach has been more extensively used in technology industries and medical system reform than in universities, there is a growing body of work that examines how the CL can be used to support radical change in HEIs (Bligh and Flood 2015). To the best of our knowledge, however, the approach has not previously been applied to specifically sustainability-related initiatives in HEIs – though it has been used to support the development of sustainable agriculture initiatives in farming communities (Mukute et al. 2018).

The CL arises from a long tradition of interventionist research commenced in the 1920s by Lev Vygotsky (Daniels 2008). Vygotsky sought, in laboratory experiments, to investigate the Zone of Proximal Development – the space between what is currently done and what can be done with extra assistance – for an individual experimental subject. The CL, by contrast seeks to help a group of practitioners explore the Zone of Proximal Development of their own real activities with assistance from an interventionist researcher. In practice, doing so involves a group of practitioners meeting together, over a period of time, to address tasks in a series of workshops.

A range of more lengthy descriptions of the CL approach, each with its own particular nuances and points of emphasis, can be found elsewhere (e.g. Daniels 2008, ch. 6; Virkkunen and Newnham 2013; Bligh and Flood 2015; Morselli 2019). But three aspects, in particular, are crucial for understanding the present project: the basis of the approach in activity theory, the use of expansive learning to provide a strategy-level structure for the intervention, and the use of the double-stimulation principle to design workshop tasks. We now describe these.

6.4.1 Activity Theory

Activity theory is an established and mature approach for understanding practice which, like the CL, has a strong heritage in the theories of Lev Vygotsky (Blunden 2010). The theory has been used in an extensive array of academic disciplines, and has, in recent times, been imported into HE studies, where it is valued for its ability to grasp the dynamics of complex situations, its emphasis on understanding how phenomena arise within a cultural and historical context, and its strong focus on change and development (Bligh and Flood 2017). While activity theory is extensive and sophisticated, the core principles of direct relevance to the subsequent narrative in this chapter are as follows (cf. Moffitt and Bligh 2021, pp. 127–128):

- *Activities* (sustained, collective projects of human *subjects*) are distinguished from *actions* (subjects' time-bound pursuit of goals), with actions understood as deriving their meaning from their broader position within the wider activities that generate them.
- Activities are *oriented* toward *objects*, meaning materially existing items that those participating in the activity derive motivation from working on.
- Activities are *mediated* by *artifacts*, meaning other items (such as tools) that subjects use to work on the object, as well as various social structures and rules that arise within the activity which guide how work on the object is undertaken.
- Activities are *changing*, with current forms of activity having arisen out of *historical* precedents and developing into new forms.
- The engine of *development* within activities are *contradictions* within and between different aspects of activity that those participating experience and try to overcome, thereby modifying the activity (importantly, their modifications do not always work in the ways that were intended).

Activity theory plays several roles in the project we describe in the present chapter. We use it to conceptualize sustainability-related reforms in HEIs as the development and change of activities, and to position the project, based on the CL, as an activity whose object is those existing activities that participants wish to change (in other words, we are creating an activity whose purpose is to work on other activities and change them). The process of the project is disaggregated, as elaborated further in Section 6.4.2, into a series of actions which derive their purpose from the wider change effort. Task designs, meanwhile, place considerable emphasis on the artifacts mediating participants' efforts, including the use of diagrammatic means to represent activity structures to participants.

6.4.2 Expansive Learning

Expansive learning is a notion developed, within the scholarship on activity theory, by Engeström (1987), for the purposes of conceptualizing radical change in activities. For Engeström, ruptural change in activity is characterized by subjects experiencing and identifying acute contradictions in enacting the activity and, as a consequence, changing it in ways that involve qualitatively transforming – "expanding" – its object. For Engeström, it is ongoing attempts at such radical change in activities that construct novel ideas and practices within particular cultures, to the extent that expansive learning can be characterized as "learning what is not yet there" (Engeström 2016). Such a form of learning is seen as increasingly important, in the activity theory tradition, given that societal challenges increasingly require subjects to go beyond the acquisition, replication, and application of predetermined knowledge toward conceptual and practical innovation.

It is important to acknowledge that not all attempts at such radical change are even remotely successful in achieving their aims. Yet, where expansion of the object *is* achieved in practice, Engeström's (2016) work suggests that subjects will have undertaken a range of actions whose goals can be categorized into the following ideal-types (pp. 47–48):

1) **Questioning**: Rejecting or criticizing established aspects of activity.
2) **Analysis**: Investigating, representing and explaining (i) the structure of the present activity and (ii) the earlier activities that have led to the present ways of working.
3) **Modeling**: Devising simplified but explanatory models of new ways of working that might overcome present contradictions.
4) **Examination:** Exploring the dynamics, potential, and limitations of proposed models by debating their application and considering test cases.
5) **Implementation**: Applying models in practice at small scale and identifying how they work in concrete terms.
6) **Process reflection**: Evaluating the progress of attempts at change and how those attempts align with the motivations of the people participating.
7) **Consolidation and generalization**: Embedding models as new forms of practice at wider scale.

Engeström's work suggests that actions of the above types do not occur in a linear fashion, but instead form cycles as change initiatives move forward, encounter stumbling blocks, and revisit earlier decisions and proposals.

While expansive learning does occur in the wild, the CL approach that underpins the project we describe in this chapter is an explicit attempt to nurture or accelerate it; indeed, Moffitt and Bligh (2021) have called the CL a "pedagogy of expansive learning" precisely because it involves researcher-interventionists designing a microcosm environment for the purposes of stimulating expansive learning and thus changing real activities. In the project we describe in this chapter, the typology of expansive learning actions we have listed were used as the basis of the project's strategy – for example, a specific task for a workshop might be designed to address a goal related to *questioning*.

6.4.3 Double-Stimulation

The other important principle for the project we describe is *double-stimulation*, an approach to designing tasks which also originates in the tradition of Vygotsky (Sannino 2015).

Double-stimulation involves introducing a problem, known as the *first stimulus*, which subjects are given the goal of addressing. Yet the problem is of such a type (and has been formulated in such a way) that obvious solutions are absent, and participants experience it as conflicting. Subsequently, another artifact, known as the *second stimulus*, is introduced, which provides participants with a framework for addressing the goal of the problem.

Such task structures have long been understood, as Sannino (2015) says, as a way of promoting volitional action in experimental subjects. Indeed, doing so was the focus of Vygotsky's original experiments, in which the double-stimulation principle was first developed. In the CL, double-stimulation is used as the basis for collective task designs (Virkkunen and Newnham 2013; Bligh and Flood 2015) and considerable attention has been devoted to understanding the kinds of first and second stimuli that participants in change efforts might address. Given that CL tasks are typically carried out by stakeholders in group meetings, the first and second stimuli of double-stimulation tasks are usually accompanied by mirror data – concrete examples of the kind of dilemmas and problems being discussed. Moffitt and Bligh (2021), for example, report extensive use of video footage to fulfill this function, though a range of other alternatives are possible, such as institutional documents, graphs, statistical reports, and photographs. Importantly, as the project goes on, resources developed by participants themselves in earlier sessions (such as a map of a proposed new activity) are often brought back to serve as components of new tasks, thereby contributing toward cumulative knowledge building in the project and reinforcing participant influence over the initiative.

It is these principles – a CL research design, using activity theory for conceptual framing and analysis, expansive learning for strategy, and double-stimulation for the design of particular tasks – that formed the underlying basis of the project we describe in this chapter.

6.5 Research Design

6.5.1 The Research Site

Projects based on the CL approach start out by choosing an intervention unit to be the focus of the change (Virkkunen and Newnham 2013). It is understood that any intervention unit can generate concepts and practices, whose later generalization will be a stepwise, active, and contested process. But the starting point for a research-intervention is, nonetheless, consequential, and needs to be considered strategically. In HE settings, the choice of intervention unit can be difficult: ideally it is one "where there is recognition of a need for change, an organisationally strategic position, and sufficient stability to cope if matters become intense"; yet it might also be a unit where the researcher has access, or where they already work, with the selection therefore strongly constrained (Bligh and Flood 2015, p. 155).

For the present project, the intervention unit selected was a whole campus in the West of Ireland; this was considered manageable because the site was a small, auxiliary campus (c. 1000 students) within a multicampus Institute of Technology (total student population

12,000). The research site was chosen because a number of programs focused on particular aspects of sustainability were already delivered there; for example, the outdoor education program has a focus on environmental management and sustainability. The range of programs offered meant that there was wide range of disciplinary expertise available on-site which is often considered essential for success of sustainability related initiatives. Correspondingly, a strong staff interest in sustainability was already evident on the campus. One of the researchers was, at the time, also working there as a member of the academic staff, and thus had access to the staff and management. A prior interest in sustainability was also held by some members of campus management and this created a fertile environment in which to explore a more integrated approach to embedding sustainability into the practices and activities on the campus.

The campus had previously established a track record on environmental issues in 2011, by becoming the first Institute of Technology (IoT) campus in Ireland to achieve a "Green Flag" for Waste and Water under the national "Green Campus" program. The campus has since been awarded three additional Green Flags – for Energy, Biodiversity, and Transport.

6.5.2 Conceiving the Project

As we have outlined, sustainability and the environment were issues that attracted a lot of interest and activity from certain members of the staff in the campus. This manifested itself through involvement in Green Campus programs and the inclusion of sustainability related topics in the curriculum of some programs on the campus. Yet, prior to the present project, these activities were, in the main, bottom-up initiatives: instigated and driven by individual lecturers who were interested in particular aspects of sustainability and who sought to incorporate it into their own modules and programs. There were no formal sustainability policy or plans anywhere in the wider institute and, aside from the Green Campus initiative, there were no sustainability-focused inter-/cross-disciplinary activities being carried out on the intervention unit campus. Thus, in spite of a groundswell of support for sustainability, sustainability-related activities were being carried out in isolation and were not having the desired impact on the wider institute or on the students. This is in line with Appleton's (2017) observation, discussed in this chapter's Introduction, that fragmentary approaches lacking practical coordination or overall vision are common, but problematic.

6.5.3 Recruiting Stakeholders

An early step for the project involved considering participant recruitment. We referred to Virkkunen and Newnham's (2013) criteria, which suggest, firstly, striving to include an appropriate range of voices (from a range of roles, including both management and staff) and, second, trying to ensure that they "are dealing with the same object in their daily work and are involved in realizing the same final outcome despite differences in their occupation, task or hierarchical position" (p. 65). While these criteria are often seen as potentially conflicting (ibid.), in this project there were indeed common objects and outcomes that a variety of members of staff and management were each seeking to achieve: attracting students to the campus to ensure its viability (given widespread reorganization in the sector within Ireland) and making sustainability a focus of the practices on the campus. Thus, we attempted to recruit participants who would be aligned with these objects.

Participation in the CL process was made open, in principle, to all staff from the campus (an email was circulated among staff, outlining that a research project on ESD and sustainability was going to take place on the campus, and requesting expressions of interest in taking part), though in practice most participants were enlisted through direct contact by the researcher. The selection of candidates was based on previously exhibited interest in the general area of sustainability and environmental issues. Participants were contacted individually, with recruitment prioritizing the following criteria, all of which included both staff and management:

1) Membership of the Green Campus Committee.
2) Membership of the (informal) environmental and sustainability group.
3) Staff teaching subjects directly related to the environment or who had a previous record (on the campus) of environmental or sustainability-related activities.

Virkkunen and Newnham (2013) suggest a typical figure of 20 participants, and once there were 22 participants confirmed, further recruitment activities stopped.

6.5.4 Designing Stakeholder Workshops

CL interventions typically involve 5–12 workshops and, at the outset, it was anticipated that eight sessions would be needed to complete the process. The CL sessions were designed to guide the participants through cycles of expansive learning actions which, as described in Section 6.4.2, is part of the strategic backbone of the CL methodology. Correspondingly, in the initial plan, tasks within each workshop were designed to engage with appropriate goals of expansive learning actions and to do so using double-stimulation principles.

The planned schedule and initial design intentions (in terms of expansive learning actions) are presented in Table 6.1, along with the actual stages of the expansive learning cycle (ELC) observed during the intervention. As for many intervention projects of this type, it was only possible to plan in detail the tasks and stimuli for the first one or two sessions, because the outcomes of these sessions will influence the direction and subject matter of the following sessions. Nonetheless, it is possible to prepare an outline plan of the project from the beginning, which is often useful for thinking strategically about the change initiative even if the plan needs to be amended as action unfolds in the project. Prior to the first formal CL workshop, an introductory session was held, which provided an introduction to the research project, a description of the methodology, and an outline of what was expected from the volunteers, should they agree to participate.

In line with the concept of expansive learning, the primary intention of the first session was to get the participants questioning and criticizing existing sustainability related practices on the campus. The focus on questioning carried over into session 2, where the participants started to analyze why current practices were as they were, in terms of historical reasons, as well as the inner systemic nature of the practices. That analysis, in turn, carried over into session 3, and with participants subsequently starting to model new practice solutions, which continued in session 4. This process of designing workshops to correspond to expansive learning actions continued until the end of the project. An overview of the design for each session is provided in Table 6.2, which provides details of the main tasks (first stimuli), solution frameworks (second stimuli) and concrete examples (mirror data) used.

After each session, the researcher reviewed the recordings and prepared minutes and notes, and an agenda for the following session, using the expansive learning to support strategic thinking about the ongoing direction of the project. The researcher then emailed the minutes, agendas, and any additional material needed for the next session to all participants, thus ensuring that all were kept up to speed even if, as occasionally happened, they missed a session.

As it turned out, the intervention consisted of eight sessions and, as discussed in this chapter's Introduction, resulted in a number of significant practice outcomes for the campus. For the purposes of this chapter, we focus in on one of those outcomes in particular – the

Table 6.1 Actions of the expansive learning cycle mapped onto the CL research workshops.

Mapping the stages of the expansive learning cycle to the sessions		
Description of planned stage and initial design intention	Session number, dates and intervals	Actual focus of action when judged against the expansive learning cycle
Type 1 Questioning: people reject established wisdom, current practices, and existing plans;	**Session 1** Planned 11 Jan. 2016 Actual 13 Jan. 2016	Type 1: Questioning and criticizing
Type 1 Questioning: people reject established wisdom, current practices, and existing plans;	**Session 2** 2-week interval Planned 25 Jan. 2016 Actual 27 Jan. 2016	Type 2: Analysis
Type 2 Analysis: people investigate and represent the structure and history of the present situation;	**Session 3** 2-week interval Planned 8 Feb. 2016 Actual 10 Feb. 2016	Type 3: Modeling
Type 3 Modeling: people pose a new, simplified model that aims to explain the situation in a public form and to suggest potential solutions;	**Session 4** 2-week interval Planned 22 Feb. 2016 Actual 24 Feb. 2016	
Type 4 Examination: people work with the model to better comprehend its dynamics, potential and limitations;	**Session 5** 3-week interval Planned 7 Mar. 2016 Actual 16 Mar. 2016	Type 4: Examining
Type 5 Implementation and Reflection: people render the model more concrete by applying it practically and conceptually, so enriching and extending it;	**Session 6** 3 weeks Planned 4 Apr. 2016 Actual 6 Apr. 2016	
Type 6 Process reflection: people evaluate their current process, generating critique and identifying further requirements;	**Session 7** 4 weeks Planned 18 Apr. 2016 Actual 3 Apr. 2016	Type 5: Implementation Type 6: Process reflection
Type 7: Consolidation and generalization: people attempt to embed stable forms of new practice.	**Session 8** 3 weeks Planned 3 May 2016 Actual 30 May 2016	Type 5: Implementation Type 6: Process reflection Type 7: Consolidation and generalization

development of a CSS. Below, we shall examine how this particular outcome influenced, and was influenced by, the development of stakeholders' transformative agency during the process.

6.5.5 Data Generation and Analysis

CL research-interventions typically generate a lot of raw data, including video footage, the associated notes and minutes, flip-chart materials, and full transcripts from each session. In this project, additional transcripts from post-intervention semi-structured interviews were also generated. The data is effectively processed and analyzed three times: (i) initially, during the sessions, participants' work constitutes an ongoing, collaborative analysis of data that unfolds in real time alongside the generation of new data (we call this form of collaborative knowledge production *intersession analysis*); (ii) the researcher-interventionist then examines

Table 6.2 Summary of Change Laboratory session design.

Stage of the ELC	Session: no	First stimulus or session tasks	Second stimulus	Mirror data
	Introduction 60 minutes, 15 participants			
Questioning	13 Jan. 2016 Session 1 133 mins, 15 p.	Discuss the concepts of sustainability in HE. How does ESD relate to you own practices? What is the status of SHE on the campus?	Visual prompts Hard copies of a range of SHE documents and journal articles	Answers given by individual participants recorded and displayed on flipchart sheet for others to reflect on
	27 Jan. 2016 Session 2 97 mins, 11 p.	What would a sustainable IoT look like? Identify SHE practice priorities for the campus. What are the barriers to SHE on the campus?	Visual prompts Hard copies of a range of institutional SHE documents and journal articles	PowerPoint presentation and printed summary of session 1 material
Analysis	10 Feb. 2016 Session 3 110 mins, 14 p.	Develop a mission statement for the Campus. Discuss the potential of the practice proposals identified in session 2.	Sample definition of HE for sustainable development Reference to examples of how other HEIs implement SHE	Hard copy summaries of the SHE related activities of the participants provided
Modeling	24 Feb. 2016 Session 4 91 mins, 12 p.	Consider and develop the proposals made in the previous session, the "Mission Statement," institute strategy and new program development.	Expansive learning diagram, Institute Strategy, A previous SHE related proposal for the campus	Hard copy summary of material generated in previous sessions
Examination	16 Mar. 2016 Session 5 86 mins, 11 p.	Sense-check purpose of the mission statement. How can the models be operationalized?	Outlining the main research objective	Material generated in the previous session.
	6 Apr. 2016 Session 6 64 mins, 10 p.	How can the models be operationalized?	Reference to examples of how other HEIs implement SHE	Material generated in the previous session
Implementation/Process reflection	3 May 2016 Session 7 49 mins, 12 p.	Reflect on the proposed wording of the CSS Reflect on the proposed sustainability paragraphs How can the (CL) process be built upon	Summary of materials from early in the project (Reflecting on how the statement and the paragraphs address the task identified earlier)	The CSS statement The program sustainability paragraphs Summary of outputs
Implementation/Process reflection/Consolidation		Review the work and outcomes of the process and reflect on how these might be continued.	Expansive learning cycle diagram (emphasis on reflection in the context of expansive learning)	The wording of the proposed statement, and program sustainability paragraphs

data from a given session afterwards, to support and facilitate the ongoing design of the project (we call this work, which must be completed in time for the next workshop, *intrasession analysis*); and (iii) subsequently, a *post-intervention analysis* is undertaken for the purpose of producing research outputs (and, often, institutional reports).

In this case, the initial inter-/intrasession analysis of the video footage and notes served the design of the intervention by identifying and summarizing the outcomes from each session, which were necessary in order to design and produce the tasks, tools, and activities required for the following workshops. The video footage from each session, in particular, was analyzed between sessions by the researcher and used to create detailed minutes which recorded the significant outcomes from each session. These were then circulated to participants via email, in a timely manner, along with an appropriately designed agenda/plan for the following workshop. It is important that participants can see how the design for upcoming workshops has been influenced by their working in earlier sessions. It is also worth noting that, in addition to carrying out the session tasks, participants were actively encouraged to take part in the intrasession analyses and, in practice, made many significant contributions which were recorded and distributed alongside the project minutes.

The post-intervention analysis of the video footage and transcripts, on the other hand, forms the direct basis of the account we present in the Section 6.6. For the purposes of this chapter, that analysis was carried out with the intention of identifying and extracting information relating to the following:

1) Turning points in the development of the CSS which influenced the development of the stakeholders' agency.
2) Manifestations of expressions of transformative agency (see the framework in Section 6.3.2).
3) Relationships between the stakeholders' transformative agency and the development of the CSS.

For the purposes of the analysis presented in this chapter, it is worth highlighting that the relevant sections of the videos and the associated transcripts were reviewed with the single purpose of discerning their place in the typology of transformative agency expressions, using the previously outlined framework. Doing so involved making judgments about both the content and context in which the dialogue occurred. This process required a number of repeat viewings of the footage as well as reviews of the transcripts.

6.6 Findings

In CL research-interventions, the development of stakeholders' transformative agency is part of a process that also encompasses the development of new concepts and practices. In this case, to assist the illustration of our narrative, we specifically home in on the development of that agency as it co-occurred with the conception and design of the CSS. For that reason, Section 6.6.1 sets out how the CSS was developed in the project, which, our analysis highlights, occurred via five turning points. The subsequent sections (6.6.2–6.6.6) document, in turn, the forms of stakeholder agency that were influential on the process at each of those five turning points.

6.6.1 Development of the Campus Sustainability Statement

In order to provide a chronological framework for the development of the CSS, we now map the process in terms of turning points identified during particular sessions. The notion of turning points was described in Section 6.3.3; it refers to events that can change the focus or perspective of an initiative and mark a distinct change in the quantity and/or category of discursive expressions of agency. In relation to the development of the CSS, we identified five such turning points:

1) Recognizing the lack of a sustainability framework.
2) The idea of a mission statement as a shared framework.
3) A proposal for a mission statement that encourages students to think for themselves.
4) Determining a suitable title for the statement and seeking inclusion of all campus stakeholders.
5) Emphasizing the importance of expressing commitment.

Each turning point represents a key event in the development of the CSS. In Table 6.3 we present the session timeline showing the turning points, the session in which they occurred, and a brief summary of the context in which they arose.

In the following section we use these five turning points as a framework to describe and analyze the development of participants' transformative agency, as it was observed during the intervention in the lead up to each turning point.

The manifestations of the various types of participants' transformative agency in relation to the development of the CSS, as observed during the intervention are mapped against the session timelines and presented in Table 6.4. To place the events in the context of the design intentions for each of the session, we include reference to the types of expansive learning actions for the overall intervention.

Table 6.3 Timeline and key events in the formation and development of the Campus Sustainability Statement.

Session no	Turning point	Development context
1	(TP1) Recognizing the lack of a sustainability framework	Exploring the range of meanings and interpretations of the term sustainability and how people understand it in relation to their own practices.
2	(TP2) The idea of a mission statement as a shared framework	The idea of a mission statement is first suggested as an alternative framework to detailed descriptions and definitions of sustainability.
3	(TP3) A proposal for a mission statement that encourages students to think for themselves	The idea of the mission statement is expanded and developed into a mission statement for the campus; wordings are proposed, reviewed and revised.
4		Further revisions to the proposed CSS wording
5	(TP4) Determining a suitable title for the statement and seeking inclusion of all stakeholders	The concept develops from a "mission statement" to a "Campus Sustainability Statement." Draft wordings are agreed by the group and issued to all staff for comment and feedback.
6		No development action on the CSS
7		Feedback from wider staff received, selection of a particular wording option agreed by participants.
8	(TP5) Emphasizing the importance of expressing commitment	The concept is further refined and commitment to action is made explicit through the inclusion of terms such as "committed to" and "endeavors" in the statement. The final wording is agreed for submission to management for consideration and adoption at a staff meeting.

Table 6.4 The development of participants' transformative agency mapped against the session timeline in the development of the Campus Sustainability Statement.

ELC action	Quest. and Criticizing	Analysis	Modeling	Examining	Implementation Reflection Consolidation
Turning point	TP1 Recognizing the lack of a sustainability framework	TP2 The idea of a mission statement as a shared framework	TP 3 A proposal for a mission statement that encourages students to think for themselves	TP4 Determining a suitable title for the statement and seeking inclusion of all campus stakeholders.	TP5 Emphasizing the importance of expressing commitment
TA Type *Resisting*			R.1 Mission statements are too corporate	R.2 Duplication of a mission statement	
Criticize	Cr.1 relating to lack of agreement on terminology Cr.2 relating to diversity of views Cr.3 the lack of a framework	Cr.1 relating to lack of agreement on terminology Cr.2 relating to diversity of views Cr.3 the lack of a framework	Cr.4 How the mission statements could help accomplish the aims. They should: express beliefs, have meaning, guide actions, be honest and realistic	Cr.6 The title Cr.7 The lack of campus wide collaboration Cr.8 Mission statements as having little impact	Cr.5 The wording as not strong enough
Explicate		Ex.1 A mission statement			
Envision			En.1 A statement that is phrased in terms of student opportunities. En.2 The specific wording, initial draft	En.3 An appropriate title. En.4 A collaboratively developed campus wide vision	En.2 The specific wording of the statement, agreeing the final wording.
Commit					Co.1 Committing to commit. Wording to signal commitment
Conseq. Action					
Session No	1	2	3	4	5 6 7 8

6.6.2 Recognizing the Lack of a Sustainability Framework

The focus of the first session in the intervention (subsequently running into session 2) was on questioning and criticizing the existing practices on the campus. Doing so immediately resulted in a lot of discussions about sustainability terminology and how different terms are defined. It became obvious that there were different understandings and beliefs in the group about what sustainability is and how it should be dealt with in the HE context. Conversely, it also became apparent that there was a lot of interest in "sustainability" (howsoever defined) and that many of the participants were already carrying out sustainability related activities in their practices.

The first turning point identified in the intervention was a recognition that, while there was a lot of interest in and activity around sustainability, there was no formal framework to work with to build capacity on the campus.

The expressions of transformative agency that were observed in the lead up to this turning point are each expressions of criticizing. Given that the design of the session had been intended to support questioning actions (see Table 6.2), then finding such evidence is perhaps unsurprising. Yet it is noticeable that, at this stage, participants did not feel able to resist the direction of the intervention or suggest ways forward of their own. Instead, at this early stage, their agency was nurtured by allowing them to criticize a range of concepts – in practice, as it turned out, the target of much criticism was the very notion of *defining sustainability.* Three expressions of transformative agency, all forms of criticizing, dominated proceedings at this point.

6.6.2.1 Cr1: Criticizing Relating to the Lack of Agreement on Terminology

One target of criticizing, in relation to how the participants understood sustainability terminology, was evident from the first session, which started off with one of the participants asking:

> Are we all starting with a common definition of sustainability?
> *S1 Management participant A*

This was the first of many engagements in the first two sessions where the participants problematized and also sought clarification regarding the issues of terminology and definitions. Such expressions attempted to raise the point that it would be difficult to begin the project without clarity on the key definitions that would be used.

6.6.2.2 Cr2: Criticizing Relating to the Diversity of Views

It quickly became apparent that different participants had diverse views on what sustainability is and how it can be dealt with: whether through teaching practice and/or in programs as a whole.

In session 1, participants tended to build on expressions of Cr1 by articulating that they had personal views that were clear to them but unlikely to be shared by all others in the group. One participant, for example, observed:

> …in terms of applying it to myself, I am aligned with environmental sustainability… and there are things I teach specifically such as the idea of cultural sustainability…traditions and crafts and the importance of the built heritage…
> *S1 Heritage Lecturer B*

Other participants, by contrast, suggested that they were focused on social or community aspects of sustainability:

> ...we take the three strands environment, economic and community and I really think that if we were looking at the programe as a whole, a lot of it is around compassion rather than passion, and I think that is very much the social element or the community element.......and we try to include that in the whole program.
>
> *S1 Social Care Lecturer A*

Subsequently, participants came to explicitly criticize this diversity of views, and to notice that some views were irreconcilable with others:

> that could end up leaving you with some tension between irreconcilable concepts, between trying to teach business students, for example, sustainability, and trying to teach them a certain type of economics at the same time.
>
> *S2 Social Care Lecturer B*

While the diversity of the participants' views, and the associated lack of agreement on sustainability terminology and definitions were recognized in session 1 (S1), they came to be more prominently identified as problematic in session 2 (S2), when the participants started to seek common ground to agree on a shared understanding.

6.6.2.3 Cr3: Criticizing the Lack of a Framework or Formal Structure

The first expression of criticizing practices (as opposed to definitions) directly related to the development of the CSS, was observed in session 1, where participants acknowledged that, even though there was a lot of sustainability activity being carried out on the campus (including by participants themselves), it was occurring in the absence of any structured plan or framework. The range of sustainability-related teaching activities was highlighted, as was the fact that they were independent of any formal institute framework, and this was acknowledged as problematic.

6.6.3 A Mission Statement as a Shared Framework

In session 2, many of the same issues that arose in session 1 reappeared and were discussed and debated again by the participants. Yet the intended focus for the session, as manifest in the task design, was on analyzing why the situation was as it was, and, moreover, the participants were asked to imagine what a sustainable IoT might look like. Doing so resulted in the following episode of explicating – the first time that new potential had been identified in the intervention.

6.6.3.1 Ex1: Explicating the Potential of a Mission Statement

The idea for the development of a mission statement as something that could guide practice and provide a framework within which to work arose in the context of the prevailing discussions about definitions of sustainability and the lack of an institutional framework. The idea was only mentioned in one exchange by the group during session 2, with the following extract an abbreviated illustration:

> ...we felt that there should be a mission statement....it would be useful, in that it would provide a framework, by which we are the individuals that drive it, and you are open to interpret that mission in terms of your own practices.
>
> *S2 Outdoor Education Lecturer B*

After the session, during the process of inter-session analysis, the researcher-interventionist highlighted this concept as worth developing in later sessions. Since the mission statement idea was being discussed as potentially providing a framework, as something open to individual interpretation, as something individuals could drive, and as something that seemed to be an achievable outcome, it was highlighted within the analysis at this point as a potential solution that might provide for a shared frame of action for sustainability.

6.6.4 A Proposal for a Mission Statement that Encourages Students to Think for themselves

Turning point 3, which was in many ways *the* pivotal point in the development of the CSS, occurred in session 3. As the following subsections elaborate, an initial – and robust – bout of resisting led to an oscillation between moments of envisioning and criticizing.

6.6.4.1 R1: Resisting Mission Statements as Corporate

At the start of session 3, the idea of a mission statement, which had only recently been put forward, was strongly resisted because of the perceived corporate nature of the term and the associated terminological and conceptual duplicity:

> ...if we have a mission statement saying that we are committed to sustainability... how can you run a business program on the campus? Or how can the campus fulfill its regional mission, which is to support "economic development" when development inherently means growth economics, which is not a sustainable concept?
>
> *S3 Social Care Lecturer B*

Members of the group were resisting the use of a tool, which is strongly associated with corporate identity, to promote sustainability in a HE context. The resistance focused on a number of features of mission statements, such as their actual function (i.e. are they meaningful, or just purely emblematic public presentations?). Recalling earlier criticizing, resistance was also encountered in relation to the need that such a statement would present for conceptual clarity (specifically regarding the concept of sustainability). Two examples were offered to illustrate this: how could an organization that states that it is committed to sustainability either run business programs or fulfill its local and regional remit to support economic growth? Both of these undertakings, it was suggested, are based on the growth economics model, which is seen by some as being an unsustainable economic model.

After some preliminary exploration and discussion, the initial resistance was, to some extent, replaced with criticizing what mission statements *are* (see Section 6.6.4.3), which seemed a bid to react to these moments of resistance.

6.6.4.2 En1: Envisioning a Statement that is Phrased in Terms of Students' Opportunities

The first expression of envisioning was prompted by the first task set in session 3, which asked the participants to develop a mission statement that the group could support. This focus on envisioning was driven by the researcher, who hoped that the group might be able to develop a statement that could be adopted in some way by the campus. It was hoped that it might be able to generate some form of conceptual alignment around sustainability among the participants.

The following speech occurred in the early part of session 3 and responded to the previous resistance expressed about mission statements:

> I am not a fan of mission statements but it might be something that might focus the group, but the other side of it is, instead of saying we are one extreme or the other . . .it's just to say that what we are offering students, is the ability *to look at things in a different way*, and not just in what could be the mainstream way, but enabling them to think for themselves and make a choice, and maybe in the future, make a decision, so we are not like, trying to convert them to one way or the other, but enabling people to make an informed choice.
>
> *Green Campus/Administration A*

This proposal changed the focus of the discussion to what the participants could collectively offer the students (i.e. encouraging their critical thinking), rather than the participants' own opinions or beliefs. The proposal received broad agreement from the participants on that basis, as the following extract demonstrates:

> I agree with that, what is good about that, is that it is more realistic, it's actually more accurately saying what we would do. It's not making a claim that we are going to be sustainable, or that we are going to commit ourselves to sustainability education . . . we are not, but we could do that, it's more realistic and more modest. . . . I suppose, this is as good as it gets.. . . .
>
> . . .We should be quite rigorous about our concepts and make sure that they are meaningful. . .now I think a modest one [mission statement] makes perfect sense to me. Instead of a big mission we have a tiny little mission, with a really modest claim. Our claim is modest, but the mission is a dramatic concept. . . another contradiction, but it can also be a signal of aspiration
>
> *Social Care Lecturer B*

This proposal, then, represented a pivotal moment in the development process. It provided a way to express an academic/pedagogical aspiration without either compromising values or committing to something that would have been considered unachievable by some of the participants.

6.6.4.3   Cr.4: Criticizing How the Mission Statement Could Help Accomplish the Aims of the Group

It was only after the proposal to "look at things in a different way" was made that the language of resistance gave way, to be replaced by criticizing, mainly manifest as critical commentary about the form the mission statement would take and whether this could achieve the aspirations of the group within the existing realities of the institution.

There were many individual instances of criticizing observed which we categorized under this heading, including:

- Discussions of participants' beliefs and how these would be projected (some participants felt that, while the statement should be about what they believed in, it was also important to acknowledge that there were many different beliefs about sustainability, and these others should be reflected too).
- Expressions of feeling that the statement should have meaning that could guide definite actions if the prevailing institutional lack of coordination was to be overcome.
- Arguments that the statement should articulate a common purpose within the institution.
- Reiterations that any mission statement should be honest and realistic or risk not being taken seriously given the institution's existing priorities.
- Arguments that only a general and simple statement would stand any chance of gaining traction and therefore being effective.

Such instances proceeded from a tacit assumption that the mission statement idea was gaining traction in the group, and the attendant criticizing involved jockeying to ensure that certain broad aims would be embedded in whatever mission statement was going to emerge. Earlier conversations in the project about the consequences of bottom-up initiatives in the institution were referred to and used to justify many of the points being made.

6.6.4.4   En2: Envisioning the Specific Wording of the Statement

As a consequence of the preceding bouts of criticizing, the development of precise wording for the statement came to be considered as very important by the participants. The development of that wording was observed in separate episodes of envisioning throughout the project, the first of which arose at this point in the intervention.

The development of the initial wording of the statement occurred in a two-step process, the first focusing on student engagement and second on the campus operations. It resulted in an initial draft, as follows:

> All our students will critically engage with sustainability in their program of study. The campus will endeavor to make sustainability a core value of its operation.

By the end of session 3, the draft of the statement contained two aims – a clear development from the initial proposal for a mission statement, which had referred only to student engagement. This development was the result of a discursive process that allowed the participants to explore what they felt was important about sustainability, and how it could be supported through the creation of a mission statement.

6.6.4.5   Cr5: Criticizing How the Statement Wording Would Be Understood

Subsequently, criticizing the specific wording of the statement was observed on two separate occasions. On each occasion, such criticism was made with regard to the prevailing situation in the institution, and doing so prompted the participants to propose slightly new wordings (which we categorized as further instances of En2).

6.6.5   Determining a Suitable Title for the Statement and Seeking Inclusion of all Campus Stakeholders

Once the idea of a mission statement had gained broad acceptance by the group, they turned their attention to refining it. Doing so, in particular, meant focusing on its title and what that meant for themselves and for the wider campus. This led to series of expressions of transformative agency which started out with resistance to the title "mission statement" and ended up with a concept whose new title acknowledged that the intended stakeholders included the wider campus staff. In terms of transformative agency, this is the first time that the group acknowledged and took responsibility for working and acting on behalf of staff from the campus as a whole.

6.6.5.1   R2: Resisting Duplication of the Term "Mission Statement"

The second instance of resisting, like the first (R1), related to the very idea of a mission statement. Yet, this time, the basis of the resistance was that the institute already had a mission statement. It was therefore felt that it would be inappropriate for the campus to develop its own mission statement or charter.

> The mission statement that is there, is institute-wide. . ... But what we have been trying to develop here is something that probably is specific for this campus. . .?
>
> *S5 Researcher*

> I'd agree with [Management Participant B] that the [existing] mission statement is for the institute, so having separate mission statements for different campuses probably won't have value for it, in terms of communicating it...
>
> *S5 Management Participant A*

Such resistance served to foreground the idea that the group's activities were oriented toward the campus, rather than the institution as a whole.

6.6.5.2   Cr6: Criticizing the Title

In session 5, as a consequence of the above resistance to the idea of a mission statement (R2), the previously proposed statement was again discussed by participants, this time on the basis that the title would be unsuitable given the existing institutional situation.

> Is it a campus charter specific to sustainability, like a mission statement or a charter, is that a bit broad? I'd be a bit confused, which is the actual campus one? Very specific to sustainability and green...
>
> *Social Care Lecturer A*

Such criticizing ultimately led to the envisioning of a new title.

6.6.5.3   En3: Envisioning a more Appropriate Title

Much of the time spent on envisioning at this point involved exploring what the participants wanted the statement to represent and, therefore, considering what the title should be to reflect this intention. The proposed title went through a series of iterations. The term "charter" had been mentioned in a previous session, and one participant asked if the statement might be a "campus charter" specific to sustainability.

> I think a charter (rather than mission statement) might be one that might reflect the group, you know, it's meaningful rather than a mission.
>
> *S5 Management Participant A*

Members of the group subsequently explored series of possible options, including a "charter for sustainability" and a "campus sustainability charter" (a momentarily important distinction), and "a sustainability proclamation." It was eventually decided that the group should put forward a "sustainability statement for the campus," subsequently shortened to "Campus Sustainability Statement." Doing so seemed to capture the advantages of the statement that had been proposed earlier, while avoiding the pitfalls identified in R1.

6.6.5.4   Cr7: Criticizing the Lack of Campus-Wide Collaboration

Proposing the concept of a "Campus Sustainability Statement," however, was consequential for how the group perceived themselves and related the change initiative to existing institutional practice. In sessions 4 and 5, a number of participants commented on the fact that the group was not representative of the whole staff on the campus. The group, it was suggested, could not impose a new mission statement for the campus without replicating the existing pattern of bottom-up initiative which failed to garner engagement from other stakeholders:

> We can't as a self-selecting group say, by the way, so that all the rest of you know, we have decided that the new mission for the campus is X. . .. . .people will likely say whoa what is this? We can't do it that way.
>
> *S4 Social Care Lecturer B*

In session 5, this was again articulated as criticizing, as follows, (see also Section 6.6.5.5 En.4.)

> I think Judd had more points about this the last time, about his concern about it being a mission for the campus, as opposed to . . .. not everyone would subscribe to that
>
> *S5 Management Participant A*

6.6.5.5   En.4: Envisioning a Collaboratively Developed Campus-Wide Vision

In session 5, in response to those expressions we have categorized as Cr7, it was envisioned to get input into the CSS from wider campus stakeholders. A number of options for sharing the content of the statement with the staff were explored, including organizing a face-to-face staff meeting, creating a sharefile on the intranet of the institution, and sending an email to all staff. One such contribution was set out as follows:

> So maybe we could set up a sharefile, put it there for people to contribute to, and close it out maybe at a wider meeting. Just be a long enough time for people to be able to think about and understand, and, I suppose, they might say what's the impact with that, to understand what we're proposing there, what we're trying to take forward, and that they have a chance to . . . Just whatever format works for them to contribute or voice concerns in that way. Sometimes, at staff meetings people might not like to stand up and speak up about something in front of a whole group. . .
>
> *Management Participant A*

6.6.5.6   Cr8: Criticizing of Mission Statements as Having Little Impact

Another expression of criticizing that arose at this point reiterated earlier opprobrium at the very notion of statements. In particular, one of the participants, who had previously been through numerous strategic review processes where institutional statements had been developed, expressed his concern that even though he thought the proposed statement was positive, in his experience, statements do not necessarily have much impact or elicit strong responses from staff members:

> I think it's a lot better than the amount of spin-out meetings we've had about making a mission statement for this college, which have gone on and on, I've gone through about five mission statements for this college at this stage so. . ..
>
> . . ..They've been put through . . .you know . . ..we have a mission statement appearing, and then. . .. life goes on as normal, so, I'd be surprised if you get many big dissenters to the mission statement.
>
> *IT Lecturer A*

That it took several sessions of discussion on the topic before anyone commented on the fact that the institute already had a mission statement is perhaps proof of this point. Such criticizing, and the discussion that it prompted, served in this instance to reinforce a decision that had already gained traction: that it would be important to try to get input from a wider set of institutional stakeholders about then proposals being developed by the group.

As a consequence of these discussions the proposed wordings, along with a short overview of the project and its aims, were shared via email with all campus staff.

6.6.6 Emphasizing the Importance of Expressing Commitment

The final turning point observed in the development of the CSS occurred in the last session and was because of a further episode of criticizing (similar to those under Cr5 above) aimed at questioning the level of commitment expressed in the existing wording of the statement. That criticizing led to envisioning (type En2) of a new wording. On the surface, the changes might appear to be modest and subtle, yet they are significant in terms of agency because of what they represent in terms of the *expression of commitment* that they indicate.

In session 8, the participants considered whether the wording was simply not "strong" enough to express the sentiment that they wished to communicate:

> Sorry, can I just make one comment on it. . .? Just, do you want to go with "endeavors" or something a bit more. . .. I suppose, it softens the ability that "endeavors to embed." Whereas if you said "it embeds sustainability" is that too pushy?
>
> *S8 Nursing Lecturer*

This led to a short discussion about the detail of wording and resulted in the final expressions of envisioning, when the wording of the statement was changed from:

> The Mayo Campus *endeavors to* embed sustainability into the core of its activities and operations. We *aspire to* provide a teaching and learning space that promotes critical engagement with sustainability.

to

> The Mayo Campus *is committed* to embedding sustainability into the core of its activities and operations. We *endeavor to* provide a teaching and learning space that promotes critical engagement with sustainability.

6.6.6.1 Co1: Committing to Commit

During the intervention, there were many expressions of committing observed, such as the formation of a number of subcommittees; however, only one episode was related to the development of the CSS specifically. We argue that "committing to taking concrete actions" was demonstrated when the proposed wording of the statement was changed in the final session to include the words, "committed," and "endeavors." These changes, in relation to campus operations and teaching and learning activities, were intended as an unequivocal expression of commitment by the participants to taking concrete, new actions, in relation to embedding sustainability on the campus.

While this manifestation is aspirational and somewhat vicarious (in that the CSS had yet to be approved and adopted by the campus staff, and then enacted by them, rather than just by the participants) we believe that it demonstrates a commitment to taking concrete action in the future so long as the CSS is eventually approved and adopted. The following quotations evoke the wider enthusiasm of the participants for including the new words and their meaning:

> Yeah, "commits." There's a commitment, whether people act on it or not, that's why "commit" would be better.
>
> *S8 Outdoor Education Lecturer A*

I prefer "committed" of course. . . .. I far prefer "committed."

S8 Environment Lecturer

6.6.7 Consequential Actions

The final wording of the mission statement was agreed at the last CL session and so expressions of consequential actions were not observed during the project workshops. Many consequential actions were taken after the process, most of which were led by participants in the research-intervention, but these fall outside the dataset whose analysis forms the basis of this chapter.

6.7 Discussion

Let us now step back and consider what these findings tell us about stakeholder agency in HE sustainability initiatives.

We have outlined, from the beginning of the chapter, that pursuing sustainability-related change within HEIs is viewed as increasingly urgent – a moral imperative underpinned by the requirement to maintain credibility with external stakeholders and to fulfill the educational remit of the institution. The existing literature, for good reason, has focused on the problematic nature of many change initiatives, and there has been some debate on the different kinds of problems encountered by top-down, bottom-up, and middle-out approaches. Yet such literature has largely remained blind to process and, therefore, has failed to appreciate how stakeholder agency is expressed in different ways and at different times.

One way in which our findings contribute, therefore, is in showing that the capacity-building element of these institutional change initiatives is dependent upon the extent to which participants are able to define the problems being addressed for themselves and guide the direction of the outcomes that are being developed. As we have demonstrated, the eventual outcome of the CSS arose initially from a critical discussion between stakeholders about the meaning of the term sustainability – a discussion in which it became clear that agreement would not be forthcoming. Had the lack of agreement been taken as a sign that the intervention was becoming directionless, then a decision could have been taken to enforce a decision or close down the project. Instead, the disagreement and passion of the group were harnessed, even at the risk of frustrating some of the stakeholders, and the urge to impose tidy resolution was resisted. As a consequence – and through a series of intervening turning points – the concept of the CSS was developed by the participants themselves. While this chapter has focused on the CSS in particular, similar narratives could have been unfolded about the various other outcomes that were generated from the wider initiative. We contend that the key distinction between sustainability-related change initiatives within HEIs, therefore, should be seen not so much in terms of a categorization of the institutional origins of the initiative (such as top-down) but, rather, in terms of how time and resources are provided to support and nurture an ongoing inquiry by the participants concerned. A similar point could be made concerning the tendency – mentioned in this chapter's Introduction – to categorize initiatives based upon which institutional functions they focus on. Had our project commenced from the starting point that it was focused on "educational provision," for example, then many of the actual outcomes that were developed would have been judged, very quickly, to have been out of the scope of the intervention, to the detriment of the influential and coordinated set of strategies that did emerge from the project as it unfolded.

Our literature review also highlighted how prominently the issues of barriers and challenges are discussed in the literature on sustainability-related change initiatives. It is worth emphasizing that many of the barriers and challenges described in that literature concern issues that were encountered fairly directly in the project we have described in this chapter. Take, for example, the widely acknowledged issue that institutional stakeholders lack an agreed definition or understanding of sustainability. That challenge was prominently encountered during this project, and indeed how it was overcome has been documented above at considerable length. Our project also encountered problems with disciplinary communication and collaboration, pessimistic views about whether the institution was really committed to taking action, and lack of resourcing. What this chapter demonstrates, however, is that opening up such issues to debate and critique can be hugely productive. That approach contrasts sharply with how these challenges are typically discussed in the literature, where agreeing definitions is seen as a good way of avoiding confusion, clarity of communication is seen as essential for generating action, and resourcing is seen as something that should be agreed at the outset of a project. Such impulses speak to a tendency to try to over-prescribe the remits of projects and over-determine their directions. The approach we document here, by contrast, demonstrates the productivity of providing tasks (and supporting resources) which allow participants to explore their differences; of using mutual disagreement as a springboard for creativity; and of generating ideas (such as that for a research center) even where funding is not yet in place and where acquiring it may seem ambitious.

Finally, our chapter makes a distinctive contribution to the issue of stakeholder engagement. As our literature review documents, engagement is seen as an important issue, due to the moral and ethical responsibilities of HE stakeholders, and the discourse that HEIs are training future leaders who might take forward sustainability agendas outside the sector as well as within their institutions. Yet the existing literature typically considers such engagement in ways that are individualistic and reflective of traditional divisions of labor existing within universities. Senior academics, for example, are positioned as thought-leaders; those from particular disciplines are set up to find solutions; and administrators are positioned as facilitating awareness and supporting others. Our approach, by contrast, highlights the centrality of building a collective agency – a transformative agency – as a core part of the capacity building that the literature already recognizes as a key element of educational change. Individuals were engaged as people, rather than merely as employees, and encouraged to treat the project's meetings as a safe space where they could talk in ways that did not respect prevailing institutional ranks, roles, and divisions. People adopted new roles within the project, and subsequently changed their views and those roles as the initiative developed; seeing that their resistance and criticism had a good chance to change the direction of the project encouraged people to step up and take ownership of the new ideas that were generated. Such interactions are increasingly challenged where HEIs come to operate in ways more reminiscent of corporations, but such "relatively democratized" knowledge production was central to the initiative and can be taken to explain the repeatedly encountered willingness to overcome obstacles and engage with solutions at length.

6.8 Conclusion

This chapter has reported on a CL research-intervention designed to foster sustainability-related capacity building among the staff of a small, third-level, multidisciplinary HEI campus. The intervention sought to explore how sustainability could be embedded in the practices of staff across the campus, through a process in which the creation of new concepts and the development of the participants' transformative agency were dovetailed.

The process resulted, among other outcomes, in the development of a CSS, which was subsequently adopted by staff and campus management and launched at a high-profile public event. The CSS has subsequently helped influence and reinforce the development of a number of other sustainability related initiatives on the campus, many of which are led by members of the project described in this chapter.

The underlying study demonstrates the potential that the CL methodology has in relation to exploring how sustainability can be embedded in an HE setting, and how it can produce tangible results which can have a significant impact on practice. This chapter has highlighted the potential and benefits of harnessing stakeholder input (and enthusiasm) within a structured, collaborative development processes, where the participants are allowed to identify, examine, and iteratively re-envisage the underlying issues and develop their own solutions.

In relation to the applicability of the CL as a methodology for designing, enacting, and exploring sustainability-related change initiatives in HE, we propose the following conclusions:

1) The CL is an effective methodology for the development of sustainability-related practices and initiatives in HE settings.
2) The process promotes robust, open, and frank discussions and stimulates resolution of the issues that may arise. This is essential when dealing with contentious and emotive subjects where participants have a wide range of potentially opposing views.
3) The capacity building aspect of the process is crucial and is nurtured where people feel that they are genuinely heard – even if their contributions are uncomfortable and contentious.
4) Terminological issues, whether due to beliefs or disciplinary background, can be overcome through the structured collaborative development of new ideas and concepts understood as bespoke to the institutional setting.
5) The process facilitates cross- and transdisciplinary collaboration, which is essential for the development of successful sustainability initiatives.
6) The process can be used to harness participants' existing enthusiasm about sustainability and address skepticism about institutional practices and regimes.
7) The process develops participants' willingness to express commitment and pursue objectives.

Based on the results of this study we believe that there is significant scope for further projects like this in other institutions where staff and management are interested in developing sustainability-related practices and activities.

References

Adams, C.A. (2013). Sustainability accounting. *Management and Policy Journal* 4 (13): 384–392.

Akins, E., Giddens, E., Glassmeyer, D. et al. (2019). Sustainability education and organizational change: a critical case study of barriers and change drivers at a higher education institution. *Sustainability* 11 (2): 501. https://doi.org/10.3390/su11020501.

Aleixo, A.M., Leal, S., and Azeiteiro, U.M.d.M. (2018). Conceptualization of sustainable higher education institutions, roles, barriers, and challenges for sustainability: an exploratory study in Portugal. *Journal of Cleaner Production* 172: 1664–1673. https://doi.org/10.1016/j.jclepro.2016.11.010.

Amaral, A.R., Rodrigues, E., Gaspar, A.R., and Gomes, Á. (2020). A review of empirical data of sustainability initiatives in university campus operations. *Journal of Cleaner Production* 250: 119558. https://doi.org/10.1016/j.jclepro.2019.119558.

Appleton, E. (2017). *Next Generation Sustainability Strategy and Structure: Whole-Institution Approaches to Sustainability in Universities and Colleges*. Cheltenham, UK: Environmental Association for Universities and Colleges.

Baker-Shelley, A., van Zeijl-Rozema, A., and Martens, P. (2017). A conceptual synthesis of organisational transformation: how to diagnose, and navigate, pathways for sustainability at universities? *Journal of Cleaner Production* 145: 262–276. https://doi.org/10.1016/j.jclepro.2017.01.026.

Barrett, C.B. (1996). Fairness, stewardship and sustainable development. *Ecological Economics* 19 (1): 11–17.

Berchin, I.I., Sima, M., de Lima, M.A. et al. (2018). The importance of international conferences on sustainable development as higher education institutions' strategies to promote sustainability: A case study in Brazil. *Journal of Cleaner Production* 171: 756–772. https://doi.org/10.1016/j.jclepro.2017.10.042.

Bligh, B. and Flood, M. (2015). The change Laboratory in Higher Education: research-intervention using activity theory. In: *Theory and Method in Higher Education Research* (ed. J. Huisman and M. Tight), 141–168. Bingley: Emerald Group Publishing.

Bligh, B. and Flood, M. (2017). Activity theory in empirical higher education research: choices, uses, and values. *Tertiary Education and Management* 23 (2): 125–152.

Blunden, A. (2010). *An Interdisciplinary Theory of Activity*. Leiden: Brill.

Brundtland, G. H. (1987). Our common future (the brundtland report). In *Report of the World Commission on Environment and Development: Our Common Future (The Brundtland Report)* 4(1). https://sustainabledevelopment.un.org/content/documents/5987our-common-future.pdf (accessed 25 November 2021).

Cheeseman, A., Wright, T.S.A., Murray, J., and McKenzie, M. (2019). Taking stock of sustainability in higher education: a review of the policy literature. *Environmental Education Research* 25 (12): 1–16. https://doi.org/10.1080/13504622.2019.1616164.

Christensen, P., Thrane, M., Herreborg Jørgensen, T., and Lehmann, M. (2009). Sustainable development. *International Journal of Sustainability in Higher Education* 10 (1): 4–20. https://doi.org/10.1108/14676370910925217.

Cortese, A.D. (2003). The critical role of higher education in creating a sustainable future. *Planning for Higher Education* 31: 15–22.

Dahle, M. and Neumeyer, E. (2001). Overcoming barriers to campus greening. *International Journal of Sustainability in Higher Education* 2 (2): 139–160. https://doi.org/10.1108/14676370110388363.

Daniels, H. (2008). *Vygotsky and Research*. Oxford: Routledge.

Djordjevic, A. and Cotton, D.R.E. (2011). Communicating the sustainability message in higher education institutions. *International Journal of Sustainability in Higher Education* 12 (4): 381–394. https://doi.org/10.1108/14676371111168296.

Dlouhá, J., Glavič, P., and Barton, A. (2017). Higher education in central European countries – critical factors for sustainability transition. *Journal of Cleaner Production* 151: 670–684. https://doi.org/10.1016/j.jclepro.2016.08.022.

Engeström, Y. (1987). *Learning by Expanding: An Activity-Theoretical Approach to Developmental Research*. Helsinki: Orienta-Konsultit Oy.

Engeström, Y. (2016). *Studies in Expansive Learning: Learning What Is Not Yet There*. New York: Cambridge University Press.

Eteläpelto, A., Vähäsantanen, K., Hökkä, P., and Paloniemi, S. (2013). What is agency? Conceptualizing professional agency at work. *Educational Research Review* 10: 45–65.

Evangelinos, K.I. and Jones, N. (2009). An analysis of social capital and environmental management of higher education institutions. *International Journal of Sustainability in Higher Education* 10 (4): 334–342. https://doi.org/10.1108/14676370910990684.

Ferrer-Balas, D., Adachi, J., Banas, S. et al. (2008). An international comparative analysis of sustainability transformation across seven universities. *International Journal of Sustainability in Higher Education* 9 (3): https://doi.org/10.1108/14676370810885907.

Figueiró, P.S. and Raufflet, E. (2015). Sustainability in higher education: a systematic review with focus on management education. *Journal of Cleaner Production* 106: 22–33. https://doi.org/10.1016/j.jclepro.2015.04.118.

Findler, F., Schönherr, N., Lozano, R. et al. (2019). The impacts of higher education institutions on sustainable development: a review and conceptualization. *International Journal of Sustainability in Higher Education* 20 (1): 23–38. https://doi.org/10.1108/IJSHE-07-2017-0114.

Fischer, D., Jenssen, S., and Tappeser, V. (2015). Getting an empirical hold of the sustainable university: a comparative analysis of evaluation frameworks across 12 contemporary sustainability assessment tools. *Assessment & Evaluation in Higher Education* 40 (6): 785–800.

Flavin, C. (2010). Preface. In: *State of the World Transforming Cultures from Consumerism to Sustainabilty*, 1e (ed. L. Starke and L. Mastny), xvii–xxi. W.W. Norton.

Fullan, M. (2016). *The New Meaning of Educational Change*, 5e. New York, NY: Teachers College Press.

Gale, F., Davidson, A., Wood, G. et al. (2015). Four impediments to embedding education for Sustaianbility in higher education.PDF. *Australian Journal of Environmental Education* 31 (2): 248–263.

Gibson, R. (2000). *Specification of Sustainability-Based Environmental Assessment Decision Criteria and Implications for Determining "Significance" in Environmental Assessment*. Canadian Environmental Assessment Agency.

Godemann, J., Bebbington, J., Herzig, C., and Moon, J. (2014). Higher education and sustainable development. *Accounting, Auditing & Accountability Journal* 27: 218–233. https://doi.org/10.1108/AAAJ-12-2013-1553.

Green, T.L. (2015). Lecturers' perspectives on how introductory economic courses address sustainability. *International Journal of Sustainability in Higher Education* 16 (1): 44–56. https://doi.org/10.1108/14676371311312905.

Haapasaari, A., Engeström, Y., and Kerosuo, H. (2016). The emergence of learners' transformative agency in a change laboratory intervention. *Journal of Education and Work* 29 (2): 232–262. https://doi.org/10.1080/13639080.2014.900168.

Holden, E., Linnerud, K., and Banister, D. (2014). Sustainable development: our common future revisited. *Global Environmental Change* 26 (1): 130–139. https://doi.org/10.1016/j.gloenvcha.2014.04.006.

Hoover, E. and Harder, M.K. (2015). What lies beneath the surface? The hidden complexities of organizational change for sustainability in higher education. *Journal of Cleaner Production* 106: 175–188. https://doi.org/10.1016/j.jclepro.2014.01.081.

Johnston, P., Everard, M., Santillo, D., and Robèrt, K.-H. (2007). Reclaiming the definition of sustainability. *Environmental Science and Pollution Research* 14 (1): 60–66.

Karatzoglou, B. (2013). An in-depth literature review of the evolving roles and contributions of universities to education for sustainable development. *Journal of Cleaner Production* 49: 44–53. https://doi.org/10.1016/j.jclepro.2012.07.043.

Leal Filho, W. (2011). About the role of universities and their contribution to sustainable development. *Higher Education Policy* 24 (4): 427–438. https://doi.org/10.1057/hep.2011.16.

Leal Filho, W., Shiel, C., do Paço, A., and Brandli, L. (2015). Putting sustainable development in practice: campus greening as a tool for institutional sustainability efforts. In: *Sustainability in Higher Education* (ed. J.P. Davim), 1–19. Chandos https://doi.org/10.1016/B978-0-08-100367-1.00001-9.

Lozano, R. (2006). Incorporation and institutionalization of SD into universities: breaking through barriers to change. *Journal of Cleaner Production* 14: 787–796.

Lozano, R. (2008). Envisioning sustainability three-dimensionally. *Journal of Cleaner Production* 16 (17): 1838–1846. https://doi.org/10.1016/j.jclepro.2008.02.008.

Lozano, R. (2018). Proposing a definition and a framework of organisational sustainability: a review of efforts and a survey of approaches to change. *Sustainability (Switzerland)* 10 (4): https://doi.org/10.3390/su10041157.

Lozano, R., Lukman, R., Lozano, F.J. et al. (2013). Declarations for sustainability in higher education: becoming better leaders, through addressing the university system. *Journal of Cleaner Production* 48: 10–19.

Lozano, R., Ceulemans, K., Alonso-Almeida, M. et al. (2015). A review of commitment and implementation of sustainable development in higher education: Results from a worldwide survey. *Journal of Cleaner Production* 108: 1–18. https://doi.org/10.1016/j.jclepro.2014.09.048.

Mader, C., Scott, G., and Razak, D.A. (2013). Effective change management, governance and policy for sustainability transformation in higher education. *Sustainability Accounting, Management and Policy Journal* 4 (3): 264–284. https://doi.org/10.1108/SAMPJ-09-2013-0037.

Meadows, D., Randers, J., and Meadows, D. (2004). *The Limits to Growth: The 30 Year Update*. Eathscan.

Moffitt, P. (2019). Transformative agency for the collaborative and future-oriented redesign of activity in military higher education; empowering participants to change their boundary-crossing technology enhanced learning. PhD thesis. Lancaster University.

Moffitt, P. and Bligh, B. (2021). Video and the pedagogy of expansive learning: insights from a research-intervention in engineering education. In: *Video Pedagogy: Theory and Practice* (ed. D. Gedera and A. Zalipour), 123–145. Cham: Springer.

Morselli, D. (2019). *The Change Laboratory for Teacher Training in Entrepreneurship Education: A New Skills Agenda for Europe*. Cham: Springer.

Mukute, M., Mudokwani, K., McAllister, G., and Nyikahadzoi, K. (2018). Exploring the potential of developmental work research and change laboratory to support sustainability transformations: a case study of organic agriculture in Zimbabwe. *Mind, Culture, and Activity* 25 (3): 229–246.

Müller-Christ, G., Sterling, S., Van Dam-Mieras, R. et al. (2014). The role of campus, curriculum, and community in higher education for sustainable development – a conference report. *Journal of Cleaner Production* 62: 134–137. https://doi.org/10.1016/j.jclepro.2013.02.029.

Omazic, A. and Zunk, B.M. (2021). Semi-systematic literature review on sustainability and sustainable development in higher education institutions. *Sustainability* 13 (14): 7683. https://doi.org/10.3390/su13147683.

Orr, D.W. (2009). *Down to the Wire: Confronting Climate Change*. Oxford University Press.

Owens, K.A. and Legere, S. (2015). What do we say when we talk about sustainability? Analyzing faculty, staff and student definitions of sustainability at one American university. *International Journal of Sustainability in Higher Education* 16 (3): 367–384. https://doi.org/10.1108/14676371211211809.

Pattison, E. (2020). In-service teachers as relational and transformative agents: a study of primary school teachers' professional learning during a Change Laboratory formative intervention. PhD thesis. Lancaster University.

Ralph, M. and Stubbs, W. (2014). Integrating environmental sustainability into universities. *Higher Education* 67 (1): 71–90. https://doi.org/10.1007/s10734-013-9641-9.

Sannino, A. (2015). The principle of double stimulation: a path to volitional action. *Learning, Culture and Social Interaction* 6: 1–15.

Sidiropoulos, E. (2010). The role of HEIs in society's transformation to sustainability. The case for embedding sustainability concepts in business programs. In: *Proceedings of the 10th Australasian Campuses Towards Sustainability Conference*, 45–53. Melbourne: https://doi.org/10.13140/2.1.2698.1768.

Sidiropoulos, E. (2012). Synergising sustainability initiatives across a tertiary institution – building momentum for institutional transformation. *Workshop presentation at the Asia Pacific Association for International Education (APAIE) 2012 Conference*, Bangkok, Thailand https://www.researchgate.net/publication/265251328_Synergising_sustainability_initiatives_across_a_tertiary_institution_-_building_momentum_for_institutional_transformation.

Steiner, G. and Posch, A. (2006). Higher education for sustainability by means of transdisciplinary case studies: an innovative approach for solving complex, real-world problems. *Journal of Cleaner Production* 14 (9–11): 877–890. https://doi.org/10.1016/j.jclepro.2005.11.054.

Sterling, S., Maxey, L., and Luna, H. (2013). *The Sustainable University*. New York: Routledge.

Thogersen, J. and Crompton, T. (2009). Simple and painless; the limitations of spillover in environmental campaigning. *Journal of Consumer Policy* 32 (2).

Too, L. and Bajracharya, B. (2015). Sustainable campus: engaging the community in sustainability. *International Journal of Sustainability in Higher Education* 16 (1): 57–71. https://doi.org/10.1108/IJSHE-07-2013-0080.

UNESCO (2006). Drivers and barriers for Implementing sustainable development in higher education. In: *Education for Sustainable Development in Action* Technical Paper No 3 (ed. J. Holmberg and B.E. Samuelsson), 1–130. UNESCO http://unesdoc.unesco.org/images/0014/001484/148466E.pdf (accessed 22 April 2017).

UNESCO Education Sector (2005). *Framework for the UNDESD International Implementation Scheme*. UNESCO.

Vargas, L., Mac-Lean, C., and Huge, J. (2019). The maturation process of incorporating sustainability in universities. *International Journal of Sustainability in Higher Education* 20 (3): 441–451. https://doi.org/10.1108/IJSHE-01-2019-0043.

Verhulst, E. and Boks, C. (2014). Employee empowerment for sustainable design. *Journal of Corporate Citizenship* 55: 73–101.

Verhulst, E. and Lambrechts, W. (2015). Fostering the incorporation of sustainable development in higher education. Lessons learned from a change management perspective. *Journal of Cleaner Production* 106: 189–204. https://doi.org/10.1016/j.jclepro.2014.09.049.

Viegas, C.V., Bond, A.J., Vaz, C.R. et al. (2016). Critical attributes of sustainability in higher education: a categorisation from literature review. *Journal of Cleaner Production* 126: 260–276. https://doi.org/10.1016/j.jclepro.2016.02.106.

Virkkunen, J. (2006). Dilemmas in building shared transformative agency. *Activities* 3 (1): 43–66. https://doi.org/10.4000/activites.1850.

Virkkunen, J. and Newnham, D.S. (2013). *The Change Laboratory: A tool for collaborative development of work and education*. Springer https://doi.org/10.1007/978-94-6209-326-3.

Wright, T.S.A. (2002). Definitions and frameworks for environmental sustainability in higher education. *International Journal of Sustainability in Higher Education* 3 (3): 203–220. https://doi.org/10.1108/14676370210434679.

Wright, T.S.A. (2010). University presidents' conceptualizations of sustainability in higher education. *International Journal of Sustainability in Higher Education* 11 (1): 61–73.

Wu, Y.C.J. and Shen, J.P. (2016). *International Journal of Sustainability in Higher Education* 17 (5): 633–651. https://doi.org/10.1108/14676371211211809.

Velazquez, L., Munguia, N., Platt, A., and Taddei, J. (2006). Sustainable university: What can be the matter? *Journal of Cleaner Production* 14 (9–11): 810–819. https://doi.org/10.1016/j.jclepro.2005.12.008.

Sidiropoulos, E. (2011). Navigating the journey to sustainability: The case for embedding sustainability literacy into all tertiary education business programs. *The International Journal of Environmental, Cultural, Economic & Social Sustainability* 7 (3): 248–273.

Engeström, Y. (2011). From Design Experiments to Formative Interventions. *Theory & Psychology* 21 (5): 598–628. https://doi.org/10.1177/0959354311419252.

7

Technology-Enhanced Education: Improving Students' Learning Experience in the Higher Education Context

Mengting Yu

7.1 Introduction of Sustainable Higher Education Made by Technology-Enhanced Learning (TEL)

The fields of education are not immune to advances in sophisticated information and communication technology (ICT). ICT is being rapidly integrated into higher education (HE) for a variety of objectives, and the notion of technology-enhanced learning (TEL) as well as the various uses of ICT, e-resources, and pedagogical methods for improving education are discussed in scientific articles. The specific application of TEL to HE is especially relevant for countries in rapid development in order to provide quick and sustainable access to quality education (the United Nations [UN] Sustainable Development Goals [SDG] 4) (Orozco-Messana et al. 2020). Online training is the most effective way of delivering a sustainable HE, especially given the increased volume and complexity of the knowledge to be delivered, as well as the exponential growth in the need for skilled workers in emerging economies (Orozco-Messana et al. 2020).

TEL has become one of the most talked-about topics in the education debate, from preschool to HE (Daniela et al. 2018). Currently, technology is being used as a supportive educational tool. It can assist the learner in acquiring knowledge in specific fields, but more importantly, TEL can be used to improve the skills acquisition process, particularly in terms of critical thinking, civic engagement, and the overall empowering of individuals to seize opportunities and maximize their potential (Daniela et al. 2018). However, according to both 2018 and 2020 HE sustainability reports, TEL still has to be considered as a helpful way to support the learning of students through educators. Although TEL can effectively scaffold students' learning in HE, it can deviate from the UN's quality education goal at any time (Orozco-Messana et al. 2020). The integration of technology within education therefore actually offers a great promise, yet HE educators should spare no effort in monitoring and developing the direction of how TEL supports the HE in order to boost technological innovation, strengthen the economy, enhance awareness of environmental sustainability, and ultimately empower people to secure their well-being.

Nonetheless, with the rapid advancement of science and technology, TEL has become a necessary trend when combined with HE programs. It offers a platform for global teachers to share up-to-date education information, and it also assigns educational resources more fairly through the digital learning method. Overall, if teachers and educators are adequately

The Wiley Handbook of Sustainability in Higher Education Learning and Teaching, First Edition.
Edited by Kelum A. A. Gamage and Nanda Gunawardhana.
© 2022 John Wiley & Sons, Inc. Published 2022 by John Wiley & Sons, Inc.

prepared academically and collaboratively, the implementation of a TEL strategy will allow for the rapid and sustainable development of HE with a broad reach in the near future (Orozco-Messana et al. 2020).

7.2 Sustainable Higher Education and TEL

The most important aspect of sustainable HE is its ability to assist students in the knowledge-building process, supporting them in acquiring critical thinking skills and the like. Many studies have shown that TEL can be used as a tool to support higher-order learners' higher-order thinking activities (Daniela et al. 2018).

7.2.1 Mapping and Understanding the Debate on TEL

TEL has certainly become an important topic in the discussion about education, from pre-school to HE. The core of the argument is determined across the area by the topic of how technology might help or improve teaching and learning processes, as well as the obstacles or challenges that arise in this regard (Orozco-Messana et al. 2020).

Technology can serve as a supportive educational tool. It can be used to create digital educational resources and can also assist a learner in the acquisition of knowledge in highly specialized disciplines. Most importantly, technology can be used to improve the skills acquisition process, particularly in the areas of critical thinking and civic involvement, as well as empowering individuals to seize opportunities and fully exploit their potential. Even so, the use of technology in education necessitates more in-depth consideration. In other words, there is, on the one hand, considerable pressure to apply technology in teaching and learning, mainly driven by the realization that citizens should be ICT-literate. On the other hand, the education field is regarded as one of the most important technology consumers, implying that an intrinsic, albeit contentious, link exists between education and the ICT industry. Given that, the goal of the research is to broaden our knowledge and understanding of the world around us, as well as to make research findings accessible to all stakeholders. The intriguing questions are whether and how the incorporation of technology into the field of education is beneficial to our societies.

One of the SDGs approved by the UN forum in 2015 is quality education. The SDGs, in an attempt to go beyond the success of the Millennium Development Goals, include the imperative to "ensure inclusive and quality education for all and promote lifelong learning" (Daniela et al. 2018). Quality education may be the most important driver of long-term development around the world, including both developing and developed worlds. Access to, the role of, and the potential of using technology in teaching and learning, become more than a slogan. In fact, the definition of inclusive education emphasizes the critical role of technology-enhanced education in increasing technological innovation, strengthening the economy, raising awareness of environmental sustainability, and ultimately empowering people to secure their own well-being. Without a doubt, the inroad of technology in the field of education yields a great promise (Orozco-Messana et al. 2020).

7.2.1.1 TEL in Higher Education

Admittedly, technology provides immeasurable opportunities to learn, teach more effectively, and contribute to the process of knowledge construction. Also, at the same time, advancements in ICT pose challenges to the field of education.

However, literature and fieldwork suggest that TEL has two main characteristics coming from professors and students and constituting the key factors that affect the possibility of technology-enhanced approaches to teaching and learning creating value-add in education. These two factors are professors' ICT-literacy and competence to apply technology to ensure effective TEL, and students' induction to ICT and development of ICT skills to interact with technologies to learn and to construct their knowledge in the process of TEL (Daniela et al. 2018).

When it comes to professors' TEL competencies, they can be easily examined from various angles. The most important of these is their ability to assist students in acquiring critical thinking skills by assisting them in the knowledge-building process. However, research indicates that many educators are either unprepared to work with technology or have a negative attitude toward the use of technology in general. They occasionally feel that the HE institution where they work does not provide adequate administrative and technical support. It is not uncommon that professors feel that the use of technology, to some extent, increases their workload. So, these factors obviously work to the detriment of effective use of technology in the teaching and learning process (Daniela et al. 2018).

From students' or learners' angle, some studies reveal that student competence in using technology is inadequate. On a daily basis, they see that students' digital competence is not sufficiently developed. However, research has shown that the instant availability of information on the internet can have an impact on cognitive strategies. According to some studies, students' self-evaluation of their digital competence is higher than their actual digital competence. This does not, however, change the fact that students want to use technology. That is, they are motivated to actively participate in the learning process, but they require assistance in making meaningful use of technology to aid in the development of ICT competence. What follows is that, if they have ICT skills, professors can serve as those who scaffold learning. Therefore, it is worth noting that students and learners are very interested in TEL, but professors or educators have to apply themselves to become familiar with using tech to instruct them. Only in this way, can they satisfy the development requirements of students in HE (Daniela et al. 2018).

7.2.1.2 TEL for Sustainable Education

The role of educators who are prepared, committed, and willing to use various technologies to scaffold learning is central to the educational process. In recent years, different educational frameworks across countries saw agreement that digitalization of education is one of the key objectives of collaborations. By the same token, scholars and educators emphasized the need for pedagogical innovation in order to support actions conforming to the imperative of HE quality education. In this way, a direct and an indirect link were established between different countries' TEL institutions and centers and the SDG was established.

Researchers active in the TEL field have long argued that various forms of knowledge, academic development, and organizational changes are interconnected, and that synergies between teachers and students can be created. A debate about transformational learning is thriving in the same context. It is argued that the latter is the foundation for sustainable education, i.e. education in which teachers are the drivers of this process – to remain open to change, questioning the epistemological backgrounds on which they base institutional management and teaching. Some researchers point out that HE can be sustainable if organizational changes are made in the HE process as well as curriculum redesign to develop sustainable education (Daniela et al. 2018).

Consequently, supporting the development of stakeholders' digital skills and competence can ensure sustainable HE, but is a significant challenge in the transformative processes of HE systems all over the world. Meanwhile, to assist the sustainable development of the whole society beyond HE alone, the development of digital competence based on TEL skills across the society should be have more effort focused on it. (Daniela et al. 2018).

7.3 Integrating Blended Learning in Higher Education (HE)

Blended learning (BL) has prevailed globally for many years and belongs to the TEL field. Since learners became aware of tech-assisted learning, the term "blended learning" has become more common in academic and corporate circles. In 2003, the American Society for Training and Development identified BL as one of the top 10 trends to emerge in the knowledge delivery industry (Rooney 2003). Early in 2002, the president of Pennsylvania State University was quoted in The Chronicle of Higher Education saying that the convergence of online and residential instruction was the single greatest unrecognized trend in HE today (Young 2002). The editor of The Journal of Asynchronous Learning Networks was also quoted in that article, and he predicted a dramatic increase in the number of hybrid (i.e. blended) courses in HE, possibly including as many as 80–90% of all courses (Young 2002). From 2019 until today, the COVID-19 virus pandemic has swept the through countries across the globe. Large numbers of students undertake their self-quarantine study at home and BL has further upgraded to support distance learning, becoming the key learning method for all university students (OECD 2020).

7.3.1 Introduction of Blended Learning

When people hear about BL, one of the first questions they ask is, "What exactly is being blended?" While there are many different answers to this topic, the majority of the definitions are variations on a few key concepts (Driscoll 2002).

Several researchers put forward different definitions of blended learning. For instance, Driscoll (2002) defines blend learning as intermixing of any instructional forms to achieve an educational goal, whereas Garrison and Kanuka (2004) explain that to blend simply means integrating classroom teaching with online experiences. Singh (2010) views BL as combining different delivery media to promote meaningful and motivating learning. Live chats, self-paced learning, instant messaging, social networking, blogs and forums, applications, and webinars are examples of tools which instructors can use to incorporate online opportunities in their classes (Okaz 2015).

But the latest and detailed definition of blended learning is from the Clayton Christensen Institute. The definition of BL is a formal education program in which a student learns: first, at least in part through online learning, with some element of student control over time, place, path, and/or pace; second, at least in part in a supervised brick-and-mortar location away from home; and third, the modalities along each student's learning path within a course or subject are connected to provide an integrated learning experience.

All in all, BL is a fresh new type of education that combines old and new in one frame of work, preserves traditional methods, and employs technological innovation to capture the attention of students who are already addicted to digital media in their personal social life. This is also to meet the global demand to develop conventional teaching methods, for the purpose of keeping up with current trends and standards in various educational systems.

7.3.2 Pros and Cons of Blended Learning in Contemporary HE

BL provides teachers with specific opportunities and spaces to interact with small groups of students on learning objectives. Teachers can engage with small groups of students to address learning goals (individualization), enrich or extend the curriculum (rigor), or spend time evaluating student data using BL (monitoring). By providing differentiated experiences in both online and in-person circumstances, BL allows teachers to focus more on individual students as learners and access numerous data sources to measure student growth.

The exponentially increasing use of TEL in HE over the last decade has ramifications on a variety of levels both within and outside of HE institutions (Kirkwood and Price 2014). However, everything has two sides and BL, like TEL, has both positive and negative impacts on HE.

7.3.2.1 Pros of BL

The adoption of BL in education, particularly for HE institutions, has multiple advantages, and BL is regarded as one of the greatest means of education due to its numerous advantages and benefits. Benefits and advantages resulting from technology support learning in educational institutions have been offered by several studies in previous years (Klein and Ware 2003). Additionally, some studies show the advantage of tech-assisted learning as being its ability to focus on the needs of individual learners. For example, Marc (2002) in his book review, stated that one of the benefits of tech-supported learning in education is that it emphasizes the requirements of individual students as a critical aspect in the educational process (rather than the needs of instructors or educational institutions). It somewhat supports learners in personalizing their study method and motivates them to engage in different courses, increasing the flexibility of students' learning schedules.

Despite challenges in terms of the feasibility and applicability of hybrid learning in HE, a body of research supports the concept of integrating face-to-face instruction with an online delivery modality. A combination like this leads to improved learning outcomes (Garrison and Kanuka 2004). The trend of combining asynchronous internet technologies with face-to-face engagement has been linked to better pedagogy and information access (Graham 2006). Similarly, Garrison and Kanuka (2004) claim that blended education can help students learn independently and collaboratively. BL creates a community of inquiry, and a platform for open and participatory discussion. Moreover, Paechter and Maier (2010) also mention how university students advocate integrated learning. Students who are digitally literate have more chance to take their lessons and discussions outside of the classroom (Kasraie and Alahmad 2014). Students can explore the asynchronous subjects in their own time and at their own pace via instructor-led live events and webinars, which are then followed by classroom discussion or debate. Combining technology-mediated learning with classroom dialogs clearly helps students obtain a better knowledge of the subject matter while developing their cognitive and social abilities. BL could make all aspects of students' learning come true, keeping pace with today's TEL era and improved teaching pedagogy.

Furthermore, diversity is one principal characteristic of HE as classes contain different genders, cultural backgrounds, learning preferences as well as linguistic proficiencies. Differentiation is made possible by technology, which has a wide range of features that can cater to different sorts of students. Learning management systems (LMS), for example, are used to manage a learning environment in an online setting. Instructors can utilize the LMS Moodle to publish readings, videos, wikis, forums, and quizzes outside of the classroom to improve self-regulation and boost student–teacher interaction. These BL technologies can help with meaning negotiation, scaffolding, and collaboration (Carman 2002). BL or TEL use a variety of technologies to serve students with a variety of learning requirements and interests (Dias and Diniz 2014). Especially good for introverted students, BL encourages them to exchange knowledge information online and discuss study content with peers, thus accomplishing the goal of real education – inclusivity and equality.

Apart from these examples of advantages, there are more positive opinions toward BL and tech-enhanced learning by researchers and scholars. To summarize, given the ubiquitous use of social media, BL in HE academic settings can produce significant and favorable learning effects.

7.3.2.2 Cons of BL

There are a variety of reasons why people do not use blended learning. Electricity outages are at the top of the list. In most nations, educational institution facilities do not have backup generators, therefore integrating technology with face-to-face classroom instruction might not be possible.

Another disadvantage is that, in comparison to face-to-face classroom contact, there is lack of immediate response and no interaction between teachers and learners. Some students think that in a computer-mediated learning environment, they can mostly only pay attention to their personal learning mode, nearly isolated from interactive learning setting, so are unable to interact with instructors and peers effectively, resulting in a loss of their sense of classroom community (Vonderwell 2003). Thus, students can lose the feeling of belonging and group identity.

Also, due to varying socioeconomic origins or a lack of IT understanding, some students may experience difficulties accessing online classroom materials (Holley and Oliver 2010). Similarly, given the BL circumstance, instructors must be qualified and/or trained to offer IT support to troubleshoot issues. Because of the continuously changing nature of technology, they must also be adaptable in their course content. Hence, it is very difficult to require all teachers to achieve the level, and not all educators will be able to pick up new IT knowledge quickly.

Furthermore, cultural and societal factors might influence the situation, as well as students' personal reasons for being reluctant to be self-directed learners, lowering the success rate of BL. This disadvantage could be due to a lack of learners' desire to learn or a fear of taking risks or operating outside their comfort zone. Therefore, they resist the new type of learning methods/pedagogies and are unwilling to cooperate with teachers in learning.

More evidence of disadvantages might come out in future research. However, in response to the aforementioned negative opinions, Kasraie and Alahmad (2014) have argued that through the design of a good teaching mode learners could absorb knowledge better. In other words, before organizing lessons, it is critical to understand students' requirements and preferences. Before incorporating BL in courses, instructors must identify factors such as socioeconomic background, IT knowledge levels, and gender and age. This will effectively avoid the unwanted side-effects of BL.

7.3.3 Blended Learning: Improving Students' Learning Experience

Despite the fact that some early studies indicated no difference between face-to-face learning and BL in terms of attitude and success, there are a few studies that look at the impact of various BL application formats on student satisfaction, success, and other factors (Gecer and Dag 2012). In fact, as early as 1995, BL settings assisted learners in taking on their own learning responsibilities, such as time management, material selection, and so on (Chung and Davis 1995). However, at that time there was less evidence to support the idea that BL improved students' learning experiences. But nowadays more research has proven that students' learning experiences can be better with BL. According to Gecer and Dag (2012), most students stated that the combination for a specific course of face-to-face learning and the information being offered in an electronic setting greatly aided them. Meanwhile, using a BL strategy to enable individual feedback and coaching in an electronic setting can increase students' classroom or learning engagement. As a result, BL, which should be considered a teaching design approach, is a process that should be strategically designed to be implemented in a teaching institution, program, or course, since it enhanced students' engagement in classes and courses.

Additionally, Karaman et al. (2009) emphasize that creating BL surroundings with a variety of learning activities has a favorable impact on students' growth (Gecer and Dag 2012). Motteram (2006) even looked at the program design experiences of students in a three-year BL teaching knowledge course. It was discovered that a BL strategy had a good impact on students' learning experiences. It is better to permit students to have important information about the course and access to their friends regardless of time and place, allowing them to follow the course content online, and to exchange thoughts and opinions between teacher and student and between student and student. This also supports learners in better expressing themselves (Kasraie and Alahmad 2014) – BL allows students to be themselves.

In 2007, Delialioğlu and Yıldırım's study revealed that students' assignments and project programs in BL background increased their learning responsibilities (Gecer and Dag 2012). According to the students' perspectives on roles and responsibilities in the course under the research, this situation improved their awareness of the importance of taking more responsibility in their learning. Thus, BL grows and develops students' minds and responsibility, thereby improve their learning experiences.

Kasraie and Alahmad (2014) stated that students who attended BL applications reflected having positive attitudes toward BL compared with face-to-face learning, and had higher grades in examinations. In addition, Gecer and Dag (2012) found that learning course theory in a classroom environment, and the supportive accompaniment of the course website, were extremely beneficial to students' learning experience.

Consequently, from a holistic perspective, students and learners in HE can benefit greatly from a BL method/ pedagogy since it improves learning quality and increases access to knowledge. Combining technology with face-to-face training can help students both learn and collaborate more effectively. Engagement, motivation, and interaction among students are critical components of a successful learning process. Students become more intrinsically motivated when they can apply what they are studying to real life and personalize it. BL can provide some relevance to what learners' study in class. Therefore, it is time that educational institutions start adjusting to such changes and to meet the rapidly growing demands from both learners and the workplace.

7.4 Exploring Innovative Ubiquitous Learning Tools in HE Context

The evolution of multimedia and information technologies, as well as the usage of the internet as a new teaching technique, has resulted in radical changes in the traditional teaching process (Wang et al. 2003). Yang and Arkorful (1999) and Arkorful and Abaidoo (2015) have stated that advancements in information technology have provided additional options for today's education. According to the agendas of schools and educational institutions, tech-enhanced learning has been seen as having the potential to transform people, knowledge, skills, and performance, according to the agendas of schools and educational institutions (Arkorful and Abaidoo 2015). Colleges, universities, and other institutions of higher learning, according to Wang et al. (2003), are racing to increase online course capabilities in a rapidly increasing cyber-education market. Tech-enhanced learning is becoming increasingly significant in HE institutions. Several changes in HE institutions have been triggered by the introduction and spread of a variety of e-learning tools, notably in terms of educational delivery and support operations (Dublin 2003).

7.4.1 Adopting Computer-Based Technology and Internet-Based Learning in the HE Context

There are diverse ways of classifying the different types of tech-supported learning. According to Algahtani (2011), some classifications have been made based on the level of their involvement in education, others are based on the order in which interactions occur. Algahtani (2011) divided e-learning into two basic types: computer-based and internet-based e-learning. Algahtani (2011) argued that the use of a whole spectrum of hardware and software typically available for the use of ICT is included in computer-based learning, and each component can be utilized in one of two ways: computer-managed instruction or computer-assisted learning. Computers are employed instead of traditional ways in computer-assisted learning by delivering interactive software as a support tool within the classroom or as a tool for self-learning outside of the classroom. Computers are used in computer-managed instruction to support the management of education by storing and retrieving information.

According to Almosa (2002), internet-based learning is an advance over computer-based learning in that it makes content available on the internet, with the readiness of links to related knowledge sources, such as email services and references, which can be used by learners at any time and in any place. Zeitoun (2008) classified this based on the extent to which such features are used in education: mixed or blended mode, assistant mode, and completely online mode. As needed, the assistant mode supplements the traditional method. The mixed or blended mode provides for a partially traditional method. The most comprehensive improvement is the completely online mode, which involves the exclusive use of the network for learning.

Algahtani (2011) defined the completely online mode as "synchronous" or "asynchronous" based on the application of optional interaction timing. The synchronous timing includes alternate online access between teachers or instructors and learners, or between learners, and the asynchronous allows all participants to post communications to any other participant via the internet (Algahtani 2011). The synchronous type allows students to communicate with instructors as well as with one another via the internet at the same time, using tools such as videoconferences and chat rooms. This has the advantage of providing instantaneous feedback (Almosa and Almubarak 2005). The asynchronous mode also allows students to communicate with instructors or teachers as well as with one another via the internet at different times (Almosa and Almubarak 2005). It is thus not interaction at the same time but later, through the use of tools such as thread discussions and emails, and has the advantage that learners can learn at their own pace, but the disadvantage that they will not be able to receive instant feedback from instructors and fellow learners (Algahtani 2011).

In conclusion, adopting computer-based technology and internet-based learning in the HE context can support students' resources-searching and make self-learning possible, reducing time-consuming situations.

7.4.2 Adopting Augmented Reality in the HE Context

Augmented reality (AR) is a technology that is rapidly advancing and is being used in a variety of applications to improve learning efficiency (Arkorful and Abaidoo 2015). AR applications for education have not been widely used until now. Several researchers have proposed incorporating interactive media into learning. Computer-based learning systems have the potential to provide an interactive user with a variety of controls for selecting and combining images, texts, animations, audio, and video in an integrated manner to facilitate effective learning (Arkorful and Abaidoo 2015). Researchers also state that media combined with instructional design is a superior tool for meeting learning objectives (Arkorful and Abaidoo 2015). Audio, animation, and video elements have the potential to enhance learning by providing both informative and emotional aspects. For example, the "MagicBook" has an interface that allows readers to enjoy the story while viewing it as a virtual model via AR displays. The MagicBook's interface is similar to that of a traditional book, with text and images on each page (Dias 2009). These images are framed by thick black borders, which act as markers for computer vision-based tracking systems.

AR, as a learning tool, has the ability to allow students to see their surroundings in a new light by utilizing realistic issues to which students are already connected. AR that is vision-based and location-aware makes use of smartphone capabilities such as the camera, the Global Positioning System, tracking, and object recognition. These features enable a smartphone to provide students with an immersive learning experience based on data obtained from their physical surroundings. It provides educators with a powerful, transformative, and novel tool for teaching and learning. Immersion is the subjective impression that one is participating in a realistic and comprehensive experience (Arthur 2010). Today's interactive media allow for varying degrees of digital involvement. When a person is given a virtual immersive experience that focuses on design strategies like combining symbolic, actionable, and sensory factors, they are subjected to a greater suspension of disbelief that they are inside a digitally enhanced setting. According to research, being immersed in a digital environment has the potential to improve education in at least three ways (Clark 2009): multiple perspectives, situated learning, and transfer.

To sum up, adopting AR in the HE context can, to a great extent, assist students' learning, particularly remembering knowledge easily and quickly. However, overusing AR may cause over-reliance on the digital environment and cause students to detach themselves from reality.

7.4.3 Adopting Mobile Technology in the HE Context

Davison and Lazaros (2015) stated that e-learning was defined as "utilizing electronic technologies to access educational curriculum outside of a traditional classroom." In most cases, it refers to a course, program, or degree delivered completely online. Despite the fact that mobile technology adoption is increasing, the issues we have discussed earlier create real barriers to implementing mobile technology in the classroom and facilitating e-learning. When combined with the organization's implementation issues (e.g. budget, technology procurement, bandwidth, and support), mobile technology adoption is a difficult proposition. Although the barriers exist, mobile learning (m-learning) is becoming an increasingly important part of university life and education.

M-learning can be used instead of having a computer in every home, and it can provide more freedom because the learning material can be accessed from any location. Accessing learning content on a mobile device has no disadvantages when compared to accessing the content on a computer because hardware and software are advancing at such a rapid pace (Shao and Seif 2014). Students can engage in active learning through m-learning, which can lead to the development of critical thinking and problem-solving skills. M-learning enables students to combine hands-on learning with traditional course material (Granić et al. 2009).

There are additional advantages to using m-learning. Students who can interact with a course via m-learning are more likely to have fun and enjoy the course, and will pursue the content that interests them the most. Students can work at their own pace and in the environment that is most comfortable for them (Granić et al. 2009). Mobile technologies mark a shift away from knowledge acquisition toward a more interactive form of learning (Davison and Lazaros 2015). Furthermore, they can encourage the student's "self-regulation" (Davison and Lazaros 2015). There are numerous factors to consider before implementing m-learning. For example, the content should be designed so that it can be accessed by the widest possible range of students using the least advanced device (Wang and Shen 2012). It is also critical for designers to employ a variety of techniques when creating m-learning in order to appeal to a wide range of learners (Wang and Shen 2012). The potential detriments to the learning process must be taken into account. Mobile technologies have the potential to facilitate non-learning activities in the classroom while also acting as a distraction (Davison and Lazaros 2015). While m-learning technologies can improve student learning, they are not without drawbacks. They pose challenges in terms of instructor technology adoption as well as instructor facilitation of e-learning platforms (Darby 2004). In the educational environment, there are a number of barriers to technology adoption. These barriers range from infrastructure technical capabilities to policy enactment (McKay et al. 2014). The perceived usefulness of the technology is the most important determinant of adoption, according to seminal research on the technology acceptance model (TAM) in the education sector (Hu et al. 2003).

As a result, learners are keen on using mobile to study, which is not only for the convenience of learning but more likely a fashion trend. Adopting mobile technology in the HE context is the most popular method for students to use to study by far.

7.4.4 Adopting Audio Technology in the HE Context

Audio support in HE learning has often applied to class or classroom feedback from teachers to students, which is the meaningful instructor feedback that is one of the most effective ways to empower students while also improving and transforming their learning (Van der Kleij et al. 2015). In a review of research on the impact of feedback on learning and achievement, Hattie and Timperley (2007) defined feedback as "information provided by an agent (e.g. teacher, peer, book, parent, self, experience) regarding aspects of one's performance or understanding." According to the research literature and practical experiences of blended and online teaching, the ways students receive feedback from their peers and instructors need to be improved in terms of quality, detail, and timing (Dixon 2015). Emotionally engaging feedback practices must be developed as well (Crook et al. 2012). In academic settings, students' emotions play a critical role in their motivation to learn as well as academic achievement, and feedback from instructors is one of the sources of students' emotions (Rasi and Vuojärvi 2018). Positive emotions in students predict high achievement, while negative emotions like anxiety, anger, boredom, and shame predict low achievement (Pekrun and Linnenbrink-Garcia 2014). Well-timed, detailed, specific, and positive feedback can empower students during their learning processes by eliciting emotions such as joy, pride, and excitement, and can lead to better learning outcomes because instructors have the ability to step into a student's learning process and potentially change or deepen it (Rasi and Vuojärvi 2018).

Students begin to demand more personalized feedback. Because staff-to-student ratios are worsening and academic staff workloads are increasing, high-quality technology-supported pedagogical practices must be developed to assist instructors in providing feedback efficiently and in pedagogically sound ways (Mayhem 2016). In a digitized world, these practices must align with the core of m-learning, namely, the promotion of connectivity and flexibility among people, contexts, contents, times, places, and modes of learning (Crook et al. 2012). Numerous initiatives have been launched to promote audio feedback practices in HE settings, and technology-supported feedback tools as well as digital applications have been developed and/or tested to assist instructors in providing students with asynchronous multimodal feedback (Mayhem 2016). Instructors can use these applications to provide feedback to individual students, small groups of students, or even the entire class (Rasi and Vuojärvi 2018).

The use of audio feedback by instructors is nothing new, and it has been available and recommended for teachers since 1980s with the available technologies at the time (Dixon 2015). Parkes and Fletcher (2014) also revealed that asynchronous instructor audio feedback was well received by students, who preferred audio feedback to written feedback. Rasi and Vuojärvi (2018) stated that, if teachers received adequate technical support on a timely basis, audio materials could help to strengthen a social presence and connectivity between students and teachers, thereby helping students to learn better.

In summary, audio technology used in an HE context can add a friendly tightening of the teacher–student relationship. Teachers' feedback can give students intuitive suggestions, and it supports learners in gaining a relatively clearer concept of feedback.

7.4.5 Adopting Social Media and Social Platforms on the HE Context

Practitioners have taken note of the rise of social media networks and the potential they hold for HE teaching and learning in recent years. There is now a growing body of academic research that has set out to investigate the benefits of social media on the student learning experience.

The rapid rise and adoption of social media networks around the world over the last decade has been an extraordinary technological development. Two major companies – Facebook and Twitter – have transformed, shaped, and driven the digital landscape in a relatively short period of time. Social media networks like these appear to have enormous potential for teaching and learning in HE, with their core function based on connecting groups of people around the world and encouraging them to create and share information. The central premise of social media networks is to provide individuals with the opportunities and power to create, collaborate, and share ideas and information in an open manner, all of which are important aspects of fostering student development. As a result, there has been an increasing belief in recent years that social media platforms have the potential to improve teaching and learning in HE (Rasi and Vuojärvi 2018) and could play a role in the solution. Not only might they address the criticisms of lack of technology, but platforms like Facebook and Twitter have the potential to perform a number of important pedagogical functions.

In addition, the prevalence of social media is nowhere more visible than at universities. Social media are becoming more visible in HE settings as instructors look to technology to mediate and enhance their instruction while also encouraging students to participate in active learning. Many academics advocate for the intentional use of social media as an educational tool. Social media and other Web 2.0 technologies are exploding at an unprecedented rate (Rasi and Vuojärvi 2018). As users generate content, share photos, choose to "like" something, or interact in a game, social media technology has become an essential part of personal life. At the university, technology is transforming how students communicate, collaborate, and learn. Even as today's college student encounters a variety of classroom formats (bricks and mortar, virtual, and hybrid), social media use and influence vary depending on context.

Back in 2014, Graham discovered that using social media as a learning tool had a functionally positive effect on Humanities students. When the necessary conditions are in place to instill and encourage participation among the student body, there is a greater likelihood that they will interact more effectively throughout the semester (Graham 2014). Although social media has been widely accepted as a tool for personal or business purposes, the idea that it could be an effective tool for educational purposes has received only recent attention. By carefully planning tasks via social media platforms, these tools have the potential to nurture and develop increased participation and engagement for Humanities students outside of the classroom (Graham 2014).

Consequently, students, especially Humanities students, should begin to use their social media and social platforms in the HE contexts. Online public data from social platforms is currently the best and most useful resource, and students can apply the public materials into their research and study, broadening their horizons and learning in their field knowledge.

7.5 The Impact of the Tech-Enhanced Classroom to Students' Learning Experience under Various Courses

In the digital era, many researchers are attempted to develop and practice the theories of technology-supported HE. Tech-enhanced classrooms improved students' learning experiences in all kinds of class settings.

7.5.1 Tech-Enhanced Classroom in the Language Course

Research has shown that the use of instructional technology and ICT in the English language classroom, in particular, can improve and optimize students' language acquisition while also significantly motivating them to continue learning and stimulating their creativity and passion. That is, technology in language learning can increase the variety and diversity of learning environments and opportunities, as well as strengthen the quality of the learning experience. Instructors can design more varied class content and pedagogies, giving every learner more access to class learning and ensuring greater participation and engagement (Hara 2016).

ICT integration in the curriculum provides access to a variety of electronic resources such as interactive video, the internet, email, and the World Wide Web. These ICT tools can assist learners in developing linguistic skills, establishing contact and interaction with other language users, and broadening their minds about different cultural practices, values, and contemporary lifestyles in countries where English is spoken as a first or second language. It is believed that ICT-assisted teaching increases the level of activity and interaction in the English as a foreign language (EFL) classroom. Incorporating information technology into language teaching provides students with numerous advantages that increase their chances of successfully learning a foreign language. These benefits include increasing motivation, fostering critical thinking skills, encouraging innovation and creativity, establishing interaction, improving communication, promoting research and cooperative learning in the language classroom, and improving students' performance in written class assessments.

Motivating students in the language classroom is a difficult function to perform because it involves a variety of psychosocial and linguistic factors (Hara 2016). Most foreign language professionals recognize the significance and utility of motivation in optimizing language learning and achieving desired outcomes. So, to what extent can information technology boost motivation and increase student involvement in their learning? Many researchers contend that information technology can influence students' motivation to learn by increasing their interest and attention, as well as ensuring greater involvement and engagement in the classroom (Zheng et al. 2015).

When computers are used in the classroom, students are more likely to have positive attitudes, and they are more eager to communicate with native speakers from other countries (Zheng et al. 2015). The use of ICT can create a learning environment in which motivation is maintained and increased. A study of the impact of technology use in EFL classrooms revealed that technology can improve the effectiveness of EFL activities. Students insisted that technology be used in the classroom by their teachers. This has increased and maintained their motivation and engagement, and increased their involvement in the learning process (Hara 2016).

The use of blogs, podcasts, and digital videos as classroom content also boosts motivation and engagement. Hara (2016) investigated the use of blogs to motivate students to write, demonstrating the significance of providing students with a genuine audience as well as the utility of writing for a global audience. McMinn (2008) of Hong Kong University of Science and Technology chose to investigate the effect of podcasting on student motivation in the language classroom (Azmi 2017). He has concluded that podcasting, the publication of audio or video files over the internet, assists teachers in making the most of classroom time by incorporating authentic material and simulated environments into the foreign language learning curriculum. The use of podcasts provides engaging authentic learning content. Podcasts, he continues, provide learners with more opportunities to hear a speech from the specific social group that they want to learn about and possibly identify with.

Thus, it can be seen that the role of instructional technology is introduced as a facilitator of this role exchange and as a tool that many students are actually using to become autonomous learners. Azmi (2017) also stated that the more a teacher employs instructional technology, the less teacher-centered and the more student-centered a classroom will become. It has been discovered that technology-enhanced classrooms promote discovery learning, learner autonomy, and learner centeredness.

Furthermore, in many parts of the world, English teachers assign project work to students as a way to supplement and enhance classroom learning. The internet is used as a research and resource tool by the majority of students. This allows them to direct their own learning by participating in real-world projects (Azmi 2017). Within the same program, students can complete a reading assignment in the target language, consult a dictionary, study grammar and pronunciation related to the reading material, take a comprehension test on the reading content, and receive immediate feedback. This will be sufficient to maximize targeted outcomes while also providing more opportunities and facilities for autonomous learning.

Chapelle (2003) declared that computer-mediated communication "constitutes a kind of virtual immersion setting for those who choose to participate in it" (Azmi 2017). In keeping with the common wisdom that if one wants to learn English, they should live in a country where English is spoken, many internet websites for communication among English learners provide opportunities for conversation and interaction with other English speakers. By bringing students together to communicate, interact, and construct knowledge, new technologies have the potential to transform task-based language teaching into active learning (Azmi 2017).

Computer-mediated communication systems, both synchronous and asynchronous, have numerous advantages. They may improve the collaborative learning experience by reducing social pressures associated with face-to-face participation, such as turn-taking, dominating the discussion, and fear of retaliation, as well as cognitive inertia (Englund et al. 2017). Language learners do not feel compelled to provide immediate feedback and instead take their time developing appropriate responses. De Ramirez (2010) claimed that web-based platforms can also provide a safer, more anonymous space in which to practice English. Beginners can be reticent and uncomfortable speaking in class or sharing their writing with peers in a face-to-face situation (Azmi 2017).

7.5.2 Tech-Enhanced Classroom Course in the Science Department

Learners' interest in science, technology, engineering, and mathematics (STEM) subjects is currently declining, particularly after secondary school. It is critical to increase their motivation and engagement in these subjects, as well as to encourage them to pursue third-level STEM degrees, which are underrepresented in university enrollment. This can be accomplished through the use of TEL and interactive solutions, which will engage students in the learning process, motivate them, and improve their knowledge gain, thereby dispelling the myth that STEM subjects are difficult and increasing their interest in STEM-related careers. Over the last 10 years, various technologies have been implemented in the educational sector with the goal of improving the method of teaching and learning. Virtual reality (VR) is a technology with enormous potential and significant pedagogical benefits that allows for new teaching methods. VR creates an immersive multimedia 3D simulation of real life, allows for interactivity with the created environment, and enables sensorial experiences (Altmeyer et al. 2020). VR has a wide range of applications, including physics. Virtual laboratory (VL) technology is also used in education, particularly in subjects that require running experiments (e.g. physics, chemistry). VL is a highly interactive multimedia environment that immerses learners in a virtual world where they can design and conduct simulated experiments while visualizing the results in a 3D environment. This technology enables learners to improve their problem-solving, computer literacy, and practical skills, all of which are important for lifelong learning, in a fun way. The advantages of using VL technology in science education are as follows: the experimental activities are completed faster than in a real-world experiment; the same experiment can be run multiple times at no additional cost for materials; it allows for easy observation of the experiment at a time convenient for the learner; and it encourages collaboration and communication between teachers and students (Altmeyer et al. 2020).

Additionally, TEL with physical experimentation incorporates elements of multimedia learning: visual (e.g. real electric circuits constructed of cords, resistors, and power supplies; digital representation of data as needle deflection) and verbal information (worksheets, measurement data) are used in tandem for knowledge construction (e.g. guided deduction of rules). According to Faria et al. (2014), displaying AR information, in particular, helps to transform traditional learning environments into multimedia settings by literally incorporating additional external representations into the physical environment. This viewpoint enables the use of validated theoretical models on multimedia learning to predict the outcomes of AR-learning scenarios. Kapp et al. (2019) proved that cognitive load theory (Sweller 1988) and the cognitive theory of multimedia learning (Mayer 2009) predicted and explained the effectiveness of multimedia learning environments by considering memory processes, and various design principles for multimedia instruction have been deduced. Thus, TEL applied in a physics course supports students' learning by visualizing theoretical content (Altmeyer et al. 2020).

7.6 From Passive to Active: TEL Improving Students' Learning Experience in an HE Flipped Classroom

Improving student thinking abilities like creativity are a vital task in the rapidly changing digital world for HE institutions. Despite the development of applications and the capacity of technology in recent decades, traditional teaching based on lectures continues to prevail (Butt 2014). Hargrove and Nietfeld (2014) thus argue that "creativity has been marginalized to some extent within formal educational contexts." The ability of HE systems to promote meaningful learning that prepares students to meet the requirements of the twenty-first century can be problematic. In response, scholars advocate that, "carefully designed interventions can have a positive effect in increasing various creative abilities and that these outcomes extend across criteria, settings, and target populations" (Hargrove and Nietfeld 2014). The flipped classroom is one such typical intervention for instance, that has the potential to revolutionize online education and promote higher-order thinking skills (Bergmann and Sams 2012).

Two main movements can be attributed to the increase of the flipped or "inverted classrooms" (Mason et al. 2013). Bishop and Verleger (2013) have stated that the first movement is the global technology movement that facilitates "extremely cheap" integration of information technology into education. The second is the ideological movement and ideas that have spread over technology.

Some scientists argue that flipping courses are not a new educational movement because teachers encourage students to prepare themselves for their classes in order to participate effectively in classrooms (Al-Zahrani 2015). Other scientists point to the decades-long implementation of educational TV and computer-based instruction (Strayer 2012). However, the regular and systematic use of interactive technologies in the learning process integrates flipped schools (Strayer 2012). One of the major benefits of the reversed classroom is that it is not limited only to certain groups of students, a specific curriculum, or a specific field of content (Bergmann and Sams 2012).

Although flipped classrooms are an exciting topic for academics, there is lack of consensus on how to implement the flipped classroom (Abeysekera and Dawson 2014). However, most academics agree that in a flipped classroom, activities that would normally take place during traditional classes must take place prior to class, and vice versa (Strayer 2012). This strategy is defined by Bishop and Verleger (2013) as "a new pedagogical method, which employs asynchronous video lectures and practice problems as homework, and active, group-based problem-solving activities in the classroom."

Several studies on the flipped classroom in HE have been conducted to investigate various aspects of the strategy's effectiveness (Butt 2014). The majority of these studies yielded encouraging results. Students in flipped classrooms, for example, were better prepared for subsequent traditional classroom activities (McLaughlin et al. 2013); they were more excited, engaged, and satisfied (Butt 2014); they were more open to cooperative learning (Strayer 2012); they had better examination scores (Mason et al. 2013); they demonstrated better proficiency when using problem-solving techniques (Mason et al. 2013); and they were highly personalized learners (Al-Zahrani 2015). Only a few studies yielded contradictory results. (Al-Zahrani 2015) Strayer (2012) found, for example, that students in a flipped classroom were dissatisfied with how the classroom structure oriented them to learning tasks. Despite the students' positive attitudes toward this learning strategy, studies by Findlay-Thompson and Mombourquette (2014) and McLaughlin et al. (2013) found no change in academic outcomes of participants in flipped classrooms (Al-Zahrani 2015).

Different from the stereotype of HE classroom, the flipped classroom heavily relies on the use of visualization, particularly videos and presentations, and can greatly aid in the generation of creative ideas, to foster creative thinking (Martin and Schwartz 2014). The relationship between visualization and creativity is defined by Martin and Schwartz (2014): "Visualisations can create conditions for creativity, in part, because they support simple strategies that anyone can execute." And, creative thinking has been defined as a "mental process involving the generation of new ideas or concepts, or new associations between existing ideas or concepts" (Jackson et al. 2012). It means that creative thinking would assist students to generate class concepts much more easily, learning faster and more clearly than before. Furthermore, with the proliferation of digital technologies such as video games and online interaction, educators have become increasingly concerned about the potential effects of such technologies on students' creative thinking (Al-Zahrani 2015). Previous research has found that flipped classrooms can improve students' motivation, engagement, and overall achievement in HE. Based on the findings of the current study, the flipped classroom can effectively stimulate students' creativity. A well-designed flipped classroom can motivate HE students to generate novel ideas that are rich and relevant to real-world problems with the appropriate preparation at home and intensive classroom activities (Al-Zahrani 2015). It also enables them to be more elaborative, versatile, and fluent in their ideas. It seems that a TEL-supported flipped classroom learning strategy has a greater impact on HE learners, especially in terms of the development of higher-order thinking skills, such as creativity. This is due to the fact that cultivating students' creativity is a critical task for HE systems all over the world. Also, under this learning mode, HE students might be more open to change and have a greater ability to manage their study loads, especially if they use technology to support their study in their daily life. Moreover, by using flipped classrooms,

HE students can become more independent and autonomous learners, which may positively influence their creative thinking (Al-Zahrani 2015).

In conclusion, with the theoretical development of science and technology supporting HE, as well as increasing evidence emerging from the field of HE technology practice, the situation of TEL in HE is moving from passive to positive. In particular, TEL combined with the HE flipped classroom can develop students' creative thinking, cultivate their learning interests and enhance learners' study motivation, thereby improving their learning experiences in the HE stage.

References

Abeysekera, L. and Dawson, P. (2014). Motivation and cognitive load in the flipped classroom: definition, rationale and a call for research. *Higher Education Research and Development* 34: 1–14.

Algahtani, A.F. (2011). *Evaluating the Effectiveness of the E-Learning Experience in Some Universities in Saudi Arabia from Male Students' Perceptions*. Durham University.

Almosa, A. (2002). *Use of Computer in Education*. Riyadh: Future Education Library.

Almosa, A. and Almubarak, A. (2005). *E-Learning Foundations and Applications*. Saudi Arabia: Riyadh.

Altmeyer, K., Kapp, S., Thees, M. et al. (2020). The use of augmented reality to foster conceptual knowledge acquisition in STEM laboratory courses – theoretical background and empirical results. *British Journal of Educational Technology* 51 (3): 611–628.

Al-Zahrani, A.M. (2015). From passive to active: the impact of the flipped classroom through social learning platforms on higher education students' creative thinking. *British Journal of Educational Technology* 46 (6): 1133–1148.

Arkorful, V. and Abaidoo, N. (2015). The role of e-learning, advantages and disadvantages of its adoption in higher education. *International Journal of Instructional Technology and Distance Learning* 12 (1): 29–42.

Arthur, C. (2010). Augmented reality: it's like real life, but better. *The Observer*. http://www.guardian.co.uk/technology/2010/mar/21/augmented-reality-iphone-advertising (accessed 25 November 2021).

Azmi, N. (2017). The benefits of using ICT in the EFL classroom: from perceived utility to potential challenges. *Journal of Educational and Social Research* 7 (1): 111.

Bergmann, J. and Sams, A. (2012). *Flip Your Classroom: Reach Every Student in Every Class Every Day*. Washington, DC: International Society for Technology in Education.

Bishop, J. L. and Verleger, M. A., 2013.The flipped classroom: a survey of the research. *Paper presented at the 120th ASEE Conference and Exposition* (23–26 June 2013). Atlanta GA: American Society for Engineering Education. https://doi.org/10.18260/1-2-22585

Butt, A. (2014). Student views on the use of a flipped classroom approach: evidence from Australia. *Business Education and Accreditation* 6 (1): 33–43.

Carman, J. M. (2002). Blended learning design: five key ingredients. KnowledgeNet. http://blended2010.pbworks.com/f/Carman.pdf (accessed 25 November 2021).

Chung, J. and Davis, I.K. (1995). An instructional theory for learner control: Revisited. In: *Proceedings of the 1995 Annual National Convention of the Association for Educational Communications and Technology* (ed. M.R. Simonson), 72–86. Anaheim, CA: AACE.

Clark, D. (2009). *Immersive Interfaces for Engagement and Learning*. New York: Springer.

Crook, A., Mauchline, A., Maw, S. et al. (2012). The use of video technology for providing feedback to students: can it enhance the feedback experience for staff and students? *Computers and Education* 58: 386–396.

Daniela, L., Visvizi, A., Gutiérrez-Braojos, C., and Lytras, M.D. (2018). Sustainable higher education and technology-enhanced learning (TEL). *Sustainability* 10 (11): 3883.

Darby, J. (2004). eLearning as change agent. *International Journal of the Computer, the Internet and Management* 12 (2): 171–176.

Davison, C.B. and Lazaros, E.J. (2015). Adopting mobile technology in the higher education classroom. *Journal of Technology Studies* 41 (1): 30–39.

De Ramirez, L.L. (2010). *Empower English Language Learners with Tools from the Web*. Thousand Oaks, CA: Corwin.

Dias, A. (2009). Technology enhanced learning and augmented reality: an application on multimedia interactive books. *International Business and Economics Review* 1 (1): 69–79.

Dias, S.B. and Diniz, J.A. (2014). Towards an enhanced learning management system for blended learning in higher education incorporating distinct learners' profiles. *Educational Technology and Society* 17: 307–319.

Dixon, S. (2015). The pastoral potential of audio feedback: a review of the literature. *Pastoral Care in Education* 33: 96–104.

Driscoll, M. (2002). Blended Learning: Let's get beyond the hype, *E-learning* (1 March).

Dublin, L. (2003). If you only look under the street lamps or nine e-learning myths. *The e-Learning Developers Journal* 1–7.

Englund, C., Olofsson, A.D., and Price, L. (2017). Teaching with technology in higher education: Understanding conceptual change and development in practice. *Higher Education Research & Development* 36 (1): 73–87.

Faria, F.A., Dos Santos, J.A., Rocha, A., and Torres, R.D.S. (2014). A framework for selection and fusion of pattern classifiers in multimedia recognition. *Pattern Recognition Letters* 39: 52–64.

Findlay-Thompson, S. and Mombourquette, P. (2014). Evaluation of a flipped classroom in an undergraduate business course. *Business Education & Accreditation* 6 (1): 63–71.

Garrison, D.R. and Kanuka, H. (2004). Blended learning: uncovering its transformative potential in higher education. *The Internet and Higher Education* 7 (2): 95–105.

Gecer, A. and Dag, F. (2012). A blended learning experience. *Educational Sciences: Theory and Practice* 12 (1): 438–442.

Graham, C.R. (2006). Blended learning systems. In: *The Handbook of Blended Learning: Global Perspectives, Local Designs* (ed. C.J. Bonk and C.R. Graham), 3–21. Pfeiffer Publishin.

Graham, M. (2014). Social media as a tool for increased student participation and engagement outside the classroom in higher education. *Journal of Perspectives in Applied Academic Practice* 2 (3): 16.

Granić, A., Ćukušić, M., and Walker, R. (2009). mLearning in a Europe-wide network of schools. *Educational Media International* 46 (3): 167–184.

Hara, T. (2016). Analyses on tech-enhanced and anonymous peer discussion as well as anonymous control facilities for tech-enhanced learning. PhD dissertation. Technical University of Dresden, Germany.

Hargrove, R.A. and Nietfeld, J.L. (2014). The impact of metacognitive instruction on creative problem solving. *The Journal of Experimental Education* 83: 1–28.

Hattie, J. and Timperley, H. (2007). The power of feedback. *Review of Educational Research* 77: 81–112.

Holley, D. and Oliver, M. (2010). Student engagement and blended learning: portraits of risk. *Computers and Education* 54: 693–700.

Hu, P.J.-H., Clark, T.H., and Ma, W.W. (2003). Examining technology acceptance by school teachers; a longitudinal study. *Information and Management* 41 (2): 227–241.

Jackson, L.A., Witt, E.A., Games, A.I. et al. (2012). Information technology use and creativity: findings from the children and technology project. *Computers in Human Behavior* 28 (2): 370–376.

Kapp, S., Thees, M., Strzys, M.P. et al. (2019). Augmenting Kirchhoff's laws: using augmented reality and smartglasses to enhance conceptual electrical experiments for high school students. *The Physics Teacher* 57 (1): 52–53.

Karaman, S., Özen, Ü., Yıldırım, S., and Kaban, A. (2009). Açık kaynak kodlu öğretim yönetim sistemi üzerinden internet destekli (Harmanlanmış) öğrenim deneyimi. Akademik Bilişim Konferansı 2009'da sunulan bildiri, (Internet assisted (Blended) learning experience through an open source teaching management system. Paper presented at the Academic Informatics Conference 2009). Harran University, Şanlıurfa.

Kasraie, N. and Alahmad, A. (2014). Investigating the reasons institutions of higher education in the USA and Canada utilize blended learning.Mevlana. *International Journal of Education (MIJE)* 4 (1): 67–81.

Kirkwood, A. and Price, L. (2014). Technology-enhanced learning and teaching in higher education: what is 'enhanced' and how do we know? A critical literature review. *Learning, Media and Technology* 39 (1): 6–36.

Klein, D. and Ware, M. (2003). E-learning: New opportunities in continuing professional development. *Learned Publishing* 16 (1): 34–46.

Marc, J.R. (2002). Book review: E-learning strategies for delivering knowledge in the digital age. *Internet and Higher Education* 5: 185–188.

Martin, L. and Schwartz, D.L. (2014). A pragmatic perspective on visual representation and creative thinking. *Visual Studies* 29 (1): 80–93.

Mason, G.S., Shuman, T.R., and Cook, K.E. (2013). Comparing the effectiveness of an inverted classroom to a traditional classroom in an upper-division engineering course. *IEEE Transactions on Education* 56 (4): 430–435.

Mayer, R. (2009). *Multimedia learning*, 2e. New York, NY: Cambridge University Press.

Mayhem, E. (2016). Playback feedback: the impact of screen-captured video feedback on student satisfaction, learning and attainment. *European Political Science* 16: 179–192.

McKay, S.B., Seward, J.C., and Davison, C.B. (2014). Mobile technology adoption in K-12 classrooms. *Academic Exchange Quarterly* 18 (3).

McLaughlin, J.E., Griffin, L.M., Esserman, D.A. et al. (2013). Pharmacy student engagement, performance, and perception in a flipped satellite classroom. *American Journal of Pharmaceutical Education* 77 (9): 1–8.

McMinn, S.W. (2008). Podcasting possibilities: Increasing time and motivation in the language learning classroom. The Hong Kong University of Science and Technology. http://www.eife-l.org/publications/proceedings/ilf08/contributions (accessed 25 November 2021).

Motteram, G. (2006). Blended education and the transformation of teachers: A long-term case study in post graduate UK Higher Education. *British Journal of Educational Technology* 37 (1): 17–30.

OECD (2020). Education responses to COVID-19: Embracing digital learning and online collaboration. https://www.oecd.org/coronavirus/policy-responses/education-responses-to-covid-19-embracing-digital-learning-and-online-collaboration-d75eb0e8 (accessed 18 June 2020).

Okaz, A.A. (2015). Integrating blended learning in higher education. *Procedia-Social and Behavioral Sciences* 186 (13): 600–603.

Orozco-Messana, J., Martínez-Rubio, J.M., and Gonzálvez-Pons, A.M. (2020). Sustainable higher education development through technology enhanced learning. *Sustainability* 12 (9): 3600.

Paechter, M. and Maier, B. (2010). Online or face-to-face? Students' experiences and preferences in e-learning. *The Internet and Higher Education* 13 (4): 292–297.

Parkes, M. and Fletcher, P.R. (2014). Talking the talk: Audio feedback as a tool for student assessment. In: *Proceedings of the World Conference on Educational Multimedia, Hypermedia and Telecommunications*, Tampere, Finland, (23–26 June), 1606–1615.

Pekrun, R. and Linnenbrink-Garcia, L. (2014). Introduction to emotions in education. In: *International Handbook of Emotions in Education* (ed. R. Pekrun and L. Linnenbrink-Garcia), 1–10.

Rasi, P. and Vuojärvi, H. (2018). Toward personal and emotional connectivity in mobile higher education through asynchronous formative audio feedback. *British Journal of Educational Technology* 49 (2): 292–304.

Rooney, J.E. (2003). Blending learning opportunities to enhance educational programming and meetings. *Association Management* 55 (5): 26–32.

Shao, D. and Seif, H. (2014). Mobile learning a new way of learning: a survey among University of Dodoma students. *International Journal of Computer Applications* 98 (16): 1–4.

Singh, T. (2010). Creating opportunities for students in large cohorts to reflect in and on practice: lessons learnt from a formative evaluation of students' experiences of a technology-enhanced blended learning design. *British Journal of Educational Technology* 41 (2): 271–286.

Strayer, J.F. (2012). How learning in an inverted classroom influences cooperation, innovation and task orientation. *Learning Environment Research* 15: 171–193.

Sweller, J. (1988). Cognitive load during problem solving: Effects on learning. *Cognitive Science* 12 (2): 257–285.

Van der Kleij, F.M., Feskens, R.C.W., and Eggen, T.J.H.M. (2015). Effects of feedback in a computer-based learning environment on students' learning outcomes – a meta-analysis. *Review of Educational Research* 85: 475–511.

Vonderwell, S. (2003). An examination of asynchronous communication experiences and perspectives of students in an online course: a case study. *Internet and Higher Education* 6 (1): 77–90.

Wang, M. and Shen, R. (2012). Message design for mobile learning: learning theories, human cognition and design principles. *British Journal of Educational Technology* 43 (4): 561–575.

Wang, Y.S., Wang, Y.M., Lin, H.H., and Tang, T.I. (2003). Determinants of user acceptance of internet banking: an empirical study. *International Journal of Service Industry Management* 14: 501–519.

Yang, N. and Arjomand, L.H. (1999). Opportunities and challenges in computer-mediated business education: An exploratory investigation of online programs. *Academy of Educational Leadership Journal* 3 (2): 17–29.

Young, J.R. (2002). 'Hybrid' teaching seeks to end the divide between traditional and online instruction. *Chronicle of Higher Education* 48: A33.

Zeitoun, H. (2008). *E-Learning: Concept, Issues, Application, Evaluation*. Riyadh: Dar Alsolateah Publication.

Zheng, B., Niiya, M., and Warschauer, M. (2015). Wikis and collaborative learning in higher education. *Technology, Pedagogy and Education* 24 (3): 357–374.

8

Sustainability Assessment Tools in Higher Education Institutions: Comprehensive Analysis of the Indicators and Outlook

M. Mapar, P. Bacelar-Nicolau, and S. Caeiro

8.1 Introduction

Higher education institutions (HEIs) have been generally considered significant contributors to the promotion of sustainability (Karatzoglou 2013). They can act as transformative agents to shape sustainability (Findler et al. 2018; Wersun et al. 2020) among society and empower individuals to tackle social and ecological problems with entrepreneurial means to put sustainability into practice (Hesselbarth and Schaltegger 2014). The process of sustainability integration in HEIs has recently been gaining increasing attention worldwide, with a stronger interest in Europe (Moreno Pires et al. 2020). Sustainability integration is the entire process of moving from a business-as-usual university to a sustainable university, including all stages of the process along a certain time (Kapitulčinová et al. 2018). A sustainable university is defined by Velazquez et al. (2006) as an HEI that addresses and promotes, on a regional or a global level, the minimization of negative environmental, economic, societal, and health effects being generated in its use of its resources, and fulfills its functions of teaching, research, outreach, and stewardship in ways to help society make the transition to sustainable lifestyles. Several studies show developing new initiatives to integrate sustainability into the whole systems elements of HEIs, including core elements like education, research, operations, community outreach, and assessment and reporting (Lozano et al. 2015b). Kapitulčinová et al. (2018) schematized three stages of this integration process, namely (i) initiation/awakening, (ii) implementation/pioneering, and (iii) institutionalization/transformation, to shift from a business-as-usual university to a sustainable university. Given the central role of HEIs in fostering the United Nations 17 Sustainable Development Goals (SDGs), in particular SDG 4 (Quality Education) and target 4.7 (United Nations 2015), the adoption of whole-institution approaches and integrated frameworks by the academic community still appears to be in initial stages (Lozano et al. 2013).

There are several practices and initiatives adopted by HEIs to promote sustainability (Alshuwaikhat and Abubakar 2008). These practices can emerge in a wide range of areas (Caeiro et al. 2013), including the curriculum (Lozano 2010; Watson et al. 2013; Xiong et al. 2013; Stough et al. 2018); change in HEIs' assessment and management practices, e.g. through implementing management standard systems such as environmental management systems (EMS) (ISO 14001) and the EU Eco-Management and Audit Scheme (EMAS) (Alshuwaikhat and Abubakar 2008; Amaral et al. 2015; Nurcahyo et al. 2019); and assessing and

The Wiley Handbook of Sustainability in Higher Education Learning and Teaching, First Edition.
Edited by Kelum A. A. Gamage and Nanda Gunawardhana.
© 2022 John Wiley & Sons, Inc. Published 2022 by John Wiley & Sons, Inc.

reporting sustainability through applying sustainability assessment tools (Shriberg 2002; Alghamdi et al. 2017; Findler et al. 2018).

Different tools have been developed to specifically assess sustainability implementation at HEIs, for example Sustainability Assessment Questionnaire (SAQ) (ULSF 2009); Graz Model for Integrative Development (GMI) (Mader 2013), and Graphical Assessment of Sustainability in Universities tool (GASU) (Lozano 2006a) among many others. Also, there are some tools that propose ranking systems to compare the level of sustainability performance at HEIs such as Time Higher Education Impact Ranking System (THE), Three Dimensional University Ranking (TUR) (Lukman et al. 2010), and Sustainability Tracking, Assessment & Rating System (STARS) (AASHE 2019). However, HEIs assessment and ranking systems still require a specific definition of criteria and indicators developed to assess an HEI's progress toward the integration dimensions of sustainability (e.g. environmental, social, economic, academic, and institutional). As a result of usage of various indicators within the tools, the overall rankings based on diverse assessment tools are different (Lukman et al. 2010) and there are still some open questions on why a particular methodology or indicator was chosen by an HEI, how well it was structured, how the assessment and decision process was conducted, and finally what the main similarities and differences among these tools and associated indicators are. These questions are important for better overall comparison and benchmarking of sustainability implementation in HEIs, in terms not of competition but of network and collaboration.

The research aims to follow up earlier research by Caeiro et al. (2020) and critically analyze the existing tools that assess the implementation of sustainability at HEIs as well as their associated indicators and explore how the indicators emerge into the different core elements of sustainability implementation at HEIs, as well as into sustainability dimensions. More specifically, it also reveals through which thematic areas these indicators measure sustainability implementation at the HEIs.

This chapter is structured as follows: Sections 8.2 provides an overview of sustainability assessment at HEIs and describes the existing tools in HEIs and the main gaps; Section 8.3 describes the methods and the steps of the analysis; Section 8.4 presents the results and comparative analysis; Section 8.5 provide the overall discussion and the future development of the research; and finally Section 8.6 concludes the chapter.

8.2 An Overview of Sustainability Assessment and the Associated Tools at HEIs

Assessment should function as a learning and capacity-building instrument to help reflect on actions taken and improve future processes (Mader 2013). According to Lozano and Huisingh (2011), sustainability assessment is "a voluntary activity to assess the current state of an organization in triple-bottom-line of sustainable development." Sustainability is not a single discipline to be assessed but requires the equal analysis of the impact of economic, social, and environmental issues. While definitions of sustainability in the context of HEIs vary, commonalities encompass four dimensions (Moreno Pires et al. 2020): the environmental (defined as the sum of all biophysical processes and the elements involved in them); the social (intrapersonal qualities of human beings); the economic (the formal and informal economic activities that provide services to individuals and groups); and the institutional dimension (particularly within the realms of campus life including the administrative structure and policy directions of HEIs). Moreover, as pointed out in the previous literature (Lozano 2006a; Waheed et al. 2011; Berzosa et al. 2017), the sustainability dimensions in HEIs also include its main activity: academic sustainability, mainly covered by "education, research, and curriculum." Therefore, to evaluate sustainable development, all five dimensions of sustainability need to be reflected within one assessment process and with their interdependencies.

Corresponding to the development of sustainability declarations of HEIs, sustainability assessment practices at the university level have received increasing attention in the past decade (Fischer et al. 2015). As stated by Shriberg (2002), ideal sustainability assessments across institutions, in general, must address the following features: (i) contextualize appropriate issues of major importance to campus environmental, social, and economic efforts and effects; (ii) be calculable and allow for cross-campus comparisons; (iii) move beyond eco-efficiency and stress issues at the nexus of the environment, society, and economy with the goal of no negative impacts instead of focusing only on environmental performance and regulatory compliance; (iv) measure processes and motivations deep into decision-making by asking about missions, rewards, incentives, and other process-oriented outcomes; and (v) be comprehensible to a broad range of stakeholders by developing mechanisms for reporting that are verifiable and lucid.

To foster sustainable development at HEIs, there is a need to provide a tool for assessment and improvement of measures and actions taken toward sustainable development. Findler et al. (2018) defined sustainability assessment tools in the context of HEIs as "instruments that offer HEIs a systematic set of procedures and methods to measure, audit, benchmark, and communicate their sustainable development efforts." These tools allow the assessment of whether all possible dimensions to the implementation of sustainability are being implemented and whether they are doing so holistically (Caeiro et al. 2020). They do not only offer the technical support of implementation and evaluation of measures that actors in HEIs have developed to achieve outcomes that they have agreed on, but also provide a reference framework that is based on normative assumptions about what constitutes a sustainable university (Fischer et al. 2015).

A growing number of diverse assessment tools and methods have been developed and implemented by single institutions as well as alliances across different campuses. These tools are underpinned by different monitoring purposes, from ensuring compliance to predetermined standards, diagnosing the state of internal processes, and providing data for competitive performance comparisons (Fischer et al. 2015). They can be used to confirm the outcomes and impacts of the processes and activities (Smedby and Neij 2013) in a different context. They also provide the ability to decide what actions should be taken by the authorities to make HEIs more sustainable. However, since the concept of sustainability varies in different organizations – owing to differences between cultural, political, social, and economic conditions (Jones 2010) – therefore, each sustainability assessment tool should be adjusted for particular contexts, reflecting the specific conditions of each case study (Mapar et al. 2017). In the case of HEIs, the assessment tools should cover the whole system by addressing the seven core elements of sustainability implementation in HEIs that are widely accepted in the literature (Lozano et al. 2015a; Findler et al. 2018): (i) governance (i.e. the HEI commitment, policies, vision, mission, sustainable development office, and administrative structure); (ii) operations (i.e. energy use and energy efficiency, green-house gases, waste, water and water management, food purchasing, transport, accessibility for disabled people, and equality and diversity); (iii) education (i.e. courses on sustainable development, programs on sustainability issues, curricular reviews, and "educate-the-educators" programs); (iv) research (i.e. research funding, sustainable development research used in teaching, publications, patents, new knowledge, and technologies); (v) outreach and collaboration (i.e. exchange programs for students in the field of SD, joint degrees with other universities, joint research, SD partnerships such as enterprises, non-governmental organizations, and governments, and SD events open to the community); (vi) on-campus experiences (i.e. SD working group, sustainable development initiatives for students and staff, sustainable practices for students); and (vii) assessment and reporting (i.e. external assurance, reporting cycles, stakeholder identification processes). The majority of sustainability assessment tools in HEIs can be categorized into three types, as follows:

1) The first type includes a set of measurable individual indicators as the most frequent tools to assess sustainable development (Coelho et al. 2010; Ramos 2019; Mapar et al. 2020). Indicators are qualitative or quantitative bits of information that assess organizational performance and bring together multiple areas of sustainability that are generally comparable (GRI and ISO 2014). Using indicators-based methods, as compared to other assessment approaches, seek to achieve the integration of all sustainability issues by using a wide range of indicators in different domains of sustainability (Adinyira et al. 2007). Several studies have compiled a wide list of sustainability indicators at HEIs, including among many others Findler et al. (2018), Alghamdi et al. (2017), Lukman et al. (2010), and Penn State Green Destiny Council (2000).
2) The second type of assessment tool includes composite indices which means a major tool to aggregate or combined different indicators (Gasparatos 2010; Agovino et al. 2018; Mapar et al. 2020) by mathematical or heuristic functions (Ramos et al. 2004) into one single measure to evaluate complex multidimensional phenomena. One example is the uncertainty-based driving force-pressure-state-exposure-effect-action-Sustainability index Model (uD-SiM) (Waheed et al. 2011) which is a causality-based model in which the sustainability index is an outcome of nonlinear impacts of sustainability indicators in different stages of a driving force-pressure-state-exposure-effect-action (DPSEEA) framework and it used to quantitatively assess the sustainability for HEIs.
3) The third type of sustainability assessment tool has a distinct origin, in the tradition of EMSs that involve external audits and certification mechanisms (Fischer et al. 2015) such as the EMS ISO 14001 and the EMAS Regulation. There are some examples of the employment of these management-based assessment tools at HEIs as a means of achieving a sustainable campus (Alshuwaikhat and Abubakar 2008; Amaral et al. 2015; Nurcahyo et al. 2019).

However, among the three types of sustainability assessment tools, indicators are one of the approaches most used in different contexts, playing a central role in sustainability assessment (Ramos 2019), and in the context of HEIs, the various tools for assessing their sustainability are mostly based on indicators, using graphs or final rankings to communicate the results. Indicator-based tools have the advantage of being potentially more transparent, consistent, and comparable and thus useful for monitoring and decision support, although support for decision-making is not yet fully demonstrated (Caeiro et al. 2020). The indicator-based assessment approach is comprehensive and representative (Alghamdi et al. 2017), and in addition to being easily measurable and comparable (Lozano 2006a), it can convey value-added messages in a simplified and useful manner to different types of target audiences, including policy- and decision-makers as well as the general public (Ramos and Moreno Pires 2013; Alghamdi et al. 2017).

Shriberg (2002) analyzed the strengths and weaknesses of 11 sustainability assessment tools at HEIs and stated that most assessment tools do not provide mechanisms for comparing campus efforts against other institutions. Yarime and Tanaka (2012) developed a comparative analysis of 16 sustainability assessment tools and examined the recent trends in the issues and methodologies addressed in these tools, both quantitatively and qualitatively. The results demonstrated that the reviewed sustainability assessment tools focused mainly on the environmental impacts of HEIs' operation; the other aspects of integration of sustainability at HEIs are not well addressed by these tools. Another study by Fischer et al. (2015) provided a comparative analysis of around 600 indicators and criteria extracted from 12 sustainability assessment tools to find the dominance and marginalization of different fields and issues. Even though education and research are commonly referred to as crucial fields of action and key functions of universities, the results revealed a strong bias in the indicators and criteria toward the field of operations and, more specifically, to physical resource management. Alghamdi et al. (2017) reviewed 12 assessment tools of sustainability in universities by focusing on their associated indicators. The tools reviewed shared a similar pattern in terms of criteria, subcriteria, and indicators, and subsequently five benchmarks were introduced as essential elements for a holistic framework including management, academia, environment, engagement, and innovation. The most recent literature, by Caeiro et al. (2020), reviewed 27 existing tools to assess and benchmark education for sustainable development (ESD) implementation at HEIs and to discuss their applicability in two public universities in Southern Europe – one in Portugal and the other in Spain – and stated that the existing tools were too operational not evaluating the strategic processes.

However, according to several authors, the overall implementation of these tools is still low and development still at an early stage (Caeiro et al. 2020). Also, these studies have focused mainly on analyzing the characteristics of a selected number of assessment tools and there is still a lack of study exploring a comprehensive list of assessment tools, particularly exploring the associated subcriteria and indicators, as well as the similarities and differences between them. On the other hand, those few studies that have covered a comprehensive list of assessment tools (Caeiro et al. 2020) or explored the characteristics of indicators within the tools, do not include a clear picture of thematic areas covered by the indicators and do not cluster them based on sustainability dimensions. So, since there are several sustainability assessment tools across universities worldwide, as asserted by Alghamdi et al. (2017): "The next step should be moving from proposing more tools, criteria, and subcriteria to practically detailing and operationalizing the core of these tools, which is indicators. Indicators should be given more attention. Tools ought to develop indicators in easily measurable ways, clearly defined and agreed upon." Following this, an analysis is conducted to reveal the thematic areas covered by existing tools and to explore what sustainability dimensions and core elements of sustainability implementation at HEIs are covered by their associated indicators to provide a holistic picture of sustainable university.

8.3 Methods and Steps

The assessment tools in this research were identified based on a review of existing studies of sustainability assessment tools in HEIs and online research that aimed to identify recently developed tools. Thus, a systematic review of the tools for sustainability assessment in HEIs was conducted and the tools were selected based on the following conditions, by Caeiro et al. (2020) and Alghamdi et al.'s (2017) studies:

1) Tools that were specifically developed for assessing the performance of sustainability implementation in HEIs.
2) Tools covering at least two of the seven core elements of sustainability implementation in HEIs, adopted from the studies of Lozano et al. (2015a) and Findler et al. (2018): governance, education, research, outreach and collaboration, operation, on-campus experience, and assessment and reporting.
3) Tools covering at least two of the sustainability dimensions (environmental, social, economic, academic, and institutional), to guarantee that the tools, in some way, were based on a holistic and whole-university approach.
4) Tools that are, to a large degree, indicator-based assessment tools, which means that they are more easily measurable and comparable.

These selection conditions aimed to generate a maximum variety of tools to foster a comprehensive and comparative assessment. Based on these conditions, the assessment tools were searched on Google Scholar using the following keywords: "assessment tools," "higher education institution," "university," "campus," "indicator," and "evaluation"; any tool that does not meet the mentioned conditions were excluded. Each selected tool was then characterized through qualitative and quantitative content analysis based on the structure given in Figure 8.1 including (i) tool structure (ii) core elements of sustainability implementation in HEIs, (iii) sustainability dimensions, and (iv) more commonly covered thematic areas.

In the first step, each tool was explored briefly in terms of background, the main aim, the tool characteristics, and the assessment process. Also, each tool was explored succinctly to extract its existing level of hierarchy including the subjective dimensions, the subcriteria, and the associated indicators. In this research, "subcriteria" refers to the middle level of the hierarchy, namely the broad categories under which a bunch of indicators with a similar subject or objective falls. For example, in the STARS tool, "Engagement" as a subjective category is divided into two subcriteria including "Campus engagement" and "Public engagement" under which several indicators are allocated (e.g. participation in public policy, intercampus collaboration, outreach materials and publication, and outreach campaign).

In the second step, the process involved both deductive and inductive parts, adapted from the approaches proposed by Fischer et al. (2015) and Findler et al. (2018). The deductive analysis aimed to link each tool based on the subcriteria to the seven core elements of sustainability implementation in HEIs (see Section 8.2). Each tool was assigned to each core element according to a five-stage scoring system whereby the minimum link between the subcriteria and the core element was assigned 1 and the maximum link 4. Also, 0 was assigned if there was no link between the tool and the core element. Then the contribution of the core elements in the whole scale (based on percentage) was calculated by averaging the score of each core element as a share of the total.

Also, to explore the link of tools to the sustainability dimensions, each indicator was assigned to at least one of the five dimensions of sustainability: environmental, social, economic, academic, and institutional (see Section 8.2 for the definition of each dimension). However, by limiting the link of each indicator to only one dimension without considering the interlinks among them, the profiling sustainability in the tools can become problematic, particularly for

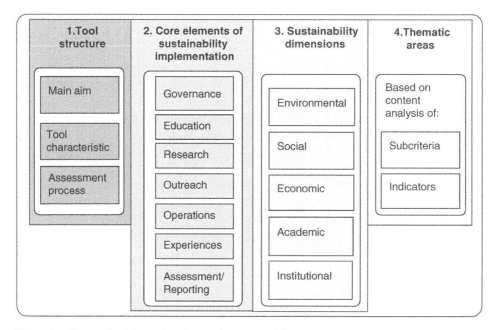

Figure 8.1 The methodology of analyzing the sustainability assessment tools in HEIs.

those indicators that reflect more than one dimension at a time. Therefore, in this research, the overlaps of the dimensions were taken into account and the indicators were assigned to more than one sustainability dimension only if they had a significant link with those dimensions. Then the profile of the sustainability dimensions in each tool (based on percentage) was calculated based on the frequency of the indicators in each dimension as a share of the total. Also, the profile of the sustainability dimension in the whole scale was calculated by averaging the obtained values in each dimension.

For the inductive part of the analysis, because several subcriteria in the selected tools were repeated or duplicated, or had the same meaning with different names, based on the approaches of Fischer et al. (2015) and Findler et al. (2018), the authors independently reviewed the descriptions of each subcriterion to combine those with the same meaning and subsequently to identify the main thematic areas covered by them. Finally, the subcriteria were summarized into thematic areas based on their frequency in the assessment tools. The thematic areas that were pointed out more than twice were included in the final list.

8.4 Results and Comparative Analysis

8.4.1 Tools Structure

A total of 27 assessment tools were selected. They are listed in Table 8.1, which represents each tool's capability to assess the sustainable development of HEIs. Also, a total of 239 subcriteria and 1033 indicators were extracted from the tools. Table 8.2 shows the details of each tool including the main structure, the assessment procedure, and the number of indicators in each tool. The results of the analysis show that, although there is a variation in the main purposes, the assessment processes and content of the tools share many commonalities. A common characteristic of the listed assessment tools is the fact that the main structure is based on hierarchical levels and largely includes the main subjective categories, subcriteria, and then indicators. In around half the tools (52%), the total number of indicators is less than 30, whereas 22% of the tools have between 30 and 50 indicators, and 26% of them assess the progress of universities toward sustainability using more than 50 indicators.

Some tools propose the assessment of the indicators as a set of questions to make it more user-friendly for audiences to assess HEIs' progress toward each indicator (e.g. ASSC, AUSP, BIQ-AUA, CTIE-AMB, ESDGC, SAQ, and SustainTool). Although the data collection process in these tools differs from those that directly measure the indicators, the main content and the assessment process do not differ.

Based on the characteristics of the tools shown in Table 8.2, the tools were critically analyzed to explore their real assessment pattern based on the core elements of sustainability implementation in HEIs (Section 8.4.2), the sustainability dimensions covered by the indicators (Section 8.4.3), and the thematic areas covered by the subcriteria (Section 8.4.4).

8.4.2 Analysis of Core Elements of Sustainability Implementation at HEIs

The overall distribution of the indicators across the seven core elements of sustainability implementation at HEIs is shown in Table 8.3. The proportion of each core element shows a strong focus on the core elements of "governance" and "operations," which stand in joint first place (25%) (Figure 8.2). This result is aligned with the study of Yarime and Tanaka (2012), which showed that among 16 sustainability assessment tools at HEIs, the operation and governance dimensions had approximately the same score (44% and 39%), standing in

Table 8.1 Overview of sustainability assessment tools included in this research.

No.	Brief name	Full name	Country	Year of construction	Main aim/application	References
1	AISHE	Assessment Instrument for Sustainability in Higher Education	Netherlands	2000	Developing a policy toward sustainable development	(Roorda et al. 2009)
2	AMAS	Adaptable Model for Assessing Sustainability in Higher Education	Chile	2014	Assessing sustainability in HEIs among different implementation stages	(Gómez et al. 2015)
3	ASSC	Assessment System for Sustainable Campus	Japan	2013	Enabling a university to discover criteria for its administrative policies	(CAS-NET Japan 2019)
4	AUSP	Assessment of University Sustainability Policies	Spain	2007	Contributing to strengthening sustainability policies in Spanish HEIs	(CRUE 2018)
5	BIQ-AUA	Benchmark Indicator Questions - Alternative University Appraisal	Asian-Pacific	2009	Self-awareness of the universities' strengths/weaknesses in the field of ESD	(Razak et al. 2013)
6	CTIE-AMB	Red de Ciencia, Tecnologia, Innovacion y Educación Ambienal em Iberoamerica	Colombia	2014	Making a diagnosis of the current situation of the institutionalization of environmental commitment in universities, mainly on the top level of universities	(CTIE-AMB et al. 2014; Caeiro et al. 2020)
7	DUK	German Commission for UNESCO	Germany	2011	Sustainability self-assessment concept for HEIs	(Yarime and Tanaka 2012; Findler et al. 2018; DUK 2011)
8	ESDGC	Education for Sustainable Development and Global Citizenship	Wales/UK	2012	Assessing the implementation of ESD in universities, specifically for HEIs in Wales, UK	(Glover et al. 2013)
9	GASU	Graphical Assessment of Sustainability in Universities	UK	2006	Comparing and benchmarking of universities' sustainability efforts and achievement by the graphical overview	(Lozano 2006b)
10	GC	Good Company's Sustainable Pathways Toolkit	US/International	2001	Evaluating the social and environmental impacts of HEIs	(Good Company 2002)
11	GM	GreenMetric University Ranking	Indonesia	2010	Assessing, ranking, and comparing campus efforts toward sustainability	(Lauder et al. 2015)

12	GMID	Graz Model for Integrative Development	Australia/International	2012	Evaluating the transformative potentials of sustainability processes on ESD by focusing on interrelations between HEIs and regional stakeholders	(Mader 2013)
13	GP	Green Plan	France	2010	Assisting HEIs in drawing up their own sustainability plans	(Alghamdi et al. 2017; Caeiro et al. 2020)
14	HE21	Higher Education 21 or Higher Education Partnership for Sustainability (HEPS)	UK	2001	Achieving strategic objectives through positive engagement with the sustainable development agenda	(Buckland et al. 2001)
15	PSIR	Penn State Indicator Report	US	1998	Evaluating the performance at Pennsylvania State University through the lens of sustainability	(Penn State Green Destiny Council 2000)
16	P&P	People & Planet University League	UK	2007	Ranking of UK universities by environmental and ethical performance	(People and Planet University League n.d.; Findler et al. 2018)
17	SAQ	Sustainability Assessment Questionnaire	US	2001	Assessing how sustainable university's teaching, research, operations, and outreach are	(ULSF 2009; Alghamdi et al. 2017)
18	SRC	College Sustainability Report Card	US/Canada	2010	Examining colleges and universities, as institutions, through the lens of sustainability	(Sustainable Endowments Institute 2011)
19	STARS	Sustainability Tracking, Assessment & Rating System	US	2010	Self-reporting of colleges and universities to measure their sustainability performance	(AASHE 2019; Caeiro et al. 2020)
20	SUM	Sustainable University Model	Mexico	2006	Visualizing and achieving a sustainable university system	(Velazquez et al. 2006)
21	SLS	Sustainability Leadership Scorecard	UK/Ireland	2016	Improving social responsibility and environmental performance through a whole-school approach in a self-assessment process	(EAUC n.d.)
22	SustainTool	Program Sustainable Assessment Tool or PSAT	US	2013	Evaluating the sustainability capacity of a program (a small set of organizational and contextual domains that can help build the capacity for maintaining a program)	(Washington University 2013)

(*Continued*)

Table 8.1 (Continued)

No.	Brief name	Full name	Country	Year of construction	Main aim/application	References
23	THE	Times Higher Education Impact University Ranking	International	2019	Assessing universities against the SDGs	(THE Impact Ranking 2021)
24	TUR	Three Dimensional University Ranking	International	2009	Comparison between universities regarding their research, educational and environmental performances.	(Lukman et al. 2010)
25	UEMS	University Environmental Management System	Saudi Arabia	2008	Achieve campus sustainability through overcoming the lack of environmental management practices	(Alshuwaikhat and Abubakar 2008)
26	USAT	Unit-Based Sustainability Assessment tool	Africa	2009	Guiding for educating and aiding the university toward sustainability by a flexible tool used at the departmental, faculty, and unit level	(Togo and Lotz-Sisitka 2009)
27	uD-SiM	Uncertainty-based quantitative assessment of sustainability for HEIs	Canada	2011	Achieving a causality-based impact assessment by using a driving force-pressure-state-exposure-effect-action (DPSEEA) framework	(Waheed et al. 2011)

Source: Adapted and built upon Caeiro et al. (2020).

Table 8.2 A review of 27 sustainability assessment tools at HEIs.

No.	Tool name	Tool characteristics	Assessment procedure	No. of indicators
1	AISHE	• Consists of five modules (Operations, Education, Research, Society, Identity)/Each module consists of six criteria • Each criterion is described by five development stages (Activity oriented/Process-oriented/System oriented/Chain Oriented/ society oriented) by incorporating the Deming cycle approach • Less emphasis on the environmental component (just one indicator); • The intended target is the university system; • For a university, or a part of it (the application domain adapts according to the university structure as an entire university, campus, buildings, or research institute) • With a wide world application across the universities; • Version 2000 and 2001 only focused on the educational role of universities, however, AISHE 2.0 has a wider scope in terms of the research, operations, and relation with the society	• Assessment is done by a group of 15 people (or less if the assessed institute is small) and it takes about one day • One person who takes notes, and who will have completed the report at the moment the assessment is done • A fee for the external certified assessor (if one is involved) • Tool not available online, only the manual	30
2	AMAS	• A model for sustainability assessment based on a four-tiered hierarchy: goal, criteria, subcriteria, indicators • Indicators with different weights and key actors' participation, allowing to be adapted by each institution but comparable in the same country • With an expert consultation system	• To calculate the 25 indicators, both qualitative and quantitative data are required; 15 indicators need quantitative data (60%), whereas just 10 need qualitative data (40%) • Tool not available online	25
3	ASSC	• Indicators are divided into four domains (Management, Education and Research, Environment, Local Community); (based on 170 questions) • Based on other tools (STARS, GM, BIQ - AUA) • Includes specificities of the country where it was developed (e.g. natural disasters) • Reported on graphical form	• Based on a questionnaire • Rating system with four levels, allowing to obtain certification: platinum, gold, silver, and bronze • Tool available online: https://www.osc.hokudai.ac.jp/en/action/assc	26

(Continued)

Table 8.2 (Continued)

No.	Tool name	Tool characteristics	Assessment procedure	No. of indicators
4	AUSP	• Based on three areas (Organization, Teaching and research, Environmental management), 11 aspects and 140 questions (indicators) based on version 2018 • Less emphasis on the social component • Graphical representation of indicators • Last updated on 2018 • Specifically, for HEIs in Spain and tested in several Spanish Universities	• Data collection by questionnaire and interviews (self-assessment) and reviewed by an external organization; • Each question has three levels of scoring (0/0.5/1) • Questionnaire available online: https://goo.gl/forms/Fol9qwVvYF2juTbC2	140
5	BIQ-AUA	• Calculate indicators for the benchmark (BIQ) and dialogue • The hierarchical level: Main criteria (4); subcriteria (with equal weight) (15); indicators (30), questions (50) • The method is to form a group that represents all users such as administrative staff, faculty staff and members, academics, and students • It does not include environmental management and social responsibility indicators • Dialogue is the component that enables institutions to share their concerns, best practices and learning about Education for Sustainable Development (ESD)	• Self-assessment process based on questions • The highest rating is 100, thus allowing comparison	30
6	CTIE-AMB	• Based on five areas (Government and environmental participation, Teaching, Research, Environmental projection, Environmental management) and 27 questions • More focus on environmental strategies and plans and less focus on the environmental component of campus infrastructure and social component • No updates available	• A questionnaire with Yes/No answers • Tool not available online	27
7	DUK	• Based on indicators in four areas (Operations, Research, Education, Community); • With a strong focus on the Education • The tool operates as a moderator in the whole-school approach • It contains 10 action field	• Each field offers five stages of implementation to which HEIs can assign themselves • Tool not available online; only a report about the tool in German is available	10

8	ESDGC	• Based on a ranking system with five Common areas (Commitment and leadership, Teaching and learning, Institutional management, Partnerships, Research and monitoring) • Open and close-ended questions • Based on evidence • Results with a semaphore system; • Adaptation of a maturity model and training usually applied to companies and the industrial sector	• Four-level categorization based upon traffic light system (no color, red, amber, and green) to statements corresponding to the depth of ESDGC material evident • Tool not available online	Five common areas (Covered by 26 questions)
9	GASU	• Based on GRI report with adaptations to HEIs; • Applied in many universities, • Five main subjective categories (Environmental/Economic/Social/Education/Inter-linking issues and dimensions) • GASU 2006 was updated in 2011 to align it with the GRI G3 (2011), as well as adding Inter-linking issues and dimensions • Graphical presentation of results	• Grading each indicator, either by choosing a number from five different choices, 0–4 • Tool not available online for free, only with a fee payment	43 aspects (covered by 174 indicators)
10	GC	• Based on subcriteria (8) and indicators (20 core +9 supplementary indicators); • The system allows benchmarking and comparison • Along with each indicator goes a benchmark suggesting a desirable performance for the respective area of application • More emphasis on operations • Without focusing two categories of sustainability implementation in HEIs, namely, Research and Stakeholder involvement	• Assessing a set of indicators through three principles: meaningful indicators (targeting those that contribute most to the overall impact or footprint of the institution), feasible action (leading the assessment to the feasible action and address areas where an institution can potentially improve) and measurable (defining quantitative and qualitative measures that can be achieved with minimal cost and time) • The final assessment report for each indicator includes the aspect, the indicator definition, the intent (the importance of and the reason for the indicator), the benchmark, and a summary of performance • Tool not available online, neither report nor update	29

(*Continued*)

Table 8.2 (Continued)

No.	Tool name	Tool characteristics	Assessment procedure	No. of indicators
11	GM	• Based on six domains (Setting and infrastructure, Energy and climate change, Waste, Water, Transport, Education & Research) with different weights; • Mainly focus on the environmental dimension, less community involvement or other social components • With a wide world application across the universities	• It collects data through an online survey. The criteria are assessed and then added up. Each specific indicator within each criterion is assessed based on a points system of awards • Tool available online: http://greenmetric.ui.ac.id	33
12	GMID	• Based on narrative and domains: It includes a set of indicators across the basic principles of five domains (Leadership, Social Networks, Participation, Education and Learning, Research) • Applicable but not specific to HEIs • Applied to the RCE, an international network of formal, non-formal, and informal education organizations, mobilized to provide ESD to the local and regional community at three levels	• Based on three levels in each category	15
13	GP	• Based on five domains (Strategy governance, Education and training research, Environmental management, Social policy, Regional presence); 18 subcriteria, 44 indicators • It can be audited and certified by internal and external stakeholders concerning the ISO 26000 (Social responsibility) • Purpose of assisting in the elaboration of sustainability plans/policies	• The framework includes definitions, indicators, supporting documents, action plan, and five levels (categories) for each indicator explaining (awareness, initiation, conformity of green plan scheme targets, control, and leadership) • Tool not available online at the present	44
14	HE21	• Based on indicators (12 key indicators and 8 strategic management indicators); • Focusing mainly on parameters of organizational management change and less emphasis on social indicators and does not encompass in a balanced way all the dimensions of ESD in HEIs (more emphasis on governance); • Difficult to benchmarking • Latest version: 2003	• No available information • Tools not available online	12 key indicators and 8 strategic management indicators

15	PSIR	• Based on indicators across 10 domains • Covering the environmental dimension of the campus, transport, decision support, research, and community • Less emphasis on social indicators and teaching and curriculum components; • To be communicated to the general public how sustainability is being implemented • Suspended in 2012	• Results of each indicator are reported in four levels of implementation and with proposals for improvement • Tool not available online, only on the report: http://www.willamette.edu/~nboyce/assessment/PennState.pdf	33
16	P&P	• Based on indicators across 13 domains • Greater focus on environmental operations • In operation for several years allowing the annual comparison and an annual ranking • Graphical presentation of results	• Data collection is carried out in the universities' webpages and the UK Higher Education Statistics Agency • Tool available online: https://peopleandplanet.org/university-league	40
17	SAQ	• Based on indicators across seven domains • Largely qualitative teaching tool aiming to raise consciousness and encourage debate about what sustainability means for higher education • With greater emphasis on operations	• Based on a questionnaire addressed to various internal stakeholders • It consists of forming a representative sample of 10–15 individuals drawn from students, faculty, staff, and the university administration; and introducing the purpose, the objectives, the definitions in advance, and facilitation of the discussion throughout the exercise. Each participant should take 30 min to fill out the questionnaire. It may take 2–3 h or so • Tool available online: http://ulsf.org/sustainability-assessment-questionnaire	35
18	SRC	• Based on indicators across five domains (Campus operations, Meal service, Donation investment, Transportation, Involvement of key stakeholders) • More focus on energy saving and less emphasis on education	• Presented through a questionnaire with a final grade from A to D • Tool not available online	52

(Continued)

Table 8.2 (Continued)

No.	Tool name	Tool characteristics	Assessment procedure	No. of indicators
19	STARS	• Based on narrative and indicators: Version 2.0: 74 indicators and version 2.2: 67 indicators, 18 subcriteria, and 5 categories with different weights (Academic, Involvement of key actors, Operations, Planning and administration, Innovation and leadership) • One of the most used tools internationally • Updated every year; • Initially developed for HEIs in the US and Canada but applicable to any region	• Five levels of final classification, allowing the ranking (reporter, bronze, silver, gold, platinum) • It is not only an assessment instrument but also a rating framework adding more value to the system as a comparison tool • The ranking process is international and external evaluators are ranked the involved HEIs based on voluntary self-reporting by universities • Tool available online: https://reports.aashe.org/accounts/login/?next=/tool	67
20	SUM	• Based on indicators across four domains (Education, Research, Dissemination and partnership, Campus sustainability) • Tested at various world universities • Without updates	• Divided into four phases (Vision development, Mission, Sustainable committee, Audit of sustainability strategies), incorporating the Deming cycle approach • Tool not available online	23
21	SLS	• Based on performance indicators; four priority areas (Leadership and governance, Partnership and Engagement, Learning, teaching and research, Estates and operations), 18 Framework areas, and each framework area include 7 activities areas • No weights in the indicators and final result in a dashboard index • Linked to SDGs	• Final scores with a range from 0 to 4 • Tool available online for free to the UK and Ireland: www.sustainabilityleadershipscorecard.org.uk/#!/login	18
22	SustainTool	• Based on indicators (Questions), focused on areas/programs or at the institution level; eight subcriteria (Environmental support, Funding stability, Partnership, Organizational capacity, Program, Evaluation, Program adaptation, Communications, Strategic planning) with low weight in the environmental component • Allows the communication, review, and development of an action plan • Available for several years with updates • Developed particularly in the North American context, but especially directed to the health area	• Self-assessment Questionnaire based on 40 multiple-choice questions, with answers being given individually or in a group • The assessment takes about 10–15 min to finish • Tool available online: https://sustaintool.org/assess	40

23	THE	- Each SDG has some indicators associated with it
- The tool covers all 17 SDGs across 75 metrics, and 227 required evidences
- Equal weight is given to each SDG, but with different weights on each metric
- The rankings are open to any university that teaches at either undergraduate or postgraduate level
- Participation in the overall ranking requires universities to submit data to at least four SDGs, one of which must be SDG 17 – Partnerships for the Goals	- The overall score is generated from the score for SDG 17 (worth up to 22% of the overall score), plus the three strongest of the other SDGs for which they provided data (each worth up to 26% of the overall score)
- The ranking process is international and external evaluators are ranked the involved HEIs based on voluntary self-reporting on each metric through evidence
- Tool available online (requesting by free registration): https://www.timeshighereducation.com/how-participate-times-higher-education-rankings	75 metrics and 227 required evidences
24	TUR	- Based on indicators across three domains (Research, Education, Environment)
- Weighted based on a participatory process and Analytical Hierarchical Process (AHP)
- Less holistic approach
- Graphical presentation of results
- Tested in the best universities, but without updates	- Allows ranking based on rankings of world universities
- Tool not available online	15
25	UEMS	- Based on EMAS/ISO14001 with a social responsibility component and indicators
- Three strategies (University EMS, Public participation and social responsibility, Teaching and research in sustainability), 8 initiatives (subcriteria), and 27 indicators	- The assessment process is based on three strategies. Each strategy has initiatives that can lead to achieving the sustainability mission at the institution. Moreover, higher
- Tool not available online	27

(Continued)

Table 8.2 (Continued)

No.	Tool name	Tool characteristics	Assessment procedure	No. of indicators
26	USAT	• Based on indicators across four domains (Teaching, Research and community services, Operation and management, Student involvement, Written policy and statement), 9 subcriteria and 75 indicators • Adapted from SAQ, AISHE and GASU • It Can be used in the department, college, or HE unit • Without updates	• Scoring system (based on 1–4) Assessment criteria including: Rating X = Don't know (no information concerning the practice) 0 = None (There is a total lack of evidence on the indicator) 1 = A little (Evidence show poor performance) 2 = Adequate (Evidence show regular performance) 3 = Substantial (Evidence show good performance) 4 = A great deal (Excellent performance) - Tool not available online but questionnaire available online on the report: www.ru.ac.za/elrc/publicationsandresources/unit-basedsustainabilityassessmenttoolusattool/	75
27	uD-SiM	• Based on indicators and the models of Driving force, Pressure, Exposure, Effects, Action (DPSEEA) and a multicriteria decision process (applying Fuzzy logic) • With different weights and normalized indicators • Indicators based on the GASU model; four areas (Environmental, Economic, Social and Education) and five categories –DPSEEA; • Applied to Canadian universities but its implementation is international	• Aggregate scores in a final index that integrates the non-linear effects of the indicators • The calculation method is complex • Tool not available online	56

Table 8.3 Distribution of core elements at HEIs on the 27 studied tools.[a]

No.	Tool (abbreviation)	Governance	Education	Research	Outreach	Operations	On-campus experiences	Assessment and reporting
1	AISHE	2	2	2	2	1	0	1
2	AMAS	4	1	1	1	2	0	2
3	ASSC	3	1	1	2	3	0	0
4	AUSP	2	1	1	1	3	0	1
5	BIQ-AUA	3	2	1	2	0	0	1
6	CTIE-AMB	3	2	2	1	1	0	1
7	DUK	2	3	2	0	2	0	1
8	ESDGC	4	2	2	1	0	0	0
9	GASU	3	1	1	1	3	1	1
10	GC	1	1	0	0	4	0	0
11	GM	0	1	1	0	4	0	1
12	GMID	2	2	2	4	2	0	0
13	GP	3	2	2	1	2	0	0
14	HE21	4	2	1	1	3	0	1
15	PSIR	1	0	1	0	4	1	0
16	P&P	3	1	0	0	4	0	0
17	SAQ	2	1	1	1	3	1	0
18	SRC	3	0	0	1	3	0	0
19	STARS	3	2	1	1	3	0	1
20	SUM	1	2	1	2	3	0	0
21	SLS	2	1	1	2	3	0	0
22	SustainTool	4	0	0	2	0	0	2
23	THE	2	3	3	2	3	2	1
24	TUR	2	3	3	0	1	0	0
25	UEMS	1	2	2	3	3	0	0
26	USAT	3	2	1	1	2	1	0
27	uD-SiM	1	2	1	0	3	0	0

[a] The minimum link with core element is allocated to one and the maximum link to four. Also, 0 is allocated if there is no link.
Source: Based on the five-stage scoring system.

first and second places. Also, other studies that reviewed some of the assessment tools at HEIs (Fischer et al. 2015; Kosta 2019) highlighted that STARS, AISHE, and SAQ have a higher incidence on the percentage of indicators for governance and operations, again aligning with our results.

However, there is still a bias in favor of the operations element over the other core elements, since operations are not the main function of HEIs. For example, the earlier study by Fischer et al. (2015) showed that even though there are some differences between the distribution of

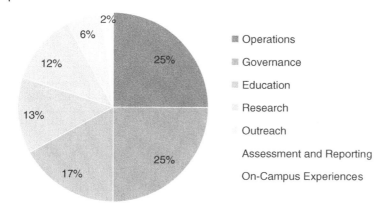

Figure 8.2 The proportion of core elements of sustainability implementation at HEIs within the tools.

core elements among the analyzed assessment tools, overall an extensive share was for the field of operations (67%), followed by the fields of education, research, and community engagement (with only 18%, 10%, and 6%, respectively). Also, it seems that in some earlier studies, the definitions of governance and operations have been combined; for instance, as defined by Ceulemans et al. (2015b), all the organizational activities supporting the creation of HEIs' services (e.g. student administration and planning, accounting, facility management, human resource management, marketing, and communication, among many others) are part of HEI's operations activity. However, based on Findler et al. (2018), "on broad-scale policies and the administrative structure of the HEIs, including, e.g. governance body structure, vision and mission statements, policies for staff and faculty hiring, budget issues, student associations, and development programs for staff and faculty" are the issues that should emerge on the governance element rather than operations. This might be the reason that in some studies the operations activities show a remarkable difference from other core elements. In the current research, the reasons behind obtaining the same score for both governance and operations might be because of: (i) addressing a more holistic assessment tools inventory in this research (N = 27) rather than the previous studies that mainly focus on the number of 8–19 tools, (ii) addressing more recent assessment tools in our final list (such as THE), which effects more accurate results on the distribution of the core elements, and (iii) the definition of each core element in this research where indicators concerning the administrative issues and policies were assigned to the governance element.

The "education" element (17%) stands in second place, closely followed by "research" (13%), and "outreach" activities (12%). Although education and research are commonly referred to as crucial fields of action and key functions of universities, we are observing a gap between postulated areas with the highest priorities in the assessment of sustainable performance in HEIs, including operations and governance, as we have already discussed. So, as stressed by Yarime and Tanaka (2012) and Fischer et al. (2015), more work is needed to further engage "education" and "research" in the sustainability assessment of HEIs.

The areas where the indicators have seen weaker use are "assessment and reporting" and "experiences" such that only 6% of the tools are associated with the assessment and reporting indicators and only 2% with the on-campus experiences. Among the tools, AISHE, STARS, and THE are those with some explicit indicators on the participatory assessment and reporting system. However, sustainability reporting in HEIs is still in its early stage (Lozano et al. 2015a; Kapitulčinová et al. 2018) due to the low number of HEIs publishing sustainability reports, the low quality of the reports, the lack of consecutive reporting, and the lack of institutionalization of sustainability reporting in the higher education system (Lozano 2011; Ceulemans et al. 2015a). So, HEIs should apply the assessment tools not only for guiding or assessing but also for comparing and reporting to make sure that they are heading in the right direction (Alghamdi et al. 2017).

8.4.3 Sustainability Dimensions

The profile of the sustainability indicators within each sustainability dimension of the analyzed tools is shown in Table 8.4. Also, Figure 8.3 shows the overall distribution of the indicators in the whole scale.

Table 8.4 Scope of the different sustainability tools analysis.

No.	Tool (abbreviation)	Sustainability dimensions covered by the tool (% based on the frequency of indicators)				
		Environment	Social	Economic	Academic	Institutional
1	AISHE	3	23	3	40	30
2	AMAS	26	23	10	13	29
3	ASSC	37	26	15	15	7
4	AUSP	40	11	4	14	31
5	BIQ-AUA	0	24	9	39	27
6	CTIE-AMB	21	16	2	26	35
7	DUK	18	9	9	45	18
8	ESDGC	0	40	0	40	20
9	GASU	20	36	13	16	15
10	GC	52	21	6	6	15
11	GM	72	7	5	14	2
12	GMID	0	40	0	40	20
13	GP	21	24	3	23	29
14	HE21	26	16	5	5	47
15	PSIR	64	19	0	11	6
16	P&P	31	31	6	9	22
17	SAQ	27	19	0	27	27
18	SRC	53	23	14	0	11
19	STARS	32	34	4	21	9
20	SUM	41	30	0	15	15
21	SLS	42	37	0	11	11
22	SustainTool	11	22	11	0	56
23	THE	24	34	6	21	14
24	TUR	6	6	6	65	18
25	UEMS	41	31	3	21	5
26	USAT	20	34	2	29	15
27	uD-SiM model	45	17	16	19	3

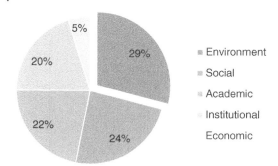

Figure 8.3 The profile of the sustainability dimensions within the assessment tools.

Overall, the "environmental" (29%) dimension is the most addressed among the assessment indicators. The "social" and "academic" dimensions jointly occupy the second and third positions in the assessment indicators (24% and 22%, respectively). As already noted by several authors (Cunningham et al. 2010; Lozano and Huisingh 2011; Mapar et al. 2017), there has been a bias when considering sustainability, where environmental issues have gained much more attention than social or economic issues. These results are also aligned with those of Blasco et al. (2019), who found, in a study conducted within Spanish universities, that more attention was given to the environmental dimension and that more holistic approaches were necessary to achieve an integrated perspective of sustainability. However, these authors also asserted that there was a correlation between the three dimensions of sustainability so that those entities with the higher environmental score also had higher social and economic scores, which would evidence that universities have been exploring an integrated concept of sustainability in their performance (Blasco et al. 2019).

Notably, there are still some differences in the profile of the sustainability dimensions among the assessment tools analyzed. For instance, in some tools, the profile relating to the social and environmental indicators is approximately the same, namely for STARS, P&P, and AMAS. Also, among the tools, there is one example where the social dimension is predominant over others, namely the GASU tool, which addresses five main categories on the social dimension, namely labor practices and decent work, human rights, society, product responsibility, and overall social issues.

Some tools exclusively focus on the assessment of the academic dimension of sustainability. As an example, TUR is a three-dimensional ranking tool that makes it possible to compare universities in respect to three main subcriteria of research, education, and environmental performances. In TUR, although one of the subcriteria is entitled "environment," most indicators belonging to this thematic area (e.g. including sustainability vision and mission, sustainability-oriented courses and programs, and office or council for sustainable development) mainly address the academic and institutional dimensions.

The "institutional" dimension covers 20% of the total indicators and is placed fourth in relation to the other dimensions. Institutionalization refers to the process in which an idea passes from individual efforts and attitudes to changes in the system, stakeholders, and the sustainability dimensions at HEIs. So, to achieve institutionalization, the whole university community (including students, academic staff, non-academic staff, and stakeholders) must receive the proper sustainable development skills to help promote a sustainable development institutionalization process by enforcing it with their attitudes and behaviors (Lozano 2006b). Among the assessment tools, SustainTool is unique by having been explicitly developed to address the institution dimension at HEIs by exploring the areas of programs and plans such as program evaluation, program adaptation, and strategic planning, with low weight on the environmental component.

The "economic" dimension is placed last, relating to other dimensions; only 5% of the total indicators addressed the economic issues directly. Among the tools, only GASU, SustainTool, and THE include specific subcriteria for financial and economic issues that mainly cover the economic performance, indirect economic impact, funding stability, decent work, and economic growth. Some tools solely assess the economic dimension of HEIs by indicators that are placed on the interlinking dimension of sustainability. As an example, AMAS assesses the number of students with low socioeconomic backgrounds on the equality subcriteria. The uD-SiM tool also shows a distinct focus on addressing economic indicators (e.g. financial and economic growth rate; increasing education, operation, and maintenance cost; percentage of expenditure, facilities and infrastructure costs; financial impacts; and effects on revenues through educational cost and investments) where the economy is addressed as one of the four performance categories of sustainability based on the DPSEEA framework (Waheed et al. 2011). However, in comparison with other dimensions, the state of development of the tool is revealed by the lack of assessment of the impact on the economic dimension of sustainability so that only 16% of the total indicators in uD-SiM are associated with economy and finance.

8.4.4 Thematic Areas

Overall, 25 thematic areas, extracted from the content analysis of the subcriteria, were identified, as shown in Table 8.5. Also, Figure 8.4 shows the contribution of the top 10 thematic areas in the tools. The heterogeneity of thematic areas of sustainability implementation in HEIs is still remarkable, with the "education" and "research" areas remaining the best addressed with the highest frequency.

Table 8.5 The thematic areas applied in the studied sustainability assessment tools at HEIs.

No.	Thematic areas	Frequency	Including but not limited to:
1	Education	34	Informal education/programs and education/education for sustainable development/quality education/subject-related teaching/interdisciplinary teaching/training/curriculum
2	Research	21	Interdisciplinary, multidisciplinary, and disciplinary research/research and development/research activities and integration
3	Management and planning	19	Management systems/Institutional management/strategic planning/policies/coordination & planning /institutional mission, structure and planning/decision making/organizational capacity/administration and planning
4	Partnership and engagement	18	Government and environmental participation/public participation and engagement/staff willingness to participate/staff and student engagement/shareholder engagement/campus engagement/national, regional, and international partnership/partnerships for the goals
5	Society and communities	13	Responsible society/development of a knowledge-based society/campus community and beyond/community learning/community services/sustainable cities and communities
6	Waste	9	Solid waste and hazardous materials/waste policy/waste minimization/waste disposal

(Continued)

Table 8.5 (Continued)

No.	Thematic areas	Frequency	Including but not limited to:
7	Energy	9	Energy management/energy sources/renewable energy/affordable and clean energy
8	Water	8	Water policy/water reduction/clean water and sanitation/life below water
9	Climate and carbon reduction	7	Air pollution policy/climate change/climate action/managing carbon/carbon reduction
10	Transportation	7	Transportation program/sustainable transportation/mobility
11	Staff and students' development	6	Development of staff sustainability skills/development of students' sustainability skills
12	Food	6	Food service/sustainable food/food and dining/zero hunger
13	Economy and finance	6	Direct economic impact/economic growth/investment and finance/ethical investment and banking/investment priority/funding stability/scholarships
14	Resources and consumption	6	Resources/consumption/responsible consumption and production
15	Social issues	5	Social network/social responsibility/social policy/peace and social justice
16	Diversity and equality	5	Diversity and affordability/equality policy for students/gender equality/reduced inequalities
17	Labor practices and decent work	5	Working rights/decent work/human rights/employee benefits
18	Commitment and leadership	5	Commitment/leadership/vision/leadership and governance
19	General environmental issues	5	General issues/environmental extension or projection/environmental support
20	Outreach	4	Outreach services/outreach support
21	Monitoring, evaluation	4	Monitoring process/program evaluation/examination of sustainability topics/impact assessment
22	Purchasing and Procurement	4	Sustainable purchasing and procurement
23	Health	3	Employee health and safety/good health and well-being
24	Land	3	Life on land/grounds
25	Infrastructure and building	3	Industry, innovation, and infrastructure/buildings/green building

The main topics covered by the "education" thematic area are informal education, ESD, quality education, subject-related teaching, interdisciplinary teaching, training, and curriculum. Also, making the curriculum more sustainable is a topic that has also been explicitly repeated seven times among studied tools. As already emphasized by Karatzoglou (2013), "greening" of the curriculum has been repeatedly included among the best practices applied by universities to enhance their sustainable standing. So, if the approach is to be achieved, sustainability should be addressed as the core theme that runs through the curriculum (Cotgrave and Kokkarinen 2010).

In the "research" thematic area, the main topics covered by the tools are focused more on interdisciplinary, multidisciplinary, and disciplinary research, research and development,

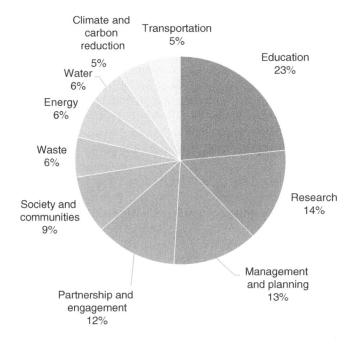

Figure 8.4 The top core thematic areas based on subcriteria in the studied sustainability assessment tools.

research activities, and research integration. Some tools (e.g. GreenMetric) apply direct quantitative indicators about the ratio of sustainability research funding relating to total research funding at university and emphasize research priorities based on the sustainability context. Another noticeable point in terms of research is the importance of sustainability research on recent international assessment tools for HEIs. One example is the research area in THE ranking systems (THE Impact Ranking 2021), which measures the proportion of the university's publications in each SDG independently through a set of exclusive indicators. Then, each SDG topic is measured against a keyword search of the Scopus database of peer-reviewed literature to reflect on the excellence of academic output. However, it is notable that still, the majority of HEIs who engage in the sustainability assessment focus more on education topics rather than research, as indicated by Wals (2014), which is also in line with our results (see Figure 8.4).

"Management and planning" and "Partnership and engagement" and thematic areas were at third and fourth place, respectively. The "management and planning" thematic area encompasses management standard systems, institutional management, strategic planning, policies, coordination, mission, and decision-making. Many HEIs adopt environmental management systems to achieve sustainability (Nurcahyo et al. 2019). Among them, ISO 14001 EMS is the most frequently used set of management standards adopted by universities in recent years. It is a framework for organizations to facilitate the implementaion of an environmental management system (Rahdari and Anvary Rostamy 2015; Zilahy 2017), and to assess the environmental impact of operations and improve their performance (Lozano and Huisingh 2011).

The partnership refers to both global and multistakeholder partnership to facilitate engagement in the implementation of sustainability, bringing together government, civil society, private sector, and other actors and work together to achieve a common purpose or undertake a specific task and to share risks, responsibilities, resources, and benefits. In HEIs, partnerships range from research and development, knowledge exchange, and technology transfer platforms to economic development and urban reform projects. HEIs should be seeking to improve the possibilities of expanding innovations out of their borders through a process of continuous learning, in collaboration with the public and the private sectors (Trencher et al. 2014; Özuyar and Moreira 2017). As an example, "collaboration with stakeholders in addressing community sustainability challenges" is addressed as one of the sustainability assessment indicators in the USAT tool (Togo and Lotz-Sisitka 2009). Also, as stated by Trencher et al. (2014), in HEIs, individual partnerships are making strong social, environmental, and sustainability impacts, with far less confidence shown for contributions to economic development. However, internal university policies are yet to prove a substantial driver for sustainability partnerships.

The next frequent thematic area is "society and communities," covering subjects such as responsible society, development of a knowledge-based society, campus community and beyond, community services, and sustainable communities. There are some initiatives in this thematic area that need the engagement of students, staff, and the whole university body to achieve a sustainable society. Voluntary community service by students related to sustainability and environment, and student groups with an environmental or sustainability focus are some examples of these initiatives applied in the tools to assess the progress of universities toward sustainable societies and communities (Togo and Lotz-Sisitka 2009).

In the field of environmental issues, there are five distinct thematic areas addressing "waste," "energy," "water," "climate and carbon reduction," and "transportation" closely following each other, to which both policy and action are addressed in these environmental clusters. However, most of the environmental indicators in these thematic areas focus more on the operations core element of HEIs, e.g. total recycling waste and recycling infrastructure (GC), and use of water-efficient appliances (GM), and indoor air quality (USAT). It is noted that there is still a distinct dedicated cluster for "general environmental issues" area in the final list (e.g. environmental extension or projection and environmental support), which assesses the environmental issues in a broader concept rather than explicit environmental themes.

8.5 Overall Discussion and Potential Areas of Improvement

The 27 tools reviewed show many similarities in their main structure. In comparing the number of indicators among the tools, it is obvious that, although the number of indicators differs in each tool, overall 74% of the tools use 50 or fewer indicators for assessing sustainability in HEIs. Even though sustainability indicators help in knowing the direction and distance from the target (Panda et al. 2016; Mapar et al. 2017, 2020), whenever a large number of indicators exists, it is more difficult to make comparisons across different systems, over time and space (Ciommi et al. 2017). Therefore, setting a list of adequate indicators for assessing the progress of an institution toward sustainability is a highly challenging task since it is difficult to measure a large number of indicators while assessing the progress toward sustainable development, due to the time limitation, high cost, and complex process of assessing sustainability when we are dealing with too many indicators (Mapar et al. 2020).

Another noticeable aspect behind the communalities in the tools is that the majority of tools are filled out through self-assessment, requiring only a leader or researcher to complete them, a point stressed by Caeiro et al. (2020). Only a few of the tools, e.g. THE ranking system and STARS, assess the performance of HEIs based on international assessment systems through collaboration with a group of international evaluators. In this case, the HEIs just provide the evidence for each indicator for further evaluation by the external evaluators.

The analysis of the tools also highlights the concrete thematic areas for sustainable development assessment at universities, currently covered by the subcriteria and indicators. The sample contains a relatively higher proportion of education, research, and management and planning thematic areas in the assessment process of HEIs, specifically those that can be measured in quantifiable units based on data readily available to HEIs, as also indicated by Findler et al. (2018). As an example, there are several indicators in the thematic areas of research and education that directly assess the current status of HEI research and education through direct quantitative measurement units, such as the amount of sustainability-related research (AMAS), the number of scholarly published papers in the different areas of sustainability (GM, THE), the ratio of sustainability courses to total courses, the ratio of sustainability research to total research (GM), and the percentage of faculty members who teach or do research on sustainability issues (SAQ), among many others.

On the top 10 thematic areas, even though the assessment indicators with an overwhelming focus on research, education, and management and planning reached the higher places, there are still several indicators associated with natural environment themes (e.g. energy, water, waste, climate and carbon reduction, and transportation; see Figure 8.4) where the total portion of the indicators in these environmental themes can be same or higher than indicators in the "management and planning" theme. The main reason for this might be that the ability to measure natural environmental issues quantitatively makes them easier to assess than many other institutional management indicators. Thus, the majority of tools focus on the indicators that can be measured based on internally available data in a quantitative way. The same trend could be also observed in the profile of the sustainability dimensions within the tools, where the proportion of environmental indicators is greater than the social one (see Figure 8.3). Again, it might be because of the simplicity of assessing the environmental performance indicators in a quantitative way rather than social ones such as HEIs' sustainability culture. So it seems the assessment tools have a tendency to focus more on the subjects that can be measured based on internally available data quantitatively, as also suggested by Findler et al. (2018).

The stakeholder participatory approach is another issue that can be discussed by reviewing the list of assessment tools. Ideally, the concepts of sustainable development should be integrated into the policies, approaches, and learning of all the university's stakeholders, including academic and non-academic staff, students, and the broad range of internal and external stakeholders; however in practice, it is almost impossible to include this approach in the first stages of sustainable development integration into the HEIs system, as stated by Lozano (2006b). Some tools, e.g. GMID and SRC, also focus on the involvement of key stakeholders and the interrelations between HEI and stakeholders as a requirement and a benefit toward the integration of sustainable development into the HEIs. As stated by Alghamdi et al. (2017):

> Applying these assessment tools through not only education and research but also operating the campus and engaging with the internal community (students, faculties and supporting employees) and with the external communities (different stakeholders) creates a culture of sustainability at universities and beyond benefiting societies and promoting living more sustainably.

Although, the majority of tools proposed equal weights for subcriteria and indicators, there are still some tools, e.g. AMAS, GM, STARS, THE, TUR, uD-SiM, that proposed different weights for the subcriteria and indicators. As an example, THE proposes the same weight for the main subcriteria of SDGs, but each metric in this tool has a different weight so that the maximum score for each metric is given as an exact percentage (here, weight) within each SDG and as an approximate percentage if the SDG was to be used for the overall ranking of that university (THE Impact Ranking 2021).

The strong focus of the tools on the operations elements needs to be further discussed in future studies since, as stated by Lozano et al. (2015a), education, research, and community outreach should be perceived as the core activities of HEIs, while operations should be realized as a supporting activity. Also, tools with open-ended questions (e.g. SAQ and ESDGC) still need to be discussed in the future development of the tools since it is difficult to apply them as a comparative tracking tool due to the lack of establishing a final score (Berzosa et al. 2017).

Using the assessment tools that cover all sustainability dimensions as well as core elements of sustainability at HEIs can open new space to integrate sustainability within HEIs. However, with the 2030 Agenda to steer global society toward sustainability, it is clear that further development of the tools should also encompass all 17 SDGs to reach a holistic integration approach at HEIs. Among the studied tools, some tools directly address the SDGs within their main structure. One example is STARS, which shares a similar intent and scope with the SDGs so that an institution's STARS score can be used to demonstrate progress toward helping deliver the SDGs. Another example is THE which is entirely built upon the SDGs framework so that each SDG is assigned to a subcriterion and then several metrics are assigned to each SDG to assess the progress of HEIs toward the whole agenda. On the other hand, a recently published report by United Nations Environment Programme (2021) highlights the transformation of humankind's relationship with nature as a defining task of the coming decades toward a sustainable future. So, all actors, including HEIs, have individual, complementary and nested roles to initiate and lead transformative changes in their domains. One illustration of the transformative change in the human relationship with nature can emerge in the social responsibility initiatives and practices in HEIs that are also covered by some assessment tools (e.g. social responsibility coordination [AMAS], social responsibility policy [BIQ], and community services and social justice as main indicators of social responsibility [UEMS], among others). However, this topic is still in its early stages and more in-depth analysis to explore the contribution of the existing tools and indicators on human relationships with nature, as well as the interlink between SDGs and the thematic areas in future studies, can enrich this research. It can also provide a better understanding of the areas that still need to be covered by the tools to comprehensively integrate the context of the SDGs within HEIs.

There are some limitations associated with these kinds of qualitative analyses. The limitations of the applied method in this research are mainly associated with the time-consuming process of content analysis, the human resources needed for content analysis to be rigorously applied, and the fact that the content analysis is a meticulous process (Maier 2017). Another limitation was data availability since some tools were suspended or there were not updated versions (e.g. HE 21 and SRC) which made it problematic to comprehensively compare them with the new tools such as THE. Another limitation of this research was the possibility that some tools missed being included during the screening process. However, selection bias was minimized by using a range of keywords to select the studies and a wide date range of multiple databases for screening and searching.

8.6 Conclusions

This research expands upon previous development of sustainability assessment tools in HEIs, which have mainly focused on how the existing tools root for an integrated approach toward sustainability rather than on what they achieve for society, the economy, and the environment distinctly. In this research, four approaches were used to analyze the 27 sustainability assessment tools at HEIs: (i) tool structure, (ii) core elements of sustainability implementation in HEIs, (iii) sustainability dimensions, and (iv) more commonly covered thematic areas. Several commonalities were found in the structure of the tools that mainly address the similarities on the levels of hierarchy (including subjective categories, subcriteria, and indicators), the total number of indicators (commonly less than 50), and the self-assessment process in the majority of tools. The top 10 underlying thematic areas in the tools are education, research, management and planning, partnership and engagement, society and communities, waste, energy, water, climate and carbon reduction, and transportation.

Among the core elements, a strong focus is jointly on the "governance" and "operations" core elements, whereas the core element that the indicators have seen having weaker use was the "assessment and reporting" and "on-campus experiences." In terms of sustainability dimensions, the environmental dimension is the most addressed among the indicators, while the economic dimension of sustainability is weak in the tools. Therefore, there is still a need to draw out economic indicators in the future development of the tools.

The increasing variety of these assessment tools makes a great potential for more tailored and structured development processes in HEIs. However, the progress of the tools is still inadequate to assess the university system in an integrated way by covering all sustainability dimensions and core elements as well as the main activities of HEIs. The results of this research can be used to modify the existing sustainability assessment tools, specifically by contributing to the indicators that were less addressed on the proposed thematic areas and sustainability dimensions. Also, sustainability assessment in HEIs should be viewed as a social construction that makes a significant contribution to the development of society. Therefore, the successful implementation of these assessment tools needs the active involvement of different stakeholders, where the various internal and external actors within and beyond the university contribute positively to the implementation of these tools.

References

AASHE (2019). STARS Technical Manual Version 2.2. Association for the Advancement of Sustainability in Higher Education. 1–322. https://stars.aashe.org/wp-content/uploads/2019/07/STARS-2.2-Technical-Manual.pdf (accessed 25 November 2021).

Adinyira, E., Oteng-seifah, S., and Adjei-kumi, T. (2007). A review of urban sustainability assessment methodologies. In: *International Conference on Whole Life Urban Sustainability and its Assessment* (ed. M. Horner et al.). Glasgow, UK: https://doi.org/10.1016/j.ecolind.2008.05.011.

Agovino, M., Cerciello, M., and Gatto, A. (2018). Policy efficiency in the field of food sustainability. The adjusted food agriculture and nutrition index. *Journal of Environmental Management* 218: 220–233. https://doi.org/10.1016/j.jenvman.2018.04.058.

Alghamdi, N., den Heijer, A., and de Jonge, H. (2017). Assessment tools' indicators for sustainability in universities: an analytical overview. *International Journal of Sustainability in Higher Education* 18 (1): 84–115. https://doi.org/10.1108/IJSHE-04-2015-0071.

Alshuwaikhat, H. and Abubakar, I. (2008) An integrated approach to achieving campus sustainability: Assessment of the current campus environmental management practices. *Proceedings of the 4th International Barcelona Conference on Higher Education, vol. 7, Higher Education for Sustainable Development*, Barcelona, Spain (March 2008). GUNI. http://www.guni-rmies.net (accessed 25 November 2021).

Amaral, L.P., Martins, N., and Gouveia, J.B. (2015). Quest for a sustainable university: a review. *International Journal of Sustainability in Higher Education* 16 (2): 155–172. https://doi.org/10.1108/IJSHE-02-2013-0017.

Berzosa, A., Bernaldo, M.O., and Fernández-Sanchez, G. (2017). Sustainability assessment tools for higher education: an empirical comparative analysis. *Journal of Cleaner Production* 161: 812–820. https://doi.org/10.1016/j.jclepro.2017.05.194.

Blasco, N., Brusca, I., and Labrador, M. (2019). Assessing sustainability and its performance implications: an empirical analysis in Spanish public universities. *Sustainability (Switzerland)* 11 (19): https://doi.org/10.3390/su11195302.

Buckland, H. et al. (2001). *The UK higher education partnership for sustainability (HEPS).* https://ulsf.org/the-uk-higher-education-partnership-for-sustainability-heps (accessed 19 July 2021).

Caeiro, S. et al. (2013). *Sustainability Assessment Tools in Higher Education Institutions: Mapping Trends and Good Practices around the World.* Springer Science & Business Media.

Caeiro, S. et al. (2020). Sustainability assessment and benchmarking in higher education institutions-a critical reflection. *Sustainability (Switzerland)* 12 (2): 1–28. https://doi.org/10.3390/su12020543.

CAS-NET Japan (2019). Good practices on campus sustainability in Japan. https://www.osc.hokudai.ac.jp/en/action/assc (accessed 15 July 2021).

Ceulemans, K., Lozano, R. and Alonso-almeida, M. M. (2015a) 'Sustainability reporting in higher education: interconnecting the reporting process and Organisational change Management for Sustainability', pp. 8881–8903. https://doi.org/10.3390/su7078881

Ceulemans, K., Molderez, I., and Van Liedekerke, L. (2015b). Sustainability reporting in higher education: a comprehensive review of the recent literature and paths for further research. *Journal of Cleaner Production* 106: 127–143. https://doi.org/10.1016/j.jclepro.2014.09.052.

Ciommi, M. et al. (2017). A new class of composite indicators for measuring well-being at the local level : an application to the equitable and sustainable well-being (BES) of the Italian provinces. *Ecological Indicators* 76: 281–296. https://doi.org/10.1016/j.ecolind.2016.12.050.

CTIE-AMB (Red de Ciencia, Tecnología, Innovación y Educación Ambiental en Iberoamér- ica) et al. (2014) 'Encuesta Para El Diagnóstico De La Institucionalización Del Compromiso Ambiental En Las Universidades Colombianas [Inquiry for Diagnosing the Institutionalisation of Environmental Committment of Colombian Universities].' Bogota: MADS.

Coelho, P., Mascarenhas, A., Vaz, P. et al. (2010). A framework for regional sustainability assessment: developing indicators for a Portuguese region. *Sustainable Development* 18: 211–219. https://doi.org/10.1002/sd.488.

Cotgrave, A.J. and Kokkarinen, N. (2010). Developing a model promoting sustainability literacy through construction curriculum design. *Structural Survey* 28 (4): 266–280. https://doi.org/10.1108/02630801011070975.

CRUE (2018). Diagnóstico De La Sostenibilidad Ambiental En Las Universidades Españolas. In *Conferencia de Rectores de las Universidades Españolas; Comisión Sectorial de Calidad.* Madrid, Spain.

Cunningham, T.R., Galloway-Williams, N., and Geller, E.S. (2010). Protecting the planet and its people: how do interventions to promote environmental sustainability and occupational safety and health overlap? *Journal of Safety Research* 41: 407–416. https://doi.org/10.1016/j.jsr.2010.08.002.

DUK (Deutsche UNESCO-Kommission e.V.) (2011). Hochschulen für eine Nachhaltige Entwicklung: Nachhaltigkeit in Forschung, Lehre Und Betrieb. https://www.hrk.de/uploads/media/Hochschulen_fuer_eine_nachhaltige_Entwicklung_Feb2012.pdf (accessed 20 October 2021).

EAUC (n.d.) Sustainability Leadership Scorecard. A transformational tool for the education sector – the Sustainability Leadership Scorecard. www.eauc.org.uk/sustainability_leadership_scorecard (accessed 11 June 2021).

Findler, F., Schönherr, N., Lozano, R. et al. (2018). Assessing the impacts of higher education institutions on sustainable development-an analysis of tools and indicators. *Sustainability (Switzerland)* 11 (1): https://doi.org/10.3390/su11010059.

Fischer, D., Jenssen, S., and Tappeser, V. (2015). Getting an empirical hold of the sustainable university: a comparative analysis of evaluation frameworks across 12 contemporary sustainability assessment tools. *Assessment and Evaluation in Higher Education* 40 (6): 785–800. https://doi.org/10.1080/02602938.2015.1043234.

Gasparatos, A. (2010). Embedded value systems in sustainability assessment tools and their implications. *Journal of Environmental Management* 91: 1613–1622. https://doi.org/10.1016/j.jenvman.2010.03.014.

Glover, A., Jones, Y., Claricoates, J. et al. (2013). Developing and piloting a baselining tool for education for sustainable development and global citizenship (ESDGC) in welsh higher education. *Innovative Higher Education* 38 (1): 75–86. https://doi.org/10.1007/s10755-012-9225-0.

Gómez, F.U., Sáez-Navarrete, C., Lioi, S.R. et al. (2015). Adaptable model for assessing sustainability in higher education. *Journal of Cleaner Production* 107: 475–485. https://doi.org/10.1016/j.jclepro.2014.07.047.

Good Company (2002). *Sustainability Assessment of the University of Oregon based on Good Company's Sustainable Pathways Toolkit*. Final report. Eugene, OR: Good Company.https://cpfm.uoregon.edu/sites/cpfm2.uoregon.edu/files/sust_assessment_-_sust_pathways_toolkit_0.pdf (accessed 25 November 2021).

GRI & ISO (2014) GRI G4 Guidelines and ISO 26000:2010: How to use the GRI G4 Guidelines and ISO 26000 in conjunction. http://www.iso.org/iso/iso-gri-26000_2014-01-28.pdf (accessed 25 November 2021).

Hesselbarth, C. and Schaltegger, S. (2014). Educating change agents for sustainability - learnings from the first sustainability management master of business administration. *Journal of Cleaner Production* 62: 24–36. https://doi.org/10.1016/j.jclepro.2013.03.042.

Jones, H. (2010) Sustainability reporting matters: What are national governments doing about it? ACCA. https://www.accaglobal.com/gb/en/technical-activities/technical-resources-search/2010/december/sustainability-reporting-matters-what-are-national-governments-doing-about-it.html (accessed 21 July 2021).

Kapitulčinová, D., AtKisson, A., Perdu, J. et al. (2018). Towards integrated sustainability in higher education – mapping the use of the accelerator toolset in all dimensions of university practice. *Journal of Cleaner Production* 172: 4367–4382. https://doi.org/10.1016/j.jclepro.2017.05.050.

Karatzoglou, B. (2013). An in-depth literature review of the evolving roles and contributions of universities to education for sustainable development. *Journal of Cleaner Production* 49: 44–53. https://doi.org/10.1016/j.jclepro.2012.07.043.

Kosta, K. (2019). Institutional sustainability assessment. In: *Encyclopedia of Sustainability in Higher Education* (ed. W.L. Filho), 1–7. Cham, Switzerland: Springer Switzerland AG, Springer https://doi.org/10.1007/978-3-319-63951-2_196-1.

Lauder, A., Sari, R.F., Suwartha, N. et al. (2015). Critical review of a global campus sustainability ranking: GreenMetric. *Journal of Cleaner Production* 108: 852–863. https://doi.org/10.1016/j.jclepro.2015.02.080.

Lozano, R. (2006a). A tool for a graphical assessment of sustainability in universities (GASU). *Journal of Cleaner Production* 14 (9–11): 963–972. https://doi.org/10.1016/j.jclepro.2005.11.041.

Lozano, R. (2006b). Incorporation and institutionalization of SD into universities: breaking through barriers to change. *Journal of Cleaner Production* 14 (9–11): 787–796. https://doi.org/10.1016/j.jclepro.2005.12.010.

Lozano, R. (2010). Diffusion of sustainable development in universities' curricula: an empirical example from Cardiff University. *Journal of Cleaner Production* 18 (7): 637–644. https://doi.org/10.1016/j.jclepro.2009.07.005.

Lozano, R. (2011). The state of sustainability reporting in universities. *International Journal of Sustainability in Higher Education* 12: 67–78. https://doi.org/10.1108/14676371111098311.

Lozano, R. and Huisingh, D. (2011). Inter-linking issues and dimensions in sustainability reporting. *Journal of Cleaner Production* 19: 99–107. https://doi.org/10.1016/j.jclepro.2010.01.004.

Lozano, R., Lukman, R., Lozano, F.J. et al. (2013). Declarations for sustainability in higher education: becoming better leaders, through addressing the university system. *Journal of Cleaner Production* 48: 10–19. https://doi.org/10.1016/j.jclepro.2011.10.006.

Lozano, R. et al. (2015a). A review of commitment and implementation of sustainable development in higher education: results from a worldwide survey. *Journal of Cleaner Production* 108: 1–18. https://doi.org/10.1016/j.jclepro.2014.09.048.

Lozano, R., Ceulemans, K., and Scarff, C. (2015b). Teaching organisational change management for sustainability : designing and delivering a course at the University of Leeds to better prepare future sustainability change agents. *Journal of Cleaner Production* 106: 205–215. https://doi.org/10.1016/j.jclepro.2014.03.031.

Lukman, R., Krajnc, D., and Glavič, P. (2010). University ranking using research, educational and environmental indicators. *Journal of Cleaner Production* 18 (7): 619–628. https://doi.org/10.1016/j.jclepro.2009.09.015.

Mader, C. (2013). Sustainability process assessment on transformative potentials: the graz model for integrative development. *Journal of Cleaner Production* 49: 54–63. https://doi.org/10.1016/j.jclepro.2012.08.028.

Maier, M. (2017). Definition of content analysis. In: *The SAGE Encyclopedia of Communication Research Methods* (ed. M. Allen), 242–245. SAGE Publications.

Mapar, M., Jafari, M.J., Mansouri, N. et al. (2017). Sustainability indicators for municipalities of megacities: integrating health, safety and environmental performance. *Ecological Indicators* 83: 271–291. https://doi.org/10.1016/j.ecolind.2017.08.012.

Mapar, M., Jafari, M.J., Mansouri, N. et al. (2020). A composite index for sustainability assessment of health, safety and environmental performance in municipalities of megacities. *Sustainable Cities and Society* 60: 102164. https://doi.org/10.1016/j.scs.2020.102164.

Moreno Pires, S. et al. (2020). *How to Integrate Sustainability Teaching and Learning in Higher Education Institutions? From Context to Action for Transformation towards SDGs Implementation: A Literature Review* (ed. M. Nicolau and M. Mapar). UA Editora: University of Aveiro, Portugal https://doi.org/10.34624/6gq8-9480.

Nurcahyo, R., Nurcahyo, R., Handika, F.S. et al. (2019). Integration of UI Greenmetric performance measurement on ISO 14001 implementation in higher education. *IOP Conference Series: Materials Science and Engineering*, Terengganu, Malaysia (27–28 August 2019) 697 (1): https://doi.org/10.1088/1757-899X/697/1/012011.

Özuyar, P.G. and Moreira, R.M. (2017). Barriers to innovation and sustainability at universities around the word. *Journal of Cleaner Production* 164: 1268–1278.

Panda, S., Chakraborty, M., and Misra, S.K. (2016). Assessment of social sustainable development in urban India by a composite index. *International Journal of Sustainable Built Environment* 5: 435–450. https://doi.org/10.1016/j.ijsbe.2016.08.001.

Penn State Green Destiny Council (2000). *Penn State Indicators Report 2000: Steps Toward A Sustainable University*. Pennsylvania. https://p2infohouse.org/ref/17/16964.pdf (accessed 25 November 2021).

People and Planet University League (n.d.) How Sustainable Is Your University? https://peopleandplanet.org/university-league (accessed 11 July 2021).

Rahdari, A.H. and Anvary Rostamy, A.A. (2015). Designing a general set of sustainability indicators at the corporate level. *Journal of Cleaner Production* 108: 757–771. https://doi.org/10.1016/j.jclepro.2015.05.108.

Ramos, B. (2019). Sustainability assessment : exploring the Frontiers and paradigms of indicator approaches. *Sustainability* 11: 1–14. https://doi.org/10.3390/su11030824.

Ramos, T. and Moreno Pires, S. (2013). Sustainability assessment: the role of indicators. In: *Sustainability Assessment Tools in Higher Education Institutions: Mapping Trends and Good Practices around the World* (ed. S. Caeiro, L. Walter, J. Charbel and U. Azeiteiro), 81–99. Cham, Switzerland: Springer.

Ramos, T.B., Caeiro, S., and de Melo, J.J. (2004). Environmental indicator frameworks to design and assess environmental monitoring programs. *Impact Assessment and Project Appraisal* 22 (1): 47–62. https://doi.org/10.3152/147154604781766111.

Razak, D. et al. (2013). Alternative university appraisal (AUA). Reconstructing universities' ranking and rating toward a sustainable future. In: *Sustainability Assessment Tolls in Higher Education in Higher Education Institutions: Mapping Trends and Good Practices Around the World* (ed. S. Caeiro, W. Leal Filho, C. Jabbour and U.M. Azeiteiro), 139–158. Cham, Switzerland: Springer.

Roorda, N. et al. (2009). 'AISHE 2.0 Manual – Assessment Instrument for Sustainability in Higher Education. www.eauc.org.uk/theplatform/aishe (accessed 25 November 2021).

Shriberg, M. (2002). Institutional assessment tools for sustainability in higher education: strengths, weaknesses, and implications for practice and theory. *International Journal of Sustainability in Higher Education* 3 (3): 254–270. https://doi.org/10.1108/14676370210434714.

Smedby, N. and Neij, L. (2013). Experiences in urban governance for sustainability: the constructive dialogue in Swedish municipalities. *Journal of Cleaner Production* 50: 148–158. https://doi.org/10.1016/j.jclepro.2012.11.044.

Stough, T., Ceulemans, K., Lambrechts, W. et al. (2018). Assessing sustainability in higher education curricula : a critical re flection on validity issues. *Journal of Cleaner Production* 172: 4456–4466. https://doi.org/10.1016/j.jclepro.2017.02.017.

Sustainable Endowments Institute (2011). *The college sustainability report card*. http://www.greenreportcard.org/report-card-2011/indicators.html (accessed 25 May 2021).

THE Impact Ranking (2021) Impact Rankings Methodology 2021. https://www.timeshighereducation.com/sites/default/files/breaking_news_files/the_impactrankings_methodology_2021_v1.3_final.pdf (accessed 25 November 2021).

Togo, M. and Lotz-Sisitka, H. (2009) Unit based sustainability assessment tool. A resource book to complement the UNEP Mainstreaming Environment and Sustainability in African Universities Partnership. http://www.unep.org/training/mesa/toolkit.asp (accessed 25 November 2021).

Trencher, G. et al. (2014). University partnerships for co-designing and co-producing urban sustainability. *Global Environmental Change* 28: 153–165. https://doi.org/10.1016/j.gloenvcha.2014.06.009.

ULSF (2009). Sustainability Assessment Questionnaire (SAQ) for Colleges and Universities. Association of University Leaders for a Sustainable Future. 1–12. http://ulsf.org/wp-content/uploads/2015/06/SAQforHigherEd09.pdf (accessed 25 November 2021).

United Nations (2015) Sustainable development goals (SDGs). https://sdgs.un.org/goals (accessed 25 November 2021).

United Nations Environment Programme (2021) Making peace with nature: a scientific blueprint to tackle the climate, biodiversity and pollution emergencies. Nairobi. http://doi.org/10.18356/9789280738377.

Velazquez, L., Munguia, N., Platt, A. et al. (2006). Sustainable university: what can be the matter? *Journal of Cleaner Production* 14: 810–819. https://doi.org/10.1016/j.jclepro.2005.12.008.

Waheed, B., Khan, F., Veitch, B. et al. (2011). Uncertainty-based quantitative assessment of sustainability for higher education institutions. *Journal of Cleaner Production* 19: 720–732. https://doi.org/10.1016/j.jclepro.2010.12.013.

Wals, A.E.J. (2014). Sustainability in higher education in the context of the UN DESD : a review of learning and institutionalization processes. *Journal of Cleaner Production* 62: 8–15. https://doi.org/10.1016/j.jclepro.2013.06.007.

Washington University (2013). The program sustainability assessment tool V2. St .Louis, MO: Washington University. www.sustaintool.org (accessed 19 July 2021).

Watson, M.K., Lozano, R., Noyes, C. et al. (2013). Assessing curricula contribution to sustainability more holistically : experiences from the integration of curricula assessment and students' perceptions at the Georgia Institute of Technology. *Journal of Cleaner Production* 61: 106–116. https://doi.org/10.1016/j.jclepro.2013.09.010.

Wersun, A. Klatt, J., Azmat, F., *et al.* (2020) *Blueprint for SDG integration into curriculum, research and partnerships*. PRME (Principles for Responsible Management Education). https://d30mzt1bxg5llt.cloudfront.net/public/uploads/PDFs/BlueprintForSDGIntegration.pdf (accessed 25 November 2021).

Xiong, H., Fu, D., Duan, C. et al. (2013). Current status of green curriculum in higher education of mainland China. *Journal of Cleaner Production* 61: 100–105. https://doi.org/10.1016/j.jclepro.2013.06.033.

Yarime, M. and Tanaka, Y. (2012). The issues and methodologies in sustainability assessment tools for higher education institutions: a review of recent trends and future challenges. *Journal of Education for Sustainable Development* 6 (1): 63–77. https://doi.org/10.1177/097340821100600113.

Zilahy, G. (2017). *Environmental Management Systems-History and New Tendencies, Encyclopedia of Sustainable Technologies*. Elsevier https://doi.org/10.1016/B978-0-12-409548-9.10529-9.

9

COVID-19 Disruptions to SDG 4 in Higher Education Institutions
Luis Velazquez

9.1 Introduction

Education for sustainable development (ESD) is at the core of SDG 4, Sustainable Development Goal 4: Quality Education, which is one of the top priorities for higher education institutions. In particular, SDG 4 in higher education settings aims at providing inclusive and sustainable education on campuses. Sustainability is a topic that has existed in higher education for at least 30 years. However, the progress toward SDG 4 has been slower than it was supposed to be. Regrettably, since the emergence of the coronavirus SARS-CoV-2, the chances of meeting this aim are fading. In this context, the purpose of this chapter is to provide an overview of how higher education institutions worldwide are implemented sustainability initiatives while returning to the *new normal* safely.

Before visioning how universities can help ensure inclusive and equitable higher education for all, it is necessary first to better understand the educational background of the United Nations (UN) 2030 Agenda and the genesis of SDG 4: Quality Education. There is now an increased recognition at the international policy level that education is essential to sustainable development. Many countries are committed to continuing to work to advance ESD at the national and local levels. To be inclusive and to be sustainable are the main characteristics of SDG 4 and both are briefly debated in specifics sections in this chapter. Finally, COVID-19 disruptions to SDG 4 are discussed to generate insights about how these disruptions will affect higher education institutions' sustainability, particularly among the most vulnerable communities.

9.2 The Educational Background of the 2030 Agenda

To analyze in detail the complexities associated with fostering post-COVID-19 initiatives in higher education, it is necessary first to better understand the educational background of the 2030 Agenda. In particular, the genesis of SDG 4: Quality Education. Reorienting education toward sustainability was first visioning in a comprehensive plan of action within chapter 36 of Agenda 21 at the Rio Earth Summit in 1992. Chapter 36 comprised 27 items addressed at promoting education, public awareness, and training. It should be highlighted that sustainability education was a complementary theme in the rest of Agenda 21 (Sitarz 1993). Another exciting landmark UN event related to sustainability education was the UN 2000 summit. Eight Millennium Development Goals (MDGs) aimed to eliminate the gravest problems confronted in human life, mainly those regarding the African continent. Among the eight goals, one addressed universal primary education (UN General Assembly 2000). It is precisely under the umbrella of this objective that the term "education for sustainable development" begins to be used in the literature concerning higher education. Two years later, during the 2002 World Summit on Sustainable Development, a Decade of Education for Sustainable Development (DESD) was adopted. This decade started in 2005 and finished in 2014. The DESD had the purpose of "integrating the principles and practices of sustainable development into all aspects of education and learning, to encourage changes in knowledge, values, and attitudes with the vision of enabling a more sustainable and just society for all" (UN General Assembly 2003). Unfortunately, both the MDGs and the DESD came to an end without achieving the expected results.

Nevertheless, the concept of ESD had been institutionalized in many universities through congresses, project implementation, greening the curriculum, sustainability research, and many other sustainability initiatives (UNESCO 2014). These achievements led to the UN 2030 Agenda, comprising 17 SDGs, with SDG 4 aiming to ensure inclusive and equitable quality education and promote lifelong learning opportunities for all. It includes 10 targets (UN General Assembly 2015), seven outcome targets and three means of implementation:

Outcome targets

1) **Universal primary and secondary education by 2030**: Ensure that all girls and boys complete free, equitable, and quality primary and secondary education leading to relevant and effective learning outcomes.
2) **Early childhood development and universal pre-primary education by 2030**: Ensure that all girls and boys have access to quality early childhood development, care, and pre-primary education so that they are ready for primary education.
3) **Equal access to technical, vocational, and tertiary education by 2030**: Ensure equal access for all women and men to affordable and quality technical, vocational, and tertiary education, including university.
4) **Relevant skills for decent work by 2030**: Substantially increase the number of youth and adults who have relevant skills, including technical and vocational skills, for employment, decent jobs, and entrepreneurship.
5) **Gender equality and inclusion by 2030**: Eliminate gender disparities in education and ensure equal access to all levels of education and vocational training for the vulnerable, including persons with disabilities, indigenous peoples, and children in vulnerable situations.
6) **Literacy and numeracy by 2030**: Ensure that all youth and a substantial proportion of adults, both men, and women, achieve literacy and numeracy.
7) **Education for sustainable development and global citizenship by 2030**: Ensure that all learners acquire the knowledge and skills needed to promote sustainable development, including, among others, through education for sustainable development and sustainable lifestyles, human rights, gender equality, promotion of a culture of peace and non-violence, global citizenship, and appreciation of cultural diversity and of culture's contribution to sustainable development.

Means of implementation

1) **Effective learning environments**: Build and upgrade education facilities that are child disability and gender sensitive and provide safe, non-violent, inclusive, and effective learning environments for all.

2) **Scholarships**: By 2020, substantially expand globally the number of scholarships available to developing countries, in particular, least developed countries, small island developing States and African countries, for enrolment in higher education, including vocational training and information and communications technology, technical, engineering, and scientific programmers, in developed countries and other developing countries.
3) **Teachers and educators**: By 2030, substantially increase the supply of qualified teachers, including through international cooperation for teacher training in developing countries, especially least developed countries and small island developing states.

In general, the UN's perseverance in fostering the 2030 Agenda has not rendered the expected results. Data in the Sustainable Development Goals Report 2020, issued by the UN Department of Economic and Social Affairs (United Nations 2020) recognized three critical issues about the SDGs:

1) SDGs require immense political will and ambitious action by all stakeholders.
2) Progress remains uneven, and we are not on track to meet the SDGs by 2030.
3) The COVID-19 is making the achievement of SDGs even more challenging.

Specifically, the same report suggested that worldwide education developments have meant that many countries are further away from ensuring inclusive and equitable quality education for all. Moreover, since the emergence of the coronavirus SARS-CoV-2, the chances of reaching the goal are fading. According to a recent UN policy brief, more than 1.5 billion children and youth worldwide have been affected by COVID-19 measures and socioeconomic impacts; as a result, the consequences of disruptions in their education are hard to predict (UNICEF 2020). Yet, UNESCO estimates that over 100 million children will not reach the minimum proficiency level in reading (UNESCO 2020b). Scholars also suggest that the large-term impacts of the pandemic on education will be lost in the development of human capital (Sachs et al. 2020).

The following sections will address SDG 4 in the context of higher education, specifically in the context of more sustainable higher education institutions.

9.3 The Genesis of SDG 4 in Higher Education

At this stage, it is important to understand the genesis of what drove higher education institutions to be involved in sustainability initiatives. Decades ago, long before sustainable development was an essential part of political discourses, environmental programs were established in a few universities to offer technical education to professionals in the environmental field (EPA 1997). These programs found inspiration in the Declaration of the UN Conference on the Human Environment, held in June 1972 in Stockholm, Sweden, which mandated to educate youngers and adults in environmental subjects (UNEP 1972). The environmental movement at universities started to gain momentum in 1987 when the World Commission on Environment introduced, in the renowned Brundtland Report, the phrase "sustainable development." In this report, sustainable development was defined as "development that meets the needs of the present without compromising the ability of future generations to meet their own needs" (WCED 1987). The Brundtland Report set the path universities should follow from that point onward. Higher education institutions have adopted several more university-oriented declarations and charters to frame their sustainability initiatives. The most notable among them are the Talloires Declaration; the Halifax Declaration; the Blueprint for a Green Campus: The Campus Earth Summit Initiatives for Higher Education; the University Charter for Sustainable Development; CRE-Copernicus; and the International Declaration on Cleaner Production.

The content of these declarations encourages sustainability promoters to implement and maintain sustainability policies about strategies on campuses. Individuals such as professors, students, or staff might sign some declarations, but the most recommended action is that a higher authority endorses them. It is important to note that all manifestos state principles that are adopted voluntarily and are subject to no penalties. We should be cautiously optimistic about the signature of declarations and not raise expectations very high. Years ago, colleagues warned us that signing manifestos without showing evidence of performance was not enough to move toward sustainability in higher education (Lans 2000). Some universities and colleges sign a declaration to boost their institutional image without showing objective evidence of their sustainability performance. This practice is known as "greenwashing," which consists of declaring an interest in sustainability while not being interested. At present, manifestos have continued to grow, but not with the same intensity and enthusiasm with which the first manifestos were adopted. Although manifestos are rarely updated over the years to reflect new world events, they continue to inspire university leaders. However, the current state of sustainability in higher education demands more than simple motivation. After reflecting on this, and other critiques, we can conclude that having signed a declaration does not mean that universities will have immediate success in incorporating sustainability into the university activities. Still, it means a commitment to support the implementation of sustainability initiatives on campus.

The above might generate mistrust and suspicion among university community members and external stakeholders about hidden intentions. For the sake of transparency, rectors and presidents choose to conduct sustainability audits on campus. Audits examine the environmental policies and practices on campus. They also comprise procedures to periodically assess the institution's sustainability performance to compare them against pre-established criteria (EPA 2000). For higher education institutions, there are specific audit frameworks to evaluate the performance of their sustainability initiatives. For instance, the College Sustainability Report Card was an audit tool to assess operations in higher education institutions. Developed by the Sustainable Endowments Institute, it assigns a subjective grade to universities in several areas, and then an overall grade average is given on the audited items. This framework was used to compare environmental performance in American and Canadian universities and colleges (Sayed et al. 2013; Ebrahimi and North 2017). Despite being a successful project, it is currently suspended, and it is unlikely that updated versions of the audit instrument will be developed (Sustainable Endowments Institute 2011). Another popular auditing framework is the Campus Environmental Audit Response Form, a comprehensive guide to assessing environmental quality, which creates strategies for change. It contains 200 questions about different topics and is intended to help students compare and share information, monitor changes, and evaluate their programs (Smith 1993). Our third and final item is the Sustainability Assessment Questionnaire (SAQ), an instrument designed to help colleges and universities assess their sustainability in their teaching and practice. Twenty items, divided into seven critical dimensions of higher education, form this document. It does not include a rating/scoring system (ULSF 2001).

The effectiveness of these audit formats for evaluating the environmental performance of universities depends on the data available and the way that information is collected and presented. Sustainability assessment in universities is undertaken under more considerable uncertainty; in this sense, sustainability indicators are among the most critical elements in an audit. Ideally, metrics should provide reliable, relevant, and valuable information about one or several features to be audited in the system (Rammel et al. 2016). In the end, conducting an audit should help universities better understand the sustainability state of their operations according to compliance criteria (Cahill 1991). In addition, it could enhance the university's image and be an instructional tool to teach students about environmental management principles (Campus Earth Summit 1995).

9.4 SDG 4 in the Context of Inclusive Higher Education

In the context of transformation, higher education institutions must catalyze broader initiatives to meet SDG 4 (Ferguson and Roofe 2020). SDG 4 comprises a twofold aim: to be inclusive and to be sustainable. One of the significant challenges facing most universities is coverage. According to a forecast by the Organisation for Economic Co-operation and Development (OECD), the number of higher education students will be about 263 million by 2025 (Tremblay et al. 2012). In many countries, the demand surpasses the offer, leaving many prospective students without the opportunity to enroll.

Years before the pandemic emerged, the global education community issued a call to action by adopting the Incheon Declaration for Education 2030. This declaration is consistent with the provisions set out in SDG 4 (Agbedahin 2019). As noted in the declaration's seventh paragraph:

> Inclusion and equity in and through education is the cornerstone of a transformative education agenda, and we therefore commit to addressing all forms of exclusion and marginalization, disparities and inequalities in access, participation and learning outcomes. No education target should be considered met unless met by all. We therefore commit to making the necessary changes in education policies and focusing our efforts on the most disadvantaged, especially those with disabilities, to ensure that no one is left behind (UNESCO 2015).

Considering inclusive education as that measure of the integration of groups designated as disabled of any kind (Mamah et al. 2011), the development of strategies to harmonize controversial elements such as those related to politics, race, gender, and even religion is appropriate (Nakidien et al. 2021). Without a doubt, this task cannot be carried out by one specific university; indeed, the only way is to reach a partnership agreement that considers as many universities as possible willing to take joint actions (Boeren 2019). For inclusive and equitable quality education to succeed, professors with more flexible and dynamic training should be involved in the reengineering process (Zhu and Liu 2020). Reengineering educational programs in higher education toward inclusive education must address themes related to interdependence, citizenship, future generation needs, diversity, equity, justice, sustainable change, and uncertainty and precaution (Goodman 2011); but it must also fit into sociocultural, political, and environmental structures prevailing at any given time (Aktan 2021).

Advancing in line with SDG 4 requires a paradigm shift on educative systems to focus on leaving no one behind (Grob-Zakhary 2020). However, the paradigm shift will not happen if everything possible is not done to prevent and eliminate the current obstacles preventing access to higher education, particularly the university admission of the most vulnerable people without regard to race, color, religion, or national origin (IESALC 2020). Bangert et al. (2017) assert that despite the effort made for SDG 4 to ensure quality and inclusive education, there are still challenges to be achieved to provide quality education at all educational levels and include the most critical groups.

9.5 SDG 4 in the Context of Sustainable Higher Education

The second aim of SDG 4 is to foster ESD, which is an integral element of the 2030 Agenda, not only for SDG 4 also the entire set of SDGs (UNESCO 2020a). Universities have played a consistent role in driving society toward sustainability through their substantive activities

(Leal Filho et al. 2019). According to Weiss et al. (2021), sustainability initiatives in higher education could be initiated under any of the following six patterns, collaborative paradigm change, bottom-up, evolving institutional change, top-down, mandated institutional change, externally driven initiatives, isolated initiatives, and limited institutional change. Hence, how universities promote sustainability is very diverse, from simple activities to recycling materials to strategic initiatives involving the institution's positioning on sustainability, for example, in the statement of the vision, mission, and policies (Beringer and Adomssent 2008). Higher education institutions embed sustainability best practices in teaching, research, outreach and partnership, and operational activities (Velazquez et al. 2006).

Universities fostering education for sustainability aim to change attitudes and behaviors of students that are affecting the quality of life in the world. They aim to meet SDG 4 through formal, non-formal, and informal education. Greening the curriculum is perhaps the oldest and most popular practice among all alternatives that universities choose in order to become a more sustainable institution. Inspired by the 1990 Taillores Declaration, higher education institutions are incorporating sustainability knowledge into the curriculum as a way to enable students to make responsible decisions in favor of the environment of both the present and future generations (Khan 2013). This sustainability educational commitment gained momentum in awareness and action with the promulgation of Agenda 21 (Leal 2000; Paraschivescu and Radu 2012; Okanović et al. 2021). Since then, sustainability leaders have developed theories to refine the curriculum (Chiu and Chai 2020). In response, universities have implemented changes in their structures to help society move toward more sustainable lifestyles (Junyent and de Ciurana 2008). The process of integrating ESD into the curriculum required a wide range of innovative educational approaches to facilitate learning processes to empower students for a more sustainable future (Cincera et al. 2018). Although the acquirement of credits characterizes formal education, sustainability is taught in universities at three levels: undergraduate, graduate, and certificate programs. In the past, courses were primarily elective, but today it is possible to find entire sustainability programs at all levels. There is a diversity of contents for sustainability programs depending on the discipline where the class is taught. Sustainability instruction might be offered face-to-face in classrooms and laboratories, but it is also possible to find sustainability distance learning.

Distance learning started to be present in education about the mid-nineteenth century, when the printed media, the postal service, and some years later, the telephone served to develop the educational process (Peters 2002). Arguably, this learning modality stems from the invention of technologies such as compact disks, videodisks, and others that began to be incorporated into education. Still, it was not until the emergence of the internet and the development of information technology that higher education institutions started to transmit knowledge as part of the sustainability teaching-learning process (Velazquez et al. 2015a). Since then, the evolution of distance learning to support sustainability education has been unstoppable and challenging because the advance of technology demands a continuous process of change and innovation (Bell et al. 2017). In addition, from an energy efficiency perspective, distance learning courses result in energy expense savings and the generation of fewer emissions (Roy et al. 2008).

Universities make operational the social dimension of education for sustainability by stressing its importance among relevant community stakeholders through a participatory approach (Disterheft et al. 2015). Therefore, sustainability engagement is promoted in the frame of formal education, but also through non-formal and informal education initiatives. Universities develop non-formal education courses to provide sustainability knowledge among the greater university community, such as other schools or other institutions in their vicinity or even farther (Reimers 2021). This education model comprises a series of workshops, seminars, training sessions, meetings, and pilot projects. These initiatives are short-term and are scheduled depending on the capacity and needs of the institution.

Furthermore, non-formal education is often complemented by informal education. Higher education institutions use this alternative to raise sustainability awareness among the external community. Commonly, informal education initiatives only inform the audience about a specific topic in speaker sessions, cultural events such as the Earth Day celebration, rallies, and demonstration projects.

Beyond education for sustainability, universities conduct sustainability research within their departments or affiliated research center. This strategy aims to increase the current stock of knowledge in this field under economic, social, environmental, and political approaches on both regional and global scales. Sustainability research is traditionally carried out in most universities worldwide. However, only those universities with a long tradition in sustainability research understand the importance of being at the field's cutting edge in order to gain valuable knowledge about a particular subject. Traditionally, research centers maintain interdisciplinary teams to search for solutions to prevent or eliminate unsustainability problems.

Owning to the diversity of sustainability themes, it is hard to determine a single dominant field. Still, scholars usually conduct research associated with global climate, pollution prevention, sustainable consumption, toxic use reduction, industrial ecology, regional development, hazardous waste, and environmental justice. Recently, however, the emergence of a novel scientific niche called "sustainability sciences" has rapidly embraced previously separated sustainability research clusters (Kajikawa et al. 2014). Sustainability science suggests transdisciplinarity, community-based, interactive, or participatory research approaches to solve real-world problems (Lang et al. 2012). However, the transdisciplinarity approach demands new skills for researchers because it implies the suppression of disciplines (Zen 2017).

Sustainability research is a solid link to develop outreach and partnership with industries, governmental agencies, educational institutions, and non-governmental organizations, among other groups. This strategy poses a particular challenge to universities. It aims to collaborate with communities, agencies, and organizations to improve the quality of life of its members. These activities coordinate and enhance communities, workers, churches, and other organizations by advising services and technical assistance. Among the preferred tasks of people participating in these sustainability initiatives are grassroots movements, creating networks that address poverty, health, environmental and social justice, and the design of educational materials for all education level students, teachers, and community leaders.

Although, in general, the purpose of each initiative is very diverse and linked with university-wide policies, the most consistent sustainability policies in higher education institutions aim to improve their sustainability in all of their operations (Vaughter et al. 2016). The path toward a more sustainable university includes sustainability on campus because students and professors are using university campuses as a living laboratory to research and learn (Pretorius et al. 2019). Currently, international students consider sustainability as a decisive criterion when selecting an overseas university (Manzoor et al. 2020). Perhaps, for this reason, they become champions of reducing environmental impacts on campus by top-down on bottom-up change efforts (Brinkhurst et al. 2011).

From all the projects undertaken by students, professors, researchers, and staff over the last decades, energy efficiency, energy conservation, and energy consumption stand out. It perhaps is because "campus energy costs typically constitute 30% of a university's total operations and maintenance budget" (Hogan and Flanigan 1996). However, universities have already reaped the advantages of implementing information and communication technologies in gathering and analyzing electricity and energy data (Popoola et al. 2018). Energy audits, energy-efficient lighting retrofit or upgrade, buildings insulation, high-efficient equipment installation and maintenance, movement sensors and timers installation, energy awareness, solar panel installation, are some of the practices used to fulfill the goals of this alternative. As a result of the combination of these measures, universities have saved many dollars on their energy bills (Bughio et al. 2021).

In parallel to energy-efficiency initiatives, students also show interest in climate change. All kinds of issues related to climate change have raised students' interest in implementing their climate change initiatives on campus (Helferty and Clarke 2009). The genuine interest of university students in climate change has forced presidents and rectors to react by preparing long-term agendas to tackle climate change on-campus (Ellard and Swieter 2015). In addition, projects strive to predict the effects of climate change generated on university buildings (Fathi et al. 2020) and disseminate knowledge to educate and raise awareness among university members about the consequences of climate change and reduce the emission of greenhouse gases on-campus.

Climate change often links to water consumption initiatives because universities are large-scale water users (Johnson and Castleden 2011). For that reason, the conservation of this natural resource is one of the biggest concerns in universities and colleges worldwide, and university staff seek windows of opportunity to conserve water on-campus (Cockerill and Carp 2009). Water initiatives are diverse and can comprise some of the following: water audits, repairing or replacing leaky faucets and other plumbing repairs, pipe maintenance, low-flow showerheads and toilets retrofit, flush valves installation, automatic faucet retrofit, improvement of irrigation practices, high-efficiency cooling system installation, sewage treatment facilities, water conservation awareness, sprinkling systems installation, and water use policies (Velazquez et al. 2013).

Recycling organic waste is being done in universities either on-site or off-campus at external composting facilities. There are several ways to organically compost material. The most convenient methods for on-campus composting are the trench, vermicomposting, and composting toilets. These methods are developed on a small scale; besides that, they aim to encourage university members to compost their organic waste at home. However, others have the goal of producing enough compost to be used in their university green areas. Food, wood, and yarn, and animal wastes are the organic material often composted in universities (Waliczek et al. 2016). In particular cases, sewage sludge is also composted for fertilizer (Fei-Baffoe et al. 2016).

As the university community grows, universities cope with transportation and environmental problems (Alshuwaikhat and Abubakar 2008). Several strategies have been tried to encourage students and faculty to reduce the use of particular vehicles on-campus. These strategies are aimed at stimulating walking, the use of bicycles, and public transportation (Velazquez et al. 2015b). Among the best practices are the purchase of highly efficient vehicles, running shuttle services, car-pooling programs, installation of bicycle parking racks, raising the awareness among the campus, creating policies, replacing fuel vehicles with electric vehicles, using alternatives to fossils fuel, discussions with public officials to improve public transportation, financial incentives to use mass transit to get to work, creation of transportation policies, and introducing university parking fees (Balsas 2003).

Most of the environmental and health problems created on-campus have to do with chemical exposures. In particular, accidents in chemistry laboratories represent a great risk for students, professors, and staff (Álvarez-Chávez et al. 2019). European or North American governmental agencies have drawn increased attention to hazardous waste generated in universities (Callao et al. 2019; Brainard 2002). However, in other countries, the enforcement can be different and it is, therefore, hard to generalize a specific set of initiatives for higher education institutions to reduce the risk that hazardous materials pose to the university community.

Nevertheless, universities are constantly trying to reduce, reuse, and recycle the dangerous waste produced in their labs, research centers, janitorial services, or other university sources (Yekkalar et al. 2015). Hazardous waste-related initiatives on-campus are diverse and can include, but are not limited to, the following aims: sharing material between labs, making audits for getting comprehensive data, improving chemicals storage practices, coordinating material purchasing, using micro-scale methods in chemistry lab courses, doing chemical tracking, creating policies, and substituting hazardous materials with non- or less-dangerous materials (Hassanvand et al. 2011). In addition, due to the pollution potential of hazardous waste transportation, special attention is paid to the amount of material carried, the type of material, the routes, and the types of trucks that transport the material (Liu et al. 2011).

Finally, among the initiatives most implemented by students on-campus are those aimed at non-hazardous materials management initiatives. These initiatives promote reduce, reuse, recycle techniques for managing the waste generated o- campus (Smyth et al. 2010). The recycling of inorganic materials, such as office paper, newspaper, aluminum, glass, plastic, batteries, cardboard, and metal, is the most chosen technique to deal with non-hazardous waste, followed by reusing and then reducing (Baeyens et al. 2010).

As was observed in this section, the trend shows that many universities have reached a stage of maturity concerning SDG 4 in the context of ESD. In summary, higher education institutions have set the foundation to motivate present and future generations to be more committed to their environment (Leicht et al. 2018). However, the current unprecedented health and economic crises are testing worldwide higher education institution's resilience to the limit because they have caused significant disruptions to their sustainability initiatives. In the following sections, we will debate COVID-19 disruptions to SDG 4, both general and relating to sustainability in higher education.

9.6 COVID-19 Disruption to SDG 4, at a Glance

The spread of the coronavirus SARS-CoV-2 further exacerbated the already dispiriting impression that achieving the 2030 Agenda and the SDGs appear unlikely (United Nations 2020). Education systems worldwide canceled traditional face-to-face teaching and relied on information technologies to strengthen their resilience; however, this response has had the cost of leaving behind many children and youth, especially in developing countries (Hörisch 2021). At the K-12 level, professors wonder if they can maintain teaching quality standards that are as high as possible and whether teaching will worsen if children do not return to school soon (Catalano et al. 2021). Even for those who succeed in shifting to distance education, the shift has been a long and torturous experience because technology is not an adequate substitute for traditional education (Powers et al. 2020). Stopping attending schools interfered with children's learning and development, and the interruption of social relationships among children, youth, and teachers is considered to have been a significant disruption at this education level. Children's socialization is deemed to be necessary for forging their development, values, and attitudes; for this reason, schools are adjusting their teaching models, offering both synchronous and asynchronous sessions to compensate for the social disadvantage of remote communication technologies in elementary and middle school (Murai and Muramatsu 2020).

With online education, educational institutions for children and youth started to rely increasingly on parents to the extent that parents were asked to follow schedules and tasks previously performed by professors, which is not advisable in the long term (Formosinho 2021). Working parents started to face the challenge of mentoring and supervising their children and youth through their online courses and, at the same time, themselves working from home. The latter is has been stressful for the children's parents who have seen their role change from being a complementary one to a primary one in the support their children's education, as if they were teachers (Iyengar 2021). This stress is particularly exacerbated in parents whose children have developmental difficulties because of the specific needs of these children (Brklja and Lu 2020). Gender scholars have also pointed out the disproportionate impacts of COVID-19 on working women who have suffered a lot of tension when balancing their work and domestic roles, such as their children's school assignments (Adisa and Adekoya 2020).

High school teachers are doing their best during COVID-19 times, but they are not having a good time either. Further, the pandemic's stressors themselves, teachers are coping with new challenges and demands as a result of their online teaching experience, increasing the chances of suffering from stress, anxiety, depression, insomnia, and anger (Truzoli et al. 2021). Having to adapt or learn quickly to use web platforms such as Microsoft Teams or Zoom is the first source of stress because many have not been used to information technology environments (Adedoyin and Soykan 2020). As a response, professors worldwide have reacted, encouraging mentoring and collaboration among peers, mainly related to distance learning, which did not frequently happen before the pandemic (Darling-Hammond and Hyler 2020). Grading is another of the crucial teaching activities that have changed to reflect current academic conditions. For instance, in California, to deliver accurate and reliable assessments, some high school professors adjusted weighing criteria to considering more homework completion and exams over practical work. As a result, grades have increased overall (Schramm et al. 2021).

9.7 Higher Education During the COVID-19 Pandemic

Early experiences on campuses have demonstrated many opportunities and many problems with the successful implementation of sustainability programs; unfortunately, many obstacles prevent the success of sustainability initiatives on campuses around the world (Velazquez et al. 2005). Now, the COVID-19 pandemic is causing chaos and forcing universities to rethink how to foster sustainability on-campus. Unlike the COVID-19-related effects on education at the elementary and upper secondary levels, higher education institutions experienced even broader affectations that compromise other activities inherent to its substantive activities such as research, outreaching, and partnership with the private sector and society. The COVID-19 pandemic seriously disrupted face-to-face instruction in higher education to the extent that many universities were forced to experiment with digital education, which has left many behind, especially the poorest (Pittman et al. 2020). The UNESCO International Institute for Higher Education in Latin America and the Caribbean (IESALC 2020) predicts various scenarios at the institutional level to return to the classroom, among which the following stand out:

1) Anticipate an extended suspension, focusing efforts on ensuring training continuity and guaranteeing equity, creating governance mechanisms, monitoring, and efficient support.
2) Design pedagogical measures to evaluate and generate mechanisms to support learning among disadvantaged students.
3) Document the pedagogical changes introduced and their impacts.
4) Learn from mistakes and scale-up digitization, hybridization, and ubiquitous learning.

According to a global survey conducted on the impact of COVID-19 on higher education around the world by the International Association of Universities (Marioni et al. 2020), 98% of 424 universities participating in the survey faced COVID-19-associated disruptions in their teaching and learning activities. However, 67% of them shifted to distance learning as soon as possible. Research activities were reported to have been disrupted by 80% of the respondents.

They indicated that nearly 50% of the research projects were compromised to a certain extent, and 21% claimed that scientific research was stopped. In addition, international student mobility was canceled in nearly 90% of the higher education institutions. In general, university partnership was disrupted in about 64% of responding universities.

The fear of catching COVID-19 and also social distancing have caused mental disorders in university students. The mental health of university students has always been important on campuses (Brewer et al. 2021), but as a result of the pandemic, building the students' resilience became a priority since many experienced emotional distress (Cicha et al. 2021). During the pandemic, students have faced multiple daily stressors that might cause psychological distress. For example, students are experiencing poor sleep quality and dietary risks (Du et al. 2021) caused by high anxiety levels due to academic delays, economic stressors, and SARS-CoV-2 infections (Dhar et al. 2020). However, addressing the demands of current students has become problematic for professors because it implies an increased workload in preparing online teaching and mentoring of students (Troshani 2021). Therefore, higher education institutions are focusing on building resilience to the COVID-19 crisis by implementing innovative approaches to support and encourage their students in their adaptation to the new normal.

One of the most widely implemented strategies to maintaining teaching was implementing a mix of synchronous and asynchronous online learning (Kyne and Thompson 2020). Some researchers have successfully adapted to online meetings and online resources, and the current COVID-19-related situation is an opportunity to collaborate in the reduction of carbon emissions (Leal et al. 2021). International mobility offices have found ways to keep this activity alive. Studying abroad is a unique opportunity to experience learning from different perspectives, explore other cultures, try ethnic cuisine, and learn a new language. Unfortunately, visa restrictions for foreign visitors and students imposed by many countries make this learning option unavailable. However, virtual mobility programs, such as the Virtual Mobility Space in Higher Education (eMOVIES) and the Erasmus Mundus NetACTIVE program, represent an attractive alternative to maintaining international mobility students and academics (Quintero-Goris 2020).

Higher education institutions tried to achieve the best input from professors and stakeholders to provide essential alternatives to keep the institutions open (García-Morales et al. 2021). As restrictions begin to lift and universities reopen their campuses, the lessons learned should not be forgotten: it should not be overlooked that a participatory curricular approach is a safe bet in generating more sustainable solutions to the challenges of contemporary education (Alexander and Hjortsø 2019). Moreover, adequate monitoring of the innovative approaches will allow the anticipation of significant adverse pedagogical outcomes generated by changes without affecting the stability of the education system (Cucuzzella et al. 2010).

9.8 Wrap up

Sustainable Development Goal 4: Quality Education is one of the top priorities for higher education institutions. Some progress had been made in advancing toward more sustainable universities. Still, however, the state of maturity in many universities concerning ESD is not enough. Regrettably, SDG 4 initiatives on-campus have been seriously disrupted by the unprecedented COVID-19 pandemic. What is currently most concerning is the people being left behind in the higher education system. Therefore, this chapter aimed to provide an overview of how higher education institutions worldwide are implementing sustainability initiatives while returning to the new normal safely.

The level of disruption that the lockdowns and health restrictions caused by the COVID-19 pandemic have caused to SDG 4 is simply incalculable. In general, we know that due to full school closures during the first year of the pandemic, the 2020–2021 academic period was lost for many children and adolescents. Moreover, for the vast majority, the year turned out to be unproductive. The COVID-19 experience has taught us that radical inclusion should be the next normal. It has also taught us the need for collective engagement and mutual accountability. This new normal is a pivotal time toward a fairer, more equitable, and sustainable education for all (Silva and Sá 2018). Currently, sustainability initiatives on-campus refer in most cases to environmental efforts. However, it is necessary to add the social and economic dimensions of sustainability to those initiatives.

No one knows for sure how long the consequences of the pandemic will last, yet the disruption caused so far makes it unlikely that SDG 4 will be met by 2030. Indeed, there will be inequalities in how COVID-19 will affect the sustainability of higher education institutions, mainly among the most vulnerable communities. Nevertheless, envisioning an inclusive and sustainable higher education is a goal that will be on official universities' agendas for a long time. Leaving no one behind in education implies facing an enormous challenge, perhaps the most significant compromise on the 2030 Agenda. This unprecedented situation has allowed us to value sustainability initiatives on-campus; hopefully, the acquired knowledge has built a worldwide resilience in higher education institutions to significant COVID-19 disruptions to SDG 4. The approach of "build back better together" must drive our post-COVID sustainability initiatives to act as a catalyst that speeds up the progress toward inclusive and sustainable higher education for all.

References

Adedoyin, O.B. and Soykan, E. (2020). COVID-19 pandemic and online learning: the challenges and opportunities. *Interactive Learning Environments* https://doi.org/10.1080/10494820.2020.1813180.

Adisa, T.A. and Adekoya, O.D. (2020). The work–family balance of British working women during the COVID-19 pandemic. *Journal of Work-Applied Management* 13 (2): 241–260. https://doi.org/10.1108/JWAM-07-2020-0036.

Agbedahin, A.V. (2019). Sustainable development, education for sustainable development, and the 2030 agenda for sustainable development: emergence, efficacy, eminence, and future. *Sustainable Development* 27 (4): 669–680. https://doi.org/10.1002/sd.1931.

Aktan, S. (2021). Waking up to the dawn of a new era: reconceptualization of curriculum post Covid-19. *Prospects* https://doi.org/10.1007/s11125-020-09529-3.

Alexander, I.K. and Hjortsø, C.N. (2019). Sources of complexity in participatory curriculum development: an activity system and stakeholder analysis approach to the analyses of tensions and contradictions. *Higher Education* 77 (2): 301–322. https://doi.org/10.1007/s10734-018-0274-x.

Alshuwaikhat, H. and Abubakar, I. (2008). An integrated approach to achieving campus sustainability: assessment of the current campus environmental management practices. *Journal of Cleaner Production* 16 (16): 1777–1785. https://doi.org/10.1016/j.jclepro.2007.12.002.

Álvarez-Chávez, C.R., Marín, L.S., Perez-Gamez, K. et al. (2019). Assessing college students' risk perceptions of hazards in chemistry laboratories. *Journal of Chemical Education* 96 (10): 2120–2131. https://doi.org/10.1021/acs.jchemed.8b00891.

Baeyens, J., Brems, A., and Dewil, R. (2010). 'Recovery and recycling of post-consumer waste materials'. Part 2. Target wastes (glass beverage bottles, plastics, scrap metal and steel cans, end-of-life tyres, batteries, and household hazardous waste). *International Journal of Sustainable Engineering* 3 (4): 232–245. https://doi.org/10.1080/19397038.2010.507885.

Balsas, C.J. (2003). Sustainable transportation planning on college campuses. *Transport Policy* 10 (1): 31–49. https://doi.org/10.1016/S0967-070X(02)00028-8.

Bangert, M., Molyneux, D.H., Lindsay, S.W. et al. (2017). The cross-cutting contribution of the end of neglected tropical diseases to the sustainable development goals. *Infectious Diseases of Poverty* 6 (1): 1–20. https://doi.org/10.1186/s40249-017-0288-0.

Bell, S., Douce, C., Caeiro, S. et al. (2017). Sustainability and distance learning: a diverse European experience? *Open Learning* 32 (2): 95–102. https://doi.org/10.1080/02680513.2017.1319638.

Beringer, A. and Adomssent, M. (2008). Sustainable university research and development: inspecting sustainability in higher education research. *Environmental Education Research* 14 (6): 607–623. https://doi.org/10.1080/13504620802464866.

Boeren, E. (2019). Understanding sustainable development goal (SDG) 4 on "quality education" from micro, meso and macro perspectives. *International Review of Education* 65 (2): 277–294. https://doi.org/10.1007/s11159-019-09772-7.

Brainard, J. (2002). 3 universities cited on hazardous waste. In: *The Chronicle of Higher Education*, vol. 49(13). Gale Academic: OneFile.

Brewer, M., van Kessel, M., Sanderson, B. et al. (2021). Enhancing student resilience by targeting staff resilience, attitudes and practices. *Higher Education Research and Development* 1–15. https://doi.org/10.1080/07294360.2021.1877622.

Brinkhurst, M. et al. (2011). Achieving campus sustainability: top-down, bottom-up, or neither? *International Journal of Sustainability in Higher Education* 12 (4): 338–354. https://doi.org/10.1108/14676371111168269.

Brklja, T. and Lu, L. (2020). Effects of COVID-19 related restrictive measures on parents of children with developmental difficulties. *Journal of Children's Services* 15 (4): 229–234. https://doi.org/10.1108/JCS.

Bughio, M., Khan, M.S., and Mahar, W.A. (2021). Impact of passive energy efficiency measures on cooling energy demand in an architectural campus building in Karachi, Pakistan. *Sustainability* 13: 1–35. https://doi.org/10.3390/su13137251.

Cahill, L.B. (ed.) (1991). *Environmental Audits*, 7e. ISBN-13: 978-0865875258s. Rockville, Maryland: Government Institute.

Callao, C., Martinez-Nuñez, M., and Pilar Latorre, M. (2019). European countries: Does common legislation guarantee better hazardous waste performance for European Union member states? *Waste Management* 84: 147–157. https://doi.org/10.1016/j.wasman.2018.11.014.

Campus Earth Summit (1995). The Blueprint for a Green Campus: The Campus Earth Summit initiatives for higher education. The Heinz Family Foundation: Yale University. https://www.sustainable.org/living/education-training-and-lifelong-learning/758-blueprint-for-a-green-campus-the-campus-earth-summit-initiatives-for-higher-education (accessed 25 April 2021).

Catalano, A.J., Torff, B., and Anderson, K.S. (2021). Transitioning to online learning during the COVID-19 pandemic: differences in access and participation among students in disadvantaged school districts. *International Journal of Information and Learning Technology* 38 (2): 258–270. https://doi.org/10.1108/IJILT-06-2020-0111.

Chiu, T.K.F. and Chai, C.S. (2020). Sustainable curriculum planning for artificial intelligence education: a self-determination theory perspective. *Sustainability (Switzerland)* 12 (14): https://doi.org/10.3390/su12145568.

Cicha, K. et al. (2021). Covid-19 and higher education: first-year students' expectations toward distance learning. *Sustainability (Switzerland)* 13 (4): 1–20. https://doi.org/10.3390/su13041889.

Cincera, J., Biberhoferb, P., Binka, B. et al. (2018). Designing a sustainability-driven entrepreneurship curriculum as a social learning process: a case study from an international knowledge alliance project. *Journal of Cleaner Production* 172: 4357–4366. https://doi.org/10.1016/j.jclepro.2017.05.051.

Cockerill, K. and Carp, J. (2009). Leveraging opportunities for campus sustainability: a case study of water resources. *Sustainability: Science, Practice, and Policy* 5 (2): 28–37. https://doi.org/10.1080/15487733.2009.11908033.

Cucuzzella, C., Pearl, D., and Mertenat, C. (2010). Greening the Curriculum: A Canadian Academic National Forum. *Engineering Education in Sustainable Development (EESD)*. 1–5. Gothenburg, Sweden (September 2010). http://eesd10.org/wp-content/uploads/2010/10/2A-Mertenat.pdf

Darling-Hammond, L. and Hyler, M.E. (2020). Preparing educators for the time of COVID . . . and beyond. *European Journal of Teacher Education* 43 (4): 457–465. https://doi.org/10.1080/02619768.2020.1816961.

Dhar, B.K., Ayittey, F.K., and Sarkar, S.M. (2020). Impact of COVID-19 on psychology among the university students. *Global Challenges* 4: 1–6. https://doi.org/10.1002/gch2.202000038.

Disterheft, A., Azeiteiro, U.M., Leal Filho, W. et al. (2015). Participatory processes in sustainable universities – what to assess? *International Journal of Sustainability in Higher Education* 16 (5): 748–771. https://doi.org/10.1108/IJSHE-05-2014-0079.

Du, C., Chong, M., Cho, M.J. et al. (2021). Health behaviors of higher education students from 7 countries: poorer sleep quality during the COVID-19 pandemic predicts higher dietary risk. *Clocks & Sleep* 3 (1): 12–30. https://doi.org/10.3390/clockssleep3010002.

Ebrahimi, K., Leslie, A., and North, L.A. (2017). Effective strategies for enhancing waste management at university campuses. *International Journal of Sustainability in Higher Education* 18 (7): 1123–1141. https://doi.org/10.1108/IJSHE-01-2016-0017.

Ellard, P. and Swieter, K. (2015). Preparing and adapting our campuses for the effects of climate change. *Planning for Higher Education* 44 (1): 27. https://scholarworks.merrimack.edu/tolle/133.

Environmental Protection Agency (2000). *The Small Business Source Book on Environmental Auditing*. Washington, DC: EPA Small Business Division.

Environmental Protection Agency, Pollution Prevention (1997). A national progress report. 169. Office of Pollution Prevention and Toxics: Washington, DC.

Fathi, S., Srinivasan, R.S., Kibert, C.J. et al. (2020). AI-based campus energy use prediction for assessing the effects of climate change. *Sustainability (Switzerland)* 12 (8): 1–22. https://doi.org/10.3390/SU12083223.

Fei-Baffoe, B., Osei, K., Agyapong, E. et al. (2016). Co-composting of organic solid waste and sewage sludge – a waste management option for university campus. *International Journal of Environment* 5 (1): 14–31. https://doi.org/10.3126/ije.v5i1.14562.

Ferguson, T. and Roofe, C.G. (2020). SDG 4 in higher education: challenges and opportunities. *International Journal of Sustainability in Higher Education* 21 (5): 959–975. https://doi.org/10.1108/IJSHE-12-2019-0353.

Formosinho, J. (2021). From schoolification of children to schoolification of parents? – educational policies in COVID times. *European Early Childhood Education Research Journal* 29 (1): 141–152. https://doi.org/10.1080/1350293X.2021.1872677.

García-Morales, V.J., Garrido-Moreno, A., and Martín-Rojas, R. (2021). The transformation of higher education after the COVID disruption: emerging challenges in an online learning scenario. *Frontiers in Psychology* 12: 1–6. https://doi.org/10.3389/fpsyg.2021.616059.

Goodman, B. (2011). The need for a "sustainability curriculum" in nurse education. *Nurse Education Today* 31 (8): 733–737. https://doi.org/10.1016/j.nedt.2010.12.010.

Grob-Zakhary, R. (2020). COVID-19 is an opportunity to reset education. Here are 4 ways how. World Economic Forum. https://www.weforum.org/agenda/2020/10/covid-19-education-reset (accessed 25 April 2021).

Hassanvand, M., Naddafi, K., Nabizadeh, R. et al. (2011). Hazardous waste management in educational and research centers: a case study. *Toxicological and Environmental Chemistry* 93 (8): 1636–1642. https://doi.org/10.1080/02772248.2011.602683.

Helferty, A. and Clarke, A. (2009). Student-led campus climate change initiatives in Canada. *International Journal of Sustainability in Higher Education* 10 (3): 287–300. https://doi.org/10.1108/14676370910972594.

Hogan, B. and Flanigan, T. (1996). *Comprehensive Energy and Resource Management*, 4. Buffalo, NY: State University of New York at Buffalo.

Hörisch, J. (2021). The relation of COVID-19 to the U.N. sustainable development goals: implications for sustainability accounting, management and policy research. *Sustainability Accounting, Management and Policy Journal* https://doi.org/10.1108/SAMPJ-08-2020-0277.

IESALC (2020). COVID-19 and higher education: Today and tomorrow. https://www.iesalc.unesco.org/en/publicaciones-2 (accessed 27 October 2021).

Iyengar, R. (2021). Rethinking community participation in education post Covid-19. *Prospects* 2021: https://doi.org/10.1007/s11125-020-09538-2.

Johnson, L. and Castleden, H. (2011). Greening the campus without grass: using visual methods to understand and integrate student perspectives in campus landscape development and water sustainability planning. *Area* 43 (3): 353–361. https://doi.org/10.1111/j.1475-4762.2011.01001.x.

Junyent, M. and De Ciurana, A.M.G. (2008). Education for sustainability in university studies: a model for reorienting the curriculum. *British Educational Research Journal* 34 (6): 763–782. https://doi.org/10.1080/01411920802041343.

Kajikawa, Y., Tacoa, F., and Yamaguchi, K. (2014). Sustainability science: the changing landscape of sustainability research. *Sustainability Science* 9 (4): 431–438. https://doi.org/10.1007/s11625-014-0244-x.

Khan, T. (2013). Sustainability accounting courses, Talloires declaration and academic research. *International Journal of Sustainability in Higher Education* 14 (1): 42–55. https://doi.org/10.1108/14676371311288949.

Kyne, S.H. and Thompson, C.D. (2020). The COVID cohort: student transition to university in the face of a global pandemic. *Journal of Chemical Education* 97 (9): 3381–3385. https://doi.org/10.1021/acs.jchemed.0c00769.

Lang, D.J. et al. (2012). Transdisciplinary research in sustainability science: practice, principles, and challenges. *Sustainability Science* 7 (Suppl. 1): 25–43. https://doi.org/10.1007/s11625-011-0149-x.

Lans, H. (2000). The Dutch sustainability award for higher education 1998. In: *Sustainability and University Life* (ed. W. Leal Filho), 213. Frankfurt am Main, Berlin, Bruxelles, New York, Oxford, Wien: Peter Lang.

Leal Filho, W. (2000). Dealing with misconceptions on the concept of sustainability. *International Journal of Sustainability in Higher Education* 1 (1): 9–19. https://doi.org/10.1108/1467630010307066.

Leal Filho, W., Shiel, C., Paço, A. et al. (2019). Sustainable development goals and sustainability teaching at universities: falling behind or getting ahead of the pack? *Journal of Cleaner Production* 232: 285–294. https://doi.org/10.1016/j.jclepro.2019.05.309.

Leal Filho, W., Azul, A.M., Wall, T. et al. (2021). COVID - 19: the impact of a global crisis on sustainable development research. *Sustainability Science* 16: 85–99. https://doi.org/10.1007/s11625-020-00866-y.

Leicht, A., Heiss, J., and Byun, W.J. (2018). *Issues and Trends in Education for Sustainable Development*. Paris: UNESCO.

Liu, K.H., Shih, S.Y., and Kao, J.J. (2011). Planning for hazardous campus waste collection. *Journal of Hazardous Materials* 189 (1–2): 363–370. https://doi.org/10.1016/j.jhazmat.2011.02.046.

Mamah, V. et al. (2011). University teachers' perception of inclusion of visually impaired in Ghanaian universities. *International Journal of Special Education* 26 (1): 70–79.

Manzoor, S.R., Ho, J., and Al Mahmud, A. (2020). Revisiting the 'university image model' for higher education institutions' sustainability. *Journal of Marketing for Higher Education* 1–20: https://doi.org/10.1080/08841241.2020.1781736.

Marioni G., van't Land, H., and Jensen, T. (2020) The impact of COVID-19 on higher education around the World. IAU global survey report. Paris, France. https://www.iau-aiu.net/IMG/pdf/iau_covid19_and_he_survey_report_final_may_2020.pdf (accessed 15 April 2021).

Murai, Y. and Muramatsu, H. (2020). Application of creative learning principles within blended teacher professional development on integration of computer programming education into elementary and middle school classrooms. *Information and Learning Science* 121 (7–8): 665–675. https://doi.org/10.1108/ILS-04-2020-0122.

Nakidien, T., Singh, M., and Sayed, Y. (2021). Teachers and teacher education: limitations and possibilities of attaining SDG 4 in South Africa. *Education Sciences* 11 (2): 1–13. https://doi.org/10.3390/educsci11020066.

Okanović, A., Ješić, J., Djakovic, V. et al. (2021). Increasing university competitiveness through assessment of green content in curriculum and eco-labeling in higher education. *Sustainability* 13 (2): 1–20. https://doi.org/10.3390/su13020712.

Paraschivescu, V. and Radu, C.E. (2012). The universities and Agenda 21. *Economy Transdisciplinarity. Cognition* 15 (1): 1–8. www.ugb.ro.

Peters, O. (2002). *La educación a distancia en transición. Nuevas tendencias y retos [Distance Education in Transition. New Trends and Challenges]*. Mexico: Universidad de Guadalajara. Guadalajara.

Pittman, J., Severino, L., DeCarlo-Tecce et al. (2020). An action research case study: digital equity and educational inclusion during an emergent COVID-19 divide. *Journal for Multicultural Education* https://doi.org/10.1108/JME-09-2020-0099.

Popoola, S.I., Atayeroa, A., Okanlawon, T.T. et al. (2018). Smart campus: data on energy consumption in an ICT-driven university. *Data in Brief* 16: 780–793. https://doi.org/10.1016/j.dib.2017.11.091.

Powers, J.M., Brown, M., and Wyatt, L.G. (2020). SPARK-ing innovation: a model for elementary classrooms as COVID-19 unfolds. *Journal of Professional Capital and Community* 5 (3–4): 307–320. https://doi.org/10.1108/JPCC-06-2020-0036.

Pretorius, R.W., Anderson, R., Khotoo, A. et al. (2019). Creating a context for campus sustainability through teaching and learning: the case of open, distance and e-learning. *International Journal of Sustainability in Higher Education* 20 (3): 530–547. https://doi.org/10.1108/IJSHE-02-2019-0066.

Quintero-Goris, J.A. (2020). How will COVID-19 affect International Academic Mobility? IESALC. https://www.iesalc.unesco.org/en/2020/06/26/how-will-covid-19-affect-international-academic-mobility (accessed 15 April 2021).

Rammel, C., Velazquez, L., and Mader, C. (2016). Sustainability assessment in higher education institutions. In: *Routledge Handbook of Higher Education for Sustainable Development*, 1e (ed. M. Barth, G. Michelsen, M. Rieckmann and I. Thomas). Routledge https://doi.org/10.4324/9781315852249.

Reimers, F.M. (2021). The role of universities building an ecosystem of climate change education. In: *Education and Climate Change - The Role of Universities* (ed. F.M. Reimers), 1–44. Cham, Switzerland: Springer https://doi.org/10.1007/978-3-030-57927-2_1.

Roy, R., Potter, S., and Yarrow, K. (2008). Designing low carbon higher education systems: environmental impacts of campus and distance learning systems. *International Journal of Sustainability in Higher Education* 9 (2): 116–130. https://doi.org/10.1108/14676370810856279.

Sachs, J., Schmidt-Traub, G., Kroll, C., et al. (2020). Sustainable Development Report 2020. The Sustainable Development Goals and COVID-19. Cambridge: Cambridge University Press.

https://s3.amazonaws.com/sustainabledevelopment.report/2020/2020_sustainable_development_report.pdf (accessed 5 April 2021).

Sayed, A., Kamal, M., and Asmuss, M. (2013). Benchmarking tools for assessing and tracking sustainability in higher educational institutions: Identifying an effective tool for the University of Saskatchewan. *International Journal of Sustainability in Higher Education* 14 (4): 449–465. https://doi.org/10.1108/IJSHE-08-2011-0052.

Schramm, H., Rubin, I., and Schramm, N. (2021). Covid-19 and high school grades: an early case study. *Significance* 18 (2): 6–7. https://doi.org/10.1111/1740-9713.01500.

Silva, E. and Sá, A.A. (2018). Educational challenges in the Portuguese UNESCO Global Geoparks: contributing for the implementation of the SDG 4. *International Journal of Geoheritage and Parks* 6 (1): 95–106. https://doi.org/10.17149/ijg.j.issn.2210.3382.2018.01.007.

Sitarz, D. (1993). *Agenda 21: The Earth Summit Strategy to Save Our Planet*. Boulder, CO: Earth Press.

Smith, A.A. (1993). *Campus Ecology: A Guide to Assessing Environmental Quality and Creating Strategies for Change*. Venice, California: Living Planet Press.

Smyth, D.P., Fredeen, A.L., and Booth, A.L. (2010). reducing solid waste in higher education: The first step towards 'greening' a university campus. *Resources, Conservation and Recycling* 54 (11): 1007–1016. https://doi.org/10.1016/J.RESCONREC.2010.02.008.

Sustainable Endowments Institute (2011). *2011*. Green Report Card: The billion dollar green challenge https://www.endowmentinstitute.org/our-initiatives (accessed 26 October 2021).

Tremblay, K., Lalancette, D., and Roseveare, D. (2012). *Assessment of Higher Education Learning Outcomes - Feasibility Study Report, Design and Implementation*, vol. 1. OECD https://doi.org/10.1007/978-94-6091-867-4.

Troshani, I. (2021). Organisational learning mechanisms in the age of pandemics: the case of accounting research. *Accounting, Auditing and Accountability Journal* 34 (2): 281–306. https://doi.org/10.1108/AAAJ-09-2020-4940.

Truzoli, R., Pirola, V., and Conte, S. (2021). The impact of risk and protective factors on online teaching experience in high school Italian teachers during the COVID-19 pandemic. *Journal of Computer Assisted Learning* 37: 1–13. https://doi.org/10.1111/jcal.12533.

UN General Assembly (2000). United Nations Millennium Declaration, Resolution Adopted by the General Assembly, (18 September), A/RES/55/2. https://www.refworld.org/docid/3b00f4ea3.html (accessed 10 June 2021).

UN General Assembly (2003). United Nations Decade of Education for Sustainable Development, Resolution Adopted by the General Assembly (21 February), A/RES/57/254. https://undocs.org/en/A/RES/57/254 (accessed 10 July 2021).

UN General Assembly (2015). Transforming our world: the 2030 Agenda for Sustainable Development (21 October), A/RES/70/1. https://www.refworld.org/docid/57b6e3e44.html (accessed 24 March 2021).

UNESCO (2014). Shaping the future we want- U.N. Decade of Education for Sustainable Development (2005–2014) Final Report. Paris, France. https://sustainabledevelopment.un.org/content/documents/1682Shaping the future we want.pdf (accessed 29 April 2021).

UNESCO (2015). *Incheon Declaration and Framework for Action for the implementation of Sustainable Development Goal 4*. http://uis.unesco.org/sites/default/files/documents/education-2030-incheon-framework-for-action-implementation-of-sdg4-2016-en_2.pdf (accessed 29 April 2021).

UNESCO (2020a). Education for Sustainable Developement- A roadmap. UNESCO. Paris, France. https://www.gcedclearinghouse.org/resources/education-sustainable-development-roadmap (accessed 2 July 2021).

UNESCO (2020b). Education: From disruption to recovery. https://en.unesco.org/covid19/educationresponse (accessed 5 April 2021).

UNICEF (2020). Policy Brief: The impact of COVID-19 on Children. United Nations. https://www.unicef.org/zimbabwe/media/2631/file/Policy Brief: The Impact of COVID-19 on children.pdf (accessed 10 July 2021).

United Nations (2020). The Sustainable Development Goals Report 2020. https://unstats.un.org/sdgs/report/2020/The-Sustainable-Development-Goals-Report-2020.pdf (accessed 5 April 2021).

United Nations Environmental Programme. (1972). Report of the United Nations Conference on the Human Environment: Stockholm, Sweden.

University Leaders for a Sustainable Future. (2001). Sustainability Assessment Questionnaire. http://ulsf.org/sustainability-assessment-questionnaire (accessed 5 April 2021).

Vaughter, P., McKenzie, M., Lidstone, L. et al. (2016). Campus sustainability governance in Canada: a content analysis of post-secondary institutions' sustainability policies. *International Journal of Sustainability in Higher Education* 17 (1): 16–39. https://doi.org/10.1108/IJSHE-05-2014-0075.

Velazquez, L., Munguia, N., and Sanchez, M. (2005). Deterring sustainability in higher education institutions: an appraisal of the factors which influence sustainability in higher education institutions. *International Journal of Sustainability in Higher Education* 6 (4): https://doi.org/10.1108/14676370510623865.

Velazquez, L., Munguia, N., Platt, A. et al. (2006). Sustainable university: what can be the matter? *Journal of Cleaner Production* 14 (9–11): https://doi.org/10.1016/j.jclepro.2005.12.008.

Velazquez, L., Munguia, N., and Ojeda, M. (2013). Optimizing water use in the University of Sonora, Mexico. *Journal of Cleaner Production* 46: https://doi.org/10.1016/j.jclepro.2012.09.005.

Velazquez, L., Munguia Vega, N.E., Gabriela, A. et al. (2015a). Designing a distance learning sustainability bachelor's degree. *Environment, Development and Sustainability* 17 (2): 365–377. https://doi.org/10.1007/s10668-015-9622-5.

Velazquez, L., Munguia, N.E., Will, M. et al. (2015b). Sustainable transportation strategies for decoupling road vehicle transport and carbon dioxide emissions. *Management of Environmental Quality* 26 (3): 373–388. https://doi.org/10.1108/MEQ-07-2014-0120.

Waliczek, T., McFarland, A., and Holmes, M. (2016). The relationship between a campus composting program and environmental attitudes, environmental locus of control, compost knowledge, and compost attitudes of college students. *HortTechnology* 26 (5): 592–598. https://doi.org/10.21273/HORTTECH03320-16.

Weiss, M., Barth, M., and von Wehrden, H. (2021). The patterns of curriculum change processes that embed sustainability in higher education institutions. *Sustainability Science* 16: https://doi.org/10.1007/s11625-021-00984-1.

World Commission on Environment and Development (1987). *Our Common Future*. Oxford/NY: Oxford University Press.

Yekkalar, M., Panahi, S., and Nikravan, M. (2015). *Evaluation of current laboratory waste management: a step towards green campus at Amirkabir University of Technology*. In: *Implementing Campus Greening Initiatives*, World Sustainability Series (ed. F.W. Leal, N. Muthu, G. Edwin and M. Sima). Cham: Springer https://doi.org/10.1007/978-3-319-11961-8_17.

Zen, I.S. (2017). Exploring the living learning laboratory: an approach to strengthen campus sustainability initiatives by using sustainability science approach. *International Journal of Sustainability in Higher Education* 18 (6): 939–955. https://doi.org/10.1108/IJSHE-09-2015-0154.

Zhu, X. and Liu, J. (2020). Education in and after COVID-19: immediate responses and long-terms visions. *Postdigital Science and Education* 2: 695–699. https://doi.org/10.1007/s42438-020-00126-3.

Part II

Transforming the Curriculum – Discipline-Specific Initiatives

10

Integrating Harmonious Entrepreneurship into the Curriculum: Addressing the Sustainability Grand Challenge

David A. Kirby, Iman El-Kaffass, and Felicity Healey-Benson

10.1 Introduction

Since the publication of the research of Birch (1979) in the US showing that half of all gross job gains in the US between 1969 and 1976 were from new ventures, at a time when larger firms were downsizing, governments around the world have encouraged their education system to introduce entrepreneurship to the curriculum. Although there is no agreed definition of what entrepreneurship is in 2008, the European Commission (2008, p. 7) suggested that:

> the benefits of entrepreneurship education are not limited to start-ups, innovative ventures and new jobs [but to] an individual's ability to turn ideas into action and is therefore a key competence for all, helping young people to be more creative and self-confident in whatever they undertake.

Traditionally, however, programs have focused on teaching students how to write a business plan (Cannavacciuola et al. 2006; Gailly 2006) and while this remains a key objective of many programs (Al-Dairi et al. 2012), there has developed, over the years, an ongoing debate not just over whether entrepreneurship can be taught (Henry et al. 2005) but over the nature and purpose of entrepreneurship education. Is it about new venture creation and equipping students with the functional skills to start a business or is it a much broader concept that recognizes entrepreneurship as a way of thinking and behaving – about seeing opportunities and harnessing the resources to bring such opportunities to fruition, in the process bringing about change? (Kirby 2006; Fayolle and Gailly 2008). Increasingly it is being recognized that effective entrepreneurship education should engage students with the various thinking styles and behaviors associated with the entrepreneur, not just with a set of business tools (Kirby 2003) and it is this latter, broader concept that is being adopted and an appropriate definition might be:

> Entrepreneurship is about seeing new opportunities and/or finding new, innovative solutions to problems, it is about harnessing the resources to bring them to fruition and it is about instigating measurable change and improvement.

This would very much fit with Schumpeter's (1943) view of entrepreneurship as creative destruction – resulting from "new combinations" (innovations) that disturb the status quo.

The Wiley Handbook of Sustainability in Higher Education Learning and Teaching, First Edition.
Edited by Kelum A. A. Gamage and Nanda Gunawardhana.
© 2022 John Wiley & Sons, Inc. Published 2022 by John Wiley & Sons, Inc.

As such, entrepreneurship might be expected to have the potential to address the sustainability[1] challenge (Villar and Miralles 2019) and is regarded by some as a panacea hypothesis. However, while entrepreneurship is a global phenomenon and is not new, there remains, as Hall, et al. (2010, p. 440) acknowledge, "considerable uncertainty regarding the nature of this role and how it will unfold." Indeed, questions have been raised as to whether entrepreneurship is compatible with sustainability (Gawel 2012).

Hence the purpose of this chapter is to analyze the problem, and not just propose a solution, but to explore how entrepreneurship and sustainability might be integrated into the curriculum in higher education in order to change mindsets and bring about the requisite change.

10.2 The Challenge

Essentially the challenge is twofold and revolves around the way entrepreneurship is both taught and applied or implemented.

10.2.1 The Teaching Challenge

Equipping students with the entrepreneurial mindset and skills required to bring about change and improvement requires (Kirby 2006, 2007) a move away from the narrow paradigm for entrepreneurship that equates it with new venture creation and the tools to start and run a business. If the education system is to develop more entrepreneurial attitudes and behaviors in its students, then in most institutions of higher education there needs to be a "very significant transformation in not only what is taught but how it is taught" (Kirby 2006). Indeed, there needs to be a change in the purpose, content, process and place of learning (Kirby 2007) and it is possible to agree with Chia (1996, p. 40) that what is needed is a "deliberate strategy which privileges the weakening of thought processes so as to encourage and stimulate the entrepreneurial imagination."

How this is to be done is the subject of increasing debate and numerous volumes have been produced (Fayolle 2007a,b; Fayolle and Klandt 2006; Greene and Rice 2007: West et al. 2009) to address the issue and provide exemplification. However, it is generally agreed that there needs to be a more experiential approach to learning and the creation of enterprising environments and approaches that enable entrepreneurial aptitudes (such as creativity, need for achievement, calculated risk-taking, autonomy, etc.) to be developed, alongside business acumen and understanding and the more traditional skills of the graduate student (critical thinking, communication, problem-solving, time management, etc.). This requires a change in not only what is taught, but the purpose of learning and pedagogy, as well as the development of right-brain as well as the traditional left-brain analytical, objective thinking skills (Kirby 2007). Developing the student's right-brain thinking skills is important. Not only have successful entrepreneurs been found to have a right-brain learning preference (Nieuwenhuizen and Groenwald 2004), but rather than being logical and results oriented, right-brain thinking is creative, lateral, imaginative, and emotional, resulting, through association, in more than one solution (De Bono 1970). The two ways of thinking are complementary and it is apparent that in order to develop entrepreneurial capability, both critical and creative thinking are needed. As with critical thinking, students can be trained to think creatively and to cope with ambiguity and

---

[1] The 1987 World Commission on Environmental Development definition of sustainability is "development that meets the needs of the present without compromising the ability of future generations to meet their own needs."

uncertainty (Bragg and Bragg 2005), but perhaps of most importance is the ability to maintain, at all times, an open and enquiring mind. This should be the role of education but all too frequently, however, it is not.

In many institutions the introduction of entrepreneurship education has been resisted or confined solely to the study of business administration. There are several reasons for this, including the fact that many educators do not see the role of education as preparing young people for the world of work and have opposed entrepreneurship education in particular for this reason. However, there has been a further, possibly more fundamental, objection that has hindered its adoption. This has resulted from the fact that the whole enterprise agenda has been perceived as a right wing inspired initiative to promote capitalism (Erkkila 2000), something that many educators are opposed to politically. Also, and perhaps even more fundamental, is the fact that the word "enterprise" is used in different ways, "sometimes referring to an individual ability considered amenable to improvement and at other times to a form of economic activity, usually in small businesses" (MacDonald and Coffee 1991, p. 30). However, even when it is clearly relating to the former many educators find it confusing as there is no tightly defined, agreed, and unitary concept. Rather, according to MacDonald and Coffield (op. cit. 30) it comprises "a Farrago of 'Hurrah' words like 'creativity', 'initiative' and 'leadership.'"

On top of this, universities are notoriously slow to change. They are not the most entrepreneurial of institutions and many university managers are concerned about the likely negative impact on their institution's research performance if their leading academics become involved in entrepreneurial activity. Thus, although some of the leading research universities are among the most successful entrepreneurially, in terms of spin-outs (Etzkowitz 2003), for many in higher education the concept provokes "an image of shady villainy, a fifth column gnawing away at the basic values that define a university, a wolf masquerading as a milch-cow" (McNay 2002, p. 20).

This is important as it has become recognized, increasingly, that entrepreneurial education itself will not be effective unless there is both a change in the teaching paradigm, as just outlined, and the educational institutions themselves become entrepreneurial. Not only are the traditional, passive methods of learning required to be changed but, as Jonathan Ortman (Senior Fellow at the Kauffman Foundation) has observed "universities can only effectively become incubators of entrepreneurship and innovation if they themselves practice entrepreneurship." While the concept of the Entrepreneurial University has emerged (Etzkowitz 2003) it is not widely developed despite the numerous measures that have been introduced to encourage universities to change. In the UK, for example, these have included, government funding incentives (Kirby 2007), capacity building programs (NCEE 2020), recognition schemes such as Entrepreneurial University Leaders Programme (www.eulp.co.uk) and The Times Higher Education Outstanding Entrepreneurial University of the Year Award (the-awards.co.uk). Elsewhere, international initiatives have included:

- The International Accreditation Council for Entrepreneurial and Engaged Universities (www.aceeu.org) intended not only to recognize and promote entrepreneurial and engaged universities but to enable the necessary culture change to facilitate their formation.
- HEInnovate (www.heinnovate.eu), the EU/OECD tool that enables universities to evaluate themselves against eight key criteria.

As a result, the 2020 Report of the National Council for Entrepreneurship in Education in the UK indicates that the provision of enterprise education in the country's universities has increased in recent years so that "90.5 per cent of institutions have credit-bearing entrepreneurship and enterprise courses within at least some degree programmes." However, as the finding implies, the provision is not uniform either across universities or the country. This appears to be the case globally as, according to Potter (2008) there is a "need to expand existing entrepreneurship efforts and introduce more creative and effective approaches, building on best practices highlighted from around the world."

10.2.2 The Implementation Challenge

Since they were first introduced, there has been a proliferation of Entrepreneurship Education programs across the globe (Vesper and Gartner 1998), coupled with a broadening of the concept to include not just wealth and job creation (economic entrepreneurship), but issues to do with the environment (ecopreneurship), society (social entrepreneurship) and, most recently, people (humane entrepreneurship). While there are valuable and growing cases of eco[2] and social[3] entrepreneurship rarely do they address both environmental and social aspects[4] and the most recent "theory" of humane entrepreneurship, which focuses on the management of people within enterprises, "presents a new perspective on how to create 40 million quality jobs each year and helps address global challenges" (Kim et al. 2018, p. 10). This has led Schaltegger et al. (2016, p. 5) to observe that "while extant research on sustainable business models has often been rooted in ecological sustainability, other scholars have seen business models as tools for addressing social needs."

This disaggregated approach to entrepreneurship has meant that it has had relatively little impact on the sustainability challenge and has led some to question whether entrepreneurship and sustainability are, indeed, compatible (Gawel 2012). According to Kirby and El-Kaffass (2021) this results from the systemic nature of the problem. The planet is a system composed of interconnected subsystems which means that any solution to the problem needs to adopt the principles of general systems thinking (Von Bertalanffy 2015). Thus, given this interconnectivity and multifaceted nature of the sustainability problem, any solution will need to adopt Ashby's (1968) law of requisite variety. This implies that only variety can absorb variety – that it is not possible to address the problem by addressing just one facet. The solution must be equal to or greater than the number of factors involved.

As an example:

SEKEM Holding (Abouleish and Kirchgessner 2005; Mair and Seelos 2006) is an Egyptian agricultural business that introduced biodynamic agriculture to Egypt and turned 70 acres of desert located 37 mi northeast of Cairo into a thriving, fertile oasis. Its 150 products, including organic foods, herbal teas, medicines, and organic cotton products, are produced by 10 companies, and sold nationally and internationally through four subsidiaries:

- ISIS Organic Food (vegetables, honey, dates, oils, beverages)
- Lotus Organic Herbs and Spices
- NatureTex Organic Textiles (Baby and children's wear, dolls, toy, home textiles)
- PharmaAtos (pharmaceuticals)

It was founded in 1977 by Professor Ibrahim Abouleish (1937–2017), an Egyptian pharmacologist, to help address the poverty encountered in Egypt and the parlous state of Egyptian agriculture. However, instead of focusing solely on business growth, he addressed the much

---

2 Ecopreneurship may be defined as entrepreneurship that addresses and finds innovative sustainable solutions to environmental problems.
3 In social entrepreneurship the aim is not to create wealth, but to find innovative solutions for community-based problems.
4 Under some definitions of social entrepreneurship the environment is considered, but usually the focus is on only one aspect of the problem, social or environmental.

broader interconnected issues, building a thriving rural community in which the profits generated by the holding company are used to fund social and cultural projects through the Co-operative of SEKEM Employees, which has responsibility for all aspects of the human resources development of the workforce, and the SEKEM Development Foundation, which is responsible for all cultural matters and which receives 10% of all company profits.

In total the holding company employs some 2000 people and has a network of over 3000 farmers who produce for the Group. To help meet its objectives of promoting sustainable agriculture it has trained some 477 Egyptian farmers in biodynamic agricultural methods which are applied on approximately 4600 acres of land. Since 2000, around 1000 students have graduated from the Company's Vocational Training Centre and in 2012 it opened a not-for-profit university that specializes in sustainability and offers knowledge transfer opportunities to farmers, employees, and the community. In addition, employees are entitled to reduced fees for the education of their children at SEKEM's Steiner or Waldorf schools,[5] while free courses are provided for illiterate employees. Healthcare is available for employees in SEKEM Health Centers.

Professor Abouleish's vision was to create a comprehensive holistic business venture, based on a synthesis of the Islamic values of equitable business and social responsibility and the anthroposophy of Rudolf Steiner[6] that would promote sustainable agriculture and enable employees and farming communities to improve their living conditions, health, education, and quality of life. When the project was first launched, he planted 120,000 casuarina, eucalyptus, and Persian lilac seedlings, engaged the internationally renowned Egyptian architect, Hassan Fathy, to design traditional adobe housing, and engaged and housed the native Bedouin residents. Some 43 years later, his vision has resulted in 684 acres of desert being reclaimed and converted to agricultural use with a 90% reduction in artificial fertilizers and pesticides and a 30% increase in the production of Egyptian cotton.

In 2003, Dr. Abouleish received the Right Livelihood Award (also known as the Alternative Nobel Prize) from the King and Queen of Sweden in recognition of his creation of a twenty-first-century business model that provided a practical and exemplary solution to one of the challenges of the twenty-first century. Clearly the solution Dr. Abouleish identified and adopted combined business, eco, humane, and social entrepreneurship[7] and Kirby and El-Kaffass (2021) argue that this is the way entrepreneurs will need to operate in the future if the mistakes of earlier generations are not to be repeated. Given the interconnectivity of all elements in the economic system, it is inevitable that any change in the state of one element will require or bring about change, to a greater or lesser extent, in the other connected elements. Dr. Abouleish recognized this as did the Right Livelihood Award Foundation. In its award citation, the foundation stated:

> Sekem (Egypt) shows how a modern business can combine profitability and engagement in world markets with a humanistic and spiritual approach to people and respect for the natural environment. The Jury sees SEKEM as a business model for the twenty-first century in which commercial success is integrated with and promotes the social and cultural development of society through the "economics of love."

Thus, the SEKEM initiative very much accords with the Harmony principles espoused by His Royal Highness The Prince of Wales (HRH The Prince of Wales 2012). The prince argues that

---

5 These schools provide a holistic approach to education by developing the intellectual, artistic, and practical skills of their pupils.
6 A system of teaching and helping people to become as mentally and physically healthy as possible.
7 In 2004, the Schwab Foundation selected Dr Abouleish for its Outstanding Social Entrepreneur Award.

many of the modern challenges the world is facing are the result of disharmony with nature and contends that the solution lies in our ability to regain a balance with the world around us. It is not just nature and the environment that is important but the physical well-being of the human population – its health, nutrition, living conditions, education, spirituality, etc.

The future of entrepreneurship is to see problems and opportunities more holistically and harmoniously, rather than as unrelated elements in what is a highly interconnected system. This has led Kirby and El-Kaffass (2021) to introduce the concept of *harmonious entrepreneurship*, whereby entrepreneurship addresses the sustainability challenge by adopting a systems approach to the problem and applying the principles of harmony. The result is a more integrated, holistic business model that provides:

> a vision for the future that is rooted in ethical innovation that results in change and improvement in economy and society while not harming or damaging people or the environment. Preferably, it improves and replenishes them and leads to development that is both long-term and sustainable.

The solution adopted by SEKEM is thus clearly a harmonious business model. Larsen (2000) points out that

> we are accustomed to thinking of business in terms of discrete units with clear boundaries between them. We forget that these boundaries exist primarily in our minds or as legal constructs.

For this change to occur, the research into SEKEM shows that entrepreneurs of the future will not only have to be highly rated on the five dimensions of Caird's General Enterprising Tendency test (Caird 1991) and possess all 19 of the characteristics or traits identified by Timmons (1989), but possess additional attributes, such as the ability to see opportunities, courage, self-belief, persuasiveness, and networking capability. However, Villar and Miralles (2019) have concluded that sustainability entrepreneurs (as they call them) differ from more conventional entrepreneurs, particularly in their desire to change the world and it is necessary, therefore, "to acknowledge the orientation and motivation of the entrepreneur to include non-economic goals in the entrepreneurial ventures" (op.cit., p. 106). Additionally, the SEKEM case demonstrates the entrepreneur's

- Ability to think strategically
- Interdisciplinary competence (including commercial awareness)
- Understanding of systems thinking and the interconnectivity of the ecosystem
- Action orientation and practical capability
- Interest in recycling and saving waste
- Ability to motivate and empower others
- Spirituality

To educate students to become entrepreneurs capable of creating new harmonious models of business that address the sustainability challenge requires a change in both the content and pedagogy of learning, as Lans et al. (2014) and Ploum et al. (2018) have demonstrated. It is necessary not just to develop in the participants the attitudes and competences of the harmonious entrepreneur or to educate them in how to launch and grow a harmonious venture, but to introduce them to such issues as sustainability and its importance, the concept of systems thinking, harmonious entrepreneurship and the characteristics of the harmonious entrepreneur. Such topics have to be added to the traditional entrepreneurial education content/curriculum with the students developing their understanding and capability experientially and becoming "pragmatist" and "activist" learners as well as "reflectors" and "theorists" (Honey and Mumford 1986).

Learning does need to be experiential, however, and rather than working individually and in isolation, it needs to take place, preferably, in multidisciplinary teams. Not only does this educate the course participants in how to develop and manage an entrepreneurial team, but it creates a rich learning experience that enhances creativity, (Kirby 2003). As Penaluna et al. (2014) have acknowledged, students need to learn not only how to generate creative ideas but to sustain them. This requires the students to make lateral connections and engage in divergent thinking and the brain needs to be challenged to enable the student to express, ideational, expressional, and divergent fluency. They can do this by contextualizing the problem, using readily available materials, and linking different sources of information to help problem-solve.

As an example, following an introduction to harmonious entrepreneurship and sustainability, the first stage in the process is to learn about team formation, including selecting a leader and identifying the different team roles each member will play. This stage involves various self-assessment exercises including the Durham University General Enterprising Tendency test (Caird 1991, 2006) and Belbin's Self-Perception Inventory (Belbin 1981).

In the second phase the focus is on creativity (Bragg and Bragg 2005) and the teams begin to identify the sustainability challenge and their proposed entrepreneurial solution to the problem they have identified. This is often referred to as the ideation phase, a medical term referring to the forming of mental images. During this stage they start to pass through the storming phase of Tuckmann's (1965) five phases of team development. By the end of this stage, they have usually navigated the "forming" and "storming" phases, and reached the "norming" third phase before embarking on the "performing" phase. This involves:

- Undertaking the requisite research to construct a rigorous, realistic plan for the venture to determine its feasibility and commercial viability.
- Identifying the resource needs of the venture including potential sources of funding.
- Raising finance and launching the venture.

Throughout this stage the teams, which are basically self-managed (Kirkman and Rosen 1999), are monitored and mentored, required to network and keep records of their contacts, and encouraged to monitor on a "feel wheel" the periodic emotions of their members.

Once this stage has been reached it is not the intention that the teams will pass into the "adjourning" phase of Tuckman's cycle, but many teams do. Whether they break up or continue, the final stage is reflection – what has been learned, what skills have been acquired, and what are the members' plans for the future? Wherever possible a variety of performance evaluations is used, including peer appraisal, presentations to expert panels, and formal assessment of the written components of the program, particularly the business plan. Sometimes, especially in accredited award-bearing programs, this is not possible and more traditional assessment methods have to be adapted to measure the learning outcomes, requiring ingenuity on the part of program leader.

The ventures that are launched have the opportunity to be further monitored and supported with the aid of a negotiated learning contract (Stephenson and Laycock 1993) or agreement that becomes the action or learning plan for the next stage in the venture's development (Kirby 2007, pp. 34–43). It outlines what needs to be done or learned, and how and by when it will be, thereby giving the founder(s) ownership of the learning and ensuring it is relevant and timely.

While this is one example of the type of program that is required, it is not the only one. Addressing the problem from the perspective of sustainability educators, Hermann and Bossle (2020) recognize that research on education for sustainability has neglected to integrate entrepreneurial skills. Using content analysis, they then proceed to produce "a program for entrepreneurial-oriented sustainability education, providing a description of the educational focus, teaching-learning approaches, main themes, and external collaboration." The point to be recognized, however, is that different teaching models can and should be developed to suit the local circumstances – there is no one size fits all. The key, however, is for the educator to feel free to experiment and try new approaches. Some will work, some might not but it is only through the creation of a learning community where all of the members (both staff and students) feel able to innovate that progress will be made.

10.3   Barriers to Integration into the Curriculum

The intention is that this new approach to entrepreneurship and the sustainability challenge should be introduced into the curriculum not just for students of business administration or environmental studies but for all students, irrespective of discipline. As with entrepreneurship education, this will not be easy and will take time. Given the experience gained from introducing entrepreneurship into the curriculum, it might be expected that academics will argue that there is no room in the curriculum for such a study, that they will point to the fact that promotion is based in most instances on research not teaching, that they are not trained and/or equipped to teach the subject, and that it is not the purpose of higher education to do so. This resistance has to be acknowledged and overcome.

Unlike entrepreneurship education, education for sustainability is relatively new. Although recognized in the nineteenth century, the problems of global warming were not taken seriously until the last quarter of the twentieth century when the concept of corporate social responsibility was introduced in the US (Aqudelo et al. 2019), together with the first training courses. However, the term "sustainability" was not defined until the publication of the UN's Brundtland Report in 1987. After that, the first courses in sustainability began to emerge but it was not until May 2001 that the *Journal of Teacher Education and Training* (renamed *Journal of Teacher Education for Sustainability* in 2007) was introduced and 2003 before the first international sustainability educators conference was held in Latvia. So, it would seem that higher education has been similarly slow to respond, also, to the sustainability challenge, citing in the UK a crowded curriculum, irrelevance, limited staff awareness and expertise, and limited institutional commitment as the main barriers (Dawe et al. 2005).

Again, as with entrepreneurship education, commitment is found to be growing and an emerging imperative, though the response has again been patchy and not always based on the experiential learning approaches that are necessary to teach the subject effectively. This point has been recognized in Australia where it was found that the innovative pedagogies recommended for the effective teaching of sustainability were not practiced, the academics preferring and utilizing more traditional pedagogies such as lectures and tutorials (Christie et al. 2013). In a later study examining the slow take up of education for sustainability in Australian universities, Christie et al. (2015) discovered that Australian academics are supportive of education for sustainability for all university students but that it needs to be "framed within their disciplinary worldviews." By comparison, in a UK study of the attitude of sustainability educators their attitude toward entrepreneurship was found to be mixed though predominantly negative, the educators not seeing the contribution entrepreneurship can make to sustainability (Wyness and Jones 2019). In contrast, a study of UK entrepreneurship educators (Wyness et al. 2015) identified much good practice, but discovered that "embedded sustainability practice was typically limited and it was more typically regarded as an 'add on' to traditional entrepreneurial teaching." However, as Christie and Higgins (2020) contend such interdisciplinary learning opportunities need to be encouraged as they offer "a holistic view of learning and teaching that creates opportunities to engage in deep questioning that provokes each of us to consider what it means to live well and how we may continue to do so while facing contemporary complex global challenges."

10.4 Overcoming the Barriers

As Higgins and Thomas (2016) have recognized, "change in universities is commonly acknowledged as a complex process." However, given our knowledge and understanding of entrepreneurship in general and intrapreneurship in particular, it should be possible to create the sort of environments in which harmonious enterprise can flourish. For example, cognitive theory (Ajzen 1991) would suggest that for the changes to be made, it is necessary for "society" to have a favorable attitude toward such an objective, and for academics to believe that it is intrinsically rewarding and they have the ability to do it. Therefore, if these conditions can be created within our universities, then it should be possible to harness the enterprise that exists within the academic community. Although academics have been found to be, perhaps somewhat surprisingly, similar to entrepreneurs (Caird 1991; Hay et al. 2003), there needs to be a culture that is supportive of enterprise and they need to believe they have the ability to do it. Almost inevitably this will involve training in how to design, deliver, and assess such programs either as part of their induction program or through national or even international programs as occurred in the 1990s with entrepreneurship (Urbano et al. 2008).

Intrapreneurship theory (Pinchot 1985) suggests how a "favorable attitude" and a culture that is supportive of entrepreneurship might be developed and demonstrated within universities. On top of ensuring the academic staff has the knowledge and skills to develop and deliver such programs, it stresses the importance of formulating and implementing a high-level strategy that demonstrates the university's intent, makes it clear that this form of behavior is encouraged and rewarded, and creates and provides an environment that reduces the risks involved but encourages experimentation. To be effective, such a strategy needs to be endorsed by the university's governing body, incorporated into the strategy for the university, and, importantly, communicated to the staff. Ideally the academic staff should be involved in its formulation or, at the very least, consulted.

The theory also stresses the importance of senior management commitment and the need to identify and appoint champions within the organization. However, words are not sufficient. Not only do senior management need to model the behavior they wish to promote, but action on the part of the government will probably be necessary. Government should make it clear to management that it wants its universities to engage in the enterprise-sustainability agenda by educating and training its students in how to address the challenge, as well as by conducting research into the issues. It should also stress, possibly through its funding regimes, that these changes should not be bolt-on or short-term, but core and permanent, applying to all aspects of the curriculum and all the activities of the institution. Linked to this will be the need to move to multidisciplinary research and teaching, thereby breaking down the concept of the single disciplinary silos that tend to prevail in higher education.

While such intervention is necessary, universities should be free from close government regulation and encouraged to interact with their local communities, addressing the economic, environmental, humane, and social sustainability challenges they are facing. Through their research and teaching they should find local solutions to local problems and should develop, as a consequence, special institutional identities. However, this would suggest the need also to change the way university research and teaching is evaluated, assessed, and ranked.

10.5 Conclusion

The aims of this chapter were to examine the issues involved in introducing entrepreneurship and sustainability to the curriculum in higher education. As HRH The Prince of Wales (2012) has recognized "the many environmental and social problems that now loom large on our horizon cannot be solved by carrying on with the very approach that has caused them." A new approach to entrepreneurship and sustainability is required and Kirby and El-Kaffass (2021) have proposed that it is necessary to recognize the systemic nature of the problem and integrate not just the four main approaches to entrepreneurship (economic, eco, humane, and social) but the principles of harmony to produce a new business model that is not just about making as much money as possible (Friedman 1970) but about addressing Elkington's (1999) *triple bottom line of profit-planet-people*.

The resultant model, harmonious entrepreneurship, is based on the actual case of SEKEM Holding in Egypt. It demonstrates that entrepreneurship and sustainability are compatible and that entrepreneurship can impact positively on the sustainability challenge, and can address the UN's 17 Sustainable Development Goals. This has been recognized subsequently in the "Terra Carta" a 10-point sustainability charter intended to harness "the transformative innovation and resources of the private sector" (Terra Carta 2021). It was introduced by HRH The Prince of Wales at the One Planet Summit held in Paris on 11 January 2021 but though supported in practice, like harmonious entrepreneurship it is not widely accepted, yet, in academia. Like harmonious entrepreneurship, also, it recognizes the need to ensure a skilled workforce and "a cadre of leaders that are prepared to participate in a fair, inclusive, equitable and just transition towards a sustainable future." The message could not be clearer. The workforce of the future needs to be educated about the sustainability challenge and equipped with the knowledge and entrepreneurial skills to bring about change and improvement through enterprise. The resistance to entrepreneurship education and education for sustainability has to be overcome as does the failure of academics to appreciate that the two have to be taught together and incorporated into all disciplines not just environmental science and business administration.

This clearly has implications for universities, their role in the country's economy and society, and the way they are organized and managed. Entrepreneurship and sustainability have to be incorporated into the core mission of the university, traditional subject boundaries have to be blurred, and the product champions will have to be not just supported but recognized and rewarded. For this to happen governments might have to intervene to make clear what is expected of the university sector with respect to the sustainability challenge, and while this might involve incentive funding, it should lead to long-term change and not be short-term, bolt-on initiatives that end with the termination of the funding.

The COVID-19 pandemic has brought to the fore issues relating to sustainability and awareness of the need for a more sharing and caring economy and society (Ashan 2020). At the same time, it has demonstrated the leading role that universities can play in addressing such issues (Universities UK 2020) and illuminated the need for educated young people who can cope with uncertainty and find innovative solutions to contemporary problems. Thus, "the COVID-19 pandemic has not necessarily shown universities what they should do, but it has certainly shown universities what is possible" (O'Kane 2020) and hopefully this will have helped overcome the internal academic resistance to the concept of the entrepreneurial university and the changes that are needed if universities are to address the sustainability challenge, change public attitudes, and bring about the very necessary solutions to help resolve "the many environmental and social problems that now loom large on our horizon."

As this is a completely new approach to the sustainability challenge, there is clearly scope for further research. While the sort of paradigm changes required to achieve this have been recognized in entrepreneurship education for some time, their impact remains under investigation (Vanevenhoven and Liquori 2013), while in sustainability education the concept of learning for sustainability "as an integrated holistic concept is under-researched...and... further research is encouraged" (Christie and Higgins 2020). Further research is necessary also to explore and test the efficacy of the proposed approach in different socioeconomic contexts and physical environments. Perhaps, however, the most urgent need is for action research since, as Tilley and Young (2009, p. 91) have acknowledged, there has been an "explosion of sustainability rhetoric but far too little absolute progress in reducing (never mind improving) the environmental and social problems society faces today."

At all times, though, it should be remembered that, as the late Nelson Mandela acknowledged, "Education is the most powerful weapon which you can use for changing the world."

References

Abouleish, I. and Kirchgessner, M. (2005). *Sekem: A Sustainable Community in the Egyptian Desert*. Edinburgh: Floris Books.

Ajzen, I. (1991). The theory of planned behavior. *Organisational Behavior and Human Decision Processes* 50: 179–211.

Al-Dairi, A., McQuaid, R., and Adams, J. (2012). Entrepreneurship training to promote start-ups and innovation in Bahrain. In: *World Sustainable Development Outlook 2012: Change, Innovate and Lead for a Sustainable Future* (ed. A. Ahmed). Brighton: World Association for Sustainable Development (WASD).

Aqudelo, M.A.L., Johannsdottir, L., and Davidsdottir, B. (2019). A literature review of the history and evolution of corporate social responsibility. *International Journal of Corporate Social Responsibility* 4 (1): 1–23.

Ashan, M. (2020). Entrepreneurship and ethics in the sharing economy: a critical perspective. *Journal of Business Ethics.* 161 (10): 19–33.

Ashby, W.R. (1968). Variety, constraint and the law of requisite variety. In: *Modern Systems Research for the Behavioural Scientist* (ed. W. Buckley). Chicago ill: Aldine Publishing Co.

Belbin, M. (1981). *Management Teams: Why they Succeed or Fail*. Oxford: Butterworth-Heinemann.

Birch, D.L. (1979). *The Job Generation Process*. Massachusetts: MIT Program on Neighbourhood and Regional Change.

Bragg, M. and Bragg, A. (2005). *Developing New Business Ideas: A Step-by-Step Guide to Creating New Business Ideas Worth Backing*. FT/Prentice Hall.

Caird, S. (1991). The enterprising tendency of occupational groups. *International Small Business Journal.* 9 (4): 75–81.

Caird, S. (2006). Appendix: GET test 2. In: *Entrepreneurship and Innovation: A Manager's Perspective* (ed. T. Mazzarol), 247–266. Prahan, Vic: Tilde University Press.

Cannavacciuola, L., Capaldo, G., Esposito, G. et al. (2006). To support the emergence of academic entrepreneurs: the role of business plan competitions. In: *International Entrepreneurship: Issues and Newness* (ed. A. Fayolle and H. Klandt). Cheltenham: Edward Elgar.

Chia, R. (1996). Teaching paradigm shifting in management education: university business schools and the entrepreneurial imagination. *Journal of Management Studies* 33 (4): 40.

Christie, B. and Higgins, P. (2020). The educational outcome of learning for sustainability: A brief review of literature. University of Edinburgh Moray School of Education: Outdoor and Environmental Education.

Christie, B.A., Miller, K., Cooke, R., and White, J.G. (2013). Environmental sustainability in higher education how do academics teach? *Environmental Education Research.* 19 (3): 385–414.

Christie, B.A., Miller, K., Cooke, R., and White, J.G. (2015). Environmental sustainability in higher education; what do academics think? *Environmental Education Research.* 21 (5): 655–686.

Dawe, G., Jucker, R., and Martin, S. (2005). *Sustainable Development in Higher Education: Current Practice and Future Developments: A Report for the Higher Education Academy.* York: Higher Education Academy.

De Bono, E. (1970). *Lateral Thinking: Creativity Step-by-Step.* New York: Harper and Row.

Elkington, J. (1999). *Cannibals with Forks: The Triple Bottom Line of 21st Century Business.* Capstone.

Erkkila, K. (2000). *Enterprise Education: Mapping the Debates in the United States, United Kingdom and Finland.* London: Garland.

Etzkowitz, H. (2003). Research groups as "quasi firms"; the invention of the entrepreneurial university. *Research Policy* 32: 112.

European Commission (2008). *Entrepreneurship in Higher Education, Especially within Non-business Studies: Final Report of the Expert Group.* Brussels: The Commission.

Fayolle, A. (2007a). *Handbook of Research in Entrepreneurship Education, Volume 1: A General Perspective.* Cheltenham: Edward Elgar.

Fayolle, A. (2007b). *Handbook of Research in Entrepreneurship Education, Volume 2: Contextual Perspectives.* Cheltenham: Edward Elgar.

Fayolle, A. and Gailly, B. (2008). From craft to science. *Journal of European Industrial Training.* 32 (7): 569–593.

Fayolle, A. and Klandt, H. (2006). *International Entrepreneurship Education: Issues and Newness.* Cheltenham: Edward Elgar.

Friedman, M. (1970). The social and ethical responsibility of business is to increase its profits. *New York Times* (13 September) pp. 122–126.

Gailly, B. (2006). Can you teach entrepreneurs to write their business plan? An empirical evaluation of business plan competitions. In: *International Entrepreneurship: Issues and Newness* (ed. A. Fayolle and H. Klandt). Cheltenham: Edward Elgar.

Gawel, A. (2012). Entrepreneurship and sustainability: do they have anything in common? *Poznan University of Economics Review.* 12 (1): 5–16.

Greene, P.G. and Rice, M.P. (2007). *Entrepreneurship Education.* Cheltenham: Edward Elgar.

Hall, J.K., Daneke, G.A., and Lenox, M.J. (2010). Sustainable development and entrepreneurship: past contributions and future directions. *Journal of Business Venturing.* 25 (5): 439–434.

Hay, D.B., Butt, F., and Kirby, D.A. (2003). Academics as entrepreneurs in a UK University. In: *The Enterprising University: Reform, Excellence and Equity* (ed. G. Williams). Buckingham: The Society for Research into Higher Education and Open University Press.

Henry, C., Hill, F., and Leitch, C. (2005). Entrepreneurship education and training: can entrepreneurship be taught? Part II. *Education + Training.* 47 (3): 158–169.

Hermann, R.R. and Bossle, M.B. (2020). Bringing an entrepreneurial focus to sustainability education: a teaching framework based on content analysis. *Journal of Cleaner Production* 246: https://doi.org/10.1016/j.jclepro.2019.119038.

Higgins, B. and Thomas, I. (2016). Education for sustainability in universities: challenges and opportunities for change. *Journal of Environmental Education* 32 (1): 91–108.

Honey, P. and Mumford, A. (1986). *Using your Learning Styles.* Maidenhead: Peter Honey.

HRH The Prince of Wales (2012). *Harmony: A New Way of Looking at our World.* London: Harper Collins.

Kim, K., El Tarabishy, A., and Bae, Z. (2018). Humane entrepreneurship: how focusing on people can drive a new era of wealth and quality job creation in a sustainable world. *Journal of Small Business Management* 56 (Suppl. 1): 10–29.

Kirby, D.A. (2003). *Entrepreneurship.* Maidenhead: McGraw-Hill.

Kirby, D.A. (2006). Entrepreneurship education: can business schools meet the challenge? In: *International Entrepreneurship Education: Issues and Newness* (ed. A. Fayolle and H. Klandt). Cheltenham: Edward Elgar Publishing Ltd.

Kirby, D.A. (2007). Changing the entrepreneurship education paradigm. In: *Handbook of Research in Entrepreneurship Education, Volume 1: A General Perspective* (ed. A. Fayolle). Cheltenham: Edward Elgar Publishing Ltd.

Kirby, D.A. and El-Kaffass, I. (2021). Harmonious entrepreneurship – a new approach to the challenge of global entrepreneurship. *World Journal of Entrepreneurship, Management and Sustainable Development* 17 (4): 846–855.

Kirkman, B.L. and Rosen, B. (1999). Beyond self-management. Antecedents and consequences of team empowerment. *Academy of Management Journal* 42: 58–74.

Lans, T., Blok, V., and Wesselink, R. (2014). Learning apart together: towards an integrated framework for sustainable entrepreneurship competence in higher education. *Journal of Cleaner Production* 62: 34–47.

Larsen, A. (2000). Sustainable innovation through an entrepreneurship lens. *Business Strategy and the Environment.* 9 (5): 304–317.

MacDonald, R. and Coffee, F. (1991). *Risky Business: Youth and the Enterprise Culture*. London: Routledge.

Mair, J. and Seelos, C. (2006). The SEKEM initiative: a holistic vision to develop people. In: *The New Social Entrepreneurship: What Awaits Social Entrepreneurial Ventures?* (ed. F. Perrini). Cheltenham: Edward Elgar.

McNay, I. (2002). The E-factors and organisation cultures in British universities. In: *The Enterprising University: Reform, Excellence and Equity* (ed. G. Williams). Buckingham: The Society for Research into Higher Education and Open University Press.

NCEE (2020). *Unlocking Entrepreneurship in Education: University Heads of Enterprise Report 2020: An Annual Survey of Enterprise in Higher Education*. Coventry: NCEE.

Nieuwenhuizen, C. and Groenwald, D. (2004). Entrepreneurship training and education needs as determined by the brain preference profiles of successful, established entrepreneurs. Paper presented at the Internationalising Entrepreneurship Education and Training Conference (IntEnt 2004), Naples (5–7 July 2004).

O'Kane, C. (2020). Universities' chance to practise what they teach. *Newsroom Opinion Piece* (8 May, updated 8 October). https://www.newsroom.co.nz/ideasroom/1156977/universities-chance-to-practise-what-they-teach (accessed 25 November 2021).

Penaluna, K., Penaluna, A., Jones, C., and Matlay, H. (2014). When did you last predict a good idea. Exploring the case of assessing creativity through learning outcomes. *Industry and Higher Education* 28 (6): 399–410.

Pinchot, G. (1985). *Intrapreneuring*. New York: Harper and Row.

Ploum, L., Blok, V., Lans, T., and Omta, O. (2018). Towards a validated competence framework for sustainable entrepreneurship. *Organization & Environment.* 31 (2): 113–132.

Potter, J. (2008). *Entrepreneurship and Higher Education*. Paris OECD.

Schaltegger, S., Hansen, E.G., and Ludeke-Freund, F. (2016). Business models for sustainability: origins, present research and future avenues. *Organization & Environment.* 29 (1): 3–10.

Schumpeter, J.A. (1943). *Capitalism, Socialism and Democracy*. London: Allen and Unwin.

Stephenson, J. and Laycock, M. (1993). *Using Learning Contracts in Higher Education*. London: Kogan Page.

Terra Carta (2021). Terra Carta: For nature, people & planet. https://www.sustainable-markets.org/TerraCarta_summarium_Jan11th2021.pdf (accessed 25 November 2021).

Tilley, F. and Young, W. (2009). Sustainability entrepreneurs–could they be the true wealth generators of the future? *Greener Management International* 55: 79–92.

Timmons, J.A. (1989). *The Entrepreneurial Mind*. Andover MA: Brick House Publishing.

Tuckmann, B.W. (1965). Development sequence in small groups. *Psychological Bulletin.* 63: 384–399.

Universities UK (2020). *How Universities Are Helping Fight COVID-19.* London: Universities UK.

Urbano, D., Aponte, M., and Toledano, N. (2008). Doctoral education in entrepreneurship: a European case study. *Journal of Small Business and Enterprise Development.* 15 (2): 336–334.

Vanevenhoven, J. and Liquori, W. (2013). The impact of entrepreneurship education: introducing the entrepreneurship education project. *Journal of Small Business Management.* 51 (3): 315–328.

Vesper, K. and Gartner, W. (1998). *University Entrepreneurship Programs Worldwide.* Los Angeles: The University of South Carolina.

Villar, E.B. and Miralles, F. (2019). Sustainable entrepreneurship in response to grand challenges: what do we know and how do we move forward? *DLSU Business and Economics Review.* 28 (3): 102–111.

Von Bertalanffy, L. (2015). *General Systems Theory: Foundations, Development, Applications.* George Brazillier.

West, G.P., Gatewood, E.J., and Shaver, K.G. (2009). *Handbook of University-Wide Entrepreneurship Education.* Cheltenham: Edward Elgar Publishing Ltd.

Wyness, I. and Jones, P. (2019). Boundary crossing ahead: perspectives of entrepreneurship by sustainability educators in higher education. *Journal of Small Business and Entrepreneurship.* 31 (3): 183–200.

Wyness, L., Jones, P., and Klapper, R. (2015). Sustainability: what the entrepreneurship educators think. *Education + training* 57 (8/9): 834–852.

11

Sustaining Place Transformations in Urban Design Education: Learning and Teaching Urban Density, Mix, Access, Public/Private Interface, and Type

Hesam Kamalipour and Nastaran Peimani

11.1 Introduction

In this chapter, we discuss how urban design education can effectively engage with the key concepts of density, mix, access, public/private interface, and type in relation to how places work. We begin from the view that sustaining place transformations relies on a sophisticated understanding of not only each of these urban design concepts but also the complex relations between them. The main question is about the ways in which learning and teaching these concepts can be incorporated in urban design education. In what follows, we first reflect on urban design as a field in the process of becoming, with a focus on the dynamics of its education and its multiple pedagogies. Following a brief discussion of certain key concepts in urban design, including density, mix, access, public/private interface, and type, we draw on our experience of teaching the Urban Design Foundation module as a part of the MA (Masters) Urban Design program at Cardiff University to elaborate on how these key concepts can be incorporated in urban design education.

A range of urban design concepts can be potentially discussed in relation to urban design education. Yet, it is beyond the scope of this chapter to provide comprehensive coverage in this regard. In this chapter, we draw on our experience of addressing the concepts of urban density, mix, access, public/private interface, and type, among others, in the context of urban design education. We primarily build upon the works of Dovey (2016), Dovey et al. (2018), and Dovey and Pafka (2020) regarding the discussion of these key urban design concepts. The relations between density, mix, and access have been previously articulated as "the urban DMA" by Dovey and Pafka (2020). Our attempt here is to further develop this articulation by incorporating the concepts of public/private interface and type. We will then draw on our experience of deploying these concepts in the context of urban design education to discuss the ways in which built environment professions can effectively engage with sustaining place transformations. We argue that a nuanced understanding of density, mix, access, public/private interface, and type, as well as their synergies and interrelations, can play a key role in enabling urban design scholars and practitioners to critically engage with place transformations.

This chapter is related to the United Nations Sustainable Development Goal 11 (Sustainable Cities and Communities) with a particular focus on urban design education. Our attempt here is to cautiously approach the concept of sustainability. Considering its broad scope and the

The Wiley Handbook of Sustainability in Higher Education Learning and Teaching, First Edition.
Edited by Kelum A. A. Gamage and Nanda Gunawardhana.
© 2022 John Wiley & Sons, Inc. Published 2022 by John Wiley & Sons, Inc.

range of issues it aims to incorporate, we begin from the view that sustainable development can be considered as a "contested concept" (Jacobs 1999). Our use of the term "sustain" as a verb in this chapter is primarily to highlight the ways in which place transformations can be enhanced by providing a better understanding of how urban density, mix, access, public/private interface, and type work in cities. Sustainability, like place, can be considered as a work-in-progress. We argue that while contextual dimensions such as economic, political, social, and cultural aspects have impacts on how different places work, we cannot simply reduce place transformations to such underlying factors. Valorizing the macro scale and assuming such underlying processes as the key factors often run the risk of taking space for granted and further overlooking the spatialities of place transformations. We argue that space is by no means instrumental when it comes to urban design interventions.

We adopt assemblage thinking as a theoretical lens, which can work as a toolkit to explore how different places work across scales and contexts with the view to avoiding forms of reductionism, including macro and micro reductionism, and explore the relations between different elements. There is an emerging body of knowledge adopting assemblage thinking in relation to urban design (Dovey 2010; Dovey 2016; Kamalipour and Peimani 2015). Assemblage thinking can be articulated at the intersections between the two axes of territorialization/deterritorialization and spatiality/sociality. Each axis can then resonate with a set of twofold conceptions. For example, the axis of territorialization/deterritorialization can resonate with other twofold conceptions, including informal/formal, network/hierarchy, smooth/striated, rhizome/tree, becoming/being, and destabilization/stabilization, among others. The spatiality/sociality axis can also resonate with materiality/expression, among others. When it comes to transforming places, assemblage thinking reminds us to avoid reducing places to essences and/or a set of imagined causal relationships at a given scale. In their seminal works, Alexander (1965) argued against reducing cities to tree-like structures and Jacobs (1961) elaborated on the significance of exploring the relations between different elements to provide a nuanced understanding of how cities work. Sustaining place transformations can be considered as a process working along the axis of spatiality and sociality on the one hand and the axis of territorialization/deterritorialization on the other.

11.2 Urban Design and Its Multiple Pedagogies

Urban design is an evolving yet contested field subject to appropriation and modification by a broad range of disciplines. It is an evolving field in the sense that its domains and territories gradually develop and adapt over time. It is also a contested field in the sense that it inevitably has some overlapping interests and challenges with a range of other related fields such as architecture, landscape architecture, urban planning, urban studies, and geography. Urban design can arguably become many things to many people. Depending on the variety of departure points, urban design is also subject to forms of appropriation and modifications by a variety of disciplines and scholars. In this chapter, we begin from the view that urban design is a multiplicity and a field in the process of becoming (Kamalipour and Peimani 2019). We also point to how urban design works inevitably as a transdisciplinary field of intersecting disciplines.

Urban design can be explored in relation to its multiple dimensions. The morphological dimension and functional dimension are among the key dimensions of urban design (Carmona et al. 2003). Exploring the ways in which *urban morphology* and *functional mix* work has also been among the primary trajectories of research in urban design. A sophisticated understanding of the ways urban morphology and functional mix work in cities is critical in developing effective approaches to place transformations. There is an extensive body of knowledge focusing on urban morphology and typology (Kropf 2017; Moudon 1997; Scheer 2017). There are also substantive relations between urban morphology and urban design. Our engagement with certain aspects of urban morphology in this chapter is primarily related to the critical role of space in generating and sustaining social, environmental, cultural, and economic values. It has been discussed that urban design can potentially add value by strengthening economic viability, reinforcing social benefits, and fostering environmentally concerned initiatives (Carmona et al. 2002, p. 80).

We begin from the view that the urban design process, thinking, and practice are interrelated, and urban design education can prepare future urban design scholars and practitioners to effectively engage with urban transformation processes by developing a range of relevant skills. Urban design is a relatively new discipline struggling to justify its scope, specify its role, and outline its territories in relation to theory and practice. As an evolving field, urban design has also been appropriated by a range of other disciplines. It is critical to respond to its ambiguities by reaching a relatively broad definition of urban design as a conscious process and a multidisciplinary activity that engages with how the built environment can be shaped and managed across different scales (Madanipour 1997). The articulations of urban design either as a large-scale architecture or small-scale planning can be problematic, as urban design interventions often cut across multiple scales and dimensions.

The challenge of defining the scope of urban design has also been reflected in the ways in which its education and pedagogy have been framed over time. Urban design education has primarily engaged with those urban issues related to quality that could not be effectively addressed by other professions (Butina Watson 2016, p. 545). An articulation of urban design focusing on its architectural and artistic aspects can potentially put more emphasis on studio teaching and forms of creative design research. Approaching urban design from a geography and planning perspective can also be reflected in a mix of lecture, workshop, and seminar modes of teaching delivery with a particular focus on critical thinking, urban theory, policy, governance, and development, among others. An engineering approach to the field can also put more emphasis on its scientific relevance and rigor using a mix of lecture, workshop, and seminar modes of teaching delivery. Approaching urban design from a landscape approach can also be reflected in the studio teaching with a thematic engagement with public open space, green infrastructure, and ecological design, to name a few. As a field of intersecting disciplines, urban design pedagogy is inevitably multiple as its education extends across different fields such as architecture, urban planning, and landscape, as well as multiple disciplines such as politics, urban studies, economics, and sociology.

11.3 The Urban Density, Mix, Access, Public/Private Interface, and Type

11.3.1 Density

The concept of density in urban research primarily indicates the relationships between an area and certain entities such as dwellings, people, and floor space (Berghauser Pont and Haupt 2010). Density has been largely addressed in urban theory and practice, yet poor understanding and confusion about this concept have led to various applications (Berghauser Pont and Haupt 2010; Nes et al. 2012). As one of the keys 5 Ds – density, design, distance to transit, destination accessibility, and diversity – density has also gained popularity over the past decade for investigating the ways in which the built environment can have impacts on travel behavior (Ewing and Cervero 2010). Nevertheless, it has been argued that despite the wide range of research on density, there have been fewer attempts that could compare different measures of urban density and connect them with urban design research (Dovey and Pafka 2014). The work of Jacobs (1961) has been seminal to the understanding of the links between dwelling, internal, and streetlife densities. In her work, density is identified as a key condition for urban diversity. She takes this further by arguing that a density of nearly 250 dwellings per hectare is a necessary yet insufficient condition that encourages a high volume of streetlife and walkable access to mixed-use urban developments. She also suggests a high lot coverage of 60–80%, suggesting that densely built, low-rise urban morphologies can bring more people out into the streets relative to high-rise modern developments.

"Spacematrix" has been proposed as a three-dimensional model of density with a view that a single measure of density cannot fully describe city areas (Berghauser Pont and Haupt 2010). In this definition, urban density has been identified as a multiscale and multivariate phenomenon, incorporating the correlations between network density, floor area ratio, and land coverage. These measures describe the typomorphology of urban areas, capturing the building types and street patterns. Berghauser Pont and Haupt (2010) use a two-dimensional representation of the model (Spacemate) as the three-dimensional projection was not useful. Hence, they added a set of co-dependent measures including building height, open space ratio, and the size of urban blocks to the FSI/GSI Spacemate, which could facilitate the representation of the correlations between built density and urban form. The key issue here indicates that density is not a single measure that matters, but rather is a part of a larger assemblage wherein formal, functional, and social mixes as well as access networks and sociocultural contexts are of great significance. In this sense, Dovey and Pafka (2014) conceptualize urban density as a multiplicitous assemblage that cannot be reduced to any particular entity such as populations, buildings, or public open space.

11.3.2 Mix

Functional mix, or what is often considered as mixed-use or land-use mix, is about the key question of emerging flows and synergies between different uses of housing, working, and amenities (Dovey and Pafka 2017; Hoek 2008; Nes et al. 2012). Functional mix patterns in buildings cannot be conceived as independent from their forms. This resonates with how Conzen identifies functional mix as a basic layer in town plan analysis (Moudon 1994). The relevant literature has seen the call for exploring the potential positive or negative impacts of the various degrees and types of the functional mix, building age, and lot size on urbanity and socioeconomic productivity of cities. For Jacobs (1961), a mix of primary and secondary uses and different forms of co-functioning between them are necessary to enable streetlife vitality as it assures the flow of pedestrians over a given streetscape at different times over the course of the day. She elaborated on this, criticizing how spatial sorting and functional divisions were carved into the cityscape by the modernist urban zoning and design ideas, paralleled with economic segmentation and environmental inequity as more people seek to sustain their lives and livelihoods in largely polarized and poorly served cities. Notably, such modernist planning and spatial design that separated land uses also seemed to overlook the needs and desires of pedestrians, giving high priority to vehicles and, in the process, destroying the public space as a multifunctional, fluid, and relational space in many cities of the global North.

The thinking of Jacobs motivated a wave of urban planners such as new urbanists who stressed the significance of functional mix among the hallmarks of urban form that were believed to encourage local retail and transit connectivity across the metropolitan scale (Knaap and Nelson 1992) and foster pedestrian use within North American planning (Grant 2002). Since then, there has been an increasing interest in transport planning and public health to outline functional mix as a key condition for creating walkable neighborhoods that can also encourage physical activity (Cervero and Kockelman 1997; Frank et al. 2005). In the context of transit urbanism, a high degree of functional mix and a better integration of that with transport nodes have consistently been associated with more use of active transportation and fewer vehicle miles of travel in transit precincts (Belzer and Autler 2002; Chatman 2013; Krizek 2003; Peimani and Kamalipour 2020; Renne 2009). Urban precincts in proximity to transit nodes and corridors with the high density of retail activities are correlated with the greatest proportion and incentive for walking (Loutzenheiser 1997). As such, a sophisticated understanding of the functional mix patterns across different scales (i.e. from buildings and streets to the neighborhoods) and within various transit-oriented morphologies can contribute to a greater capacity to modify car-dependent cities and their public spaces. To design for transit accessibility is first and foremost to design for functional mix as it is linked to microspatialities and urban morphologies. Designing for functional mix in this framework then focuses on close proximity and intermixing of land uses.

11.3.3 Access

The question of accessibility is about the ways in which people navigate the urban movement network. Accessibility is a quality of the built environment shaped over time by a range of actions, including collective and individual as well as public and private (Handy 2019). Such actions might enable accessibility or constrain it. To design for accessibility primarily indicates designing for function. Nevertheless, function here cannot be seen as independent from form. This resonates with what has been called "movement economies" (Hillier 1996) where the visibility and nature of spatial relations condition movements, with the latter generating social and economic activities. The way in which the spatial configuration of street networks mediate urban flows and movements contributes to socioeconomic initiatives in the shaping of the built environment. The quality of accessibility differs markedly across different scales. At the neighborhood scale, a mix of different mobility modes, including pedestrian movement, become important. It is at this scale that building footprints, public open space networks, and bicycle and pedestrian facilities mediate accessibility. In this sense, Marshall (2005) outlines permeability as the degree to which a particular urban area is "permeated" by publicly accessible space. This concept refers to the ease of pedestrian movement within the urban fabric and ensures that pedestrians have multiple route choices between any two places. Accessibility has also been defined according to the two components of "travel impedance" and "destination attractiveness," where the former is about the cost of reaching a destination, and the latter is about the value of the activity at the destination (Handy and Niemeier 1997). Accessibility for Jacobs (1961) answers how permeability is enabled by short blocks, which allows for convenient access to diverse destinations. For Jacobs, public spaces with intensive interconnections promote visually diverse and varied streetscapes and economic productivity.

The quality of accessibility is also linked to the notion of "pools of use" coined by Jacobs (1961). This notion refers to the functions accessible within a walkable catchment of a certain place measured by time or distance. This is parallel to Handy's (2019) argument that accessibility is geared first and foremost to the functional mix patterns, the spatial distribution of human activities. In this sense, functional mix patterns mediate proximity to possible places of different types and as such have impacts on both the impedance and attractiveness aspects of accessibility (Handy 2019). The focus on accessibility and pools of use comes to the fore in transit urbanism research (Porta and Renne 2005; Schlossberg and Brown 2004; Vale 2015). Here, transport systems work in association with functional mix patterns to determine the travel time and distance between certain activities. In addition, transport systems also determine the range of possible modes to travel from one location to another.

11.3.4 Public/Private Interface

Public/private interface is primarily about the micro-scale relationships between private and public realms when it comes to how places work. It has long been established as seminal to the socioeconomic productivity of public space and embodied in urban design principles such as "edge effect" (Appleton 1975), "activity pockets" (Alexander et al. 1977), "active edge," (Gehl 1987) and "eyes on the streets" (Jacobs 1961). There is also emerging literature on public/private interface typologies (Bobić 2004; Gehl et al. 2006; Dovey and Wood 2015; Kamalipour 2017). Gehl (1987) and Jacobs (1961) outline the intervisibility of entries and building frontages as a formula to enable vibrant streetscapes and vitality in urban environments. This also lends itself well to the point made by Alexander et al. (1977, p. 600) that "if the edge fails, then the space never becomes lively." Such a transitional place is infused with human-environment relations at thresholds where human use and occupation interact with material form (Habraken 1998). It is a complex setting in its own right (Stevens 2007) with varying spatial porosity and permeability levels, which encompass forms of affordance – a set of capacities for use, control, and appropriation. Such public/private interfaces are therefore distinguishable from building facades as their sociospatial nature defies any reduction to material form and esthetic qualities. It is important to note that these urban street edges do not necessarily indicate physical boundaries or breaks in continuity, but rather they are spaces of becoming, a loose mix of two different realms: where private becomes public, the interior becomes exterior, enclosed becomes open, and the like.

11.3.5 Type

The notion of type is central to the understanding of building blocks and the language of urban morphology. What Moudon (1994) sets forth as "typomorphology" is primarily about the study of the built form based on the classification of typical structures and spaces across scales and over time. In urban design, the built environment demonstrates a rich set of recurring arrangements or configurations of certain elements such as street networks, the mix of plots and blocks, and the like. Such recurring patterns are broadly referred to as "types of form," which together with the process and hierarchy of interrelated forms, identify the morphological approach to the urban built environments (Kropf 2017). Scheer (2017, p. 89) discusses the ways in which types provide urban designers with "a common vocabulary, customary relationships, even materials and modes of expression." Type is an aggregation of interrelated parts that has emerged and evolved in a way that has certain formal characteristics or configuration of elements in common. A type resists any reduction to singular parts as it is the whole that makes any particular type distinguishable (Dovey 2016, pp. 69–70). Kropf (2017, p. 14) makes a distinction between a configuration and a type, where the former is about the "arrangement of parts" and "set of relationships," the latter has a level of "modularity and integration as a cultural habit." While each example of a type is relatively different, the configuration remains consistent regardless of the changes made to the singular parts of a certain artifact (Kropf 2017).

11.4 Case Study

Urban Design Foundation is a key module offered to urban design students at the postgraduate level in the MA Urban Design program at Cardiff University, which is jointly delivered by the Welsh School of Architecture and the School of Geography and Planning. The MA Urban Design program enables students to learn by deploying design, theory, and development and design control practices, which inform urban design processes. The aim of the Urban Design Foundation module is to provide an introduction to urban design analysis and thinking. It has typically been an intensive module running for about four weeks right at the beginning of the MA Urban Design program in the Autumn (Fall) semester. Lectures, small group workshops, and seminars have been among the key modes of delivery in this module. Urban analysis and mapping have also become integral to this module. As a part of this module in the 2020/2021 academic year, students undertook a comparative urban design analysis and individually submitted it as a structured report with a range of illustrations, including maps and photos, for summative assessment. Through assessed work, students could develop urban analytical skills and communicate urban analysis in relation to key urban design concepts using a mix of textual and visual presentations. The following were the learning outcomes of this module in the 2020/2021 academic year:

- Undertaking urban analysis using certain urban design concepts and analytical tools and drawing on relevant literature in urban design.
- Communicating urban analysis and mapping in relation to key urban design concepts through textual and visual presentations.
- Undertaking independent critical reading in the field of urban design.
- Critically discussing some key urban design theories and/or concepts.

In this section, we draw on our experience of delivering this module in the 2020/2021 academic year through a blended format, which incorporated a mix of face-to-face and online teaching and learning. The module started in November 2020 with over 80 students, the last teaching week was in December 2020, and the final submission was in January 2021. An innovative interim review was also designed and implemented in the last teaching week of the module to provide students with equal opportunities to receive timely, focused, and constructive formative feedback on their work-in-progress so that they could most effectively develop their work for summative assessment. Students were allocated specific time slots for individually presenting a copy of their work-in-progress and receiving feedback from the module tutors paired with staff members. The provided formative feedback was as much as possible aligned with the assessment criteria outlined and communicated in the assessment proforma. The interim review sessions took place live online via Zoom and in parallel to each other. There were two staff members and two tutors involved in the process of delivering the live online review sessions over two days. As such, each student presentation was followed by feedback from two members of the teaching team.

As mentioned, the module was delivered through a mix of face-to-face and online modes of delivery. The face-to-face component included small group seminars, and the online component incorporated a mix of asynchronous and synchronous learning activities and materials. A range of urban design topics was introduced in lectures and further discussed live online in small group workshops. Core lectures were the primary means for the online delivery of the academic content of the module. In addition, the module leader delivered small group seminars face-to-face with a particular focus on the discussion of the summative assessment of the module. Students were also provided with opportunities for formative feedback throughout the module to receive feedback on their work-in-progress from their tutors in small group workshops. In addition to lectures, workshops, and seminars, specific live online weekly discussion sessions were designed to further support students and address possible questions. A weekly drop-in session was also allocated for individual questions and informal discussions to support individual learners throughout the process.

Cardiff University's online platform, Learning Central, and Zoom were among the primary digital learning and teaching platforms used in the online delivery of this module. Learning

Central was mainly used for asynchronous learning and teaching activities, whereas Zoom was particularly used for synchronous learning and teaching activities. Module materials, including lectures slides, recordings, library resources, reading lists, schedule outline, and other supporting documents and links, became available on Learning Central to facilitate asynchronous learning. Students were able to review the key learning materials at their own pace. All live online sessions took place on Zoom during the teaching weeks of the module. Using such platforms for live online sessions provided individual learners with opportunities to use a mix of text-based and oral communications. In addition to a mix of online asynchronous and synchronous learning, face-to-face sessions were also designed and delivered in this module for students to enhance their learning experience.

The module incorporated a mix of formative feedback and summative assessment. The summative assessment of this module was designed to enable constructive alignment with the related learning activities and outcomes. The summative assessment was primarily about undertaking comparative urban analysis and mapping at a particular scale using the key urban design concepts of density, mix, access, public/private interface, and type, and further communicating the comparative urban analysis in relation to the relevant literature. A list of key references was provided, and students could access the related reading materials through the university library using reading lists on Learning Central. Students were expected to individually select two case studies in Cardiff and comparatively analyze them at the same scale in relation to urban density, mix, access, public/private interface, and type. It was critical to avoid reducing the urban analysis to a graphic presentation exercise. Instead, students were expected to demonstrate a sophisticated understanding of the key concepts, critically engage with the related learning materials, including the relevant lectures and readings, and discuss the comparative analysis in the context of related literature.

The summative assessment was eight pages in total. An indicative layout outlining the overall structure and order was also provided. The internal layout design was up to students, which helped to provide opportunities for creativity regarding the internal layout design and presentation. In addition to the comparative urban analysis and mapping at a particular scale using the specified key concepts, the assessment included discussing the relations between density, mix, access, public/private interface, and type in the context of the relevant references in the selected case studies. In the comparison and conclusion section, students were expected to critically compare the selected case studies based on the discussion of the relations between density, mix, access, public/private interface, and type, provide a concise summary of the key findings of their comparative urban analysis, and address the question of "so what?" in the context of the related literature. Students could virtually explore the selected case studies using Google Earth, Google Maps, Digimap, and Google Street View.

A detailed coursework brief document called "Assessment Proforma" was provided to outline and communicate the key information, including the mode and type of assessment, length of assessment, and its percentage contribution to the module, marking criteria, learning outcomes assessed, date of submission, marker, moderator, as well as feedback return date and method. It also provided specific instructions regarding case study selection, submission, structure, format, and referencing conventions. Providing such detailed and specific instructions could at once support students in developing their work for summative assessment and enable a degree of consistency in terms of the overall structure and format when it comes to assessment. The key references for this assessment were also listed in this document, and they were available through the university library. The Assessment Proforma document was made available on Learning Central prior to the commencement of the module so that all enrolled students could access it from the beginning of the module. In addition to an interim review to provide formative feedback before summative assessment, written feedback was also provided as part of the summative assessment using a consistent structure with a focus on substance, structure, style and presentation, sources/referencing, and considerations for future assessments.

In addition to the core learning materials of the module, key documents called "Weekly Module Maps" were also developed to support students on a weekly basis by outlining the primary learning and teaching activities in relation to indicative time commitments per week and specifying where the related material is located on Learning Central, what the primary takeaways are, and how the outlined learning activities are related to the assessment and learning outcomes of the module. The Weekly Module Maps were made available before the beginning of the module so that students could navigate through the module content, schedule, and the associated learning and teaching activities. They could also plan as appropriate and reflect on their progress and learning experience, particularly in relation to the module learning outcomes and activities. To enhance readability, the key learning and teaching activities were also mapped using consistent color codes across the relevant documents of the module.

11.5   Concluding Discussions

Place, as Dovey (2010) points out, can be considered as a sociospatial assemblage in the process of becoming. Change is often inevitable and at times required, and the agents of change are multiple. There is scope for the built environment professions, including urban design, to become critically engaged at the intersections of top-down and bottom-up processes of place transformation. The capacity of urban design, among others, is geared to its flexibility and adaptability and the ways in which it has become an evolving field. Urban design can also be understood as a contested field. It cannot be reduced to a large-scale architecture, and its engagement with urban form and morphology makes it distinctive from other fields such as urban planning and geography. Hence, urban morphology plays a key role in shaping urban environments, dealing with the spatial composition, access networks, and emergent urban intensity at different scales, generally through the instruments of design and planning codes. Urban morphology, in its broad explanation, involves the articulation of both urban form and structure, as argued by Marshall and Çalişkan (2011). When it comes to urban design interventions and transforming places, a sophisticated understanding of urban morphology is critical. There is often a link between poor design interventions and a limited understanding of how urban morphology works. In this chapter, we pointed to a range of key concepts, including density, mix, access, public/private interface, and type, which are specifically related to how urban morphology works in the processes of place transformation. Drawing on our experience of focusing on these concepts in the context of urban design education, we also discussed how different places could be comparatively analyzed against the key concepts of density, mix, access, public/private interface, and type. While our focus in this chapter has primarily been on the spatial aspects of place, it is critical to note that spatiality and sociality are interrelated in transforming places. In this sense, assemblage thinking has been a useful theoretical lens to understand the underlying processes of continuity and change in the city where various forces come together to make different places work. Such an integrative multidisciplinary approach cuts across any separation of sociality and spatiality and defies any reduction to the confines of any single discipline or research method.

While density, mix, access, public/private interface, and type can be explored in isolation from each other, the key point is that they work in relation to each other. In addition to understanding how each concept works, we argue that exploring the relations between them in urban design education is particularly important. Providing a nuanced understanding of these concepts in relation to each other can enable urban design scholars and practitioners to adopt a sophisticated approach to place transformation. What we have discussed in this chapter can also be considered as an example of a constructive alignment between learning outcomes, content, and assessment concerning these key urban design concepts. In this sense, we argue that integrating these key concepts in urban design education and enabling a constructive alignment in relation to assessment and learning outcomes can foster a critical engagement with urban design theory, process, and practice. Learning urban design in the context of studio teaching can also benefit from discussing these key concepts and the connections and synergies between them.

Understanding how different places work can also be linked to a range of underlying social, cultural, political, and economic dimensions, among others. It was beyond the scope of this chapter to discuss such underlying processes. Building upon the works of Dovey (2016), Dovey et al. (2018), and Dovey and Pafka (2020), our attempt in this chapter has been to extend the articulation of "the urban DMA" to incorporate the concepts of public/private interface and type as well. We also pointed to the significance of the urban density, mix, public/private interface, and type concepts in relation to each other. Drawing on our experience of teaching in the MA Urban Design program at Cardiff University, we have discussed how we addressed these key concepts in the context of urban design education. Regarding the urban design pedagogy, we have also pointed to the development of an innovative critique strategy to further support students by providing formative feedback on their work-in-progress before the summative assessment. This critique strategy to feed forward in urban design education has been discussed in further detail elsewhere (Kamalipour 2021).

In addition to the opportunities provided for formative feedback throughout the module, a specific interim review session was also designed and delivered in the last teaching week of the module with the view to provide students with opportunities to present their work-in-progress and receive feedback from their tutors and another member of staff. While the interim review session can work as an effective critique strategy to support students further to develop their works and receive timely and focused feedback and advice before summative assessment, such review sessions can be particularly resource-intensive and somewhat challenging to design and deliver in large cohorts. Two module tutors and two staff members were involved for two days to deliver this critique strategy. Although the review sessions were designed to be delivered in parallel, they still took two days in total. The parallel review sessions took place live online using Zoom, and this was initially considered in the design of this critique strategy. Delivering such parallel sessions face-to-face can be challenging, particularly when it comes to timetabling and booking appropriate physical spaces for such parallel learning and teaching activities.

While designing and delivering such critique sessions can be considerably resource-intensive in large cohorts, the value of such interim review sessions to provide timely and focused formative feedback cannot be overlooked. The importance of timely and clear formative feedback has been acknowledged in relevant studies (Shute 2008). For Sadler (1989), formative feedback can enable individual learners to reflect on their progress and performance. It is also critical to provide timely feedback that is constructive with a balanced mix of both positive and negative comments (Ramsden 2003). The capacities and limitations of formative assessment and feedback are yet to be explored in the context of urban design education. Reflecting on the progress being made would be as important as feeding forward in the context of urban design pedagogy with a particular focus on some key points that need to be addressed moving forward so that students can effectively develop their projects further before the summative assessment.

It is also important to address the challenge of the COVID-19 pandemic in this context. The Urban Design Foundation module was adapted accordingly and redesigned for blended delivery, incorporating face-to-face and online teaching and learning activities. The face-to-face component included several small group seminars. The online component included a mix of synchronous and asynchronous learning and teaching activities. While the core content of the module remained unchanged, the mode of delivery was adapted accordingly in response to the related policies, frameworks, and changing circumstances. The module was well received by the MA Urban Design students, particularly in terms of its content and delivery. The highlights regarding the module content include the range of learning materials about urban design analysis and thinking as well as reading lists. The key points regarding the module delivery are primarily about communication, style, and structure.

While face-to-face learning might be preferable over online learning in specific circumstances, certain aspects of online learning were also well received in the evaluation of the module. Online learning and teaching provided an opportunity for communication using a mix of writing and speaking in live online discussions and workshops. The availability of both synchronous and asynchronous learning materials and activities provided flexibility regarding how online learning and teaching could take place and the module materials could be accessed. It was also possible to watch and review the key learning and teaching materials, such as lectures, over and over if needed. The key learning materials were all accessible on Learning Central, which was the main digital platform hosting this module. Live online sessions took place using Zoom as the primary platform. Reading lists were also accessible online through the university library.

The challenge of access to the field was among the key limitations of this experience. It was impossible to undertake field site visits due to the COVID-19 pandemic and subsequent restrictions. Digital tools such as Google Earth, Google Maps, Digimap, and Google Street View have become the primary tools for exploring certain aspects of how the selected case studies worked in the city. While there might be critical limitations concerning the extent to which one could learn about how places work by merely relying on such digital tools, they can work as valuable resources shedding light on certain aspects of how different places work. They can also enable comparative studies focusing on the spatiality of place across different case studies and scales. While there were some critical limitations for exploring the sociality of place using such tools, one could still explore certain physical traces visible in the public realm.

The challenge of the COVID-19 pandemic has raised a range of critical questions regarding the ways in which learning and teaching activities can most effectively adapt in a state of uncertainty. Drawing on the experience of delivering the Urban Design Foundation module as a part of the MA Urban Design program at Cardiff University, we outline the following key considerations. Both online and face-to-face learning and teaching activities incorporate a range of capacities and limitations. We cannot simply establish a dichotomous distinction between online and face-to-face learning and teaching and select one over the other. The questions of communication, visibility, equity, and digital literacy are particularly at stake in this context. Online learning and teaching using digital platforms can enable simultaneous use of textual, verbal, and visual communications. However, the associated learning experience and engagement are yet to be explored before jumping to any conclusion in this regard. Visibility plays out in different ways across online and face-to-face learning and teaching, and the question of equitable access and digital literacy regarding digital technologies are paramount here.

The dynamics of visibility in online and face-to-face learning and teaching activities are particularly related to how the rights to see and to be seen can be negotiated in urban design pedagogy. The rights to see and to be seen are often taken for granted in face-to-face learning and teaching activities, as one seems to be inevitably inseparable from the other. In the physical classroom setting, one cannot often see others without being seen. Nevertheless, this is somewhat different in the context of online synchronous learning and teaching, where teachers and individual learners can select to see others without being seen. While this configuration may work in large-group live online lectures or discussions, it can become particularly problematic in small-group online workshops as it constrains the capacity to establish eye contact with students, which has been deemed as important for a successful online learning experience (Rapanta et al. 2020).

Equity in the context of online and face-to-face learning and teaching is about the extent to which individual learners and the teaching team have equitable access to the essential means and opportunities for effective engagement, particularly concerning digital technology and its literacy. Ensuring equitable access to a stable internet connection, appropriate hardware, and required software can become a significant challenge, particularly in synchronous online learning and teaching. As argued elsewhere (Peimani and Kamalipour 2021), face-to-face learning and teaching cannot be simply considered a more just option. Individual differences can still be overlooked, and preexisting inequalities can also become normalized or even intensified. While online learning and teaching might work as a more equitable alternative for those with limited access to face-to-face learning and teaching activities, on-campus and face-to-face learning can become a more equitable option for those with limited access to appropriate hardware and software as well as stable internet connection. This might also be the case for those with limited digital technology literacy.

While it might not be possible to entirely replace in-person field study visits with internationally accessible platforms such as Google Earth and Google Street View, there is much to learn about how places work using such online platforms. They can be particularly useful in at least two ways in relation to urban design learning and teaching activities. They can facilitate comparative studies across different contexts and work as a key source for analyzing urban form and streetscapes, among others. Nevertheless, the dynamics of visibility and coverage can be an issue of concern as one explores the extent to which different places have become visible through Google Earth and Google Street View. For example, informal urbanism has generally remained invisible on official maps (Kamalipour and Dovey 2019). Hence, there are limitations in terms of the types of places that can be explored using Google Street View, and the resolution may not be consistent across different places in Google Earth. Nevertheless, urban design education can become more effectively engaged with the capacities and challenges of such online platforms in addition to in-person field study visits.

Undertaking comparative urban analysis can pave the way for exploring how different places work in a global context across multiple scales. Sustaining place transformations relies on a sophisticated understanding of how density, mix, access, public/private interface, and type work in relation to each other in urban environments. Undertaking comparative urban analysis with a focus on these key concepts can provide a nuanced understanding of the complex dynamics of urban density, mix, access, public/private interface, and type across different places. Adopting such a theoretical framework for comparative urban analysis at given scales can provide a consistent structure for undertaking urban design analysis across different places in a global context. When physical access to fieldwork is impossible, certain publicly accessible tools, such as Google Earth and Google Street View, can be used as primary tools to ensure a degree of consistency regarding data collection. Such tools might be more useful to facilitate comparative urban analysis across cities of the Global North. Undertaking comparative urban analysis between cities of the Global North and those of the Global South might be more challenging using such tools due to variations and inconsistencies in terms of data coverage, resolution, and the like.

Similar to urban design as a field of intersecting disciplines, its education has become a work-in-progress being pushed to a range of directions depending on the ways in which the field itself is being defined. We argue that we cannot discuss urban design education in isolation from how the field is being defined and how various definitions might be contested. The scope and focus of urban design education are inevitably geared to the imagined boundaries and agenda of the field itself. Multiple articulations of urban design remind us that there are multiple urban design pedagogies as well. We argue here that it is critical to provide a nuanced understanding of the key concepts of density, mix, access, public/private interface, and type as well as how they are related to each other across different scales. To provide alternative scenarios and develop sound spatial design interventions, it is critical for urban designers to study and analyze how cities work. Exploring how cities work cannot simply overlook the dynamics of density, mix, access, public/private interface, and type as well as their interrelations across multiple scales. Nevertheless, it is important to note that such an understanding is necessary but by no means sufficient when it comes to sustaining place transformations.

Acknowledgments

The assessment discussed as a part of the case study section in this chapter was designed based on the multi-scale DMA analysis assignment in the Urban Design Theory subject, which was initially developed and led by Professor Kim Dovey and further by Dr. Elek Pafka at the University of Melbourne. The authors would also like to acknowledge the contributions of Lotte Hoeijmakers, Guanyu Wang, and Monisha Peter to the delivery of the Urban Design Foundation module at Cardiff University in the 2020–2021 academic year.

References

Alexander, C. (1965). A city is not a tree. *Architectural Forum* 122 (1): 58–61.
Alexander, C., Ishikawa, S., and Silverstein, M. (1977). *A Pattern Language: Towns, Buildings, Construction*. New York: Oxford University Press.
Appleton, J. (1975). *The Experience of Landscape*. London: Wiley.
Belzer, D. and Autler, G. (2002). *Transit Oriented Development: Moving from Rhetoric to Reality*. Washington, DC: Brookings Institution Center on Urban and Metropolitan Policy.
Berghauser Pont, M. and Haupt, P. (2010). *Spacematrix: Space, Density and Urban Form*. Rotterdam: NAi Publishers.
Bobić, M. (2004). *Between the Edges: Street-Building Transition as Urbanity Interface*. Bussum: Thoth Publishers.
Butina Watson, G. (2016). An international perspective on urban design education. *Journal of Urban Design* 21 (5): 545–547.
Carmona, M., De Magalhães, C., and Edwards, M. (2002). What value urban design? *Urban Design International* 7 (2): 63–81.
Carmona, M., Tiesdell, S., Heath, T., and Oc, T. (2003). *Public Places—Urban Spaces: The Dimensions of Urban Design*. Oxford: Architectural Press.
Cervero, R. and Kockelman, K. (1997). Travel demand and the 3Ds: density, diversity, and design. *Transportation Research Part D: Transport and Environment* 2 (3): 199–219.
Chatman, D.G. (2013). Does TOD need the T? *Journal of the American Planning Association* 79 (1): 17–31.
Dovey, K. (2010). *Becoming Places: Urbanism/Architecture/Identity/Power*. London: Routledge.
Dovey, K. (2016). *Urban Design Thinking: A Conceptual Toolkit*. New York: Bloomsbury.
Dovey, K. and Pafka, E. (2014). The urban density assemblage: modelling multiple measures. *Urban Design International* 19 (1): 66–76.
Dovey, K. and Pafka, E. (2017). What is functional mix? An assemblage approach. *Planning Theory & Practice* 18 (2): 249–267.

Dovey, K. and Pafka, E. (2020). What is walkability? The urban DMA. *Urban Studies* 57 (1): 93–108.

Dovey, K. and Wood, S. (2015). Public/private urban interfaces: type, adaptation, assemblage. *Journal of Urbanism: International Research on Placemaking and Urban Sustainability* 8 (1): 1–16.

Dovey, K., Pafka, E., and Ristic, M. (ed.) (2018). *Mapping Urbanities: Morphologies, Flows, Possibilities*. New York: Routledge.

Ewing, R. and Cervero, R. (2010). Travel and the built environment. *Journal of the American Planning Association* 76 (3): 265–294.

Frank, L.D., Schmid, T.L., Sallis, J.F. et al. (2005). Linking objectively measured physical activity with objectively measured urban form: findings from SMARTRAQ. *American Journal of Preventive Medicine* 28 (2): 117–125.

Gehl, J. (1987). *Life between Buildings: Using Public Space*. New York: Van Nostrand Reinhold.

Gehl, J., Kaefer, L.J., and Reigstad, S. (2006). Close encounters with buildings. *Urban Design International* 11 (1): 29–47.

Grant, J. (2002). Mixed use in theory and practice: Canadian experience with implementing a planning principle. *Journal of the American Planning Association* 68 (1): 71–84.

Habraken, J. (1998). *The Structure of the Ordinary: Form and Control in the Built Environment*. Cambridge, MA: MIT Press.

Handy, S. (2019). Accessibility-oriented Urban Design. In: *The New Companion to Urban Design* (ed. T. Banerjee and A. Loukaitou-Sideris), 585–596. London: Routledge.

Handy, S. and Niemeier, D.A. (1997). Measuring accessibility: an exploration of issues and alternatives. *Environment and Planning A* 29 (7): 1175–1194.

Hillier, B. (1996). Cities as movement economies. *Urban Design International* 1 (1): 41–60.

van den Hoek, J.W. (2008). The MXI (mixed-use index) as tool for urban planning and analysis. In: *Corporations and Cities: Envisioning Corporate Real Estate in the Urban Future*, 1–15.

Jacobs, J. (1961). *The Death and Life of Great American Cities*. New York: Random House.

Jacobs, M. (1999). Sustainable development as a contested concept. In: *Fairness and Futurity: Essays on Environmental Sustainability and Social Justice* (ed. A. Dobson), 21–45. Oxford: Oxford University Press.

Kamalipour, H. (2017). Mapping urban interfaces: a typology of public/private interfaces in informal settlements. *Spaces & Flows: An International Journal of Urban & Extra Urban Studies* 8 (2): 1–12.

Kamalipour, H. (2021). Feeding forward in Urban Design pedagogy: a critique strategy. In: *Effective Design Critique Strategies across Disciplines* (ed. S.W. Zollinger and J. Nyboer). Minneapolis, MN: University of Minnesota Libraries Publishing https://doi.org/10.24926/edc.107.

Kamalipour, H. and Dovey, K. (2019). Mapping the visibility of informal settlements. *Habitat International* 85: 63–75.

Kamalipour, H. and Peimani, N. (2015). Assemblage thinking and the City: implications for urban studies. *Current Urban Studies* 3 (4): 402–408.

Kamalipour, H. and Peimani, N. (2019). Towards an informal turn in the built environment education: informality and Urban Design pedagogy. *Sustainability* 11 (15): 4163.

Knaap, G. and Nelson, A.C. (1992). *The Regulated Landscape: Lessons on State Land Use Planning from Oregon*. Cambridge, MA: Lincoln Institute of Land Policy.

Krizek, K.J. (2003). Operationalizing neighborhood accessibility for land use-travel behavior research and regional modeling. *Journal of Planning Education and Research* 22 (3): 270–287.

Kropf, K. (2017). *The Handbook of Urban Morphology*. Chichester: Wiley.

Loutzenheiser, D. (1997). Pedestrian access to transit: model of walk trips and their design and urban form determinants around bay area rapid transit stations. *Transportation Research Record: Journal of the Transportation Research Board* 1604: 40–49.

Madanipour, A. (1997). Ambiguities of urban design. *Town Planning Review* 68 (3): 363–383.

Marshall, S. (2005). *Streets and Patterns*. London: Spon Press.

Marshall, S. and Çalişkan, O. (2011). A joint framework for urban morphology and design. *Built Environment* 37 (4): 409–426.

Moudon, A.V. (1994). Getting to know the built landscape: Typomorphology. In: *Ordering Space: Types in Architecture and Design* (ed. K.A. Franck and L.H. Schneekloth), 289–311. New York: Van Nostrand.

Moudon, A.V. (1997). Urban morphology as an emerging interdisciplinary field. *Urban Morphology* 1: 3–10.

Nes, A., Berghauser Pont, M., and Mashhoodi, B. (2012). Combination of space syntax with spacematrix and the mixed use index: The Rotterdam South test case. Paper presented at the Eighth International Space Syntax Symposium, Santiago, Chile (3–6 January 2012).

Peimani, N. and Kamalipour, H. (2020). Access and forms of urbanity in public space: transit Urban Design beyond the global north. *Sustainability* 12 (8): 3495.

Peimani, N. and Kamalipour, H. (2021). Online education and the COVID-19 outbreak: a case study of online teaching during lockdown. *Educational Sciences* 11 (2): 72.

Porta, S. and Renne, J.L. (2005). Linking urban design to sustainability: formal indicators of social urban sustainability field research in Perth, Western Australia. *Urban Design International* 10 (1): 51–64.

Ramsden, P. (2003). *Learning to Teach in Higher Education*, 2e. London: Routledge Falmer.

Rapanta, C., Botturi, L., Goodyear, P. et al. (2020). Online university teaching during and after the Covid-19 crisis: refocusing teacher presence and learning activity. *Postdigital Science and Education* 2: 923–945.

Renne, J.L. (2009). From transit-adjacent to transit-oriented development. *Local Environment* 14 (1): 1–15.

Sadler, D.R. (1989). Formative assessment and the design of instructional systems. *Instructional Science* 18 (2): 119–144.

Scheer, B.C. (2017). *The Evolution of Urban Form: Typology for Planners and Architects*. New York: Routledge.

Schlossberg, M. and Brown, N. (2004). Comparing transit-oriented development sites by walkability indicators. *Transportation Research Record* 1887: 34–42.

Shute, V.J. (2008). Focus on formative feedback. *Review of Educational Research* 78 (1): 153–189.

Stevens, Q. (2007). Betwixt and between: building thresholds, liminality and public space. In: *Loose Space: Possibility and Diversity in Urban Life* (ed. K. Franck and Q. Stevens), 73–92. London: Routledge.

Vale, D.S. (2015). Transit-oriented development, integration of land use and transport, and pedestrian accessibility: combining node-place model with pedestrian shed ratio to evaluate and classify station areas in Lisbon. *Journal of Transport Geography* 45: 70–80.

12

Sustainability of Innovations in Health Professions Education

Gominda Ponnamperuma, Asela Olupeliyawa, Madawa Chandratilake, and Kosala Marambe

12.1 Introduction

Education needs to change, depending on the needs of the learners, demands of the society, our evolving understanding of how humans learn, and the technology that delivers learning. Innovations have been the driving force behind such change. Innovations related to the planning, organization, delivery, and assessment are not unusual in health professions education. Some of these innovations have stood the test of time; some have not. In this chapter, health professions education innovations are categorized broadly into innovations in curriculum development and evaluation, teaching and learning, and assessment. The chapter first describes these innovations, tracing them back to their historical roots. Then, why they came into being, how popular and sustainable they were, and what led to their acceptability/sustainability or demise are analyzed. In doing so, an attempt has been made to highlight the typical features that contribute to the sustainability of innovations in health professions education.

12.2 Curriculum Development and Evaluation

The word curriculum literally means a track on which a chariot travels. Similarly, in education, the curriculum defines the pathway followed by educational programs. A curriculum is more than a syllabus, which usually defines the topics and related learning outcomes. The curriculum encompasses the educational strategies, teaching-learning and assessment methods, education environment, and almost anything related to the learning experience of students (Prideaux 2003). Curriculum design and development is a process of mixing theoretical underpinnings and pragmatism. It is influenced by cultural factors, resources, and attitudes and caliber of people involved. The success of the design and its sustainability depends heavily on the achievement of the right balance between these components. Curriculum evaluation, on the other hand, determines the effectiveness of the curricula, and the findings largely influence sustainability.

The Wiley Handbook of Sustainability in Higher Education Learning and Teaching, First Edition.
Edited by Kelum A. A. Gamage and Nanda Gunawardhana.
© 2022 John Wiley & Sons, Inc. Published 2022 by John Wiley & Sons, Inc.

12.2.1 Curriculum Development

In recent history, three major paradigms in curriculum development in medical education could be observed: Flexner model, problem-based approach, and outcome-based education. The inception of these innovation paradigms, their theoretical underpinnings, the key features, and the sustainability aspects are discussed in this section.

12.2.1.1 The Flexner Model

Until the nineteenth century, medical education was largely apprenticeship-based and the application of common standards to measure the competence of individual doctors was challenging (Barzansky 2010). Medical practice, on the other hand, was about remembering signs and symptoms and treating patients based on one's "experience" (Barzansky 2010). In an era where infectious disease is the major burden, several scientific advancements, e.g. the discovery of causative agents, the introduction of diagnostic investigations, and examination instruments like ophthalmoscopes, took place. These helped make hospitals scientific institutions and community-based medical care became institutionalized from its traditional form of "home visits" (Barzansky 2010). Doctors were expected to demonstrate a more scientific approach to patient management, higher diagnostic accuracy, and better patient outcomes than their "experience-based" practice. The apprenticeship-based model of medical education did not support the changing expectations and increasing demands. A need for a more systematic approach to medical education led to the formulation of curricular models with comparable standards. A curriculum is essential when standards are in place to measure success. Flexner's report, which was published in 1910, was the response to this felt need (Flexner 1910). Although the consideration of educational theories was less, Flexner's model catered to the need for standardization and systematization. With the implementation of this educational model, the number of institutions that produced doctors in the US was reduced considerably; these institutions could not withstand the standards expected (Barzansky 2010). The Flexner model identified three blocks in the content to be delivered in undergraduate medical education, namely basic sciences, applied sciences, and clinical sciences, which Flexner proposed to be built sequentially (Dornan 2005). Growing medicine into disciplines and subdisciplines started during the same period and this element was reflected in his curriculum model (Barzansky 2010). From an educational point of view, guiding teachers on defining the process of education, and determining the information to be delivered appeared to be the main role of the Flexner model curriculum.

The systemic and pragmatic approach of the model helped its existence for decades as the most popular framework for designing undergraduate curricula (Barzansky 2010). It was compatible with the parallel developments in medicine, e.g. development of disciplines, which was more familiar and understandable to medical practitioners than educational theories. On the other hand, the Flexner model largely focused on providing information. Many subject experts found it easier to identify the components to be included in the curriculum from their respective disciplines and to teach them to their students. The major drawback of this model, however, was the poor integration of subjects and limitless accommodation of the ever-advancing knowledge base of medicine. Integration of subjects and translating knowledge into practice were largely the responsibility of the learner under this model. The subject experts tended to expand their subject areas without knowing or considering their overall impact on the macro curriculum. The curricula tended to be overloaded and deviated from developing practitioners to subject expertise. The model tended to take the path of a disease-oriented approach to medical education rather than a patient-oriented approach, which is more useful in medical practice.

12.2.1.2 Problem-Based Model

In a problem-based approach to curriculum development, the curriculum is defined through a series of practice-based problems and the learning of basics through applied to clinical sciences takes place around these problems (Barrows 1996). The conventional approach of "rule and example" was transformed to "example and rule" in this model (Wood 2003). It was the first prominent paradigm change in curriculum design in health professions education after the Flexner model. It was introduced with no support of educational theory but a strong hunch of experienced medical practitioners who identified the importance of emphasizing the relevance and integration in medical education (Neville et al. 2019). These aspects had been poorly reflected in the Flexner model (Barzansky 2010). After its inception at McMaster University in 1967, it was embraced by 40 medical schools over 20 years with the approval of governing and professional bodies. This could be an indication of the acceptance of integration, and relevance, as some of the key principles of medical education. Later, some of the educational theories, which support this conceptual framework have been described, which included constructivist theory, social learning theory, experiential learning philosophy, adult learning theory, self-determination theory, and information processing theory (Onyon 2012).

One of the main features of the problem-based curriculum model is shifting the responsibility of learning from teachers to learners. This appeared to be a paradigm shift and, in the new paradigm, guiding the learner was the main role of the curriculum and facilitation of learning was the main role of teachers (Barrows 1996). The problem-based approach to curriculum design has helped improve the self-learning skills of learners (Aziz et al. 2014). It appeared to promote higher-order thinking and students' ability to apply theoretical knowledge in practice (Albanese and Mitchell 1993). It has improved the retention of knowledge among medical students (Dochy et al. 2003) and developed certain social skills relevant to medical practice (Albanese and Mitchell 1993). Problem-based curricula appear to develop the application of knowledge as opposed to the acquisition of knowledge (Hung et al. 2008). The problem-based approach to curriculum design has given rise to newer modes of assessment such as progress testing (van der Vleuten et al. 1996), which may be used more effectively for the development of knowledge than the traditional models of assessments. However, experimenting with newer assessments modalities that are compatible with the philosophy of problem-based model appear to have been scarce or at least to have progressed at a snail's pace (Gijbels et al. 2005). The change of assessments, especially at the national level, was key to determining the effectiveness of the new approach.

Students and graduates of programs who followed problem-based models, however, had underperformed in conventional institutional and national level examinations (Hartling et al. 2010). This resulted in reputational issues for institutions and acceptability issues about the program among existing and potential students. The sustainability of this curricular model was severely challenged by political, social, and societal pressures, which eventually led to the weaning away from the problem-based approach to curriculum design in some countries. The basic assumption of cognitive readiness of students for self-learning might not always be true in certain settings, which might also have contributed to their underperformance. In addition, the adoption of the concept without considering the cultural factors appeared to have affected its sustainability in some countries and contexts (Frambach et al. 2012). The essence of the problem-based model was about dealing with uncertainty, which did not appear to go down well by students from certain cultures (Frambach et al. 2012). In addition, cultural dimensions such as tradition – e.g. traditional roles of a "teacher" and a "student"; respecting and maintaining the power gap (hierarchy) – appeared to challenge the philosophy of this model (Frambach et al. 2012). As a result, although the problem-based approach has become less popular currently as a model for curriculum design, it has maintained its usefulness as a valued teaching and learning modality (see Section 12.3.1).

12.2.1.3 Outcome-Based Education Model

The emergence of outcome-based education in the mid-twentieth century was related to the behaviorist movement in education (Morcke et al. 2013). However, due to its reductionist approach, it failed to emerge as an approach to curriculum development (Morcke et al. 2013). In the late twentieth century, outcome-based education reemerged with a different theoretical outlook. The implementation of this model was triggered by the Carnegie report, which influenced many governing bodies around the world (Morcke et al. 2013). The need for addressing multiple dimensions in medical practice in education and accountability toward the public were the basic triggers for the adopting this approach (Morcke et al. 2013). Although the theoretical underpinning of the contemporary version of outcome-based education is still under debate, some authors claim that outcome-based education is based on developmental and constructivist theories (Brady 1996). Competency-based education could also be regarded as an alternative discourse for outcome-based education, as the two concepts have little or no conceptual differences (Morcke et al. 2013). Unlike the two previous paradigms discussed in Sections 12.2.1.1 and 12.2.1.2, outcome-based education in the new form defines the product and not the process (Frank et al. 2010a). The product defined different components of the curriculum such as selection of students, content, teaching and learning, and assessment methods (Frank et al. 2010a). The confusion about the old and the contemporary versions of outcome-based education can still exist. Some authors suggest that old and contemporary versions belong to three levels of defining outcomes (Donnelly 2007 citing Spady 1993).

- **Traditional outcome-based education**: The outcomes are defined at the level of subjects mostly similar to behavioral objectives. They are delivered in discipline-based teaching and students are assessed against them.
- **Transitional outcome-based education**: The outcomes are defined as higher-order competencies, such as critical thinking, problem-solving and communication skills, by moving away from teaching subjects.
- **Transformational outcome-based education**: The outcomes are focused on graduates' ability to perform complex tasks in the real-world setting that are related more directly to life. This is more futuristic and the transformational outcomes are not directly related to subjects or the curriculum.

The contemporary version of outcome-based or competency-based education is related to transitional and transformational levels (Donnelly 2007 citing Spady 1993). It claims to uphold some of the education principles which were observed in the problem-based approach: self-directed learning, integration, and practice orientation (Frank et al. 2010a). It appears that the models have been revised and re-revised in many contexts and cultural applicability has been explored (Frank et al. 2010b). This model is still in its implementation stage and more concrete evidence is yet to emerge. The sustainability of the outcome-based model is assumed to be compatible with evolving educational theories, pragmatism, and expectation of the public.

The concept of Entrustable Professional Activities (EPAs) has been introduced as a means of improving outcome-/competency-based medical education (Ten Cate et al. 2015). In EPA, tasks that a doctor is expected to perform in real practice are identified. These tasks can be related to one or more of the competencies of the program. For each task, the level of competence needed at different stages of training are defined in terms of performance indicators or milestones. When learners progress in the training program, they are assessed against the level of supervision. For example, while a novice is expected to develop into an expert in a particular task with one-to-one supervision, an advanced trainee might gain a similar level expertise with no supervision, by passing through the relevant, predefined levels of entrustability. EPAs have existed in postgraduate education in medicine for more than a decade and have helped translate competency-based education into practice (O'Dowd et al. 2019). The role of EPAs in the undergraduate health professions education, where performance of clinical tasks independently is not an expectation of a medical graduate, has been debated for a while. However, EPAs have been adapted for undergraduate medical education in certain contexts (Shorey et al. 2019). EPAs and similar developments provide promising signs of sustainability, as they improve the pragmatism of the concept.

As the above account shows, during the last century, three paradigms in curriculum development and innovation could be observed. The innovations are mostly triggered by the recommendations of the governing bodies and cater to the political or societal needs more than the evolution of educational theory. These innovations have proposed a change in educational culture and philosophical perspective. Poor compliance with these aspects, lack of consideration to cultural and contextual factors and ineffectiveness demonstrated by less appropriate evaluations have contributed to the poor sustainability of some of those models. On the other hand, pragmatism and support from governing bodies appear to be the key facilitators of sustainability.

12.2.2 Curriculum Evaluation

Curriculum evaluation is an important aspect of determining effectiveness and sustainability. The evaluations should not necessarily be conducted at the end a program. Rather, an evaluation plan should be formulated together with the curriculum and appropriate points of data collection should be determined prospectively (Nouraey et al. 2020). The basic steps of evaluation are very similar to research. However, the individualization of the methodological approach and case-specificity of findings occur more in evaluations than in research. Various models of evaluation combine these steps of evaluation into theoretical frameworks (Table 12.1) and a model that suits the plan of evaluation should be appropriately selected (Nouraey et al. 2020).

Every evaluation model aims to figure out the extent to which the program meets its goals. Models of evaluation have been studied to varying degrees and their strengths and weaknesses have been reported (Nouraey et al. 2020). Recently, how program evaluation models are conceptualized, designed, and manifested has changed; evaluators are more interested in concepts such as adequacy, effectiveness, efficiency, value, and competency than the cause-and-effect relationship between expectations and outcomes of the program (Rossi et al. 1993) which has led to an increased complexity of evaluation (Brewer 2011). For instance, Phillips' model (Phillips 2012) would be more appropriate for evaluating the effectiveness and efficiency of a professional development program conducted using the staff development funds in an organization, as it calculates the cost–benefit or the return on investment (ROI). This ROI model may not be appropriate to measure the effectiveness of an undergraduate program.

In terms of sustainability, certain models have gained more reputation than others, as they have been subjected to constant scrutiny of evaluators for their strengths and weaknesses (Nouraey et al. 2020). For example, evaluators have recognized that level 3 of the Kirkpatrick model (Kirkpatrick and Kirkpatrick 2006) is "forgotten and neglected," as professionals are focused on the first two levels, over which they have control, and the program managers are focused on level 4.

12.3 Teaching and Learning

Teaching and learning in health professions education has been well established from the time of Hippocrates, who mentored and taught his apprentices in the fourth century BCE by demonstration and example in the practice and ethics of medicine. Over the years, these teaching

Table 12.1 Commonly used models of program evaluation in medical education.

Model	Main components	Focus	Remarks
Summative and formative evaluations (Scriven 1991)	Summative evaluation (Purpose: to pass a judgment on the program)	On program design/ implementation/ process	An evaluation of the program should include both components as they are complementary.
	Formative evaluation (Purpose: to improve the program)	On the effectiveness of the program	
Kirkpatrick's four-level model of learning evaluation (Kirkpatrick and Kirkpatrick 2006)	Reaction	What do participants think and feel about the program?	The model has been used widely in health professions education for program evaluation. It has gone through several revisions to improve some of its aspects. However, the basic elements of the model remain the same.
	Learning	What have participants learned?	
	Behavior	Has what has been learned been transferred to practice?	
	Results	What is the impact at the macro level?	
Phillips' model of learning evaluation (Phillips 2012)	Cost and benefits	Return on investment	This model is also considered the fifth level of the Kirkpatrick model.
CIPP model (Stufflebeam 2003)	Context evaluation	What needs to be done?	This model incorporates both planning and implementation of the evaluation. It has been used widely in medical education.
	Input evaluation	How should it be done?	
	Process evaluations	Is it being done?	
	Product evaluation	Did it succeed?	

methods became formally established within institutions of learning, with a focus on classroom-based didactic training. However, in line with the saying by the famous Canadian physician and educator Sir William Osler, "To study the phenomenon of disease without books is to sail an uncharted sea, while to study books without patients is not to go to sea at all" (Osler 1901), apprenticeship-based clinical training also became a mainstay of medical education. As explained in Section 12.2.1.1, the famous Flexnerian reforms in North America during the early twentieth century (Flexner 1910) standardized medical education and made it university-based, while emphasizing the focus on biomedical sciences and laboratory-based training. It is with this foundation of long-held traditions and historical context that innovations in teaching and learning have evolved in health professions education, during the last century.

This section will introduce innovative teaching and learning strategies that have prevailed in health professions education after the time of Flexnerian reforms. It will outline their pedagogical underpinnings and relate these to the current evidence on their educational impact. Some key strategies that will be discussed are problem-based learning (PBL), work-based learning, reflective practice, community-based learning, and e-learning. It will also propose how some of these strategies may be useful to promote the theme of sustainability and planetary health in health professions education.

12.3.1 Problem-Based Learning (PBL)

PBL was introduced as a complete curriculum approach in McMaster University Faculty of Health Sciences by Howard S. Barrows in the 1960s, over 50 years ago (Schmidt 2012). The defining characteristic of PBL is a "problem," commonly a patient presentation. A small group of students is presented with the problem and a structured approach, to acquire new knowledge through analyzing and solving the problem. It has continued primarily as an effective teaching/learning strategy not only in the health professions but also in other fields such as engineering.

Based on theories of constructivism, where the learner constructs their own knowledge, some of the key educational principles that underpin PBL are to do with active student-centered learning, including collaborative learning and self-directed learning. These concepts are promoted through the structured approach used in PBLs. For instance, in the Maastricht 7-jump process, students are presented with the problem (the trigger) and are required to identify the key words of the trigger and subsequently discuss the learning issues related to the trigger. Then students collaboratively brainstorm and formulate possible explanations, summarize and systematically classify such information, and identify learning outcomes that they have already achieved and those they need further study on. Prior to a follow-up PBL session, students will engage in self-study to consolidate their learning and address the learning outcomes that have not been met. These processes activate prior learning of the students and promote deep learning in an active, collaborative, self-directed manner. The clinical relevance of the material discussed would promote integration of basic and clinical sciences and enhance student motivation. The teacher acts as a facilitator of learning, for instance guiding learners in identifying the learning issues, supporting them in building up the explanations, and providing appropriate learning resources. As evident in the above approach, the PBL process corresponds to the work of Jerome Bruner on discovery learning (Bruner 1961), where a problem can be the starting point of learning, and on scaffolding (Wood et al. 1976), where support from teachers and peers is necessary to focus learning.

Many evaluations comparing PBL to traditional instructional methods have been conducted in health professions education over the past few decades. They have evaluated outcomes related to scientific knowledge as well as generic skills post-intervention as well as after graduation, and many such findings are summarized in several narrative and systematic reviews (Albanese and Mitchell 1993; Gijbels et al. 2005). A synthesis of such reviews finds that the PBL process produces sustained improvements in students' long-term retention, clinically relevant knowledge, cognitive skills development, and self-directed learning and motivation (Strobel and Van Barneveld 2009).

PBL holds much promise as an effective teaching and learning method for sustainability education in the health professions. The value of using real-world problems to address sustainability issues is quite evident, and PBL has been proposed as a key strategy in preparing medical students to address climate change (Hamel Green et al. 2009; Bell 2010). For instance, during a PBL session where non-communicable disease risk factors in a person with a sedentary lifestyle are being discussed (e.g. driving to work), triggers and tutor guidance can focus learners on the environmental co-benefits that can be achieved by encouraging lifestyle changes that would reduce greenhouse gas emissions (e.g. cycling to work). The "problems" used as PBL triggers need not be limited to patient presentations. Scenarios based on natural disasters, such as the Indian Ocean tsunami, or diseases such as Dengue, can extend their focus beyond immediate management and mitigation to discuss the possible effects of climate change on such environmental phenomena.

12.3.2 Work-Based Learning

Experiential learning is critical for health professions education, particularly as much of the learning is situated in the clinical workplace. Traditionally, clinical training has been apprenticeship-based as explained in Section 12.2.1.1 with opportunistic teaching provided by senior physicians in the "medical firm," and likewise within their professional silos in other health professions. However, the culture in the clinical workplace is changing, where health professions students and postgraduate trainees learn while observing and working with members of a healthcare team. Many of the teaching and learning practices related to modern clinical training, including learning through supervised work-based tasks and interprofessional education, can be discussed under the umbrella term "work-based learning."

A key pedagogical principle in work-based learning is the social constructivist concept of the "zone of proximal development" (Vygotsky 1978). The basic premise by Vygotsky is that when assisted by a "knowledgeable other," such as a parent, learning takes place in the wider zone of proximal development as opposed to in the narrower "zone of actual development" or what the learner at that developmental stage can do unassisted. The value of near-peer learning in health professions education, for instance trainees or senior students teaching junior students, as well as educationally sound practices in clinical supervision, such as identifying learner needs and scaffolding accordingly (see Bruner 1961), are related to this concept. Based on ethnographic studies of apprenticeships Lave and Wenger (1991) developed two concepts on "situated learning" that are more appropriate to adult learning, and to the complex clinical learning environment where working and learning take place simultaneously. They identified that learning requires "legitimate peripheral participation" or meaningful involvement in professional activities where the learner is gradually allowed to participate in that activity. They also observed the cultural aspect where learning occurs in a "community of practice" as a member of an identified community involved in these professional activities. Since the community of practice in a clinical setting can be extended to the overall healthcare team, this is an important consideration for interprofessional education as well. Models of supervised task-based learning in the workplace, such as EPAs (Ten Cate et al. 2015; see Section 12.3.1.3), are related to these concepts. Another key teaching and learning strategy through which work-based learning is operationalized in health professions education is workplace-based assessment (WPBA; discussed later in Section 12.4.3), where trainees are observed in samples of clinical tasks and provided with feedback (Norcini and Burch 2007).

The sustained impact of work-based learning is difficult to measure due to its complexity, but several systematic reviews on WPBA suggest the positive effects of feedback on learning. In particular, a type of WPBA, multisource feedback (MSF), has resulted in identification of underperformance (Barrett et al. 2016) and had positive effects on clinical practice (Saedon et al. 2012). We have found that WPBAs can support a process of legitimate peripheral participation with the healthcare team among medical students (Olupeliyawa et al. 2014).

Sustainability in health professions education can be promoted through work-based learning tasks. For instance, involvement of trainees in quality improvement projects that are based on the principles of communities of practice have been suggested as an effective learning strategy for integrating sustainability in postgraduate medical education (Gandhi et al. 2020). Furthermore, since learning takes place while performing clinical care with a lesser focus on dedicated time and resources for classroom-based teaching, the carbon footprint itself would be reduced.

12.3.3 Reflective Practice

Reflective practice is recognized as an effective educational strategy to optimize experiential learning throughout the continuum of medical education, from undergraduate education to continuous professional development, as a practicing healthcare professional. The commonly used instructional tool in reflective practice is the portfolio (noted later in the Section 12.4.3), where evidence of the learning based on reflective practice and the accompanying reflections are collated and mapped to the expected learning outcomes.

The philosophy in reflective practice was first explained by John Dewey (1910), who coined the term "reflective thought" to signify how people's beliefs can be shaped by analysis of the situations and experiences they find themselves in. Donald Schön (1987) extends this idea in professional practice by proposing that professionals can reflect on a particular situation during the experience (reflection-in-action) as well as afterwards (reflection-on-action), and that this reflection-on-action based on self-evaluation, others' feedback, and sources of evidence is critical for learning through experience. David Kolb (1984) explains the steps in the reflective practice process as having a concrete experience, reflecting on the experience, forming new concepts, and responding based on these concepts, which in turn leads to a new experience and a new beginning to the cycle. These conceptualizations highlight the learning processes of critical thinking and self-assessment that are inherent in reflective practice. They also indicate the potential for individualized learning through learner identified needs. Concepts in reflective practice is related to the social constructivist approach of learning through others and learning through feedback discussed earlier in Section 12.3.2. Moreover, reflective practice extends these concepts by incorporating critical analysis and self-assessment processes. These additions are critical for learning in the clinical workplace to overcome the hidden curriculum and influence of negative role models.

Systematic reviews have found that the process of reflection, and portfolio development that is based on Kolb's experiential learning cycle, result in sustained improvements in deeper understanding, feedback processes, self-awareness, and student–teacher relationships (Buckley et al. 2009; Mann et al. 2009). Considering that the patient context, clinician expertise, and the best external evidence need to be integrated in the practice of evidence-based medicine (Sackett et al. 1996), reflective practice offers an invaluable opportunity toward such learning.

The critical analysis of context in reflective practice can include the environmental context and sustainability. For instance, reflective journals during clinical training in rural and remote settings have been suggested as a learning method among health professions students to identify the environmental factors shaping health issues (Bell 2010). In postgraduate education, sustainability-related tasks can be incorporated within trainee portfolios as well (Gandhi et al. 2020).

12.3.4 Community-Based Learning

Training health professions learners in the community or in primary care settings (community-based medical education), and/or integrating a community approach to a patient's problems (community-oriented medical education), have been in practice for over 50 years (Margolis 2000). All stakeholders in these learning environments including members of the community, healthcare professionals, and professionals in other related sectors (e.g. agriculture, sanitation) are involved in the student learning experience.

The pedagogical processes work-based learning and reflective practice (see Sections 12.3.2 and 12.3.3) are applicable to community-based learning as well. In addition, the community orientation provides the opportunity for students to see a much more diverse range of health problems and engage in disease prevention and health promotion activities. For instance, in the *family attachment* for medical students at the University of Colombo, Sri Lanka, students assigned longitudinally to families become involved in all health-related aspects of the family's life and take a holistic approach to health, including health promotion.

Several studies provide compelling evidence on the sustained effects of community-based learning. A systematic review finds that this service-learning approach, in a context of resource limitations and exposure to the many aspects of health, enables the learner to develop the skills, values, and confidence to work in similar situations in the future and appreciate the wider determinants of health (Hunt et al. 2011). Other sustained effects include enhanced social responsibility, improved communication skills, and the opportunity to work and learn with primary healthcare professionals in a team, which is a key goal of interprofessional education (Strauss et al. 2010).

Learning in the community provides an invaluable opportunity for health professions learners to experience and reflect on sustainability. In a recent study within a similar longitudinal clerkship in the US, it was found that students are well aware of the impact of environmental issues on health, and that focused teaching on sustainability further improves students' preparedness to discuss and address environmental health issues with the community (Kligler et al. 2021). Furthermore, patient empowerment and self-care, disease prevention, and streamlined clinical pathways with appropriate primary care management have been identified as the key strategies to reduce human activity and thereby reduce the carbon footprint while improving health (Mortimer 2010). Community-based learning will make health professions students aware of the importance of such strategies, and thereby promote sustainability.

12.3.5 E-Learning

The current COVID-19 pandemic has made e-learning, or the use of internet-based technologies for learning, a necessity in health professions education. However, well before the pandemic, e-learning initiatives, appearing a few decades ago, had become well established in medical education (Ellaway and Masters 2008). In e-learning, the interactions between the learner and the teacher can either be synchronous (e.g. real-time sessions via videoconferencing) or asynchronous (e.g. learning activities in a learning management system), but the key consideration is to ensure learner engagement. E-learning can be combined with face-to-face sessions and in many situations such blended learning innovations are preferred, e.g. the flipped classroom. E-learning has the potential to address large numbers of learners across diverse geographical contexts, for instance through massive open online courses (MOOCs). It also allows for learning material to be reused in different contexts, e.g. reusable learning objects (RLOs).

The pedagogical approaches to e-learning focus on student-centeredness and adaptive learning. E-learning strategies allow learners flexibility and control over learning content/sequence and the pace of learning, while designed to encourage collaborative learning and self-directed learning based on individualized learner needs (Ruiz et al. 2006; Ellaway and Masters 2008). If appropriately designed, e-learning also allows the teachers to transition from content delivery to facilitation of learning (Ruiz et al. 2006). However, care needs to be taken in instructional design of e-learning to minimize learner fatigue and maximize learner engagement, for instance through chunking of information for optimal cognitive processing. In a context where health professions curricula are overloaded with information considered as core and teachers are overburdened with content development, e-learning strategies provide opportunities to pool resources and offer elective courses according to learner needs, thus enhancing sustainability of the educational strategy itself (Tun 2019).

Although the positive effects of e-learning are evident as noted earlier in this section, the challenge lies in its usefulness within resource-constrained settings. A recent systematic review (Barteit et al. 2020) found that in resource-constrained settings logistical challenges for e-learning such as connectivity and under-resourcing for material development are common, while failed e-learning innovations may result in poor motivation and limited sustainability. However, this review found that innovations such as offline-based blended learning approaches, student-created e-learning content, and use of social media may improve the sustainability of e-learning worldwide.

E-learning initiatives are being increasingly used to promote sustainability and planetary health in health professions education. As we have noted, pooled e-learning resources and online courses can offer health professions students the flexibility in learning, particularly in areas such as sustainable healthcare (Tun 2019). In postgraduate medical education and continuing medical education, online short courses on climate change and sustainable healthcare would attract healthcare professionals who are increasingly concerned about the impact of global health disasters, such as the COVID-19 pandemic (Gandhi et al. 2020). Furthermore, e-learning instructional processes can lead by example in promoting sustainability, particularly by reducing the carbon footprint that would otherwise be produced through paper-based face-to-face teaching methods.

In summary, many of the teaching and learning innovations that have prevailed in health professions education over the years, and that have had sustainable educational impact, use a constructivist, student-centered approach and are situated in context. Likewise, sustainability in health professions education can be better promoted through contextual learning where the learners are motivated and engaged. Therefore, one can argue that sustainable teaching and learning strategies complement, and are even necessary to promote, sustainability in health professions education.

12.4 Assessment

Assessment is one of the core functions of education. The reason for this is that it is a way, perhaps the only way, to find out whether learners have learned what they should have. For this purpose, there is a multitude of assessment methods used in health professions education. A model called "Miller's pyramid" (Miller 1990) has classified all these methods into four levels or tiers, namely knows, knows how, shows how, and does. The first or the lowermost tier of Miller's pyramid is for the assessment of factual knowledge (knows), the second is for application of knowledge (knows how), the third is for skills under examination conditions (shows how), and the fourth is for skills in real-life settings (does).

The first two tiers employ written assessment methods. In the first tier, multiple-choice questions (MCQs), essays, short answer questions, and structured essay questions are the assessments of choice to assess factual knowledge. In the second tier, questions developed based on practical scenarios are employed to assess application of knowledge. Hence, most of the assessments used in the first tier are also suitable for the second tier, provided they are constructed based on practical scenarios, i.e. usually patient or clinical scenarios. For the third tier, assessments such as the objective structured clinical examination (OSCE) and standardized or actual patient-based clinical assessments are currently preferred. Traditionally, however, this tier has been dominated by long-case and short-case examinations. Finally, the fourth tier represents a relatively new class of assessment, focusing on how the candidates conduct themselves in the workplace, known as workplace-based assessment (WPBA see Section 12.3.2). These assessments use rating scales, marked by supervisors, colleagues, and patients, to assess samples of the workplace performance of candidates. Some of the popular assessment tools used for this purpose are mini-clinical evaluation exercise (mini-CEX), directly observed procedural skills (DOPS), case-based discussion (CbD), and multisource feedback (MSF). A candidate can include the results and the feedback from all the WPBAs within a portfolio to demonstrate how they have used them to improve practice.

The above assessments can serve two essential functions: formative and summative. The trend is to describe these two functions as "assessment *for* learning" and "assessment *of* learning," respectively. While the former (i.e. formative assessment) is primarily concerned with giving feedback, the latter (i.e. summative assessment) is principally concerned with passing a judgment on candidate ability. Though the formative function attracted much attention and emphasis in the recent past, the distinction between these two functions has diminished lately, mainly due to the advent of programmatic assessment (Ponnamperuma and Schuwirth 2021). Programmatic assessment views all assessments as constituents within a system of assessment, thus allowing the incorporation of information from all assessments when judging candidate ability (van der Vleuten and Schuwirth 2005).

How sustainable have the above assessments been? Over the years, changes in assessment have taken place for a variety of reasons. Consequently, some assessments have fallen out of favor while others have emerged as the mainstay. The reasons for these changes have, by and large, been the quest for improving the utility of assessment. From its original concept (van der Vleuten 1996b), the utility of assessment has evolved into a model consisting of six factors. They are validity, reliability, educational impact, acceptability, practicability, and cost-effectiveness. Validity is the extent to which an assessment assesses what it purports to assess. Out of the many types of validities, content validity is the type that has functioned as the principal determinant when selecting and sustaining assessments. Content validity implies the ability of an assessment to sample all the contents or subject areas that an assessment is supposed to cover. Reliability is how much an assessment is error-free so that the assessment results are reproducible. Educational impact denotes the extent to which an assessment drives the students to learn practically helpful knowledge, skills, and attitudes. Acceptability is concerned with the endorsement of the assessment by its stakeholders, e.g. candidates, examiners, teachers, accreditation bodies, employers, patients, etc. Practicability refers to the relative ease of conducting an assessment. Finally, cost-effectiveness serves as a measure of the returns when compared with the expenses of an assessment.

This section discusses how each of the above factors has contributed to the advancement of assessment within the four tiers of Miller's pyramid. In doing so, we identify the shared features that have contributed to the sustainability of assessments in health professions education.

12.4.1 Assessment of Knowledge at "Knows" and "Knows How" Levels

Since the middle of the twentieth century, there have been changes in written assessments assessing these two tiers and, at the turn of the century, the predominant assessment mode was essay questions. As the quantum of knowledge in health professions education was relatively small at that time, it was possible to sample the curriculum adequately in a three-hour written paper of essay questions. However, with the expansion of health professions knowledge, essay questions became too time-consuming to cover everything that needs testing. So, first, there was an issue of content validity with essay-type assessment. That apart, essays attracted other validity concerns, such as assessing the candidates' writing ability rather than their cognitive ability. Second, different examiners interpreted candidates' answers variably and applied variable standards when marking the essay questions. So, it was hard to produce reproducible results, even with tightly worded marking schemes. Thus, the reliability of this form of assessment was at stake. Third, most essays assessed recall of knowledge. That was not a welcome finding, as health professions graduates need to make decisions related to patient problems. However, essay questions were not capable of assessing a candidate's problem-solving or higher-order thinking capacity. As a result, the candidates resorted to memorizing facts to pass examinations. Thus, the educational impact of essay questions was suboptimal. Fourth, for all these reasons, essay questions, once a well-established form of assessment, were no longer enjoying the acceptability that they used to. Fifth, although the essay questions were cheap and easy to produce, marking answer papers was resource-intensive. Despite this heavy investment in resources, mainly in terms of examiner hours, the results of essay questions were not readily comparable due to the reliability issues we have discussed. Hence, this type of assessment was not considered feasible anymore. Sixthly, due to all the above shortcomings, the returns on investment of essays were too meager for an assessment of factual recall. Thus, essay-type assessments were not considered cost-effective.

To address these issues, the essay-type question papers had to be replaced by question types that required a shorter answer, like the short answer/essay or structured essay questions (Hayes 2013). Structured essay questions, in particular, were an attractive choice, as they not only managed to increase the content areas assessed within a unit time, but also managed to assess higher-order thinking through scenario-based questions. Nevertheless, the marking still had to be performed with human invention. Also, the number of content areas tested within a unit time was not sufficient, given that the students had to construct an answer of at least a few sentences.

However, question formats that only require the candidates to select an answer from a list of options could adequately overcome the above disadvantages of short essay and structured essay questions. Hence, the MCQs became popular, as they are a convenient option to assess a vast extent of content matter within a relatively short time. Thus, the content validity issues that the essay-type question formats posed were almost entirely circumvented. Additionally, like structured essay questions, it was easy for MCQs to incorporate scenarios, thereby facilitating the assessment of higher-order thinking. Since the MCQs could be marked by a machine, as opposed to an examiner, the issues related to reliability, acceptability, feasibility, and cost were also successfully overcome.

Nonetheless, MCQs have had their share of problems. The list of options from which the candidate must select the correct answer is not the most authentic way of assessing the preparedness for practice, as no patient comes with a list of solutions to their problem. Linked with the list of options are the issues of cueing and guessing. Writing questions that avoid the ill effects of cueing and guessing when selecting the correct answer, demands considerable skill on the part of the question writer. So, the current efforts are toward finding a written assessment that minimizes the above disadvantages of MCQs while retaining its advantages of sampling the curriculum widely and adequately and assessing higher-order thinking skills uniformly and consistently. In this regard, recent evidence favors a type of written assessment called "very short answer questions," where the candidate constructs an answer of not more than two to three words in response to each question. These answers are marked by computer software fed with all possible answer combinations. Although this type of written assessment is still at an experimental stage, emerging evidence indicates that the very short answer questions could challenge the current popularity of MCQs (Sam et al. 2019).

The above account, tracing the evolution of written assessment from long essays through structured essay questions/MCQs to very short answer questions, indicates that the sustainability of this form of assessment is determined primarily by its:

1) Ability to sample the curriculum widely and adequately within a unit time.
2) Ability to assess higher-order thinking.
3) Capability of assessing candidate ability precisely, uniformly, and consistently.
4) Authenticity or closeness to practice.
5) Ease of developing and marking questions with minimal human intervention.
6) Relative inexpensiveness given the richness of information gathered.
7) Absence of unwanted effects such as the assessment of writing ability or the effects of cueing and guessing.

These features essentially support the utility criteria we have described. While doing so, this form of assessment has also emerged as being more environmentally sustainable. For example, long essay questions consumed piles of paper both as question papers and answer scripts. However, even with the same pencil-and-paper format, the MCQs could assess much more with fewer paper resources. Also, the long essays involved considerable examiner time in marking answers, consuming additional energy in terms of lighting, air-conditioning, etc. Moving from long essay questions to MCQs has minimized the consumption of these resources. However, it is noteworthy that moving from MCQs to very short answer questions does not compromise the gains accrued by moving from essays to MCQs.

12.4.2 Assessment of Behavior at "Shows How" Level

The long-case and short-case examinations dominated assessment at the "shows how" level, until the last decades of the twentieth century. In a long-case examination, the candidate takes a comprehensive history and conducts a complete physical examination, on a single patient, within 30–45 minutes. For the next 15–30 minutes, a pair of examiners interviews the candidate, based on the patient information that the candidate reports. The short case, on the other hand, assesses the candidate ability in taking a brief, focused history (e.g. history of the presenting complaint) or conducting a part of physical examination (e.g. general examination, examination of the cardiovascular system or just listening to heart sounds) using few patients – typically four to six patients. Another crucial feature in the short case is that the examiners observe the candidate. At least traditionally, in both long- and short-case examinations, the candidates are marked without using a structured marking scheme. Also, the patients and the examiners are allocated to candidates by draw. In many ways, the long case and the short case are analogous to the long essay and the short answer questions discussed in Section 12.4.1, in relation to "written assessment." Thus, the long case has the same issues as the long essay questions.

Like the long essay questions, the long case takes a considerable amount of time to assess a single disease condition or content area in the curriculum. Usually, this is the only content area assessed by this form of assessment. Hence, it essentially boils down to a long essay examination with a single question. As such, the content validity of the long case is severely constrained, given that the extent to which one disease condition can sample the curriculum is minimal. Additionally, the technique of history-taking and physical examination not being observed by the examiners, and examiners asking random questions from the candidates and awarding marks without using a structured marking scheme have led to fundamental validity criticisms leveled against this assessment format. A modified version of the long case, the objective structured long examination record (OSLER), mitigates some of these criticisms. In the OSLER, the examiners observe the candidate and use a structured, predetermined marking scheme, with checklists and rating scales, to assess the candidate (Gleeson 1997). However, its inability to sample a wide array of disease conditions and patients within a reasonable amount of assessment time remains. Various scientific publications have also queried the reliability and the comparability of its results, as the examiners and patients are assigned to candidates by draw (Wilson et al. 1969; Norcini 2002). Since the traditional long case does not allow the examiners to observe the candidates, they would not be motivated to perfect their history-taking and physical examination techniques. Hence, the long case does not offer much educational impact. However, since it was a traditional form of assessment handed over from generation to generation, its acceptability was not queried until some high-ranking scientific journals did so (Dugdale 1996; van der Vleuten 1996a; Norcini 2002). Finally, since assessing a candidate with a single patient takes at least 30–60 minutes, the practicability and cost-effectiveness concerns over the long case have also emerged.

Most of these concerns relating to the long case do not apply to the short case, except for three. First, the allocation of patients and examiners to candidates is by draw. However, the ill effects of this randomness in patients and examiners are not adequately compensated for by their numbers. Second, just four to six disease conditions are not sufficient to cover the curriculum. Third, the use of an unstructured marking scheme to award marks does not offer a uniform, consistent, and fair assessment of candidate competence. Of these three criticisms, the second is the most crucial in hampering its continued use, as the first and third could be addressed, at least to an extent, with careful planning.

To address these criticisms, the OSCE was introduced in the 1970s (Harden et al. 1975). Since then, the OSCE and its derivatives have grown in popularity to replace almost entirely the long and short cases in all major clinical assessments (Ponnamperuma et al. 2009). The reasons for this are that, in an OSCE:

1) All candidates are assessed using the same or similar patients (either standardized or real) and other examination material.
2) All candidates are assessed by the same or similarly trained examiners.
3) Examiners observe the candidate performance.
4) Examiners mark candidates using standardized marking schemes.

    Although all these features are desirable, it is not these that hallmarked the supremacy and sustainability of the OSCE at this "shows how" level. Instead, it is the sampling ability of the OSCE, such that:
5) A wide range of curriculum content or disease conditions is assessed during a reasonable time.

As in written assessment, all the above are educational reasons. However, the steps taken to implement them have also served environmental sustainability. For example, conducting an OSCE can accommodate more candidates per unit time. That saves energy, in terms of lighting, air-conditioning, refreshments, and transport, as what took several days in the past now takes only one or two days.

12.4.3 Assessment of Behavior at "Does" Level

Assessment at this level, denoted under the umbrella term WPBA, was unheard of in the past. Before WPBA, logbooks were the only assessments that served this level, and that too in a very rudimentary form. Therefore, there is no assessment that the WPBA had to replace. Although no assessment method gave way to WPBA, its emergence has mainly been due to two reasons. First, there is evidence that clinical assessment, as practiced in the twentieth century, lacked feedback. That was despite growing evidence on the usefulness of feedback for professional improvement. Thus, the imbalance of health professions education favoring summative assessment over formative assessment is the first reason for the introduction of WPBA (Norcini and Burch 2007). Such formative assessment can then be used for candidates to reflect upon the feedback they have received to initiate self-improvement activities and for educational authorities to monitor candidate progress over time. Second, there is convincing research evidence indicating a skills loss when moving from the "shows how" level to the "does" level (Rethans et al. 2007) and, therefore, not assessing a candidate at the "does" level before certifying their ability endangers patient safety.

Although these two are the primary reasons for the introduction of WPBA, the educational rationale for its sustenance is somewhat different from why the OSCE has been sustainable at the "shows how" level. Unlike the OSCE, WPBA does not offer standardized, uniform, and consistent assessment material or conditions. Since the test material comes from a candidate's workplace within a routine workplace exercise, it leads to an authentic and valid assessment. However, candidates are assessed by different examiners using different patients. How can such an assessment be defended in terms of reliability, consistency, and fairness? The answer lies in its insistence on a large number of assessment episodes or encounters. If a candidate is assessed by many examiners using many patients, then the individual variations in examiner strictness and patient difficulty are sufficiently attenuated. This essentially creates a level playing field, provided the number of assessment encounters is sufficient.

Although the above may be the reasons for the introduction and initial sustenance of WPBA, its present persistence and popularity are attributable to yet another reason. That is, its ability to contribute to programmatic assessment or be a part of a system of assessment. The results of different assessment encounters of WPBA and those of other forms of assessment can be collated within a portfolio to create a more informative picture of a candidate's ability (Ponnamperuma 2013). Not only can a candidate's ability be portrayed this way, but the improvements in it, based on feedback and reflective practice, can also be more realistically captured through a portfolio.

All this means the sustainability of WPBA is due to its amenability to:

1) Giving instant feedback to the candidate.
2) Provision of ongoing opportunities for self-improvement through reflective practice.
3) Monitoring candidate progress over time.
4) Accounting for the skill loss when moving from "shows how" level to "does" level.
5) Evening out examiner and patient discrepancies by involving many examiners and many patient encounters.
6) Being part of a system of assessment, allowing the interpretation of its results in combination with those of other assessments.

As at previous levels, it is evident that all the above reasons for the sustainability of WPBA are educational. However, the way that WPBA is practiced currently in many places – as a paperless exercise, using electronic platforms and e-portfolios – also contributes to environmental sustainability. Additionally, since all WPBAs are performed within the workplace and during routine work, the consumption of dedicated resources that are energy-draining and environmentally damaging, such as lighting, air-conditioning, transport of persons and equipment, is avoided.

12.5 Conclusion

In conclusion, this chapter draws on past sustainability trends to enunciate the features that indicate the long-term viability of innovations in health professions education. Given the trends observed throughout history, it is clear that purely educational reasons have rarely been the sole determinant of the sustainability or demise of all the innovations in health professions education. Instead, societal needs and contextual reasons have also played their role in determining the sustainability of educational innovations. Additionally, it is also clear that technology has played a vital role in the continuance of sustainability in each of the three educational processes discussed in this chapter. With the current dominance of and emphasis on technology, this trend will continue to prevail in the predictable future. However, a noteworthy aspect that this chapter highlights is that, although the motives and reasons behind sustainability and change in health professions education have mostly been a combination of educational and other imperatives, they have also contributed to environmental sustainability in no small measure. This trend, too, will continue to grow in the foreseeable future.

References

Albanese, M.A. and Mitchell, S. (1993). Problem-based learning: a review of literature on its outcomes and implementation issues. *Academic Medicine* 68: 52–52.

Aziz, M.S., Zain, A.N.M., Samsudin, M.A.B., and Saleh, S.B. (2014). The effects of problem-based learning on self-directed learning skills among physics undergraduates. *International Journal of Academic Research in Progressive Education and Development* 3 (1): 126–137.

Barrett, A., Galvin, R., Steinert, Y. et al. (2016). A review of the use of workplace-based assessment in identifying and remediating underperformance among postgraduate medical trainees: BEME guide no. 43. *Medical Teacher* 38 (12): 1188–1198.

Barrows, H.S. (1996). Problem-based learning in medicine and beyond: a brief overview. *New Directions for Teaching and Learning* 68: 3–12.

Barteit, S., Guzek, D., Jahn, A. et al. (2020). Evaluation of e-learning for medical education in low-and middle-income countries: a systematic review. *Computers and Education* 145: 103726.

Barzansky, B. (2010). Abraham Flexner and the era of medical education reform. *Academic Medicine* 85 (9): S19–S25.

Bell, E.J. (2010). Climate change: what competencies and which medical education and training approaches? *BMC Medical Education* 10 (1): 1–8.

Brady, L. (1996). Outcome-based education: a critique. *The Curriculum Journal* 7 (1): 5–16.

Brewer, E.W. (2011). Evaluation models for evaluating educational programs. In: *Assessing and Evaluating Adult Learning in Career and Technical Education* (ed. V.C.X. Wang), 106–126. IGI Global.

Bruner, J.S. (1961). The act of discovery. *Harvard Educational Review* 31: 21–32.

Buckley, S., Coleman, J., Davison, I. et al. (2009). The educational effects of portfolios on undergraduate student learning: a best evidence medical education (BEME) systematic review, BEME guide no. 11. *Medical Teacher* 31 (4): 282–298.

Dewey, J. (1910). *How We Think*. Boston, MC: D.C.Heath.

Dochy, F., Segers, M., Van den Bossche, P., and Gijbels, D. (2003). Effects of problem-based learning: a meta-analysis. *Learning and Instruction* 13 (5): 533–568.

Donnelly, K. (2007). Australia's adoption of outcome based education: a critique. *Issues in Educational Research* 172: 183–206.

Dornan, T. (2005). Osler, Flexner, apprenticeship and 'the new medical education'. *Journal of the Royal Society of Medicine* 98 (3): 91–95.

Dugdale, A. (1996). Letters: long-case clinical examinations. *The Lancet* 347: 1335.

Ellaway, R. and Masters, K. (2008). AMEE guide 32: e-learning in medical education part 1: learning, teaching and assessment. *Medical Teacher* 30 (5): 455–473.

Flexner, A. (1910). *Medical Education in the United States and Canada*. Washington, DC: Science and Health Publications, Inc.

Frambach, J.M., Driessen, E.W., Chan, L.C., and van der Vleuten, C.P. (2012). Rethinking the globalisation of problem-based learning: how culture challenges self-directed learning. *Medical Education* 46 (8): 738–747.

Frank, J.R., Snell, L.S., Cate, O.T. et al. (2010a). Competency-based medical education: theory to practice. *Medical Teacher* 32 (8): 638–645.

Frank, J.R., Mungroo, R., Ahmad, Y. et al. (2010b). Toward a definition of competency-based education in medicine: a systematic review of published definitions. *Medical Teacher* 32 (8): 631–637.

Gandhi, V., Al-Hadithy, N., Göpfert, A. et al. (2020). Integrating sustainability into postgraduate medical education. *Future Healthcare Journal* 7 (2): 102–104.

Gijbels, D., Dochy, F., Van den Bossche, P., and Segers, M. (2005). Effects of problem-based learning: a meta-analysis from the angle of assessment. *Review of Educational Research* 75 (1): 27–61.

Gleeson, F. (1997). Assessment of clinical competence using the objective structured long examination record (OSLER), AMEE medical education guide no. 9. *Medical Teacher* 19: 7–14.

Hamel Green, E.I., Blashki, G., Berry, H.L. et al. (2009). Preparing Australian medical students for climate change. *Australian Family Physician* 38 (9): 726–729.

Harden, R.M., Stevenson, M., Downie, W.W., and Wilson, G.M. (1975). Assessment of clinical competence using objective structured examination. *British Medical Journal* 1: 447–451.

Hartling, L., Spooner, C., Tjosvold, L., and Oswald, A. (2010). Problem-based learning in pre-clinical medical education: 22 years of outcome research. *Medical Teacher* 32 (1): 28–35.

Hayes, K. (2013). Workplace-based assessment. In: *Oxford Textbook of Medical Education* (ed. K. Walsh), 549–563. UK: Oxford University Press.

Hung, W., Jonassen, D.H., and Liu, R. (2008). Problem-based learning. In: *Handbook of Research on Educational Communications and Technology*, vol. 3 (ed. J.M. Spector, M.D. Merrill, J. van Merrienboer and M.P. Driscoll), 485–506. Erlbaum.

Hunt, J.B., Bonham, C., and Jones, L. (2011). Understanding the goals of service learning and community-based medical education: a systematic review. *Academic Medicine* 86 (2): 246–251.

Kirkpatrick, D. and Kirkpatrick, J. (2006). *Evaluating Training Programs: The Four Levels*. Berrett-Koehler Publishers.

Kligler, B., Zipp, G.P., Rocchetti, C. et al. (2021). The impact of integrating environmental health into medical school curricula: a survey-based study. *BMC Medical Education* 21 (1): 1–6.

Kolb, D.A. (1984). *Experiential Learning: Experience as the Source of Learning and Development*, vol. 1. Prentice-Hall, NJ: Englewood Cliffs.

Lave, J. and Wenger, E. (1991). *Situated Learning: Legitimate Peripheral Participation*. New York, NY: Cambridge University Press.

Mann, K., Gordon, J., and MacLeod, A. (2009). Reflection and reflective practice in health professions education: a systematic review. *Advances in Health Sciences Education* 14 (4): 595–621.

Margolis, C.Z. (2000). Community-based medical education. *Medical Teacher* 22 (5): 482–484.

Miller, G.E. (1990). The assessment of clinical skills/competence/performance. *Academic Medicine* 65 (Suppl): S63–5S67.

Morcke, A.M., Dornan, T., and Eika, B. (2013). Outcome (competency) based education: an exploration of its origins, theoretical basis, and empirical evidence. *Advances in Health Sciences Education* 18 (4): 851–863.

Mortimer, F. (2010). The sustainable physician. *Clinical Medicine* 10 (2): 110.

Neville, A., Norman, G., and White, R. (2019). McMaster at 50: lessons learned from five decades of PBL. *Advances in Health Sciences Education* 24 (5): 853–863.

Norcini, J.J. (2002). Death of a long case. *British Medical Journal* 324: 408–409.

Norcini, J. and Burch, V. (2007). AMEE guide no. 31: workplace-based assessment as an educational tool. *Medical Teacher* 29: 855–5871.

Nouraey, P., Al-Badi, A., Riasati, M.J., and Maata, R.L. (2020). Educational program and curriculum evaluation models: a mini systematic review of the recent trends. *Universal Journal of Educational Research* 8 (9): 4048–4055.

O'Dowd, E., Lydon, S., O'Connor, P. et al. (2019). A systematic review of 7 years of research on entrustable professional activities in graduate medical education, 2011–2018. *Medical Education* 53 (3): 234–249.

Olupeliyawa, A., Balasooriya, C., Hughes, C., and O'Sullivan, A. (2014). Educational impact of an assessment of medical students' collaboration in health care teams. *Medical Education* 48 (2): 146–156.

Onyon, C. (2012). Problem-based learning: a review of the educational and psychological theory. *The Clinical Teacher* 9 (1): 22–26.

Osler, W. (1901). Books and men. *Boston Medical and Surgical Journal* 144 (3): 60–61.

Phillips, J.J. (2012). *Return on Investment in Training and Performance Improvement Programs*. Routledge.

Ponnamperuma, G. (2013). Workplace-based assessment. In: *Oxford Textbook of Medical Education* (ed. K. Walsh), 537–548. UK: Oxford University Press.

Ponnamperuma, G.G. and Schuwirth, L.W.T. (2021). Section 4: how can I assess my trainee to perform better? In: *Educate, Train and Transform: A Toolkit on Medical and Health Professions Education* (ed. D.D. Samarasekera and M. Gwee), 77–5124. Singapore: World Scientific.

Ponnamperuma, G.G., Karunathilake, I.M., Mcaleer, S., and Davis, M.H. (2009). The long case and its modifications: a literature review. *Medical Education* 43: 936–941.

Prideaux, D. (2003). ABC of learning and teaching in medicine: curriculum design. *British Medical Journal* 326 (7383): 268.

Rethans, J.-J., Gorter, S., Bokken, L., and Morrison, L. (2007). Unannounced standardised patients in real practice: a systematic literature review. *Medical Education* 41: 537–549.

Rossi, P.H., Freeman, H.E., and Lipsey, M.W. (1993). Programs, policies, and evaluations. In: *Evaluation: A Systematic Approach*, 13. Sage.

Ruiz, J.G., Mintzer, M.J., and Leipzig, R.M. (2006). The impact of e-learning in medical education. *Academic Medicine* 81 (3): 207–212.

Sackett, D.L., Rosenberg, W.M.C., Gray, J.A.M. et al. (1996). Evidence based medicine: what it is and what it isn't. *British Medical Journal* 312 (7023): 71–72.

Saedon, H., Salleh, S., Balakrishnan, A. et al. (2012). The role of feedback in improving the effectiveness of workplace based assessments: a systematic review. *BMC Medical Education* 12 (1): 1–8.

Sam, A.H., Westacott, R., Gurnell, M. et al. (2019). Comparing single-best-answer and very-short-answer questions for the assessment of applied medical knowledge in 20 UK medical schools: cross-sectional study. *British Medical Journal Open* 9: e032550.

Schmidt, H.G. (2012). A brief history of problem-based learning. In: *One-Day, One-Problem* (ed. G. O'Grady, E.H.J. Yew, K.P.L. Goh and H.G. Schmidt), 21–40. Singapore: Springer.

Schön, D.A. (1987). *Educating the Reflective Practitioner: Toward a New Design for Teaching and Learning in the Professions*. New York: Jossey-Bass.

Scriven, M. (1991). Beyond formative and summative evaluation. *Teachers College Record* 92 (6): 18–64.

Shorey, S., Lau, T.C., Lau, S.T., and Ang, E. (2019). Entrustable professional activities in health care education: a scoping review. *Medical Education* 53 (8): 766–777.

Strauss, R.P., Stein, M.B., Edwards, J., and Nies, K.C. (2010). The impact of community-based dental education on students. *Journal of Dental Education* 74: S42–S55.

Strobel, J. and Van Barneveld, A. (2009). When is PBL more effective? A meta-synthesis of meta-analyses comparing PBL to conventional classrooms. *Interdisciplinary Journal of Problem-Based Learning* 3 (1): 4.

Stufflebeam, T.K.D.L. (2003). *International Handbook of Educational Evaluation*. US: Taylor & Francis.

Ten Cate, O., Chen, H.C., Hoff, R.G. et al. (2015). Curriculum development for the workplace using entrustable professional activities (EPAs): AMEE guide no. 99. *Medical Teacher* 37 (11): 983–1002.

Tun, M.S. (2019). Fulfilling a new obligation: teaching and learning of sustainable healthcare in the medical education curriculum. *Medical Teacher* 41 (10): 1168–1177.

van der Vleuten, C.P.M. (1996a). Making the best of the 'long case'. *The Lancet* 347 (3): 704–5705.

van der Vleuten, C.P.M. (1996b). The assessment of professional competence: developments, research and practical implications. *Advances in Health Sciences Education* 1 (1): 41–567.

van der Vleuten, C.P.M. and Schuwirth, L.W.T. (2005). Assessing professional competence: from methods to programmes. *Medical Education* 39: 309–5317.

van der Vleuten, C.V.D., Verwijnen, G.M., and Wijnen, W.H.F.W. (1996). Fifteen years of experience with progress testing in a problem-based learning curriculum. *Medical Teacher* 18 (2): 103–109.

Vygotsky, L.S. (1978). *Mind in Society: The Development of Higher Psychological Processes*. Cambridge, MA: Harvard University Press.

Wilson, G.M., Lever, R., Harden, R.M., and Robertson, J.I. (1969). Examination of clinical examiners. *The Lancet* 1 (7584): 37–40.

Wood, D.F. (2003). Problem based learning. *British Medical Journal* 326 (7384): 328–330.

Wood, D., Bruner, J.S., and Ross, G. (1976). The role of tutoring in problem solving. *Journal of Child Psychology and Psychiatry* 17 (2): 89–100.

13

Sustainability in Energy Systems Analysis and Design

J. McKellar, H. Gaber, and D. Hoornweg

13.1 Introduction

The supply and use of energy are ubiquitous in societies around the world, in myriad forms and applications. The links between energy availability and quality of life are well-established (e.g. Pioro et al. 2019 with respect to electricity; Steinberger 2016). Also well-established are the challenges energy supply and use can present to the environment, to equality within societies, and to economics on international, national, and individual scales. While all energy carriers have some negative sustainability implications (environmental, economic, and/or social), some perform worse than others. Consequently, there is broad recognition of the need to transition the world's energy systems to more sustainable forms.

The challenges and opportunities presented by energy transition are as varied as energy systems themselves. It will be crucial to have a workforce capable of leading and executing this widespread change.

This chapter presents factors to support successful undergraduate educational programs in postsecondary institutions in the area of energy systems analysis and design. First, the chapter will discuss energy systems more broadly. Next, it will introduce attributes required of our energy professionals and the components of energy systems programs that will enable their achievement. The chapter will include barriers and challenges and best practices to offer successful energy programs. Aspects related to engineering accreditation processes will be discussed. Finally, the chapter will summarize some of the changes recommended to existing curricula and program governance to ensure we are able to meet the growing demand for energy systems professionals.

13.2 Energy Systems

13.2.1 Definition of a "System"

All aspects of energy supply and use need to be considered for improvement as part of the energy transition. However, examining an individual technology or energy carrier in isolation can mean missing important information. For example, planning for the use of hydrogen

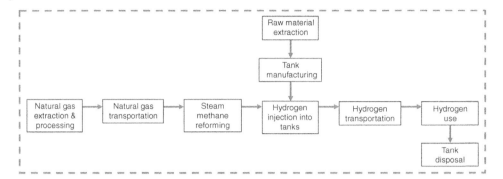

Figure 13.1 Simplified process flowchart for hydrogen life cycle. Depending on the LCA scope, it can be appropriate to include, for example, the hydrogen-fueled vehicle, as well.

without considering how the hydrogen is produced, or mandating the use of electric vehicles without considering the mode of electricity generation can result in significant, unexpected impacts. The entire system must be considered.

There are many ways to define an "energy system," from the heating, ventilating, and air-conditioning (HVAC) system of a single dwelling, to the global production and trade of petroleum. In this chapter, we use "system" more in the latter context. However, in all instances, the scope of the system must be defined.

A useful way of describing a system is in terms of life cycles. Life cycle assessment (LCA; CSA 2006a, b) is a method for evaluating environmental impacts of a product or process. As part of the analysis, it is necessary to define all of the unit processes between extraction of raw materials, through conversion and use, to final disposal of wastes i.e. the life cycle. In terms of hydrogen, for example, the life cycle would include the extraction and processing of natural gas and the steam methane reforming process, as well as the life cycle of the hydrogen storage tanks and potentially, for instance, the vehicle in which the hydrogen is used, depending on the scope of the analysis. Figure 13.1 shows a simplified life cycle flowchart for hydrogen. Although not formally a part of traditional LCA, the life cycle concept is applicable to economic (i.e. life cycle costing; Trigaux et al. 2017) and social (i.e. social LCA; McManus and Taylor 2015) perspectives, as well.

13.2.2 Energy Systems, Economics, Society, and Climate Change

Energy systems link closely with the concept of sustainability. Traditionally, energy sectors have been major drivers of many economies, with the extraction, conversion, and sale of energy carriers employing significant numbers of people and funding many of society's needs, from education to roads. The link between energy and sustainability has been codified among the United Nations (UN) Sustainable Development Goals. Goal 7 is to "ensure access to affordable, reliable, sustainable and modern energy for all" (UN 2021a), with the rationale linked to economic, social, and environmental issues (UN 2021b).

The economic implications of energy supply and use cannot be overstated, on international, national, and individual scales. For example, in 2019 energy contributed about 10% of Canada's nominal gross domestic product (GDP) and accounted for just over 4% of employment (NRCan 2020). A recent report by Clean Energy Canada (2021) attributes 22% of Canada's 2020 "total energy GDP" to "clean energy"; a figure they expect to grow to 29% by 2030. It is worth noting that on a global scale, the relationship between energy use and GDP declined over the period 1981–2016 (IEA 2019). While energy use has been increasing since at least 1990 (IEA 2021), in higher-income countries we have become better at using our energy more efficiently.

On an individual basis, energy economics become important in terms of energy poverty, or conversely, ensuring everyone has equal access to an adequate level of energy services. Energy accessibility is not an end in itself; energy is only valuable in terms of the services it supplies. This ranges from lighting to allow students to do homework at night, to adequate home heating and cooling, to the ability to travel to access employment and healthcare.

Energy supply and use also clearly impact human health and well-being, both positively and negatively. Indeed, a major driver of growth in global energy demand is to improve quality of life. It has been shown (e.g. Pioro et al. 2019 with respect to electricity; Steinberger 2016) that there is a positive, logarithmic relationship between the Human Development Index (HDI) and energy demand. Although, Steinberger (2016) also notes an upper limit on this relationship: at low rates of energy use, small increases can have large gains for HDI, while at high rates of energy use, increases in HDI are marginal at best. On the other hand, the use of energy can result in negative impacts on human health. For example, the combustion of transportation fuels in vehicles emits particulate matter, a significant contributor to morbidity and mortality, globally (Sofiev et al. 2018; Mueller et al. 2017; Davis 1997).

The reduction of negative impacts on human health is one of the co-benefits often cited in support of switching away from fossil fuel combustion (e.g. Shindel and Smith 2019). Another argument in favor is mitigation of climate change. Climate change mitigation is one of the primary drivers for improving the sustainability of energy systems. Not only are energy supply and use a significant contributor to climate change, they have the potential to be significantly impacted by climate change, including variations in temperature and extreme weather events. For example, a recent study by Oak Ridge National Laboratory (ORNL; Allen-Dumas et al. 2019) found that over the period 2000–2012 "increased severity of extreme weather events" led to longer electricity outages; increasing severity and frequency of extreme weather events has been likened to climate change (e.g. Hoegh-Guldberg et al. 2019). The Canadian Electricity Association (CEA 2016) has also warned that "climate change presents considerable risk to service reliability."

13.2.3 Scale of the Challenge

Overall, our goal is to improve sustainability. The Brundtland Commission defined sustainable development as: "development that meets the needs of the present without compromising the ability of future generations to meet their own needs" (WCED 1987). In terms of energy, this means striving toward a point where everyone has access to energy they can afford and use efficiently, in quantities sufficient to achieve a high quality of life, and where that energy is supplied in a way that minimizes negative impacts on the environment and human health, both now and into the future.

In some societies this will require greenfield expansion of energy systems: building new infrastructure to supply (and use) energy. In other societies, this will require changing existing infrastructure (physical, regulatory, social, etc.) to support different energy conversion technologies, carriers, and users.

The energy transition will involve a substantial redistribution of funds, jobs, and people, sectorally and geographically. There have been significant calls for a "just transition" (e.g. Caranci and Fong 2021), essentially ensuring that no one is left behind. In a just transition, a coal-sector worker is not simply left unemployed as coal use ends, but is supported through retraining and a shift to a new job.

Working within this broader economic transition will be energy systems specialists (see Box 13.1). Workers who not only understand the energy technologies being phased in and out, but who are cognizant of the environmental, social , and economic impacts of those

> **Box 13.1 Employers of Energy Systems Designers and Analysts**
>
> Regulators, licensing agencies, technology providers, electricity generators, energy resource companies, natural gas distributors, oil and gas companies, electricity distribution and transmission companies, municipalities, provincial and federal governments, environmental non-governmental organizations, think tanks, energy storage technology and system providers, energy management companies, insurers, consultancies, data analytics specialists, energy planning agencies, and standards organizations.

technologies, and who are comfortable with a continually evolving workspace. The US, for example, in 2018 had 6.7 million workers in the energy sector (out of a total 147 million workers, or about 5%) (EFI and NASEO 2021). One forecast (Clean Energy Canada 2021) estimates employment in Canada's "clean energy sector" will increase by 4% each year, to 2030. Energy systems engineers and analysts will constitute a subset of this, but the demand is clear.

Training the workers to meet this need will be a challenge on its own. Educational programs continually evolve as new knowledge is generated, but it would be valuable for the changes discussed here to be made quickly. Figure 13.2 shows an exaggerated characterization of how energy systems analyses were approached in the past, and how they must be approached in the future (currently, we are somewhere in between). Broadly speaking, it can be argued that, in the past, economic concerns were largely dominant; not just profits for energy companies, but job creation and the economic benefits that extend from a successful project. Energy systems were often planned centrally. Availability of inexpensive energy was good for industrial development, and politically. Environmental concerns were not ignored, but tended to be approached from an end-of-pipe perspective. That is, negative environmental impacts were something to be mitigated in the final stages of project development as opposed to being designed out early on.

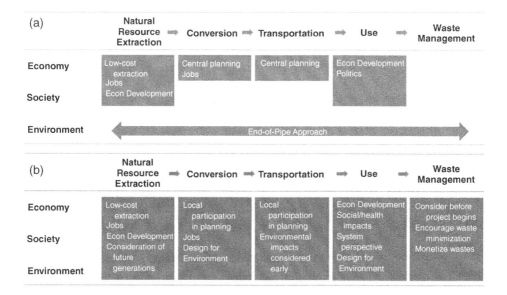

Figure 13.2 A simple representation of energy systems analysis and design from (a) an exaggerated conventional approach and (b) a sustainability-oriented approach. Develop't = Development.

In the future, energy systems analysis and design should take a more holistic approach, with maximum gains in sustainability sought during all stages of an energy process' life cycle. "Maximum net gains" is one of the "trade-off rules" put forth by Gibson (2006) in his discussion of sustainability assessment. Recognizing that a project is likely to involve at least some trade-offs, Gibson (2006) recommended that "any acceptable trade-off or set of trade-offs must deliver net progress toward meeting the requirements for sustainability." In the Figure 13.2 example, this would mean ensuring that project planning considers the entire project life cycle (raw material extraction to waste management), and the performance of each life cycle stage in terms of economics, social impacts, and the environment. While it is unlikely to achieve net positive performance everywhere, maximizing net gains can be prioritized.

13.3 Requisite Learning Outcomes

Sustainability is conceptually broad. Notably broader than most traditional, postsecondary technical training. In order to transition people from high school students to professionals in the field of energy systems, we must give them the tools and skills they will need to manage sustainable development. In part that will mean ensuring their education extends beyond traditional silos and that they are comfortable working in interdisciplinary teams, but it will also mean ensuring graduates have the requisite skills for lifelong learning.

13.3.1 Requirements of Jobs and Careers

The impacts of the energy transition will be felt across economic sectors and around the world. The energy sector itself will certainly undergo changes, from the companies extracting energy resources, to transmission grid operators, to retailers of energy carriers to individuals. However, the effects will also be felt by manufacturers required to supply different components and machinery, resource developers required to supply different base materials, financiers examining investments in emerging technologies, retailers looking at different markets, etc.

It is not easy to forecast what skills and competencies will be in demand in the future. Thürer et al. (2018) indicated that industry requirements related to sustainability are still unclear and listed identifying those skills as a key "future research question." In a recent TD Economics report (Caranci and Fong 2021), determining the skills required by the clean energy sector was one of the primary recommendations toward achieving a just transition. From one perspective, this could be a challenge for educators: trying to meet the unknown needs of employers in transition. From another perspective, it is an opportunity to lead: to educate future energy sector specialists with the skills to lead the energy transition as it continues.

We are not entirely without guidance. There was an entire decade devoted to incorporating sustainability into education (Thürer et al. 2018) and, for example, "key competencies" have been proposed (Wiek et al. 2011). As well, the energy transition is underway and professional bodies do have guidance available. For example, Engineers Canada (2016) has developed a set of ten guidelines for practicing engineers to follow in their work. Ensuring graduating engineers have the skills and abilities necessary to practice within Engineers Canada's framework would seem to be a clear first step. Of course, what those skills and abilities are, might be open to interpretation. Beyond academia and professional bodies, consultancies also have advice for how businesses should manage personnel in order to succeed in the energy transition (e.g. PwC 2020; Oosterhuis et al. 2020). For example, Accenture (Oosterhuis et al. 2020: 12) describes how learning will differ in the new operating environment for energy companies; it seems the company is expecting employees with a propensity for lifelong learning.

Ultimately, careers in the energy sector will require technical knowledge and analytical skills, an appreciation for the economic, social and environmental performance of energy systems (i.e. a sustainability mindset), the ability to work well in multidisciplinary teams, and the capacity for lifelong learning. These attributes, and how they may be acquired by students, are discussed next.

13.3.2 Program Outcomes

The focus here is on educating the next generation of technical specialists who will work specifically in energy systems analysis and design. More, as we have suggested, we have the opportunity to educate those who will lead the energy transition. On the design side, these will largely be engineers, subject to professional licensing, and educated in systems that are often accredited by professional bodies. On the analysis side, the workforce can be much broader, including people with expertise in data management, artificial intelligence (AI), project management, and finance, to name a few. In order for these energy systems specialists to lead us into a more sustainable energy future, their technical training must be complemented with skills in analysis, social issues, economics, and teamwork.

13.3.2.1 Technical Knowledge

Regardless of which specific job the energy systems designer or analyst holds, they will be well-served by an understanding of how various energy systems work. While engineers and project managers will clearly need different levels of understanding and differing skill sets, both will benefit from understanding not only how a specific technology works, but how it fits into the broader system. Their ability to problem-solve and to think creatively will be enhanced when the technologies and systems are understood.

To support this learning, students will need to acquire at least a basic understanding of some technical fundamentals, such as fluid mechanics, heat transfer, and electrical concepts (see Box 13.2). These fundamentals can then by applied to understand how conventional and unconventional energy systems work (see Box 13.3). By starting with the fundamentals, students will be better placed to learn about emerging technologies as they are developed; a strong understanding of the fundamentals is a good foundation for the lifelong learning we discuss.

The systems-level perspective is the first step toward taking a holistic view of an energy technology. For example, recognizing that while a technology has few to no on-site emissions during operations, it relies on large quantities of a rare metal that is mined at great environmental and social impact. The environmental and social aspects are discussed further later in this

---

Box 13.2 Samples of Fundamental Knowledge Requirements

Physics, math, materials, statistics, data science, thermal hydraulics, electric circuits, power systems, computer-aided design, engineering design (engineering programs).

Box 13.3 Energy Technologies and Carriers

Renewable energy (solar, wind, small-scale hydroelectric), fossil fuels (oil, natural gas, coal), waste-to-energy, energy-transportation (pipelines, wires, trains, etc.), energy storage technologies (electrical, thermal, and chemical; batteries, flywheels, ultracapacitors, hydrogen, molten salts), smart grid integrated energy systems.

chapter, but recognizing that a particular technology is part of a larger system is fundamental to the pursuit of sustainability. "Systems thinking" was one of the "key competencies" identified by Wiek et al. (2011).

13.3.2.2 Multidimensional Analytical Skills

Analytical skills will be of particular importance in the energy transition. It is imperative that those working to support and lead the transition have a wide, objective perspective on the options available to them. They must have the ability to critically assess new proposals before them, and the ability to solve new problems as they arise. Standard engineering analytical techniques will continue to be valuable for assessing technical performance, as well as environmental, social, and economic performances, to an extent.

These traditional techniques will need to be augmented with analytical methods that focus explicitly on the environmental and social performances of projects (not just technologies) and their associated systems. Further, these techniques must not be afterthoughts, similar to the end-of-pipe remedial approaches of the past. Systems-level, multidimensional analyses must be applied throughout the design stage of a technology and from the very start of the planning stage of a project. It is important this aspect be internalized by students. Analogously, the best way to teach students how, when, and why to apply these methods, might be to introduce them early and consistently throughout their degree studies. This is one element of the sustainability framework that energy specialists must apply.

Tools such as LCA (CSA 2006a,b), sustainability assessment (e.g. Gibson 2006), and energy system optimization models, including the use of AI, decision-making with uncertainties, fuzzy logic, and game theory (e.g. Liu et al. 2013; Tan et al. 2021), are all valuable. It is not necessary (or possible) for graduating students to be experts in all useful tools, but they should be familiar with them – sufficiently familiar that they could have a knowledgeable discussion with a practitioner.

13.3.2.3 Non-technical Skills

It is important that students understand that they will not be experts in all aspects necessary for the successful implementation of an energy technology or project. Just as important as students' technical and analytical capabilities, will be their ability to work as part of interdisciplinary teams. Gone are the days when engineers can solve a problem in isolation. A "solution" generated in that way is likely to fail in today's environment. Indeed, it has been argued that "sustainable development [is] a wicked problem" (Pryshlakivsky and Searcy 2013) and that concept (or something similar; Yearworth 2016) has been discussed in relation to energy (e.g. Pacquet 1989). In its definition of wicked problems, the Design Dictionary (Anon. 2007) states that a monodisciplinary approach to solving such a problem is destined to simply exacerbate the problem.

Engineers and energy systems analysts will be required to consult with economists, social scientists, indigenous and community groups, and politicians in order to identify system-appropriate solutions to the problems we currently face. Teamwork and external consultations will require strong communication skills, as we will discuss. The ability to work in multidisciplinary teams, and further, understanding the value (and, frankly, necessity) of that approach, is another aspect of the sustainability mindset we need our energy systems specialists to espouse.

Additionally, students must be taught to apply their fundamental knowledge, their systems-perspective and their analytical skills to situations that will continue to evolve over their careers. As economies shift to new energy systems, problems may not be solvable based on historical precedents; we will likely run into challenges we do not yet expect. Consequently, our workforce must also have the ability to adapt; this was also noted by Ruiz-Rivas et al. (2020). Educating workers to perform one job for their entire working careers is no longer a viable option; emphasis must be placed on lifelong learning. This is already evident in the information being shared with current energy industry companies, centered on upskilling and reskilling their workforce (e.g. Oosterhuis et al. 2020). The implication is that this will not happen once; workers will not take a single course and be set for the rest of their careers. Instead, a career may contain many twists and turns, each with a different learning requirement attached. The learning may be informal, and perhaps self-directed. For example, an engineer reading the specifications and technical bulletins about a new type of solar panel hitting the market. The learning may be more structured and measurable. For example, the Province of Ontario in Canada has recently been pursuing the development of microcredentials targeted at providing workers with in-demand skills (MCU 2021). In order to be successful at lifelong learning, energy system designers and analysts will require a strong understanding of the fundamentals, a reliable analytical and problem-solving toolbox, and a perspective that is both open to new ideas and critical in their assessment. These are attributes that can be taught.

13.3.3 Teaching Toward Learning Outcomes

In much the same way as sustainability integrates environmental, social, and economic perspectives, these varied perspectives should be integrated into an undergraduate program of study. Having students complete a course on environmental science, a course on social welfare, and a course on economics would seem to simply reinforce the siloed approach to energy that we must overcome. Instead, the holistic nature of sustainability should be reinforced at each opportunity, including in curricular design. It should be noted that various approaches of incorporating sustainability into curricula have been implemented and discussed, and the "best" approach is still an open question (Thürer et al. 2018). However, the integrative approach will be prioritized here.

While industry requirements of energy specialists are still unknown, or at the very least, evolving, that does not mean industry should be excluded from program development or oversight. Engagement with employers in the form of an advisory board, invited talks, and/or student project advisors, can be invaluable for ensuring and maintaining the strengths of the program and graduates.

13.3.3.1 Engineering Programs

Modifying an existing, running program is a large undertaking for a university and relatively smaller changes (replacing a course here or there) are easier than a broad-based reconceptualization of how material is organized and shared with students. At the same time, however, many engineering programs are accredited by external, professional bodies. As well, students who ultimately become working professional engineers will bear a considerable degree of responsibility to society, necessitating that they attain rigorous learning outcomes. This can limit the flexibility available to instructors to incorporate sustainability concepts into the curriculum.

The best-case scenario would be for the accrediting agencies to recognize the importance of sustainability concepts and facilitate their incorporation into curricula across engineering disciplines. Based on their literature review, Thürer et al. (2018) identified the need for accreditation bodies to be a "driving force" behind the integration of sustainability into engineering curricula. In Canada, for example, the Canadian Engineering Accreditation Board (CEAB) is a committee of Engineers Canada (Engineers Canada 2021) which, as we have mentioned, has issued guidance on the inclusion of sustainability in engineering practice. As well, the CEAB mandates that all engineering programs "must include studies in...sustainable development and environmental stewardship" (CEAB 2020). Similarly, the accrediting agency in the US, ABET (2021), requires that graduates "consider the impact of engineering solutions in global, economic, environmental, and societal contexts" in their decision-making. From an instructional perspective, the challenge can arise from trying to incorporate these elements along with all other requirements into the relatively limited time and space of an undergraduate degree. Siller et al. (2009) also noted this challenge [as cited by Thürer et al. (2018)].

However, anecdotally, one of the elements that engineering students most enjoy is solving real-world problems. Emphasizing for students that real-world problems require sustainable solutions and requiring them to take a systems-level, multi-disciplinary approach to their work, should help them internalize the concept of sustainability and make its consideration second nature. Indeed, Thürer et al. (2018) noted the importance of active learning in students' "retention" of sustainability concepts. Problems and case studies should range in scale from community-based to questions with international implications to ensure students are exposed to the full breadth of issues surrounding energy.

In terms of making room within an engineering degree, it may be time to shift away from the traditional structure. Typically, engineering programs begin with one-to-two years of basic math, science, and applied science, in whatever discipline is being studied. Beginning in third year, knowledge becomes more applied, and by fourth year, students are expected to be able to integrate the concepts they have previously covered to address more complex problems. With an ever-increasing body of background knowledge to learn (and teach) and increasing restrictions on the academy (reductions in instructional time, rising tuition costs for students, changes to the ways in which students learn and the skills expected by industry), it may be time to reorganize courses to focus more on applications, with a just-in-time-delivery of fundamental knowledge. For example, rather than teaching a first-year course on chemistry to energy systems engineers, teach the chemistry they need in a course devoted to fossil fuel energy conversion and pollution control. Students may learn and retain the knowledge and skills better, by seeing a stronger emphasis between the theory and the application. This approach was taken in the development of a Bachelor of Technology in Sustainable Energy Systems degree at Ontario Tech University. This is a natural analogue of the discussion of teaching sustainability: rather than having a course on sustainability, teach it where it is needed/used, with the intent of emphasizing the connections between it and other content students are learning to improve their understanding and retention.

In order to develop comprehensive energy systems educational programs, it is crucial to ensure that the learning outcomes are clearly established to ensure a smooth and successful link to target careers and market needs. The collective set of graduate attributes utilized by the CEAB (2020) is as follows:

- A Knowledge Base for Engineering (KB)
- Problem Analysis (PA)
- Investigation (Inv.)
- Design (Des.)
- Use of Engineering Tools (Tools)
- Individual and Teamwork (Team)
- Communication Skills (Comm.)
- Professionalism (Prof.)
- Impact of Engineering on Society and the Environment (Impacts)
- Ethics and Equity (Ethics)
- Economics and Project Management (Econ.)
- Lifelong Learning (LL)

Figure 13.3 Learning outcomes and energy systems engineering education.

The proposed mapping between graduate attributes and layers of an energy systems engineering program is shown in Figure 13.3.

The proper and balanced mapping between graduate attributes and main themes of the program as well as key courses will enable smooth flow of learning from early years of the program until final years, as shown in Figure 13.4. Ruis-Rivas et al. (2020) present a discussion of the proposed contents for "sustainable energy engineering" programs.

At Ontario Tech University, engineering programs are organized around "streams" (Kishawy et al. 2014). Each stream can be thought of as a thread through the program in a particular subfield, along which students progressively build their skills. A program may have streams in design engineering, thermo fluids, and solid mechanics, for example (Kishawy et al. 2014). Within each stream, various CEAB graduate attributes are "introduced, developed, and applied" (Kishawy et al. 2014). Since engineering programs must retain these core competencies, the learning outcomes related to sustainability could be added in as a new stream. An example stream, based on the program structure in Figure 13.4, is laid out in Figure 13.5, along with sample learning outcomes and suggested teaching tools.

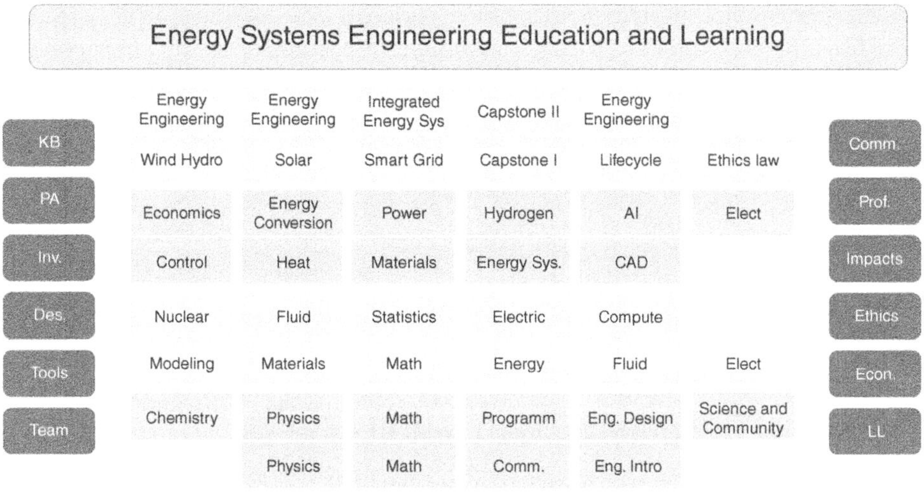

Figure 13.4 Main themes of an energy systems engineering program.

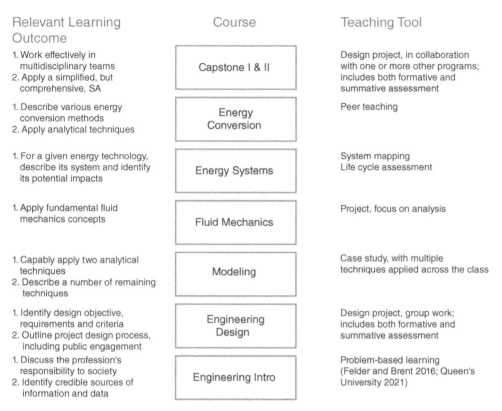

Figure 13.5 Proposed sustainability stream within an engineering program, leading to the achievement of the requisite learning outcomes.

The stream is a sequence of eight courses (Capstone I and II are offered in consecutive semesters in fourth year). In each course, students work toward at least one of the desired learning outcomes: technical knowledge and analytical skills; an appreciation for the economic, social, and environmental performance of energy systems (i.e. a sustainability mindset); the ability to work well in multidisciplinary teams; and, the capacity for lifelong learning. The courses selected here are for the most part examples or suggestions; however, Capstone in particular, is highly recommended to be included, as discussed in Section 13.3.3.1.7.

13.3.3.1.1 Engineering Intro
This course is students' first introduction to the field of engineering, a glimpse of what they will be studying for the next four years, and potentially of their future careers. It is also an excellent opportunity to lay the groundwork for the sustainability mindset and capacity for lifelong learning. The first learning outcome suggested here is for students to be able to discuss the engineering profession's responsibility to society. This is a fundamental element of engineering and arguably equivalent to the need for a sustainability mindset, if it is accepted that achieving sustainable development is necessary for global society. It is not uncommon for engineering students to take a course on ethics (Newberry 2004). If this is taken at a late stage of their studies, students are more mature and are more seriously contemplating their careers and what it means to be a licensed engineer. Introducing this concept earlier, however, allows for more opportunities to train students and to encourage ethical practice and consideration throughout their undergraduate career. The University of Windsor (2021), for example,

requires their first year, first semester, engineering students to take Engineering and the Profession, wherein they learn about the links between engineering and society, and specifically "sustainability considerations." This first course is also a great opportunity to lay the foundation for lifelong learning. Specifically, teaching students how to seek out information, how to assess the credibility of a source, and even where to look for information. In this first semester, students have no real engineering knowledge or skills. What they do have is their knowledge of fundamental math and science from secondary school. In some ways, this is analogous to a situation they may face as practicing engineers faced with an emerging technology. One way of achieving the learning outcome may be through problem-based learning (PBL; Felder and Brent 2016 p. 207; Queen's University 2021). This approach involves active learning to engage students' interest and allows them the independence to guide their own learning. However, a fairly large supervisory element should be maintained, appropriate to students just beginning their postsecondary education. Indeed, while PBL could encompass an entire course (Queen's University 2021), at this stage, more tightly constrained problems are more likely appropriate.

13.3.3.1.2 Engineering Design

It is important that engineering students recognize the interdisciplinary implications of design, right from the start of their education. To do otherwise would be to reinforce the misconception that social and environmental impacts of a project are secondary elements, to be managed once the technology and economics have been specified. Learning outcome (1) in this course in Figure 13.5 is somewhat standard; the intention is that the design objectives, requirements, and criteria cover not only technical and economic considerations, but also environmental and social performance. It is also important that when introducing a typical engineering design process, stakeholder engagement is emphasized, whether the design is for a technology or a project (e.g. installation of an energy technology in a specific location). Having the students complete a group design project is a natural option here. If outside participation can be achieved, so much the better, although it is noted that might be difficult given the students' early stage of study and therefore low expected expertise. Having alumni or even upper year students act as stakeholders can be an option.

13.3.3.1.3 Modeling

This course gives students the opportunity to focus on developing and honing their analytical skills. As in Section 13.3.2.2, it may be best if systems-level, multidimensional analytical tools are introduced early and consistently throughout a program. As such, it is not intended that this be "the" course on analytical tools. Indeed, application could begin in first year, at an appropriate level. However, this course could give students the chance to become expert in one or two key tools. Recalling that the purpose of a stream is for students to sequentially improve their skill level, this course could build on techniques introduced in first year and set students up for subsequent applications and exposure to other tools. Depending on instructor expertise and instructional resources generally (software availability, teaching assistant availability and expertise, etc.), it may be desirable to have students select from a set of approved techniques, to better align with in dividual interests, and to reinforce the idea of a broad field and equitable importance across the field. Indeed, it may be instructive to assign the class a single case study, but have students analyze it in multiple ways, using multiple techniques (e.g. each student or group of students conducts a unique analysis). Students would then see not only the functioning of the different techniques, but the importance of applying multiple techniques and conversely the danger of applying only one technique, as well as the need to critically assess a model's output.

13.3.3.1.4 Fluid Mechanics

Fluid mechanics was chosen as an example of a traditional engineering course, wherein scientific principles are put to practical use. An energy system engineering program would need such a course to teach students the basics of pressure, forces exerted by fluids, energy balances, momentum transfer, and internal and external fluid flows, for example. These are basic concepts covered by many engineering disciplines and establish some of the fundamental knowledge students will be able to rely on throughout their careers. When presented with a new energy technology, they will be able to fall back on their second-year mechanical energy equation as a first check on the feasibility of the technology and/or the veracity of the developer's claims. As a first step toward developing student's abilities in this area, a project could be introduced. This approach was employed in a second-year, fluid mechanics course at Ontario Tech University in 2020. Students were asked to apply concepts they had learned in class to an actual engineering project, either operating or in development. For example, they could identify a specific hydro dam, look at the head difference between the reservoirs, make appropriate assumptions and calculate a potential power output, which they could then compare against the rated power of the plant. The intent was to help students learn and increase their enthusiasm by applying what could be fairly theoretical course content to a real-life scenario.

13.3.3.1.5 Energy Systems

An energy systems course is an opportunity for students to focus on the systems aspect. Again, applying the stream approach, they would have been introduced to this concept previously, and are expected to be experts by their fourth-year capstone projects. The learning outcome identified in Figure 13.5 is course-specific, but it contributes to students attaining the sustainability mindset and expanding their analytical skills. As suggested in Section 13.2.1, life cycles are a helpful way of conceptualizing an energy system. While teaching LCA can constitute an entire course, its principles can be conveyed to upper-year undergraduate students fairly easily. This not only helps them describe an energy system, it gives them another analytical technique for their toolbox (perhaps not something they are able to apply, but certainly something in which they could be sufficiently knowledgeable to converse with a practitioner). Another activity that may help students conceptualize an energy system may be to map it geographically. For example, installing a solar panel on a residential rooftop may seem likely a fairly small action. However, when one considers that the panel might have been manufactured in China and shipped to North America, that the metal for the frame might have been mined elsewhere, the global reach of energy systems, and their impacts, can quickly become clear. The importance of considering impacts in this course may open up another avenue for learning: encouraging students to seek out the perspectives and insights of non-engineers to explore how energy systems are perceived by others, would be a first step toward understanding the value of a multidisciplinary team.

13.3.3.1.6 Energy Conversion

This course gives students the ability to strengthen their discipline-specific technical knowledge. In terms of the stream, it performs an intermediary function, linking the fundamental courses like fluid mechanics and heat transfer, and the more technology-specific courses, such as solar and wind/hydro. It also gives students the opportunity to apply some of their learned analytical techniques, essentially practice in advance of the summative capstone project in fourth year. A teaching technique that may be valuable here is peer-teaching. Each student or pair of students could be assigned an energy conversion to explore (thus also contributing to their propensity for lifelong learning) and then present to the class (improving communication skills, as well). In order to develop their multidisciplinary teamwork skills, students work with others to better integrate various types of energies and energy conversion.

13.3.3.1.7 Capstone

Capstone projects are a common, summative assessment in engineering programs. They are generally intended to require students to make use of "everything" they have learned through their studies in order to solve a problem, as close to a real-world problem as possible. In an energy system engineering program this might be for example: "Design an energy system to supply electricity, heat, and transportation to a remote community," with some additional information around location, budget, etc. In terms of the sustainability stream, the capstone project gives students the opportunity to showcase their:

- **Technical knowledge and analytical skills**: This is done by them actually designing an appropriate energy system to meet the established need.
- **Sustainability mindset by applying a sustainability assessment**: While this would normally be a huge project on its own, expectations could be set such that the assessment could touch on key aspects, while being suitably constrained so as to be achievable with the resources available.
- **Multidisciplinary teamwork skills**: As discussed further in Section 13.3.3.2, developing the capstone courses (across two semesters) to explicitly require the participation of students in programs outside of engineering would be an excellent way of giving the students the opportunity to learn how to work effectively with people from other disciplines. It would be important, however, that this not be students' first experience with this type of work.
- **Capacity for lifelong learning**: Generally, capstone projects should be predominantly student-led. In order to successfully solve their assigned problem, they will be required to seek out information on their own, to overcomes challenges as they arise, and likely to move themselves beyond what they have learned in their courses, in terms of technical knowledge and analytical tools.

13.3.3.2 Energy Analyst Programs

Non-engineering degrees allow for more flexibility in approach. Although, in the area of energy, not too much will change relative to an engineering degree. While not designing energy systems, to be a competent professional it will be important for graduates to understand how energy systems work. This will necessitate coursework on energy systems specifically, but also many of the applied fundamentals important to engineers, such as fluid mechanics and heat transfer. In this case, though, the potential for just-in-time-delivery of content becomes even greater: teaching only those fluid mechanics concepts students need, at the time they need to apply them, rather than a full course in the fundamentals.

By removing some of the technical requirements there is more program space to place greater emphasis on skills such as communication, and some of the softer elements of sustainability, such as social implications. The importance of communication in the field of energy should not be underestimated. Energy projects require the cooperation of industry, governments, and the public. Each of these entities has different goals, levels of expertise, and requirements and expectations regarding communications. Failing to meet these communications needs with any one group can spell disaster for an energy project. This relates to the "social license" of energy; the necessary buy-in from taxpayers, consumers, nearby property-owners, environmentalists, chambers of commerce, etc. Engineers have a reputation for being weak communicators, although this is, of course, not always the case. For those engineers and their instructors who would like to strengthen communication skills, there is not always time in an undergraduate program; it is one of 12 graduate attributes listed by the CEAB (2020). Consequently, if an energy analyst degree is better able to incorporate communication skills, that will be an invaluable asset to multidisciplinary energy teams.

There are many traditional approaches to teaching communication skills, both written and oral. These can include collaborations with institutional writing offices, formative assessments, and class presentations. These are all valuable. However, it is also important that graduates are proficient in more modern and perhaps casual modes of communication, such as blogs, vlogs, and social media. The energy field often interfaces with the general public and it is important to relate to people on their own terms. A graduate course in the Faculty of Energy Systems and Nuclear Science at Ontario Tech University, for example, has students follow the social media postings of companies, environmental non-governmental organizations (ENGOs), commentators, etc.

In addition to fostering strong communication skills, non-engineering programs may be better able to encourage energy-focused students to integrate with non-energy and non-technical students. An excellent way to understand the importance of a sustainability approach is to interact with people who have limited knowledge of, and interest in, energy. These are the people with whom energy project proponents will be communicating. People who care deeply for their communities, their family and friends, their environment, their local economy, etc., and who do not understand why it is important that an electricity generating station be developed on the edge of town, or why they must switch from the gasoline-fueled car they understand to an electric one they are unfamiliar with, or even to switch to transit for their daily commute. One of the strongest aspects of a university education, in any discipline, is exposure to ideas and values that differ from your own.

Providing these opportunities for multidisciplinary interactions are not always easy. Universities themselves can easily become siloed. The issue of energy, however, so explicitly cuts across so many fields that it may be easier to find instructors in non-technical programs who are looking for opportunities for their students to interact with technical experts, just as technical program instructors seek the opposite. Such interactions could begin informally, through student groups or interdepartmental workshops. Integrating a course from a non-technical field (e.g. sociology) into a technical energy degree would certainly immerse the technical students into a different culture. While valuable, that may not necessarily prompt the dialogue that we are seeking. Requiring students to work on a multidisciplinary project would seem to offer the best chance for them to learn how to communicate with each other and to learn the value of their colleagues' perspectives and expertise. Regardless of the program, engineering or not, no graduate is going to be able to be expert in all aspects of sustainability. As we have noted, this is where the importance of teamwork comes in. Developing a class project that cuts across programs may be challenging logistically, but worth the effort in the end.

In terms of degree nomenclature, non-engineering degrees of this type are somewhat difficult to name. Given the focus on technology and the applied nature of the material, a Bachelor of Science is not quite appropriate. Bachelor of Applied Science is an option, but in Canada at least, that is sometimes used for engineering degrees. Another option to consider is Bachelor of Technology (BTech). Programs such as BTechs can also require shifts in public perception and preferences as the popularity for these degrees seen in some countries, e.g. India, does not yet translate to other countries, such as Canada, where less than a handful of BTech programs exist. Going forward, energy systems education lends itself well to a more fluid approach where technological comfort in graduates is key, even if specific technologies will change. Also, when social aspects are often the largest driver of energy trends, graduates need to understand the system complexities between technology and its shifting interaction with society.

13.4 Summary and Recommendations

Globally, we are in the midst of an accelerating energy transition. Society needs an expert workforce that understands not only the energy technologies available to us, but the economic, social, and environmental impacts of their use, on a systems-scale. It is insufficient to analyze a specific energy technology or project in isolation, without considering how it was manufactured, how it will be decommissioned, and where it fits into the larger energy system surrounding it.

These are high-level goals and aspirations. They are not necessarily actionable. Further, while employers may agree they need such people, they too are in flux. Employers are not yet entirely sure which skills will be most required. This gives educators and students the chance to lead: to update and implement new postsecondary programs that help students attain the knowledge and skills they will need to lead the energy transition.

The proposal here is that our energy systems analysts and designers will require technical knowledge and analytical skills, a sustainability mindset, the ability to work well in multidisciplinary teams, and the capacity for lifelong learning.

How these learning outcomes are to be achieved will vary by the type of program. In all cases, it is our recommendation that sustainability thinking be integrated throughout the curriculum. Not only is this expected to help students internalize the concept of sustainability, but it will reinforce the integrative nature of sustainability.

It is further recommended that accrediting bodies for engineering programs encourage and facilitate the integration of sustainability thinking into engineering curricula. Both the Canadian and American bodies, for example, have already recognized the importance of students understanding sustainability concepts. Providing clear guidance on how the concepts can (should) be incorporated into already crowded curricula would be an efficient means of reaching all engineering students in a timely manner.

Finally, the ability to work effectively in multidisciplinary teams, and a propensity for lifelong learning need to be fostered in both engineering and non-engineering students.

The energy transition is a global challenge, and an opportunity. It is also a perfect example of a field where sustainability expertise is required. We need experts with strong fundamental knowledge and analytical skills who are able to adapt quickly and capably to changing circumstances, and to work confidently with experts across sectors and with laypeople. Finally, we need to ensure these experts see the whole picture, a picture that will be clearer when viewed through the lens of sustainability.

References

ABET Engineering Accreditation Commission (ABET) (2021). *Criteria for Accrediting Engineering Programs*. E001 12-28-2020. ABET: Baltimore, MD https://www.abet.org/wp-content/uploads/2021/02/E001-21-22-EAC-Criteria.pdf (accessed 10 July 2021).

Allen-Dumas, M.R., KC, B., and Cunliff, C.I. (2019). Extreme weather and climate vulnerabilities of the electric grid: a summary of environmental sensitivity quantification methods. *ORNL/TM-2019/1252*. Climate Change Science Institute, Oak Ridge National Laboratory. https://www.energy.gov/sites/prod/files/2019/09/f67/Oak%20Ridge%20National%20Laboratory%20EIS%20Response.pdf (accessed 6 June 2021).

Anon. (2007). Wicked problems. In: *Design Dictionary* (ed. M. Erlhoff and T. Marshall), 434–434. Birkhäuser: Berlin, Boston.

Canadian Electricity Association (2016). Adapting to climate change: state of play and recommendations for the electricity sector in Canada. https://electricity.ca/wp-content/

uploads/2016/02/Adapting_to_Climate_Change-State_of_Play_and_Recommendations_for_the_Electricity_Sector_in_Canada.pdf (accessed 6 June 2021).

Canadian Engineering Accreditation Board (CEAB), Engineers Canada. (2020). Questionnaire for evaluation of an engineering program – 2021/2022 visit cycle. https://engineerscanada.ca/accreditation/accreditation-resources/2021-2022-accreditation-cycle (accessed 10 July 2021).

Canadian Standards Association (CSA) (2006a). *Environmental management — life cycle assessment — principles and framework (CAN/CSA-ISO 14040:06 (ISO 14040: 2006))*, 2e. Canadian Standards Association: Mississauga, Ontario.

Canadian Standards Association (CSA) (2006b). *Environmental management — life cycle assessment — requirements and guidelines (CAN/CSA-ISO 14044:06 (ISO 14044:2006))*. Canadian Standards Association: Mississauga, Ontario.

Caranci, B., Fong, F. 2021. Don't let history repeat: Canada's energy sector transition and the potential impact on workers. 6 April. *TD Economics.* http://economics.td.com (accessed 6 July 2021).

Clean Energy Canada. 2021. The new reality. Tracking the energy transition 2021. June. http://cleanenergycanada.org (accessed 3 July 2021).

Davis, D.L. (1997). Short-term improvements in public health from global-climate policies on fossil-fuel combustion: an interim report. *The Lancet (British edition).* 350 (9088): 1341–1349.

Energy Futures Initiative (EFI) and National Association of State Energy Officials (NASEO) (2021). The 2019 U.S. energy & employment report: A joint project of NASEO & EFI. https://www.usenergyjobs.org/2019-report (accessed 15 July 2021).

Engineers Canada (2016). National guideline on sustainable development and environmental stewardship for professional engineers. *National guideline.* https://engineerscanada.ca/national-guideline-on-sustainable-development-and-environmental-stewardship-for-professional-engineers (accessed 6 July 2021).

Engineers Canada (2021). Accreditation board. https://engineerscanada.ca/accreditation/accreditation-board (accessed 16 July 2021).

Felder, R.M. and Brent, R. (2016). *Teaching and learning STEM, a practical guide.* In: *Jossey-Bass.* San Francisco, CA.

Gibson, R.B. (2006). Beyond the pillars: Sustainability assessment as a framework for effective integration of social, economic and ecological considerations in significant decision-making. *Journal of Environmental Assessment Policy and Management.* 8 (3): 259–280.

Hoegh-Guldberg, O. et al. (2019). The human imperative of stabilizing global climate change at 1.5°C. *Science* 365: 1263.

International Energy Agency (IEA) (2019). Changes in global energy intensity in energy per unit of GDP, 1981–2016, IEA, Paris. https://www.iea.org/data-and-statistics/charts/changes-in-global-energy-intensity-in-energy-per-unit-of-gdp-1981-2016 (accessed 15 July 2021).

International Energy Agency (IEA) (2021). Total final consumption (TFC) by sector, World 1990–2018. Data and statistics, data tools, data browser. https://www.iea.org/data-and-statistics/data-browser?country=WORLD&fuel=Energy%20consumption&indicator=TFCShareBySector> (accessed 15 July 2021).

Kishawy, H.A., Sidhu, T., Pop-Iliev, R. et al. (2014). Meeting the outcome-based CEAB accreditation criteria: engineering programs at UOIT. In: *Proceedings of the 2014 Canadian Engineering Education Association (CEEA14) Conference*, 43. Canmore, AB (8–11 June 2014). https://ojs.library.queensu.ca/index.php/PCEEA/article/view/5885/5607 (accessed 27 July 2021).

Liu, J., Lin, Q.G., Huang, G.H. et al. (2013). Energy systems planning and GHG-emission control under uncertainty in the province of Liaoning, China – A dynamic inexact energy systems optimization model. *International Journal of Electrical Power & Energy Systems* 53: 142–158.

McManus, M.C. and Taylor, C.M. (2015). The changing nature of life cycle assessment. *Biomass and Bioenergy.* 82: 13–26. https://doi.org/10.1016/j.biombioe.2015.04.024.

Ministry of Colleges and Universities, Government of Ontario (MCU) (2021). Micro-credentials from Ontario's postsecondary schools. https://www.ontario.ca/page/micro-credentials-ontarios-postsecondary-schools (accessed 16 July 2021).

Mueller, N., Rojas-Rueda, D., Basagaña, X., and e.a. (2017). Urban and transport planning related exposures and mortality: a health impact assessment for cities. *Environmental Health Perspectives.* 125 (1): 89–96.

Natural Resources Canada, Government of Canada (NRCan) (2020). Energy and the economy. https://www.nrcan.gc.ca/science-data/data-analysis/energy-data-analysis/energy-facts/energy-and-economy/20062 (accessed 15 July 2021).

Newberry, B. (2004). The dilemma of ethics in engineering education. *Science and Engineering Ethics.* 10: 343–351.

Oosterhuis, I., Van Singel, J., Datta, A., et al. (2020). Reinventing the energy workforce for a net-zero world. *Accenture.* https://www.accenture.com/ca-en/insights/energy/reinventing-energy-workforce (accessed 6 July 2021).

Paquet, G. (1989). A social learning framework for a wicked problem: the case of energy. *Energy Studies Review* 1 (1) article 5.: Available at: http://digitalcommons.mcmaster.ca/esr (accessed 14 July 2021).

Pioro, I., Duffey, R.B., Kirillov, P.L. et al. (2019). Current status and future developments in nuclear-power industry of the world. *Journal of Nuclear Engineering and Radiation Science.* 5: 024001–024001.

PricewaterhouseCoopers LLP (PwC) (2020). Forward together, What's ahead for Canada's oil and gas industry. 3. New world. New skills. Preparing your workforce for the energy transition. *Energy visions 2020.* https://www.pwc.com/ca/en/industries/energy/energy-visions-2020/new-world-new-skills-preparing-your-workforce-for-the-energy-transition.html. (accessed 11 July 2021).

Pryshlakivsky, J. and Searcy, C. (2013, 2013). Sustainable development as a wicked problem. In: *Managing and engineering in complex situations. Topics in safety, risk, reliability and quality 21* (ed. S.F. Kovacic and A. Sousa-Poza). Springer Science+Business Media Dordrecht. Ch. 6.

Queen's University, Centre for Teaching and Learning. (2021). Teaching support, instructional strategies, problem-based learning. https://www.queensu.ca/ctl/teaching-support/instructional-strategies/problem-based-learning (accessed: 30 July 2021).

Ruiz-Rivas, U., Martinez-Crespo, J., Venegas, M., and Chinchilla-Sanchez, M. (2020). Energy engineering curricula for sustainable development, considering underserved areas. *Journal of Cleaner Production.* 258: 120960.

Shindell, D. and Smith, C.J. (2019). Climate and air-quality benefits of a realistic phase-out of fossil fuels. *Nature* 573: 408–411. https://doi.org/10.1038/s41586-019-1554-z.

Siller, T.J., A. Rosales, J., and Haines, A. (2009). Benally Development of undergraduate students' professional skills. *J. Prof. Issues Eng. Educ. Pract.*, 135 (3): 102–108.

Sofiev, M., Winebrake, J.J., Johansson, L. et al. (2018). Cleaner fuels for ships provide public health benefits with climate tradeoffs. *Nature communications* 9 (1): 406–406.

Steinberger, J.K. (2016). Energising human development. http://hdr.undp.org/en/content/energising-human-development (accessed 15 July 2021).

Tan, C., Geng, S., Tan, Z. et al. (2021). Integrated energy system – Hydrogen natural gas hybrid energy storage system optimization model based on cooperative game under carbon neutrality. *Journal of Energy Storage.* 38: 102539.

Thürer, M., Tomašević, I., Stevenson, M. et al. (2018). A systematic review of the literature on integrating sustainability into engineering curricula. *Journal of Cleaner Production.* 181: 608–617.

Trigaux, D., Wijnants, L., De Troyer, F. et al. (2017). Life cycle assessment and life cycle costing of road infrastructure in residential neighbourhoods. *Int J Life Cycle Assess.* 22: 938–951. https://doi.org/10.1007/s11367-016-1190-x.

United Nations, Department of Economic and Social Affairs, Sustainable Development (UN) (2021a). Goals, 7, Ensure access to affordable, reliable, sustainable and modern energy for all. https://sdgs.un.org/goals/goal7 (accessed 15 July 2021).

United Nations, Department of Economic and Social Affairs, Sustainable Development (UN) (2021b). Topics, Energy. https://sdgs.un.org/topics/energy (accessed 15 July 2021).

University of Windsor, Faculty of Engineering, WINONE – Office for First-Year Students (2021). *Course Information, Course Descriptions*. https://www.uwindsor.ca/engineering/674/course-descriptions (accessed 30 July 2021).

Wiek, A., Withycombe, L., and Redman, C.L. (2011). Key competencies in sustainability: a reference framework for academic program development. *Sustainability Science.* 6: 203–218.

World Commission on Environment and Development (WCED) (1987). Report of the World Commission on Environment and Development: Our common future. https://sustainabledevelopment.un.org/content/documents/5987our-common-future.pdf (accessed 15 August 2021).

Yearworth, M. (2016). Sustainability as a 'super-wicked' problem; opportunities and limits for engineering methodology. *Intelligent Buildings International.* 8 (1): 37–47.

Part III

Global Trends – Country Specific Initiatives

14

Sustainability Teaching in Higher Education and Universities in Spain

Sergio Nogales Delgado, Silvia Román Suero, and Beatriz Ledesma Cano

14.1 The Shift Toward More Sustainable Practices: Global Framework

Values, skills, and abilities in the frame of energy saving, efficiency, and good practices to decrease the human footprint on the environment are essential in our current society. These skills are a key factor in relation to sustainable development and governments all over the world, at regional, national, or international levels, have moved into action to favor research initiatives, to effect changes in the model of management of energy and wastes and, to a lesser extent, to modify the curricula of educational systems to provide these skills.

An increasing number of national and international regulations are pushing our society to shift the ways of managing resources, as we discuss; these have been essential to agreeing the context for the subsequent educational landmarks (see Figure 14.1).

A highlight starting point for initiatives targeted to foster practices that preserve the environment was the first Human Environment Conference in Stockholm, Sweden, in 1972. For the 20th anniversary, the Rio Summit (United Nations (UN) Conference on Environment and Development), marked a blueprint for international action on the environment, in 1992; in this event, a global forum of non-governmental organizations was also held, and a common vision on the world's future in relation to environment and socioeconomic development was settled.

The Kyoto protocol was also very representative. It was signed in the 1997 UN Framework Convention on Climate Change that was linked to the reduction of greenhouse gases in order to prevent global warming. Although this event was a milestone that brought up the commitment that all nations should have about their emissions, the associated carbon dioxide markets were a drawback toward real changes related to the environment.

The UN 2000 Millennium Summit led to the Millennium Declaration of the Millennium Development Goals (MDGs). Two years later, in 2002, the World Summit on Sustainable Development (Johannesburg Summit), would focus on how to face the difficult challenges associated with the rising rate of population growth of the planet. The World Summit in 2005, at the UN headquarters, in New York, was a follow-up of the 2000 Millennium Summit and involved a review of the MDGs.

In 2008, the UN Environmental Programme (UNEP) launched the Green Economy Initiative (GEI) to enhance the development of environmental initiatives, in a context of sustainable

---

The Wiley Handbook of Sustainability in Higher Education Learning and Teaching, First Edition.
Edited by Kelum A. A. Gamage and Nanda Gunawardhana.
© 2022 John Wiley & Sons, Inc. Published 2022 by John Wiley & Sons, Inc.

Figure 14.1 Significant landmarks on policies and education in the context of sustainability.

development. This was the seed to launch other plans in the same frame and, as a consequence, the "green economy in the context of sustainable development and poverty eradication" was included in the agenda of the Rio+20 summit, held in 2012, and was recognized as a tool to reach sustainable development (United Nations 2011).

The GEI concept seeks the wellness of people and social equality, at the same time that environmental risks and economical restrictions are improved. This strategy has evolved toward the concept of an inclusive green economy, characterized by being low-carbon economy, efficient, and clean with regard to production processes, but also inclusive in terms of consumption and based on circularity, solidarity, resilience, opportunity, and interdependence. Therefore, the main aim of the GEI is not only to generate employment and wealth, but also to improve our health, environment, and future, within the limits of a fragile and finite planet.

After the Rio Earth Summit (Rio+20 2012), the first Partnership for Action on Green Economy (PAGE 2021) was created to give support to those countries aiming to take part in greener and more inclusive projects. The commitment of this initiative was to place sustainability at the center of politics and economics of countries, with the target of contributing to the 2030 Agenda for Sustainable Development (United Nations 2019). This was the seed that facilitated the UN Summit for Sustainable Development in 2015; more than 150 countries embraced the cited 2030 Agenda, which included 17 objectives requiring urgent action from all countries (both developed and developing ones) in a common alliance. These objectives stated that ending poverty has to be linked to strategy management, improving health and education, reducing inequalities, and fostering economic development (UNESCO 2012).

A very important milestone on the path toward the settlement of green practices was the Paris Agreement in 2015, signed by 190 member states, which established the basis of the current situation and forecast possible scenarios about global temperature, based on the expected carbon dioxide emissions, and pointed out the urgent need to take measures at a global scale. The dramatic consequences of anthropogenic activities on Earth were visualized.

In Europe, the Europe 2020 strategy, based on the premise of an intelligent, sustainable, and integrating growth, aimed to reduce greenhouse gas emissions by 20% with respect to the values obtained in 1990, and to increase by 20% the participation of renewable energies and energy efficiency. This was then moved into the Europe 2030 strategy that emphasized industrial innovation and efficiency to foster sustainable growth.

In addition, the European Green Deal set the target of making Europe climate neutral by 2050 and also set a greenhouse gas emission reduction target (by 2030) of at least 50% and toward 55% compared with 1990 levels. This action plan also emphasizes the conversion of wastes into added-value products and their linkage to the potential of creating employment and contributing to the adherence to the UN's Sustainable Development Goals (SDGs) shown in the Agenda of Sustainable Development previously described, especially in reference to SDG 12, to guarantee sustainable models of production and consumption (European Union 2021).

At a national level, "The Circular Economy in Spain" report of 2017 drew attention to the "incipient character" of this strategy in the country. So far, the measures that have been taken have been mostly focused on environmental politics devoted to the final product life cycle. An example is the case of waste management and the National Plan for the Management of Wastes (Plan Estatal Marco de Gestión de Residuos, PEMAR, 2016–2022). In addition, new perspectives for bioprocesses have also been opened with the Spanish Strategy of Bioeconomy (Estrategia Española de Bioeconomía Horizonte, 2030). The report gives an analysis of the situation in Spain in relation to the consumption of resources and the evolution and trends of the main economic sectors with relation to circular economy – such as tourism, industry, agriculture and, in particular, those sectors managing biological resources (agrarian, fish, food, and forestry) – on the sustainable and efficient use of products, byproducts, and their corresponding wastes (MITECO 2016; Ministerio de Agricultura 2021).

In 2018, the Spanish Strategy of Circular Economy 2020 was launched. This document reported that Spain aimed to become an international reference for the effective establishment of the circular economy, fostering green growth by means of the development of companies, the optimal use of raw materials, and competitiveness. However, in the ranking on this field for European Union countries, Spain was ranked tenth. This strategy was articulated around five action lines and three transversal axes, and encompassed five sectors: construction, agroalimentary industry, industrial manufacture, consumer products, and tourism. The subsequent initiative, the Spanish Strategy of Circular Economy 2030, was briefly explicated as follows: "In parallel, the role of the consumer has to be strengthened through education and sensibilization, to make him/her appreciate and distinguish between products and services that are respectful with the environment, and that guarantee health protection" (MITECO 2020).

None of these plans and priorities has been clearly addressed at the educational level, as there is no correspondence about the abrupt change that we are facing in terms of research, innovation and business models, and the modifications that might be expected in the contents related to this approach at schools, high schools, or universities. Paris, Rio, Green Deal, Circular Economy, and the like have addressed as main topics: land use, oceans and coastal zones, water, human settlements, transport, energy, and industry, but what about education? Can not the greatest wars be won through education? As we have stated, the circular economy has talked of the power of education in this transition, but only by means of campaigns and isolated actions.

14.2 Changes in Educational Policies: The Specific Case of Spain

As discussed in Section 14.1, Spanish education policies have reacted to global environmental and educational policies regarding many aspects, including sustainability and the circular economy. In this sense, the search for new educational strategies to conserve and protect the environment has existed in Spain since the early 1980s.

In 1983, the First Environmental Education Conference was held in Sitges, organized by the General Director of the Environment of the Ministry of Public Works and Urban Planning and the Barcelona Provincial Council. Later, in 1987, the National Center for Environmental

Education was created in Segovia. Some years after that, in 1992, the White Book on Environmental Education in Spain was published by the Ministry of the Environment; this was quite important, but not at the academic level for which it was intended. In it, the general framework and the basic objectives and principles that justified environmental education (EE) were collected.

A summarized version was then made – the "White Book of environmental education in a few words" – to facilitate its application at educational centers, making the most important principles that motivated it available to students in a simple way. All these events marked a starting point related to the field of EE that was interrupted in a particularly abrupt way by the crisis that hit the world in 2008. With it, EE programs and activities in the key areas of sustainability and ecology were lost, and a high percentage of unemployment in this field occurred.

Apart from the actions carried out by different institutions and professionals from the environmental sector, it was not until 1990, under the LOGSE (Organic Law for the Management of Education), when the respect due to the environment was discussed for the first time in terms of educational legislation (Ministerio de Educación 1990).

In successive educational reforms, some nuances were introduced so that students could catch up with environmental issues and even develop skills in knowledge and interaction with the physical world. One of the purposes envisaged by the LOE (Organic Law of Education) was "Training for peace, respect for human rights, life in common, social cohesion, cooperation, and solidarity among people, as well as the acquisition of values that promote respect for living beings and the environment, in particular, the value of forest spaces and sustainable development" (Ministerio de Educación 2006). However, it was still easy to demonstrate that, for all these organic laws, there was an important disagreement between what was postulated in the introduction that justified them, referring to environmental and sustainability issues, and the learning contents that were proposed for each course and knowledge area. Even so, it was understood that there was a good resolve among teachers and management teams about the need to develop sustainability policies in general and also awareness actions, such as the creation of environmental events or green weeks, participation in networks, etc., to promote education for sustainability (Marcén-Albero 2018).

Although EE was considered in Spanish classrooms, the economic crisis that took place in 2008 made this long-awaited field a secondary issue at the investment level. This caused the disappearance of many environmental awareness programs and activities, as well as a high percentage of unemployment, not only in the field of EE, but in the environmental sector in general.

Later, in 2013, the LOMCE (Organic Law for the Improvement of Educational Quality) defined the separation of knowledge of the environment into the subjects of Social Sciences and Natural Sciences, thereby neglecting the dependence between nature and society (Ministerio de Educación 2013).

Finally, on 19 January 2021, the Organic Law 3/2020, of 29 December, which modified Organic Law 2/2006, came into force. The preamble included sustainability as one of the key points on which the law is based, attending to sustainable development in accordance with the provisions of the 2030 Agenda and in compliance with the UN's fourth SDG of "guaranteeing inclusive education, quality and equitable quality and promote lifelong learning opportunities for all" by 2030, even if this implies the need to increase public spending on education (Ministerio de Educación 2020).

On the other hand, given that the educational system cannot be indifferent to the climate challenge of the planet, educational centers have to become sites of conservation and care of the environment. Therefore, they must promote a culture of environmental sustainability and social cooperation, developing sustainable lifestyle programs and encouraging recycling and contact with green spaces (Ministerio de Educación 2020). In that sense, Article 110 was modified to introduce sustainability and relationships with the environment, making the consolidation of administration necessary to coordinate, promote, and guarantee, at least, the following:

- Sustainability culture
- Social cooperation to protect biodiversity
- Sustainability in educational centers
- Relationship with the natural environment
- Adaptation to the consequences of climate change
- Safe school roads
- Sustainable transport and travel

If a thorough analysis of the content of this law continues, good intentions and a large set of modifications are envisaged with respect to the Organic Law 2/2006, aimed at consolidating more environmentalist practices. However, until the curriculum is written, we will not know whether the climate emergency is being considered in a transversal way or if it remains as an isolated content within a specific subject.

At the primary education stage, according to Article 18, environmental contents would be included in the subject "Education in Civic and Ethical Values," to be taken only in a third cycle course. However, in Articles 19 and 121, transversality is included, first when working on education for responsible consumption and sustainable development and then to include sustainable development in the educational project of the center. LOMLOE (the Organic Law Amending the Organic Law of Education) opens up the possibility for each center to have autonomy and be able to expand this education for sustainability as much as it wishes. As far as early childhood education is concerned, Section 3 of Article 14 has been altered and includes education for responsible and sustainable consumption, among other values.

Concerning secondary education, letter k) of Article 23 is modified by adding "respect for living beings, especially animals, and the environment, contributing to their conservation and improvement." Similarly, Section 7 of Article 25 mentions that "in some course of the stage all students will take the subject of Education in civic and ethical values paying attention, among others, to education for sustainable development."

Regarding new proposals for the Baccalaureate, a new subsection, o), was added to Article 33, stating the following: "To promote a responsible and committed attitude in the fight against climate change and in the defense of sustainable development."

In reference to vocational training, Section 3 of Article 42 also proposed improvements and strengthened its commitment to sustainable development.

Regarding sports education, a new letter i) was added to Section 3 of Article 66 in the following terms: "Develop attitudes and acquire knowledge related to sustainable development and the effects of climate change and environmental, health, or economic crises and promote health and healthy eating habits, reducing sedentary lifestyle."

Also, within the powers of the school council, the conservation and renovation of school facilities and equipment was promoted to improve quality and sustainability, being included in Article 127.

To finish with this analysis, some additional provisions were added, at the end of the text, which encouraged the regulation of sustainability and EE.

Regarding teacher training, the sixth additional provision included education for sustainable development, global citizenship, and the 2030 Agenda in the processes of training and access to the teaching function. The necessary and urgent training of teachers is considered in all these aspects and especially in the SDGs, which is a considerable improvement.

And finally, the fourth final provision modified Article 83.1 of the Organic Law 3/2018, of 5 December, on the protection of personal data and guarantee of digital rights, was that the educational system will guarantee, among other things, the learning of responsible consumption, the critical and safe use of digital media, and the need to be respectful of environmental sustainability.

In the university context, some courses specifically devoted to the environment were created in the early 1980s. In 1992, the Degree in Environmental Sciences was created, and other scientific degrees incorporated some subjects involving sustainable awareness, although only isolated cases can be cited; most of the physics, chemistry, or engineering degrees were still forgetting sustainability, focusing on process productivity. The appearance of a social commitment contributed to economic, social, and cultural modifications toward sustainable development. Since then, a significant change has taken place; nowadays, there are specific degrees or masters on sustainability and green economy, and many different awareness initiatives are held, such as meetings, actions of environmental voluntary service, programs focused on ecological agriculture, sustainable fashion, etc. However, and coming back to the university framework, apart from specific subjects on the environment, the only way to work on environmental efforts is through their inclusion as transversal skills (as explained in the following sections), which has so far depended on the commitment of teachers.

14.3 Skills in Education: Focus on Environmental Good Practices

As will be explained in the following sections, the relationship between educational systems and entrepreneurship is vital in many educational or social aspects, with regard to companies' demands on many occasions for a correct curricular program. The Organisation for Economic Co-operation and Development (OECD) Skills for Job Report is a compilation of the most important skills currently valued by companies, for all countries belonging to the OECD. Figure 14.2 shows these skills in the case of Spain, with an estimate of the importance they are given in professional networks. No skill regarding environmental management has yet been included (OECD 2021).

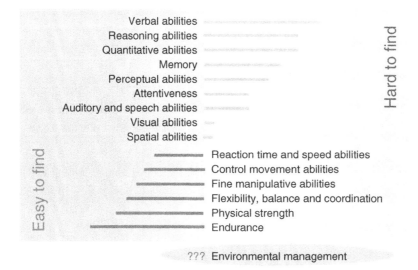

Figure 14.2 Most valued skills in Spain according to OECD Skills for Job Report, where skills related to environmental management are missing (OECD 2021).

Transversal skills have to prepare students for professional life. In this frame, transferable skills include analyzing problems and reaching appropriate solutions, communicating ideas, being creative, showing leadership, dealing with others in teams and demonstrating entrepreneurial capabilities. Some authors have referred to these skills as "soft," "transferable," "non-cognitive," or "twenty-first-century" skills (Pellegrino and Hilton 2021), and have included more and more items, such as factors associated with physiological health or emotional stability, and have associated them with personality factors.

Those skills associated with respect and good practices regarding the environment were more difficult to find in the list (Pellegrino and Hilton 2021), where the skills were included in clusters. If the work/ethic conscientiousness cluster is considered, citizenship has been reported, but there were no references related to appropriate environmental management.

Conscientiousness on suitable environmental management in order to respect other living beings (including social activism) is not so clearly stated in the curricula, especially in some subjects, because it is sometimes difficult to fit these values into subjects. These skills are related to "feelings" rather than "know-how," and therefore their inclusion involves the design of very specific activities in which the teacher has to combine pieces of information related to specific subjects and data about real-life situations of concern.

14.4 Real Implementation at Higher Education and University Levels

It is evident from the previous sections in this chapter that there is a constant trend to promote sustainability and environmental protection in Spain, as in many other countries around the world. This fact is mainly due to the transposition of legislation or policies from international agencies, which have been making an effort for years in that sense.

However, on many occasions willingness does not go further than kind words, mainly because of a confusing and heterogeneous implementation of these policies, especially concerning education, where all the agents involved (from institution to teachers or students) have a wide range of laws, regulations, or clauses related to the promotion of environmental issues (including circular economy or sustainability) without any specific guideline for its implementation or customization to take into account the circumstances in real education.

It has been an issue of concern for years, and some early studies in Spain pointed out the need for collaboration among all areas of knowledge to preserve and improve environmental conditions, as well as a reorientation in higher education (especially university studies) toward sustainability (Junyent and De Ciurana 2008). As a consequence, although sustainability has been a recurring term included in the curriculum for years, some signs indicate that the implementation of sustainability in everyday life is not complete (Larrán Jorge et al. 2015). That is the reason why many Spanish researchers from different fields or disciplines (from pure didactics or cognitive psychology to its application in technical subjects such as mathematics, chemical engineering, or statistics) have paid attention to educational issues regarding sustainability.

As a consequence, as can be seen in Figure 14.3, research activity in this specific field has considerably increased in recent years in Spain. Thus, in Scopus, the largest database of peer-reviewed literature Scopus (2021), there was a steady increase in published documents for "Environment" (with "environment," "education," and "Spain" as keywords) from 2005, whereas this trend was not observed for "Sustainability" (with "sustainability," "education," and "Spain" as keywords) until 2015. In other words, there is a relatively recent concern about sustainability

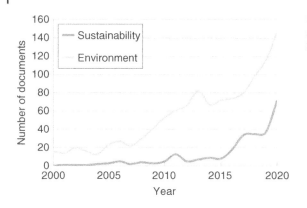

Figure 14.3 Research publications about sustainability and environment education in Spain. Data from Scopus(2021).

education, although other more general or global terms like the environment have been dealt with in this field previously.

These figures reveal that the interest in sustainability education might be an important research subject in the future, possibly due to different factors like the fact that researchers are facing a real problem (the real implementation of sustainability in general education) with multiple solutions (with the possible collaboration of many and multidisciplinary educational teams), which is going to provide a considerable amount of research works in these fields in the coming years. Thus, education (and its research) for sustainable development will play a very important role in the near future, as many authors forecast (Veiga Ávila et al. 2018; Glavič et al. 2021), as opposed to other surveys which claim that the environment and human health are the most considered concepts for Spanish citizens in science education, focused on secondary schools (Charro 2021).

Specifically, and taking into account a thorough analysis of the research works carried out by Spanish institutions, the interest of researchers has evolved considerably, focused on three main aspects about sustainability in education (especially in higher education), as follows:

- Knowledge of the current situation, trying to identify the main challenges for correct implementation of sustainability, circular economy, or the environment, among other subjects.
- Proposal of appropriate measures for a suitable implementation of sustainability at all educational levels, where transversality plays a vital role.
- Exhibition of specific and successful examples, indicating the need for explicit knowledge of each specific educational environment.

A detailed explanation of each trend in research will be addressed in the following sections, pointing out specific examples in the case of Spanish education at higher education.

14.5 Main Challenges for Sustainability Implementation in Spanish Education

Regarding the current situation in Spain, when it comes to the implementation of concepts such as circular economy or sustainability most authors agree on one fact: the goodwill shown by governments and institutions does not necessarily imply a correct or clear implementation in everyday education. Additionally, this problem does not seem to be easily identified, as it is more complicated than it first appears. The identification of these issues is vital in order to take the most appropriate steps to really implement EE. As many researchers have pointed out,

Figure 14.4 Main barriers for sustainability education implementation.

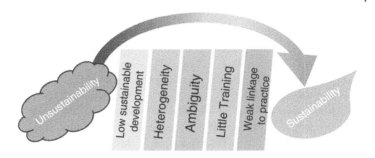

there are many challenges in Spain in promoting and implementing sustainability (see in Figure 14.4), and these are usually barriers to successful sustainability education. It is interesting to note that most of these barriers are usually found in industry (Sharma et al. 2021), confirming the difficulty of putting concepts such as circular economy into practice (Alonso-Almeida et al. 2021). Therefore, communication between educational institutions and entrepreneurship is vital to identify these shared problems, as the students of today will become the workers (and leaders) of tomorrow.

It should be noted that many of these problems can be found in other countries or contexts but, in the case of Spain, some specific barriers can be observed or, at least, be more prominent, such as heterogeneity.

In this case, many studies have found that the implementation of sustainability can be different depending on the area of study, and include other factors such as gender, age, or social status. Also, a low sustainable development can hinder the implementation of sustainability at all educational levels.

According to recent studies at university level, many influential factors on the environmental habits of students can be found, such as the field of study, gender, or perceived environment commitment (Chuvieco et al. 2018). Especially interesting is the fact that females showed higher sustainability values in general, regardless of the years of study or the country studied (including Spain). This trend is also supported by other surveys about secondary students in Spain whose results showed that women had greater knowledge of environmental issues and more sensitivity, with a greater commitment to recycling and changing lifestyles, if necessary (Cifuentes-Faura et al. 2020). Moreover, concerning higher education in Spain, some studies have pointed out that female teachers tend to teach sustainable development in a more balanced way (Lozano and Barreiro-Gen 2019). As another study stated, many environmental attitudes (including sustainability or circular economy) had, as a consequence, an influence on recycling, reducing, and reusing packaging materials in Spain, with women, older individuals, and highly educated people engaging more in these positive habits (Escario et al. 2020). This is the reason why a homogeneous, but at the same time customized, education could play a vital role for real sustainability implementation.

In the Spanish context, the territorial organization is based on autonomous regions (or communities), and each region (up to 17) can decide how it implements education policies, which makes heterogeneity more pronounced. Even though the European Union is the main reference point concerning sustainability policies in Europe, setting common objectives to be calibrated depends on the context of each member country, and in the case of Spain, different economic, social, and environmental contexts are found depending on the region considered. Consequently, policies devoted to sustainable development have been more considered in northern regions than in southern regions, equally affecting sustainability education at all educational levels (Paolotti et al. 2019). This same pattern was observed by other researchers, where social, economic, and environmental sustainability was considered by assessing these parameters at a local scale (in 31 Spanish cities) through multiple indicators. As a result, there were considerable differences in this study, especially between the north and the south of Spain (Rama et al. 2020). Some of these differences in sustainability implementation or education can explain, again, the different behavior of individuals regarding specific aspects, such as waste generation. In general, according to recent research, northern regions showed lower waste ratios whereas the insular and Mediterranean coastal regions had the highest waste generation per capita terms, mainly due to economic factors like the dependence of the tourism industry (Alcay et al. 2020). Another factor, as some studies have concluded, was the possibility of students to be connected to nature, which can equally affect their knowledge about circular economy or sustainability, promoting pro-environmental behaviors (Solano-Pinto et al. 2020).

In that sense, continuous improvement processes should be considered, paying attention to the adoption of issues such as circular economy or sustainability at regional level (where different behaviors were observed) and making greater efforts in regions with low implementation levels, especially when it comes to the education of these subjects (Silvestri et al. 2020).

Concerning ambiguity, the main reason for this barrier is the lack of information or guidance, although there are plenty of laws or regulatory decrees regarding sustainability and environmental education. Nevertheless, many higher education institutions in Spain have started to develop academic curricula, research capacity, and outreach activities related to circular economy, but some studies have pointed out that this transition is confusing, requiring guidance to help universities develop a circular strategy to improve efficiency and environmental sustainability in university management systems and their campus operations (Mendoza et al. 2019a).

Furthermore, lack of training seems to be another important barrier for sustainability education in Spain. Thus, teachers should be at the forefront of many aspects related to the environment, circular economy, or sustainability, which is not always the case. As was observed in a study about a master's degree in secondary education, it is important to train future teachers through holistic and interdisciplinary visions about sustainability, focusing on the UN 2030 Agenda. Thus, this study pointed out the need to promote collaborative work across disciplines to engage teachers in the transition to sustainability and encourage them to participate in the research process (Aznar et al. 2018), following a holistic approach and exploring specific issues such as the promotion of eco-responsible use of information and communication technologies, which is something relatively unknown (Baena-Morales et al. 2020). Accordingly, specific training is vital (for teachers and students), requiring specific and transversal competencies throughout the whole curriculum (Zamora-Polo et al. 2019).

Another important challenge is the weak linkage to practice, which is a fact that is equally reported by the business community and the education sector.

Regarding the former, which is closely linked to education as one of the direct beneficiaries of educational policies (whose interconnection with educational institutions pressures the education systems to introduce modules and curriculum to support sustainability and circular economy), many studies have focused on the room for improvement of practical usage related to environmental issues such as sustainability or circular economy (Lanz et al. 2019). In these cases, a need to link theory to practice is vital, especially when it comes to recycling or energy use, for instance, pointing out the important role of higher education in achieving the SDGs (Barreiro-Gen and Lozano 2020; Rokicki et al. 2020). Indeed, there are some examples in Spain (such as chemical engineering degrees) where there are external advisory committees with several stakeholders (including companies that collaborate in internship programs) that have demanded short-term challenges like the improvement of main skills (e.g. sustainability, circular economy, resilience, communication capacity, and information management), suggesting the formation of multidisciplinary professionals including the environmental aspects we have mentioned (Feijoo et al. 2019).

Concerning education, these problems can be clearly observed in curricula or the content in textbooks at all educational levels. For instance, a study about the content of textbooks in higher education related to sustainability in Spain proved that, although there was an abundance of cognitively simple activities about sustainability, there was a shortage of complex activities focused on practice, and the typical subjects were environmental problems and recycling, which covers a reduced part of sustainability issues (Martínez-Medina and Arrebola 2019). This fact has been equally supported by other studies that highlight considerable room for improvement in environmental education, especially in curriculum and textbooks (for instance, dealing with subjects such as geography), where many environmental problems that surround us are not properly covered (García-González et al. 2021). In higher education institutions, students have usually shown low competencies related to SDGs, and some researchers have pointed out that specific training linked to case studies could play an important role so that their level can be improved (Zamora-Polo et al. 2019). All these reports point in a single direction, where adaptation to specific cases and transversality are vital to try to solve all the above-mentioned problems. In Section 14.6, these options are explained thoroughly.

14.6 The Role of Curricular Adaptation and Transversality

Once the main problems have been identified, it is easier to implement solutions. As can be imagined, there are plenty of proposals to foster, promote, or implement sustainability in educational programs or tasks (as many as research works found in the literature), which are adapted to specific cases (depending on the region, educational level, classroom, teachers' training, etc.). Obviously, the first key measure to be carried out is adaptation or customization. In this sense, in most studies, the first step has been to study the specific situation to introduce a specific and appropriate set of solutions, which can be variable. Specifically, the implementation of a circular economy in higher education sector cannot be understood without a thorough analysis of the university's sustainability policies (Mendoza et al. 2019b). Nevertheless, some common topics have been found to go further, with transversality standing out.

Regardless of the kind of study carried out about sustainability education in Spain, many research articles have pointed out one important aspect (which is also equally important for other issues, such as gender equality or social awareness), that is, transversality, which affects all the educational actors, disciplines, and levels involved in sustainability and environmental education. Many researchers have focused on at least one of the three axes included in the "three-dimensional space for sustainability education" represented in Figure 14.5.

As can be observed in this figure, these three factors (educational stage, discipline, and actors involved) are interrelated, and each of them can play an important role at almost every level. For instance, for secondary education, all the disciplines can take part in teaching environmental awareness (including sustainability promotion), with important roles reserved for teachers or companies, among others. On the other hand, local administration or agencies can promote the inclusion of these subjects in many disciplines at any educational level. Another interesting aspect of this transversality network is that the more interactions between disciplines, educational level, and agents there are, the stronger and steady foundations for correct implementation of sustainability (or any other subject) there are. Consequently, these interactions can contribute to breaking down most of the barriers explained discussed in Section 14.5 (see Figure 14.4), fostering higher sustainability development from education, obtaining

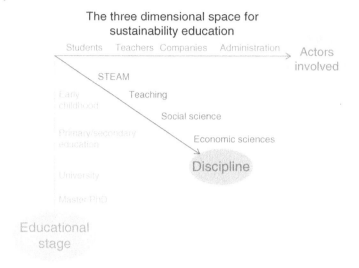

Figure 14.5 Transversality for sustainability education.

homogeneous educational environments (even at a national level, in spite of regional heterogeneity), creating more specific or realistic goals, and promoting real sustainability training that is truly linked to practice or real situations. These steps are only possible with as many studies or research works as possible, many of them setting an example from local to global. Many researchers have contributed with their wide experience, showing some specific and successful cases that can be inspiring for other colleagues or for future generations. In Section 14.7, we address many of these cases, concluding with a recurring topic in the context of Spain: the important role of universities as a transforming agent for sustainability implementation in society.

14.7 Success Stories

All the studies considered in this chapter have provided important lessons, based on success stories which are equally inspiring and encouraging for other education professionals. The reasons why most of these stories have shown good results seem to follow a similar pattern, as follows:

- Experienced working teams
- Multidisciplinary cooperation
- Focus on specific problems or contexts
- Adjustment to current policies

Many researchers have broad experience in their corresponding teaching field, always linked to a teaching approach (mainly due to their teaching tasks at any educational level). In addition, the members of teaching staff at schools, high schools, or universities are collaborative, coming from different contexts, which could explain the multidisciplinary nature of the resulting works or initiatives (which is linked to the transversal solutions explained in Section 14.6). Finally, one very interesting point about these professionals is their focus on specific problems (in this case related to the lack of sustainable culture in Spanish society), paying attention to local, regional, national, and international policies so that their work can comply with the corresponding requirements.

Accordingly, there are plenty of successful cases when it comes to sustainability education in Spain, covering a wide range of different aspects dealing with this cornerstone. The following is a non-exhaustive list of some examples:

- Use of practical cases such as biorefineries, which is a highly recurring subject in sustainability or circular economy, mainly due to the sustainable nature of the process and the use of concepts such as recycling, reusing, natural feedstocks, etc. Some studies about the adaptation of curricula to different kinds of audiences, underlining sustainability at all educational levels (including higher education or even graduate education) have been carried out (Nogales-Delgado and Encinar 2019). On the other hand, another study revealed the successful use of computer activities to teach biorefinery concepts, showing better grades in questionnaires compared with traditional lessons, suggesting this technique for the promotion of sustainability concepts, and highlighting, again, the vital role of transversality (Martín-Lara and Ronda 2020).
- Development of collaborative project-based learning, where students take responsibility for their knowledge process. For instance, in the case of engineering students in Spain, it was a rewarding experience, where students with previous knowledge valued the relevance of circular economy, whereas different knowledge was acquired (eco-design, product planning, reuse, recycling, etc.). Most students considered that these subjects should be a complementary discipline and with transversal competence (González-Domínguez et al. 2020).
- Use of guides, such as a sustainability matrix for engineering careers, which was successfully implemented at university and master's degree levels. This was a good opportunity to check the sustainability competencies developed during the career, including degree theses. The main questions were about project development, exploitation, and risks involved. Also, this guide helped students to carry out sustainable projects and allowed teachers to assess how sustainability was incorporated intto the degree theses (Sánchez-Carracedo et al. 2020).
- The role of massive open online courses (MOOCs), which are an interesting tool to promote self-paced learning and transversality, was a useful way to teach sustainability and digital skills for high-school students (Carrera and Ramírez-Hernández 2018).
- Education in other contexts, at all educational levels. For example, National Parks would be another interesting supplement to sustainability and environmental education, and some initiatives have shown good results as they promote enjoyment and pro-environmental behavior among users through different activities such as snorkeling (Piñeiro-Corbeira et al. 2020).

As was pointed out earlier, universities play a vital role when it comes to sustainability promotion, also propelling circular economy approaches into reality (Nunes et al. 2018), as observed in Figure 14.6. It is clear that the educational function of universities is the most important aspect for this purpose, mainly through teaching students, training teachers, and adapting the curriculum to meet new challenges like those stated by international agencies (the 2030 Agenda, for instance). Apart from that, universities can contribute in different ways. For instance, researching to find more sustainable ways of energy production, replacing petroleum derivatives for bioproducts, or even finding new prospects for teaching and promoting sustainability, the main subject of this chapter. In other words, universities create new knowledge in a wide range of fields which can be useful for this purpose. But there are other subtle aspects that should not be skipped, such as communication with companies or the labor market and the possibility of setting an example as an institution. In the first case, there are many examples of companies that have turned to the services offered by universities to adapt their current

Figure 14.6 Main actions taken by universities concerning sustainability.

working lines to a more sustainable practice. Specifically, in the case of chemical engineering in Spain, many companies collaborate in training, demanding chemical, environmental, and energy competencies for future professionals (Feijoo et al. 2019). Moreover, the promotion of sustainability in future professionals will imply, sooner or later, higher visibility of sustainable behavior in professional environments. In the second case, universities, as institutions and employers, should set an example and foster sustainability in every single action, including plans to promote improved environmental behaviors of staff (and also students) (Nunes et al. 2018). Thus, for instance, recycling (implementing recycling points and carrying out correct waste management in their facilities) or energy- and water-saving are currently key points at universities, facilitating these tasks for students, teachers, and any worker or person related directly or indirectly with the institution (see Figure 14.6). Indeed, from university students' point of view, simple steps toward sustainability are really appreciated, such as parking control, promotion of bicycle use, pedestrianization of campuses, and agreements with public transport companies, according to a recent study (Bayas Aldaz and Sandoval Hamón 2019). Finally, communication with companies, as explained earlier, is vital, and universities should act as a catalyst to promote circular economy by working with businesses to improve eco-effectiveness and eco-efficiency (for instance, decreasing carbon footprint, improving water efficiency, recycling) through pilot projects, for instance (Nunes et al. 2018).

In conclusion, universities, as in the case of other relevant influential aspects (such as equality or inclusion), play a significant role as a change agent in our society, and this role should be equally important for environmental issues such as sustainability or environmental protection.

14.8 Conclusions and Future Trends

After a comprehensive review of the current situation of teaching subjects related to sustainability in Spain, the main findings were the following:

- There is an incipient interest from international agencies and organizations to promote a sustainable culture, and the Spanish government has engaged with these policies for years.
- Based on new approaches, it can be thought that a real change in sustainability is underway and that it will be in accordance with Article 31 of Chapter VIII of the recently approved Law Against Climate Change, which makes a direct reference to education: "The Spanish educational system will promote the involvement of Spanish society in response to climate change."
- However, and even though there are clear signs which show a positive trend concerning sustainability performance, greater efforts should be made in order to promote a green and sustainable culture. So far, what has been achieved should have a good outcome, thanks to an adequate curricular reformulation.
- In order to achieve this goal, many educational measures have been taken in Spain, from school to university; this chapter has paid attention to studies and proposals focused on higher education and university level, in different disciplines.

- Thus, these measures have been mainly focused on students, but the training of teachers, along with rewriting curricula and university policies, have been equally important to achieve this goal.
- Transversal competencies in education are needed in order to foster sustainability at all educational levels. Thus, the involvement of different disciplines from different fields, along with different partners (from children/students, parents, and teachers to entrepreneurs, companies, or agencies) is needed, at every educational level (from early childhood to university), to facilitate the implementation of a real sustainable policy with specific and realistic results in our society.
- To sum up, we should go further. Apart from teaching main environmental problems and recycling, we should include further contents and practical or specific activities at all educational levels. Good sustainable management must be carried out, including sustainable trips to centers, reduction of water consumption, sustainable energy use, correct waste treatment, air quality promotion, etc., at schools, institutes, and universities. Finally, the role of governments and political administrations in facilitating the development of these actions is vital.

References

Alcay, A., Montañés, A., and Simón-Fernández, M.B. (2020). Waste generation in Spain. Do Spanish regions exhibit a similar behavior. *Waste Management* Elsevier Ltd 112: 66–73. https://doi.org/10.1016/j.wasman.2020.05.029.

Alonso-Almeida, M.d.M., Rodriguez-Anton, J.M., Bagur-Femenías, L., and Perramon, J. (2021). Institutional entrepreneurship enablers to promote circular economy in the European Union: impacts on transition towards a more circular economy. *Journal of Cleaner Production* 281: 124841. https://doi.org/10.1016/j.jclepro.2020.124841.

Aznar, P., Calero, M., Martínez-Agut, M.P. et al. (2018). Training secondary education teachers through the prism of sustainability: the case of the Universitat de València. *Sustainability (Switzerland)* 10 (11): https://doi.org/10.3390/su10114170.

Baena-Morales, S., Martinez-Roig, R., and Hernádez-Amorós, M.J. (2020). Sustainability and educational technology – a description of the teaching self-concept. *Sustainability (Switzerland)* 12 (24): 1–20. https://doi.org/10.3390/su122410309.

Barreiro-Gen, M. and Lozano, R. (2020). How circular is the circular economy? Analysing the implementation of circular economy in organisations. *Business Strategy and the Environment* 29 (8): 3484–3494. https://doi.org/10.1002/bse.2590.

Bayas Aldaz, C.E. and Sandoval Hamón, L.A. (2019). 'Perceptions of students' representatives towards sustainable mobility on Spanish university campus. *Transportation Research Procedia*. Elsevier B.V. 41: 70–72. https://doi.org/10.1016/j.trpro.2019.09.015.

Carrera, J. and Ramírez-Hernández, D. (2018). Innovative education in MOOC for sustainability: learnings and motivations. *Sustainability (Switzerland)* 10 (9): https://doi.org/10.3390/su10092990.

Charro, E. (2021). A curricular Delphi study to improve the science education of secondary school students in Spain. *Journal of Research in Science Teaching* 58 (2): 282–304. https://doi.org/10.1002/tea.21655.

Chuvieco, E., Burgui-Burgui, M., Da Silva, E.V. et al. (2018). 'Factors affecting environmental sustainability habits of university students: Intercomparison analysis in three countries (Spain, Brazil and UAE). *Journal of Cleaner Production*. Elsevier Ltd 198: 1372–1380. https://doi.org/10.1016/j.jclepro.2018.07.121.

Cifuentes-Faura, J., Faura-Martínez, U., and Lafuente-Lechuga, M. (2020). Assessment of sustainable development in secondary school economics students according to gender. *Sustainability (Switzerland)* 12 (13): https://doi.org/10.3390/su12135353.

Escario, J.J., Rodriguez-Sanchez, C., and Casaló, L.V. (2020). The influence of environmental attitudes and perceived effectiveness on recycling, reducing, and reusing packaging materials in Spain. *Waste Management* 113: 251–260. https://doi.org/10.1016/j.wasman.2020.05.043.

European Union. (2021). EU Green Deal. For a cleaner and more competitive Europe. European Comission. https://ec.europa.eu/info/strategy/priorities-2019-2024/european-green-deal_es (accessed 20 May 2021).

Feijoo, G., Ibáñez, R., Herguido, J. et al. (2019, 2009). Reprint of: Education of chemical engineering in Spain: A global picture. *Education for Chemical Engineers* 26: 2–7. https://doi.org/10.1016/j.ece.2019.01.003.

García-González, J.A., Palencia, S.G., and Ondoño, I.S. (2021). Characterization of environmental education in Spanish geography textbooks. *Sustainability (Switzerland)* 13 (3): 1–22. https://doi.org/10.3390/su13031159.

Glavič, P., Pintarič, Z.N., and Bogataj, M. (2021). Process design and sustainable development – a European perspective. *Processes* 9 (1): 148. https://doi.org/10.3390/pr9010148.

González-Domínguez, J., Sánchez-Barroso, G., Zamora-Polo, F., and García-Sanz-Salcedo, J. (2020). Application of circular economy techniques for design and development of products through collaborative project-based learning for industrial engineer teaching. *Sustainability (Switzerland)* 12 (11): 7–9. https://doi.org/10.3390/su12114368.

Junyent, M. and De Ciurana, A.M.G. (2008). Education for sustainability in university studies: a model for reorienting the curriculum. *British Educational Research Journal* 34 (6): 763–782. https://doi.org/10.1080/01411920802041343.

Lanz, M., Nylund, H., Lehtonen, T. et al. (2019). Circular economy in integrated product and production development education. *Procedia Manufacturing*. Elsevier 33: 470–476. https://doi.org/10.1016/j.promfg.2019.04.058.

Larrán Jorge, M., Herrera Madueño, J., Calzado Cejas, M.Y., and Andrades Peña, F.J. (2015). An approach to the implementation of sustainability practices in Spanish universities. *Journal of Cleaner Production* 106: 34–44. https://doi.org/10.1016/j.jclepro.2014.07.035.

Lozano, R. and Barreiro-Gen, M. (2019). Analysing the factors affecting the incorporation of sustainable development into European Higher Education Institutions' curricula. *Sustainable Development* 27 (5): 965–975. https://doi.org/10.1002/sd.1987.

Marcén-Albero, C. (2018). Medioambiente y escuela. Octaedro. https://octaedro.com/libro/medioambiente-y-escuela (accessed 20 May 2021).

Martínez-Medina, R. and Arrebola, J.C. (2019). Analysis of sustainability activities in Spanish elementary education textbooks. *Sustainability (Switzerland)* 11 (19): 5182. https://doi.org/10.3390/su11195182.

Martín-Lara, M.Á. and Ronda, A. (2020). Implementation of Modeling tools for teaching biorefinery (focused on bioethanol production) in biochemical engineering courses: dynamic modeling of batch, semi-batch, and continuous well-stirred bioreactors'. *Energies* 13 (21): 5772. https://doi.org/10.3390/en13215772.

Mendoza, J.M.F., Gallego-Schmid, A., and Azapagic, A. (2019a). 'A methodological framework for the implementation of circular economy thinking in higher education institutions: towards sustainable campus management. *Journal of Cleaner Production*. Elsevier 226: 831–844. https://doi.org/10.1016/j.jclepro.2019.04.060.

Mendoza, J.M.F., Gallego-Schmid, A., and Azapagic, A. (2019b). 'Building a business case for implementation of a circular economy in higher education institutions. *Journal of Cleaner Production*. Elsevier 220: 553–567. https://doi.org/10.1016/j.jclepro.2019.02.045.

Ministerio de Agricultura, P. y A. (2021). Estrategia Española de Bioeconomía Horizonte, 2030. https://www.mapa.gob.es/es/desarrollo-rural/temas/innovacion-medio-rural/estrategiaenbioeconomia23_12_15_tcm30-560119.pdf (accessed 12 Aug 2021).

Ministerio de Educación, C. y D. (1990). Ley Orgánica 1/1990, de ordenación general del sistema educativo (LOGSE). https://www.boe.es/buscar/doc.php?id=BOE-A-1990-24172 (accessed 12 Aug 2021).

Ministerio de Educación, C. y D. (2006). Ley Orgánica 2/2006 de Educación (LOE). https://www.boe.es/buscar/act.php?id=BOE-A-2006-7899 (accessed 12 Aug 2021).

Ministerio de Educación, C. y D. (2013). Ley Orgánica 8/2013 para la mejora de la calidad educativa (LOMCE). https://www.boe.es/buscar/pdf/2013/BOE-A-2013-12886-consolidado.pdf (accessed 12 Aug 2021).

Ministerio de Educación, C. y D. (2020). Ley Orgánica 3/2020, por la que se modifica la Ley orgánica 2/2006 (LOMLOE). https://www.boe.es/diario_boe/txt.php?id=BOE-A-2020-17264 (accessed 12 Aug 2021).

MITECO (2016). Plan Estatal Marco de Gestión de Residuos (PEMAR 2016-2022). https://www.miteco.gob.es/es/calidad-y-evaluacion-ambiental/planes-y-estrategias/pemaraprobado6noviembrecondae_tcm30-170428.pdf (accessed 12 Aug 2021).

MITECO (2020). *España Circular 2030. Estrategia Española de Economía Circular*. https://www.miteco.gob.es/es/calidad-y-evaluacion-ambiental/temas/economia-circular/espanacircular2030_def1_tcm30-509532.PDF (accessed 20 May 2021).

Nogales-Delgado, S. and Encinar, J.M. (2019). Environmental education for students from school to university: case study on biorefineries. *Education in Science* 9 (3): 202. https://doi.org/10.3390/educsci9030202.

Nunes, B.T., Pollard, S.J.T., Burgess, P.J. et al. (2018). University contributions to the circular economy: professing the hidden curriculum. *Sustainability (Switzerland)* 10 (8): 1–24. https://doi.org/10.3390/su10082719.

OECD. (2021). Skills for Jobs. http://www.oecdskillsforjobsdatabase.org/imbalances.php#ES/_/_/_/[%22abilities%22]/co (accessed 20 May 2021).

PAGE (2021) Partnership for action on green economy. https://www.un-page.org (accessed 20 May 2021).

Paolotti, L., Del Campo Gomis, F.J., Agullo Torres, A.M. et al. (2019). Territorial sustainability evaluation for policy management: the case study of Italy and Spain. *Environmental Science and Policy*. Elsevier, 92 (September 2018): 207–219. https://doi.org/10.1016/j.envsci.2018.11.022.

Pellegrino, J.W. and Hilton, M. (2021). *Education for life and work: Developing transferable knowledge and skills in the 21st century*. National Academies Press.

Piñeiro-Corbeira, C., Barreiro, R., Olmedo, M., and De la Cruz-Modino, R. (2020). Recreational snorkeling activities to enhance seascape enjoyment and environmental education in the Islas Atlánticas de Galicia National Park (Spain). *Journal of Environmental Management* 272: 111065. https://doi.org/10.1016/j.jenvman.2020.111065.

Rama, M., González-García, S., Andrade, E. et al. (2020). 'Assessing the sustainability dimension at local scale: case study of Spanish cities', *Ecological Indicators. Ecol. Indic.* 117: 106687. https://doi.org/10.1016/j.ecolind.2020.106687.

Rio+20 (2012). Rio+20: El futuro que queremos. https://www.uclg.org/es/temas/rio20. (accessed 20 May 2021).

Rokicki, T., Perkowska, A., Klepacki, B. et al. (2020). The importance of higher education in the EU countries in achieving the objectives of the circular economy in the energy sector. *Energies* 13 (17): https://doi.org/10.3390/en13174407.

Sánchez-Carracedo, F., López, D., Martín, C. et al. (2020). The sustainability matrix: a tool for integrating and assessing sustainability in the bachelor and master theses of engineering degrees. *Sustainability (Switzerland)* 12 (14): 1–23. https://doi.org/10.3390/su12145755.

Scopus (2021). Scopus preview. https://www.scopus.com/home.uri (accessed 20 May 2021).

Sharma, N.K., Govindan, K., Lai, K.K. et al. (2021). The transition from linear economy to circular economy for sustainability among SMEs: a study on prospects, impediments, and prerequisites. *Business Strategy and the Environment* 30 (4): 1803–1822. https://doi.org/10.1002/bse.2717.

Silvestri, F., Spigarelli, F., and Tassinari, M. (2020). Regional development of circular economy in the European Union: a multidimensional analysis. *Journal of Cleaner Production* 255: 120218. https://doi.org/10.1016/j.jclepro.2020.120218.

Solano-Pinto, N., Garrido, D., Gértrudix-Barrio, F., and Fernández-Cézar, R. (2020). Is knowledge of circular economy, pro-environmental behavior, satisfaction with life, and beliefs a predictor of connectedness to nature in rural children and adolescents? A pilot study. *Sustainability (Switzerland)* 12 (23): 1–13. https://doi.org/10.3390/su12239951.

UNESCO (2012). Youth and skills: Putting education to work. *EFA Global Monitoring Report*. https://en.unesco.org/gem-report/report/2012/youth-and-skills-putting-education-work (accessed 20 May 2021).

United Nations (2011). Towards a green economy: Pathways to sustainable development and poverty eradication. A synthesis for policy makers. https://sustainabledevelopment.un.org/content/documents/126GER_synthesis_en.pdf (accessed 20 May 2021).

United Nations (2019). Sustainable Development Goals. https://www.un.org/sustainabledevelopment (accessed 20 May 2021).

Veiga Ávila, L., Rossato Facco, A.L., Dos Santos Bento, M.H. et al. (2018). Sustainability and education for sustainability: an analysis of publications from the last decade. *Environmental Quality Management* 27 (3): 107–118. https://doi.org/10.1002/tqem.21537.

Zamora-Polo, F., Sánchez-Martín, J., Corrales-Serrano, M., and Espejo-Antúnez, L. (2019). What do university students know about sustainable development goals? A realistic approach to the reception of this UN program amongst the youth population. *Sustainability* 11 (13): 3533. https://doi.org/10.3390/su11133533.

15

Sustainability in Higher Education in Egypt: Perception, Challenges, and Way Forward

Marwa Biltagy

15.1 Introduction

Human capital investments are activities that affect future real income streams of individuals. There are many examples of human capital investments; one of the most important is education (Becker 1962). Investment in education improves the quality of life for millions of people. In other words, education is the most powerful tool for achieving economic growth, reducing poverty, and improving living standards. The education system in Egypt has many problems, for example, low levels of quality of education, high rates of dropping out of school, and a big misallocation of resources between pre-university and university education. The quality of education in Egypt is considered another sizable challenge; it is unequally distributed among different areas, leading to inequality of educational outcomes.

It is estimated that the average years of schooling of the total population aged 15 years and over in Egypt was 7.4 years in 2020 (UNDP 2020). Furthermore, the mismatch between the outputs of the education system and the requirements of the job market represents one of the key causes of a high rate of unemployment of 15–64 years in Egypt, which was estimated at 7.2% in the fourth quarter of 2020 compared to 7.9% in 2019 (CAPMAS, Egypt in Figures 2021).

Unemployment is particularly high among university graduates. In Egypt, graduates of technical intermediate and higher education face the highest unemployment rates. It is estimated that technical intermediate education graduates represent 41% of the total workforce (Nassar and Biltagy 2021).

The key objective of this chapter is to identify the concept of sustainability in higher education by introducing the cultural perception of sustainability and education and proposing the principal challenges and opportunities. The main research questions that the chapter aims to answer are: What is the structure of the Egyptian education system? What is the relationship between sustainability and education? What is the concept of higher education for sustainable development (ESD)? And what are the main challenges and the way forward?

Higher education institutions are those that conduct studies, training, and research at the postsecondary level. These include public and private universities, institutions affiliated to them, other research centers, and educational establishments that are approved as institutions of higher education. Higher education systems should respond to what society expects from them. Institutions of higher education must play a leading role in making the transition to

---

The Wiley Handbook of Sustainability in Higher Education Learning and Teaching, First Edition.
Edited by Kelum A. A. Gamage and Nanda Gunawardhana.
© 2022 John Wiley & Sons, Inc. Published 2022 by John Wiley & Sons, Inc.

sustainability. Higher education can realize sustainability through policy-making, technology transfer, capacity building, science, and research on its campuses. Universities can support a sustainable society by teaching and transferring knowledge through research. Despite increased awareness of the human impact on the environment and a greater focus on personal as well as global consequences of individual lifestyle choices, sustainable development and sustainable consumption are still not central topics in educational systems today (UNESCO 1998).

This chapter consists of six main sections, including an introduction and conclusion. The second section addresses the structure of the Egyptian education system, the third introduces the cultural perception of sustainability and education and the fourth proposes an overview of higher ESD. The fifth section presents the challenges and opportunities.

15.2 The Structure of the Education System in Egypt

The Egyptian educational structure consists of kindergarten[1] stage for two years, then primary and preparatory education (elementary stage of education). It is followed by secondary school, but some of the children do not complete this level of education because they prefer to work in order to support their families. These stages of education are called "pre-university education." The last stage is the higher education system.

Educational enrollment rates have improved during the last few years. However, they remain low in some poor areas, for example, Upper Egypt governorates and rural areas in Lower Egypt governorates. The number of students enrolled in primary, preparatory, and secondary education amounted to approximately 23.6 million in 2021, excluding Al Azhar education.[2] The total number of schools amounted to approximately 56 600 and the total number of classrooms was 509 500 (CAPMAS, Egypt in Figures 2021).

The types of schools in Egypt consist of public schools and private schools. There are also international schools in which curricula are taught in the mother language of foreign countries; the Ministry of Education does not supervise these schools and they offer different certificates, for example, International General Certificate of Secondary Education (IGCSE) and American Diploma. In addition, Al Azhar schools present another kind of education, which contains the Qu'ran and other Islamic studies; Al Azhar Al Shareef is responsible for the teaching staff and employees of Al Azhar schools (Biltagy 2012).

Higher education in Egypt consists of university and non-university education. University education includes 28 governmental universities as illustrated in Table 15.1, including Al Azhar University. In addition, there are 26 private universities. In 2019/2020, the total number of students enrolled in private universities was 207 154 students (95 249 females and 111 905 males).

This number represents a small percentage of the total number of university students (see Figure 15.1). On the other hand, the number of students enrolled in governmental universities was 2 441 645 students in 2019/2020 including 382 306 students enrolled in Al Azhar University (CAPMAS, Egypt in Figures 2021).

Non-university higher education includes higher education in some academies, faculties, and institutes, for instance, police academies and military colleges. Moreover, non-university higher education includes higher institutes under the direct supervision of the Ministry of Higher Education (MOHE). The total number of graduates of higher institutes and some academies in 2019/2020 was 92 365 (28 225 females and 64 140 males),[3] while the total number of

---

1 This stage of education is called "preschool education," an independent educational stage for children aged four to five years old.
2 Al Azhar Education includes approximately 1.8 million students.
3 These estimates include Police Academy records.

Table 15.1 Students enrolled in governmental universities in 2019/2020.

University	Total
Cairo	215 007
Alexandria	166 438
Ain Shams	238 191
Asyout	86 213
Tanta	114 425
El Mansura	166 060
El Zagazig	136 866
Helwan	178 298
El Menia	62 269
El Menoufia	78 699
Suez Canal	33 175
Ganoub el Wadi	54 812
Al Azhar	382 306
Fayoum	34 874
Beni-Suef	87 628
Banha	87 956
Souhag	57 631
Kafr El Sheikh	64 977
Damanhor	58 094
Port Said	24 427
Suez	14 394
Damietta	30 064
Aswan	25 847
Sadat	25 886
Arish	6 741
El-Wadi El-Gidid	5 168
Matrouh	3 066
Luyxor	2 133

Source: Created by the author based on the data of CAPMAS, Egypt in Figures, 2021.

graduates of intermediate technical institutes was 55 269 (31 281 females and 23 988 males) (CAPMAS, Egypt in Figures 2021).

Government expenditure on education has grown significantly in the past period. The amount of the government's budget[4] directed to education increased from approximately 116 billion Egyptian pounds (LE) in 2018/19 to LE132 billion in 2019/2020. This indicates high levels of public spending on education. However, this remarkable increase in public educational spending did not achieve a higher quality of education. This is not only a question of high

---

4 As a percentage, the amount of total public expenditure directed to education increased from 8.1% in 2018/19 to 8.4% in 2019/2020.

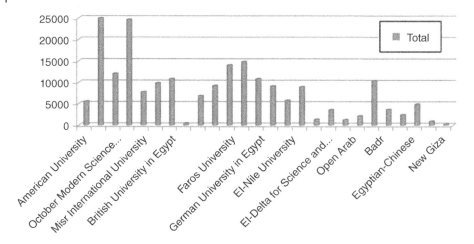

Figure 15.1 Students enrolled in private universities in 2019/2020. *Source:* Created by the author based on the data of CAPMAS, Egypt in Figures, 2021.

Table 15.2 The distribution of public educational expenditure by educational stage in 2019/2020.

Item/stage	Pre-university education	Higher education	Other aspects of expenditure on education	Total
Public expenditure on education (in millions)	81 399.6	32 561.5	18 077.4	132 038.5
% of total public expenditure on education	61.6	24.7	13.7	100

Source: Created by the author based on the data of CAPMAS, Egypt in Figures, 2021.

amounts of spending or resources being allocated to the education sector, but also a question of the appropriate allocation of these resources.

In Egypt, spending on education is biased against pre-university education, as Table 15.2 demonstrates. The number of students enrolled in pre-university education represents a great percentage of the total number of students enrolled in the Egyptian education system; however, public expenditure on pre-university education compared to the total expenditure on education is 61.6% in 2019/2020. On the other hand, higher education gets 24.7% of the total public expenditure on education in the same academic year (CAPMAS, Egypt in Figures 2021).

The higher education system is controlled mainly by the MOHE in addition to some other governmental institutions, for example, the Ministry of Finance and the Supreme Council of Universities. This kind of centralized control represents the main challenge for the Egyptian education system (Biltagy 2013).

15.3 Sustainability and Education: Cultural Perception

15.3.1 The Concept of Education for Sustainability

The goal for most countries is to change their target from development to sustainable development. This means that the emphasis is to widen the economic view of development to a larger vision that includes the other important components of sustainability, i.e. social, economic, and environmental. Knowledge-based economies call for new levels of learners, teachers, and skills, while insufficient opportunities to access higher levels of learning and acquire skills are resulting in a knowledge divide among and within countries, with major economic and employment consequences. These challenges need an ambitious, transformative, and inclusive post-2015 education agenda of universal relevance applicable to all countries, irrespective of their development status. The international community has come a long way since the worldwide movement Education for All (EFA), which was initiated in Jomtien, in 1990, and reaffirmed in Dakar in 2000. While exceptional progress has been made, the journey to achieving EFA is not over.

The Sustainable Development Goals (SDGs) proposed by the Open Working Group (OWG) of the General Assembly in July 2014 included a separate goal on education. The international education community, co-led by the United Nations Educational, Scientific and Cultural Organization (UNESCO) and the United Nations Children's Fund (UNICEF), began a broad and intensive consultation to define the future education agenda. This extensive process concluded in the Muscat Agreement adopted at the Global EFA Meeting in Oman in May 2014, representing a shared vision of education for the future (Sarabhai 2015).

The concept of sustainable development was introduced at the first Earth Summit in 1972 in Stockholm. During this conference, education was introduced as an essential element in achieving sustainable development. There are many definitions of sustainable development, but the most famous one is that introduced by the United Nations (UN) in 1987 as "Development which meets the needs of the current generation without compromising the ability of future generations to meet their needs." In 2005, the UN adopted a Decade of Education for Sustainable Development (DESD). The objective of the DESD is to relate the principles and values of sustainable development to all aspects of education (UNESCO 2005).

Many international organizations are urging educational institutions to tackle sustainability issues and endorse sustainable development due to the surge of unique environmental problems worldwide. ESD can be defined as an active and extensive learning process where every person has the chance to benefit from educational opportunities while studying the required norms, values, and lifestyles to build a sustainable future. It is for everyone, at all stages of life within any learning context. It involves multiple stakeholders and employs all means of public awareness-raising, training, and education to endorse a broad understanding of sustainable development by addressing its three pillars (society, environment, and the economy) while taking into consideration the cultural dimension (Deshmukh 2017), and by balancing the three pillars while conserving the planet's natural resources for future generations. Thus, it is closely related to the SDGs, as its mission is outlined in SDG 4. This mission in higher education institutes is to create a better world to live in and to produce graduates who can help solve urgent societal needs (Glavic 2020). Therefore, ESD can be perceived as a transformed educational paradigm which highlights learning features that improve the transition toward sustainability because it transforms sustainability research outcomes into educational practices. Consequently, it helps individuals reflect on their own actions through assessing their current and future environmental and social effects in a sustainable manner. It aims to improve individuals' capabilities to allow them to take part in sociopolitical processes and move their society toward sustainable development (Barth et al. 2016).

Three models of ESD learning were recognized by Moore (2005). The first is the cooperative learning model, which is defined as a structured process that necessitates learners sharing information, working together on a task, and supporting and encouraging each other. This model is like the conventional learning model in the sense that the instructor is in control of the learning context and guides students to learn. The second model is the collaborative learning model in which students are dynamic learning agents and the educator acts as a class member and learning organizer without firm authority. The third is the transformative learning model, which supports learners to modify their references and structures, whereas educators in this model apply instructional methods that emphasize critical reflection to allow learners to develop reflective and critical thinking to adjust habits and mindsets (Khalil et al. 2013). Transformative learning in ESD allows for a structural modification of the thoughts, feelings, values, paradigms, beliefs, assumptions, and view of the world that guide students' thinking with the aim of altering their consciousness toward the world; this necessitates self-exploration and self-location of their relationships with other humans and the natural world. The transformation process is unique, personal, and context-oriented. It is considered an iterative rather than a direct process that requires time and space and might lead to further transformation (Forster et al. 2019).

To define the process of education for sustainability, some important questions need to be identified. For example:

- What are the learning values and curricula that should be formulated?
- How can assessment methods support the learning process?
- What are the required educational planning and resourcing systems?
- What are the suitable approaches of learning needed for decent and sustainable work?
- What is the role of international support in achieving sustainability in education?

Learning at all ages plays a vital role in the development of sustainable futures. At Rio+20 1 – The United Nations Conference on Sustainable Development – countries agreed to establish an intergovernmental process to develop a set of SDGs to help in implementing sustainable development. It was emphasized that education is fundamental in achieving sustainable development and is the most effective way to reduce poverty, by concentrating on the quality of education, innovation, and lifelong learning. Elmassah et al. (2020) report that in the past few years, there have been many studies on the impact of education in building students' sustainable development literacy, attitudes, behavior, and competencies.

Higher education is in a unique position to lead the transition process to sustainability. Higher education in particular is considered fundamental to the strategy for achieving sustainability because of its direct influence on graduates. Universities have the means to influence students by providing these individuals – tomorrow's planners, teachers, doctors, engineers, business leaders, scientists, journalists, and politicians – with the necessary skills to change existing societies into sustainable cultures.

The challenge of incorporating sustainability into university curricula is significant and involves sitting on curriculum committees, developing student learning outcomes, and creating new academic programs. In addition to educating students, institutionalizing sustainability includes creating new knowledge through research and promoting sustainability through community engagement. There are many attempts to implement sustainable practices into higher education institutions, for example, the Talloires Declaration, an international agreement signed by over 350 university presidents in more than 40 countries all over the world (ULSF 1990). Other programs include the International Sustainable Campus Network (ISCN) and the Global Higher Education Sustainability Partnership (GHESP), which provide forums for institutions to exchange good practices and improve current practices.

15.3.2 Sustainability and Education: Literature Review and Cultural Perception in Egypt

There is a close connection between education and culture as both affect, complement, and supplement each other, in that education plays the role of reserving, transferring, and advancing the culture of a society. Hence, international organizations advocate and promote ESD to change society's cultural perception (Glavic 2020; Deshmukh 2017). This was clearly manifested in chapter 36 of Agenda 21 adopted by the UN Conference on Environment and Development (1992) which discussed promoting education, public awareness, and training and clearly stated that education is crucial for endorsing sustainable development and enhancing peoples' capacity to tackle environmental and development issues. It called for incorporating ESD as a vital part of learning in formal and non-formal education. Hence, ESD was perceived as a prerequisite to achieve ethical and environmental awareness, creating sustainability values and attitudes as well as skills and behavior to allow for capable public participation in decision-making.

It called for countries to allow accessibility of education about both the environment and sustainable development from primary school age through adulthood for all people to ensure awareness in all sectors of society and it endorsed the incorporation of environmental and developmental concepts in all educational programs to help explore the reasons for major environmental and development issues within a local context. Moreover, countries were encouraged to enable and enhance non-formal education activities at the local and national levels in cooperation with non-formal educators and community-based organizations. Agenda 21 identified four areas of interest for ESD: improving basic education, modifying current education to tackle sustainability, raising people's awareness of sustainability, and training leaders across the society (Abozaied 2018).

UNESCO is considered the main advocate for ESD and works on facilitating entry to quality education on sustainable development at all levels and in all social backgrounds to support people in improving the needed knowledge, skills, behaviors, and values for sustainable development. This was expressed in the Muscat Agreement (UNESCO 2014), which confirmed that education is a central human right for everyone. It is an indispensable condition for decent work, gender equality, peace, sustainable development, economic growth, and responsible global citizenship. It helps in eliminating inequalities and eradicating poverty through building fair, sustainable, and inclusive societies. Accordingly, it should be positioned at the core of the global development agenda. Thus, the agreement called for ensuring equitable and inclusive quality education and lifelong learning for all by 2030 as the main goal of the post-2015 education agenda and set the target of learners to obtain the needed knowledge, values, skills, and attitudes to create sustainable and peaceful societies through ESD and global citizenship education by 2030.

Furthermore, the 2030 Agenda for sustainable development stressed the importance for all learners to obtain the needed knowledge and skills to endorse sustainable development that can be achieved through ESD and sustainable lifestyles (Lovren 2017). In addition, UNESCO disseminated a draft framework for ESD beyond 2019 with three main messages: the need for transformative action from individuals, the need for a structural change in the relationship between economic growth and sustainable development, and the need to ensure a technological future through endorsing critical thinking and green skills (Glavic 2020).

Students are the center of focus in ESD. Nevertheless, studies on students' cultural knowledge and perception of sustainability are scarce. The available studies have revealed a lack and a deficiency in the perception of sustainable development in a number of countries. Indeed, a study by Darnton (2004) demonstrated awareness of the sustainable development concept in the UK general public as being below 30%. Azapagic et al. (2005) concluded that despite a narrow knowledge of the sustainable development concept among undergraduate engineering students, they perceived it as significant especially for future generations even though students only knew of the environmental aspects of sustainable development. Stir (2006) revealed the superficial knowledge of the aspects of sustainable development among students enrolled in pre-service teacher education at Griffith University in Australia. A study by Lourdel et al. (2007) employed the cognitive map technique to calculate students' perception of sustainable development after joining training on this concept; the results showed that students had a changed perception after the training as they became able to link a wide range of terms to sustainable development.

The concept of ESD in Egypt is still new. Strategies that tackle the issue of education still focus on the notion of quality education such as the long-term socioeconomic development vision (2002/2003–2021/2022) which aimed at advancing human capital through education and raising the employment rate (Miyakoshi 2016).

The Sustainable Development Strategy (SDS): Egypt's Vision 2030 tackled education and training in its seventh pillar under the social dimension, stating that the country aims at providing quality education and training without discrimination for all citizens in pre-university and university education to equip students with the necessary skills to think in a creative way and be empowered technically and technologically; the aim is to produce responsible, creative, and competitive citizens who tolerate changes and diversity. The strategy set specific targets and plans to be accomplished by 2030 for each type of education: pre-university, technical, and university level education.

For pre-university education, the strategy set programs with specific targets to develop an education investment strategy with new finance mechanisms for education at the school level, create a proper preschool system, advance teachers' technical and professional skills, apply an inclusive curriculum reform system, adopt an illiteracy and dropout eradication program, construct a system for accredited schools, implement a program to incorporate slightly disabled students in schools and another support program for distinguished and talented students, create a subsidy system to support poor families, and establish a periodic assessment system for students based on international standards. As for technical education and training, it set programs to improve the quality of educational and training facilities, encourage the private sector's engagement in developing technical education, adopt the attractive school project as well as a specialized development program for teachers and trainers, increase awareness to improve the social perception of this type of education, set an effective information system about the needs of the labor market, implement the Egyptian national qualifications framework for technical education and vocational training, and have specialized faculties for technical and vocational education and provide a professional practicing license for graduates of vocational and technical education.

Regarding higher education the program aims at improving the quality of higher education institutions while entering into partnerships with the private sector and civil society to establish more institutions. It also aims at creating curricula based on the national qualifications framework while enhancing the human capital of the teaching staff and modernizing the admission system for higher education, approving the Egyptian diplomas equivalence system, as well as approving higher education certificates, stimulating research centers' role, and creating a link between graduates and employment institutions at local, regional, and international levels (Ministry of Planning, Monitoring and Administrative Reform 2016).

Some sustainability initiatives were presented in a report by the Arab Republic of Egypt reviewing the SDGs inputs in 2016. In academia, three main initiatives were identified. The first was the establishment of the "EduCamp: ESD beyond the campus," which is an Egyptian–European project aimed at promoting and applying ESD nationwide and through all education levels, with an emphasis on public schools, by integrating key values of sustainable development into the teaching and learning process. EduCamp applied four principles to integrate ESD into the Egyptian education system:

1) Sharing responsibilities among different stakeholders.
2) Altering educational practices.

3) Raising public awareness and acceptance of sustainability.
4) Developing teachers' capacities through training of trainers.
5) The project resulted in positive outcomes, such as the creation of ESD resource kits that enabled educational institutions to offer teachers and students activities related to agriculture, energy, biodiversity, and water to connect the curriculum with the local community. The application of the training program for teachers allowed them to apply ESD and utilize the kits in their teaching activities. In addition, seven ESD Centers of Excellence were created to approve ESD in the educational system and deliver training programs for teachers.

The second initiative was the organization of a Mega Projects Conference by the British University in Egypt with the Centre for Sustainability and Future Studies (CSFS). Its aim was to concentrate on sustainable development ideas and model an approach to support governmental concerns and initiatives. The third initiative was the development of an MSc program in Sustainable Development at the American University in Cairo (AUC) to benefit from sustainable development as an opportunity to achieve further economic growth. The MSc program aimed at producing a new generation of business and social entrepreneurs with the appropriate skills to introduce innovative projects and products and green businesses, and to formulate public policy and social entrepreneurship innovations that satisfy the new environmental challenges. In addition, the civil society had an important initiative reflected in the establishment of the Egyptian Sustainable Development Forum (ESDF) as a think tank that works to enable discussions among different stakeholders to define policy gaps in strategies, legislations, and national planning to attain sustainability, while providing action-oriented recommendations to enable the incorporation of sustainability in different policies. It acts as a communication tool between government representatives, politicians, the private sector, non-governmental organizations (NGOs), trade unions, universities, and research centers, media, and other sectors of society. Sustainable education was set as one of the activities of the ESDF.

15.4 Higher Education for Sustainable Development: An Overview

15.4.1 A General Outlook

Universities have an important role as generators and transferors of relevant knowledge and educators of future decision-makers. The concept of sustainable development allows universities to recognize and face up to complexities and handle uncertainty. Hence, the research on higher ESD became prominent and a number of research initiatives and postgraduate programs worldwide became involved in this area (Barth et al. 2016). Higher education institutions play an imperative role in advocating the goal of a sustainable society. Raising sustainability issues forms the values and behaviors of students in universities, which can lead to better conservation of natural and financial resources (Deshmukh 2017).

The role of universities is to produce future professionals, policy-makers, and leaders able to deal with current and future economic, social, and environmental issues. Consequently, universities have a moral responsibility toward attaining sustainability. Universities have a high potential to apply ESD due to their nature as teaching and research institutes that are able to construct innovative systems that are in harmony with the ecological system. Nevertheless, the business-oriented educational approach that merely targets production, consumption, and profit maximization with minimal account for the environment is still dominant (Abozaied 2018).

The UN DESD (2005–2014; see Section 15.3.1) directed the debate on how to transform university curricula to enable students to build a more sustainable future. It called for the integration of sustainable development principles in national education curricula as a tool to realize sustainability and validated the role played by ESD as a significant element in shifting people's behavior and outlook toward building and nourishing more sustainable societies. ESD endorses a complete learning approach that differs from the traditional discipline-based education that led to the current social, environmental, and economic threats. It confronts the leading and conventional model that teaches students only to follow the behavioral standards of society and achieve economic growth. ESD is favored by many educators as it raises students' awareness of the links between the economy, society, and the environment, making them knowledgeable citizens fit to take proper economic and social decisions taking into consideration their impact on the environment (Fonseca et al. 2018; Abozaied 2018). Accordingly, to ensure proper ESD in higher education, curricula must be formulated according to the SDGs and the UNESCO World Program of Action on ESD (2015–2019) (Nolting et al. 2020).

Gardanova et al. (2021) stated that, in order to find sustainable solutions to the challenges of the future, it is a must to modify the roles of the major players, i.e. the government, the industrial sector, and universities, in the innovation process in which universities' role must include offering research and development and practical ideas for application. Hence, higher education institutions should become leaders in creating and executing regional economic plans that incorporate the needs of the local economy, such that higher education institutions act as knowledge and know-how hubs in addition to being active players in the government–industry–university connection. Fonseca et al. (2018) stated that higher education institutions must work on developing skills such as critical thinking and moral reasoning.

A university's institutional potential to speed up transformation toward sustainability necessitates considering new teaching approaches and modifying the role of teachers. In order for universities to assume the role of leaders and facilitators of the move toward sustainability, teachers must be actors for learning, not just distributors of information and knowledge. Recent experiences in many countries show that a successful tool for incorporating sustainability in universities is that of creating networks of academics, students, staff, and local communities' representatives to enlarge their scope at national and international levels and to transfer their role from teaching to researching and greening the infrastructure inside and around their institutions (Lovren 2017).

Nolting et al. (2020) have suggested that higher education institutions can apply sustainability through teaching and research. Accordingly, it is important to transfer those ideas, knowledge, and technologies to society to be applied directly and quickly in practice to meet particular societal needs. Sustainability transfer can be defined as a precise form of transfer that helps in achieving sustainable development in society by having a tangible impact on sustainable development through concepts, projects, or discussions about sustainability. It is carried through joint exchange between the university and practitioners. Transfer actors inside higher education institutions include teachers, researchers, students, and university administration and management staff, while non-university partners for transfer consist of companies, public administration, policy-makers, civil society organizations, and citizens. There are four phases of the sustainability transfer process:

1) Beginning the transfer process and recognizing the actors.
2) Identifying the concept and goals of the transfer activity.
3) Applying the transfer activity.
4) Collecting and recording results.

5) A number of studies attempted to explain the link between sustainable development and education. Gardanova et al. (2021) have suggested that there is a strong correlation between the number of universities and the rate of economic development in the region as they perceive that the growth of the higher education sector helps in increasing the economic growth rate. Although universities have direct and indirect impacts on development, little attention has been given to the role of universities in knowledge development even though recent global crises have shown the need for sustainable solutions and the utilization of higher education as a tool for achieving sustainable development through advocating and approving entrepreneurial teaching and activities. This entrepreneurial education will allow people to develop the required skills for new entrepreneurial ventures that aim at achieving sustainability. Holm and Martinsen (2015) stated that the key to realize sustainable development is education. They suggested four distinct approaches to explain the relationship between sustainable development and higher education. The first two approaches are necessary knowledge and demanded qualifications for sustainable development, which constitute the education discourse that focuses on which type of knowledge or qualifications ought to be the primary target for learning. The other two approaches are formation and lifelong learning of skills for sustainable development that create the learning discourse.

The first field in the education discourse is the necessary knowledge for sustainability which is defined as the level of knowledge that a student acquires through schooling, while the demanded qualifications for sustainable development focus on a certain type of knowledge that the students receive from a specific curriculum in higher education institutions that can be applied to develop a sustainable society. The formation approach deals with the formation of personality through education, which entails that sustainable development in higher education is not dominated by a certain view of sustainable development but rather should turn into a supporting theme across universities. The lifelong learning skills contribute to higher education on sustainable development through the continuous development of lifelong learning skills, such as sustainable assessments skills that lead to a resilient life.

Several countries have attempted to reform their educational systems in the context of sustainable development. For example, in Germany, a sustainability-related educational program (the BLK program) was applied (1999–2004) which included a large number of educators and schools that had positive results by providing students with vital ESD competencies (Miyakoshi 2016).

Kukeyeva et al. (2014) stated that in the past, education was regarded as an issue that was isolated from economic and environmental sustainability in Kazakhstan. However, in recent years, a range of reforms has been taken by the Kazakhstani government to align the country's education system with international standards. This began in 2006 when the country approved a document on the state's transition to a model of sustainable development. It acknowledged that the transition is unmanageable without reforming the education system to create a new generation of workers capable of understanding the demands for this transition. In 2010, the country approved a state program on the development of education (2011–2020) with the goal of enhancing the country's human capital through quality education to ensure sustainable growth of the economy. Nevertheless, higher education in Kazakhstan remains ineffective and needs to be further integrated in Kazakhstan's model for sustainable development. This entails stable and steady investment in science and academia to enhance the capabilities and skills of the national workforce by transforming the concept of teaching to learning by doing in addition to reconsidering and forming new educational standards by collaborating with all relevant stakeholders, including industry representatives, educators, foreign experts, and government representatives.

Another study by Fonseca et al. (2018) examined the Portuguese BSc and MSc courses in the top eight higher education institutions (four universities and four polytechnic institutes) to classify those that tackled sustainability, social responsibility, or ethics issues. Results have shown an average of seven BSc and MSc courses and 12.5% of curricular units addressed sustainability in their syllabi, with three main fields that incorporate sustainability-related syllabus in their curricula: social sciences 40%, engineering and science 35%, and management and economics 23%. There is an average of 49 teaching hours covering sustainability-related topics. In addition, the results of an online survey conducted on the students in the School of Engineering of the Polytechnic Institute of Porto, one of the five largest engineering schools in Portugal, revealed that most respondents viewed the implementation of production systems that utilize used products and recycling as a beneficial step for the environment and the economy, supporting the selective collection of waste and the implementation of a zero-waste economy.

15.4.2 Education for Sustainable Development in Egyptian Higher Education Institutes

Some efforts have been taken to incorporate sustainability in Egyptian higher education systems. Egypt was part of the Reorient University Curricula to Address Sustainability (RUCAS) project, which aimed at helping the academic and administrative staff in universities in Egypt, Lebanon, and Jordan to integrate ESD in higher education curricula (Ramzy and Wahieb 2012).

In particular, among higher education institutions in Egypt, there are three universities known for truly engaging in sustainability. The first one is Cairo University (CU); Elmassah et al. (2021) have stated that CU has a clear strategic direction that takes into consideration sustainable development. However, CU did not consider sustainable development as one of its main concepts in its vision or mission statements; it did, however, consider it as an end result, which it could achieve through education and research. Moreover, CU identified only the key performance indicators (KPIs) as monitoring ways of their overall plan, without setting a specialized system for auditing and reporting for sustainable development practices within the university. Elmassah et al. (2021) mentioned that CU did not set any obligatory standards to integrate the concepts of sustainability in the curriculum. However, there are courses that, by their nature, address sustainable development related topics, such as CU's Professional Masters in Gender and Development.

CU highlighted the importance of student activities and communities in building the students characters as a non-formal way of educating students. Such activities included simulation models, initiatives, employment fairs, competitions, international student associations, student clubs/circles, local communities, and on-campus events. While CU did not have specialized student activities that were created mainly with an aim of adopting the sustainable development agenda. Yet, there were student activities that implicitly addressed sustainable development issues, such as the "Model of United Nations – Women," and the "Model of the European Union." Furthermore, CU displayed great efforts in building its faculty competencies by providing them with different development and training programs. CU's Faculty and Leadership Development Center (FLDC) provides training programs that work on developing one or more of four faculty competencies: teaching and education systems competency, scientific research competency, management and leadership competency, and group communication and interaction competency. CU took steps to transform its campus into a sustainable one. It reduced the use of printed papers and replaced them with electronic copies. In addition, it reduced energy consumption by replacing the normal lamps, used in lighting the buildings, with LED energy-saving lamps. Other steps are still under discussion including a recycling project and using solar energy to light the university's street lamps (Elmassah et al. 2021).

The second Egyptian university truly engaging in sustainability is Heliopolis University (HU), declaring sustainable development in its mission and vision as a main theme and as value applied in all its disciplines. Accordingly, every educational program aims to tackle sustainability in diverse ways. The third university is the AUC, which also started to incorporate the sustainability concept in both its curricula and campus. It was one of the partner universities in the EduCamp project and it supported the project-related training program for teachers through the Center of Sustainable Development (CSD) in the university. In addition, the university has a graduate program in sustainable development which delivers in-depth education on sustainability and its application in the economy, environment, and society to improve students' literacy in sustainability issues (Abozaied 2018).

A study by Khalil et al. (2013) measured students' perception of ESD in HU as a non-profit university in Egypt. It showed a satisfactory understanding of the concept and its applications among students who were able to recognize solutions, list examples, and express their ability to apply sustainable development in their own lives through daily activities.

Abozaied (2018) investigated how university faculty members in a language department in a private university in Egypt identify sustainable development and ESD and how these diverse perceptions have affected their teaching methods. It revealed that attending a workshop on development enhanced academics' understanding of sustainable development and its interconnected dimensions, as well as clarifying perception of their roles as educators toward ESD. Nevertheless, the workshop did not result in a transformation in teaching approaches to meet ESD because of time constraints, discouraged students, and complications of implementing an ESD approach.

15.5 Higher Education for Sustainable Development: Challenges and the Way Forward

15.5.1 A Global Insight

Wade (2008) noted that one of the biggest challenges for ESD is the current structures in the formal education system, which usually hinder interdisciplinary approaches and actively work against them. Similarly, Lovren (2017) stated that the challenges that higher education face in promoting sustainable development are linked to the traditional culture of the academic institutions, for example, the perception that the traditional role of universities is being only scientific producers of knowledge. Additionally, sometimes the nature of the structure of universities hinders the application of a new sustainability paradigm through different elements of the university, leading to a structural trap. Hence, teaching has a great role in filling that gap, linking these separate elements of the university structure, and endorsing its new function of giving for the economy, cultivating values, and improving the intellectual value of sustainability. This can be applied within the university context by transforming it into a green campus, advocating ESD, and endorsing sustainability science.

Hargreaves (2008) listed some obstacles in applying ESD, such as inadequate teaching methods, inefficient teacher training, and the lack of a positive vision. Hargreaves also cited a common conviction that individual teaching is unable to create a difference due to time and resource constraints coupled with overcrowded curricula and the partial implementation of limited features of ESD as extras to the curriculum. In addition, leadership challenges were identified as obstacles to the application of a complete ESD approach. This was confirmed by Fernandez-Sanchez et al. (2014) who proposed that the main challenges encountered by higher education institutions in applying ESD are the lack of proper guidance, knowledge, resources, interest, and support of university administration and top management to appropriately integrate ESD, in addition to non-existent teacher training, deficiency of funds, centralization of training activities, and the absence of real commitment on an institutional level toward ESD. They also observed that the integration process itself greatly affects the success of ESD, whether it is a top-down or a bottom-up approach.

Tudor et al. (2020) stipulated that one of the main challenges in applying sustainability in higher education institutions is related to adopting suitable measures to implement several sustainability standards while assessing the related costs and benefits. Hence, higher education institutions need to adopt economically effective sustainability measures that help in acknowledging those sustainability efforts at regional and international levels. This was noted by Ssossé et al. (2021) who suggested that the challenges are not only associated with the application of ESD, but with evaluating the impact and efficiency of ESD. They expressed two main concerns: first, a concern of ESD validity by questioning how to calculate the real outcomes of ESD and, second, how to measure whether ESD outcomes can be truly credited to it alone.

Many universities that attempt to adopt an ESD approach fall into the trap of merely greening the campus rather than creating real transformation in education. In addition, the process of integrating ESD into the educational programs is generally carried out by a small number of faculty staff on a course level isolated from the systems dominating the university; this is not adequate as ESD needs alteration to the policies, systems, and philosophies of the university. Furthermore, ESD manifests in some fields (e.g. environmental science), while it remains almost non-existent in other fields (e.g. psychology), which necessitates an examination of how faculty members responsible for curriculum modification perceive and understand sustainable development to allow for proper integration of ESD in all curricula. Additionally, faculty members' beliefs and perceptions of sustainable development can either help or impede the incorporation of ESD in curricula as ESD is subject to personal interpretation of the concept, which affects the content and the learning process (Abozaied 2018).

Forster et al. (2019) identified the proper implementation of transformative teaching (see Section 15.3.1) as another challenge that faces ESD in higher education institutions, as this type of education requires the willingness and engagement of both students and teachers in a transformative learning process that questions whether their perceptions contribute to a sustainability-related transformation or must be changed. It requires learning on both the cognitive and emotional levels. Accordingly, three main challenges manifest in applying transformative learning:

1) Identifying the learning edge, which questions how teachers, given the uniqueness of each person, can identify and accommodate different learning edges to allow for transformative learning among individuals and groups.
2) Recognizing ethical and feasibility considerations, which questions what type of intentional trigger for transformative learning are ethically suitable and feasible to build a safe space for transformation?
3) Knowing the quality assurance considerations, which requires investigating how the learning process is facilitated, bearing in mind learners' norms and emotions while guaranteeing to deliver quality and competence-oriented teaching.

All these challenges that confront the implementation of ESD can be turned into opportunities. Hargreaves (2008) suggested that applying a whole approach to ESD is a great opportunity for the formal education sector as it improves the environmental performance of educational institutions while enhancing the quality of education and shaping a more sustainable future. This approach can be applied by moving ESD from the border to the core by integrating sustainability as a fundamental goal of the educational process and applying sustainability principles across all aspects of higher education institutions, leading to a competitive edge for institutions that adopt this approach.

Tudor et al. (2020) listed some opportunities that stem from applying sustainability in higher education institutions, such as improving the recruitment process for high-level students, staff, and administration, publishing innovative researches, creating new employment opportunities for graduates, improving funding opportunities, as well as raising the willingness of future students to join the university.

Wade (2008) suggested that non-formal education processes that support lifelong learning for sustainability offer a great opportunity for endorsing ESD. Hence, higher education institutions can utilize this form of education by offering non-credit courses on sustainability for community members and by engaging with NGOs in designing workshops and seminars on sustainability.

15.5.2 Challenges and Opportunities in Egypt

Since the beginning of the 1990s, educational reform has been on the top of the government's agenda. However, the higher education sector in Egypt faces many problems, including:

- Low quality of higher education sector, with many graduates unable to meet the requirements of the labor market.
- Overcrowded universities and low levels of per capita expenditure.
- Low levels of internal/external efficiency.
- Limited funds devoted to scientific research.
- A lack of sustainability awareness – even though the SDS 2030 was declared to be achieved; the sustainability concept is still not integrated in society.
- Accordingly, teaching can play a vital role in influencing citizens' knowledge of sustainability and its effect on society. A major challenge for ESD in Egypt is that the current school system provides universities with students who lack the basic understanding of ESD principles which creates a challenge for educators to guide students to think from a sustainable development perspective (Abozaied 2018).

A study by Ramzy and Wahieb (2012) on branding green and sustainable education in Egypt suggested that limited cultural resources in Egypt create great difficulty for students and parents in understanding ESD. The study concluded that a positive relationship exists between access to good cultural resources in early childhood and the level of acceptance and integration of ESD, while a negative relationship exists between ESD integration and the level of satisfaction with the conventional curriculum. In addition, inadequate resources and materials devoted to sustainable development in Egypt create a challenge in integrating ESD. As a result, parents and students lack the proper understanding of the significance of ESD (Khalil et al. 2013).

Since the 1960s, the free tuition policy in public universities has led to large student enrollment ratios in those universities, causing a number of problems such as high student-staff ratio, substantial teaching loads, the inadequacy of professors' support for students, as well as minimal time for professors to advance their own capabilities. Also, the scope for modernizing programs and courses is limited, with little enhancement in the infrastructure. In addition, in some cases, teaching assistants (TAs) assume the responsibility of some courses to reduce professors teaching load; this results in TAs having a reduced amount of time for their own studies, hence prolonging the time taken to complete their master's degree to five to seven years (Miyakoshi 2016).

Applying ESD in Egypt can be perceived as both a challenge and an opportunity. Introducing ESD in Egyptian schools requires a total transformation of teaching techniques into participatory active learning and student-centered teaching practices; this creates a major challenge to ESD implementation due to the solid link between teachers' educational practice and their values and views of teaching that developed long before they became teachers in classrooms. Moreover, teachers in Egypt are faced with large class sizes, rigid curricula, and inadequate resources, as well as the lack of significance placed on ESD in Egypt. Furthermore, teachers' development, which is usually carried out through the training of trainers, is another challenge as it permits variances in the objective and subjective notion of change that the trainer and the teacher assign to the educational initiative. Accordingly, teachers can apply a modified version of the activities as they were initially intended (Sewilam et al. 2015).

There are great opportunities in applying ESD in higher education institutions in Egypt. The surge of private universities with innovative missions and flexible structures allows for incorporating ESD as a core element in the educational process. These universities can build their unique curricula by adopting cutting edge, innovative, active, participatory, and transformative learning approaches. By doing so, they can be branded as green and sustainable universities and benefit from having a competitive edge that will help in attracting sustainability-passionate staff and students, as well as attracting funds from sustainability-oriented investors. Furthermore, ESD can be further developed in the form of creating innovative interdisciplinary degrees and programs that incorporate the different dimensions of sustainability.

Another opportunity for ESD is presented in the adoption of informal education activities in Egyptian higher education institutions to disseminate sustainable development principles to the community. In this way, higher education institutions will fulfill their social responsibility toward the society, while enhancing the cultural perception of sustainable development, which will be in turn be reflected on the quality of education in the future. In addition, there is an untapped potential lying in the research centers across higher education institutions in Egypt. These centers, by engaging in sustainability-related research and by forming coalitions with the private sector and NGOs, can affect the creation of sustainability hubs across the country that can act as incubators for environmental and green start-ups working on attaining the country's sustainability goals.

15.6   Conclusions and Recommendations

Sustainability requires a transformation of the entire educational paradigm rather than a mere change to the existing one. Therefore, the idea of sustainable education must focus on educational thinking, policy, and practice (Wade 2008). Accordingly, the full integration of ESD in education requires a transformation not only in higher education institutions, but also in schools. As suggested by Hargreaves (2008) a whole-school approach to ESD ensures holistic incorporation of sustainability in formal sector curricula rather than it being taught separately. On-the-job training for teachers is required to enable educators acting as active implementers of ESD. In addition, all stakeholders, from educators and policy-makers to grassroots activists, should commit and collaborate on all levels to ensure that ESD becomes a catalyst for change.

There is a need for networking and for creating associations between educational institutions to shift education so that it is value-based and intercultural, and allows for the dissemination of success stories and best practices at all levels of the education system. Accordingly, higher education institutions need redesigning, shifting from being bureaucratic and disciplinary organizations to become entities that advocate teamwork and adopt group activities (Deshmukh 2017).

Scherak and Rieckmann (2020) stated that there are 12 core ESD competencies that faculty members in higher education institutions should have in order to help students better understand and realize sustainability. Those skills are refined from the competencies proposed by the UN Economic Commission for Europe (UNECE). The 12 skills were classified into four main categories:

1) **Integration**: This includes the competencies of systems, futures, and participation.
2) **Involvement**: This consists of attentiveness, empathy, and values competencies.
3) **Practice**: This contains creativity and action skills.

4) **Reflexivity**: This incorporates criticality, responsibility, and decisiveness skills.
5) Kankovskaya (2016) suggested that the realization of sustainable development is closely connected to the appropriate development of a national innovation system in any country. This system comprises three main sectors: the business sector, the higher education sector, and the research and development sector. The system needs adequate economic incentives, excited policy-makers who stimulate innovation, less bureaucratic activities, strong connections between all the system elements, and enhanced education-related laws and regulations

Multiple efforts have been taken by Egypt to encourage ESD and incorporate it in diverse curricula. However, the country remains only at the initial phase of implementing ESD. Egypt, like other Arab countries, encounters many complications in integrating ESD in higher education institutions, which can be attributed to lack of awareness and inadequate ESD curriculum. Accordingly, the main target for ESD in Egypt should be attracting cultured students to ensure its full realization. Education quality and the type of education are the most attractive features for students in choosing a university. Consequently, Egyptian universities that apply ESD as a distinctive education type can use it to attract moderate and highly cultured students and enhance the university's reputation. ESD as a distinct type of education must be promoted in cultural centers and other places, such as libraries and culture events, popular among moderate and highly cultured students. Additionally, it is recommended that new private universities that offer ESD should target conventional/public school graduates while well-established universities that apply ESD should target international and upscale school graduates in Egypt. ESD in Egypt requires not only incorporating sustainable development topics in classes, but also altering the educational approaches adopted by Egyptian teachers.

To conclude, Egypt is in a dire need of a major transformation of the current education system to allow for the integration of ESD as a distinctive field of education. This entails innovations on the policy, educational, and administrative levels. At the policy level, there is a need for a clear policy framework for ESD that sets specific targets and time frames for implementing ESD across all educational levels. This framework must be accompanied by an attractive set of economic and administrative incentives to encourage educational institutions to adopt ESD. There is also a need for a strong monitoring system to assess the progress of ESD through these institutions. On the educational level, specialists in ESD should be in charge of the process of curriculum development to ensure that the principles of sustainable development are truly embedded, allowing for the establishment of ESD-oriented degrees and programs to produce future ESD specialists. Moreover, teachers and faculty staff need to have extensive training and workshops that not only teach them about ESD, but also develop their teaching techniques to ones suited for ESD. On the administrative level, the rigid structures associated with educational institutions in Egypt need to change to allow for the integration of sustainable development principles and for cross-sectoral collaboration in ESD-related activities. In addition, the media should assume their role in presenting and advocating the concepts of sustainable development and ESD through awareness campaigns that will help in eradicating citizens' illiteracy on sustainability and in changing the cultural perception of the significance of sustainable development for Egypt.

References

Abozaied, H., (2018). Perceptions of education for sustainable development in Egypt: Prospective changes in teaching practices. Master's thesis. The American University in Cairo.

Azapagic, A., Perdan, S., and Shallcross, D.C. (2005). How much do engineering students know about sustainable development? The findings of an international survey and possible implications for the engineering curriculum. *European Journal of Engineering Education* 30 (1): 1–19.

Barth, M., Michelsen, G., Rieckmann, M., and Thomas, I. (2016). Introduction. In: *The Routledge Handbook of Higher Education for Sustainable Development* (ed. M. Barth, G. Michelsen, M. Rieckmann and I. Thomas), 1–7. Routledge.

Becker, G.S. (1962). Investment in human capital: a theoretical analysis. *Journal of Political Economy* 70: 9–49.

Biltagy, M. (2012). Quality of education, earnings and demand functions for schooling in Egypt: An economic analysis. *Procedia – Social and Behavioral Sciences* 69 (2012): 1741–1750.

Biltagy, M. (2013). Higher education in Egypt between financing constraints and development strategies. Cairo, Egypt: Partners in Development (PID). (In Arabic).

CAPMAS. (2021). Egypt in figures. Arab Republic of Egypt: Central Agency for Public Mobilization and Statistics.

Darnton, A. (2004). The impact of sustainable development on public behavior. Report 1 of Desk Research Commissioned by COI on behalf of DEFRA. Andrew Darnton Research and Analysis, pp. 1–23. https://www.yumpu.com/en/document/read/32650293/the-impact-of-sustainable-development-on-public-behaviour-report-

Deshmukh, V. (2017). Achieving resiliency through sustainable literacy. In: *Handbook of Theory and Practice of Sustainable Development in Higher Education*, vol. 4 (ed. W.L. Filho, U.M. Azeiteiro, F. Alves and P. Molthan-Hill), 3–14. Switzerland: Springer.

Elmassah, S., Biltagy, M., and Gamal, D. (2020). Engendering sustainable development competencies in higher education: the case of Egypt. *Journal of Cleaner Production* 266: 121959.

Elmassah, S., Biltagy, M., and Gamal, D. (2021). Framing the role of higher education in sustainable development: a case study analysis. *International Journal of Sustainability in Higher Education* https://doi.org/10.1108/IJSHE-05-2020-0164.

Fernandez-Sanchez, G., Bernaldo, M.O., Castillejo, A., and Manzanero, A.M. (2014). Education for sustainable development in higher education: state-of-the-art, barriers, and challenges. *Higher Learning Research Communications* 4 (3): 3–11.

Fonseca, L.M., Portela, A.R., Duarte, B. et al. (2018). Mapping higher education for sustainable development in Portugal. *Management and Marketing Challenges for the Knowledge Society* 13 (3): 1064–1075.

Forster, R., Zimmermann, A.B., and Mader, C. (2019). Transformative teaching in higher education for sustainable development: facing the challenges. *GAIA Ecological Perspectives on Science and Society* 28 (3): 324–326.

Gardanova, Z., Nikitina, N., Grebennikova, V., and Ilgov, V. (2021). Role of higher education in sustainable development of regions. *E3S Web of Conferences* 250: –04005. http://doi.org/10.1051/e3sconf/202125004005.

Glavic, P. (2020). Identifying key issues of education for sustainable development. *Sustainability* 12 (6500): 1–18.

Hargreaves, L.G. (2008). The whole school approach to education for sustainable development: from pilot projects to systemic change. In: *Policy & Practice: A Development Education Review* (ed. J. Coriddi), 69–74. Lisburn: Impression Print and Design NI Ltd.

Holm, C. and Martinsen, A. (2015). Mapping the relationship between higher education and sustainable development. *Studia Paedagogica* 20 (4): 71–84.

Kankovskaya, A.R. (2016). Higher education for sustainable development: Challenges in Russia. In: *Procedia CIRP, 23rd CIRP Conference on Life Cycle Engineering*, vol. 48, 449–453.

Khalil, D., Ramzy, O., and Mostafa, R. (2013). Perception towards sustainable development concept: Egyptian Students' perspective. *Sustainability Accounting, Management and Policy Journal* 4 (3): 307–327.

Kukeyeva, F., Delovarova, L., Ormyshevac, T., and Davar, A. (2014). Higher education and sustainable development in Kazakhstan. *Procedia - Social and Behavioral Sciences* 122: 152–156.

Lourdel, N., Gondran, N., Laforest, V. et al. (2007). Sustainable development cognitive map: a new method of evaluating student understanding. *International Journal of Sustainability in Higher Education* 8 (2): 170–182.

Lovren, V.O. (2017). Promoting sustainability in institutions of higher education: the perspective of university teachers. In: *Handbook of Theory and Practice of Sustainable Development in Higher Education*, vol. 4 (ed. W.L. Filho, U.M. Azeiteiro, F. Alves and P. Molthan-Hill), 475–490. Switzerland: Springer.

Ministry of Planning, Monitoring and Administrative Reform (2016). *Sustainable Development Strategy: Egypt's Vision 2030*. Egypt: MPMAR.

Miyakoshi, M. (2016). Higher education and development in Egypt: Exploratory case study of the perception of E-JUST students and graduates. Master's thesis in Sustainable Development. Uppsala University.

Moore, J. (2005). Barriers and pathways to creating sustainability education programs: policy, rhetoric and reality. *Environmental Education Research* 11 (5): 537–555.

Nassar, H. and Biltagy, M. (2021). Human resource competitiveness and digital economy in Egypt. In: *The Egyptian Economy in the Twenty-First Century: The Hard Road to Inclusive Prosperity*. American University Press.

Nolting, B., Molitor, H., Reimann, J. et al. (2020). Transfer for sustainable development at higher education institutions – untapped potential for education for sustainable development and for societal transformation. *Sustainability* 12 (7): 2925.

Ramzy, O. and Wahieb, R.M. (2012). Branding the green education: challenges facing implementation of education for sustainable development in Egypt. *Discourse and Communication for Sustainable Education* 3: 83–99.

Sarabhai, K. (2015). ESD for sustainable development goals (SDGs). *Journal of Education for Sustainable Development* 9 (2): 121–123.

Scherak, L. and Rieckmann, M. (2020). Developing ESD competences in higher education institutions – staff training at the University of Vechta. *Sustainability* 12 (24): 10336.

Sewilam, H., McCormack, O., Mader, M., and Abdel Raouf, M. (2015). Introducing education for sustainable development into Egyptian schools. *Environment, Development and Sustainability* 17: 221–238.

Ssossé, Q., Wagner, J., and Hopper, C. (2021). Assessing the impact of ESD: methods, challenges, results. *Sustainability* 13 (5): 2854.

Stir, J. (2006). Restructuring teacher education for sustainability: student involvement through a "strengths model". *Journal of Cleaner Production* 14 (9–11): 830–836.

Tudor, A.T., Zanellato, G., and Moise, E.M. (2020). Higher education Institution's sustainable development: *performance and reporting*. *Journal of Environmental Protection and Ecology* 21 (1): 211–221.

ULSF (University Leaders for a Sustainable Future) (1990). Report and Declaration of the Presidents Conference. Washington, DC: ULSF.

UNDP. (2020). Human Development Report 2020, "The next frontier: Human development and the Anthropocene". New York: UN Development Programme.

UNESCO. (1998). Higher education in the twenty-first century: Vision and action. World Conference on Higher Education, UNESCO, Paris.

UNESCO. (2005). *UN Decade of Education for Sustainable Development: 2005–2014*. UNESCO - Education for Sustainable Development.

UNESCO (2014). *Global Education for all Meeting*. Muscat, Oman: UNESCO.

United Nations Conference on Environment and Development. (1992). AGENDA 21. Rio de Janerio, Brazil. United Nations Division for Sustainable Development.

Wade, R. (2008). Education for sustainability: challenges and opportunities. In: *Policy & Practice: A Development Education Review* (ed. J. Coriddi), 30–48. Lisburn: Impression Print and Design NI Ltd.

16

Youth Communicators as an Engine for Sustainable Development: A Case Study for Achieving SDGs in Remote Higher Education Institutions

Saira Ahmed, Amir Qayyum, Azza Malik, and Hassan Ali

16.1 Introduction

It is often seen that urban institutions of higher learning are able to attain and exploit exemplary exposure and opportune advantages. However, the institutions in far-flung areas lack the cutting-edge facilities and resources required in the centers of learning of today. This creates an imbalance of sustainable development in the country. Demographic differences are seen as a reason to contribute to a country's uneven growth and volatility in sustainable development indicators (Johnston et al. 2016). Pakistan, too, is trying its best to minimize and curtail differences in patterns of its uneven growth and development.

Indeed, higher education has a key role in the shrinking of such differences for sustainable development due to demographic and geographical dimensions. The 17 United Nations (UN) Sustainable Development Goals (SDGs) are achievable through changes in perception, behavior, and nudging positive psychology – all that is potentially achievable through steps that lead to making a population more conscious of, aware of, and responsible for its actions (Zaleniene and Paulo 2021). Shackleton and Luckert (2015) state that it is imperative to note that rural areas and semi-urban cities are coping desperately with pressures on health systems due to poor health indicators, a situation exacerbated by successive Covid-19 waves leading to an unprecedented pandemic causing an influx of patients. To make matters worse, the government has been implementing a resource cut on higher education since 2019 due to increased fiscal pressures of ongoing International Monetary Fund (IMF) stabilization measures and interest and loan repayments on outstanding international debts (*Samaa News* 2021).

This budget cut has now led public sector higher education institutions (HEIs) to look into business models for running universities and to look for in-house methods of raising funds. One such method is to encourage faculty and students to introduce sustainability (as a long-term goal) and the knowledge of SDGs into curricula, in order to become active actors for community development. This not only generates funds and employment, but also contributes to the attainment of the SDGs.

The Wiley Handbook of Sustainability in Higher Education Learning and Teaching, First Edition.
Edited by Kelum A. A. Gamage and Nanda Gunawardhana.
© 2022 John Wiley & Sons, Inc. Published 2022 by John Wiley & Sons, Inc.

16.1.1 Assessment of Current Curricula

In Pakistan, the Higher Education Commission (HEC) is the apex regulatory body formulating the respective National Curriculum Revision Committees (NCRCs) for almost all fields and disciplines. These NCRCs give non-binding curriculum advisory guidelines for the facilitation and guidance of faculty in universities all over the country. HEC is the top entity that formulates policies, principles, and priorities for HEIs for promoting socioeconomic development of Pakistan. It designs guidelines via thorough consultations with the various institutions for the advancement of learning and teaching and voices its opinions on all matters pertaining to new issues and challenges in design and quality enhancement. It also prescribes minimum conditions under which institutions, including those that are not part of the state educational system, must operate to impart higher education. The HEC is also responsible for setting up national or regional evaluation councils or authorizing existing councils or similar bodies to carry out accreditation of institutions, including their departments, faculties, and disciplines, by giving them appropriate ratings (Figure 16.1).

HEC was established in 2002 and its initial aims included supporting and building capacity of existing councils or bodies for the purpose of enhancing the reliability of the evaluation carried out by the HEC itself. Pakistan, being a rising knowledge-based economy, has emerged as a leading hub of research and development in higher education and steps taken by the HEC and its governance of the higher education sector deserve the credit for this. The HEC has also ensured crucial reforms to promote quality assurance (QA) initiatives for ensuring the quality of non-tertiary and tertiary education. The knowledge-based economy is being promoted

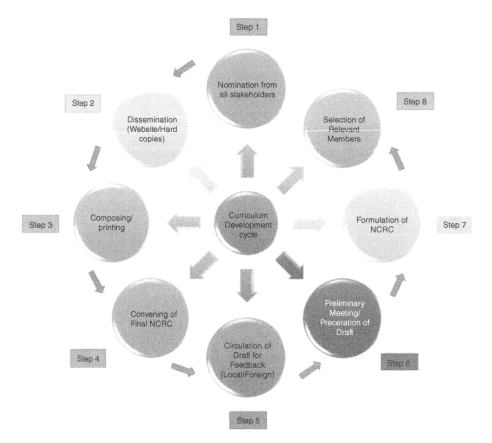

Figure 16.1 Circular steps for curriculum development by NCRC, HEC.

through novel measures, such as awarding doctoral scholarships for education both in Pakistan and abroad and grants for the presentation of research papers at international forums.

HEC programs and projects also include the running of the following innovative programs aligned with the United Nations (UN) 2030 Agenda:

- Capacity building of faculty under the National Academy of Higher Education (NAHE).
- Undertaking of revision of curriculum.
- Development of infrastructure of HEIs.
- Award of indigenous scholarships.
- Grant of foreign scholarships.
- Patent filing support.
- Travel grants for participation in national and international conferences.
- Increasing collaboration between industry and university research.

Moreover, the following is a list of technology reforms – also known as e-reforms – that have been brought into the system:

- Development of a countrywide educational research network.
- Bringing to the reach of the scholars the use of digital sources.
- Developing a research repository for the potential researchers.
- Making learning possible through e-resources.
- Making available the opportunity of videoconferencing.

Bringing increased reforms to the technology sector has been key in times of Covid-19. With several smart lockdowns in almost all cities of the country, these technology initiatives have kept the process of online learning and teaching alive during 2020 and 2021.

16.1.2 Youth Development at HEIs

The current medium of instruction, the efforts behind the training of teaching faculty, the process of students having discussions with their respective teachers outside of the classroom, the discussions students have with their peers during their free time, and university-specific policies on disseminating happenings and news headlines on bulletin boards are all examples of variations in training interactive youth. In metropolitan regions and in government institutions, class sizes tend to be bigger. The majority of lessons are taught in the national language i.e. Urdu (English translated versions are, however, available), but a number of courses are taught in English. Except at elite institutions or at urban universities, even when the language of instruction is mainly English, teachers present the explanation of the content in Urdu or translate it to help students understand it better (Hussain and Khan et al. 2021).

It has also been observed across government, semi-government, private, and not-for-profit universities, that the assigned textbook reigns supreme. This is not very surprising, especially because examinations are based solely on textbooks. Teachers are teaching almost solely focusing on the exam, ensuring that students learn or memorize the content verbatim. They go though the textbooks two or three times over the course of the academic semester or term and give multiple tests and assignments to ingrain memorization. Untrained and inexperienced teachers usually impart a portion of the full chapter of the textbook in each lecture, constantly rewording the same phrases and sentences in the textbook and delivering very little explanation and no extra teaching materials. Moreover, the validity or newness of the materials taken from the textbook are not challenged or questioned by learners. Neither the teacher nor the learners engage in any evaluation or critical testing of the information in the books. Classes hardly ever steer away from the theme under discussion. It has also been ironic to note that in some cases the teachers have been teaching materials from the older editions of the prescribed textbook.

Some teachers do, however, refer to examples from current news or from history to add further explanations of the topic. Habib et al. (2021) continues to add insightfulness by adding that "the additional material or examples brought in are generally no more controversial or radical than the material in the textbooks." Some differentiation is indeed notable: teachers in not-for-profit or private institutions that work on upgrading of teaching methodology are inclined to use creative, graphic diagrams and examples. This allowed them to keep the students creatively engrossed in the materials. Moreover, they assign problems and questions that are, for instance, from outside the textbook. It is interesting to note that the (male) teacher at prestigious private schools asks the students to read up further on the material independently and on the internet by using Google tools and Wikipedia. In public sector universities, the male faculty members are more inclined toward introducing examples from current affairs, news websites, and historical content. Their female counterparts, however, seem less likely to deviate from the textbook and simply comply with the requirement that their students rote-learn the material. Obviously, this is alarming, as faculty needs to be more proactive in bringing awareness about SDGs to the students via print media and social media, such as Facebook, Instagram, and Twitter.

In comparison with private HEIs, the faculty in government universities remains closely attached to the books prescribed in the curriculum and does not encourage interaction between the teacher and student in the lecture or beyond. Among students, too, gender is a key determinant: boys generally seem to have more internet access in comparison to girls, and girls studying in private universities are likely to have much more access to the internet than girls in public sector universities. Exposure to television is not very different: almost all students are exposed to it. Newspaper readability is, however, limited across the board.

16.1.3 Using Sustainability Lens for Evaluation of Pakistan HEIs

"Sustainability in higher education has gained the attention of researchers and academia; however, there is still a need to explore and assess it from different perspectives that are unexplored" (Habib et al. 2021). It is important to see that education for sustainable development has not been fully understood in the national policy on teacher training education. A meager 5% of the syllabus of Bachelors of Education refers indirectly or directly to sustainability. Moreover, "National Professional Standards for Teachers and Standards for Teacher Education Programs" were found to be very poor in terms of their emphasis on sustainability education. The research findings indicate a dire need for inclusion of knowledge about sustainable development in the faculty development curriculum of Pakistan. A recent UN study reveals that although teacher education reform in Pakistan occurred during the UN Decade of Education for Sustainable Development, it was inadequate in its scope, in that it failed to incorporate aspects of sustainability. This raises doubts and concerns about the implementation and execution of international reforms across all of Pakistan.

Teacher education is a key space in the implementation of sustainability education. Sustainability themes have been advocated in various domains of manufacturing, management, and business, including technological education, software development, and information communication technology (ICT). Education can assist students to understand how to implement the components of sustainability, such as in the economic, social, and environmental domains; they can do this by incorporating sustainability concepts into technology. Students' capacity to incorporate sustainability into technological development may be hampered by a lack of understanding and education about sustainability. As a result, developing student competence across the technology education curriculum is critical for long-term sustainability (Lorente et al. 2020).

HEIs are one of the most powerful vectors for putting sustainability and sustainable development ideals into practice. As we know, manufacturing industries of all types are important stakeholders, relying on universities to meet the demand for qualified workers. Universities are also expected to educate young people and contribute to their self-development by reaching saturation of scientific and intellectual information. Among all these goals, colleges are now attempting to build sustainability curricula in order to raise sustainability consciousness and provide undergraduate students with a toolbox that will give them a competitive edge in the labor market. A multidisciplinary approach is required to create such a program.

16.2 Do HEIs Complement Community Needs?

Currently, the mode of the population is in the 15–24-year-old age bracket. The country is at a crossroads, where it can use the demographic dividend to achieve transformational and long-term socioeconomic progress (Ashraf et al. 2013). Formerly, HEIs have not functioned well, but due to advancements in ICT they have improved at various levels, the first being the research level. It appears that for a host of reasons, such as digital reforms, availability of e-sources, favorable HEC policies, university-led initiatives, and investment in current ICT infrastructure, the growth in research volume has been quite exponential in Pakistan. Furthermore, the HEC has actively taken many initiatives in the past two decades to enhance the digital as well as research milieu in universities in order to improve the quality and volume of research. This has been done by setting up e-databases and offering a variety of information technology (IT) facilities. Since 2004, the "HEC Digital Library" has been helping the research community by providing access to thousands of peer-reviewed scholarly journals in all disciplines to all universities in Pakistan. During this period, the number of PhDs has multiplied three times.

An often-used definition of the internationalization of higher education is "the process of integrating an international, intercultural or global dimension into the purpose, functions or delivery of post-secondary education" (Knight 2003). Internationalization is viewed at its worst as an economic ploy to drum up student numbers and tuition and at its best as a way to positively influence universities' global outlook (Rose and McKinley 2017). A more positive view of internationalization relates to noted benefits that internationalization can have for a university's reputation, research quality, teaching quality, and graduate employability (Delgado-Márquez et al. 2013). Tange and Jenson (2012) observe a difference in perception of internationalization of higher education between native English-speaking nations and many non-English speaking nations, especially those in Europe. Rather than looking at international students as a source of income, Shen (2008: p. 223) argues that many European universities see internationalization as a way of "attracting and keeping the best brains from around the world to help develop their own knowledge economies." A study by Frølich (2006) on the internationalization of higher education in Norway adds support to Shen's assertion by concluding that the moves to internationalize were driven by academic, rather than financial motivations.

There are currently 195 recognized and registered degree-awarding institutes in Pakistan (Habib et al. 2021). In all areas of HEIs (curriculum, research, faculty, stakeholder involvement, and governance), the findings reveal a minimal indication of sustainability. Campus (operations) sustainability was obvious, as were, to some extent, outreach initiatives. Teaching and research are the primary goals of HEIs; however, in Pakistan, these goals have yet to be met. Pakistan's HEIs are at the early and initial stages of sustainability. For the attainment of sustainability in HEIs, comprehensive planning and internal governance are required.

16.3 A Pilot Project for Pakistan's Rural Universities

Education is the key to improving development in some of the world's poorest communities. SDG 4 calls for inclusive, equitable, and quality education for all. To integrate this goal into society the Directorate of Sustainability and Environment (DSE) at the Capital University of Science &

Table 16.1 Details of the project.

Client	Pakistan Poverty Alleviation Fund (PPAF)	
Sponsor	Agency for Italian Development (AICS)	
Partners	1. Luiss Business School, Italy	Consultant
	2. Bahria University, Pakistan	ICT Partner
Project Coordinator	Directorate of Sustainability and Environment- CUST, Pakistan	
Local Universities (in Pakistan)	1. University of Chitral 2. University of Malakand 3. University of Swat 4. Lasbela University of Agriculture, Water and Marine Sciences 5. University of Turbat	
Duration of the project	23 November 2020 – 24 March 2021	

Technology (CUST – Pakistan) has worked with the Italian Agency for Development Cooperation (AICS) in collaboration with the Pakistan Poverty Alleviation Fund (PPAF). It involved Luiss Business School as the consultant and Bahria University as an ICT partner (Table 16.1)

In this project, the DSE acted as a mediator for communication. The role of the DSE was to provide smooth and efficient communication between clients, sponsors, partners, the local community, and all stakeholders of the project. It did not only coordinate the activities of the project, but also ensured that each student could understand the basic goal of the project by integrating it into the classes held by Luiss facilitators with online ICT support from Bahria University in Pakistan. The ICT support was crucial in carrying out this project, especially during times of Covid-19.

16.3.1 Project Goal

The overall goal of this project is to contribute to creating sustainable community self-development through youth engagement and communication initiatives based on a Pakistani-Italian liaison. The project, through training, aims to promote youth participation in the social and economic context of the rural and poor areas of Chitral, Swat, Malakand, Lasbela, and Kech. It broadly targets SDGs 5, 8, 9, 11, and 12. That is to say, reduced inequalities and responsible consumption and production are the way forward in raising sustained livelihoods in sustainable cities of Pakistan.

The specific community approaches for the youth leaders and communicators of the project are listed in Table 16.2:

16.3.2 Training Modules

The following highly relevant training modules were conducted for the capacity building of faculty and students at the five local HEIs in the remotest parts of Pakistan. The training was entitled Youth Communicators for Development (YCD) and was conducted by Luiss Business School instructors and facilitators. The following subsections give brief descriptions of the training modules.

16.3.2.1 Social Communication

This course was based on simple and authentic communication tools. The main focus was on social communication for local communities, working on a full range of SDGs. In this course,

Table 16.2 Community approaches for the youth leaders and communicators of the project.

Approach	Key goals	Participant groups
Advocacy	Focuses on policy environment and seeks to develop or change laws, policies, and administrative practices	Policy-makers and decision-makers Program planners Community leaders
Social mobilization	Focuses on uniting partners at the national and community levels for a common purpose Emphasizes collective efficacy and empowerment to create an enabling environment	National and community leaders and groups Public and private partners
Social change communication	Focuses on enabling groups of individuals to engage in a participatory process to define their needs, demand their rights, and collaborate to transform their social system	Groups of individuals in communities
Behavior change communication	Focuses on individual knowledge, attitudes, motivations, self-efficacy, skills building, and behavior change	Individuals Families/households Small groups

the students were taught how to manage non-profit sector communication in any context along with empathy, feedback, and audience management. Also, light was shed upon the assessment of the correct media mix along with its respective purpose. In addition, students were taught how to create impactful awareness in their territories and develop campaigns on specifically targeted SDGs. The expected outcome was to become an effective public communicator and to master communication techniques for non-profit projects which would culminate in becoming a strategic communication planner.

16.3.2.2 Planning and Monitoring

The main purpose of this module was to introduce students to the full-fledged planning and monitoring of projects as part of the project management discipline. Projects addressed were meant to meet the needs of a community, with specific reference to communities of interest to Pakistan. In the introductory part, the course addressed how to start a project and make it fit the economic constraints in alignment with relevant SDGs. The core of the course focused on developing a comprehensive project plan, using effective tools to oversee and monitor a project and bring it to successful completion. Particular attention was given to stakeholder management aligned to the respective SDG and the needful project communication activities.

16.3.2.3 Information and Communication Technology

The strategic aim of the course was to stimulate the participants to acquire the necessary digital mindset to embrace "the innovation change" with enthusiasm and equanimity. The course aimed to enable self-awareness as one of the key drivers for the motivation to change and innovate and to foster a successful digital mindset. It discussed how to create effective social media and multimedia content and how to define e-social media strategy. It introduced the application of new methods, techniques, and tools to produce and set up sharing systems and content dissemination strategies. It further embedded the comparison of strategic and operational insights to make the most of new resources available on the web and to integrate traditional communication activities with innovative digital ones. It also integrated and evaluated the provided toolkit in the project work in order to apply it to professional life.

16.3.2.4 Community Organization and Institutional Framework

Participants attending this module were interactively taught the theoretical framework of local development study combined with practical tools for community organization and the promotion of community building to develop knowledge and skills; they were supported in setting a working plan supported by scenarios analysis, SWOT (strengths, weaknesses, opportunities, and threats) analysis, and logical frameworks. After completing this course, students are primarily expected to be familiar with the engagement process, able to describe the duration, breadth, and intensity of actions foreseen and matched to specified passages within the process.

16.3.2.5 Environmental Communication

From the very beginning, this module highlighted the importance of SDGs 13, 14, and 15. The objective of this course was basically to identify, assess, and evaluate environmental information sources and to develop critical thinking. Students focused on the nature and scope of issues and explored the evidence, support, and framing of values, challenges, assumptions, and opportunities embedded in environmental communication.

It integrated learning from multiple disciplines that focus on environmental communication. Students were asked to consider and communicate learning from other disciplines that are relevant to the discussion, including anthropology, marketing, psychology, and environmental science.

16.3.2.6 Rural Development and Olive Crop

The objective of this course was to speak about SDG 3: Good Health and Well-being. The aim was to explain first generally what rural development is, and then what the main principles and issues are of olive culture in terms of farm management, cooperation, technical assistance, environmental, social, economic, and health impacts, etc. This course provided students with the ability to understand the current policies, programs, action plans, strategies, sector studies, economic potentialities of the value chain, etc., all aligned to the rural development and socio-economic uplift of rural territories. After completing this course, students were expected to understand the main aspects of a sustainable agro-food system and the olive sector. They were able to analyze the main instruments of national and regional policies including multitier strategic plans, action plans, rural development programs etc., and understand their formation and implementation. They were also able to conduct projects for rural development and for business and social improvement.

16.3.2.7 Public Health and Nutrition

In light of a post-pandemic world, this course was very important, especially for rural faculty and students. The objective of the course was to introduce students to the main concepts of public health and nutrition issues, which are challenges to the science and art of preventing disease, prolonging life, and promoting health, via SDG 3, through the organized efforts of society. After this course, the students were able to understand various aspects of health and nutrition needs, analyze various aspects of health status and needs assessment, and support public health policies/initiatives.

16.3.2.8 Sustainable Tourism and Cultural Heritage

This course aimed at defining sustainable development, sustainable tourism, and the marketing perspective for sustainable destination development. It also focused on cultural heritage and sustainable tourism development with tangible and intangible attractors. Furthermore, it helped in identifying the key actors and the key factors of competitiveness of the local tourism systems, along with defining the value concept and the value co-creation processes via SDG 11.

16.3.3 The Fieldwork

The courses mentioned in Section 16.3.2 were taught to give important insights into community and to show how an individual can communicate with the inter- and intra-environment. The students were then divided into groups to carry out the project, which had to be sustainable and meet the needs of the local community. Here, project coordinators helped students to understand their action plans and keep the facilitators updated with the students' activities. Students were highly encouraged by facilitators and the PPAF to perform all the activities physically.

The students were divided into 15 teams. They were allotted respective district supervisors and facilitators by LUISS. It started with team one, whose project title was "Promoting Girls Education in District Lasbela & Lower Dir." Students and facilitators found this a sustainable act because Lower Dir and Lasbela are among the backward areas of Pakistan and most of the people there are illiterate and poor peasants and laborers. The major reason is the fact that the girls have to leave school just after 5th Grade; sometimes they are not allowed to study further and sometimes there are financial issues. Women's mobility is considered a bad omen in society, and therefore parents do not usually allow their daughters to go very far to school.

To solve this issue students took several steps, such as building awareness campaigns to highlight the importance of female education and its role in society. Students also worked for the rehabilitation of government schools in the target union council (UC) by mapping damaged schools and conducting a technical survey for needs analysis and provision of missing facilities. The also established innovative ICT labs in government schools, peer coaching, and innovation workshops for IT teachers.

Team 2 had worked on a similar project as team 1, focusing on SDG 4 – Quality Education. The community theme-based topic was; "Community involvement in school's education in District Kech, Balochistan." The main problem seen there was the sheer lack of awareness among the parents and lack of funding by the government to educational institutes. The students carried out surveys and built strategies to: involve maximum parent/guardian engagement in education in UC Jinnah and Kalatuk; promote quality education, school infrastructure, and primary and secondary facilities in schools; enroll the maximum number of students, especially girls, in schools; provide for the basic needs of female students; bring benefits to 500 students through the intervention of PPAF in the shape of educational kits, e.g. books, notebooks, and uniforms.

The team noted the following:

> There is negligible community involvement in education. From the field visits, we concluded that there is no attention toward the community involvement in education. It is because of lack of awareness in the people, poverty, and negligible community involvement in the learning process of the students which affect the quality of learning. The community people in district Upper Dir are not aware of the importance of their involvement in education. In district Upper Dir every school has a PTC (Parent Teachers Committee) but they are not actively involved in the educational interventions. During our visits to the community, we observed that every school has PTC but these PTCs are not actively involved in educational decisions. We wish to functionalize the PTC of every school. We will try our level best to involve maximum community people in education. We have to encourage the parents to regularly visit their schools., Communication & Technologies are the need of the day for improvement of education but there were no ICT facilities.

Important questions asked included:

Q: Why does the problem exist?
A: Lack of awareness in the people Poverty
Q: Who is causing the problem?
A: The problem is caused by the illiterate, poor, and unaware parents of the areas.
Q: Who is affected by it?
A: Children are most affected by it as negligible community involvement in the learning process of the students affects the quality of learning.
Q: How significant is the problem?
A: The problem is quite significant because the community involvement in education in the targeted district is very less.

To recap, we show the basic issues and challenges facing the parents in their involvement in education.

- The parents are busy with their duties.
- Most of the parents are outside the towns for work-related reasons.
- Most of the people are poor.
- There are no ICT facilities to connect parents with teachers.

The communication strategy was to arrange awareness sessions about community involvement in education at the community level. We arranged 20 sessions in different places at UC level. Each activity will have 20 to 35 participants. The participants will include parents, elites of the local area, religious scholars, and members of local support organizations (LSOs). We will arrange combined meetings of parents and teachers at the schools.

Team 3 worked on the topic "Raising Awareness against Drug Addiction." The reason for choosing this problem was a significant rise seen in drug addiction, especially among youth (aged 26–30) and rising by greater levels in Khyber Pakhtunkhwa (KPK). This is leading to deterioration in the mental, as well as the physical, health of people and preventing them from living healthy lives. The major activities on which students worked were in designing campaigns to communicate to the audience through different media (physically, social media, radio, and television) at the societal level, they also did counseling on a personal level.

Team 4 worked on a project titled "Smart-bin Garbage Monitoring System in Tourist Areas." As the tourism industry of Pakistan is flourishing, the need for sustainable tourism is increasing in communities residing in tourist regions of the country. To work for sustainable tourism, the project aims to provide improvements to the bin to enable timely waste disposal. The innovative smart-bin is based on the internet of things which helps the user by automatically opening the lid. An ultrasonic fill level sensor is embedded inside to detect bin status. Incorporating odor detection to protect public health, the sensor constantly senses air quality and the data is seen in real-time via the Blynk, a platform with IOS and Android apps to control Arduino, Raspberry Pi, and the like over the internet. The smart-bin is ideal for busy locations such as campuses, theme parks, railways, and shopping malls. The action steps for this project targeting SDG 12 were as follows:

Step 1: From the very first we needed to visit various spots to identify favorable points and plan how to install the bins.
Step 2: Collect information from the possible stakeholders about the importance of the project and conduct focus-group consultations with the local people.
Step 3: Design the final bins final for installation.
Step 4: Educate the people about the use of the bin through awareness campaigns and chart diagrams.

Team 5 worked on "Women's Empowerment." The area targeted in their project was Turbat, Balochistan. This area contains a male-dominant society and has few or no opportunities for education and employment for women. Women do not have any role in decision-making bodies and also are never seen in the committees of UC-based bodies of the local system. They are seen working only in the education and health sectors, again in very small numbers. The students developed strategies, such as the promotion of women's participation through capacity building and skills training, for the women to be independent. They also worked to advance gender equality, equity, and empowerment of women, ensuring the elimination of all kinds of violence against women through participation in social, economic, and political spectra at all levels, and bringing women into the mainstream of development.

Team 6 worked on SDG 3, emphasizing the SDG topic "Iron Deficiency in Teenagers and Children." The statistics show that in relation to iron deficiency, 22% of the cases are found in girls, 20% in children, 17% in preschool children, 16% in adolescents, 13% in adult females, and 12% in boys. This is causing significant deterioration in the health of the population. The students' targets were to spread awareness about iron deficiency in children and teenagers, and to provide sufficient iron supplements in collaboration with local support organizations at UC Balambat District Dir, lower province KPK. Parents must be made aware of what iron deficiency is and how important it is to have the required amount of iron in our bodies.

Team 7 carry out an analysis of the drinking water of government-based water supply systems in UC Gokdan, Kech, and Lasbela regarding waterborne diseases in the community. The students carried out several surveys to collect data on the quality of water and how it is being sanitized, and also had meetings with the National Rural Support Programme (NRSP), water-based department, and LSOs to get more information regarding water suppliers' problems and solutions. The objective of this analysis was to promote the importance of clean water and knowledge of how the population in rural areas can get access to sanitized water and improve their health.

The action steps for this team are as follows:

- Ensure the availability of safe and clean drinking water.
- Promote awareness regarding the restoration of the filtration plant.
- Ensure healthy lives and promote well-being for all at all ages.
- Support better and improved socioeconomic development as a result of good health.
- Engage local government to take steps for this cause.

Restoration of the farmland, especially karez, was practiced by team 8. Karez are a marvel of traditional engineering with a "mother well" at the base of the hills and a number of other wells connected through tunnels – with an outlet near the valley floor with culturable lands (Steenbergen et al. 2015). The team's main idea was to bring modern agriculture to Balochistan and embed the sustainability aspect by installing solar panels. The basic purpose is to move toward sustainable farming, which can only happen if we move toward solar energy. The students carried out studies to gain insights into systems and their findings stated that karez are being destroyed due to tubewells and pumping technology. The findings about the conditions were shared with farmers, including information about the likely reduction More than 100 karez are installed, but only 24 are in working condition.in water levels in future, if appropriate remedial measures were not taken. The action steps projected by the university youth included:

1) Estimate the total number of karez (functional and non-functional).
2) Rehabilitation of the mother well of non-functional karez.
3) Analyze the water quality of karez.
4) Adopt climate-based agriculture practices.
5) Design policies for the protection of karez irrigation and modern agriculture methods.

6) Train farmers to utilize modern techniques in agriculture.
7) Support farmers with appropriate water resources by installing tanks and canal systems.

The problems that were being faced in the adoption of the karez irrigation method were also identified:

- Widespread droughts.
- Collapsed materials from the underground tunnels.
- Lowering of water tables.
- Unsatisfactory water flow and supply because of siltation of channels due to deferred maintenance.
- Soil erosion affecting the mother well and the vertical shafts.
- Lack of support from the government and non-governmental organizations regarding rehabilitation and restoration for the karez systems.

The issue of water non-availability has impacted farmers immensely. Approximately 70% of the farmers in Balochistan are facing this issue (Pakistan Economic Survey 2019–2020). Hence, cultivation has reduced and people are suffering from the insufficient water supply. A barren situation has emerged because of the lack of availability of water for agriculture and living, as a result of the non-functionality of the karez system of irrigation. Productivity and cultivation output are less than expected and people are migrating to other places. These are all grave issues that touch on several of the SDGs and thus require immediate remedial action.

Team 9 specifically worked on the promotion of aquaculture, fish breeding, and fish farming. The main areas of concern identified were the lack of awareness about aquaculture practices, unavailability of funds, and the technical expertise required. The communication goals of the youth communicators included raising awareness about aquaculture to local community people, and applying principles of aquaculture for appropriate site selection, for design and pond construction, and for selection of suitable fish species for sustainable aquaculture. Maintenance of aquaculture was also discussed and suitable techniques were imparted to the target community audience. This target audience basically included brokers, wholesalers, retailers, hotels and restaurants, and consumers at large.

Team 10 decided to work on a theme of common interest to both Italy and Pakistan. The theme of the study was "Rural Development through Agriculture and Olive Crop in Northern Pakistan." The aim was to help the local communities in their development, especially in the field of agriculture and the olive crop. This would not only promote the SDG on good health, but would also provide opportunities for decent work and economic growth. Under YCD training, the communication goals for this team were first emphasized in face-to-face meetings with the community stakeholders concerned. Apart from this, social media was actively used along with live radio broadcasts.

A unique feature of all YCD teams is consultation with the provincial government, the local government, and the relevant education, health, water, and agriculture department. No project can be a success without the support and endorsement of government and regulatory bodies. Therefore, YCD obtained due endorsements from the HEC and the National Vocational and Technical Training Commission (NAVTTC), and state permissions were fully obtained prior to running the training in remote public universities.

16.4 The Role of TVET toward Community Development

Community development is not restricted to higher education. HEI students require vocational training as well. For students, occupational training has become an important element of their education, and they expect HEIs to provide the appropriate practical training. Universities have begun to consider it as well, as they must comply with the SDGs. Technical and vocational education and training (TVET) programs are key contributors to skill and talent development for nations worldwide, as aligned with the UN's SDGs (Jay and Zarestky 2021). A gap exists between economic feminist theory, human resource development, and vocational education and training (VET) practices. Beyond VET programs, Jay and Zarestky claim that instructor preparation and practice do not effectively contribute to equal workplaces. VET programs face ongoing challenges in creating inclusive environments that assist women while challenging masculinized areas and workplace practices. VET advisors and instructors are influential in contextualizing vocational fields for students and influencing students' career trajectories. Women need more accessible training and employment in traditionally masculine industries.

In both Finland and Sweden, the main societal motive for organizing women's education has been a process of nation-building, addressing issues of poverty and health on one hand, and women's voice in society on the other (Broberg et al. 2021). This process has also encompassed other societal motives underpinning the emergence, establishment, and development of domestic education as vocational education in both countries:

1) Vocational education as a means for economic development and societal prosperity.
2) Making the population healthier by educating women in issues relating to science (hygiene, health, and nutrition). This fits well into the growing interest in point 3:
3) Developing educational possibilities for women in particular but also social groups other than the upper classes.

This is a clear indication of a societal motivation to advance gender equality. Domestic education became a concept, concealing a large quantity of VET that taught for occupations that ensured human survival. Domestic education developed courses and programs for the production and preparation of food, clothing, housing, and caring, among other things, and it is reasonable to assume that women's education also contributed to the development of the welfare state in both Finland and Sweden, with women carrying out the daily use of this knowledge. The societal motive behind equality in education has, in general, relied on general subjects, not vocational ones.

The imperative to suit employers' needs would be replaced with curricula designed to increase participants' social, economic, and political capacities under an agenda based on access to VET (Avis et al. 2020). This agenda would abandon the performative litanies that define narrow pedagogies of competence in favor of a public pedagogy in which VET contributes to societal, community, and individual well-being, as well as a post-COVID renewal that promotes the development of all members of society, particularly the excluded, and addresses the climate emergency.

YCD pushes the NAVTTC and HEC agenda of creation and promotion of new jobs, particularly because the youth communicators are now the engine for change via effective communication about solving the problems faced by the community. This will allow them to become consultants of their own remote territories and enable them to bring sustainable change.

16.5 Conclusion

The situation seen thus far after the global pandemic shows that lack of internet connectivity, or almost non-existent internet connectivity, in educational centers in the world's poorest geographic areas remains a concern. University closures have become common practice in almost every country, causing long-term damage to education and disrupting the teaching-learning process. To combat the negative effects of this, several remote education alternatives have been developed. On the other hand, the technological gap between developed and developing countries exacerbates the large gaps in educational opportunities between them. For children in the most destitute societies, as well as those belonging to the most disadvantaged and vulnerable groups, ranging from women to pupils with special educational needs, the right to education, including distant learning, is once again a threatened and unrealized right (Lorente et al. 2020). Furthermore, this inequality is doubly harmful because of the added lack of internet access and shortages of computers in universities and homes.

The YCD pilot project is a clear testimony to the fact that international experiences and exposure can be brought about via ICT partnerships. With the cooperation of the Italian aid agency, youth in Pakistan's remotest parts were not only trained in various trades, but were also given the confidence to deliver in their own communities. This will go a long way in reversing the trend to migrate to urban centers in search of greener pastures, which in itself is a major problem in South Asia.

The youth of the country are a huge force for the attainment of SDGs if given the right skillset and community drivers to work with, even in the remotest of communities and in the most difficult of geographical terrains.

The world is certainly a global village. In spite of the isolation brought about by frequent quarantining and lockdowns, the COVID-19 pandemic has taught us to use ICT and operate independently in the most efficient manner. YCD multistakeholder, multitier international pilot training on some of the most pressing issues facing our communities was aimed at precisely that, even in the toughest of economic situations. It is now hoped that using our pilot project, the HEC and NAVTTC will both come forward and create a pool of overseas Pakistani and foreign experts, who will contribute their time at least once a year to talk to students in the remotest parts of the country and share with them their experiences and knowledge. This knowledge will then allow us to embrace the new-normal world.

Acknowledgment

The authors remain grateful to the intellectual support by Dr. Emanuela Benini, Country Director of Italian Agency for Developemnt Cooperation (AICS) in Pakistan, Prof. Dr. Roberto Dandi at Luiss Business School, and Mr. Muhammad Waseem at the Pakistan Poverty Alleviation Fund (PPAF).

References

Avis, J., Atkins, L., Esmond, B., and McGrath, S. (2020). Re-conceptualizing VET: responses to covid-19. *Journal of Vocational Education & Training* 73 (1): 1–23.

Broberg, Å., Lindberg, V., and Wärvik, G. (2021). Women's vocational education 1890–1990 in Finland and Sweden: the example of vocational home economics education. *Journal of Vocational Education & Training* 73 (2): 217–233.

Habib, M., Khalil, U., Khan, Z., and Zahid, M. (2021). Sustainability in higher education: what is happening in Pakistan? *International Journal of Sustainability in Higher Education* 22 (3): 681–706.

Jay, S. and Zarestky, J. (2021). Gender in vocational education and training: an integrative review. *European Journal of Training and Development* .

Knight, J. (2003). Updated internationalization definition. *International Higher Education* 33.

Rose, H. and McKinley, J. (2017). Japan's English-medium instruction initiatives and the globalization of higher education. *Higher Education* 75 (1): 111–129.

Lorente, L.M.L., Arrabal, A.A., and Pulido-Montes, C. (2020). The right to education and ict during covid-19: An international perspective. *Sustainability* 12 (21): 9091.

Pakistan Economic Survey (2019–2020). *Ministry of Finance, Government of Pakistan*. Islamabad: Ministry of Finance, Government of Pakistan.

Hussain, S. and Khan, H.K. (2021). Translanguaging in pakistani higher education: a neglected perspective! *Journal of Educational Research and Social Sciences Review* 1 (3): 16–24.

Johnston, L., Liu, X., Yang, M., and Zhang, X. (2016). Getting rich after getting old: China's demographic and economic transition in dynamic international context. In: *China's New Sources of Economic Growth*, vol. *1* (ed. L. Song, R. Garnaut, C. Fang and L.A. Johnston), 215–245. *Reform, Resources and Climate Change*. ANU Press.

Ashraf, D., Ali, T., and Hosain, A. (2013). Youth development and education in Pakistan: exploring the relationship. *Sisyphus. Journal of Education* 1 (2): 162–192.

Delgado-Márquez, B.L., Escudero-Torres, M.A., and Hurtado-Torres, N.E. (2013). Being highly internationalised strengthens your reputation: an empirical investigation of top higher education institutions. *Higher Education* 66 (5): 619–633.

Frølich, N. (2006). Still academic and national – Internationalisation in Norwegian research and higher education. *Higher Education* 52 (3): 405–420.

Samaa News (2021). Shaukat Tarin assures IMF about implementing program goals. *Webdesk* (27 September 2021). https://www.samaa.tv/news/2021/09/shaukat-tarin-assures-imf-about-implementing-program-goals

Shackleton, S. and Luckert, M. (2015). Changing livelihoods and landscapes in the rural Eastern Cape, South Africa: Past influences and future trajectories. *Land* 4 (4): 1060–1089.

Shen, W. (2008). International student migration: The case of Chinese "sea-turtles". In: *World Yearbook of Education 2008: Geographies of Knowledge, Geometries of Power: Framing the Future of Higher Education* (ed. D. Epstein, R. Boden, R. Deem, et al.), 211–232. New York: Routledge.

Tange, H. and Jensen, I. (2012). Good teachers and deviant learners? The meeting of practices in university level international education. *Journal of Research in International Education* 11 (2): 181–193.

van Steenbergen, F., Kaisarani, A.B., Khan, N.U., and Gohar, M.S. (2015). A case of groundwater depletion in Balochistan, Pakistan: Enter into the void. *Journal of Hydrology: Regional Studies* 4: 36–47.

Žalėnienė, I. and Pereira, P. (2021). Higher Education for Sustainability: A Global Perspective. *Geography and Sustainability* 2 (2): 99–106.

17

Streamlining Higher Education in the Maldives: Issues and Challenges
Abdul Hannan Waheed

17.1 Introduction

Higher education is conventionally regarded as a public good (Tilak 2008). Hence, it is important to provide quality education for students. Applying international standards is one of the main principles of standardization of education adapted by the international community (Popkova et al. 2015). The provision of higher education in the Maldives is at a critical juncture where a relatively recently introduced system is shaping up to be established. This chapter looks at the current landscape of higher education in the Maldives and provides a detailed examination of various aspects and elements currently being adopted in the country. With this information, the author also tries to provide a comparison with global standards of such practices.

The chapter is structured into four main sections. This section presents an introduction, providing a background to the topic and information about the establishment of higher education as well as the system of higher education in the Maldives. Section 17.2 provides a discussion of emerging issues and challenges in streamlining higher education in the Maldives up to global standards. Section 17.3 presents solutions to address the issues and challenges identified in Section 17.2. Section 17.4 provides conclusions to the chapter.

17.1.1 Background

The Maldives is a small island nation situated in the Indian Ocean. It is a highly dispersed country consisting of around 1200 islands in total and 188 inhabited islands, with a population of around 400,000. The geographic and demographic features of the Maldives present challenges in terms of delivery of higher education across the country (Di Biase and Maniku 2020). These challenges might be major reasons for streamlining higher education practices in the Maldives.

The growth of higher education across the globe has been immense in recent times. Student numbers in tertiary education increased 200-fold to 100 million between 1900 and 2001 (Schofer and Meyer 2005). As in many countries, higher education provision has been expanding rapidly in the Maldives and two public universities were – for the first time –created recently. One is the National University, which was transformed from the College of Higher Education in 2011. The other is the Islamic University of Maldives (IUM), which was transformed from the College of

---

The Wiley Handbook of Sustainability in Higher Education Learning and Teaching, First Edition.
Edited by Kelum A. A. Gamage and Nanda Gunawardhana.
© 2022 John Wiley & Sons, Inc. Published 2022 by John Wiley & Sons, Inc.

Islamic Studies in 2015. However, most of the expansion is by private providers, with nine private colleges, established during the past 10 years (Ministry of Education 2019).

It is widely acknowledged that higher education has expanded significantly since the 1998 UNESCO World Conference on Higher Education. However, while the expansion of higher education has provided new opportunities for many students, it has also created many problems. This might be because of the manifestations of globalization – such as the massification of higher education – seen in almost every country, and other factors, such as the impact of information and communications technology and its impact on higher education, the "public good/private good debate," and the rise of the global knowledge economy (Altbach et al. 2010). The same trend is seen in the Maldives.

Even though higher education qualifications have been delivered in the Maldives only recently compared with many countries, the expansion of higher education, in terms of providers as well as student numbers, has been relatively steady. According to the data on approved academic programs by the Maldives Qualifications Authority (MQA), there are around 98 active higher education providers offering academic programs – including two universities, colleges, and institutes (MQA 2021a,b). However, it should be noted that out of these 98 higher education institutions (HEIs) who have been given approval to conduct Maldives National Qualifications Framework (MNQF) compliant academic programs, only two universities, 12 colleges (Ministry of Higher Education 2020) and a few institutions are really that active with continuous and consistent student enrollment. Yet, these numbers suggest there is a steadily increasing number of private providers.

While the number of HEIs is relatively respectable for the size of the country and population, recent data suggest that student numbers have also been increasing. The gross enrollment ratio (GER) in higher education rose from only 6% in 2001 to 29.2% in 2015. As this number depends on the number of school leavers from secondary education, the net enrolment ratio at lower secondary was 90.2% in 2015, and the figure was much lower at higher secondary, at only 44.5% (Ministry of Education 2019). It is worth noting that in the case of the Maldives, it is not only higher secondary leavers who enroll in higher education programs, but a lot of those students who finish lower secondary also enroll in them – or rather, to be specific, tertiary level programs – due to a loophole in the allowed minimum entry criteria for MNQF qualifications (MQA 2017), in which those students who exit Grade 10 or lower secondary – even without a single pass – can enroll in a bachelor's degree after two years of work experience and completion of what is called a University Preparatory Program. Because of this loophole, many lower secondary leavers are able to bypass higher secondary or Grades 11 and 12.

It is questionable if enough is done to guide students to complete the whole of secondary education. By observing the behavior of the people, it can be said that there is also a misconception by many parents that completing Grade 10 or lower secondary is actually completion of school education, and therefore they do not guide their children to complete Grade 12 or higher secondary education. This trend, which does not appear to be being rectified, is in direct contravention of the United Nations Sustainable Development Goal (SDG) number 4, in which the target is to ensure that, by 2030, all girls and boys complete primary and secondary education (United Nations Development Programme 2021).

The huge disparity in the number of students who finish higher secondary and lower secondary can give the impression that enrollment in higher education is fed by higher secondary completion; therefore, low. However, this is not the case in the Maldives. Many of those who complete Grade 10 or lower secondary also enroll for qualifications for which they are eligible – which can be as high as a bachelor's degree, after two years of work experience or directly with at least a Certificate 3 or a Certificate 4/Advanced Certificate. It is important to note that this reality was not captured in earlier data collections about GER in higher education.

While the GER in higher education in 2011 was 21% and improved to 29.2% in 2015, the low figures of 6% in 2001 and 10% in 2005 might have been misleading, failing to capture the relatively higher number of lower secondary leavers who enroll in higher education (Ministry of Education 2019).

17.1.2   Establishment of Higher Education in the Maldives

Although some scholars trace back the initial step toward establishing a higher education system in the Maldives to the creation of Allied Health Services Training Centre in 1973 (Ministry of Education 2019), the qualifications offered at that point fitted more into tertiary education, with qualifications only below the bachelor's degree level. The same can be said about other postsecondary institutions that were created later. These include the Vocational Training Centre (VTC), which was created in 1975, the Institute of Teacher Education (ITE), which was created in 1984, the Maritime Training Centre, which was established in 1987, the School of Hotel and Catering Services, which was also created in 1987 (Amir 2017), and the Maldives Centre for Management and Administration (MCMA) in 1991 (The Maldives National University 2021a,b).

As such, it can be argued that the real establishment of a higher education system in the Maldives was the formation of the Maldives College of Higher Education (MCHE) in 1998 by an amalgamation of a number of postsecondary education institutions that offered tertiary education level academic programs. It is important to note that, even after the formation of this college, bachelor's degrees were not taught there, nor in the whole Maldives. So, it is hard to argue that there was a proper higher education system in the country when there was no bachelor's degree offered.

The first bachelor's degree delivered in the Maldives was the Bachelor of Arts (Dhivehi Language) offered at the MCHE in 2000 (The Maldives National University 2021a,b). Therefore, it has only been 21 years since the real establishment of higher education in the Maldives. With the Maldives being a small state and having an infant-stage higher education system, it is very important to learn from more established countries and streamline the system in accordance with the best practices worldwide. However, it is acknowledged by some scholars, such as Altbach et al. (2010), that higher education remains a national phenomenon and universities function within the nation and largely serve local, regional, and national interests. Despite this national orientation, some others point to the fact that HEIs strive for internationalization – in terms of faculty, students, and curriculum (Pucciareli and Kaplan 2016), thereby serving global interests.

In the early 2000s, there was only one HEI in the Maldives, the public college MCHE. However, since the creation of the Maldives Accreditation Board (MAB) in 2000 (MQA 2021a,b), private higher education providers have gradually started increasing in number. It appears that the establishment of a higher education quality assurance regulatory body in the form of MAB actually facilitated the expansion of higher education, rather than stifling development of the sector – as some might think would happen with a regulatory regime in place.

Though the universities in the Maldives are expected to dominate the provision of postgraduate academic programs, private colleges seem to be offering a relatively higher proportion of postgraduate programs compared with undergraduate or qualifications even lower than diploma. Naseer and Al-Hibadi (2019) point out that more than 30% of graduates from private colleges are pursuing postgraduate programs. This figure is quite different when applied to all HEIs. According to the Higher Education Statistics 2019 released by the Ministry of Higher Education in 2020, out of the total 843 academic programs conducted in at all HEIs, most of the programs at 30% are Level 7 bachelor's degree level programs. Postgraduate programs (master's degrees, postgraduate diplomas, postgraduate certificates – excluding doctoral degrees) conducted at colleges and universities account for 13% of the programs (Ministry of Higher Education 2020), which is much lower than the 30% at private colleges. Hence, questions arise as to why this proportion of postgraduate students are enrolled at private colleges. What is the percentage of students who enroll without a bachelor's degree or under alternative entry criteria? It should be noted that under the alternative entry criteria set by the MQA, holders of a diploma or advanced diploma are admitted into postgraduate certificates, postgraduate diplomas and master's degrees after some years of work experience.

17.1.3 System of Higher Education in the Maldives

As discussed in Section 17.1.2, the establishment of higher education in the Maldives has been quite recent. As per the initial regulation of the Ministry of Education for registration education providers (Ministry of Education 2000), education providers are categorized into eight types of providers, as follows:

- Schools that provide general education.
- Classes that provide education or training before enrolling to schools.
- Tuition classes.
- Classes that teach a certain subject.
- Centers that specialize in a specific field or fields.
- Postsecondary education providers.
- Mobile training centers.
- Open learning and distance education providers.

It should be noted that at the time of this regulation, the function was handled by the Ministry of Education because the affairs of higher education were a mandate of that Ministry. Therefore, most of the categories of education providers at that time, did not fall into the higher education sector.

When we look at the current registration form for higher education providers, titled the "Form for Registration of Tertiary Institutions" (Ministry of Higher Education 2021), there are five types of providers: (i) university, (ii) college, (iii) polytechnic, (iv) tertiary institute, and (v) institute of a government/state organization. However, in reality, there are three types/levels of HEIs in the Maldives: universities, colleges, and institutes (Ministry of Education 2019), in terms of levels of the academic programs they are allowed to conduct.

Institutes are allowed to deliver academic programs lower than MNQF Level 6 advanced diploma/associate degree. Colleges can deliver academic programs up to MNQF Level 9 master's degree. Only universities can deliver all levels of academic programs including MNQF Level 10 doctoral degree (Ministry of Education 2019).

A dedicated government ministry for education in the Maldives was first created on 22 December 1932 with the name Wuzarathul Ma'arif, which means Ministry of Education. The first Minister of Education was Ahmed Kamil Didi. Since then, for many years, all matters related to education were handled by the Ministry of Education. A separate ministry for higher education (MoHE) was first created during the era of President Maumoon Abdul Gayyoom in the name of the Ministry of Higher Education, Employment, and Social Security. The first minister appointed to that portfolio was Mr. Yameen Abdul Qayyom, who later became the President of the country in 2013. The separate MoHE was abolished by the next government led by President Mohamed Nasheed.

The government of President Ibrahim Mohamed Salih again created a MoHE in the name of the Ministry Higher Education on 17 November 2018 at the beginning of his term of office. The new separate ministry basically took over the functions of the Department of Higher Education, which was under the Ministry of Education. The creation of a dedicated Ministry to manage and regulate higher education is another indication of the expansion of higher education as discussed in Sections 17.1.1 and 17.1.2.

With a renewed focus on the regulation and management of higher education in the Maldives, the system of higher education has also been shaping up with strengthened features. In addition to overseeing higher education quality assurance agencies – the MQA, Maldives National Skills Development Authority (which was initially Technical and Vocational Education and Training Authority) and the Maldives Polytechnic – the Ministry of Higher Education has notable functions that are directly related to the public. Management of higher education scholarships as well as loans for higher education are probably the two most prominent traditional functions of MoHE (Ministry of Higher Education 2018), carried out since the days of MoHE's predecessor Department of Higher Education (DHE).

With traditional loan and scholarship schemes in place, the current Ministry of Higher Education was also mandated to implement an audacious pledge made by the incoming government of President of Ibrahim Mohamed Salih. The pledge, which has been successfully implemented, is the First Degree Grant Scheme, which is commonly referred to as a "free degree" (Ministry of Higher Education 2019). Registration of HEIs is also a key function of the Ministry of Higher Education.

17.2 Emerging Issues and Challenges in Streamlining Higher Education in the Maldives up to the Global Standards

As we have pointed out, higher education provision in the Maldives is quite recent compared to many countries. Traditionally in the early days, Maldivians chose to pursue their higher education abroad as it was not possible to do so in the Maldives. Still, students who are serious about their studies follow the same path. One can argue that when the opportunity was available abroad, obtaining higher education was a privilege of the elite or of a few who were really lucky.

In the 22 or so years since higher education provision arrived in the Maldives, many Maldivina students have been pursuing their higher education in their own country. As HEIs in the Maldives compete against each other in recruiting students for their academic programs, there are instances in which questions are raised about the quality of provision. Some concepts are defined and used in ways that are detrimental for the overall upholding of quality standards and traditional global norms. The survival of private providers or those who are referred to as for-profit providers, largely depends on the fees collected from students. Hence, it is acknowledged that such a business model is probably the practical way for sustaining the operations of private providers (Pucciareli and Kaplan 2016). However, the increase of for-profit providers, coupled with infiltration of cross-border practices, along with other factors, such as massification of higher education or what is referred to as mass higher education (Altbach et al. 2010), present challenges and issues. As an official in the higher education quality assurance regulation in the Maldives, the author of this chapter is in a position that allows observation of higher education practices in the Maldives – as discussed in the following sections.

17.2.1 Lack of Understanding of Basic Terminologies and Concepts

There are globally accepted key terminologies and concepts, as well as processes, in higher education that shape the whole system. Lack of understanding of these key terms and concepts will be a major hindrance in properly delivering higher education. Recognized good universities in the world provide higher education without compromising quality. In fact, high-ranking universities thrive on the continuation and consistency in maintaining the quality provision of higher education qualifications. Countries such as the Maldives – where higher education provision is in the early stages – would benefit from learning and adopting such global standards in higher education.

Key features of higher education provision include concepts such as mode of study, delivery modality, credits, credit hours, and contact hours. Each of these terms will be further discussed in this chapter.

17.2.2 Link Between School Education and Higher Education

It is widely accepted in the world that schools feed students into higher education. Elementary, primary, lower secondary, and higher secondary education is delivered in schools. The situation is no different in the Maldives. Studies and surveys show that successful school education leads to successful higher education. A correlation is seen between the number of students successfully completing higher secondary education and student enrollment in higher education (Hoffman et al. 2007). Recent studies show that the same trend is seen in the Maldives (Ministry of Education 2019).

In some school systems, secondary is one level/stage of three to four years, starting from either Grade 8 or Grade 9. One example is the Arabic system in which lower secondary is not separated. While some Arabic countries have three years of secondary, some others have four years. In both variations, there is no lower secondary and the exit qualification is titled "Shahada Sanaviyaa" (secondary certificate). Comparable models are seen in other regions and in countries such as India and Thailand (Cheney et al. 2005; Jangdecha and Larpkesorn 2018). Currently, Shahadha Sanaviyya is only offered at one public school in the Maldives, Al-Madhrasathul Arabiyyathul Islamiyya in the capital Malé.

Another model is one in which secondary has two terminal examinations: lower secondary and higher secondary. One example familiar in the Maldives is the English system as it is the school system most widely used in the country, or the country's national school system. Terminal examinations are named General Certificate of Education (GCE) Ordinary (O) Level at lower secondary and GCE Advanced (A) Level at higher secondary (The StateUniversity.com 2021).

Even though some argue nowadays that entry qualification does not matter in learning and it is the exit level or learning outcomes that matter in higher education learning, many academics are still convinced that entry criteria and entry qualifications do matter. Hence, the successful completion of higher secondary by as many students as possible is important for the success of higher education. In other words, the better the quality of students who enroll in higher education the better the quality of higher education graduates.

As pointed out in Section 17.1.1, the higher education GER improved gradually in the Maldives. Other figures show that the enrollment and results of lower secondary, as well as higher secondary, also improved in the same period (Ministry of Education 2019). It can be argued that one big challenge for the Maldives in terms of school education is the perception by many that completing Grade 10 or lower secondary is completion of schooling. Hence, many students exit from Grade 10 without actually completing schooling. However, many of those who exit from Grade 10 tend to enroll in higher education programs. Thus, many of those who enroll in higher education qualifications such as diplomas, advanced diplomas and bachelor's degrees do not really possess the prerequisites for successful completion of these qualifications.

17.2.3 Mode of Study

Mode of study is defined as "the study load of the student, whether full-time or part-time" (OECD 2003, p. 1). Full-time mode is the mode that involves a maximum number of hours per week, generally seen as being 25–30 hours per week. On the other hand, part-time involves studying a few hours a week for one's chosen program (Teachmint@wp 2021). While there is a clear understanding of the application of full-time and part-time study on a global level, the usage and application of both full-time and part-time lack clarity in the Maldives.

When looking at the usage of full-time and part-time study modes in the Maldives, a number of differences can be noticed. It appears that many people in the Maldives, including students, parents, and lecturers, do not fully understand the concept of full-time study and part-time study. An overwhelming majority of the full-time students in the Maldives are full-time employees in government offices or private companies and businesses. Hence, there are serious concerns about the extent of knowledge acquisition of graduates when they are fully employed while simultaneously studying full-time.

Regarding the mode of part-time study in the Maldives, though there are academic programs approved by MQA as part-time, very few programs are actually conducted as part-time due to lack of interest by students to undertake part-time programs. The main reason is that, even though they might be employed full-time, a vast majority of the students want to get the qualification in a period not longer than the full-time study. Another observation about the notion of part-time study is the misconception that attending a class in the afternoon and at night is part-time, even though the particular provider might not say the program is part-time and, in fact, say it is full-time. This is an indication of a lack of understanding of the difference between full-time and part-time study modes.

One practice used in the Maldives in delivering higher education is the so-called "block mode." Internationally, when looking at the websites, apart from a few exceptions, we cannot usually see the term used at traditional universities. A Google search of the term "block mode" on 13 May 2021 (Google 2021), did not show much on block mode, except for the Maldives Business School, Victoria University, and University of Sydney, Australia. University of Sydney uses block mode as one of the modes of attendance (MoA) (University of Sydney 2021) and as a mode of delivery (University of Sydney 2020).

In the case of the Maldives, those HEIs that offer block mode courses, do so in a way that students do not have to study continuously over a semester in a full-time load., but rather for a few days over a long period. For example, one college in the Maldives describes block mode as "study just 3 days every 9 months" (Maldives Business School 2021). On the other hand, in the case of Australia, study during the block mode is still full-time. For example, Victoria University, Australia, describes the block model – not mode – in a positive way and defines it as a mode in which students get to focus on one subject at a time over a four-week block, instead of multiple subjects at the same time over a semester (Victoria University 2021). Hence, there is a huge difference in the way teaching and learning takes place in both modes. Also, the concept of block mode is interpreted differently in the Maldives than that of the block model by the University of Sydney.

While in the case of Maldives, serious questions are raised as to whether the required credits and learning hours are achieved in just three days in nine months. Most alarming is that the block mode in the Maldives is still said to be a full-time mode of study – even with less than part-time contact time over the study period. Also, analysis of the information published by MQA shows that this practice is not approved by MQA. In the case of Victoria University, there is continuous study and the university promotes its mode as very successful. However, even this model is criticized in the sense that research on effective learning shows learning multiple subjects, as in a traditional semester, is more effective than focusing on shorter subjects one at a time (Lodge 2018). It should be noted that the concept of block mode in the Maldives is different as it focuses on having just a few days of study and teaching one or more subjects in those few days; not a four-week period mentioned by the Victoria University.

17.2.4 Delivery Modality

There are differences in the way the terminology of the concept of delivery modality or methods of higher education is used. Some refer to it as a learning method; some refer to it as a delivery method; some refer to it as a delivery mode, and some others refer to it as a delivery modality. A delivery modality or method of a course or a program is "the way in which educational content is conveyed from instructor to students" (Top Hat 2021). Traditionally, there were two delivery modalities: face-to-face and distance learning. However, with the advent of the internet and world wide web as well as various learning and videoconferencing platforms, distance education has become more diverse, with the introduction of e-learning and blended learning.

Traditionally, distance education has been an opportunity facilitated for disadvantaged people unable to attend a university or a college (Plessis 2019), but conventional wisdom says that there is nothing like being in an actual classroom with an actual professor in face-to-face delivery (Harden 2013). Hence, it can be argued that face-to-face delivery modality is the mainstream or the standard delivery modality in higher education. Even with the recent surge in the use of e-learning as a form of distance education, universities do not seem to regard it as the dominant delivery modality. Considering the extent of physical and human resources as well as financial facilities in place at universities to cater for teaching and learning of students who attend, it is inconceivable that universities will opt for e-learning as the dominant delivery modality at the expense of face-to-face delivery modality. Generally, e-learning is used as complementary to the face-to-face learning in which students attend universities.

When looking at the delivery modalities used in the Maldives, as in other countries, face-to-face delivery modality remains the dominant modality. However, due to the nature of the country as an island nation, HEIs have increased their offering of e-learning programs, especially with the availability of the internet and online learning platforms. The speed of the extent of migration from face-to-face delivery to e-learning may be a cause for concern for educators and regulators.

17.2.5 Medium of Instruction in Higher Education

The medium of instruction in higher education can be argued as a key factor in learning. In this globalized world, the English language has become a popular medium of instruction for reasons such as the role of the English language as an international language, the global tendency to internationalize educational policies and practices, and the desire to cope with the global academic environment (Kir and Akyuz 2019). Over the years, the medium of instruction in the Maldives has been English as well.

Traditionally, in early eras, Maldivians used to learn various subjects such as religion, languages, mathematics, and astrology from individual scholars by attending their residences. The methodology used the most was the teaching of lessons from certain books. These books were mostly in Arabic, with a few also in Urdu. These were higher-level studies in terms of the subjects and lessons. Hence, it can be argued that the medium of education at higher levels in the Maldives in early or ancient times, or the traditional medium, was Arabic and Urdu. Arabic was the major language of education after the Maldives converted to Islam because the main references for Islamic Studies are the Holy Qur'an and Prophetic Tradition, which are in Arabic. At that time, Arabic was regarded at the major foreign language, and was highly valued due to the link to Islam. Urdu was also learned as a foreign language. English became regarded as the main foreign language slowly after the introduction of the English language as the medium of instruction in schools and the use of the London GCE O Level exam as the terminal examination after Grade 10 at schools in the Maldives during the 1960s.

Strangely, as the Maldives progressed with a full-fledged school education system in the English medium, access and completion rates increased and the results of students improved considerably, but some people started lobbying to use the local language Dhivehi as the medium for instruction in higher education. The main argument of such people is that when the medium of instruction is Dhivehi, students understand and learn better. However, logically speaking, as more successful students finish schooling in the English medium, the natural expectation would be that there will be more students who are relatively proficient in English who are well-positioned or prepared to pursue their higher education in the English language.

Another argument being leveled by those who advocate for the use of Dhivehi as a medium of instruction in higher education is that, in order to protect and improve the local language, it is important to teach higher education programs in Dhivehi. The rationale behind linking protection of the mother tongue and the issue of the medium of instruction in higher education is questionable. Or it is questionable that there is any rationale at all. Having English as the medium of instruction gives many benefits to students. In fact, there are many scholarly articles and research papers that stress the importance of having English as the medium of instruction in higher education. Even in much bigger countries such as India – though there are 15 main languages and hundreds of other languages and dialects – English plays a crucial role in higher education and helped India to become a global economic powerhouse (Cheney et al. 2005).

As Dhivehi is only spoken in the Maldives, with a small population of around 400 000 people, and Minicoi, an island in the Indian Ocean currently under the Indian administration and with a population of around 10 000, the reach and influence of Dhivehi are very limited in this globalized world. This means there is little use of the Dhivehi language in commercial activities. Hence, serious questions are raised about the benefit for students in pursuing higher education programs in Dhivehi.

Arguably, students benefit most when academic programs are conducted in an appropriate language in terms of availability of international references, pathways for higher qualifications, and use of that language in related professions and workplaces. If the studies of qualifications in areas such as STEM and many areas in Arts and Social Sciences, except the local language itself, are in Dhivehi, it is questionable whether the objectives we have mentioned will be achieved.

17.2.6 Time of Teaching at Universities, Colleges, and Institutes

In terms of teaching, study, or class times at universities around the world – as for schools – what we see is that timetables or class schedule are set to be carried out in the morning, or at least starting in the morning. This means that most of the students attend in the morning. On a global scale, one almost never hears of a university opening and starting classes in the afternoon or at night. However, the situation seems to be a bit different in the Maldives.

While schools operate normally, starting in the morning like other countries, most higher education students in the Maldives start their classes in the afternoon or even at night. The situation seems better handled at two public universities. However, as pointed out in Section 17.2.3, due to the fact that most full-time students are also full-time employees at either government offices or private companies, class schedules or timetables are usually arranged for times at which students can attend. Hence, instead of students having to attend classes according to timetables set by HEIs, these providers are setting timetables according to student demands.

As most of the students enrolled in higher education programs in the Maldives are full-time employees, it can be argued that such students are not dedicated students. Though they are enrolled in full-time programs, it is hard to comprehend that such students can focus enough on their studies and get enough time for a full-time academic program. In terms of knowledge acquisition, it is questionable whether students can get the full benefits of study when studying full-time programs in a part-time capacity.

17.2.7 Library

The library is defined by Nirala et al. (2018, p. 287) as "building homologue to a repository, which contains Books, Research papers, Thesis, Journals, Magazines, Periodicals, Newspapers, Digital resources, etc." The importance of a library for getting information and for learning has never been disputed. Libraries across the globe are major providers of information services. Types of libraries may have changed over the years and offering print or electronic formats. However, the roles of libraries remain the same, which is acquiring, organizing, and disseminating information resources to users (Omeluzor et al. 2013).

The status of a library in university education or higher education is not in dispute as many have the perception that the library is at the heart of education. For a university or college, a good physical library is so crucial. Apart from knowledge flow, libraries are multidimensional platforms with multifaceted sides that provide a soulful ambience to students (Nirala et al. 2018). Hence Nirala et al. (p. 292) argue that "without a good library and information centre, it is highly impossible to ensure quality education and research." Furthermore, they assert that, just like "a body is nothing without a soul, an educational institution has no existence without a library" (p. 287).

While libraries are key in educational institutions, HEIs, apart from a few, in the Maldives do not seems to give priority to having a good physical library in place. Hence, it is questionable how students can experience a full academic atmosphere at their learning places as libraries are places of knowledge creation and sharing (Omeluzor et al. 2013). Also, it is hard to comprehend how an educational institution maintains its status without a proper library, as scholars argue that a library plays a vital role in raising its quality of education (Nirala et al. 2018).

Actually, institutions might not agree that they do not have a library. In fact, even without having a physical library, many boast of having digital libraries, downplaying the significance of having a physical library. While there is no denying the benefits of digital libraries, they cannot entirely replace traditional physical libraries. Digital libraries have numerous benefits, but traditional libraries offer additional social and educational benefits that digital libraries cannot offer (Kaur and Kaur 2018).

17.2.8 Issues with Assessment

Assessment, in all its types, is an integral part of learning. While it is the same for school education, in this chapter the focus is on the assessments used in higher education. Scholars such as Brown (2004) who focus on student assessment as a field, argue that assessment is probably the most important thing for students' learning and should be able to evaluate the extent of the students' learning, which is its real purpose.

If students progress in higher education without proper assessments, one assumption would be that the extent of their learning is not evaluated or not known or not identified. That would be a huge challenge for educators who aim to graduate students who have really learned and thus contribute in their workplaces with what they have learned. Also, it would be hugely immoral and unethical on the part of HEIs if assessments were designed to or aimed to pass students, not to evaluate their learning outcomes.

When we look at assessment methods of higher education students, many educators complain that there is a trend to use too many assignments or to have too much weighting on the assignments, even for students of lower-level qualifications. Therefore, the impression of some people is that the assessment methods deployed do not always evaluate students' learning.

17.2.9 For-Profit Provision of Higher Education

The terms "for-profit provision" or "for-profit providers" refer to private provision or providers in higher education. For-profit providers are often pitched against public universities or public providers. The term has been used for around fifty years and came to be used after an exponential increase in the number of private providers in higher education across the world (Knobel and Verhine 2017). While the term for-profit indicates profit-making, traditionally, higher education was not regarded as such when public universities were the only providers of higher education in countries around the world.

As discussed in Sections 17.1.1 and 17.1.2, private higher education providers that function as for-profit providers have been active in the Maldives since early the 2000s. There is no denial of the importance of private universities, colleges, and HEIs. The same is true for the Maldives as elsewhere. In fact, it is not expected that any country will move to exclude private providers from the higher education sector. What we need to do is enforce proper regulation of the higher education provision, in order that the quality of higher education is not compromised for the sake of profit.

17.2.10 Neglect of Standard Entry Criteria

Entry criteria or admission requirements for higher education qualifications is an important standard adhered to in higher education. The standard entry criteria to enroll in a university has been higher secondary education to enroll for a bachelor's degree; a bachelor's degree to enroll for a master's degree; and a master's degree to enroll for a doctoral degree. Perhaps the neglect of adhering to standard entry criteria for higher education qualifications – especially higher secondary as the entry criterion for a bachelor's degree, and a bachelor's degree as the entry criterion for a master's degree – is related to the thinking that admission models should aim at achieving equity in education access, rather than quality (Wong and Shulruf 2013).

Universities in good standing around the world adhere to published minimum entry criteria in the admission of students for various qualifications. A review of websites of a number of universities (Oxford University 2021) reveals that the standard entry criteria for a bachelor's degree is a good result in higher secondary education, and the entry criteria for a master's degree is a bachelor's degree.

Although, traditionally, certain standard entry criteria have been used for university admission, some people lobby for less stringent entry criteria or even open entry for qualifications such as a bachelor's degree or a master's degree. Such people claim that entry criteria are not important as long as learning outcomes are achieved, which may be very difficult to uncover. However, by looking at the entry criteria or admission requirements utilized by most universities, it can be argued that there is a belief among academia that for successful learning, a certain threshold of prior learning is necessary.

Education and learning have always been a gradual process. Generally, one cannot learn a lot of content or knowledge in a short period of time. Also, as knowledge level is from very low to advanced, one has to have elementary and/or lower-level education in order to properly understand and learn higher-level knowledge. One very obvious example is learning the alphabet of a language as the first step to becoming literate and able to start reading, writing, and comprehending. No one will argue that people should be allowed or would be able to start reading, writing, and comprehending without learning the alphabet and becoming literate. Hence, it is quite logical and rational to set certain entry criteria for higher education qualifications. Indeed, as discussed, this is the standard practice in higher education in major universities.

It is important to note that since the inception of the higher education quality assurance system in the Maldives in the name of the MAB in 2000, national minimum entry criteria for qualifications – to be used for both qualifications recognition as well approval of academic programs/courses – was developed and implemented. The first entry criteria were incorporated within the MNQF. Later, the entry criteria were amended twice: once in 2010 and again in 2017 (MQA 2017). In all three versions, in addition to the standard entry criteria, there were also what are referred to as the "alternative entry criteria." It is worth noting that alternative entry criteria have been getting more lenient with these revisions. For example, the lowest qualification accepted under the alternative entry criteria for a master's degree – for those who do not hold a bachelor's degree – in the initial entry criteria was advanced diploma. However – though it was amended to be a diploma in the latest version – in the second version, it was changed to just an advanced certificate, which is the standard entry criteria for a bachelor's degree apart from higher secondary education. Similarly, the alternative entry criteria for a bachelor's degree have also been lowered. The reasons could be the pressure exerted on MQA by people with a vested interest in enrolling as many students as possible in higher education. In other words, it can be argued that is an impact of massification of higher education

17.2.11 Negative Impact of Cross-Border Higher Education

There are numerous benefits for developing countries from cross-border higher education, by learning from the experiences of other countries – especially developed countries – in higher education. Indeed, conducting academic programs in affiliation with more established universities is an ideal approach promoted by scholars to be utilized by aspiring universities in less-developed countries across the globe. Cross-border higher education is linked to the growth in the mobility of students, programs, and providers across borders and it provides new opportunities to increase access to higher education (Knight 2007). However, much of the debate and discussion by scholars has been on the dangers and risks to students and others of poor-quality cross-border higher education (Blackmur 2007).

For many countries, the biggest challenge for regulating cross-border provision of higher education in their countries is a lack of regulatory systems in place to register foreign providers operating in their countries (Knight 2007). However, that is not the case in the Maldives. That does not mean all is safe for the Maldives with regards to cross-border higher education, and there are risks and challenges.

17.2.12 Challenges and Implications

Though there are no foreign higher education providers operating in the Maldives, the cross-border influence is immense in the Maldives. Most of the risks for the Maldives through cross-border higher education is related to the market forces that make the profile and reputation of a provider and its programs more and more important, as pointed out by Knight (2007). As a result, major campaigns are being carried out by various providers for marketing and branding in order to get name recognition and to increase student enrollment. These marketing efforts are increasingly made by foreign providers, not necessarily operating in the Maldives, but trying to attract Maldivian students to study abroad. One alarming issue is that more marketing is done by those non-traditional and private for-profit cross-border providers who often operate outside a national higher education system of education. On one hand, poor practices of such foreign providers are sometimes adapted by local providers in delivering their academic programs. On the other hand, some Maldivian students are being taken in by marketing gimmicks carried out by unregulated foreign providers who deliver substandard qualifications. These qualifications might not be approved or accredited by competent bodies in the operating counties or they might be offshore cross-border programs in another country, but delivered with compromised quality compared to the onshore programs.

In both these scenarios, the MQA is under immense pressure in its efforts to assure quality, whether it is in recognizing foreign qualifications obtained by Maldivians or in monitoring the conduct of approved academic programs. The pressure is displayed in the sense that those involved in these practices often lobby for acceptance and recognition of such substandard qualifications and poor practices.

17.2.13 Challenges for Maintaining Quality Higher Education

The issues highlighted in Sections 17.2.1–17.2.11 indicate that there are numerous challenges for assuring quality higher education in the Maldives. Lack of understanding of basic terminologies in higher education is dangerous in the sense it allows poor practices in delivery of higher education. Provision of higher education cannot be sustained properly without proper understanding of the basic terms and concepts – like any other field.

While school education lays the foundation for higher education and prepares students for higher studies, it is very important to have a school education system in which many students finish Grade 12 or higher secondary education. Without certain prerequisites, students often struggle to cope with the level of knowledge in higher education studies. Some officials of universities and colleges in the Maldives are concerned by the increased number of students who enroll in higher education qualifications, such as bachelor's degrees, under alternative entry criteria, which means without successfully completing higher secondary education.

While concepts such as mode of study and delivery modality are key concepts in the provision of higher education, if those who are involved do not properly understand these concepts, the quality of teaching and learning will be affected. Conducting a part-time study in the name and duration of full-time, and allowing full-time employees to do full-time study instead of part-time study, is destructive for higher education. For-profit providers of higher education might support these arrangements, but a vast majority of academics oppose such practices as we cannot see them carried out by mainstream high-ranking universities.

Not every language is academic, in the sense that a lot of international research, books, and papers are not written in them. Dhivehi is one such language. That does not mean the native language of the Maldives is useless. Quite the contrary, as Dhivehi is the mother tongue of all Maldivians and has its own alphabet, unlike many languages in the world. However, only around 400 000 people speak Dhivehi and it is never used regionally or internationally. Therefore, teaching high-level programs in fields that have an international dimension in Dhivehi might not be helpful for students in their careers in a long run. Thus, delivering such programs in Dhivehi to provide an easy way to obtain a higher education qualification is against the sanctity of knowledge.

It is a norm to start studies at schools, universities, and colleges in the morning. As discussed in Section 17.2.6, a lot of higher education classes in the Maldives are held in the afternoon and even at night. At many HEIs, there is no tradition of starting classes in the morning, which is not what we see in other countries. Hence, it is questionable whether holding classes in the afternoon or at night can be detrimental to learning.

As discussed in Section 17.2.7, a library is an integral element of a higher education provider. Hence, planning and arranging teaching and learning activities without a proper library will have a negative impact on the quality of education. Similarly, assessment of students, as discussed in Section 17.2.8, is a determinant of quality and learning outcomes. Hence, if there are no genuine assessment methods to evaluate students, this will affect the quality of learning.

As discussed in Section 17.2.9, with the increasing involvement of private providers in higher education, for-profit provision of higher education is also increasing. While this development is inevitable in the current higher education landscape, it is also true that making higher education merely a profit-making venture will be detrimental. That is why higher education quality assurance bodies such as the MQA are so important.

Possibly related to the for-profit interest in higher education, some people are calling for relaxing standard entry criteria for university qualifications. Some people even lobby for what they call "open entry." However, as discussed in Section 17.2.10, relaxing entry criteria could have a negative impact on the learning capacity of students.

While cross-border higher education has numerous benefits, depending on the type of practice adopted, there are risks associated as well. International bodies such as UNESCO-OECD and regional bodies such as Asia Pacific Quality Network (APQN) have been working to address the issue by advising higher education quality assurance bodies to be vigilant of risks and dangers of cross-border higher education (Stella 2006).

17.3 Addressing the Issues for Embedding Sustainability in Higher Education

The issues highlighted in this chapter, raise serious questions. Some of these issues might be unique to the Maldives, but many are also prevalent in other countries. As discussed, the Maldives is a small state, unlike many countries, and its higher education system is in its early stages. Therefore, it is more likely to be exposed to and impacted by bad practices. Hence, it is very important to address these issues, in order to establish a higher education system that is on a par with the best practices worldwide.

If there are questionable issues, these can be solved by learning from good systems and standard institutions across the world. This is important for the sustainability of the higher education system in the Maldives. A system cannot be improved by ignoring its defects. However, with a proactive approach, by addressing the current issues, the higher education system in the Maldives can be improved.

17.3.1 Distinguishing Between Malpractices and Best Practices

In all aspects of the issues highlighted in this chapter, it is important to realize the problems. Ignoring the issues and going forward without addressing them would spell disaster for the future of the quality of higher education. Hence, distinguishing between malpractices and best practices is important. Some might not realize that there are issues in their approach and in the practices in higher education provision.

It can be argued that these malpractices happen because of the exponential expansion of higher education in the Maldives, especially with the increase of private for-profit providers. Expansion of higher education and providing access to more students is progress. However, academics such as Gaikwad and Solunke (2013, p. 58) stress that "merely growth of higher education will not serve the basic policy of higher education." It is also acknowledged that the rapid change that occurred in the twenty-first century also impacted higher education. With this change, the traditional system of education is also under threat.

Even though higher education provision involves profit-making, it is not a typical business such as running a shop or selling goods. Higher education is an academic endeavor, which involves highly advanced knowledge and experience (Hongjie 2009). Indeed, some higher education qualifications, especially postgraduate qualifications like PhDs and research master's degrees, equip students with capabilities of knowledge creation (Grønhaug and Olson 1999; Saunders et al. 2016) Therefore, it is paramount to adopt worldwide best practices in the provision of higher education.

17.3.1.1 Malpractices in Higher Education in the Maldives

In comparison to the best practices adopted by mainstream universities across the globe, there are discrepancies observed in the practices used in the Maldives in higher education provision, and are subject to public debate (Naseer and Al-Hibadi 2019). Some perceive these issues as a threat to the nation. Indeed, the debate has come to the attention of media and journalists as well.

A local newspaper called *MIhaaru* published a report that highlighted many malpractices in the provision of higher education (Ali 2018), including most of the issues discussed in this chapter, namely, conducting full-time programs in part-time arrangements (specifically the so-called "block mode"), full-time employees studying in full-time academic programs, low quality of lecturers, and a lack full-time lecturers employed at local universities, colleges, and institutes. Overall, the major concern of those who were interviewed for the report was, due to these malpractices, the quality of graduates is becoming so low to the extent that employers are raising the issue that the qualifications earned are, through easy modes and modalities, alas, being rendered useless. The author of the report claimed that his arguments are supported by many academics and intellectuals in the Maldives. Maybe it is a global issue. Martin (2016) argues that corruption and malpractices are a major concern in almost all the countries around the world.

17.3.2 Respect of Knowledge Acquisition

As this chapter has argued, higher education is about knowledge, both knowledge acquisition through all academic programs or qualifications and knowledge creation through research degrees. This noble process of learning or knowledge acquisition is extremely important for human development, and knowledge acquisition has been increasingly linked to the economy (hence the widely used term "knowledge economy") and development, as argued by Naidoo (2010) and should not be taken for granted.

Ali (2018) argues that massification of higher education is not beneficial for a small state such as the Maldives and merely increasing certificate holders is not enough. According to his report, experts stress the importance of maintaining quality in order to produce quality people. The impression from these concerns is that focusing on quantity without quality is detrimental to the development of the country.

Another issue raised by Ali (2018) in his investigative report is contract cheating by higher education students with the help of those who sell the service of writing assignments for money.

Such malpractices undermine knowledge acquisition and act as breeding grounds for a host of issues that affect the quality of higher education. This is an issue widely written about by researchers in the field, and many authors even refer to it as corruption in higher education, as pointed out by Golunov (2014).

17.4 Conclusions

The issues raised in this chapter are based on the well-known practices in the provision of higher education in the Maldives. Indeed, one can argue that it is the public – especially intellectuals – who are concerned about such malpractices. These practices are compared to the traditional good university practices as we know them; both from what the author of this chapter has gained from first-hand experience while studying face-to-face at different well-established universities around the world (a bachelor's degree at Al-Azhar University, Egypt; a master's degree at the University of Sussex, UK; a PhD Queensland University of Technology, Australia) and based on good practices at leading universities around the world.

Some authors acknowledge that technology is driving a huge change in higher education, which is true. However, some seem to be exaggerating the extent and the nature of that change. For example, Harden (2013, p. 55) claimed that the future of higher education will have five major changes as following.

- Access to college education will be free for everyone.
- The residential college campus will become largely obsolete.
- Tens of thousands of thousands of professors will lose their jobs.
- Bachelor's degrees will become increasingly irrelevant.
- Ten years from now, Harvard will enroll ten million students.

However, eight years from that prediction, none of the above seems to have happened or to be true. It is also important to note that, claiming that college classrooms are about to go virtual at the same time, Harden pointed out that in this change, for-profit colleges or low-level non-profit colleges, which he describes as bottom feeders, will disappear in the midst of stiff competition among universities. This is an indication that providing higher education merely for profit-making has consequences, not only for the quality, but also for the survival of such providers.

As discussed in Sections 17.1.1 and 17.1.3, the Maldives is a small state and the higher education system in the country is not yet fully established. As noted by Ali (2018), in his report in *Mihaaru Daily*, some qualifications are offered and delivered without the required capacity existing, in terms of the availability of qualified lecturers. One example noted by Ali's report is that of offering PhDs without having qualified local professors, which is one of the concerns of those whom he interviewed. It is important to note that as the higher education system in the Maldives is not yet fully established, it cannot logically be a trendsetter in higher education in changing the way it is done traditionally. Instead, it would be more useful for the country at this early stage of the higher education system, to learn from good university practices from more established higher education systems in the world.

It is important to note that the malpractices highlighted in this chapter are not necessarily carried out by all higher education providers in the Maldives. Institutions such as the Maldives National University are working hard to learn good university practices from around the world and to establish a quality higher education system in the Maldives (Maldives National University 2021a,b). However, it is a concern of many, especially academics, that malpractices are taking place and need to be addressed through a robust quality assurance regime.

While these issues are a concern for many, it is also important to note that some concrete steps are already being taken by the Government of the Maldives to tackle such issues by strengthening the legislative framework in the country for higher education as a whole. Indeed, the Maldivian parliament, which is called the "Citizens' Majlis," has recently passed the Maldives Higher Education and Training Act, which was ratified by President Ibrahim Mohamed Salih on 16 May 2021 (President's Office 2021).

It is important to note that one of the main objectives of this is to strengthen the higher education quality assurance regulatory system in the Maldives by empowering the MQA as well as by addressing many issues that undermine the quality of higher education provision in the country. One of the provisions in the Act includes imposing penalties on those who breach rules and regulations (Naeem 2021) by committing acts that undermine the quality of higher education, in addition to setting up legal boundaries for many of the processes and practices in higher education in the Maldives. Hence, it is expected that with the implementation of provisions in the Maldives Higher Education and Training Act, many of the gaps that allow infiltration of malpractices into higher education provision can be filled.

References

Ali, A.S. (2018). Mathee Thauleemuge Fenvaraamedhu Suvaalu. https://mihaaru.com/news/35801 (accessed 29 May 2021).

Altbach, P.G., Reisberg, L., and Rumbley, L.E. (2010). *Trends in Global Higher Education: Tracking an Academic Revolution*. Paris: UNESCO.

Amir, M.N. (2017). Faculty of Hospitality and Tourism Studies: 30 years of training hospitality professionals. https://hoteliermaldives.com/faculty-hospitality-tourism-studies-30-years (accessed 18 April 2021).

Blackmur, D. (2007). A critical analysis of the UNESCO/OECD guidelines for quality provision of cross-border higher education. *Quality in Higher Education* 13: 117–130.

Brown, S. (2004). Assessment for learning. *Learning and Teaching in Higher Education* 1 (1, 1): 81–89.

Cheney, G.R., Ruzzi, B.B., and Muralidharan, K. (2005). *A Profile of the Indian Education System*. s.l. National Centre on Education and the Economy.

Di Biase, R. and Maniku, A. (2020). Transforming education in the Maldives. In: *Handbook of Education Systems in South Asia. Global Education Systems* (ed. P.M. Sarangapani and R. Pappu), 1–29. Singapore: Springer.

Gaikwad, B.R. and Solunke, R.S. (2013). Growth of higher education in India. *International Research Journal of Social Sciences* 2 (8): 58–60.

Golunov, S. (2014). *The Elephant in the Room: Corrption and Chating in Russina Universities*. Stuttgart: ibidem.

Google (2021). Block mode. https://www.google.com/search?q=block+mode&ei=WWmdYOvyNKic4-EPkdOGkAI&oq=block+mode&gs_lcp=Cgdnd3Mtd2l6EAMyAggAMgIIADICCAAyAggAMgIIADICCAAyAggAMgIIADICCAAyAggAOgcIABBHELADOgyIABAHEB46CAgAEAgQBxAeOgYIABAIEB46BggAEBYQHlC_hgZY7KoGYJq6BmgBcAJ4AIAB2gOIAZoWkgEJ (accessed 20 May 2021).

Grønhaug, K. and Olson, O. (1999). Action research and knowledge creation: merits and challenges. *Qualitative Market Research* 2 ((1): 6–14.

Harden, N. (2013). The end of the university as we know it. *The American Interest* 8 (3): 1–8.

Hoffman, N., Vargas, J., Venezia, A., and Miller, M.S. (2007). *Minding the Gap: Why Integrating High School with College Makes Sense and how to Do it*. Cambridge: Harvard Education Press.

Hongjie, C. (2009). On advanced knowledge and higher education. *Frontiers of Education in China* 4 (1): 56–65.

Jangdecha, C. and Larpkesorn, P. (2018). The structure of Thai education. In: *Education in Thailand. Education in the Asia-Pacific Region: Issues, Concerns and Prospects* (ed. R. Maclean and L.P. Symaco), 79–92. Singapore: Springer.

Kaur, V. and Kaur, A. (2018). *Digital Librares and their Future*, 162–170. Hyderabad: PS Publications.

Kir, E. and Akyuz, A. (2019). An exploration of perceptions of faculty members and students: the effects of English-medium instruction on language ability. In: *Internationalising Learning in Higher Education: The Challenges of English as a Medium of Instruction* (ed. M.L. Carrió-Pastor), 155–178. Valencia, Spain: Palgrave Macmillan.

Knight, J. (2007). Cross-border higher education: issues and implications for quality assurance and accreditation. In: *Higher Education in the World 2007: Accreditation for Quality Assurance: What Is at Stake?* Global University Network for Innovation Series, 134–146. Basingstoke, UK: Palgrave Macmillan.

Knobel, M. and Verhine, R. (2017). Brazil's for-profit higher education Dilema. *International Higher Education* 89: 23–24.

Lodge, J.M. (2018). Why block subjects might not be best for university student learning. *The Conversation*. https://theconversation.com/why-block-subjects-might-not-be-best-for-university-student-learning-102909 (accessed 29 March 2021).

Maldives Business School (2021). Block mode classses. https://www.businessschool.mv/home/blockmodecourses (accessed 10 May 2021).

Maldives National University (2021a). Vision & Mission. https://mnu.edu.mv/vision-mission (accessed 21 May 2021).

Maldives National University (2021b). History. https://mnu.edu.mv/history (accessed 18 April 2021).

Maldives Qualifications Authority. (2017). Entry criteria for MNQF qualifications. http://mqa.gov.mv/static/uploads/Entry-Criteria-for-MNQF-Qualifications-with-effect-from-01st-Jan-2017-7_11_2-16-BM9_2018-06-26T00-43-32.pdf (accessed 22 April 2021).

Maldives Qualifications Authority (2021a). About MQA. http://mqa.gov.mv/about (accessed 22 April 2021).

Maldives Qualifications Authority (2021b). Approved local courses. http://mqa.gov.mv/institutes/local (accessed 19 April 2021).

Martin, M. (2016). External quality assurance in higher education: how can it address corruption and other malpractices? *Quality in Higher Education* 22 (2016-1): 49–63.

Ministry of Education (2000). Resources – Regulation for registration of education providers. https://mohe.gov.mv/resources (accessed 24 April 2021).

Ministry of Education (2019). *Education Sector Analysis Maldives*. Malé, Maldives: Ministry of Education.

Ministry of Higher Education (2018). *About us*. Ministry of Higher Education.

Ministry of Higher Education (2019). More than 5000 students enrolled in free degree program. https://mohe.gov.mv/news/more-than-5000-students-enrolled-in-free-degree-program (accessed 28 April 2021).

Ministry of Higher Education (2020). *Higher Education Statistics 2019*. Malé: Ministry of Higher Education.

Ministry of Higher Education (2021). Form for Registration of a Tertiary Institution. https://mohe.gov.mv/images/resources/resources/New%20form%20edited%2002.09.2019.pdf (accessed 24 April 2021).

Naeem, I.M. (2021). Higher Education Bill to include hefty fines for students who pay to get assignments done. https://timesofaddu.com/2021/04/18/higher-education-bill-to-include-hefty-fines-for-students-who-pay-to-get-assignments-done (accessed 20 May 2021).

Naidoo, R. (2010). Global learning in a neoliberal age: implications for development. In: *Global Inequalities and Higher Education: Whose Interests Are we Serving?* (ed. E. Unterhalter and V. Carpentier), 66–90. Palgrave Macmillan: Eastbourne.

Naseer, M.S. and Al-Hibadi, D.A.Y. (2019). Quality Assurance in Higher Education in the Maldives: past, present and future. *Intellectual Discourse* 27 (2): 353–272.

Nirala, R., Bharti, S.K., Sinha, R.R.K., and Yashveer, V. (2018). *Importance of Library in Educational Institutions*, 286–293. Hyderabad: BS Publications.

OECD (2003). Glossary of statistical termshttps://stats.oecd.org/glossary/detail.asp?ID=5389 (accessed 20 April 2021).

Omeluzor, S.U., Bamidele, I.A., Ukangwa, C.C., and Amadi, H.U. (2013). The relevance of a library in the 21st century: Students' perception. *International Journal of Library and Information Science* 160–166.

Oxford University (2021). Admission requirements for 2022. www.ox.ac.uk/admissions/undergraduate/courses/admission-requirements/admission-requirements-table (accessed 10 May 2021).

Plessis, E.D. (2019). The voices of student teachers on e-learning initiatives in a distance education community of practice. *Journal for New Generation Sciences* 15 (1): 260–277.

Popkova, E.G., Chechina, O.S., and Abramov, S.A. (2015). Problem of the human capital quality reducing in conditions of educational unification. *Mediterranean Journal of Social Sciences* 6 (3 S6): 95.

President's Office (2021). Legal documents. www.gazette.gov.mv/gazette/page/2 (accessed 5 May 2021).

Pucciareli, F. and Kaplan, A. (2016). Competition and strategy in higher education: managing complexity and uncertainty. *Business Horizons* 59 (3): 311–320.

Saunders, D.B., Kolek, E.A., Williams, E.A., and Wells, R.S. (2016). Who is shaping the field? Doctoral education, knowledge creation and postsecondary education research in the United States. *Higher Education Research and Development* 35 (5): 1039–1052.

Schofer, E. and Meyer, J.W. (2005). The world-wide expansion of higher education in the twentieth century. *American Sociological Review* 70: 898–920.

Stella, A. (2006). Quality assurance of cross-border higher education. *Quality in Higher Education* 12 (3): 257–276.

Teachmint@wp (2021). Mode of study. https://www.teachmint.com/glossary/m/mode-of-study (accessed 8 May 2021).

The http://StateUniversity.com (2021). Maldives secondary education. https://education.stateuniversity.com/pages/937/Maldives-SECONDARY-EDUCATION.html (accessed 11 May 2021).

Tilak, J. (2008). Higher education: a public good or a commodity for trade? *Prospects* 38: 449–466.

Top Hat (2021). Course delivery method. https://tophat.com/glossary/c/course-delivery-method (accessed 12 May 2021).

United Nations Development Programme (2021). Goal 4: quality education. https://www.undp.org/content/undp/en/home/sustainable-development-goals/goal-4-quality-education.html#targets (accessed 19 April 2021).

University of Sydney (2020). Arts and social sciences postgraduate handbook 2021. www.sydney.edu.au/handbooks/arts_PG/subject_areas_eh/human_community_services_descriptions.shtml (accessed 15 May 2021).

University of Sydney (2021). University of sydney. www.sydney.edu.au/students/selecting-units-in-sydney-student.html (accessed 14 May 2021).

Victoria University (2021). VU block model. https://www.vu.edu.au/study-at-vu/why-choose-vu/vu-block-model (accessed 23 April 2021).

Wong, G. and Shulruf, R. (2013). Admission model and equity in higher education. *The Asia-Pacific Education Researcher* 22: 111–117.

18

Embedding Sustainability into the Education Process in the Faculty of Horticulture and Landscape Engineering, SUA in Nitra, Slovakia

Tatiana Kaletová, Ivana Mezeyová, Ján Mezey, Mária Bihuňová, Roberta Štěpánková, Andrej Tárník, Ján Horák, and Kristína Candráková

18.1 Introduction

The first complex information about sustainable development appeared during the Earth Summit in Rio de Janeiro, Brazil in 1992. Much earlier, unions, countries, and local communities had dealt with this topic based on their own knowledge and possibilities. In Slovakia, several good practices had been applied before, but their continuance was not always managed properly. Even after the Summit in Rio de Janeiro, a lot of communities continued their daily activities without any information about the plan of action, just managing conditions for themselves and their future generation. Our (great)grandparents used to live in line with nature. Developments in society and technologies gave young generations different lifestyles, away from traditional and sustainable ways of living. Currently, thanks to the great efforts of educators, activists, and government, achieving goals presented in the document "Transforming our World: The 2030 Agenda for Sustainable Development" (UN 2015) from 2015 is going to be a success. Together with the changes in society, changes in education and universities' structures have been made. New study programs have been developed, and interest in traditional study programs has decreased. Therefore, it became necessary to improve these important traditional study programs and forms of education and make them new, modern, and more attractive.

Almost at the same time as the Summit in Rio de Janeiro took place, the process of establishing the Faculty of Horticulture and Landscape Engineering (FHLE) at the Slovak University of Agriculture (SUA) in Nitra, Slovakia, started. From the beginning, the faculty focused on improving human lives and environmental protection. The main goal was to create study programs which would: (i) bring enough and healthy vegetables and fruit for all, (ii) create optimal conditions for crop production and land use for people and living organisms, and (iii) create healthy and pleasant urban sites for people.

Here we present the activities provided by employees of the FHLE to educate the university students and the public on how to achieve goals of sustainable development, and especially, how to keep up the practice in future.

The Wiley Handbook of Sustainability in Higher Education Learning and Teaching, First Edition.
Edited by Kelum A. A. Gamage and Nanda Gunawardhana.
© 2022 John Wiley & Sons, Inc. Published 2022 by John Wiley & Sons, Inc.

Table 18.1 Study programs offered by the FHLE.

Study program	Level of education[1]	Language of study
Landscape Engineering	Bc, Ms, PhD[2]	Slovak
Land Consolidation and Information Systems in Agriculture	Bc	Slovak
Garden and Landscape Architecture	Bc, Ms, PhD	Slovak
Biotechnics of Gardens and Landscape Designs	Ms	Slovak
Horticulture	Bc, Ms, PhD	Slovak
International Master of Horticulture Science	Ms	English

[1] Bc – bachelor's degree; Ms – master's degree; PhD – doctoral degree.
[2] Doctoral study programs are also available in English.
Source: Data from Igaz and Štěpánková 2020.

18.2 Education System in the FHLE, SUA in Nitra, Slovakia

The need to establish a new faculty at SUA in Nitra was determined by the lack of specialized studies in horticulture and landscape architecture in Slovakia. Therefore, the FHLE was established in 1995 and, since then, students have had an opportunity to choose from several study programs (Table 18.1), implemented by the European Credit Transfer System. The priority areas of activities include science and research, which are a prerequisite for fulfilling the mission in the field of education (Igaz and Štěpánková 2020).

Currently, the faculty consists of:

- **Institute of Landscape Engineering**: Education process and research activities are focused on water resources and landscape management, including waterworks, river modification, land consolidation, soil water management and climate change, and using geographic information systems (GIS), computer-aided design (CAD) software, and several mathematical models.
- **Institute of Landscape Architecture**: Activities are focused on garden and landscape design in urban and rural spatial settings, especially public (green) space design, special, institutional, and recreational open space design, revitalization of historical parks and villages, and principles of establishment and maintenance of different types of greenery.
- **Institute of Horticulture**: This is focused on the education of professionals specializing in vegetable and fruit production, viticulture and viniculture, and floriculture.
- **Project Grants and Lifelong Learning Centre in the FHLE.**
- **Information and Communication Technologies Centre.**

Important cooperation has been set up with the AgroBio Tech Research Centre, Botanical Garden of SUA and University Farm in Kolíňany (Nitra region, Slovakia). The FHLE also enjoys intensive collaborations with other domestic and foreign universities, entrepreneurs, research institutes, professional and state organizations, ateliers and design studios, municipalities, plant nurseries, and non-governmental organizations to improve teaching processes and enable students to gain specific knowledge and practical skills, which will improve their social and professional status as graduates in today's society.

Apart from the main standard method of teaching (i.e. lecturing), other methods have started to be increasingly incorporated into the education process over the past few years, especially project, experiential, and blended types of learning. Brainstorming, debates, individual and group projects, art-based projects, excursions, field trips, and laboratory experiments are the most used methods. Theory is interconnected with practical skills, which can be obtained at specialized courses at international and national summer schools (SS) and workshops, professional seminars, conferences, and guided excursions in Slovakia and abroad.

18.3 Embedding Sustainability into the Landscape Engineering Program

18.3.1 Setting the Study Subjects

The study program for Landscape Engineering focuses on the management and engineering solutions of soil, water, and air issues. In addition to the sustainable development and conservation of these elements, land consolidation and land ownership are the essential components of the studies. The study program consists of general subjects, e.g. chemistry, botany, and mathematics, which start in the first year of the bachelor's degree and continue toward the specialized subjects in the last year of the doctoral studies (Igaz and Štěpánková 2020).

Students have an opportunity to learn about biological and technical solutions to water and wind erosion processes, with emphasis on the vegetation cover of the surface soil with a mixture of domestic flowers, grasses, bushes, and trees. Loss of soil biodiversity, natural soil textures, and fertility is one of the biggest problems of agriculture. One of the solutions is to use biochar (a lightweight black residue, made of carbon and ashes) for the soil. Students, therefore, obtain information related to the biochar application in soil, its effects on the soil characteristics, and the production of gas emissions from the soil. Hand in hand with the gas emission from the soil, students study climate, biometeorology, and air quality.

Water-related issues are part of almost every subject throughout all the studies, from the first to the third level. As we know, water is an important component of all elements of our lives. Therefore, students start with water management, continue with hydrology and hydraulics, and then at the end, they learn about the application of knowledge in the specialized subjects related to the water quality monitoring and assessment, water-holding capacity of soil and the landscape, and sustainable management of water in a landscape using new irrigation techniques and drainage systems. Floods are an increasing problem and, thus, several possibilities for protecting against flood are presented and solved by the design of water reservoirs and river modification and restoration. Water is important not only for the landscape, but also for humans. Therefore, the appropriate design of water supply and sewage systems and of wastewater treatment plants are included in the study program.

As we can see, Sustainable Development Goals (SDGs) related to the sustainable development of water and soil are presented to students in parts in several subjects during the studies. To understand the whole topic of sustainable development and the related goals better, students must pass a couple of subjects, joining soil, water, air, and land ownership, as well as the environmental impact assessment, environmental quality assessment, or land consolidation.

18.3.2 Setting the Practical Training

Theoretical knowledge has to go hand in hand with practical training. Therefore, students take courses related to different techniques of environmental monitoring – water, air, and soil quality parameters – as well as their evaluation processes. Of course, students have an opportunity to apply the knowledge from the education process, both theoretical and practical, in public and private companies during training (Igaz and Štěpánková 2020).

There are two main practical training courses at the bachelor level: (i) a course in environmental monitoring, and (ii) a course in hydropedology. Both focus on the practical knowledge of sampling, analysis, and decision-making about issues related to the quality and quantity of air, soil, and water.

The practical training course on environmental monitoring gives students an opportunity to practice sampling and measurement of water, soil, and air quality parameters (Figure 18.1). Based on the obtained data, they evaluate the current state of the environment and discuss possible recovery activities for the future. One day of the course focuses on waste management, where students analyze the amount of the produced waste in the municipality – they sort it into groups (paper, plastic, glass, biodegradable waste, etc.), and weigh and calculate the proportion of each waste group (Figure 18.2). Their analyses and reports are used by the municipality in

Figure 18.1 Students taking water quality measurements. *Source:* Kaletová (2017).

Figure 18.2 Waste analysis in a small municipality. *Source:* Kaletová (2017).

Figure 18.3 Measurement of water velocity in a stream during the practical course of hydropedology. *Source:* Tárník (2017).

the future waste management decision-making process. Students can apply the skills obtained from the course during the monitoring and evaluation of water and air quality. These also form the basis for the bachelor and diploma theses related to water or landscape management.

The practical course of hydropedology enables students to practice the soil and soil-water properties analysis. They learn how to take disturbed and undisturbed soil samples and use them for analysis, and are able to do measurements of soil moisture, soil hydraulic conductivity, or infiltration intensity for the analysis of the soil-water dynamic in the landscape. Measuring water velocity in a stream and calculating the discharge or spring richness (Figure 18.3) are other important parts of the course for the appropriate water and land management plan. Students apply knowledge from the course during the field experiments for their final thesis related to soil-water management, soil water-holding capacity, water erosion processes, or biochar application in soil.

18.4 Embedding Sustainability into the Landscape Architecture Program

18.4.1 Setting the Study Subjects

The study program for Landscape Architecture combines technical and biological knowledge with art and creativity. It is based on humanities in combination with natural and technical sciences, garden and landscape theory, and graphic design. It deals with different types of spaces in urban and peri-urban environment up to the open landscape. The emphases are on designing functional and esthetical places, derived from detailed analyses of the sites, inventory of the greenery, and historical or current potential of the site (Igaz and Štěpánková 2020).

There are several types of greenery, which are analyzed and redesigned during the atelier classes:

- Public open spaces
- Special types of greenery
- Historical gardens and parks

- Private gardens and areas
- Peri-urban recreational landscape
- Agricultural landscape, historical landscape, vineyards, and forest parks

The study program for Landscape Architecture reflects the current requirements of society for high-quality, multifunctional public spaces, with regard to climate change. During the design process, new materials and technologies are implemented; also, alternative forms of greenery are designed, together with possible ways of improving its growing conditions in the urban environment. The core aspects of the landscape design are the greenery, support of the biodiversity, and sustainability. Even rainwater collection and management in the area of interest is being taken into consideration. The main focus is on improving the life quality of people and increasing the esthetic, functional, and biological parts of places (Figure 18.4).

The structure of the program is focused on the detailed knowledge of deciduous, coniferous, and evergreen trees and shrubs, knowledge of perennials, bulbs, and annual plants, and ornamental grasses. It is not only about the detailed information on the species, their characteristics, and requirements, but also about the appropriate management of the site and suitable combinations of species. The support for biodiversity, and new materials and species that are suitable for changing climate conditions, are studied. Also, the trends in planting design in urban areas are presented, using structural substrates, flower meadows, different management of the grass maintenance, permeable materials, rainwater collection in rain gardens or various ground depressions, and so on, which help to increase the long-term function and sustainability of the areas.

18.4.2 Setting the Practical Training

At the master's level, there are subjects as Revitalisation of the Greenery in the Villages and Rural Landscape, Design Principles of Public and Recreational Areas, and Principles of the Greenery Management. Landscape Design Studio, and Design Studio I, II, are aimed at open landscape and urban landscape on different scales. The topics of the Design Studios are chosen

Figure 18.4 Presentation of Biotope City, Vienna, as a contribution to sustainable, climate-sensitive urban open spaces. *Source:* Candráková (2019).

in cooperation with municipalities, which enable students to solve real problems and design the sites, interact with the community, and obtain new presentation skills. It is a great opportunity to come into contact with the requests and demands of the investors, answer the questions under discussion, and get to know the administrative process involved in planning and approval.

Students have an opportunity to evaluate and understand the processes related to the open landscape and to propose suitable solutions. The assessment of the landscape is in the field of landscape structure – natural and artificial elements, ecosystem services (ES), cultural and natural values, and socioeconomic services. The proposals support the landscape ecological network of the sites, appropriate traffic structure, water management, biodiversity, and the selection of appropriate functional and recreational equipment. The proposals also take into consideration changing climate conditions and existing protected areas.

18.5 Embedding Sustainability into the Horticulture Programs

18.5.1 Setting the Study Subjects

Within the study program of the Horticulture, the subjects at bachelor's degree level are aimed at obtaining a general overview of the profile subjects in fruit production, vegetable production, viticulture, and enology (Igaz and Štěpánková 2020). Sustainability is the main denominator at several levels.

Within the area of soil care, emphasis is placed on tillage systems that do not contribute to the soil's degradation by water or wind erosion. In fruit growing and viticulture, ground cover systems are used in the interrows, protecting the soil from drying out, and from wind and water erosion and compaction. We use mixtures that resemble meadow plants and consist of 13–16 species of grasses, especially herbs, which have additional positive effects on soil structure, and contribute to insect diversity and pollinators in orchards and vineyards, the latter presenting as biological predators of animal pests of fruit trees and vines.

Water management is another level. Irrigation systems with drip irrigation, which is very gentle on water resources and is applied in the form of drops, are essential parts of orchards and vineyards, but also vegetable areas. Within the subject, which deals with designing orchards and vineyards, large-capacity water tanks, whether in the form of ponds or retention tanks, are now a necessary part of the project and subsequently of the plantings themselves. Water for the ponds and tanks is collected from local wells, periodic water resources, and also the roofs of the surrounding buildings or warehouses.

The plant protection subject emphasizes integrated and ecological protection systems, or more precisely, plant production. Students learn to understand how the individual components of the environment work in relation to pathogens. Great emphasis is placed on ensuring the optimal conditions for plants, which we achieve by optimizing the cultivation technologies, and by applying accurate doses of water, fertilizers, and nutrients based on several analyses. If the plant is in optimal condition, it does not suffer from stress and, therefore, it is less susceptible to diseases and pests. In the plant protection systems themselves, we place great emphasis within the curriculum on preventive measurements that can prevent disease or damage very effectively. This includes, for example, appropriate agro-climatic regionalization, including determination of the suitability of species and varieties in terms of soil type, but also the choice of tree shape, spacing of trees, and system of tree training and pruning. Direct preventive protection methods depending on the pathogen can be used to effectively reduce the incidence of diseases and pests below the threshold of economic harmfulness. The aim is not on the complete eradication of the pest, but on the reduction of its population to such an extent that is does not cause significant damage to the crops but at the same time remains as food for beneficial organisms. As part of the eradication measurements, if possible, we first select biological protection and then chemical protection methods. In the case of chemical protection, it is applied based on signaling by means of an automatic meteorological station equipped with appropriate software, exclusively, that indicates the date of the intervention. This applies to both diseases and pests. As part of the final thesis, students address topics that contribute to the improvement or fine-tuning of the existing software for signaling specific pests by collecting effective temperature values, based on insect attack raids in pheromone traps and accurately determining flight activity, depending on individual generations of the pests.

As part of the sustainable practices, the institute focuses not only on the production of agricultural crops but also on their impact on human health. Knowledge from the institute's scientific research activities is applied in the agricultural practice. The focus is on the verification of new cultivation technologies of selected species and subsequently on monitoring the impact of nutrition and fertilization on quantitative and qualitative parameters of the crop, with an emphasis on their importance in human nutrition. The aim is to provide students with knowledge about the substances present in the plant production products with bioactive effects, ways to influence their content during cultivation and technological processing, and their positive impact on human health. Finally, the study program focuses on food safety, where the aim is to present knowledge about soil pollution problems, mechanisms of transformation of pollutants, and risks of growing agricultural crops on contaminated soils, and to show ways of solving this situation using remedial techniques to eliminate hazardous substances.

The International Master of Horticulture Science (IMHS) is an international joint degree program at master's level, which our faculty offers in English. The IMHS program has been set up as a joint program with three universities: University of Agriculture in Krakow, Poland; Mendel University in Brno, Czech Republic; and Slovak University of Agriculture in Nitra, Slovakia. The main goal of the studies is to inform students about the current situation in the field of horticultural production, with regard to international aspects. It is focused on education and training of students for their future activities in the spheres of management, trade, and services, as well as in governmental services at the European level. Within the framework of the studies, great emphasis is put on the current problems of modern horticulture that concern vegetable production, pomiculture, viticulture, greenhouse production, plant biotechnologies, and storage of horticultural products and their quality.

18.5.2 Setting the Practical Training

Within the practical exercise, the projects of planting fruit orchards and vineyards for specific localities are theoretical at first and then, in some cases, also solved in practice. Students design an orchard or vineyard for a specific location. The project usually includes agro-climatic regionalization; pre-planting soil preparation; fertilization design, based on agrochemical soil testing results; design of specific species, varieties, lengths, and numbers of rows; growing shapes, pruning, and training systems; protection, nutrition, and fertilization. A separate part of the project is dedicated to the design of irrigation systems or covering of plantings. Similar projects are also solved within the vegetable production subjects, where students propose a sowing procedure. In cooperation with local governments, fruit orchard projects have been developed for towns and villages such as Nitra, Trnava, and Rohožník and also for the Bishop's Office in Nitra.

A relatively large space is dedicated to the practical side of pruning and training fruit trees, bushes, and vineyards (Figure 18.5). Students participate in pruning at different stages of age

Figure 18.5 Practical training in fruit tree pruning. *Source:* Candráková (2019).

and condition of the plants, but also at different times of the year. Consequently, they can observe how the trees respond to the selected system of pruning.

Within grape, vine, and wine production subjects, students can participate in the processing of grapes and wine production, and they also produce wine as part of their final thesis. Furthermore, they participate in the organization of wine competitions, exhibitions, and festivals, where they peek behind the scenes of such events, for example the Nitra Wine Festival, Wine of SUA. Of course, as part of the practical exercises, they undergo sensory evaluation of wine, where, in addition to the smelling typical types from various winemaking styles, they can also smell if wines have a flaw or defect.

Students verify their theoretical knowledge in the experimental part of the botanical garden in field conditions and greenhouses. Several beds of plants are available, from spices and aromatic herbs, through vegetable and fruit stands, to lesser-known vegetable and fruit species and edible mushrooms. As a part of increasing the teaching efficiency, streamlining its quality, and improving the practical readiness of graduates in the field of horticultural sciences, the teaching process is supplemented by a hitherto absent didactic element – an interactive classroom. This consists of a collection of cultivars – spices and aromatic plants and lesser-known horticultural crops interactively connected via a QR code with a web page containing details about their basic characteristics, photographic material, and the basics of a suitable cultivation technology (http://plants.bauercreative.sk). Translation into English with proven terminology being available for foreign students and visitors is highly beneficial. Finally, in the current situation, changes in the Slovak labor market are coming to the fore and the needs of individual sectors of the economy are being influenced by innovation, digitization, and new technologies, and the modern interactive cultivar collection is contributing to the popularization of the agro-sector, education, and training of the young generation. This is all in line with current trends and the Strategy for the Development of Human Resources in Agriculture, for the period up to 2030.

Students are also acquainted with the latest cultivation technologies during their practice and excursions to the partner companies in Slovakia and abroad. Hydroponic greenhouses are examples of sustainable forms of subsistence (Figure 18.6). Due to modern measures and computer-controlled lighting, stands are grown out of the normal growing season and in conditions of strict hygiene comparable to laboratory conditions. The plants receive a computer-controlled dose of nutrition, everything is controlled via Wi-Fi (including pollination by bumblebees), water management is carefully guarded, and electricity is produced from the biogas station. After cultivation, the used substrate is composted and utilized for lawn

Figure 18.6 An excursion of Horticulture study program students to the most modern hydroponic companies. *Source:* Mezeyová (2018).

renovation or as a source for the biogas station. Despite the high initial costs, this type of cultivation is finding its way to the Slovak market and if a graduate has education in this field, it is easier to implement the ideas of sustainable forms of cultivation in practice.

18.6 Further Education Activities for Students, the Public, and Professionals

In addition to the standard education process, the university and faculty offer further forms of education, which are available for students, professionals, and the wider public.

SUA has been a member of the Baltic University Programme for more than 15 years. Since 1 October 2018, the Slovak National Centre of the Baltic University Programme has been operating in SUA in Nitra; its task is to join together organizations in Slovakia interested in the issue of the sustainable development. Further, the membership allows students and teachers of the faculty to actively participate in all activities like conferences (including those on sailing boats), and courses focused on the sustainable development.

In 2017, we started intensive cooperation with selected high schools and the faculty offered and organized SSs for their students. There were four main topics of the SS: (i) landscape engineering, (ii) landscape architecture, (iii) horticulture, and (iv) viticulture. In addition to these SSs, teachers and PhD students participate in selected lectures over a long-term period as supervisors of the high school students' scientific theses or as members of committees for high school students' science activities. Theoretical lectures focus on climate change, water management, soil erosion control, land consolidation, GIS, and the importance of fruit, grapes, wine, and vegetable production. The lectures also include practical demonstrations of water quality monitoring and analysis, pruning and training techniques, and tasting of horticultural crops and wine evaluation.

The university offers open courses for the wider public in the over 45-year-old age group – the University of the Third Age. The length of courses varies from a couple of months up to three years. Members of the faculty together with colleagues from other faculties and from practice currently participate in the following courses: eco-horticulture; medicinal and aromatic plants (MAPs); practical horticulture; flower tying and arranging; and basics of garden and park design. All courses are highly appreciated, and the number of applicants is higher than the course capacity. Therefore, several courses are offered every year.

18.6.1 Further Education Programs for Professionals

The FHLE provides and organizes further education, which continues from school education and enables acquisition of partial or full qualifications; this allows supplemental qualifications and also renews, deepens, or extends acquired qualification. At present, five modular and non-modular programs and further education courses are accredited. They are taught by teachers and researchers of the faculty in cooperation with experts from the practice.

The further education programs for professionals comprise the following:

Arboriculture in the management and maintenance of green areas: This is designed for local government employees in the field of tree administration and maintenance. Education is composed of five thematic modules: (i) biological properties of woody plants, (ii) assessment of the conditions of trees, (iii) operational safety of trees in settlements, (iv) cut trees and bushes, and (v) protection of trees during the construction activities (http://www.fzki.uniag.sk/sk/arboristika-v-sprave-a-udrzbe-zelene).

Knowledge from the course is important for the sustainable management of open public spaces, private parks and gardens, and special types of greenery.

Design of the automatic irrigation systems: This suitable for designers of automatic irrigation systems, landscape architects, implementers of automatic irrigation systems, green administrators (private and public sector), and workers in the field of environmental protection. The aim of the course is to present new knowledge and processes in irrigation systems focused on the sustainable use of water for irrigation – to select and design safer water technologies based on the modern techniques and technologies. Education is composed of five thematic modules: (i) hydraulic bases of water movement in pipes, (ii) elements and composition of the automatic irrigation systems, (iii) wells, pumps, and pumping irrigation water, (iv) design of the automatic irrigation systems, and (v) implementation and installation of the automatic irrigation systems (http://www.fzki.uniag.sk/sk/navrhovanie-automatickych-zavlazovacich-systemov).

Water management: This program is offered to employees of the state sector, local government, commercial companies, as well as third sector organizations and individuals operating in the field of water management. Knowledge of physical laws, as well as technical, biological, and legislative possibilities enables rational use of water for the needs of both human society and the landscape as a natural environment with its biotic and abiotic elements. We are currently witnessing ongoing climate change processes and their impacts on the socio-economic development of society. These factors are also reflected in new requirements for the operation and construction of water structures. The aim of the course is to upgrade the qualification of people who work directly in water management, as well as in the areas that affect water management in the landscape. The topics of the course are prerequisite for managing this issue in terms of quantity, quality, and protection against adverse consequences of scarcity or surplus. Therefore, the course brings current scientific knowledge to professionals who do not have enough time to study a wide spectrum of literature (http://www.fzki.uniag.sk/sk/vodne-hospodarstvo).

Principles of enology: This offers information to growers of grapevines, producers and sellers of wine, sommeliers, people in gastronomy, and wine assessors, as well as to graduates of secondary vocational schools of horticulture. Only quality grapes can be used to make flawless, competitive wine. The ideal state is a closed system, when someone can grow quality grapes, make flawless wine from it, present this product in an engaging way, and finally introduce it to the market. The aim of the program is to provide the target group with comprehensive knowledge about the cultivation of grapevines, grape processing, and wine production technology in line with the SDGs. Participants also undergo training in sommelier and presentation skills in wine services (http://www.fzki.uniag.sk/sk/fundamenty-enologie).

Basics of the open-source GIS: This is designed for employees of commercial enterprises or non-profit organizations, employees in public or state administration, students, employees in the military sector, police, and staff in rescue services. GIS tools are increasingly used in commercial and public applications, where they help collect, process, visualize, and publish spatial data, and thus enable the implementation and improvement of service delivery in the areas of public sector, urban management and municipalities, and design tasks, as well as in the fields of crisis management, decision-making, and records. Knowledge of the possibilities of these tools will enable the solving of design, analytical, or management tasks without the need to invest a significant amount of money in order to achieve quality outputs and analytic results, and will help in better sustainable decision-making and solutions design (http://www.fzki.uniag.sk/sk/zaklady-open-source-gis).

18.7 Projects Focused on the Sustainability Application into the Study Programs

18.7.1 Projects Funded by the Cultural and Educational Grant Agency in Slovakia

The Cultural and Educational Grant Agency supports projects focused on increasing the educational process of educational institutions. The faculty actively participates with thematic areas such as: (i) new technologies, methods, and forms in education, (ii) content integration and diversification of the university studies, and (iii) development of culture and art. Thanks to these specific grants, we can develop and spread a wide spectrum of information to the university students and the public.

Several projects implemented by the faculty have been supported. However, not all of them had a direct relation to the goals of sustainable development and it was important to create better study conditions for students. Table 18.2 gives a list of all the supported SDG-related projects and this section presents some of them in detail.

Aimed at meeting the subobjectives of sustainable development (production of functional foods in terms of prevention and improvement of health of population), "Addressing the shortage of bioactive substances through differentiated mineral nutrition of the horticultural crops" was one of the grant-funded projects that was approved and successfully conducted; commonly available crops were selenized (i.e. a solution of sodium selenate was applied by foliar spraying on the selected horticulture crops) to create and increase the content of biologically important substances, as well as the overall antioxidant activity in the horticultural crops.

Another project, "Less-known horticultural crops utilization for processing foodstuffs with increased content of bioactive compounds" was oriented to growing crops that are less-known, but are rich in bioactive compounds and antioxidants that can be used as alternatives in the preparation of baked products (bread, biscuits), e.g. product enhancement by adding gluten-free flour substitutes (sweet potato, butternut squash) and seeds (basil) for improving taste and antioxidant properties of gluten-free baked products.

Table 18.2 List of supported education projects related to sustainable development.

Name of the project	Year of start	Year of end
Survey of historic greenery objects in southwestern Slovakia	2010	2012
Gene pool of woody vegetation in Nitra region from its revitalisation and landscape creation	2011	2013
Waste management - study program, creation of study plans and textbooks	2011	2013
Terrestrial laser scanning and digital 3D-models creation in cultural heritage objects documentation	2011	2013
Program of lifelong learning for arborists in Slovakia	2013	2015
Green infrastructure and urban agriculture	2014	2016
Non-forest woody vegetation in the landscape, and its biodiversity, gene pool, and landscape architectural significance	2014	2016
Addressing the shortage of bioactive substances through differentiated mineral nutrition of horticultural crops	2014	2016
Innovation of technological advancements through large-scale fruit growing improvements	2015	2017
Interactive experimental garden	2016	2018
Multimedia support of education in river modification and restoration	2016	2018
Development and implementation of standards for urban greenery management	2017	2019
Ecosystem services of green infrastructure	2017	2019
Innovative application of the optical method in soil science: soil texture laser diffraction analysis	2017	2019
Memorial places and cemeteries as part of cultural heritage in landscape and garden architecture	2017	2019
Monitoring of elements of the environment: practical course	2017	2019
Open educational and information cycle on land consolidation and its aspects under interdepartmental umbrella	2017	2019
Course of practical skills in irrigation system construction in gardens and parks	2017	2019
Upgrade of education process in the field of hydropedology with implementation of center of excellence in the learning process	2017	2019
Less-known horticultural crops utilization for processing of foodstuffs with increased content of bioactive compounds	2017	2019
E-learning in teaching of planting and maintenance of verdure technologies	2019	2021
Green infrastructure of the urban environment: landscape design regarding measures for adapting to climate change	2019	2021
The cultural historical value of the vineyard landscape, development, and current use	2019	2021
Climate change and its impact on temperature conditions in Slovakia	2020	2022
Development of theoretical knowledge and practical skills of students for teaching of subject vegetable production	2020	2022
Education in the field of proactive urban tree management	2020	2022
Interactive learning as a tool for analysis and solutions design for water modeling training in the landscape	2020	2022
UNI:ARCH – Slovak Agricultural UNIversity in Nitra: ARCHitectural values	2020	2022
ZEL:IN:KA - Integration of green infrastructure into landscape architecture	2020	2022
Creation and implementation of the discipline "Green Infrastructure" into the study programs of the Department of Landscape Engineering	2021	2023

Source: Data from Faculty of Horticulture and Landscape Engineering.

The projects "Green infrastructure and urban agriculture" and "Ecosystem services of green infrastructure" focus on analysis of urban and rural green infrastructures in the context of historical development and structural metamorphoses of the landscape. Detailed knowledge of historical and current landscape structures of a settlement is essential for defining spatial visions for further sustainable development of a spatial unit. Using landscape architectural and planning tools, the sites are analyzed taking into consideration environmental, economic, and social points of view.

The goal of the project "Green infrastructure of the urban environment: landscape design regarding measures for adapting to climate change" is to create a publication that will not only be a study guide for university students, but also a guide for local authorities, non-profit and non-governmental organizations, and the public. The publication will answer questions about how to create green space that are of high quality, how to implement nature-friendly solutions, and how to effectively manage rainfall. It will also present guidelines on how to design urban open spaces with due regard to climate change, and will offer a list of suitable tree species, present information about new types of planting, new materials, and the importance of greenery and water features in all their forms in cities. The emphasis will be on the application of permeable materials, alternative solutions for greenery, and sustainable urban design.

The main aim of the project "Interactive experimental garden" (IEG) was to create a practical platform, and experimental and interactive site for students and public. The garden was designed, created, and planted by students, and is also being maintained by students of different study degrees. It is a dynamically changing space that offers various examples of six types of planting concepts in one place (Figure 18.7). It is possible to study the newest species and varieties of the perennials, bulbs, annuals, and their combinations.

The IEG has its own web page (www.interaktivnazahrada.sk), where you can find detailed information about plants and seasonal works. It serves as an archive of all activities that have been done, but at the same time is updated with recent events from the garden. Teachers prepare workshops that are open to the public twice a year (Spring and Autumn [Fall] workshops). It is also possible to download a publication, available in Slovak and English, that describes the garden composition, construction process, plant selection in each segment of the garden, care, and maintenance in detail. The project was awarded a special prize, Garden of the Year 2018, by the Slovak Association for Garden Design and Landscaping.

Figure 18.7 Interactive experimental garden. *Source:* Candráková (2021).

Other research performed within the IEG includes, for example: (i) smart honey hives, which monitor the activities of bees using the Dadant system and also evaluate insects and coleoptera, (ii) assessment of the increasing biodiversity at the site, and (iii) dynamic changes of plant species through the years.

18.7.2 Projects Funded by the EU Related to the Education Process

The Ministry of the Environment of the Slovak Republic is the managing authority for the Operational Program Quality of Environment. One of its calls for project proposals also supports the information activities related to adaptation of the unfavorable consequences of climate change by focusing on flood protection. Our faculty is solving such a project under the title "Support for information activities aimed at reducing the risk of floods and objectively informing about the adverse effects of climate change" during years 2019–2021 (project code: ITMS 2014+: 310021R571). Thanks to this project, we can objectively inform the target group (high schools, university students, teachers, experts in the affected areas, government authorities and the public) about the adverse effects of climate change, such as heat waves, droughts, heavy rains, floods, landslides, and soil erosion. The project also addresses the awareness in the issue of adaptation to these emergencies. The relevant information related to the project issues is formed through information programs. These include competitions, lectures, and practical environmental education in the form of field trips, information days at schools, conferences, brochures, and especially practical demonstrations during the information activity summer school. These activities are supported by creating a website covering the issues and preparing audio-visual documents (documentary videos).

"Support for increasing the quality of education at the FHLE, SUA in Nitra" (ITMS project: 26110230094) was another project supported by the Operational Program education. The main project activities consist of (i) innovation and creation of new study programs with a focus on the current conditions of work environment, (ii) support for new PhD students of the FHLE, (iii) creation of the study module in English, and (iv) increase of competence profiles and support for teachers' and PhD students' mobility. Within the project, several activities for teachers and students were created to increase their knowledge in different topics, such as sustainable development, water management, climate change, tree planting, biological protection, sustainable urban areas, urban water management, and others. Activities supported by the program included professional excursions for teachers and students in Slovakia and abroad, training for teachers and PhD students abroad, study mobility for master's students in Poland and the Czech Republic, and selected lectures by professionals and training courses for teachers.

During a professional excursion, students and teachers had an opportunity to gain knowledge about the teaching process at the Institute of Fruit Growing, Mendel University in Brno, Czech Republic. Students completed a professional tour of the institute's demonstration garden with an explanation of the ongoing research and diploma theses. Participants of the excursion saw modern intensive planting of apple trees in the shape of a slender spindle, which was installed with a system of protective nets against hail. They also attended a lecture on biological protection complexes for fruit trees; learned about the production of fruit tree planting material from the point of view of the maximum quality of the nursery stocks; obtained an overview of the cutting systems used by a private company and were presented with a wide range of cultivated fruit species and grapevines.

Teachers visited waterworks in the Netherlands (a historical water mill that was used to drain the agricultural soil and served as protection against floods, part of an initiative in the Netherlands called "Room for water"); Germany (a green roof company that was harvesting rainwater in Stuttgart and the surrounding area); and flood protection by weirs in Austria. Teachers still use the knowledge and photographs in the education process. Other excursions focused on rainwater harvesting in urban areas and children's playgrounds, and the recreational use of rural areas from ancient times up to the present was explored in various cities in France.

18.7.3 Educational Activities with International Cooperation

Teachers and researchers of the faculty have set up close cooperation with colleagues from several countries, mostly the Czech Republic, Poland, and Hungary. In addition to several others, we also cooperate with associates from Austria, Finland, the Netherlands, Russia, Serbia, and Uzbekistan. Foreign teachers usually present new trends related to water and soil protection, usage of rural and urban areas, gardens, parks and landscape architecture, cultivation, and processing of medicinal, aromatic, and spice plants, cultivation of seed stands, processing and distribution of vegetable seeds – all increasing knowledge levels about the techniques of cultivation and content of the bioactive substances to be determined in the selected horticultural crops, spice plants, etc.

The Central European Exchange Program for University Studies (CEEPUS) is mainly used for the organization of SSs and excursions for university students. For this purpose, the network "Landscape management – Sustainable land use perspectives in the Central European Region" was created. The interdisciplinary approach in landscape management led to establishment of an active network with partners who have great knowledge in landscape architecture, spatial planning, horticulture, and environmental science (mainly in soil, water, and air systems). Therefore, the main topics on which the network is built are:

- Landscape architecture
- Environmental protection
- Landscape and spatial planning

Almost every year, we have organized short-term excursions abroad for our students, and for foreign students and teachers in Slovakia (Table 18.3). The excursions reflect the actual topic of the studies and are highly valued by all the participants.

The university is a member of the ICA (the Association for European Life Science Universities) Regional Network for Central and South Eastern Europe (CASEE). The CASEE is a regional network of higher education institutions related to the life science disciplines, because such universities are the basis for sustainable, ecological, and economic development of the region. The faculty, together with the members from Serbia (the coordinator) and Hungary, prepare an SS "Ecosystem Services within an Agricultural Landscape" for university students to strengthen education and collaboration among the CASSE network universities. The topic of the SS is focusing on the importance of ES within agricultural areas of the Danube region.

The roles of ES are especially valuable in the areas where anthropogenic influence is significant. Within the Pannonian Plain, a huge land where, in most cases, intensive agriculture has been practiced, is a dominant feature of the landscape. Such landscapes dominate in southern Slovakia, Hungary, and especially in the northern part of Serbia where, in the Province of Vojvodina, around 85% of the land is arable. In these areas, agriculture is the major driver of energy and matter flow within the cultivated ecosystems, while natural ecosystems are marginalized and their diversity is depleting. In turn, this leads to deterioration of water and soil resources, soil erosion, and pest outbreak. Therefore, reexamining and assessing the potentials of ES is urgently needed. People are not often aware how strong the impact of biodiversity and the service offered by nature are and how important they are for our existence. Therefore, this SS contributed to deepening the understanding of ES through interactive education, combining lectures, field work, and workshops. Such content enables students to gain basic knowledge

Table 18.3 List of short-term international CEEPUS excursions organized by SUA.

Year	Name of excursion
2014	New life of Brownfields
2015	Water quality assessment
2015	Public open spaces in the protected urban zones and landscape in Tekov and Hont regions
2016	Water quality monitoring
2016	Landscape proposal for the recreational area in the city of Banská Štiavnica
2017	Landscape formed by water
2018	Waste management in landscape
2018	Moravia 2018 – focused on cultivation and processing of medicinal, aromatic and spice plants; cultivation of seed stands, processing, and distribution of vegetable seeds
2019	Environmental problems of the catchment used in agriculture
2019	Water retention in landscape

Source: Data from Faculty of Horticulture and Landscape Engineering

on ES, master practical tools for their assessment, and solve practical problems presented during the field trips. In this way, by applying active learning, students can obtain comprehensive experience in both theory and practice.

In addition to the short-term Erasmus+ staff mobilities, the faculty is involved in the Erasmus+ K2 Strategic partnership. The "Learning Landscapes (LeLa)" project builds on the idea that the local landscape is a place where urban communities and space users create a vision for the future through processes of democracy and inclusion. Together with partners from Croatia, the Netherlands, and Poland and through numerous workshops, lectures, round tables, mapping activities, field visits to project the defined areas, and interactive platforms, we will seek to open the academic community and connect it with local users and other target groups, actively shape knowledge processes and landscape values, influence mainstream thinking through critical reflection and questioning competencies, and explore connections of social capital, collaboration, and innovation. The project involves students and the future generation of European planners and designers, through inclusive learning processes. It also creates and shares knowledge by documenting the methodology of learning through landscape as an open educational resource (https://www.landscape-portal.org/learning-landscapes-2).

18.7.4 Projects Supported by the Visegrad Fund

Slovakia, as a part of the Visegrad region (V4: Slovakia, Poland, Hungary, and the Czech Republic), also has an opportunity to obtain financial support from the Visegrad Fund. Our faculty cooperates in several Visegrad projects focused on sustainable education and sustainable development.

The main goal of the project "Sustainable water management and hydrological security in V4 group and Ukraine" is increasing the awareness of water resources and water security in partner countries. The aim of the project was to integrate the V4 community in regard to new methods of integrated and sustainably managed reservoirs and watersheds. The project was dedicated to young people (students and high school pupils). Activities of the project included an SS focused on sustainable water management in the Visegrad countries (25 students) and a Visegrad festival in the form of discussions with experts and organized for students from every country.

Another project, directly focused on students and their environmental habits and behavior, was "Visegrad green universities." This project connects universities from Hungary, Slovakia, the Czech Republic, Serbia, and Ukraine that are interested in green topics. An international workshop about the universities' sustainable program was part of this project. Workshops provide a platform where universities can share their experience and examples of good practice in sustainability and environmental solutions. There was also a contest for students where they made videos about their sustainability ideas for their homes or universities. The best videos were awarded with various e-motion devices.

The project "Lesser-known species of vegetables, medicinal plants and edible mushrooms: New growing trends in the context of the V4 countries cooperation" was focused on the exchange of materials and information in the growing of MAPs as well as lesser-known vegetables. The output of the partial project processes was represented by creating a cultivar collection with these MAPs and less-known vegetables, and edible mushrooms, followed by a workshop – a scientific seminar on the topic and under the professional guarantee of the submitter and the project partners (Figure 18.8). The cultivar collection was created in and around the Botanical Garden (SUA, Nitra) and is used for educational purposes. Since the botanical garden is open to the public, there is also an assumption of interest in growing the named crops, which are increasingly popular in terms of nutrition and economy. The cultivar collection is interactively connected to the network with the help of QR codes (http://plants.bauercreative.sk), with references to the page where taxonomy, botanical, and possible culinary uses (recipes) of the mentioned species (varieties) are described in Slovak and English.

The project "GAP – Green and blue infrastructure in post-USSR cities: Exploring legacies and connecting to the V4 experience" is about the legacies (physical, institutional, academic) of the communist era city design concepts and practical approaches, when related to green & blue (G&B) infrastructure. The project partners represent local communities, open society, and academia of Belarus and Ukraine and all the V4 countries.

G & B was a big topic back in the USSR, and many ideas and designs even from the 1970s appear to be still very fresh. For instance, the "green and water diameter" of Minsk (arguably the best implemented and preserved) was an amazing project demonstrating a lot of strategic foresight. Many more interesting designs can be found across the former USSR (although not properly implemented and/or not maintained in most cases) while concepts, approaches, and methods for the development of G&B were extensively discussed in university textbooks. However, it can be noticed that although the cities in the formerly USSR countries, such as Belarus or Ukraine, were planned by people from the same school (or even the same people who participated in the development of the "green and water diameters"), one cannot see anything innovative and progressive there, even in the proposals for the master plans of the cities. At the same time, new concepts, such as nature-based solutions, emerged over time, and one could expect them to evolve with the old school and produce some interesting outcomes (and this is not really happening, except for a couple of funded pilots). Nevertheless, the V4 countries, having had very similar starting conditions in terms of the urban planning policies and implementation strategies as Belarus and Ukraine at the collapse of the USSR, have gone a long way in reflecting their planning legacies and choosing development paths. When it comes to the development and management of G&B infrastructure, there were both vivid successes and failures; recent development has focused on nature-based solutions, smart G&B, use of participatory approaches, and crowdsourcing techniques.

The aim of "Smart and Green – the future of the Visegrad cities" and "Smart and Green – on the spot in the Visegrad countries" was to give decision-makers and city administration representatives an opportunity to visit/learn about smart and green innovations in the V4 countries. The uniqueness was in bringing the implementers together with the public sector and enabling a direct discussion. Good examples and innovations cannot be copied in the same way from

Figure 18.8 International cooperation for the purpose of creating an interactive cultivar collection within an innovative project supported by the Visegrad Fund. *Source:* Mezeyová (2016).

city to city, but they could be a great inspiration. Results enabled a long-term impact on raising awareness of environmental protection, climate change, and sustainable development.

18.7.5 Activities Supported by the Non-governmental Grants

Several private and non-governmental organizations offer support for the public, schools, and universities to improve conditions for environment, educational process, and leisure time of students and citizens. Students and employees of the faculty have been involved in projects, the results of which have brought possibilities for improving the conditions of public spaces and localities for all inhabitants of and visitors to Nitra city. They have also provided a unique opportunity for practical teaching about edible and medicinal mushrooms, increased the possibility of better use of GIS in landscape planning, and supported better indoor conditions for students of the faculty.

The project "Chill out zone" (Grant program: I am Changing My City) created a background in the SUA campus for students and the public. It was realized by FHLE students under the leadership of the faculty employees. The aim of the program announced by the city of Nitra in cooperation with the Nitra Community Foundation was to improve the quality of the public spaces and localities, by restoring or reviving them. The green relaxation zone was built from natural materials in the context of the environment – stylish pallet seating with planted herbs and ornamental flower beds and fruit trees (about 200 plants). The pallet seating consists of six modules, symbolizing the six faculties of SUA. The created area also had the ambition to educate visitors passively; thus, for example, information labels have been placed on the planted trees and herbs.

The aim of the project "MushROOM" (supported by the Tatrabanka Foundation) as to support the practical teaching about edible and medicinal mushrooms and other related subjects, to create space for students to solve their own experimental tasks and final theses, and present modern ways of cultivating edible and medicinal mushrooms. It also aimed to support students' skills building, scientific research base, and cooperation with foreign institutions; reflect the requirements of companies from practice (verification of new substrates, additives, mechanization for the production of substrates, etc.); verify laboratory results in "semi-operation"; and issue recommendations for practice in the form of scientific and professional publications in Slovakia and abroad.

The project "Modern technologies in plant design education" (The University Grant Scheme) aimed to create a virtual educational environment in the field of interior plant design in the FHLE. As part of the project, we implemented innovative technologies to increase the attractiveness of the educational process in the faculty (Figures 18.9 and 18.10). We digitized elements of the interior greenery (green walls, kokedamas, macramé, and plants in pots/containers) in the faculty to create a virtual environment that would be used for the purpose of studying and presenting the work of students on the subject of interior floristry.

18.7.6 Scientific Projects Related to the Education Process

Monitoring the quantity and quality of water is essential to ensure that all citizens have access to drinking water. In addition, water resources are also used for additional irrigation of agricultural crops or recreation, which demands different quality requirements. Therefore, it is necessary to know how much water is available for individual activities with the necessary water quality and to find out its distribution in the landscape and availability for humans. Several current projects are focused on monitoring the quality and quantity of water in the agricultural landscape, and the result will serve as a proposal for optimal landscape management, regarding ensuring enough water for humans, agricultural production, and the environment. Also, seeking new irrigation technologies and technologies necessary for efficient use of irrigation is currently being solved. Students participate in the projects by taking water samples from water reservoirs, drainage, and irrigation canals at monthly intervals and by laboratory evaluation. In addition, the results of the monitoring are incorporated into the education process and subjects. Thus, students have an opportunity to get new knowledge and see the consequences of human activities in landscape.

Today, global agriculture is facing massive challenges, such as increasing demand for food production to satisfy the growing population, while reducing the environmental footprint of the agricultural intensification brought by the "green revolution." Recently, biochar has been

Figure 18.9 Example of the green walls in the interior of the FHLE. *Source:* Candráková (2021).

Figure 18.10 Kokedams in the interior of the FHLE. *Source:* Candráková (2019).

the focus of the increasing research attention. Reflecting this trend, a field experiment was set up in our faculty to test the potential of biochar as a soil ameliorant in Slovakia in 2014. This is a collaborative effort, where local core teams from our faculty and the Slovak Academy of Sciences work together with international experts to elucidate the effects of the biochar addition. Since the beginning of the experiment, several interesting findings have been made and widely published. Both positive and negative impacts of the biochar application on the soil function and its ability to support crop production were found. Reduction of greenhouse gas (CO_2, N_2O) emissions from soil into the atmosphere after the biochar application was among the key aims of the experiment. In the future, research broadening the knowledge base of the biochar use should focus on: (i) economically cost-effective biochar production and application within Slovakia in different soil types; (ii) the nutrient content of biochar, both total content and available forms and their ratio, with a view to eliminating the negative impacts of biochar on crop yields; (iii) different types of biochar and their combinations with other organic and/or mineral fertilizers and their repeated application, and (iv) optimum biochar application rates to improve the sustainability of agricultural production.

Students are also involved in this topic and work in field experiments during their practice, and the collected data are used for the preparation of their final theses. They take samples, analyze them, and use the analyzed results for their theses. The field experiment is a base for educational material. By this, we show students the innovative approach "biochar application to soil," which is produced by the organic waste pyrolysis (not containing any harmful and hazardous substances) and contributes to lowering greenhouse gas emissions (mitigation of climate change), and improvement of soil fertility, and also supports sustainable soil management.

Many final theses devoted to monitoring the flight activity of various fruit tree pests used information from 20 automatic meteorological stations, which were installed in the most important fruit orchards in the Slovak Republic; software signaled when there was a need for intervention in terms of pest and disease protection. The results of the measurements were then handled by the software and contributed to more effective forecasts and signaling of the pests' activity.

Another network of 20 hydrometeorological stations within the Nitra River basin was installed in 2012, providing monitoring of soil moisture up to 2 m, in addition to the meteorological parameters, The dataset from the network is also used by students of climatology and biometeorology in their final theses, as it allows them to evaluate the change in climate conditions, the impact of land use on soil moisture, and differences within the Nitra basin.

18.8 Involvement of Students

There are several organizations working at the whole-university level, where students are involved. Students and student organizations in SUA have an opportunity to apply for a small financial grant offered by the university rector. The funded project usually aims to support sport, cultural, or leisure time activities of the SUA students.

The Erasmus Student Network effort creates a more mobile and flexible education environment by supporting and developing student exchange as well as providing intercultural experience to those students who are not able to travel abroad. The values of this organization are: (i) unity in diversity, diversity in the unity, (ii) students helping students, (iii) fun in friendship and respect, (iv) international dimension of life, (v) love for Europe as an area of peace and cultural exchange, (vi) openness with tolerance, and (vii) cooperation in the integration. These values, in their ultimate spirit, match with the values of healthy community growth (Gabriels and Benke-Aberg 2020).

AIESEC is an international platform for young people to discover and develop leadership potential. It is a non-political, independent, not-for-profit organization led by students and university graduates. The members are interested in global issues, leadership development, cultural understanding, and practical learning (AIESEC in Slovakia 2021). Regarding this, they organize various internships and projects around the world.

Students have also an opportunity to be a member or participate in the activities organized by:

- University sports center.
- Divadielko na Osmičke, which brings enthusiasts of acting, music, singing, and art together.
- BUTEO hunting club.
- Sokoliari sv. Svorada, which organizes students who want to renovate the falconry on the premises of SUA.
- Cynological club.
- Folklore ensemble Zobor.
- Students' media center, which provides video and audio performances (Slovak University of Agriculture in Nitra 2019).

Every year, the FHLE students organize the "Picnic of the FHLE" and "Punch of the FHLE." Both activities are open for students and the public with an interest in the informal educational activities (Figures 18.11 and 18.12). The program consists of lectures given by graduates, experts, and environmental activists. There is also a small market where students can offer products they have prepared during their leisure time, have a hot or cold drink, and give an informal speech to the employees of the faculty.

The students are actively involved every year and succeed in several competitions. One of them is "Súťaž pre vodu" (competition for water), in which our students have received awards several times, and their ideas have been highly appreciated. The presented topics have been related to soil erosion protection, harvesting of rainwater, recreational use of a small lake, and revitalization of an old marsh. Furthermore, our students received awards from the European Council of Landscape Architecture Schools in 2013 and 2016, the BigSEE Architecture Award in 2020, and several others.

Figure 18.11 Picnic of the FHLE. *Source:* Tárník (2018).

Figure 18.12 Punch of the FHLE. *Source:* Tárník (2018).

18.9 Conclusions and Recommendations

Particularly in the case of natural sciences and precisely due to the excessive technologization of modern life, it is necessary to turn back to nature. The skills and habits acquired during the field excursions and exercises with a natural theme directly connected to nature cannot be replaced by classical teaching. Therefore, the FHLE teachers use a combination of past and current procedures within the teaching process. Even the last year showed us the need to combine standard educational methods and use of new interactive techniques. This is also the best combination for involving students in topics related to sustainable development and its goals, as well as to global megatrends. As part of ensuring the continuity of education and training activities during the current pandemic situation, a wide range of educational materials is available online. Therefore, a wide spectrum of people has free access to them, and the initial reaction has been positive. Several proposals for further cooperation and problem-solving to create modern sustainable communities, cities, and landscape have been introduced. Consequently, the crucial need for educated, progressive, and nature-minded graduates has occurred. As we can see, the education and research activities of the FHLE cover all SDGs, and inform and prepare students and the wider public to achieve these goals.

Based on our experience, we have managed to:

- Continue the combination of different education methods and bring brand new knowledge from the research into the education process.
- Combine theoretical and practical skills during the courses and training in professional organizations.
- Encourage students to study abroad and participate in the activities organized by cooperating universities.
- Organize activities for high school students to present actual topics and give them relevant information at an appropriate level.
- Contribute to scientific activities, even increasing the knowledge of the FHLE educators.
- Support student and teacher mobility to bring new knowledge, good practices, and experiences from abroad to students at the FHLE.

Acknowledgment

This publication was supported by the Operational Program Human Resources within the project: Improving the quality and efficiency of lifelong learning at the Faculty of Horticulture and Landscape Engineering, SUA in Nitra, project code ITMS2014+: 312011D609, co-financed by the European Social Fund and European Regional Development Fund.

References

AIESEC in Slovakia: Activating Youth Leadership Since 1966! (2021). https://aiesec.sk (accessed 9 June 2021).

Gabriels, W. and Benke-Aberg, R. (2020). *Student Exchanges in Times of Crisis – Research Report on the Impact of COVID-19 on Student Exchanges in Europe.*

Igaz, D. and Štěpánková, R. (2020). *Študijná príručka 2020–2021.* Nitra: Slovenská poľnohospodárska univerzita [in Slovak].

Slovak University of Agriculture in Nitra (2019). *Slovak University of Agriculture in Nitra.* Nitra: Slovenská poľnohospodárska univerzita [in Slovak].

UN. Department of Economic and Social Affairs. Division for Sustainable Development Goals (2015). *Transforming our World: The 2030 Agenda for Sustainable Development.* New York: UN.

Part IV

Equity and Inclusion within Sustainability Education

19

Inclusive Education and Sustainable Development: Challenges and Opportunities in Higher Education for Students with Disabilities

Samanmala Dorabawila, Sakunthala Yatigammana, and Anoma Abhayaratne

19.1 Introduction

The importance of education in the development of any society is well recognized. It is recognized as an integral element of the United Nations (UN) Sustainable Development Goal 4 (SDG 4) and a key enabler of all other SDGs. Education empowers learners of all ages with knowledge, skills, values, and attitudes. It will enable them to address the interconnected global challenges, including equality, poverty, climate change, environmental degradation, and loss of biodiversity. SDG 4 underscores the importance of quality, equitable, and inclusive education for all in addressing global problems.

Inclusive education implies making education accessible for all categories of children, in terms of accommodating various needs of these children by finding the optimal way for their education. Inclusive education leads to creating a quality educational environment that will help people with disabilities in many ways. First, it will help to break the vicious cycle of poverty and disability. It will also foster empowering girls/women who often face double discrimination in achieving gender equality. Skills, knowledge, and self-esteem gained through education will enhance the employment opportunities for learners with disabilities. However, due to the restriction of access of children with disabilities to education, they continue to be least likely to achieve basic learning outcomes which do not meet certain perceptions and expectations of the agencies like UN, the World Bank, and Norwegian Agency for Development Cooperation (NORAD) that are committed to achieving education for all.

In many countries, children with disabilities are among the most marginalized and vulnerable and are least likely to have access to education. Many barriers prevent them from attending and benefiting from education. Children with disabilities are less likely to stay in school than their non-disabled peers (World Bank 2019). Among them, about 85% of children of primary school age have never attended school. For those who do attend school, an inaccessible learning environment and a lack of learning support hinder their education. Learning gaps between children with disabilities and their non-disabled peers have widened.

Sri Lanka has been successful in achieving high primary and secondary enrollment rates, outperforming comparable developing countries with the net enrollment rate of 99% in primary education and 84% in junior secondary, and with gender parity in both. According to the population census of 2012, around 2% of children between the ages 5 and 14 have some form

---

The Wiley Handbook of Sustainability in Higher Education Learning and Teaching, First Edition.
Edited by Kelum A. A. Gamage and Nanda Gunawardhana.
© 2022 John Wiley & Sons, Inc. Published 2022 by John Wiley & Sons, Inc.

of disability, of which around only three-fourths attend school, compared to the near-universal enrollment of other children. Further, this share falls considerably with age. According to statistics received from the 2012 census, 34% of children with disabilities in the school attending age do not receive any form of formal education. Furthermore, it has been reported that 20.3% of the children of primary education age do not attend school.

In addition, a very small percentage of children with disabilities who sit for General Certificate in Education in Advanced Level (GCE A/L) receive the opportunity to enroll for higher education. According to available statistics, currently, approximately less than 1% of individuals with disabilities are enrolled in higher education institutions in Sri Lanka (Department of Census and Statistics [DCS] Sri Lanka 2012). To involve more people with disabilities in higher education, it is necessary to create a conducive environment that enables them to carry out their studies on a par with their peers. SDG 4 ensures that both equitable and quality education, as well as inclusion, is available to all. Inclusive, learner-friendly environments are very important in education, for they lead to sustainable development.

Inclusive education is a strategy to make education universalized irrespective of any disability within the learner and to maintain equity in society. It generates thoughts and attention worldwide as a new approach in the provision of services for learners with special needs. As a result, the development of support systems in elementary and high schools has enabled more students with disabilities (SWDs) to complete relevant examinations and apply to higher education. Further, the inclusion of SWDs in higher education has been facilitated by many factors. They are policy documents, the inclusive physical environment and social environments, innovative technologies, inclusive program designs, program delivery modes, and a shared belief among SWDs regarding the positive influence of higher education for their future, including employment and well-being. Thus, the inclusion of SWDs in higher education has increased in recent years (Majoko 2018).

In Sri Lanka, since the opening of the doors of the state Universities to the SWDs, their enrollment rate in higher education has been increasing, though at a slow rate (UGC 2014). If this can be sustained, it will certainly be more favorable and create more opportunities for the students. However, the emergence of challenges together with this process is definite.

This chapter aims at examining the current situation of inclusive education in the Sri Lankan higher education sector in order to identify the challenges, opportunities, and barriers to realizing those opportunities. For that, this chapter discusses the existing policies for inclusive education for persons with disabilities (PWDs), challenges, opportunities, and implications for sustainable development. We expect that the understanding will help stakeholders, activists, and policy-makers in outlining ways to solve the challenges to ensure achieving inclusive education.

19.2 Government Policies for Inclusive Education

This section will outline the policy formulation process for inclusive education for mainly Sri Lankan SWDs, while comparing with India in order to identify the issues with the existing policy framework. Since the completion of secondary education is the stepping stone to higher education for any student, including SWDs, initially, the policies adopted for secondary education are discussed and then we critically evaluate the policies in the higher education sector for both these developing countries.

The concept of "inclusive education" with a focus on special needs education came to the education discourse in 1994 with the signing of the Salamanca Statement and Framework for Action on Special Needs Education that called for countries to adopt policies by the UN (Johnstone et al. 2020). This was followed by the UN Convention on the Rights of PWDs in

2006 (UN-CRPD 2006) for PWDs' full enjoyment of human rights and equality under the law. The Committee on the Rights of PWDs in 2016 further introduced a set of "general comments" for governments on education, under Article 24, explaining and interpreting the right to inclusive education for all PWDs. Article 24 highlights the importance of lifelong learning and states that governments should ensure that PWDs can access higher education, vocational training, adult education, and lifelong learning without discrimination and on an equal basis with others (UN-CRPD 2006). To this end, governments have to ensure that reasonable accommodation is provided to PWDs. In addition to the above, SDG 4 – achieving inclusive and quality education for all – was adopted in 2015 to ensure that all people enjoy peace and prosperity by 2030. This goal further elaborates on the aims of providing equal access to vocational training and achieving universal access to quality higher education. The majority of the developing countries, by ratifying these conventions in their countries have committed to making the required structural changes in their systems. For more than two decades, inclusive education was discussed at various stages, with special emphasis on primary and secondary education, but did not receive adequate policy-level attention for the promotion of inclusive education in higher education in Sri Lanka and some of the developing countries.

Furthermore, the 1972 Sri Lankan Constitution states that "the achievement of complete eradication of illiteracy and the assurance to all persons of the right to universal and equal access to education" is identified as one of the main principles of government policy and its fundamental duties. According to the Constitution of Sri Lanka, every person has a right to education from Grade 1 to university. When the Constitution in principle has identified the necessity of having disability-inclusive education from its inception, then what is needed as a country is to enact appropriate legislation and policies to create the anticipated outcomes. However, the disability community in the country did not feel that it was receiving adequate stimulus and momentum to engage in socioeconomic activities in the same way as other people until 2003. In response to continuous requests from various disability movements in Sri Lanka, the Ministry of Social Welfare enacted the National Policy on Disability for Sri Lanka (NPDS) in 2003 Ministry of Social Welfare (2003). The NPDS document states that the policy framework has been formulated in accordance with the Constitution of Sri Lanka, the UN Charter, and other UN guidelines. The issue at hand is to see how far the NPDS is put into operation in the country for the benefit of the disability community and how it aligns with Article 24 and the SDG 4 toward the benefit of all disability students, and particularly for SWDs in higher education.

In developing countries, especially due to lack of resources, the authorities tend to follow a neutral approach in the allocation of resources, rather than prioritizing and mainstreaming the focus toward inclusive education for SWDs in general, and they turn a blind eye to SWDs in the higher education sector. Attention is directed to such allocation or provisioning only when the desperate need arises and/or when a responsible person or a group highlights the importance. On the contrary, in developed countries, these procedures are embedded in the structures and systems and are invariably followed within the day-to-day activities. The following section will give a summary of salient features of the historical process of policies enacted to enhance disability education up to higher education for Sri Lankan SWDs, while comparing it with India in order to identify the issues with the existing Sri Lankan policy framework.

19.2.1   India

Disability education in India goes way back to the 1880s, with the start of the first schools for deaf people in 1883 and for blind people in 1887. By 2000, there were 3000 special schools in India. In the 1960s, the government initiated a program to train teachers to teach disabled children.

Similar to the Sri Lankan situation, the 1949 Constitution of India itself identifies the right to equality of status and of opportunity for everyone, where Article 45 and also the 2001 93rd Amendment state the need for the provision of free and compulsory education for all children up to the age of 14 years (Sanjeev and Kumar 2007).

The government of India has launched various programs and policy initiatives in order to provide inclusive education to all PWDs. The 1995 Act for PWDs stresses the need to provide free-of-cost education to all children in an appropriate environment until they are 18 years old. Furthermore, the Act elaborates on the following additional measures for the purpose of creating a conducive environment for learning for disabled persons: provide transport facilities or funding to attend schools; remove architectural barriers from educational institutions; supply books, uniforms, and other materials; grant scholarships; set up appropriate environments to redress parental grievances regarding the placement of their children with disabilities; alter the examination procedures to reduce the completely mathematical questions for the benefit of blind students and students with low vision, restructure the curriculum to suit SWDs. These policy initiatives indicate that the Indian education system was willing to provide inclusive education for SWDs by being flexible and accommodating.

The Education for All Movement (Sarva Shiksha Abhiyan [SSA]), an Indian Government program aimed at the universalization of primary education focuses on children with special needs (CWSN) by identifying eight priority areas of intervention for inclusive education (Singal 2010): survey for identification of CWSN; assessment of CWSN; providing assistive devices; networking with non-governmental organizations and government schemes; barrier-free access; training of teachers; appointment of resource teachers; curricula adaptation/textbooks/appropriate technology. These steps can be identified as very constructive measures which are not only applicable to primary education but also any higher educational institution focusing on inclusive education.

The Indian government is far ahead of other developing countries in terms of enacting legislative measures to accommodate PWDs as full and equal members of society. Since the 1995 Act, there have been two Rights of Persons with Disabilities Bills (RPDB), in 2014 and 2016, in India (Government of India 2016). Each of these legislative documents further attempts to make the Indian law agreeable to the UN convention. The 2016 Bill specifically highlights the need for all government institutions of higher education that are receiving aid from the government to reserve not less than 5% of seats for persons with benchmark disabilities. This is landmark legislation for PWDs of this country.

19.2.2 Sri Lanka

Disability education history, according to the Director, Non-formal and Special Education, Ministry of Education, Sri Lanka in 2009, states that the first school for SWDs in Sri Lanka started in 1912 for blind and deaf students. By the 1939 Education Ordinance No. 39, assisted special schools were absorbed into the free education system and by the 1944 Ordinance 30 (1), 75% of the funding of teacher salaries came from the government. The implementation of compulsory education for children 6–14 years in 1961 gave the opportunity to admit children who were not severely disabled. In 1969, SWDs were integrated into regular schools through special classes and more recently through inclusive education by enrollment in regular classes.

In 2006, the government had enough foresight to enforce the Disabled Persons (Accessibility) Regulations, No. 1 of 2006 (Government of Sri Lanka 2006). This law is a comprehensive document that lays out steps necessary to be taken to make a conducive environment for all PWDs in the whole country. In 2014, the government took further steps to formulate a National Action Plan for Disability – A Multisectoral Framework (Ministry of Social Services 2014), which lists the activities based on UN-CRPD 2006. It has a section that outlines the activities to be taken up by higher education institutes in Sri Lanka as well.

The New Education Act, 2009 for General Education further elaborated on the need for inclusive education, with special emphasis on the existing shortcomings; it adopted measures of inclusive education and proposed corrective measures.

In parallel to the above policy initiatives that are directly applicable for SWDs up to the completion of their secondary education, the Sri Lankan higher education system has failed to produce any policy framework with a special focus toward SWDs to facilitate inclusive education in the higher education arena. For instance, in the recent past, the Sri Lankan higher education system has produced two major policy documents within a gap of little more than 10 years with no reference at all to the needs of SWDs. These two documents are University Education Reforms, 1997 (produced by a Presidential Task Force on University Education) (National Education Commission, Sri Lanka [NEC] 1996) and National Policy Framework on Higher Education and Technical and Vocational Education, 2009 (produced by the NEC) (NEC 2009). Though the 2003 NPDS clearly states the policy requirement to achieve inclusive education in the higher education sector, none of it is included or considered in the National Policy Framework, 2009 of the NEC. This is an indication that there was no coordination between the NEC and the Ministry of Social Welfare that formulated the NPDS.

There is further evidence to show that the focus toward SWDs in the higher education sector in Sri Lanka is not the policy-makers' or administrators' priority. For example, in one of the leading state universities in Sri Lanka, in 2014, authorities diverted a huge fund that was specifically given to construct disability accessible ramps in the faculties to other capital works that the administrators felt was important. This is manifested at national-level statistics if one analyses data from the Population and Housing Census of 2012 on persons with disability, who are five years and above (see Tables 19.1 and 19.2) (DCS 2012). According to this census, 8.7% of the total population who are five years and above are identified as disabled persons. This is an increase in the country's disabled persons of 2.1% according to 2001 population census data (the big gap could be attributed to differences in the definitions used for the survey).

The country has ratified all the UN conventions, SDGs, and the Constitution from its inception, stating the importance of inclusive education for all, which includes PWDs. However, as shown in Table 19.2, 13.9% of the PWDs in the country have no schooling and only 1.3% have received some form of higher education according to the 2012 Population Census. Census data also reveals 34.6% of PWDs in the country have received only primary education, which means that 48.5% have received no education at all or only completed primary education. In 2012, 0.1% of disabled persons were enrolled in a degree program or a postgraduate degree program.

Disability prevalence in East Asian and South Asian countries is given in Table 19.1. The table shows that there is a large variation in the disability prevalence levels among the countries. The developed countries, other than Japan, have a relatively high disability prevalence percentage and developing countries have relatively low values.

19.3 Challenges and Opportunities in Higher Education for Students with Disabilities

The emergence of challenges together with this process is unavoidable. In this section, the challenges and opportunities are described under the subtopics of attitudes and society, accessibility, awareness of the needs of disabled students, lack of resources (physical and human), and employability.

Table 19.1 Disability prevalence in East Asian and South Asian countries.

Country	Prevalence (%)	Source
Australia	19	ABS Survey of Disability, Aging and Care-Givers (1998)
Cambodia	1.5	Cambodia Socio-Economic Surveys (1999)
China	5	Sampling survey in 1987 and the growth rate of the population
Fiji	1.5	1996 Census
Indonesia	0.7	Core National Social and Economic Survey (SUSENAS) 2000
Japan	4.4	Cabinet Office Annual Report 2000
Korea (Republic of)	3	National Survey of the Disabled Persons, 2000
Mongolia	4.8	Mongolian Ministry of Social Welfare and Labor, 2001
New Zealand	20	National Household Survey, 1996
Philippines	1.3	National Census 1995
Thailand	0.3/1.4/8.1	National Census in 1990/Health and Welfare Survey 1991/Ministry of Public Health Survey, 1996
Tonga	2	Fiji Disabled People's Association, 2001
Vietnam[a]	6.4	Disability survey or component in other surveys, 2005
Sri Lanka[b]	1.6	2001 Census
Bangladesh[a]	2.5	Disability survey or component in other surveys, 2005
India[a]	2.1/8.7	2001 Census/2012 Census
Bhutan[a]	3.4	2005 Census
Maldives[a]	3.4	2003 Census

[a] World Report on Disability, 2011.
[b] Population Census of Sri Lanka, 2001 and 2012.
Source: other data from Takamine (2004).

Table 19.2 Total disability persons by education level.

Total population (5 years and above)	Primary	Secondary[1]	GCE (O/L)[2]	GCE (A/L)[3]	Degree and above	No schooling	
1 617 924	558 075	547 294	182 016	83 650	21 613	225 276	100
34.6	33.8	11.2	5.2	1.3	13.9		

Source: Population Census 2012. DCS 2012.

19.3.1 Attitudes and Society

Social acceptance is directly related to the attitude of the different stakeholders in society, which directly affect the sustainable development of inclusive education. Attitude refers to predisposition or perception, or the response of an individual toward an animate or inanimate object, event, subject, or person among others (Offor and Akinlosotu 2017). According to social learning theory (Bandura 1977), attitudes are not innate and they form through social and cultural processes in which parents, teachers, peers, and significant others play important roles. The attitudes of society toward PWDs are mainly influenced by people's knowledge of the disability and their contact with individuals with disabilities (Wang et al. 2021). Concerning higher education for SWDs, the attitudes of different stakeholders may vary and have been changed from time to time. For instance, if the relevant stakeholders pay attention to the development of support systems and learning technologies that will open more opportunities for learning for SWDs, this can be seen as a positive change in their attitude toward the SWDs. This change has created a favorable learning environment in elementary and high schools, enabling more SWDs to successfully complete school examinations and enter higher education. Gradually, this influence has resulted in a growing demand for higher education by SWDs. In response, all higher education institutions began to develop support systems and learning technologies, which helped individuals with disabilities.

In the literature, the information related to the negative attitudes of the society toward the provision of education for SWDs from elementary education to higher education is common. For instance, including children with disabilities in regular schools is a challenge faced by many countries (Eleweke and Rodda 2002). Based on a study on Greek teachers' beliefs toward educational inclusion, Zoniou-Sideri and Vlachou (2006) reveal that regular teachers hold several restrictive as well as conflicting beliefs toward disability and educational inclusion. These teachers reported that although educational inclusion is necessary as a means of improving the way ordinary school functions and reducing the marginalization and stigmatization of SWDs, provision of special education separated from other students is important in providing a secure environment to those with disabilities. It also serves as a way of covering some deficiencies in ordinary education. Similarly, according to Florian (2012), many teachers in Scotland resist including SWDs in their classrooms, believing that inclusion interferes with the effective education of other students. Rao (2004) identifies the negative attitudes as one of the most powerful barriers to the inclusion of SWDs in all aspects of social belonging and functioning, including higher education. SWDs have historically been marginalized and discriminated against in higher education over the world (Madriaga 2007). For instance, before the attainment of political independence from Great Britain in 1980, most Black and Indian SWDs, and also those of color, in Zimbabwe were excluded from higher education because of the racist colonial regime (Chateau 2008; Majoko 2005). A study, conducted by the Organisation for Economic Co-operation and Development (OECD) in 2003 reported that attitudes of decision-makers and higher education professionals toward disability and SWDs as one of the barriers that are commonly encountered in this regard. Majoko (2018) noted that non-disclosure of disabilities of students for fear of stigmatization and refusal of admission and registration in higher education interfered with their participation in learning. Moreover, teachers' identification of SWDs interfered with their participation in learning as their capabilities were undermined. Similarly, previous research indicates that teachers' practices and attitudes are barriers to participation for SWDs in higher education (Chiparaushe et al. 2016). Moreover, the sympathetic behavior of teachers toward SWDs fostered negative self-perception in them which hampered their participation in learning. This finding aligns with past research which revealed that overprotection of SWDs by teachers is a barrier to the participation of these students in learning (Chataika 2008).

Attitudinal barriers include negative attitudes of students without disabilities toward those with disabilities (Chikwature et al. 2016) and disablist practices and attitudes of staff in higher education institutions (Madriaga 2007). Past studies have indicated that teachers require in-service training to be equipped with the positive attitudes, knowledge, skills, competencies, and understanding to meet the individual needs of SWDs in higher education institutions (Chiparaushe et al. 2016). Most importantly, social change in attitudes of students and faculty toward people with disabilities is necessary for social inclusion and equal opportunities for SWDs (Sachs and Schreuer 2011).

19.3.2 Accessibility

In developed as well as developing countries, postsecondary education is considered to be a decisive factor in securing a meaningful employment opportunity, while creating avenues for progression within the job. Due to various disability conditions among PWDs, the available jobs for which they will be hired are very limited. Therefore, access to inclusive secondary education as well as higher education can be crucial for a disabled person in securing any employment opportunity that will enable them to live a quality life (Sachs and Schreuer 2011).

In the general setting, according to Lewin (2015), accessibility to education requires timely enrollment for educational programs and advancement at an appropriate age, regular attendance, learning consistent with national targets, a conducive environment for learning, and opportunities to learn that are equitably distributed.

The accessibility barriers that the SWDs encounter can be mainly of three forms: structural, attitudinal, and technical (Alsalem and Doush 2018). Structural barriers include barriers in admission to programs as well as physical barriers. The solution to these barriers solely depends on the responsible authorities, such as the legislators, UGC, policy-makers, and the administrators in higher education. It is important to have proper coordination among these personnel while having a clear understanding of the SWDs' requirements. In addition, most universities in Sri Lanka as well as in other developing countries are inaccessible to SWDs.

In the context of accessibility, SWDs enrollment rates in higher education institutions are used to measure rights to inclusive education in a country. The 2012 Population Census recorded that only 0.8% of the total PWDs are engaged in post-secondary education programs in Sri Lanka.

Another source to indicate the rate of enrollment in higher education in Sri Lanka is the UGC Annual Reports. The 2012/2013 report states that, out of the 144,816 total students eligible to apply for admission to 16 universities in Sri Lanka that are funded by the government, only 24,185 (0.2% of the total eligible) of the students were admitted. Of those admitted, only 73 (0.003% of the total admitted) were blind or differently abled students (this chapter refers to both as SWDs).The UGC only admits SWDs for four areas of course of studies, namely Arts (59), Commerce (10), Biological Science (3), and Physical Science (1). This is another occasion where SWDs are deprived of their rights to equalized opportunities in higher education (UGC 2014).

As stated in the UGC Handbook for undergraduate admissions, admission criteria for SWDs are very vague. It reads that the UGC can, at the request of the universities, decide to admit a limited number of blind students to courses of study in Arts, and other SWDs who can submit a medical certificate confirming disability to courses of study in Arts, Commerce, Biological Science, and Physical Science. It clearly shows that SWDs are not allowed to be admitted to other fields of study in national universities. According to the above criteria, the decision to admit SWDs into a specific university is decided based on the university's request, not on the requirements or a policy decision. In addition, even after the SWDs secure their admissions into the specified courses of study programs, again, they are deprived of the opportunity to select their choice of the field of study program within the faculty. For instance, in the Faculty of Arts at the University of Peradeniya, the SWDs have been continuously reporting that they do not have an opportunity to select programs in their preferred fields of study, especially in certain departments (Liyanage 2017; Yatigammana et al. 2021). This is again a deprivation of the right to equalized accessibility to higher education for the SWDs. As a solution to this problem, the University of Peradeniya has recently proposed a set of special criteria that can be followed in selecting the SWDs for various programs in the faculty.

Furthermore, there is the possibility that there can be students with mental disabilities that are not disclosed to the university, or those who have developed mental conditions while undergoing the study program. There is no evidence to show that these numbers are reported or recorded in Sri Lankan universities. In this context, it should be the responsibility of the Special Needs Resource Centers (SNRC) to keep a proper track of these student numbers and their requirements.

One reads about "Pera's blind Professor with a broad vision," Wimal Weerakkody, a dedicated academician at the University of Peradeniya, who is recognized as the person who spearheaded the establishment of an SNRC at the university and maintained the Center until he retired. In this, one can observe that the Sri Lankan higher education system was not completely discriminatory toward SWDs. That is to say, there was accessibility to higher education for SWDs from as far back as 1968 when Weerakkody entered the university as an undergraduate student. He did not receive access to higher education on a special intake category as takes place now. When he was a student, SWDs had to enter the universities on the same basis as the non-disabled students, by competing on the same platform to gain admission.

It was his total dedication and motivation to see that the SWDs complete their undergraduate degree that promoted him to find funding to maintain the SNRC until his retirement. Today, the University of Peradeniya is a highly sought-after university by SWDs in Sri Lanka. This is clearly seen in the study on accessibility to tertiary education in the country (Hettiarachchi et al. 2014), which quotes SWDs expressing their opinions based on their experiences and needs. For instance, one student says, "When I saw the hill, I felt afraid...I went to the UGC four times to change my university, with no luck...I wanted to go to Pera...I lost one year staying at home trying to get to Pera." After his dedicated pioneering efforts to maintain the Center at the University of Peradeniya, one can find several centers established at several other universities in Sri Lanka.

However, gaining admission to a university is not the only barrier that an SWD will encounter in entering higher education. One of the main barriers to is maintaining regular attendance at classes in the same way as the other students. There should be a conducive environment for SWDs to learn within the university. One of the main requirements for most of them is physical accessibility to the university (Yatigammana et al. 2021). The study by Hettiarrachchi et al. (2014) is a very good source for obtaining an assessment of the extent of difficulties the SWDs encounter in terms of barriers to physical accessibility to all state universities in Sri Lanka. For instance, although the University of Peradeniya caters to the largest number of SWD admissions in the country's university system, until 2020 there was not even a disabled accessible ramp to enter a classroom for learning. Whenever an SWD enters a classroom either the parents or their peers walk them to the classroom or carry them. After submitting a proposal through a competitive bidding process for financial assistance from the World Bank, the University of Peradeniya, Faculty of Arts is, after more than 75 years, establishing disabled accessible ramps and elevators. Finally, in 2021, the University of Peradeniya, Faculty of Arts was made completely disabled accessible physically. In addition, this and several other national universities have approved a policy for SWDs for implementation.

Literature on accessibility to education states that there are more barriers for SWDs at higher education level than at secondary education level (Webster 2004; Alsalem and Doush 2018; Hettiarachchi et al. 2014). This is further substantiated in Hettiarrachchi et al.'s (2014) study in which a student states that "At the beginning, I was unhappy with how difficult it was for me to access everything. I was expecting the university to be much better than school, but there were still many obstacles to face..."

One of the main barriers for access is the unavailability of a proper functioning office for SWDs in the universities to coordinate and connect the SWDs and other academics and non-academics functioning in the universities. Many universities in developed and developing countries where the programs for SWDs function smoothly have systematically functioning SNRCs (IIBM 2012; Hector 2020). The SNRC can and should play a major role in improving and maintaining the SWDs life in the universities. Only a few of the state universities in Sri Lanka have a functional SNRC for SWDs. Their functions are very limited because there is no cadre allocation for a competent person to be hired to take responsibility for the Center. The main reason for this is that the Centers function from charity funding or ad hoc funding that comes when the need arises. It is commendable that in 2021, the UGC has taken a positive initiative to establish an SNRC in each state university while assuring the provision of required physical and human resources to sustain their functioning.

In comparing the Sri Lankan situation with the Indian situation, India seems far better in terms of the commitment from the authorities to facilitate inclusive education for the SWDs in higher education. Krishnan (2012), in proceedings from an organized by the Indian Institute of Management, Bangalore (IIMB) states that according to the 1995 Act for PWDs, public higher education institutions such as IIM and Indian Institute of Technology (IIT) reserve a 3% quota of their seats for persons with disability (IIMB 2012). But, with the 2016 bill, the quota has increased to 5%, in addition, the identified disabilities for the quota have increased from 7 to 21 disabilities, opening avenues for the SWDs to obtain medical degrees as well in India. Furthermore, this form of allocation of a specific quota for admission of SWDs to higher education institutions is imperative if the higher education system is to promote inclusive education. When the 2016 Indian Disabilities Bill was passed the government gave a two-year deadline to ensure PWDs get barrier-free access in all kinds of physical infrastructure and transport systems.

Barriers to physical accessibility are not the only barrier to access to higher education. Attitudinal barriers toward SWDs can arise from multiple sources during university life. These barriers can come from any of the stakeholders involved in the process of learning, such as the academics staff, non-academic staff, and peers in the university. And there is evidence to say that there are situations when the students themselves are reluctant to disclose their difficulties and request special consideration be given to their situation (Gilson and Dymond 2012). Especially in the South, historically, attitudes are socioculturally constructed and deeply rooted in the mindset of the people, which seems to negatively impact the integration of inclusive education for SWDs in the Sri Lankan setting as well (Liyanage 2017). One can clearly understand the extent of these attitudes from one of the experiences of Wimal Weerakkody, who, says a newspaper article:

> recalls the incident of a fellow undergraduate who went back to his room because the blind "apala" student Wimal Weerakkody had stepped onto his path while he was heading for an exam. Such incidents and attitudes are not only sad and embarrassing but also detrimental to the creation of a positive environment for the visually impaired within our country. (*Sunday Times*, 18 September 2011)

Technical barriers occur when technology cannot be adapted into another format that can be accessed by assistive devices (Whiteneck et al. 2004). Today, technology has become an important component of all our lives, particularly during the COVID-19 pandemic. During this pandemic, SWDs in the developing countries have encountered many technological barriers due to financial constraints, exposure to illness, and not having the proper training for available software and hardware when universities were closed and adopted online teaching and learning (due to emergency remote learning) and at the same time conducted online assessments. In some ways, blind students did benefit from the online teaching and the uploading of the recorded lessons, but they could not transcribe uploaded lesson materials into Braille documents because they did not have the required assistive technology or equipment in their homes or nearby. However, deaf students were at a disadvantage because the recorded or online lessons were not subtitled. A need assessments survey conducted in four universities in Sri Lanka states that 84% of the SWDs use some form of technology for their studies (Yatigammana et al. 2021). Some technological barriers that are encountered by SWDs are lack of computers; hardware such as large monitors; Braille printers; software, such as screen readers, screen magnification, or speech recognition programs); and other assistive technologies. This technological equipment should be available for the SWDs in the SNRCs, and it is the responsibility of the SNRC to ensure that all SWDs receive exposure to these during their orientation program in order to facilitate the process of smoothly blending into the postsecondary environment, which can be totally different from the SWDs' earlier experiences (IIBM 2012; Hector 2020).

19.3.3 Awareness of the Needs of Disabled Students

The idea of simply placing SWDs in a teaching or practical session with typically developing students is not enough to truly create an inclusive environment demonstrating behaviors of acceptance and positive attitude (Rillotta and Nettelbeck 2007). Thus, awareness of the needs of the disabled students helps in moderating the conventional mindset of society, while providing vast opportunities for everyone to get involved in creating a positive and inclusive society for all in higher education settings. The awareness of PWDs indicates an education in society of disabilities and how an individual could make the necessary changes. However, over the recent decades, the importance of disability awareness has been given prominence, making it easier for society to develop its consideration toward SWDs. The university students' perceptions show that SWDs often perceive that faculty, staff, and administrators lack information regarding disability issues, have "poor" attitudes toward them, and are not responsive to accommodation requests (Dowrick et al. 2005; Farone et al. 1998). Moreover, it has been identified that the lack of teaching staff awareness of the SWDs is a barrier to participation for SWDs in higher education institutions (Gibson 2012).

Considering the Sri Lankan higher education sector, the lack of awareness about the needs of SWDs could be highlighted as a major issue among all stakeholders (Yatigammana et al. 2021). This report by Yatigammana et al. emphasizes the issues that SWDs face due to the lack of awareness of other stakeholders. They are the lack of trust in SWDs in the university, the misunderstanding others have of SWDs, problems faced in classrooms, examinations and collecting and evaluating SWDs' answer scripts, providing opportunities in engaging sports activities and other extracurricular activities in the university, and allocating university funds for SWDs. Moreover, the SWDs highlighted the importance of Vice-Chancellors, Deans, and Heads of the Department, academic and non-academic staff members, students/peers, and student counselors having awareness of their needs. Moreover, in the report, the SWDs have highlighted the need and the importance of conducting continuous awareness/training programs for both academic and non-academic staff through the Staff Development Center to enhance the awareness that leads to change in attitudes in order to create an inclusive environment for the SWDs. Furthermore, the students struggle to follow classes due to the pace and mode of delivery and due to the ambient noise levels and acoustics of the lecture hall (Hettiarachchi et al. 2014).

Thus, disability awareness is important for academic staff members as a professional development strategy. Furthermore, administrators and non-academic staff members also need to be educated on disabilities in order to have a more positive attitude and to create an inclusive environment for all students. Research findings also found awareness programs to be essential for all stakeholders as they can develop positive attitudes toward SWDs (Morin et al. 2008).

19.3.4 Lack of Resources (Physical and Human)

Many countries around the world have encountered problems in providing higher education learning opportunities for SWDs in an inclusive approach, due to the non-existence of adequate physical and human resources in higher education institutes. Much research identifies as barriers to implementing inclusion inadequacies in facilities and trained personnel, ineffective and inefficient use of technology, lack of funding, and lack of support for teachers practicing inclusion (Furuta 2009). Parveen (2018) points out that India, as a developing country has many problems such as lack of well-educated teachers, ill-planned curriculum, inadequate resources, lack of good infrastructural facilities, lack of awareness, and negative attitudes, all of which act as hurdles for extending the concept of inclusive education.

A study in Kosovo by Zabeli et al. (2021) reports that SWDs experience various barriers to higher education that are related to rigid curriculum, inappropriate teaching, and assessment methods, etc. Moreover, relating to the appropriate teaching and learning approaches for SWDs, other authors demand the implementation of inclusive pedagogies that respond to the individual differences without the differentiated treatment toward some students (Florian 2014). The main barriers to the spread of this inclusive pedagogy are found in the lack of consensus among faculty members on its meaning (Stentiford and Koutsouris 2020), as well as in the poor training of faculty in inclusive education. This hampers the implementation of inclusive strategies in university classrooms (Moriña 2017). In addition, Martins et al. (2018) identify that the prevailing instructional and methodological strategies continue to be characterized by the use of standard methodologies and study plans that hinder the academic achievement of students. Furthermore, in Sweden, the biggest obstacle pointed out by the students was the negative attitude of the members of the institutions on aspects such as the veracity of the disability, teaching methodologies that do not facilitate inclusion, and the need for regular and punctual attendance in the classroom by SWDS without considering their issues (Moriña 2017). In some instances, teachers with negative attitudes toward SWDs have been identified as a key barrier. Those with a poor understanding of differing needs, limited knowledge of how to make course content accessible, and lack of willingness and/or time to make reasonable adjustments can prevent SWDs benefiting from education (Mullins and Preyde 2013).

Lack of resources is also identified as one of the major challenges faced by the SWDs in Sri Lankan universities and higher education institutions (Hettiarachchi et al. 2014). This study by Hettiarachchi et al reports that the availability of services and their convenience or user-friendliness to the students accessing them were not at a satisfactory level. Most of the SWDs highlighted that teachers were not sensitive enough toward them while delivering lectures, giving assignments, releasing results, and so forth. They also have to face some difficulties related to administrative matters due to a lack of awareness among non-academic staff toward disability. Yatigammana et al. (2021) report the following as SWDs' suggestions for enhancing the status of their university life: providing facilities to use technology; academic materials; disability access to libraries, lecture rooms, and other places; financial assistance, and opportunities to enhance English competency.

19.3.5 Employability

Securing jobs for people with a disability is a challenge, as employers are reluctant to hire them. It is not easy for them to get an opportunity to gain work experience and maximize their potential in the working world. However, the employability of a person with a disability is enhanced when they gain a bachelor's degree. Even though some of SWDs have basic learning skills and acquire vocational skills through training, employment opportunities are very limited as work experience is considered to be one of the criteria in a job application.

University education is expected to provide knowledge and skills that will assist students in the workforce; however, it appears that many educated disabled persons will not obtain the jobs they desire upon graduation (Fichten et al. 2012). Furthermore, disabled graduates are more likely to be unemployed as well as underemployed than their non-disabled counterparts (Allen and Konin 2019). Thus, these disparities highlight the need to inquire about the factors that support SWDs' employment. Very little is known about the skills and the resources that sustain SWDs through their educational career (earlier) and toward employment (later) (Madriaga et al. 2010). Therefore, it is imperative to explore required skills and resources that can enhance the potential of SWDs to obtain opportunities to gain work experience in actual work environments and employment, so that they will be able to get jobs and earn a living on their own. For example, a study carried out in Greece (Allarakhia 2019), points out that networking with professors, classmates, and business partners involved with the university can help secure an internship, while pursuing a relevant degree and this can lead to a connection with a future employer or someone else in the related field. Also, volunteering for organizations that relate to the career path one hopes to pursue is an important measure to consider in this regard.

Discrimination in advertising job vacancies arising from attitudes, misunderstandings, and poor awareness of employers is found to be another major challenge to securing jobs for SWDs. Creating awareness, enforcement of laws related to disability, providing information, guidance, and training, providing a support system, and strengthening the association of disability are some ways to improve employability.

These views are supported by evidence from Sri Lanka (Liyanage 2017). The charity perspective toward PWDs plays a crucial role, even in the higher educational setting. Evidence suggests that SWDs in higher education need empowerment to face the challenges while mobilizing with society. The university can play a crucial role in empowering them to effectively mobilize not only with the university community, but also the entire society. However, this fact has not come into the purview of the university community.

19.4 Conclusion – Achieving Sustainable Development through Inclusive Education

An inclusive education approach that makes education accessible for all by way of accommodating their various needs has many implications for sustainable development by empowering people with skills, knowledge, and self-esteem. In this final section of the chapter, we critically evaluate the current situation and extent of the implementation of inclusive education in higher education in Sri Lanka. We draw on good practices and experiences of countries discussed in previous studies to make recommendations.

Sri Lankan policy-makers had the foresight to produce the necessary policy and legal framework for inclusive education more than two decades ago by way of initially ratifying the UN Conventions to protect the rights of PWDs. Since then, several positive steps have been taken to introduce and maintain inclusive education at the school level. However, there is a certain level of observable improvements, and further improvements are possible depending on the availability of resources, commitment, and capacity development of all relevant stakeholders. In comparison with the commitment to inclusiveness in general education, the status of the same at higher education is at a very poor level. The relevant authorities have not taken any measure to create a conducive environment for SWDs for teaching and learning.

For instance, recently implemented higher education policy documents have ignored inclusive education. Furthermore, there is no coordination between and among stakeholders from the start of the formulation of higher education policies in Sri Lanka. If inclusive education for sustainable development is to be implemented successfully, it is essential to have direct links between institutions that are expected to implement the policy.

There are a lot of loopholes and vague statements in the admission criteria used for admitting SWDs to national universities under the special admission category. The proposed criteria have to be more specific and not limit the types of disabilities only to blind, deaf, and other disabilities. The other disabilities have to be clearly listed and specify the level of disability acceptable for each degree program. The system needs to identify the exact quota of students that can gain admission to national universities.

The National Higher Education Policy (NHEP) 2009 needs to be reformulated or amended to ensure the fulfillment of requirements of SWDs for higher education. This policy should make it a necessary condition for each higher education institution to formulate and implement a disability policy. In the process of reformulating the NHEP, it has to specify a time frame to make sure that, by a certain date, all higher education institutions are physically accessible to SWDs. The policy document should make it a requirement for budgetary allocations from respective universities to purchase and maintain assistive technology for SWDs. The policy document should specify as a requirement that each institution build the human capacity to match this assistive technology.

The most important aspect to activate inclusive education in the higher education system is increasing awareness of the existing national as well as institutional policies, specific needs of SWDs, and available existing assistive technologies. There should be a mechanism that identifies the level and form of transmitting this awareness among teaching and non-teaching staff.

To make inclusive education a successful goal in higher education, it is necessary to have a comprehensive national policy framework with a focus on SWDs. There should be an implementation mechanism of the policies without limiting them only to paper. In order to fulfill this, the authorities from top to bottom should be sensitized to the requirements of SWDs at every level. If all these initiatives are put into action, they will positively contribute to reaching the expected levels of sustainable development goals.

References

Allarakhia, H. (2019). Employability and college graduates with disabilities. https://www.diverseeducation.com/demographics/disabilties/article/15105185/employability-and-college-graduates-with-disabilities (accessed 19 May 19 2021).

Allen, M. and Konin, K. (2019). What happens next?: latest report on the first destinations of disabled graduates. www.agcas.org.uk/write/MediaUploads/Resources/Disability TG/What_Happens_Next_report_2019.pdf (accessed 3 June 2021).

Alsalem, G.M. and Doush, I.A. (2018). Access education: what is needed to have accessible higher education for students with disabilities in Jordan? *International Journal of Special Education* 33 (3): 541–561.

Bandura, A. (1977). *Social Learning Theory*. Englewood Cliffs, NJ: Prentice Hall.

Chataika, T. (2008). Inclusion of disabled students in higher education in Zimbabwe: From idealism to reality- A social ecosystem perspective. *Disability & Society* 23 (7): 677–678.

Chateau, A. (2008) Langues-U: A digital campus to increase students' autonomy? Language Centres at Universities: Crossing Bridges, Integrating Cultures, 115–122. https://hal.archives-ouvertes.fr/hal-00538527

Chikwature, W., Oyedele, V., and Ntini, R. (2016). Incorporating inclusive education in the pre-service teacher education curriculum in Zimbabwean Teachers' colleges. *European Journal of Research & Reflection in Educational Studies* 4 (4): 1–19.

Chiparaushe, B., Mapako, O., and Makarau, A. (2016). *A Survey of Challenges, Opportunities and Threats Faced by Students with Disabilities in the Post-Independent Era in Zimbabwe*. Harare, Zimbabwe: Solidarity Trust.

Department of Census and Statistics, Sri Lanka (2012). Disability in Sri Lanka. https://unstats.un.org/unsd/demographic-social/meetings/2016/bangkok--disability-measurement-and-statistics/Session-6/Sri Lanka.pdf (accessed 4 May 2021).

Dowrick, P.W., Anderson, J., Heyer, K., and Acosta, J. (2005). Postsecondary education across the USA: experiences of adults with Disabilities. *Journal of Vocational Rehabilitation* 22: 41–47.

Eleweke, C.J. and Rodda, M. (2002). The challenge of enhancing inclusive education in developing countries. *International Journal of Inclusive Education* 6 (2): 113–126. http://doi.org/10.1080/13603110110067190.

Farone, M.C., Hall, E.W., and Costello, J.J. (1998). Postsecondary disability issues: an inclusive identification strategy. *Journal of Postsecondary Education and Disability* 13: 35–45.

Fichten, C., Shirley, J., Havel, A. et al. (2012). What happens after graduation? Outcomes, employment, and recommendations of recent junior/community college graduates with and without disabilities. *Disability and Rehabilitation* 34: 917–924.

Florian, L. (2012). Preparing teachers to work in inclusive classrooms: key lessons for the professional development of teacher educators from Scotland's Inclusive Practice Project. *Journal of Teacher Education* 63 (4): 275–285.

Florian, L. (2014). What counts as evidence of inclusive education? *European Journal of Special Needs Education* 29 (3): 286–294.

Furuta, H. (2009). Responding to educational needs of children with disabilities: care and education in special pre-schools in the North Western Province of Sri Lanka. *Japanese Journal of Special Education* 46 (6): 457–447.

Gibson, S. (2012). Narrative accounts of university education: Socio-cultural perspectives of students with disabilities. *Disability & Society* 27: 353–369.

Gilson, C.L. and Dymond, S.K. (2012). Barriers impacting students with disabilities at a Hong Kong university. *Journal of Postsecondary Education and Disability* 25 (2): 103–118.

Government of India. (2016). The rights of persons with disabilities act 2016 – India, Government of India. https://doi.org/10.30834/kjp.33.1.2020.183.

Government of Sri Lanka (2006). The gazette of the democratic socialist of republic of Sri Lanka – disabled persons (accessibility) regulations, No. 1 of 2006.

Hector, M. (2020). Arriving at thriving. Policy connect and the higher education commission. www.policyconnect.org.uk/research/arriving-thriving-learning-disabled-students-ensure-access-all (accessed 20 June 2021).

Hettiarachchi, S., Attanayake, L.D., Ranaweera, M. et al. (2014). Accessing tertiary education: expectations and realities for students experiencing disabilities. *Journal of the Faculty of the Graduate Studies* 3: 147–170.

IIMB Indian Institute of Management, B (2012). *Enabling Access for Persons with Disabilities to Higher Education and Workplace Role of ICT and Assistive Technologies*. IIMB.

Johnstone, C., Schuelka, M.J., and Swadek, G. (2020). Quality education for all? The promises and limitations of the SDG Framework for inclusive education and students with disabilities. In: *Grading Goal Four* (ed. A. Wulff), 96–115. Brill https://doi.org/10.1163/9789004430365_004.

Lewin, K. (2015). Educational access, equity, and development: planning to make rights realities. UNESCO Digital Library. https://unesdoc.unesco.org/ark:/48223/pf0000235003 (accessed 27 May 2021).

Liyanage, C. (2017). Sociocultural construction of disability in Sri Lanka: charity to rights-based approach. In: *Inclusion, Disability and Culture* (ed. S. Halder and L.C. Assaf), 251–265. Springer https://doi.org/10.1007/978-3-319-55224-8.

Madriaga, M. (2007). Enduring disablism: Students with dyslexia and their pathways into UK higher education and beyond. *Disability & Society* 22 (4): 399–412.

Madriaga, M., Hanson, K., Heaton, C. et al. (2010). Confronting similar challenges? Disabled and non-disabled students' learning and assessment experiences. *Studies in Higher Education* 35 (6): 647–665.

Majoko, T. (2005). Specialist teachers' perceptions on the inclusion of children with disabilities mainstream school system in Zimbabwe. Unpublished BEd thesis. Masvingo State University, Zimbabwe.

Majoko, T. (2018). Participation in higher education : voices of students with disabilities participation in higher education : voices of students with disabilities. *Cogent Education* 5 (1): 1–17. https://doi.org/10.1080/2331186X.2018.1542761.

Martins, M., Borges, M.L., and Gonçalves, T. (2018). Attitudes towards inclusion in higher education in a Portuguese university. *International Journal of Inclusive Education* 22 (5): 527–542.

Ministry of Social Services (2014). National Action Plan for Disability. https://baixardoc.com/documents/draft-national-action-plan-for-disability-sri-lanka-june-2013-5cc4bbc9e8648 (accessed 26 November 2021).

Ministry of Social Welfare. (2003). '*National Policy on Disability for Sri Lanka*', Ministry of Social Welfare, Sethsiripaya, Battaramulla, Sri Lanka.

Morin, D., Rivard, M., Crocker, A.G. et al. (2008). Public attitudes towards intellectual disability: A multidimensional perspective. *Journal of Intellectual Disability Research* 57 (3): 279–292.

Moriña, A. (2017). Inclusive education in higher education: Challenges and opportunities. *European Journal of Special Needs Education* 32 (1): 3–17.

Mullins, L. and Preyde, M. (2013). The lived experience of students with an invisible disability at a Canadian university. *Disability & Society* 28 (2): 147–160. https://doi.org/10.1080/09687599.2012.752127.

National Education Commission Sri Lanka (1996). National higher education policy –1996. http://nec.gov.lk/wp-content/uploads/2014/04/National_Policy_1996.pdf (accessed 26 November 2021).

National Education Commission Sri Lanka (2009). National Policy Framework on Higher Education 2009. http://nec.gov.lk/wp-content/uploads/2014/04/national-policy-on-higher-education-2009.pdf (accessed 26 November 2021).

Offor, D.I. and Akinlosotu, N.T. (2017). Teachers' attitude towards special need students in secondary schools in north Senatorial District of Edo state, Nigeria. *Journal of Education and Practice* 8 (4): 6–12.

Parveen, A. (2018). Inclusive education and the challenges. *National Journal of Multidisciplinary Research and Development* 3 (2): 64–68.

Rao, S. (2004). Faculty attitudes and students with disabilities in higher education: a literature review. *College Student Journal* 28: 191–198.

Rillotta, F. and Nettelbeck, T.E.D. (2007). Effects of an awareness program on attitudes of students without an intellectual disability towards persons with an intellectual disability. *Journal of Intellectual and Developmental Disability* 32: 19–27.

Sachs, D. and Schreuer, N. (2011). Inclusion of students with disabilities in higher education: performance and participation in Student's experiences. *Disability Studies Quarterly* 31 (2): https://dsq-sds.org/article/view/1593/1561 (accessed 16 August 2021).

Sanjeev, K. and Kumar, K. (2007). Inclusive education in India. *Electronic Journal for Inclusive Education* 2 (2): https://corescholar.libraries.wright.edu/ejie/vol2/iss2/7 (accessed 18 June 2021).

Singal, N. (2010). Education of children with disabilities in India: a critique, *Education for All Global Monitoring Report*. UNESCO.

Stentiford, L. and Koutsouris, G. (2020). What are inclusive pedagogies in higher education? *A systematic scoping review. Studies in Higher Education* 46 (11): 1–17.

Takamine, Y. (2004). Disability issues in East Asia: Review and ways forward. Paper No. 2004-1. http://documents.worldbank.org/curated/en/985381468036886062/pdf/292990Disability0paper 0final0May02004.pdf (accessed 28 May 2021).

UN CRPD. (2006). General assembly, convention on the rights of persons with disabilities: resolution Adopted by the General Assembly (24 January 2007) A/RES/61/106.

University Grants Commission (UGC), (2014) Annual Report – University Grant Commission – 2014. University Grant Commission.

Wang, Z., Xu, X., Han, Q. et al. (2021). Factors associated with public attitudes towards persons with disabilities: A systematic review. https://doi.org/10.1186/s12889-021-11139-3 (accessed 2 June 2021).

Webster, D. (2004). Giving voice to students with disabilities who have successfully transitioned to college. *Career Development for Exceptional Individuals* 27 (2): 151–175.

Whiteneck, G., Harrison-Felix, C., Mellick, D. et al. (2004). Quantifying environmental factors: a measure of physical, attitudinal, service, productivity, and policy barriers. *Archives of Physical Medicine and Rehabilitation* 85 (8): 1324–1335. https://doi.org/10.1016/j.apmr.2003.09.027 (accessed 3 June 2021.

World Bank (2011). World report on disability : main report. https://documents.worldbank.org/en/publication/documents-reports/documentdetail/665131468331271288/main-report (accessed 17 August 2021).

World Bank (2019). Inclusive Education Initiative: Transforming Education for Children with Disabilities, Brief (12 April, 2019). https://www.worldbank.org/en/topic/socialdevelopment/brief/inclusive-education-initiative-transforming-education-for-children-with-disabilities (accessed 7 November 2021).

Yatigammana, S., Dorabawila, S., and Abhayaratne, A. (2021). Developing inclusive education for students with disabilities in Sri Lankan universities – IncEdu Need Assessment Report, Survey.

Zabeli, N., Kaçaniku, F., and Koliqi, D. (2021). Towards the inclusion of students with special needs in higher education: challenges and prospects in Kosovo. *Cogent Education* 8 (1): https://doi.org/10.1080/2331186X.2020.1859438.

Zoniou-Sideri, A. and Vlachou, A. (2006). Greek teachers' belief systems about disability and inclusive education. *International Journal of Inclusive Education* 10 (4/5): 379–394.

20

Embedding Sustainability in Learning and Teaching: Communication Barriers to Learners with Special Needs

Leena Seneheweera and Varunadatta Edirisinghe

20.1 Introduction

The first occurrence of "sustainability" in a global context is found in the Report of the World Commission on Environment and Development: Our Common Future. It describes sustainability in relation to development: "development that meets the needs of the present without compromising the ability of future generations to meet their own needs" (Brundtland 1987). The success of development, let alone sustainable development, depends on two key contributors – education and communication. Education and communication (and communication for education) are interdependent and indispensable for sustainable development. This is evidenced in the Final Report of the United Nations (UN) Decade for Education for Sustainable Development (2015–2014) and in the goals of the UN 2030 Agenda for Sustainable Development (2015–2030). Goal 4 on education aims to promote inclusive and equitable education for all, with an equal focus on the potential of individuals with disabilities (which is largely under-utilized or not used at all) comprising, according to World Health Organization estimates, 15% of the world population. The number of persons with disabilities is one billion, of which 80% live in developing countries (United Nations 2020a). To utilize the services of a quarter of the world population, effective global initiatives are crucial to ensure opportunities for education by removing communication barriers that hinder participation, and empower this population through communication to contribute to development. Moreover, global emergencies such as the coronavirus (COVID-19) pandemic causing extensive and prolonged disruptions to every aspect of life interrupt and/or discontinue correspondence between educators and persons with disabilities around the world. The enrollment of persons with disabilities in higher education today even in less than satisfactory conditions is, indeed, an encouraging trend that could pave the way for their own sustainability, independence, and lifelong learning, and their contribution to sustainable development. The sustainability of the education of persons with disabilities can be ensured through the adaptation of pedagogical approaches that focus on overcoming their barriers.

Education is not possible without communication, because communication is a tool indispensable to teaching and learning. Educators involved in teaching special needs learners (SNLs) face the additional challenge of choosing effective verbal and nonverbal communication methods to deliver course content. When embedding sustainability in the learning and teaching process of SNLs in

The Wiley Handbook of Sustainability in Higher Education Learning and Teaching, First Edition.
Edited by Kelum A. A. Gamage and Nanda Gunawardhana.
© 2022 John Wiley & Sons, Inc. Published 2022 by John Wiley & Sons, Inc.

higher education, it is crucial that creative and effective teaching and learning methods that demand learner participation are embedded in the formal education process to develop communication. This is especially significant due to interruption to educational activities because of prolonged closure of educational institutions. During global emergencies such as the COVID-19 pandemic, SNLs are among the most adversely affected by the lack of remote learning facilities (UNESCO 2021).

20.1.1 Objectives

The objective of the current study is to propose a practical expressive arts approach to supplement the discipline curricula to overcome communication barriers of SNLs in higher education when embedding sustainability in teaching and learning. This framework adopts a student-centered, short- and long-term outcome-based approach. As its short- and long-term goals, the proposal aims to discover and improve the learner's cognitive, psychomotor, and affective skills and capabilities that, respectively, facilitate learning, promote participation, and ensure their self-relevance and usefulness to the community and country at large. The tangible outcomes attained through this means in the areas of personality, character, emotional and attitudinal development, analytical and critical thinking, and team and independent work with the capability to contribute locally and nationally will ensure the sustainability of special needs teaching and learning programs in higher education.

The objectives are to:

- Identify communication barriers of SNLs in higher education when embedding sustainability in teaching and learning.
- Overcome communication barriers of SNLs through the practice of expressive arts when embedding sustainability in teaching and learning.
- Design a curriculum with assessment and evaluation criteria to overcome communication barriers of SNLs when embedding sustainability in teaching and learning. These objectives are aligned with the UN Sustainable Development Goal (SDG) 4 on Education, and cross-cutting Goals 1 (End Poverty in all its Forms), 2 (Zero hunger), 3 (Health), 5 (Gender Equality and Women's Empowerment) 6 (Water and Sanitation), 8 (Economic Growth), 9 (Infrastructure, Industrialization), 10 (Inequality), 11 (Cities), 16 (Peace, Justice, and Strong Institutions), and 17 (Partnerships). The success of most UN SDGs relies on Goal 4 and its target of an inclusive and equitable quality education for all (UNESCO 2017).

20.1.2 Methodology

The objective was realized through a qualitative research outcome from two interactive workshops comprising 03 activities, with special needs undergraduate learners (SNLs with reference to vision impaired learners (VIL), and other physical impaired learners [OPIL]) and their peers and academics from the Faculty of Arts, University of Peradeniya and University of Jaffna, Sri Lanka, and a few workshops outside the university for SNLs of the same age group in Sri Lanka. The interactive workshop activities lasted three hours each and were conducted to celebrate World Disability Day in December 2019 and January 2020. The workshop activities were recorded using audiovisual technology. For purposes of study, they were analyzed and compared with participant observations (both SNLs and academic participants) using questionnaire surveys and feedback forms. The sample for this research was 15 SNLs (N = 15) enrolled in the undergraduate degree programs, and 40 peers (university and non-university), academic and administrative staff participants (N = 40). This methodology was used to identify communication barriers of SNLs and those between SNLs and teachers in learning and teaching, and to overcome them. The questionnaire (see Table 20.1) included 10 questions and feedback was received from 9 SNLs (N = 9) and 5 teachers (N = 5).

20.2 Education and Communication of SNLs When Embedding Sustainability in Learning and Teaching

Verbal and nonverbal communication is essential for human existence. Wiemann (2003) underscored its social significance in observing that "Our ability to create and sustain our social world depends in large measure on how well we communicate. People's social skills are crucial to their well-being – individually and collectively." In therapy, Egan (2002) identified the "helper" role of communication and observed that they are more important than words in certain contexts because "nonverbal behavior influences clients for better or for worse. Clients read cues in your nonverbal behavior that indicate the quality of your presence to them." Therefore, effective helpers ought to be mindful of the nonverbal messages they communicate to their clients. Nonverbal communication also plays a crucial role in teacher–student exchanges in a formal academic setting (see Table 20.1, No. 1, S9, T1–T5; No. 2, T1 and T4). The term communication is rooted in the Latin verb *communicare*, which means "share with," "take a share in," "associate," "impart," "communicate," "discuss together," "bring into common use," and "to make generally accessible" (Glare 2006), giving rise to similar meanings in English such as "share in," "receive," and "have a common channel of passage" (Onions 1966). Lunenburg (2010) clarified the communication process as taking place between the sender encoding a message with verbal and nonverbal mediums, and a receiver decoding the message into information. In this process various obstacles, such as language barriers and attitudes etc., can interrupt the message, while success depends on the receiver returning the message to the sender. The student-centered process of communication between student and teacher in the formal academic setting is analogous to Lunenburg's description of the communication process (see Table 20.1, No.1, S6, T3, T4, and T5).

The success or failure of education depends on good or bad communication between learners and teachers. Research findings from a number of disciplines show a correlation between communication and success in areas that directly or indirectly impact education and employment. In their reiteration of communication skills, Metusalem et al. (2017) use as evidence studies, for instance, that revealed a link between good communication skills and peer acceptance, building friendships, and satisfaction of patients and positive health outcomes. They also cite studies of oral reading skills in lower grades affecting development of reading and math in upper levels. Likewise, communication anxiety negatively impacts education and increases dropout rates (Monroe et al. 1992). In the professional setting, communication skills are a main skill set, and good communication effects success in business (Wright 2016). In higher education, reading skills lead to higher grades and graduation rates. Data from the American Management Association (2012, cited in Metusalem et al. 2017) and the National Association of Colleges and Employers (2016, cited in Metusalem et al. 2017) highlight the link between good communication and job acquisition, job advancement, and the success of business organizations (Ventura et al. 2017). Ellis (2009) highlights the correlation between communication skills and career advancement and personal development (see also Table 20.1, No. 7, S1–9). The UN surveys reiterate opposite effects, among other things, of negative communication and lack of opportunities for education: "unsafe conditions, negative interactions with caregivers and lack of educational opportunities during the early years can lead to irreversible outcomes, affecting a child's potential for the remainder of his/her life" (United Nations 2020b).

In the case of the SNLs, communication barriers prevent them from taking part in spite of their right to education (see Table 20.1, No. 4, S5, S6, and S9). Article 26 of the Universal Declaration of Human Rights (1948) states that "everyone has the right to education" (UN General Assembly 1948), and a plethora of conventions and frameworks are in place to ensure the rights, opportunities, and inclusion of persons with disabilities (SNLs) in education. These

Table 20.1 Questionnaire for survey of SNLs and teachers related to the study.

Questions	Answers SNLs (S)	Answers Teachers (T)
No. 1 What is communication?	Writing and listening (S1). Listening (S2). Speech, writing (S3). Discussing (S4.) No advanced communication systems for SNLs and typical students (S5). Giving information (S6). Exchanging ideas (S7 and S8). Understanding among groups or entities by using a language, signs, or symbols (S9).	Anything that does not prevent receiving and understanding the messages others use to convey their information, ideas, and thoughts. (T1). Non-existence (T2). Teacher is the means of "communication in education", T must convey equal knowledge/ideas/information to each student in class. A barrier is when the students are unable to receive/understand the teacher's message clearly (T3). The flow of information between two or more people. With SNLs the mode of sharing this information differs and must be customized (T4). Exchange information between two parties (T5).
No. 2 Internal communication barriers experienced	Inability to read/seek assistance (S1). Cannot write, use Braille (S2). Unable to handwrite/oral communication (S3). Lack of speed to reading and writing (S4). Can manage but others think we're vulnerable – I dislike it (S5). Need assistance to read, sometimes to walk (S6). None (S7). Finding books to read (S 8) Inability to read small letters, myopia, difficulty in using the screen/monitor of debit card machine/computer in a public place etc. (S9).	Poor listening skills, inability to read, lack of interest in the message, fear, mistrust, negative attitude, problems at home, lack of common experiences and emotion (T1, T4). No problem communicating with VILs except when some have difficulty hearing (T2).
No. 3 What is currently being done to overcome them?	No solution/seek help from others (S1, S3). Talk to others to obtain information, use mobile phones (S2). Nothing, sometimes unable to read favorite books (S4). Will attempt to overcome them (S5). Make friends (S6). Don't have a problem (S7). Ask friends (S8). Use a spectacle, a lens, and a telescope, sometimes needing assistance in public places such as banks (S9).	Provide a model to emulate, context, relevance, and opportunities to build self confidence, guide, and step aside, make parents aware (T1). Read aloud and use Braille (T2). No teaching experience with SNLs; suitable classroom seating arrangement; allocate fellow students to help (not full time) as library guide, in field visits, watch videos/movies for academic purposes. Training programs/workshops/seminars for SNLs and normal students to improve knowledge, share experiences and create an equal environment; practical assignments specially focusing to SNLs (T3). For impaired vision, learn about tools that allow students to see better, accommodate requests for flexibility, arrange extra times to work with the students, position students more visibility, stand near the student and make sure diagrams and illustrations are drawn correctly. For psychological impairment ensuring that the student has required care and to give flexibility for students in completing work (T4). Providing large print, recording lecture, using tactile tools, using picture exchange communication method (PECM) (T5).

Table 20.1 (Continued)

Questions	Answers SNLs (S)	Answers Teachers (T)
No. 4 External communication barriers encountered	Through discussion (S2). Through speech, writing (S3 and S4). Ignorance of teachers, peers, and administrators, regarding SNL needs. Coordinator linked us with others and gave opportunities to meet foreign scholars to the Faculty (S5 and S6). Unable to attend classes properly due to hospitalization for dialysis, and sometimes teachers and peers ignore me (S7). Many issues, living with mother, who may be bored because of me (S8) Insufficient time allocation for assignments and exams negatively influences studies; ignored friends a lot in my childhood because of repeated bullying and changed schools because of it (S9).	Problems at home, exams insufficient time allocation for exams, tests, assignment submission during daytime (T1). Very low skills in English (T2). Lack of knowledge/awareness of teaching SNLs; insufficient reading material for VILs, on essential subjects – mathematics and English, inaccessible lecture halls (physical impaired students); unable to attend field visits etc., due to disabilities; lack of IT facilities/training programs for SNLs (software); classroom arrangement and lack of provision for seats in front area for low vision and hearing-impaired students; devices to write during field visits, workshops (T3). Lack of facilities, SNLS seen as liability, made to beg for accommodation (T4). Insufficient time allocation, ignorance of disabilities, abuse by peers (T5).
No.5 What is currently being done to overcome them?	Rely on others for information, mobile phones to overcome communication barriers (S1, S2, and S6). Try to make others understand about me as SNL (S3, and S7). Our coordinator is friendly and conducts interactive sessions (S5). Request adequate/extra time (S9).	Consult colleagues to identify problems, verify campus policies, address challenges with sense (T1). Assign special instructors (T2). No ability to influence top-down nature of decision-making (T4). Give extra time for assignments, separate classrooms to braille users, other SNLs for exams, oral tests (T5). Monthly/daily meetings with peers of SNLs and typical students, organize annual concerts, field visits, and leisure activities like singing together (T5).
No.6 Do you (i.e. teachers)/your peers, administrators understand your communication barriers?	They say I can ask for help (S1). Yes (S2, S3, S4, S5, S6, and S7). Barriers due to lack of attention to me; but in class my peers and teachers listen (S4). Pity and treat us differently, and think we can't do things like typical students (S5). A little. Have mobility issues but no elevator to enter classrooms and administration buildings; they should be aware of our inaccessibility issues (S8). Most of the time, but most peers in my childhood did not. One painful experience in university impacted me negatively (S9).	Yes (T1). Often yes, sometimes students alerted me (T2). Only a few blind and physical impaired (T3). Sometimes (T4). From physical appearance and through conversation(T5).

(Continued)

Table 20.1 (Continued)

Questions	Answers SNLs (S)	Answers Teachers (T)
No.7 Usefulness of expressive arts workshops attended	Enjoyed them, like to participate daily; can improve vocal abilities and physical movements; help to interact with society (S1, S2, S3, and S7). like them, can practice my skills and that makes me happy. Can use my fingers properly by playing an instrument; its sound gives me confidence to move my fingers; can sing well with the resource person (S4 and S6). Engage with others and understand our communication barriers, needs in daily life and in learning. Interaction with peers and teachers is very useful (S5). Communicate with others using musical notes, movements, sounds; a therapy to relieve stress also. Makes participants express inner pressures/ feelings/emotions nonverbally (S7). Useful since the first time I attended; was at a loss how to communicate sitting in the wheelchair. But I was able to! (S8). Helped me a lot to express myself. (S9).	Learned how to use expressive arts for deaf children at a workshop; very important to work with deaf children and communicate with them (T1). Right now, not teaching SNLs due to my inability to engage them in academic work (T2). Workshops build self-esteem, self-satisfaction, better communication between peers and teachers; can share experiences in writing assignments, exam answers, presentations; very useful to include normal students to remove the barrier between disabled and non-disabled community (T3). Workshops/events become a spectacle without ensuring facilities and a flexible/ accommodating administrative process; workshops not effective in changing attitudes without institutional changes to prevent systemic discrimination of SNLs (T4). Attended as organizer, practitioner, and coordinator/very important to develop SNLs' internal and external communication barriers to ensure normal academic and personal lives (T5).
No. 8 Impact of workshops attended on developing eye contact, motor, and soft skills etc.	Told parents and others that the experience removed my sadness and shyness. Learned how to express my ideas happily (S1, S2, and S7). Expressed ideas using instruments, played at a fast tempo. All participants, including myself smiled and jumped with joy although my legs didn't move properly (S3 and S4). After the faculty Dean attended and said he also had a disability, I stopped thinking about my disability, and began to think everyone is the same. Workshop took away my negative feelings and attitude about my disability(S5). Make eye contact with teachers who. recognized me, and I recognized them; friendly communication is good for my academic career (S6). A personal experience, like therapy, relieves stress; meet a friendly and helpful community(S7). Very useful. Learned to overcome my problems like typical students; forgot I had barriers; participated in events and displayed my personality and capabilities (S8). Here SNLs don't feel alone; helps a blind person to communicate with others using voice, deaf/dumb persons with movement; highlights strengths of SNLs; develops personality (R9).	Expressive arts-based workshops are beneficial: discover happiness, nurture emotional growth, social and emotional development, improve communication and concentration and can help reduce feelings of isolation. Develops leadership qualities, expression, eye contact etc. (T1). Builds fine motor and problem-solving skills, enhances communication and expression, promotes self-esteem and motivation to succeed, sharing with and caring for each other (T3). All expressive arts activities improve eye contact including vision; body movement, playing of musical instruments and molding clay develop motor skills (T5).

Table 20.1 (Continued)

Questions	Answers SNLs (S)	Answers Teachers (T)
No. 9 Will the workshop experience help to overcome communication barriers?	Yes (S1–S3). Very important for eye contact with friends, teachers to recognize them successfully (S4 and S5). Yes, through exercise I learned how to communicate artistically and esthetically (S6 and S7). Learned about my mobility capacities in using a wheelchair. Participated in music, dance, drama with peers (S8). SNLs experience stress more owing to disabilities, and workshops teach them how to do things in life despite the disability (S9).	Yes, use the experience to overcome communication barriers in the learning environment and in daily life; eye contact and expression help to communicate and understand each other (T1). Yes (T3). Definitely, relate better to their teachers and peers, practice body movement etc. (T5).
No.10 Will the artistic experience solve communication skills in future?	Learned how to organize trips by undertaking responsibilities in the workshops. Improved self-behavior and learned to communicate with verbal and nonverbal cues (S1, S2 and S3). Love music, and dramatic action. Can use my fingers now and play instruments. Can use the experience in future activities. Learned to walk quickly (S4). Can express my feelings to my life's partner one day, and to my children and at work (S5, S6, and S7). Have confidence to live and communicate with others without a helper (S8). Of course, it will (R9).	Most likely, the leadership training they have gained is important to them; learn to use the right communication skills. (T1). Will help me to facilitate their learning better (T2). Gain experience with mainstream communities and how they express love, compassion, anxiety etc.; remove their isolation and depression (T5).

include the UNESCO Convention Against Discrimination in Education (1960), International Covenant on Economic, Social and Cultural Rights (1966), Convention on the Rights of the Child (1989), World Declaration of Education for All and Framework for Action to Meet Basic Learning Needs (1990), the Standard Rules on the Equalization of Opportunities for Persons with Disabilities (1993), Salamanca Statement and Framework for Action on Special Needs Education (1994), Dakar Framework for Action, Education For All (2000), Article 24 of the Convention on the Rights of Persons with Disabilities (2006), Samoa Pathway (2014), Incheon Declaration adopted at the World Education Forum (2015), and UN Sustainable Development Goal 4 on Education (2015–2030).

The importance of information and communication for SNLs is enshrined as a fundamental right in the preamble of the Convention on the Rights of Persons with Disabilities (CRPD) (UN General Assembly 2006). The focus is both on the different methods that can be used to share information and on a person-centered approach. Article 2 explains that the term "communication" "includes languages, display of text, Braille, tactile communication, large print, accessible multimedia as well as written, audio, plain-language, human-reader and augmentative and alternative modes, means, and formats of communication, including accessible information and communication technology," and "'Language' includes spoken and signed languages and other forms of non- spoken languages." Article 8.2, iii under Awareness-Raising, pledges "to promote the recognition of the skills, merits, and abilities of persons with disabilities, and of their contributions to the workplace and labour markets." The challenge for nations and educational institutions is to turn these into concrete realities.

The reality on the ground is not always what is envisioned in theory. World data shows evidence, on the one hand, of steps taken to socially include learners with disabilities in the education process through the provision of the right to education and non-discrimination. The UN Disability and Development Report 2018 states the legal provisions enacted for inclusion and right to education and against discrimination based on disability. In 2017, 65% of 88 countries included children with disabilities in their curricula compared with 42% in 2013. Moreover, governments had also begun to collect disability data, which is a positive development. On the positive side, the Report draws attention to the provision of material and communication necessities including assistive technology, human resources including teachers, and physical environment including accessible school buildings because "without these front-line resources in place, it is practically impossible to enable children with disabilities to go to school." The Report also records person-centered expressive arts-based creative approaches that some countries have adopted for the benefit of their citizens with disabilities. They promote inclusive education through curricula using communication methods such as assistive technology, audiovisual materials, games, activities, eBooks and audiobooks, sign language, art, drama, and music as a pedagogical method (see Table 20.2 No. 3, Level 1; No. 4. Level 1 and 2). The use, for instance, of African drumming in South Africa instills creativity, drawing in Egypt makes students (with and without disability) communicate verbally, and drama, dance, and music were used in the US with students with intellectual disabilities (see also Table 20.2). Some countries focused on capacity building of teachers through training sessions and manuals (United Nations 2019).

Elsewhere, progress is slowed down by factors that are not conducive to education. The Report reiterates that "persons with disabilities are less likely to attend school, less likely to complete primary or secondary schools and less likely to be literate. Education is fundamental for social inclusion and participation in the labor market and plays a critical role in the acquisition of skills and knowledge." It reports for the year 2012 that a staggering 75% of persons with disabilities in 41 developing countries did not attend school between the ages of 15 and 29, with a gap of more than 15% in 10 of those countries in the percentages of youth with and without disabilities. It states that large percentages of children with disabilities (aged 6–11) in developing countries are more likely to be out of school than those without disabilities in the same age group (57% to 7% respectively in Cambodia, for instance). The same applies to the out-of-school rate for 12–14-year-olds (26% to 18% respectively) in most countries. It was inevitable, therefore, that persons with disabilities were less likely to complete all levels – primary, secondary, and tertiary – than their peers without disabilities in 23 countries and territories. And around 2010, the total number of years in school for persons 25 years and older with disabilities and without them differed from country to country.

The Report continues that around 2010, in all countries, communication skills in writing and reading of persons with disabilities were lower than those of their peers without disabilities. Likewise, around 2011 the percentages of persons with disabilities who had not been admitted to school is also alarming: in Oman, 31% of persons with disabilities have had basic literacy skills while those without them remained at 81%, and large gaps in the basic literacy rates between these groups are recorded also from other countries. Consequently, students with

Table 20.2 CSD course schedule for 04 semesters (a total of 12 months).

Objective	Level	Activity Teamwork: T Individual: I	Duration	Method	Assessment
No. 1 Promote interaction/confidence building/motivation (verbal, nonverbal, and physical movements)	1	Greetings Introductions (I and T) • Introduction of self • Introduction of each other	2 hours	Music	Question and answer (verbal and nonverbal expression)
No. 1	2	Same activity with invited guest students – members of clubs, societies, and associations in the faculty/school of the educational institute	2 hours	Music	Question and answer (verbal and nonverbal expression)
No. 1	3	Same activity with administrators of the educational institute/outsiders without disabilities such as inter university affiliates	2 hours	Music	Question and answer (verbal and nonverbal expression)
No. 2 Communicate emotions (verbal, nonverbal)	1	Improvisation with vocal sounds and dramatic body movements: sudden outburst of joy, fear, excitement; animals and nature in and around the educational institute (T)	2 hours	Gestures, facial expressions, movements of the body, emotions	I's repeat the same activity with the help of EAPs
No. 2	2	Performance of a short but complete dramatic act for a play on screen OR live performance (T)	2 hours	Movements of the body, facial expressions, emotions	SNIs and peers create an act
No. 2	3	Participants act out their own piece to assess their comprehension (T)	2 hours		I's repeat the performance according to their understanding (with participants) OR concert
No. 3 Overcome physical barriers (verbal, nonverbal)	1	drawing, playing musical instruments, use of clay, rhythmical (dance) movements (I and T)	2 hours	music, dance, drawing	Participants create a story
No. 3	2	Outside the classroom: Imitate nature: sounds, animals, falling leaves, rain, water, foot steps, laughter (I)	2 hours		Imitate nature, what they hear see, touch, or feel

(Continued)

Table 20.2 (Continued)

Objective	Level	Activity Teamwork: T Individual: I	Duration	Method	Assessment
No. 3	3	Sports ground: Sports activities of the participants' preference and physical activity, exercises (T)	2 hours		Preferred individual and team events
No. 4 Overcome language barriers (use of language, repetition, recitation, improvisation)	1	Repeat Objective 1, Level 1 – turn a poem into a song, and a song into a poem (I and T)	2 hours	Singing	Compare progress with 1.1
No. 4	2	Repeat objective 4.1	2 hours	Singing	Compare progress with 4.1
No. 4	3	Formal meeting with administrators of the academic institution to report and discuss problems related to learning (I and T)	2 hours	Formal presentation of grievances. Ask questions. Agree/disagree/ express gratitude.	Initiative Confidence Communication skills

disabilities were compelled to attend special schools at primary, secondary, and tertiary levels. Data for nine countries in 2012 show on average 6% attending special schools, with higher percentages in individual countries. However, around 2010 those who managed to enter schools ran the risk of dropping out of school due to "financial and/or environmental barriers." Likewise, in the same year, in four countries on average 17% of students with disabilities dropped out of school due to financial constraints, 13% due to lack of transport or the school being too far, and 4% due to communication and language barriers. At the same time, students with disabilities are left out of school due to physical and virtual barriers, such as inaccessibility of schools or due to hindrances: in 2012 an average of 22% were affected, with some countries recording higher individual percentages. Moreover, unaffordability and unavailability of assistive technology have exacerbated communication barriers and kept learners out of the classroom, as has lack of electricity (United Nations 2019).

It is evident, therefore, that in spite of national and international efforts to integrate SNLs into the mainstream of educational activity, obstacles are real and persistent. Furthermore, global calamities such as the current COVID-19 pandemic pose unexpected challenges for learners, educators, and nations. The pandemic that exposed preexisting "fissures and inequalities" in higher education institutions worldwide (Purcell and Lumbreras 2021), has also disrupted education on a global scale, affecting more than 1.5 billion learners (UNESCO 2021). The lack of data on the impact of COVID-19 on educational activities of SNLs is indeed unfortunate. Moreover, alternative learning modes such as remote learning might not be available or accessible to persons with disabilities, and they are more likely to be excluded from educational activities (UNICEF 2020). Purcell and Lumbreras in their study of the impact of COVID-19 highlight the need to sustain higher education through partnerships by reimagining it in accordance with the SDGs and to continue the shared value of contributing to an inclusive world: "By acting to protect HE [higher education] over the long-term, the sector can re-imagine itself and sustain shared values, making its fullest contribution to a world where *no-one will be left behind*" (2021). Verbal and nonverbal communication enables inclusivity and the removal of emotional, language, attitudinal, physical, and curricular barriers to learning and teaching (see Table 20.1, No. 4, S5, S6, and S9, and T5; No. 5, S5, and T1, T2, and T5, and Table 20.2, Nos.1–4.).

20.2.1 Emotion as Nonverbal Communication and its Transformative Role

The current trend in education of SNLs is to place them in an inclusive learning and teaching environment. According to Ahmad (2012), communication is among the five main barriers – time and skills, physical, attitudinal, curricular, and communication – they encounter in the inclusive classroom. His recommendation to overcome communication barriers between SNLs and teachers, administrators, parents, and peers is a well-planned program of academic activities between general and special education teachers. Communication is one of the needs Martin-Denham (2015) also identifies in SNLs: communication and interaction, cognition and learning, social, emotional, and mental health difficulties, and sensory and physical needs. In the area of communication and interaction, she mentions the barriers of speech, language, and imagination for youth with cognitive impairments. She points out that the physically impaired needs help from their peers. Generally, they face difficulties in adjusting to education, social life, and health situations that challenge them and test their strength and confidence. Moreover, vision impaired and hearing impaired learners who rely on sign language face challenges in accessing information (see Table 20.1, No. 2, S1–S9, and T1, T2, T4, and T5). Communication barriers of SNLs are mainly due to their inability to communicate verbally. In comparison with typical learners the impairments of SNLs hinder their ability to communicate thoughts and feelings in a coherent manner. Therefore, they rely on nonverbal communications. In his account of paralanguage, Pennycook (1985) cites the definition of the term in ERIC 1984 as the "study of those aspects of communication that do not pertain to linguistic structure or content, for example, vocal qualifiers, intonation, and body language," and cites other examples of nonverbal communication such as facial movements, movement of the head, shoulder, arms, and wrist, hand and fingers, hip, neck, and foot activity, and eye contact. SNLs also resort to emotion-based communications (see Table 20.1, No. 8, S1–S9, and T1, T3, and T5).

The psychotherapist Malchiodi (2005) is of the view that individuals are endowed with different expressive styles, such as visual and tactile, and notes that "action within therapy and life is rarely limited to a specific mode of expression." And she observes further that expressive arts practitioners (EAPs) are aware of individuals' different expressive styles and use them with their special needs and typical clients to communicate effectively as well as authentically. She has studied the use of expressive arts activities in therapy, such as drawings, drumming, creative movement and play with practitioners of different fields including psychology, counseling, social work, and medicine. The purpose of her study was to verify the impact of the expressive arts on individuals' expression of feelings and thoughts through nonverbal expressions. Similar studies in cognitive sciences attest to the transformational and life-changing power of emotions. The "critical role" played by "emotional contact between humans" on cognitive processes is becoming increasingly recognized (Schore 2009). Panksepp (2008 cited in Schore 2009) observed the link between cognitive-object relations and emotional experience, and noted that "now cognitive science must relearn that ancient emotional systems have power that is quite independent of neocortical cognitive processes. . .These emotional substrates promote cognitive-object relations, optimally through rich emotional experiences." Schore argued that right-brain (i.e. the seat of emotions) survival functions are crucial in relational contexts throughout a person's life, and he is of the view that "the right hemisphere is dominant for the recognition of emotions, the expression of spontaneous and intense emotions, and the nonverbal communication of emotions" (2009). He noted further that the attention of neuroscience and the interdisciplinary approaches also concentrate on the significance of implicit emotion and self-regulation of emotion. On the latter, Schore explained that "Affect regulation is usually defined as the set of control processes by which we influence, consciously and voluntarily, our emotions, and how we experience and behaviorally express them" (2009). This experience is validated by the response of a practitioner in the current study (see Table 20.1, No. 7, T5). In the same study, in fact, EAPs consisting of an expert EAP, a medical doctor and EAP, a psychologist, community health worker and EAP, as well as an expert dance therapist, have teaching-learning experience with SNLs and persons with disabilities.

Arguing the transformative power of emotions in therapy, Fosha (2009) emphasized the impact of regulated emotion on long term transformation "through a transformational process rooted in emotional experience, suffering can morph into flourishing, contraction can be motivationally reversed, and a reorientation toward growth can be achieved" because, she reiterated, "emotions are, par excellence, vehicles of change; when regulated and processed to completion, they can bring about healing and lasting transformations." On emotions and change, Damasio (1999 quoted in Schore) said the following of the power of emotion: "For certain classes of clearly dangerous or clearly valuable stimuli in the internal or external environment, evolution has assembled a matching answer in the form of emotion," and Frijda (1986 quoted in Fosha) observed how each categorical emotion accompanies a set of "adaptive action tendencies" to assist the human bodies to recover from situations that provoked the emotions. And emotions are endowed with the power to resolve problem, for, "emotion is the experiential arc between the problem and its solution" (Fosha 2009).

Moreover, transformation is appetitive because humans have the natural ability to grow and change according to Doige (2007 quoted in Fosha) who noted that the "brain. . .is not an inanimate vessel that we fill; rather it is more like a living creature with an appetite, one that can grow and change itself with proper nourishment and exercise" and the transformational power of emotions is due to recognition, "for it is the process of recognition that holds the key to how to keep going forward, riding the river of emotion without needing to apply the damming counterforce of resistance" (Fosha 2009). According to Sander (2002) quoted in Fosha (2009), recognition is a "moment of fittedness," and Fosha emphasizes that the moment of fittedness "refers to all experiences that occur whenever there is a match, a 'click' between something inside and something outside, however inside and outside are subjectively defined" (see the Activities in Section 20.2.3). And a string of fittedness creates the transformational process that Fosha noted: "Emotion and recognition are two mechanisms that bring information and energy into the system. Emotions enlarge us as we face the environmental challenges that give rise to them, and recognition transforms us as we make seemingly foreign experiences our own. Through both moments of recognition and the activation of the adaptive action tendencies, emotion, along with new information, tremendous vitality, and energy are released and made available to the organism" (2009). The long-term effects of recognition and its transformational process is evidenced in emotional changes resulting from experience with expressive arts activities (see Table 20.1, No. 10, S1–S9, and T1–T5).

Moreover, more recent developments in biological sciences focus on the role of emotions in education. The new discipline of Social and Emotional Learning (SEL) is founded on the link between emotions and personal development. The Collaborative for Academic, Social, and Emotional Learning (CASEL) in their 2020 update defines SEL as "SEL is an integral part of education and human development. SEL is the process through which all young people and adults acquire and apply the knowledge, skills, and attitudes to develop healthy identities, manage emotions, and achieve personal, and collective goals, feel, and show empathy for others, establish, and maintain supportive relationships, and make responsible and caring decisions..." They also define how it ensures educational equity: "SEL advances educational equity and excellence through authentic school-family-community partnerships to establish learning environments and experiences that feature trusting and collaborative relationships, rigorous and meaningful curriculum and instruction, and ongoing evaluation. SEL can help address various forms of inequity and empower young people and adults to co-create thriving schools and contribute to safe, healthy, and just communities." The SEL approach is participatory and extends beyond the classroom to the community. Zins and Elias (2007) observed that "Instruction in SEL is provided in the context of caring, safe, well-managed, and participatory classroom, school, and other learning environments. These learned skills are then reinforced in the school, home, and community. All children might benefit from social-emotional instruction, including those who are at risk, those beginning to engage in negative behaviors, and those already displaying significant problems. The focus of most SEL programs is universal prevention and promotion –that is, preventing behavior problems by promoting social and emotional competence – rather than direct intervention." The transformative and developmental roles of human emotions can be mediated and regulated to overcome communication barriers in SNLs and typical students (see Table 20.2).

20.2.2 Removal of Communication Barriers in SNLs through the Practice of Expressive Arts when Embedding Sustainability in Learning and Teaching

SNLs inevitably face physical and emotional barriers at some point in their academic and daily lives. Although physical barriers are mostly visible, emotional barriers cannot be easily identified. The SNLs' emotional barriers can be seen through poor performance, and absence of interaction and communication in individual and group activities. Therefore, in learning and teaching it is important to focus on SNLs' emotional engagement in such activities. A recent study reiterated the impact of emotional skills in teamwork and communication performance, and highlighted four branches of emotional intelligence: awareness of emotions, acquisition of emotional knowledge, use of emotions in decision-making, and the management of emotions (Troth et al. 2012). The team-based expressive arts workshops in the current study fall into the four categories mentioned by Troth and the research team.

The positive effect of art works for communication of SNLs are well attested. Stamou (2002) discussed the relevance and the applicability of ancient Athenian views of Plato and Aristotle on the value of music and music education. For the ancient Greeks, *Mousike* consisted of a multiplicity of expressive arts such as music, poetry, dance, and song, and was a social affair with the participation of the community. "In its commonest form," observed Murray and Wilson (2004) "*Mousike* represented for the Greek a seamless complex of instrumental music, poetic word, and coordinated physical movement. As such it encompassed a large array of performances, from small-scale entertainment in the private home to elaborate festivals in which an entire polis was involved." In its social aspect, *Mousike* represented cultural identity, and it was a mode of communication: "*Mousike* was an endlessly variegated, rich set of cultural practices, with strongly marked regional traditions that made them a valuable item of local self-definition as well as a means for exchange and interaction." The emotional appeal of drama and its cognitive import was apparent when Aristotle acknowledged its cathartic (*Poetics*, 1449b 24–28) effect both as "purging" of emotions and "intellectual refinement" (Ford 2004). Ford stresses the ethical (Greek *ethos* – character) import that critics attribute to Aristotle's view of tragedy, because it "provides its audience with something like a public education in ethics: the poet's artfully constructed 'representations' of reality can guide spectators to form and enjoy 'correct' cognitive and emotional responses to the events portrayed so that they might carry these attitudes over into real life" (2004). Stamou examined modern scholars who echoed this view. He quotes Jorgensen (1994) who maintained that "appropriately chosen music can...'elevate' and 'invigorate' the individual morally and physically." It is indeed remarkable that some individuals with psychosomatic disorders around the world have distinguished themselves nationally and internationally in the field of expressive arts. Unfortunately, however, the physical and mental well-being of most individuals with disabilities is at a low level due to their impairments. Because of them, such individuals are more likely to be backward, lethargic, and lack initiative, courage, motivation, self-confidence, and esteem that are essential to carry out day-to-day activities and, in the long run, to live productive, healthy, and contented lives. The expressive arts can play a major role in improving the communication skills of SNLs through their ability to affect emotions and expression, movement, and attitude through active engagement (see Table 20.2).

The practice of expressive arts stimulates expression and the realization of the need to interact. It can assist learners to naturally release their hitherto unexpressed feelings, moods, and thoughts and sentiments as nonverbal and invisible communications. These help to alter their cognitive impairment in a way that will facilitate learning. Stephen and Levine (2011) observed that at its inception, expressive arts were based on the idea of "intermodality" because "artistic disciplines are rooted in the different modalities of sensory experience." As we have seen, the sensory effect of the performance of expressive arts is such that it plays a transformative role on the learner. The use of the expressive arts in learning and teaching is important because of their imitative and expressive nature. For, imitative art imitates human emotions, thoughts, character, actions, sense, and mood that it uses to communicate with its listening and viewing audience. In a formal setting, the SNLs' interaction with the expressive arts can be viewed as their imitation of the verbal and nonverbal communications they hear and/or see depending on their particular impairment. Imitation can be repeated in the classroom to overcome internal and external communication barriers through interaction with art forms, and to improve communication in learning and teaching. By practicing expressive arts which stimulate communication, SNLs experience emotions, thoughts, character, actions, sense, and mood that they see as observers and as participants in a group. Troth et al. (2012) attest to the positive impact of emotions on teamwork and communication. Teamwork creates the awareness that they belong together with members of the academic community, and the feeling of belonging removes unexpressed negative emotions and facilitates inclusion in the classroom.

20.2.3 Expressive Arts as a Tool to Overcome Communication Barriers in SNLs

The following is a descriptive account of three expressive arts activity workshops held for SNLs at the University of Peradeniya and University of Jaffna, and institutions outside the university for SNLs of the same age group in Sri Lanka in 2019 and 2020. The purpose of these workshops was to understand what the SNLs thought by observing their emotions when they were unable to use language to communicate in learning and teaching. The participants also included peers, lecturers (with and without prior teaching experience with SNLs), administrators, and non-academic staff members. The study confirms the observations of EAPs on Activities 1–3, and responses of the participants obtained in the questionnaire survey in Table 20.1.

Activity 1
The use of musical activities to overcome communication barriers   **Description**   EAPs experienced in working with SNLs and other participants (N = 40) came to meet them for the first time in the room where the workshop was held. SNLs without visual impairments looked at them with no expressions (facial or verbal), or were surprised, and the reactions were videotaped for observation and analysis. SNLs made facial expressions and gestures of surprise, awe, joy, excitement, and curiosity at the creative and artistic room arrangement made according to the requirements of the workshop. And the instruments were placed prominently. Two more EAPs arrived with harmoniums, tablas (percussion instruments of Indian origin), local drums, brass instruments, and handmade musical instruments such as cymbals, bells, drums, flutes made from coconut shells, pieces of metal, plastic, and rubber bands. Their video camera was visible to the SNLs. The EAPs sat together with the SNLs and others on the floor, and gave them handmade musical instruments. They clapped their hands together, touched the instruments, and began to play them. The instruments made sounds of different kinds; some were made of coconut shells that were brightly painted in many colors, others had eye-catching human figures, yet others had flowers and animals and geometric patterns. EAPs sang songs that were familiar to everyone, and the participants kept a regular beat with their own accompaniment. They adhered to the beats, such as the regular time of a song or musical composition and the repetition of the same beat (i.e. 1 2 3, 1 2 3) and the repetition of mixed beats (i.e. 1 2,1 2,1 2 3). The songs were sung individually and in teams, and the participants engaged in improvised question and answer sessions using musical instruments: first an individual "asked" a "question" using facial expressions and a musical rhythm, and the others as a team "answered" in the same way. The individual asked the question in a slow tempo, and some teams answered in a slow tempo while others in a fast tempo. The SNLs used their fingers, movements of the body, and facial expressions during the activity. With vocal expressions, gestures, or cues (non-stop engagement with the instruments and singing), the SNLs and others indicated their desire to continue the activity. The group interacted musically without verbal communication. The EAPs also brought raw materials such as coconut shells, plastic bottles, tin cans etc., to make instruments. The SNLs engaged with the EAPs and others willingly in making musical instruments from raw materials.

EAPs' observations

When they saw the musical instruments, the SNLs' and other participants' facial expressions showed that they were familiar to them. The clapping of hands confirmed their happiness. The purpose of the entry into the room with musical instruments was to make the teachers understand how SNLs react to a creative environment and adapt to it. For the teacher, SNLs reactions are helpful to assess their communication skills and barriers to communication (see Table 20.1, No.8, T1, T3, and T5). A creative introduction can be used in student-centered learning and teaching generally, irrespective of the discipline and the audience, to build a congenial environment and a friendly relationship between the learner and teacher.

All the participants kept a regular beat with their own accompaniment when the EAPs sang songs that were familiar to them. The functions of their fingers, movements of the body, facial expressions with smiles on their faces, indicated their desire to continue the activity. They started and finished singing and playing at the same time. EAPs observed improvement in SNLs' adherence to instructions. Also, when some teams asked a question in a slow tempo, and other teams improvised in a slow tempo or in a fast tempo, this kind of improvisational melodic and harmonic process communicates with human moods, and emotions (Wigram 2004). They also used vocal expressions, gestures, or cues (non-stop engagement with the instruments and singing). Moreover, this type of communication tool makes the human mind and the body function in unison and helps to minimize communication barriers in learning and in daily life. In this activity, some of the SNLs sang and played with their eyes closed to indicate their enjoyment of the moment in all its intensity, and were completely absorbed in their experience of esthetic feeling (see Table 20.1, No. 8, S5; T5). This kind of feeling is evidence of psychological satisfaction which is a positive sign of their connection with their own musical (vocal) sounds and their attempt to familiarize themselves with a new activity (see Table 20.1, No.7, S4, S6–S9). Continued engagement indicated that in a short time they had acquired the confidence to perform with a group. Their adherence to the beats showed their natural ability to distinguish between different beats, which can be extended to introduce concepts such as order, frequency, arrangement, organization, and time management (see Table 20.1, No. 10, S1–S3). Frequent engagement in these and similar activities will help to understand concepts that can be explained logically and rationally in class. These activities will assist them in the development of their personalities, desire and motivation to learn, to be punctual and organized in academic learning and teaching, as well as time management and teamwork. The teamwork strengthened the identity of the SNLs and their teachers as a group, diminishing the barrier between teacher and student, and SNLs and their peers. Teamwork allows the teachers ample opportunities to focus on the SNLs and peers, and to understand their communication and physical barriers and treat them with respect and understanding (see Table 20.1, No. 9, S8 and S9; T1).

The pictures on the handmade instruments were hand-drawn so that the SNLs could easily imitate and copy them. The objective was to let the learners understand that they too could make these and similar instruments on their own for their own entertainment with raw materials easily and freely available. Teachers can use this activity to engage SNLs emotionally, and with sounds and gestures that help them forget their internal and external communication barriers. It will particularly help physically impaired learners to improve their motor skills as well (see Table 20.1, No. 8, S4 and S6; T3). Moreover, the creation of instruments on their own helped SNLs to forget their disabilities and negative thoughts about themselves since making the instruments and playing them did not require formal methods or techniques. Similar reactions, expressions, and interactions were visible in the typical learners.

According to their rhythmic expressions, EAPs and other participants understood the players' mental and emotional state. The SNLs and peers had the same opportunity to connect with their teachers and to respect their efforts to help them to overcome their barriers. During the session teachers also gained experience in introducing a new topic in their inclusive classroom and in how to convey it nonverbally and meaningfully.

Activity 2
The use of visual arts (drawing, painting, and clay modeling) to overcome communication barriers **Description** SNLs including visually impaired students and participants engaged in drawing and making figures. A few of them were asked to sit on the floor in a position that was comfortable for them and draw their inner feelings. They were given pencils of different colors, and they began to draw. They were given 10–15 minutes to complete the task to the accompaniment of a piece of Indian classical music. The SNLs used different colors in their drawings to represent light, shading, and texture. After completion, they were asked to hold their drawings up and display them to the others. EAPs also asked questions about their creations. There were some contradictions between the colors SNLs said they had used, and those visible on the drawings. SNLs and participants were also given clay to mold into objects of their choice individually, and were asked to make a story out of them. Some SNLs molded animal figures and presented the stories using them either verbally or nonverbally according to their ability. **EAPs' observations** SNLs and participants' sitting posture indicated that both their mind and body were relaxed, and that they were interested in their tasks. It was observed that their attention was concentrated on the tasks throughout the exercise. A correlation was also observed between the tempo changes of the music composition and the length of the lines drawn (i.e. lines are long when the tempo is slow, and vice versa, and multiple lines in quick succession are drawn when the tempo is fast) (see Table 20.1, No. 8, S3 and S4). Their self-confidence was visible when they willingly answered EAPs' questions and themselves requested the EAPs to evaluate their drawings. This exercise is useful for teachers to understand the inner feelings, and how well they engage with tasks when the SNLs are not confident enough to express themselves verbally in the class. In the instance of the contradiction in the use of exact color, it was clear to the EAPs that some of the SNLs were color-blind. This exercise is useful to teachers in recognizing the communication barrier imposed by color-blindness, and to take appropriate measures to recognize it in their teaching and find ways to work around it. The exercise shows the teachers to be vigilant about typical learners who may also suffer from color-blindness. Here also, the teacher can communicate with the SNLs verbally and nonverbally (moving signs, gestures, and language cues) to understand thoughts and ideas when they are not articulated verbally (see Table 20.1, No. 10, S1–S3). Stone (2017) says that this type of exercise in spiritual Shamanism communicates "eyes-closed seeing," i.e. "seeing" without physically functioning eyes. Similarly, EAPs observed eyes-closed seeing in the form of movements, signs, and gestures etc. in vision impaired SNLs and other participants (see Table 20.1, No. 9, S4 and S5; T1).

Activity 3
The use of theater to overcome communication barriers **Description** The participants were divided into Groups A, B, and C with peers selected randomly for each. The groups were asked to create a short play on their own under themes of their choice. The groups took approximately 30 minutes to create a short play and perform it: **Group A**: Rights of access for persons with disabilities. **Group B**: A football game. **Group C**: A social gathering.

The hearing impaired learners at the workshop communicated their expressions (except in the case of sign language) through lip-reading. In order for lip-reading to be successful as a mode of communication, dialogs in plays were recited at a normal volume. Recreations of dramatic action also included performers who were deaf or hard of hearing.

The themes were as follows:

Group A: This group enact the moment that a female student in a wheelchair is going to catch a ride on public transport. She is surrounded by peers (SNLs and typical learners) as they wait for the bus. When the bus arrives, the wheelchair user has difficulty getting in because of her disability. Her peers lift her and place her inside the bus since she can not handle her wheelchair without a ramp. Her peers decide to take the matter to the courts to seek the right of access to public transportation for persons with disabilities.

Group B: A team with SNLs and typical learners engage in a football game. The team plays well but loses the game because of a physical impaired team member. A discussion follows regarding the loss, and some SNLs say that they would have won had they communicated with others prior to the game to place their physically impaired teammate strategically in the field. They decide to train him formally to play the game, and place him strategically.

Group C: The play begins with a social gathering after the final examinations. Some students dance to a musical accompaniment, but the SNLs do not join for the fear of revealing physical impairments. The peers see them in a corner of the room and decide to talk to them. They tell the SNLs that they can forget their impairments when they interact with typical students. SNLs decide to listen to their peers, and shortly engage in rhythmical dance movements, and dance holding hands with peers.

EAPs' observations (see Table 20.1, No.9, S6–S9, and T5)

All groups picked themes related to their rights and barriers (education, communication, health, emotions, etc.) and in spite of their disabilities, the SNLs were emotionally, psychologically, and intellectually able. The activity revealed that there was not only communication barriers but also attitudinal barriers between the SNLs and typical students. The activity gave the teachers the opportunity to interact with their students, and learn and assess their physical and other impairments, and barriers to communicating with peers and teachers. Most SNLs found in this activity the opportunity to meet and introduce themselves to peers and teachers in an informal setting, share views and ideas, engage in conversation, make friends, and practice social interaction (see Table 20.1, No.9, S6–S9, and T5). The SNLs were able to interact and communicate without the use of an interpreter or a helper-companion (see Table 20.1, No. 8, S1–S9, and T1, T3, and T5; No. 9, S1–S9, and T1, T3, T5). The SNLs' personal interaction with the play's clearly defined structure gives them a sense of the ordered structure of their academic environment and surroundings, and creates awareness of themselves and the behavior expected of them. This includes for the most part communication with others in the learning environment. A good interaction with a play links SNLs' sensory, intellectual, cognitive, and communicative functions. The use of drama to develop language skills in learning and teaching performs a social function linking SNLs and the academic culture of the institution (see Table 20.1, No. 10, S1–S9). The relationship between SNLs and their academic environment plays a transformative role in the individual learners' language skills. This transformation highlights that the SNLs have come to accept the need to communicate with peers and teachers in a learning environment. Teachers could use dramatic plays with both SNLs and typical students to facilitate communication (see Table 20.1, T1–T5).

Before these interactive sessions, communication barriers such as an absence of eye contact between the SNLs, peers, and teachers was evident in their minimal engagement with each other. However, after the workshop, there was a visible improvement (see Table 20.1, No. 9, S4 and S5, T1, T3, and T5). The SNLs and peers were unable to play musical instruments, and incapable of body movements indicating self-confidence that would enable them to begin interactions with others in and outside their comfort zone (see Table 20.1, No. 10, S1–S9, and T1, T2, and T5). These activities highlight that SNLs' engagement with the expressive art forms (dramatic) are effective in addressing communication barriers, and that prolonged engagement (i.e. duration of the undergraduate career of an SNL) with these and other expressive arts will certainly prove beneficial. In an attempt to communicate, the SNLs will explore creative ways to imitate the actions, and react and engage with them emotionally, mentally, and physically; this in itself is a new first-hand experience for them. The experience is something they feel in their minds and bodies that they will begin to use and represent in their own communications with others. This kind of exercise stresses the relationship between communication and acting through a cleansing of negative emotions such as fear, shyness, and lethargy that are a barrier to communication (see Table 20.2, Objective 2, Level 2 activity, modeled on the response to the dramatic activities in the workshop).

20.3 Curriculum with Assessment and Evaluation Criteria to Overcome Communication Barriers of SNLs when Embedding Sustainability in Learning and Teaching

20.3.1 Communication Skills Development Course for SNLs

The goal of education for sustainable development (ESD) is person-centered, focused on "life-long learning, and is an integral part of quality education. ESD is holistic and transformational education which addresses learning content and outcomes, pedagogy and the learning environment" (UNESCO 2014). The UN Disability and Development Report 2018 recommends a learner-centered pedagogy and observes that an "inclusive curriculum should address all learners' cognitive, emotions, social and creative development" and endorses engagement with "civil society and local communities in inclusive education." Moreover, since it is imperative that sustainable education, and education for sustainability is inclusive, inclusive education should facilitate learner participation through communications skills development curricula. Moreover, inclusive education "requires the use of inclusive pedagogies that respect multiple means of expression, and engagement" (Ilisko 2019). The term "disability inclusion" is defined as "the meaningful participation of persons with disabilities in all their diversity, the promotion of their rights, and the consideration of disability-related perspectives, in compliance with the Convention on the Rights of Persons with Disabilities" (United Nations 2020a).

The following curriculum addresses communication needs and disability inclusion in higher education, and interactions with SNLs to overcome verbal and nonverbal communication barriers in the aforementioned expressive arts workshop activities. The communications curriculum intends to create a space for SNLs in the formal learning teaching environment to engage both formally and informally with peers, teachers, administrators, and outsiders and to recognize their barriers to expression and communication with others. It addresses communication challenges faced by SNLs and offers them creative ways through the expressive arts to overcome them, and empower them to face current and future challenges in education, employment, and life.

Course Code: CSD
Course Title: Communication Skills Development

Aims: The course aims to encourage, motivate, improve, develop, and refine verbal and nonverbal communication skills of SNLs through expressive arts without the intervention of communication technology.

Objectives: The objectives of the course are to:

1) Communicate emotions (verbal, nonverbal).
2) Overcome language barriers (use of language, repetition, recitation, improvisation).
3) Promote interaction/build confidence, motivation.
4) Overcome physical barriers (verbal, nonverbal) to enable SNLs to communicate without barriers in learning, and in daily life.

Number of participants (per session): 12

Resource persons (03): Special needs staff trained in teaching and practitioner of the expressive arts.

Duration: 04 semesters (a total of 12 months, three levels for each objective, each level is of two hours duration)
Frequency: monthly
Activities: verbal and nonverbal
Method: expressive arts based
Location: classroom, outdoors

Assessment and evaluation:

Diagnostic and formative, and student feedback forms to assess communication skills, confidence, leadership, self-esteem, ability to accept victory/defeat, emotional strength, perseverance, personality, responsibility, morals and ethics, behavior, courage, etc.

20.3.2 Course Content

This course covers selected activities using expressive arts genres in music, drumming, dance, theater, drawing, and paintings:

Music: improvise pitch, song, beat, tempo, and imitate song (popular and applied), listen to classical music, and drumming, conduct musical dialogs, create instrumental music patterns.
Drumming: improvise three levels of tempo (slow, middle, fast) by any percussion instrument accompany the drum with other instruments.
Dance: improvise rhythmical movements accompanied by any music, create movements of mindfulness and body movements.
Theater: imitate moments from daily life, and animals, create images, emotional studies, scene development, breathing, voice balance, performance of short plays.
Drawing and painting: create lines with colors and without colors, paint while listening to music, create shapes, draw nature.

20.3.3 CSD Course Schedule for 04 Semesters

Table 20.2 shows the CSD course schedule for 04 semesters (a total of 12 months).

20.4 Conclusion

The overall objective of this chapter was to present a practical expressive arts approach to overcome communication barriers of SNLs in higher education when embedding sustainability in their learning and teaching. This approach was modeled on workshop activities using music, drawing, clay molding, and theater, and it was accompanied by a four-semester curriculum on communication skills development (CSD). Among the advantages of the approach are the stimulation of sensory experiences, verbal and nonverbal communication of the learners irrespective of their physical impairments, non-use of assistive technology, interaction between participants and teachers, and teamwork and bonding that pave the way for better communication and collaboration between SNLs, typical learners, teachers, and other stakeholders. The success of the approach in stimulating communication reinforces the need for training of teaching and support staff in the practice of expressive arts in learning and teaching, communication needs assessments, and working with SNLs. The student-centered approach builds trust and confidence, and teamwork bonds participants and teachers, creating a sense of equality that facilitates better communication and the sustainability of the learning-teaching experience. Regular engagement in the proposed activities will contribute to overcoming communication, language, attitudinal, physical, and curricular barriers that will enable personal development. It is hoped that this study will encourage wider use of the expressive arts to transform individuals and enable social inclusion, which alone can contribute to sustainable development.

20.5 Recommendations

The study recommends the following for the development of SNLs' communication skills in addition to the CSD course:

1) Conduct periodic teacher education crash courses in teaching of SNLs, especially creative and expressive arts-based courses, and train all categories of university staff to work with SNLs.
2) Ensure accountability by evaluating institutions' commitment to SNL teaching and learning in the formal institutional review processes, and reward academic departments of study via a points scheme for best practices in teaching and learning of SNLs.
3) Schedule regular meetings in the institution's formal meetings agenda to include SNLs and teachers, peers, administrators, and the outside community to discuss communication barriers in their learning and teaching, their rights, sharing information, and providing emotional support, and enable SNLs to experience communicating in real-life situations, discussing their issues to overcome barriers.
4) Involve SNLs in organizing and executing institutional events (arts, expressive arts-based, and others) and celebrations to improve communication and attitudinal changes in typical students and staff toward SNLs.
5) Conduct regular SNL awareness activities/programs for the university community, focusing on student orientation, communication skills, health, advocacy, etc.
6) Encourage higher education institutions to consult SNLs, their peers, and other persons with disabilities in their institutions in future research that is focused on SDGs and community-based activities relevant to them.

References

Ahmad, W. (2012). Barriers of inclusive education for children with intellectual disabilities. *Indian Stream Research Journal* 2 (2): 1–4.

Brundtland, G. (1987). *Report of the World Commission on Environment and Development: Our Common Future*. New York: United Nations Available at https://sustainabledevelopment.un.org/content/documents/5987our-common-future.pdf.

Casel. Org. (2020). Fundamentals of SEL. https://casel.org/what-is-sel

Egan, G. (2002). *The Skilled Helper: A Problem Management and Opportunity Development Approach to Helping*. Brooks/Cole Publishing Company.

Ellis, R. (2009). *Communication Skills: Stepladders to Success for the Professional*. Bristol and Chicago: Intellect.

Ford, A. (2004). Catharsis: the power of music in Aristotle's politics. In: *Music and the Muses: The Culture of 'Mousike' in the Classical Athenian City* (ed. P. Murray and P. Wilson), 309–336. Oxford: Oxford University Press.

Fosha, D. (2009). Emotion and recognition at work: energy, vitality, pleasure, truth, desire and the emergent phenomenology of transformational experience. In: *The Healing Power of Emotion: Affective, Neuroscience Development and Clinical Practice* (ed. D. Fosha, D. Siegel and M. Solomon), 483–566. New York: WW Norton and Company.

Glare, P. (2006). Communico. In: *Oxford Latin Dictionary*, Combined ed., 369. Oxford: Clarendon Press.

Ilisko, D. (2019). Challenges to sustainable development at regional level. In: *Encyclopaedia of Sustainability in Higher Education* (ed. W.L. Filho), 190. International Publishing: Springer.

Levine, S. (2011). Art Opens to the World: Expressive Arts and Social Action. In: *Art in Action; Expressive Arts Therapy and Social Change* (ed. E. Levine and S. Levine), 21–30. London and Philadelphia: Jessica Kingsley Publishers.

Lunenburg, F. (2010). Communication: the process, barriers, and improving effectiveness. *Schooling* 1 (1): 1–11.

Malchiodi, C.A. (2005). Expressive therapies: history, theory and practice. In: *Expressive Therapies* (ed. C.A. Malchiody), 1–15. New York: Gilford Press.

Martin-Denham, S. (2015). Introduction. In: *Teaching Children & Yong People with Special Educational Needs & Disabilities* (ed. S. Martin-Denham), 1–7. New Delhi: Sage Publications India.

Metusalem, R., Belenky, D. & DiCerbo, K. (2017). Skills for Today: What we know about teaching and assessing communication. London: Pearson.

Monroe, C., Borzi, M., and Burrell, R. (1992). Communication apprehension among highschool dropouts. *The School Counselor* 39 (4): 273–280.

Murray, P. and Wilson, P. (ed.) (2004). *Music and the Muses: The Culture of 'Mousike' in the Classical Athenian City*. Oxford: Oxford University Press.

Onions, C. (1966). Communicate. In: *The Oxford Dictionary of English Etymology*, 196. New York: Oxford University Press.

Pennycook, A. (1985). Actions speak louder than words: paralanguage, communication, and education. *TESOL Quarterly* 19: 259–282.

Purcell, W. and Lumbreras, J. (2021). Higher education and the COVID-19 pandemic: navigating disruption using sustainable development goals. *Discover Sustainability* 2 (1): 1–16.

Schore, A. (2009). Right brain affect regulation: an essential mechanism of development, trauma, dissociation, and psychotherapy. In: *The Healing Power of Emotion: Affective, Neuroscience Development and Clinical Practice* (ed. D. Fosha, D. Siegel and M. Solomon), 322–404. New York: WW Norton and Company.

Stamou, L. (2002). Plato and Aristotle on music and music education: lessons from ancient Greece. *International Journal of Music Education* 39 (1): 3–16.

Stone, R.R. (2017). Nothing is missing: spiritual evaluation of a visually impaired Moche shaman. In: *Disability and Art History* (ed. A. Millett-Gallant and E. Howie), 47–59. New York: Routledge.

Troth, A.C., Jordan, P.J., Lawrence, S.A., and Tse, H.M. (2012). A multilevel model of emotional skill, communication, performance and task performance in teams. *Journal of Organizational Behaviour* 33 (5): 700–722.

UN General Assembly. Universal Declaration of Human Rights, 10 December 1948, 217 A (III). https://www.refworld.org/docid/3ae6b3712c.html ().

UN General Assembly. Convention on the Rights of Persons with Disabilities: resolution/adopted by the General Assembly, 24 January 2006, A/RES/61/106. https://www.refworld.org/docid/45f973632.html (accessed 11 July 2021).

UNESCO (2014). *UNESCO Roadmap for Implementing the Global Action Programme on Education for Sustainable Development*. France: UNESCO.

UNESCO. (2017) More than one half of children and adolescents are not learning worldwide. Fact sheet. UNESCO Institute for Statistics. UIS/FS/2017/ED/46.

UNESCO (2021). *Supporting Learning Recovery One Year into COVID-19: The Global Education Coalition in Action*, 1–95. France: UNESCO.

UNICEF. (2020). COVID-19 response: Considerations for children and adults with disabilities. https://sites.unicef.org/disabilities/files/COVID-19_response_considerations_for_people_with_disabilities_190320.pdf

United Nations (2019). *Disability and Development Report 2018: Realizing Sustainable Development Goals by, for and with Persons with Disabilities*. New York: United Nations.

United Nations (2020a). *United Nations Disability Inclusion Strategy*. New York: United Nations.

United Nations (2020b). *Policy Brief: A Disability-Inclusive Response to COVID-19*. New York: United Nations.

Ventura, M., Lai, E., and Dicerbo, K. (2017). *Skills for Today: What We Know about Teaching and Assessing Critical Thinking*. London: Pearson.

Wiemann, J. (2003). Introduction. In: *Handbook of Communication and Social Interaction Skills*, 3e (ed. O. Hargie), ix. Routledge: London and New York.

Wigram, T. (2004). *Improvisation: Methods and Techniques for Music Therapy Clinicians, Educators and Students*. United Kingdom: Jessica Kingsley Publisher.

Wright, M. (ed.) (2016). *Gower Handbook of Internal Communication*, 2e. London and NewYork: Routledge.

Zins, J. and Elias, M. (2007). Social and emotional learning: promoting the development of all students. *Journal of Educational and Psychological Consultation* 17 (2–3): 233–255.

21

Sustainable Higher Education for Disabled Students: Comprehensive and Quality Support for All Process Participants – University of Zagreb Support Model

Lelia Kiš-Glavaš

21.1 Introduction

The University of Zagreb was founded in 1669. Today, it is the oldest and largest university in southeastern Europe and the strongest teaching and scientific institution in Croatia, with 60% of the total yearly research output in Croatia. It consists of 33 faculties and three academies, and has over 70 000 students, which is 44% of all students in the Republic of Croatia. The University of Zagreb offers a wide range of academic degree courses leading to bachelor's, master's, and doctoral degrees in the following fields: Arts, Biomedicine, Biotechnology, Engineering, Humanities, and Natural and Social Sciences.[2]

As a central and leading institution, the university pays special regard to carrying out the programs of strategic interest for the Republic of Croatia and for the development of regional and local communities. All university activities promote human rights and fundamental freedoms.[3]

The social dimension of higher education is a very important part of quality higher education in Croatia and at the University of Zagreb. It has been mentioned in the framework of the Bologna process (a mechanism promoting intergovernmental cooperation between 48 European countries in higher education) in ministerial statements since 2001, and a comprehensive definition was agreed upon in 2007 in London[4] that states that the "student population that enrolls, attends, and completes higher education at all levels reflects the diversity of our society." In Croatia, at the declaratory level everyone has the right of access to all levels of the education system under the same conditions,[5] but it is necessary to take several additional measures to make higher education truly accessible to everyone, especially to vulnerable social groups.

In 2014, the Croatian Parliament adopted The Strategy of Education, Science, and Technology that stipulates: "the inclusion of underrepresented in the system of higher education is one of

---

1 Sveučilište u Zagrebu, Mission and Vision (n.d.), http://www.unizg.hr/o-sveucilistu/sveuciliste-jucer-danas-sutra/misija-i-vizija-sveucilista
2 Sveučilište u Zagrebu (n.d.), http://www.unizg.hr/homepage
3 Sveučilište u Zagrebu, Mission and Vision (n.d.), http://www.unizg.hr/o-sveucilistu/sveuciliste-jucer-danas-sutra/misija-i-vizija-sveucilista
4 London Communiqué (2007, p. 5).
5 Ustav Republike Hrvatske/The Constitution of the Republic of Croatia (1990).

The Wiley Handbook of Sustainability in Higher Education Learning and Teaching, First Edition.
Edited by Kelum A. A. Gamage and Nanda Gunawardhana.
© 2022 John Wiley & Sons, Inc. Published 2022 by John Wiley & Sons, Inc.

the priorities of development of Croatian education."[6] The strategy, in the section on higher education, lists several tasks that are aimed at enhancing the social dimension of higher education in Croatia. One of those tasks refers to the determination of under-represented and vulnerable groups in higher education, as well as factors that contribute to a weaker enrollment of students belonging to those groups in higher education.

This task was entrusted to the intersectoral National Group for the Improvement of the Social Dimension of Higher Education, which acts as an advisory body to the Government of the Republic of Croatia, the Ministry of Science and Education, the Croatian Rectors' Conference, and the Council of Universities and University Colleges of Applied Science, and whose establishment was encouraged by one of the measures of the strategy.

Since its establishment at the end of 2015, the National Group has detected several under-represented and vulnerable groups of students in higher education, as well as some of the factors that make them vulnerable. One of them is disabled students.

21.1.1 Terminology

The terms for the appropriate addressing of disabled persons are changing. Negative connotations begin to be associated with a certain term after a while. The consciousness of society is changing and developing at the same time, which is reflected in the way of addressing disabled persons.

After a discussion on the terminology of disabled persons organized by the Ombudsman for Persons with Disabilities in 2009,[7] it was concluded that the terms "persons with disabilities" and "children with developmental disabilities" will be officially used in the Republic of Croatia.

The Office of the Ombudsman for Persons with Disabilities[8] then proposed coordinating the terms for the forthcoming amendments to the Constitution of the Republic of Croatia (*Narodne novine*, 41/2001 – consolidated text; 55/2001 – edited) in such a way that in Article 57, paragraph 2 and Article 64, paragraph 3, the words "disabled persons" are to be replaced with the words "persons with disabilities." The proposed amendments of the Office of the Ombudsperson were accepted and adopted to the Constitution of the Republic of Croatia in 2010 (*Narodne novine*, 76/2010, 85/2010, 05/2014).

People First Language, as the term implies, puts the individual first and the disability second. It eliminates generalizations, assumptions, and stereotypes by focusing on the person rather than the disability.[9] It also conveys that we understand that someone is living with an issue – their disability or difference is not their whole life (Logsdon 2020).

There are, however, different views on the disability terminology. For example, the Social Model of Disability resolutely states that people have impairments and not disabilities. Disability Rights UK (n.d.)[10] adds that the term "people with disabilities" implies that disability is caused by the individual rather than by a society that is unwilling to meet the needs of people's impairments. As a result, and according to the SPECTRUM Centre for Independent Living (2018), disabled people are people with impairments who are disabled by society.

The use of the word "Disabled" before "people" denoted identification with a common cultural identity. Capitalizing the "D" emphasized the term's political significance. Using the terms "Disabled people" or "Disabled person" brings together a broad group of individuals to

---

6 Strategija obrazovanja, znanosti i tehnologije (n.d.), p. 172.
7 Pravobranitelj za osobe s invaliditetom, Pojmovnik: terminologija (n.d.), https://posi.hr/pojmovnik
8 Pravobranitelj za osobe s invaliditetom (n.d.), https://posi.hr
9 People First Language (n.d.), Texas Council for Developmental Disabilities https://tcdd.texas.gov/resources/people-first-language/#people
10 Social Model of Disability: Language, https://www.disabilityrightsuk.org/social-model-disability-language

understand the root causes of discrimination and oppression, share common experience and knowledge, and cause change.[11]

In accordance with this, this chapter will use the terminology derived from the Social Model of Disability, while the citations will use the terms in accordance both with the People First Language principle and with the official terminology in the Republic of Croatia.

21.1.2 Who Are Disabled Students?

There is no unique definition of a student with a disability/disabilities in Croatia, although a definition largely accepted in higher education was adopted by the first document in this field, "The Regulation on the Organization and Operation of the Office for Students with Disabilities of the University of Zagreb" from 2007, as well as "The Regulation on Amendments to the Regulation on the Organization and Operation of the Office for Students with Disabilities of the University of Zagreb" (Article 3) from 2013.[12,13]

According to this regulation, disabled students are:

> All students who, due to illness, impairment, or disorder, regardless of the decision about the percentage of physical disability, have permanent, occasional, or temporary difficulties in the realization of daily academic activities (students with visual and hearing impairments, physical impairments, students with chronic diseases, mental disorders and specific learning disabilities such as dyslexia, dysgraphia, and attention deficit hyperactivity disorder [ADHD], and other health conditions and difficulties that may affect the course of study).

This definition is conceptually aligned with the definition of persons with disabilities listed in The Convention on the Rights of Persons with Disabilities (United Nations 2006) and fully aligned with Minimum Accessibility Standards for Persons with Disabilities at UNICA Universities (Network of Universities from the Capitals of Europe) from 2008.[14]

21.1.3 Needs of Disabled Students in Higher Education

A group of disabled students is composed of extremely heterogeneous population; therefore, their needs in the system of higher education are diverse and individualized. Despite that, university teachers generally view disabled students in relation to the type of disability. The type of disability can range from better physical accessibility or availability to all areas and services (people with physical impairments), to an adapted approach to literature (people with visual impairment), to having a communication intermediary (people with hearing impairment), to flexibility in the set deadlines for fulfilling student obligations and sometimes in a daily rhythm of activity (students with chronic diseases and mental health conditions), to specialized teaching materials and methods of knowledge check (students with specific learning disabilities, and sometimes students with physical and sensory impairments). In addition to adjustments that

---

11 Social Model of Disability: Language, https://www.disabilityrightsuk.org/social-model-disability-language
12 Pravilnik o organizaciji i djelovanju Ureda za studente s invaliditetom Sveučilišta u Zagrebu, http://www.unizg.hr/uredssi/index.php/lang-hr/dokumenti
13 Pravilnik o izmjenama i dopunama pravilnika o organizaciji i djelovanju Ureda za studente s invaliditetom Sveučilišta u Zagrebu, http://www.unizg.hr/uredssi/index.php/lang-hr/dokumenti
14 Minimalni standardi pristupačnosti za osobe s invaliditetom na sveučilištima članicama UNICA-e, http://www.unizg.hr/studiji-i-studiranje/podrska-studentima/podrska-studentima-s-invaliditetom/dokumenti

are mainly within the jurisdiction of higher education institutions, the possibility of including people with disabilities in higher education will also depend on preparedness of the disabled person to continue with their education, adapted transportation, adapted housing, assistance in dormitories and canteens, available assistive technology, etc. (Kiš-Glavaš 2012).

Research shows (Urbanc et al. 2014) that experiences of disabled students, with regard to accessibility of individual faculties and adjustment of teaching, are diverse and uneven: from highly positive and supporting experiences, to the experiences that indicate insensitivity of the system and the lack of information of university teachers and other participants involved. Students rightfully recognize that the system is composed of people, and that it is not enough to rely on technological advancement that makes it easier to follow lectures, but it is also necessary to conduct educational training of teaching and non-teaching staff systematically (Urbanc et al. 2014).

21.1.4 Support for Disabled Students in Higher Education

The greatest impetus to the development of various support services for disabled students in the Republic of Croatia was realized through the implementation of the Tempus Project Education for Equal Opportunities at Croatian Universities – EduQuality from 2010 until 2013, which was carried out by the University of Zagreb and in which all Croatian universities participated (although not all formally).[15]

Today, most Croatian universities offer various forms of support through institutional support services to disabled students at the level of universities and their faculties and academies (Kiš-Glavaš and Nacionalna skupina za unapređenje socijalne dimenzije visokog obrazovanja/National Group for the Advancement of the Social Dimension of Higher Education 2016). According to the written sources of the heads of institutional forms of support at universities, the forms of support include direct support to students, prospective students, university teachers, and administrative and professional staff at universities. They also offer information, lectures, workshops, counseling and education, development of guides on environmental accessibility of components, provide individualized adaptations in teaching and exams, adaptations of teaching materials, production and adaptation of audio recordings of lectures, video recording and subtitling of lectures, digitization of literature, a course on accessibility for disabled students, mediation in providing adapted transport, accommodation in dormitories in adapted rooms and assistance in dormitories, education of staff in canteens, environmental adjustments and procurement of assistive technology, scholarships and awards for the most successful disabled students, peer support, educational assistance, volunteer services, and contacts with associations and line institutions (Kiš-Glavaš and Nacionalna skupina za unapređenje socijalne dimenzije visokog obrazovanja/National Group for the Advancement of the Social Dimension of Higher Education 2016).

21.1.5 Individualization, Development, Quality

It has already been pointed out that it is a very heterogeneous population when it comes to disabled students, and that only one feature of a person – impairment – is not enough in understanding their needs. This is by no means sufficient information to choose the form and level of support in higher education, which depends on the person's personal and contextual characteristics from which arise support needs for each disabled student. Thus, an individualized approach and meeting their specific needs can be the only correct way to support disabled students. "The many types of reasonable adjustment used by student participants reflect the diversity of their learning support needs" (Fossey et al. 2015, p. 20).

---

15 https://doktorski.unizg.hr/en/projects?@=5udk

Professors often wonder how to know which form of support is most appropriate for disabled students. The answer lies in open communication with the student; they know best which adaptations would benefit them most. At any time, students can contact the coordinators for students with disabilities who have been appointed at all faculties and academies, which will be further in Section 21.3.5. It is up to the university teacher to choose those adjustments that will not compromise academic standards, i.e. defined course learning outcomes. University teachers are also responsible for ensuring that disabled students and all other students have equal access to higher education and are provided with the highest educational standards and quality, which is possible only with the necessary adjustments (Kiš-Glavaš and Nacionalna skupina za unapređenje socijalne dimenzije visokog obrazovanja/National Group for the Advancement of the Social Dimension of Higher Education 2016).

However, study programs and courses, as well as teaching forms, methods, and techniques, are being developed and improved, which may also affect the diversification of the needs for adaptation for disabled students (Vulić-Prtorić et al. 2012). Therefore, a systematic evaluation of the success of the implemented adjustments is a necessity and a good guideline for developing a support system for disabled students in higher education.

21.2 Participants in Higher Education of Disabled Students

In order to provide equity to disabled students, all members of internal and external staff are needed. This includes university teachers, administrative and professional staff, fellow students, experts/institutions from practice, support services, the local community, state/ministries, and non-governmental organizations (NGOs) (Kiš-Glavaš 2018).

21.2.1 Disabled Students

Disabled students should be subjects and not objects of higher education and they have a great role and responsibility to point out the need for quality in higher education.

By applying the Q methodology, authors Salaj and Kiš-Glavaš (2018) sought to determine how disabled students see their role in higher education. Dennis and Goldberg (1996) describe Q as a method that simultaneously combines the advantages of qualitative and quantitative research because subjective viewpoints are statistically analyzed by factor analysis to obtain belief structures (Stephenson 1936; Brown 1980, 1986; McKeown and Thomas 1988), i.e. person-types or thinking patterns of people (Aitken and Palmer 1988). McKeown and Thomas (1988, p. 17) state that "participants who are closely related to a specific factor share a perspective." The results of the research indicated the existence of three different perspectives of students on their role in the implementation of educational policy: quiet and passive participants (participants who need to be strengthened and educated to act); influential participants (participants with knowledge, advocacy skills, motivation, and a certain degree of power to influence others); and isolated participants (participants who have lost motivation to act and have little power) (Salaj, Kiš-Glavaš 2018).

The results of qualitative research entitled "Perception of Higher Education Accessible to Students with Disabilities," which included younger university professors, showed that professors believe that the rights of disabled students are guaranteed, that they are an integral part of the higher education system, and that students would achieve the expected and planned learning outcomes of an individual study program (Fajdetić et al. 2013). In doing so, they believe that "the role of disabled students is crucial, in the way that students, first, face personal problems, take responsibility for themselves, take the necessary steps, seek and secure their rights and take on their student responsibilities and obligations" (Fajdetić et al. 2013, p. 36). Likewise, Urbanc et al. (2014) determined the importance of the responsibility of disabled students themselves and the reality of their expectations as a prerequisite for successful study.

The research of Bačani et al. (2015) shows that disabled students emphasize the responsibility of disabled people in the fight for their rights and equal position in society, which can be achieved by active participation in everyday life, including higher education.

21.2.2 Peers

The relationship between disabled students and their peers should be based on the satisfaction of mutual interests and respect. It is important that the personal integrity of disabled students and their peers remains intact and that their personal rights and needs are realized (Vučijević and Luković 2012).

In the Republic of Croatia, there are relatively few studies on the role of peers in higher education for disabled students. However, one study showed that peer students have little information about the system of academic support for disabled students, including the right to adjustments in teaching and exams (Kiš-Glavaš 2014).

Another study (Franjkić et al. 2014) found that, in general, non-disabled students positively perceived the ability of disabled students to meet the requirements of the study program, but also suggest the need to develop and improve relevant programs to inform and educate students about the characteristics and capabilities of disabled people.

On the other hand, Bačani et al. (2015) researched the presence of prejudices in non-disabled students toward disabled students and found that university teachers pretended not to be aware of the issue and lowered their expectations to the disabled student.

21.2.3 University Teachers

Disabled students, depending on the nature of the disability or difficulty, may have difficulty attending classes, and are entitled to certain adjustments, including assistive technology. Therefore, flexibility in teaching becomes a necessary feature of the work of university teachers who should make teaching stimulating and accessible to all students (Osiguravanje minimalnih standarda pristupačnosti visokog obrazovanja studentima s invaliditetom u Republici Hrvatskoj/Ensuring minimum standards of accessibility of higher education to disabled students in the Republic of Croatia 2012).

The results of the qualitative research for the "Perception of Higher Education Accessible to Students with Disabilities" study showed that the teaching staff working with disabled students would be helped by timely information about the participation of disabled students in the teaching process, supervision, and additional education that would enable competences for planning and realization of classes accessible to disabled students (Fajdetić et al. 2013).

When choosing alternative methods, techniques, forms of teaching, and teaching materials, one should take special care not to compromise academic standards, that is, education goals on a certain level of education. This is precisely the responsibility of university teachers (Kiš-Glavaš 2012a). On the one hand, they need to adapt the teaching process to all their students, including disabled students, to achieve defined learning outcomes. Still, at the same time, they must be careful not to ignore the issue because this approach will not ensure learning outcomes and will hurt the acquisition of professional competencies of those students. According to the research by Doolan et al. (2015) conducted with focus groups of disabled students in Zadar and Rijeka, Croatia, the emphasis was put on the importance of avoiding university teachers' double standards regarding the assessment of disabled students. However, the university teachers are prone to giving in to disabled students because some feel sorry for them (Fajdetić et al. 2013), although they are aware that they should not abuse learning outcomes by reducing the teaching content they expect disabled students to master.

They also point out the difficulties of setting "limits" of adaptation, such as teaching a foreign language or music culture to deaf students. When they talk about students with mental health conditions, they are not sure that those students will meet their future work obligations adequately.

Urbanc et al. (2014) showed that some disabled students tend to use their status to make it easier for them to master their study obligations. Namely, it has been shown that experiences regarding acceptance and attitudes toward one's own disability are very contradictory and range from a factor that contributes to personal psychosocial resilience to various difficulties to disability that contributes to the development of ineffective behavior patterns, such as learned helplessness.

Qualitative research conducted on a group of disabled students shows that students are generally satisfied with the support system provided by university teachers who treat them the same as other students, respect their abilities, and are willing to adapt to the requirements and obligations of students in academia (Milić Babić and Dowling 2015).

21.2.4 Administrative and Professional University Staff

The administrative and professional staff of the university are primarily employees of the professional services of the faculty important to students, most often employees in student offices and libraries, and other student services if they exist at the faculty and/or university.

Employees in the student offices are often the first people students meet, the first contact with the study in general when enrolling or applying for the study. Therefore, they must establish appropriate contact with disabled students. In addition to the availability of space, they also enable the availability of procedures and services, i.e. adapted access and communication following each student's possibilities and the specific needs of disabled students.

Libraries in the higher education system have a special significance, especially libraries at the faculties that are closest to the students. There, they can most easily find materials they need to study successfully. In addition to providing the materials that students need to fulfill their student obligations, library staff often have the role of informers on various topics of interest to students and have wider educational significance. Therefore, it is essential to make university libraries fully accessible to disabled students for them to use all the services offered. Author Catherine Carter (2004) from DeVry University in Chicago points to three areas where academic librarians can concentrate efforts to better meet the needs of disabled students: bibliographic instruction, web page design, and staff training. She also emphasizes that all students can benefit from increased sensitivity and understanding of different learning styles, an improved quality of library service to better enable students to conduct research independently, and easier access to information.

To this end, additional education of administrative and professional staff at universities is needed for them to acquire basic knowledge about the characteristics of people with different types of impairments, diseases, and disorders and how to best serve users with a disability (Barić et al. 2012).

It is also important to emphasize that personal responsibility is key to achieving equal opportunities for disabled students in higher education in general (Kiš-Glavaš 2012). It is up to each employee and student to do as much as possible within their capabilities and scope of work. Only such an approach will achieve the required level of standards we strive for on a global level.

21.2.5 Other Participants

For disabled students to study successfully and well, to fulfill their student life period and professional education, and to provide them with socialization and inclusion in the community, they need access to all resources – all university spaces, services, and activities – just like other students. This will be possible through the application of universal learning design (Inclusive Education n.d.[16]) and adaptations for which it is necessary to develop awareness and encourage the involvement of the wider community.

Some of the participants in this approach are directly and some are indirectly connected with the academic community. Here are some of these participants and a brief mention of their role in equalizing the opportunities of disabled students: fellow students (friendship, cooperation, support); experts/institutions from practice (exercises, practical work, fieldwork); general student support services (canteens, dormitories, services, cultural and sports facilities); local community (transport, access to facilities, universal design); state/ministries (scholarships, transport allowance, personal assistance, personal disability allowance), and NGOs (information, fight for rights, provision of services) (Kiš-Glavaš 2018).

21.3 University of Zagreb Support Model

Although some forms of support for disabled students, such as the Office for Students with Disabilities, already existed, the greatest driving force behind the development of support services of the University of Zagreb was realized through the Tempus Project Education for Equal Opportunities at Croatian Universities – EduQuality (n.d.). During the project, institutional support services were established at all universities where they did not exist, and new activities were developed that further contribute to equalizing opportunities for disabled students, thus raising student standards and quality assurance. Assistive technology for disabled students was procured at all universities, the university course "Peer Support for Students with Disabilities" was developed and launched; teaching, professional, and administrative university staff were educated on the potential of students with various disabilities and ways to adapt academic content to their abilities without compromising academic standards. One of the most significant outcomes of the project is the drafting the national document "Ensuring Minimum Standards for Accessibility of Higher Education to Students with Disabilities in the Republic of Croatia" (Ćirić et al. 2013), which the Rector's Assembly supported in 2013 (see Section 21.3.4). The same year the document was also accepted by the Senate of the University of Zagreb. The document identifies key problems that disabled students face that need to be addressed systematically. It provides specific guidelines and recommendations for solving these problems by responsible and competent institutions.

The University of Zagreb also provides several additional rights to disabled students, such as the advantage of enrolling in studies, adapting the teaching process and the manner of taking exams, and the provision of assistive technology.[17]

Candidates with 60% or more physical impairment have the right to enroll as full-time students out of the approved enrollment quota if they are not ranked within the approved quota, provided they pass the classification threshold and a possible special ability test. Unless the

---

16 https://www.inclusive.tki.org.nz/guides/universal-design-for-learning
17 Oblici potpore studentima s invaliditetom na Sveučilištu u Zagrebu (n.d.), http://www.unizg.hr/studiji-i-studiranje/podrska-studentima/podrska-studentima-s-invaliditetom/oblici-potpore

faculties determine otherwise, all passed state exams[18] determined as compulsory for enrollment will be considered sufficient for the enrollment of study. However, faculties may also prescribe additional specific criteria for assessing the specific knowledge, skills, and abilities of study candidates. In this case, the faculties are obliged to provide an individually tailored assessment method for all applicants with disabilities who have such a need.

Disabled students (including students with visual, hearing, and motor impairments, chronic illnesses, mental health conditions, and specific learning difficulties such as dyslexia, dysgraphia, and attention deficit hyperactivity disorder [ADHD]) who have such a need are entitled to an individualized approach during classes and when taking exams. The application is submitted to the Office for Students with Disabilities of the University of Zagreb or directly to the faculty.

Although students may be entitled to some assistive technology through the health insurance system,[19] the University of Zagreb has provided assistive technology to support students with visual impairments and students with specific learning difficulties. Students can use Braille notebooks, Braille printers, electronic magnifiers, handheld scanners, speech calculators, screen readers, speech units, and laptops.

Other specific sources of support that together make up the University of Zagreb Support Model will be described in the following sections.

21.3.1 University Course "Peer Support for Students with Disabilities"

An important form of support for disabled students in teaching is provided by the university course "Peer Support for Students with Disabilities," which was introduced as part of the Tempus Project EduQuality as an elective course at the University of Zagreb. Its implementation began with the academic year of 2011/2012, and to date it has been attended and passed by over 70 students. The course is available for enrollment by students from all university faculties and at all levels of study (undergraduate, graduate, and postgraduate). With this course, disabled students can get the support of their assistant peers which, depending on the type of difficulties/disabilities, they need in the academic environment (support when coming to faculty and moving around the rooms, lecture halls, offices, libraries, student canteens, etc.; support in solving some administrative procedures; support in taking lecture notes; verbal descriptions of visually presented content; support in various social situations, such as mediation in communication; personal support as needed, such as support in using toilets, etc.).

This course aims to train students to provide quality peer support to disabled students in the academic environment. Its purpose is to provide peer support or create conditions for disabled students that will overcome some obstacles that exist organizationally and objectively in higher education.[20]

Peer support emphasizes support, not help, i.e. supporting a disabled student in the form of equalizing opportunities and enabling them to perform their study obligations as independently as possible. It is provided free of charge; students are educated through 45 hours (15 hours of lectures and 30 hours of exercises; topics are: peer support, general

---

18 Nacionalni centar za vanjsko vrednovanje obrazovanja (n.d.), https://www.ncvvo.hr/kategorija/drzavna-matura/provedeni-ispiti
19 Pravilnik o ortopedskim i drugim pomagalima (n.d.).
20 Vršnjačka potpora (n.d.), http://www.unizg.hr/studiji-i-studiranje/podrska-studentima/podrska-studentima-s-invaliditetom/vrsnjacka-potpora

characteristics of disabled people, human rights, fundamentals of multiculturalism, attitudes toward disabled people, ethics of peer support, peer support skills, accessibility of higher education, and development of individual plans), followed by 30 hours of systematic two-week supervision and mandatory course evaluations. Also, according to the students' needs, additional workshops are introduced, and the availability of lecturers and associates in the course is 24 hours a day for each possible unforeseen situation. Disabled students are partly involved in the teaching hours. By the mutual signing of the semester support plan, both parties (student assistant and disabled student) must respect the agreed forms and methods of support and full cooperation.

In addition to all the above, the results of the evaluation of the course "Peer Support for Students with Disabilities" speak in favor of the usefulness and success of the course in terms of sensitivity to disabled students, ability to provide peer support, readiness and security in advocating for the rights of disabled students, the relationship of peer support in the academic and wider social environment, and others (Ferić Šlehan et al. 2013; Novak Žižić and Kiš-Glavaš 2021). The results suggest that achieving equal opportunities for disabled students in the higher education system is effective and mutually beneficial.

21.3.2 Educational Materials

An incentive to develop educational materials (manuals) has arisen from inexperience, insecurity, prejudices/misconceptions in teaching, professional, and administrative staff at Croatian universities, and lack of rules and framework for action. The result is creating clear guidelines on the need for adaptation of the academic environment for disabled students, intended for university teachers and professional and administrative staff at Croatian universities.

Finally, eight manuals were created and written by 36 authors from six Croatian universities (25 are university teachers, six are associates and employees of the university administration, and five are students), 12 editors (of which two students), six experts for a certain disability, and 12 reviewers. In total, there is material of 1489 pages, 732 references, 272 easy-to-read defined terms, and one sheet for determining environmental accessibility, as well as a series of authentic life stories of disabled students, guidelines, links and references as suggestions for further reading, additional information, ethical challenges, examples of good practice, photos, and schematic tables. It is a huge and heavy set, 5.1 kg per manual.

It is crucial to state that by overall performance (content and structure of content, prepress, printing, and equipment) this series of manuals is adapted for use by disabled persons. We made 1100 copies and distributed them to all Croatian universities. They are also available on the website in the Croatian[21] and have been translated into English.

What is essential is that these materials are not based on disabilities, but on topics or situations of everyday student life. Disabilities are mentioned through needs and adjustments, mostly through good examples. The topics are general guidelines, environmental accessibility, access to information and services, lecturing and learning outcomes, mentorship and consultations, international student mobility, leisure/free time, and psychosocial needs of students (Edukativni materijali 2012[22]).

---

21 http://www.unizg.hr/studiji-i-studiranje/podrska-studentima/podrska-studentima-s-invaliditetom/edukativni-materijali
22 Edukativni materijali, http://www.unizg.hr/studiji-i-studiranje/podrska-studentima/podrska-studentima-s-invaliditetom/edukativni-materijali

21.3.3 Education for University Teachers and Administrative and Professional University Staff

The educational workshops are based on the educational materials mentioned at the end of Section 21.3.2, namely general guidelines, access to information and services, lecturing and learning outcomes, and mentorship and consultations.

The educational workshops were created and implemented on two levels: a three-day education of educators, a two-day workshop for university teachers, and a one-day workshop for professional and administrative staff. Twenty-four educators were trained to conduct workshops for university teachers and professional and administrative staff at Croatian universities. Those educators are persons involved in university support services for disabled students and persons dealing with issues (Kiš-Glavaš i Nacionalna skupina za unapređenje socijalne dimenzije visokog obrazovanja/National Group for the Advancement of the Social Dimension of Higher Education 2016).

The topics are as follows: defining basic concepts; modern principles in access to disabled persons; laws and bylaws and rights of disabled students in higher education; system and tools to support disabled students in higher education in the Republic of Croatia; institutional and individual forms grants; disabled students and how to adapt the academic environment to them (students with visual impairments, students with hearing impairments, deaf-blind students, students with physical impairments, students with chronic diseases, students with mental health conditions, students with dyslexia, and students with ADHD); universal design for learning and academic standards; curricular approach to education – starting point for teaching, forms, methods, and techniques of teaching; teaching and learning outcomes; access to information and services; mentoring and consulting in higher education; guidelines for mentoring and consultative relationship and experiences and recommendations of disabled students.

Two-day educational workshops for university teachers and a one-day educational workshop for professional and administrative staff are offered at the University of Zagreb every semester. The educational workshops were evaluated and supplemented with topics in which the participants expressed additional interest. In addition to these workshops, regularly, on a monthly or bi-monthly basis, lectures and workshops are organized with specific topics related to disabled students and other under-represented and marginalized groups of students and intended for university teachers at the University of Zagreb (Edukativne radionice za nastavnike[23]/ Educational workshops for university teachers n.d.).

21.3.4 Minimal Standards of Accessibility of Higher Education for Students with Disabilities

To create a legal framework for equal opportunities for disabled students, the document "Ensuring Minimum Standards of Accessibility of Higher Education for Students with Disabilities" was prepared. Eight university teachers, two disabled students, the University of Zagreb Vice Rector for Students and Study Programs, and a representative from the Institute for the Development of Education[24] participated in the preparation of the document.

The expectation is that the document is endorsed at the different national levels. All the relevant institutions will use this and associated documents when creating the policies and measures for disabled persons.

---

23 http://www.unizg.hr/studiji-i-studiranje/podrska-studentima/podrska-studentima-s-invaliditetom/aktualno
24 Institut za razvoj obrazovanja (n.d.), https://iro.hr

The first step in creation of the document was providing a workshop for disabled students with the aim to identify barriers, needs, and possibilities for disabled students in higher education from their own perspective.

The document contains an analysis of the situation and the needs for ensuring the accessibility of higher education for disabled students in the Republic of Croatia, and guidelines for action. The guidelines are defined in the areas of legal, strategic, and financial framework; enrollment in higher education; teaching and learning outcomes; support services for disabled students; environmental accessibility and living conditions; financial support and other student rights; and data collection. The document also presents the guidelines are in a table indicating the problem on which the recommendation is based, the holders of activities, and the indication of possible additional costs (Osiguravanje minimalnih standarda pristupačnosti visokog obrazovanja studentima s invaliditetom u Republici Hrvatskoj/Ensuring Minimum Standards of Accessibility of Higher Education to Students with Disabilities in the Republic of Croatia 2012).

Efforts were made to offer solutions that do not require additional funding, except in the case of guidelines for securing funding for higher education activities in the social dimension of higher education. This is done under program agreements for higher education funding, and identifying and rewarding higher education institutions that provide quality and effective support to vulnerable groups – students, including disabled students. In addition, financial resources should be provided for the formation of institutional forms of support for disabled students and the necessary resources for their activities, as well as counseling and creation and implementation of prevention activities and programs. Moreover, ensuring environmental accessibility and incorporating universal design rules into the future environmental solutions are necessary, as well as ensuring adapted transport and providing accommodation and assistance in student dormitories for disabled students. Certain financial resources, according to the needs, could be required for the implementation of some adaptations for disabled students, such as: the presence of an assistant in some forms of teaching (e.g. laboratory teaching – handling chemicals or electronic devices); ensuring the use of computers in teaching; notetakers and sign language interpreters; educating staff in charge of editing the internet content of higher education institutions on e-accessibility; providing digitized literature, as well as, if necessary, audiobooks, easy-to-read books, audio newspapers and audio periodicals, video/DVD books with subtitles and/or sign language; a book in Braille and a book in large print; and provision of assistive technology.

Guidelines that do not require additional funding, but certainly require sensitization and a proactive approach, are fundamental – to include the social dimension of higher education as one of the basic principles of higher education in new laws covering higher education. The Law on Science and Higher Education must emphasize the obligation to provide support and adaptation to disabled students, emphasize the social dimension of higher education as one of the priorities of the higher education system in the "Strategy of Education, Science and Technology of the Government of the Republic of Croatia," ensure the social dimension of higher education as one of the goals, encourage the development of quality assurance procedures for higher education institutions in terms of social inclusion, and consider how to include the social dimension in the national quality assurance system (e.g. through the process of accreditation of higher education institutions).

There are also a number of "free" specific activities, such as publishing all information on higher education institutions, study programs, and study conditions to the websites of higher education institutions and their components, including information on environmental accessibility, available forms of support, and the rights of disabled students. Furthermore, ensure that information for prospective students will be available to all, including people with disabilities; design forms for students according to the recommendations for easy-to-read materials, and ensure the design of forms in electronic form; and ensure timely publication of all information intended for newly enrolled students and ensure that all this information is accessible to disabled students. There should be cooperation between services intended for disabled students and components of higher education institutions to provide candidates with disabilities with the possibility of additional information and consultation on the choice of studies; a representative of the teaching, professional, or administrative staff of the higher education institution should be available through email, telephone, or directly to ensure the systematic implementation of an individually tailored way of taking additional tests of knowledge, skills, and abilities in higher education institutions (for example, providing extended time for solving written tasks, conducting oral instead of written tests and vice versa, enlarged press, etc.), depending on the type of disability, disease, disorder, etc.

Adopted in 2013, this document has had a significant positive impact on developing the support system for disabled students in higher education in the Republic of Croatia, especially at its universities, including the University of Zagreb. Most of its guidelines have been realized in the daily practice of the university.

21.3.5 Coordinators for Students with Disabilities

Coordinators-university teachers[25] appointed for each of the university's faculties play an important role in advocating for the rights of disabled students, the implementation of the support system, and the work of the University Office for Students with Disabilities.

Those university teachers oversee implementing and realizing the support system for disabled students at faculties/academies and departments. They are the link between disabled students and the Office for Students with Disabilities operating at the university level. They are the first people that disabled candidates encounter regarding their intention to enroll in some of the study programs at the faculty, and they, along with study program leaders and Vice Deans for teaching, discuss the possible difficulties in realizing the learning outcomes of the study program with students. They offer and enroll candidates/disabled students in an available support system to help overcome possible difficulties. It is an opportunity to prevent possible obstacles related to the inability to achieve some learning outcomes of a particular compulsory course or study program, caused by possible limitations resulting from impairment, illness, or disorders in the student, and to ensure the necessary adjustments, in time.

These university teachers, based on the documentation by which disabled students prove their status, initiate the procedure for making recommendations for adjusting teaching and checking the acquired competencies of students prepared by a professional in the Office for Students with Disabilities or independently (depending on the professional competencies of each professor). They advise disabled students as needed, mediate in communication between students and professors, and ensure that disabled students are well informed and in a timely manner about all developments at the faculty and beyond. They also provide them with information on scholarships, adapted transportation, internship, and employment opportunities, and other activities within the support system for disabled students.

University teachers, coordinators for students with disabilities, work with representatives of disabled students at the appointed faculty to evaluate the existing support system and point out the needs and possible difficulties of disabled students at the faculty. Together they develop an

---

25 Koordinatori za studente s invaliditetom (n.d.), http://www.unizg.hr/fileadmin/rektorat/Studiji_studiranje/Podrska/SSI/koordinatori_ozujak_2021_2.pdf

action plan and work on improving and raising the quality of higher education for disabled students at the faculty level. To implement these activities, they need to be provided with adequate resources and working conditions.

However, it should be noted here that while they are systematically educated and supported in their efforts to provide appropriate support to disabled students, coordinators for students with disabilities, depending on their underlying profession, have not always had equal preparation for providing such support. These efforts are not stated in the norm and do not count as part of the work that is valued for promotions; they are not rewarded financially or in any other way for their additional engagement. These are enthusiasts who have decided to dedicate their time to this vulnerable group of students and must often carry out activities that include discussions with colleagues and, as a rule, strong emotional engagement through empathy for students' personal problems.

According to research conducted by Milić Babić and Dowling (2015), disabled students point out that support provided by coordinators at higher education institutions should include an initial interview with a student who addresses the coordinator, defining needs, monitoring, evaluating experiences, and developing a plan for improved practices and, above all, a general development strategy and continuous individualized approach based on the needs and experiences of young disabled adults.

21.3.6 Commission for Students with Disabilities

The university has established the Commission for Students with Disabilities, an expert body tasked with creating plans, priorities, and activities of the Office for Students with Disabilities, as well as providing expert opinions and recommendations to address difficulties faced by disabled students, their university teachers, and other university staff met during their studies.

The Commission consists of the Vice Rector for Students and Studies, the Head of the Office for Students with Disabilities, and university teachers – representatives of sciences: social sciences, humanities, arts, biomedicine, biotechnology, technical, and natural sciences. The board's mandate is four years, and the members elect a president and a deputy among themselves.

The Commission's work is crucial for developing and raising the quality of the support system for disabled students at the university level. In addition to making decisions and thus taking responsibility for equalizing opportunities for disabled students in the academic environment, the Commission systematically conducts system evaluations by its participants, primarily disabled students and their university teachers. It provides guidelines for the system's correction, following the results of these evaluations and the needs of process participants (Kiš-Glavaš 2008).

21.3.7 Office for Students with Disabilities

The oldest and most developed form of institutional support for disabled students in the Republic of Croatia is the Office for Students with Disabilities, University of Zagreb,[26] which started operating in 2007 through a decision of the University Senate. In the same year, the Regulation on the Organization and Operation of the Office for Students with Disabilities of the University of Zagreb (2007)[27] was adopted and formally regulates the organization, competencies, mode of operation, tasks, and Office activities.

---

26 Ured za studente s invaliditetom (n.d.), http://www.unizg.hr/studiji-i-studiranje/podrska-studentima/podrska-studentima-s-invaliditetom

27 Pravilnik o organizaciji i djelovanju Ureda za studente s invaliditetom Sveučilišta u Zagrebu, http://www.unizg.hr/fileadmin/rektorat/O_Sveucilistu/Dokumenti_javnost/Propisi/Pravilnici/Pravilnik_Ured_za_studente_s_invaliditetom.pdf

According to Article 3 of the Regulation on Amendments to the Regulation on the Organization and Operation of the Office for Students with Disabilities of the University of Zagreb (2013),[28] the basic tasks of the Office for Students with Disabilities are:

- Providing professional support to disabled students in connection with studying at the University of Zagreb and a systematic approach to meeting the educational and socio-psychological needs of disabled students.
- Monitoring the needs of disabled students to improve accommodation and study conditions.
- Improving international cooperation and exchange of disabled students in collaboration with the Office for International Cooperation.
- Application and implementation of projects and providing professional assistance in application and implementation of domestic and foreign projects in cooperation with the Research Office.
- Providing support to disabled students in their adaptation and full social integration into the academic community, as well as in dealing with the challenges of everyday student life and possible difficulties in mastering certain courses.
- Providing various forms of support to disabled students in the academic environment, including information, peer support, and the lending of assistive technology.
- Collecting data on disabled students who use various intended forms of higher education support and assistance, for planning and evaluating the activities of the Office, as well as improving the forms of support provided by the Office.
- Ensuring quality access to higher education for all current and future disabled students.

At the initiative of the Office for Students with Disabilities, the University of Zagreb adopted the Guidelines for Equalization of Study Opportunities for People with Dyslexia[29] in 2011. The University adopted the Guidelines for the Treatment Procedures for Students with Mental Disorders and Chronic Diseases within the Academic Environment[30] within the Instrument for Pre-accession Assistance (IPA) Project StuDiSupport in 2015 (implemented in cooperation with the University of Rijeka and the Faculty of Organization and Informatics University of Zagreb), which makes an important step forward in ensuring the rights and support of those groups of students. Also, both the Strategy for the Development of Support for the Students of the University of Zagreb from 2013–2025[31] and the Proposal of Guidelines for the Development of the Support System for Students[32] were adopted.

Today, the Office operates within the Centre for Counseling and Student Support of the University of Zagreb.[33] The Faculty of Humanities and Social Sciences of the University of

---

28 Pravilnik o izmjenama i dopunama Pravilnika o organizaciji i djelovanju Ureda za studente s invaliditetom Sveučilišta u Zagrebu, http://www.unizg.hr/fileadmin/rektorat/Studiji_studiranje/Podrska/SSI/Pravilnik_Izmjene_i_dopune.pdf

29 Smjernice za izjednačavanje mogućnosti studiranja osoba s disleksijom (n.d.), http://www.unizg.hr/uredssi/images/datoteke/smjernice_disleksija.pdf

30 Smjernice postupanja za studente sa psihičkim smetnjama i kroničnim bolestima u okviru akademskog okruženja, http://www.unizg.hr/fileadmin/rektorat/Studiji_studiranje/Podrska/Savjetovanje/Smjernice_postupanja_psi_smetnje_i_krnicne_bolesti.pdf

31 Strategija razvoja podrške studentima Sveučilišta u Zagrebu od 2013. do 2025. godine (2014), http://www.unizg.hr/o-sveucilistu/dokumenti-i-javnost-informacija/dokumenti-sveucilista/strateski-dokumenti

32 Prijedlog smjernica za razvoj sustava podrške studentima (n.d.), http://www.unizg.hr/fileadmin/rektorat/Studiji_studiranje/Podrska/Savjetovanje/Smjernice_za_razvoj_sustava_podrske.pdf

33 Centar za savjetovanje i podršku studentima (n.d.), http://www.unizg.hr/studiji-i-studiranje/podrska-studentima/centar-za-savjetovanje-i-podrsku-studentima

Zagreb established its own Office for Students with Disabilities[34] in 2015. Currently at the University of Zagreb, about 400 disabled students receive some form of support, and only one person is employed in the Office for Students with Disabilities.

Disabled students, being participants in qualitative research conducted at the University of Zagreb, emphasize the importance of systematic support for disabled students at the university level and recognize the positive role of the Office for Students with Disabilities within which they can receive necessary information and support (Bačani et al. 2015).

21.3.8 Cooperation of University Bodies

The basic idea of the support model for disabled students at the University of Zagreb is a good connection and constant cooperation of professional bodies, individuals, and the Office for Students with Disabilities at the university level. This cooperation enables the system's development, quality, and sustainability through indications of needs, giving proposals for solutions, and evaluating the system. An overview of the cooperation scheme can be seen in Figure 21.1.

As can be seen in Figure 21.1, the Office for Students with Disabilities has a central position and inputs and outputs from the Vice Rector, the Commission for Students with Disabilities, representatives of disabled students, and their university teachers must act according to the Office, vice versa. At the same time, representatives of students and university teachers, the Vice Rector, and the Commission must have an even stronger connection and cooperation.

21.3.9 Local Community Role

The local community should provide disabled students with all activities, measures, and services it provides to all other students. This primarily refers to ensuring environmental accessibility, adapted transport and accommodation, as well as scholarships for disabled students.

Environmental accessibility of higher education institutions and other public spaces is a basic prerequisite for access to higher education for many disabled students, especially those with motor impairments (Kiš-Glavaš 2012). The results of one study show that students with motor

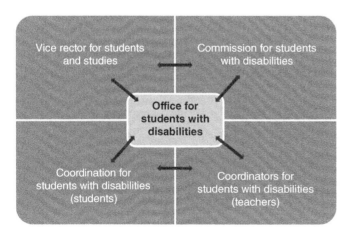

Figure 21.1 Cooperation of university bodies with the Office for Students with Disabilities.

---

34 Ured za studente s invaliditetom Filozofskog fakulteta (n.d.), http://www.ffzg.unizg.hr/ssi

impairments and wheelchair users are the most satisfied with the support system compared to other groups of disabled students (Kiš-Glavaš 2014). This is certainly the result of students' positive perception about the significant improvement of environmental accessibility in general and thus of higher education institutions (Bačani et al. 2015). Many faculties of the University of Zagreb have made great efforts to ensure environmental accessibility for disabled students (construction of ramps, elevators, conveyors, toilets for disabled students, tactile guidance lines, and markings in Braille).

Within the Tempus Project EduQuality, the manual "Environmental Accessibility"[35] was prepared and accompanied by a checklist for determining environmental accessibility which offers an assessment of existing environmental accessibility and proposals for environmental solutions. This has greatly facilitated the analysis and planning of environmental solutions that allow disabled students access to numerous spaces and services that could bring them closer to the possibilities of quality satisfaction of academic and other needs.

The local community, the City of Zagreb, has played a major role in ensuring the environmental accessibility of many public spaces (libraries, theaters, sports facilities, roads, parks, and others).

Adapted transportation is a big problem for disabled students who have difficulty moving. Namely, public city transport in Croatia is generally not adapted and, where it is (for example, in Zagreb), the access to public city transport vehicles is not completely adapted. The City of Zagreb has adapted so-called "low-floor trams," but most tram stops are designed so that the distance between the stops and the trams is so wide that disabled users cannot enter or exit the tram on their own.

That is why some disabled students use adapted vans; these vehicles in Zagreb are owned by ZET (Zagreb Electric Tram) as part of Zagreb Holding, which provides public transport. According to the Regulation on the Transport of Persons with Disabilities,[36] the adapted vans can only be used by wheelchair users and persons with severe motor impairments. The problem for students is the requirement that regular users (those who use transport at least once a month) order the date and route no later than one day in advance, and occasional users at least three days in advance. Given the sometimes-changeable schedule, gaps between lectures, unplanned consultations, and other student obligations, this mode of transportation is too rigid and impractical for some disabled students.

The Student Centre of the University of Zagreb,[37] a public institution within the University of Zagreb (Statute of the Student Centre in Zagreb[38]), currently has over 30 rooms adapted for student wheelchair users and about 10 rooms adapted for students with reduced mobility. Blind students are accommodated in single rooms. Renovation of some student dormitories is underway. About 30 rooms for student wheelchair users will be additionally adjusted. It is possible to conclude that the capacities of adapted rooms are increasing. As the need for custom rooms increases from year to year, this is extremely important.

The problem that students face outside of the academic environment, related to accommodation, is the lack of a systematic form of assistance in meeting the daily living needs of students with severe physical disabilities who are housed in a dormitory. This problem has been solved at the University of Zagreb since 2009 by organizing and financing services to help disabled

---

35 Prostorna pristupačnost, http://www.unizg.hr/fileadmin/rektorat/Studiji_studiranje/Podrska/SSI/Prostorna_Pristupacnost.pdf
36 Pravilnik o obavljanju prijevoza osoba s invaliditetom (n.d.), http://web1.zagreb.hr/default.aspx?id=21329
37 Studentski centar Sveučilišta u Zagrebu (n.d.), www.sczg.hr
38 Statut Studentskog centra u Zagrebu, http://www.sczg.unizg.hr/media/uploads/studentski_centar/zposlovi/sc_statut_30_01_2014.pdf

students who are accommodated in a dormitory. Funds for this purpose are provided from the university's own revenues and revenues from student participation in study costs. This is the need of students with severe and complex physical disabilities who desperately need the help and care of another person in performing daily life activities to realize their study obligations. Social welfare measures address these needs of disabled persons in the Republic of Croatia through the Social Welfare Act (Zakon o socijalnoj n.d.), if the persons are accommodated in their home through the right to Home Help and Care Service. This right includes organizing meals, doing household chores, maintaining personal hygiene, and doing other daily chores, which is exactly what disabled students housed in a dormitory need. The fact that the dormitory is a temporary residence for those disabled students should not be an obstacle for them to exercise this right, even though the Centers for Social Welfare carry out the procedure, in line with the law, according to the beneficiary's residence. In addition, as there are more disabled students in one student dormitory (deliberately for easier organization of assistance in meeting the daily needs of students with severe physical disabilities, and not with the intention of "ghettoizing" disabled students), the existing 24-hour provision can be an economical common solution for a larger number of students. Accordingly, it is reasonable to expect that this service should be systematically and financially handled by the ministry in charge of social welfare.

Within their regular scholarship programs, some local and regional self-government units award a certain number of scholarships to disabled students,[39] but the amounts of these scholarships differ greatly. A good example of scholarships for disabled students at the local level is provided by the City of Zagreb,[40] which annually announces a special competition for scholarships to this group of students. The amount of these scholarships is 50% of the average net salary in the City of Zagreb.

The financing of education, including higher education, in the Republic of Croatia mostly comes from the state budget, partly from the budgets of local and regional self-government units and partly from the revenues of higher education institutions. Local communities, however, vary widely, not only in terms of financial opportunities, but also in terms of development and support networks for disabled people in general. Therefore, the support system at local universities should be implemented following local resources, i.e. advantages and strengths of the local community, including NGOs.

21.3.10 Ministry of Education Role

Solutions that seek to equalize the opportunities of disabled students also come from the level of ministry, i.e. the Ministry of Science and Education.[41] This primarily refers to ensuring accessibility, adapted transport, accommodation, and scholarships for disabled students, the same as from the local community.

With the new system of participation in the cost of studies since 2012 (The Decision of the Government of the Republic of Croatia on the Full Subsidy of Participation in the Costs of Studies for Full-Time Students at Public Higher Education Institutions in the Republic of Croatia in the Academic Years 2012/2013, 2013/2014, and 2014/2015,[42] and The Decision of the Government of the Republic of Croatia on the Full Subsidy of Participation in the Costs

---

39 Portal Instituta za razvoj obrazovanja (n.d.), www.stipendije.info
40 Stipendija Grada Zagreba za učenike i studente s invaliditetom (n.d.), www.zagreb.hr
41 Ministarstvo znanosti i obrazovanja (n.d.), https://mzo.gov.hr
42 Odluka Vlade Republike Hrvatske o punoj subvenciji participacije u troškovima studija za redovite studente na javnim visokim učilištima u Republici Hrvatskoj u akademskoj godini 2012./2013., 2013./2014. i 2014./2015., http://public.mzos.hr/Default.aspx?art=11906

of Studies for Full-Time Students and Co-Financing of Material Costs for Public Higher Education Institutions in the Republic of Croatia in the Academic Years 2015/2016, 2016/2017, and 2017/2018[43]), disabled students have certain benefits. By the decision of the Government of the Republic of Croatia on full subsidy of participation in study costs for full-time students at public higher education institutions in the Republic of Croatia, disabled students who have a percentage of physical impairment of 60% or more are entitled to full subsidy for at least 30 European Credit Transfer System (ECTS) credits (unlike students who have not been diagnosed with a physical disability of 60% or more and who need to acquire at least 55 ECTS credits to exercise this right).

According to this decision,[44] public higher education institutions sign a contract with the Ministry of Science and Education, committing themselves to achieve the general and specific goals they have chosen, which serve to improve the teaching and study system in the Republic of Croatia and thus indirectly improve the quality of university management. During the first three-year term of the contract, higher education institutions were obliged to achieve at least four goals of which at least three are from the list of general goals. The University of Zagreb has chosen "Facilitating access to studies and study support for students of lower socioeconomic status and students with disabilities" as one of its general goals. Within that goal, each faculty proposed the results that it undertook to achieve over the life of the contract and also indicators to monitor those results. In the next three years, one of the mandatory general objectives of this agreement is to ensure equal access to higher education for all full-time students in the Republic of Croatia, including facilitating access to study for disabled students. For measures within this goal, the higher education institution, in agreement with student representatives, proposes to achieve results/indicators in terms of showing the share of funds spent on facilitating access to study for disabled students. This share differs from individual higher education institutions and ranges from 3% to only 0.2% of the planned funds. The University of Zagreb allocates 1% of the funds for the realization of this goal (Kiš-Glavaš i Nacionalna skupina za unapređenje socijalne dimenzije visokog obrazovanja/National Group for the Advancement of the Social Dimension of Higher Education 2016).

At the national level, the Ministry of Science and Education annually awards state scholarships to full-time university and vocational study students. They reimburse a part of the tuition costs to postgraduate disabled students.[45]

The Ministry of Science and Education also provides reimbursement of part of the transport costs for full-time disabled students in university, vocational, and postgraduate studies following the Regulation on the Conditions and Manner of Exercising the Right to Financial Support to Cover Part of Transport Costs for Full-time Students with Disabilities (Pravilnik o uvjetima i načinu ostvarivanja prava na novčanu potporu za podmirenje dijela troškova prijevoza za redovite studente s invaliditetom n.d.). One of the criteria for earning this benefit is that the student has a determined percentage of physical impairment of 60% and above.

The amount of this benefit is about 200 euros. However, the amount is too small given the increased costs of transporting disabled students who cannot use public city transport (25 euros per month). That is, students who cannot use adapted vans from public city transport or disabled

---

43 Odluka Vlade Republike Hrvatske o punoj subvenciji participacije redovitih studenata u troškovima studija i sufinanciranju materijalnih troškova javnim visokim učilištima u Republici Hrvatskoj u akademskim godinama 2015./2016., 2016./2017. i 2017./2018., http://public.mzos.hr/Default.aspx?art=13919&sec=3141

44 Odluka Vlade RH o programskom financiranju javnih visokih učilišta u Republici Hrvatskoj u akademskim godinama 2018./2019., 2019./2020., 2020./2021. i 2021./2022 (n.d.).

45 Državne stipendije – stipendije u sustavu visokog obrazovanja (n.d.), https://mzo.gov.hr/istaknute-teme/odgoj-i-obrazovanje/visoko-obrazovanje/drzavne-stipendije/162

people's NGOs must often independently organize taxi transport which increases the costs of living (Kiš-Glavaš and Nacionalna skupina za unapređenje socijalne dimenzije visokog obrazovanja/National Group for the Advancement of the Social Dimension of Higher Education 2016). On the other hand, this right is provided to all students who have a determined percentage of physical impairment of 60% or more. It is not checked whether the student is able to use public transport or not, so this benefit is realized by many who do not need it for this purpose (students with hearing or visual impairments, with physical impairments that do not affect the ability to move independently, and whose severity of impairment is 60% or more) (Kiš-Glavaš and Nacionalna skupina za unapređenje socijalne dimenzije visokog obrazovanja/ National Group for the Advancement of the Social Dimension of Higher Education 2016).

As there is obviously a big problem of providing adapted transport for disabled people in general, including disabled students, there is an initiative to specifically redirect the funds of the Ministry of Science and Education to individual disabled students. Another possibility is that the Ministry of Science and Education, through a public tender, concludes a contract on adapted transport of students where such transport is needed (Kiš-Glavaš i Nacionalna skupina za unapređenje socijalne dimenzije visokog obrazovanja/National Group for the Advancement of the Social Dimension of Higher Education 2016).

Under the decision of the Ministry of Science and Education on the criteria for distributing places in student dormitories of student centers in the Republic of Croatia,[46] and based on the Regulation on the Conditions and Manner of Exercising the Right of Full-time Students to Subsidized Housing in the Republic of Croatia,[47] students who have above 60% of physical impairment, including disabled students in postgraduate university studies, are entitled to a direct place in a student dormitory. Disabled students who have up to 60% of physical impairment earn extra points. Students who have changed their studies twice and students who have qualified for a certain study level if they re-enroll in studies at that level or are enrolled at the same level of studies a second time, are not entitled to subsidized housing. However, the decision does not define the criteria for losing the right to direct accommodation of this group of students, which may lead to a lack of accommodation capacity for newly enrolled disabled students who also exercise this right.

21.4 Is this Model Inclusive and Sustainable?

Following Goal 4 of the 17 United Nations Sustainable Development Goals[48] (SDGs), "Ensure inclusive and equitable quality education and promote lifelong learning opportunities for all," the University of Zagreb has taken several measures and procedures to ensure inclusive and sustainable higher education for disabled students. This is visible through the success of everyday practice, the level of satisfaction of students with the support system, and the constantly growing number of disabled students in higher education in the Republic of Croatia, especially at the University of Zagreb.

According to the Office for Students with Disabilities,[49] about 200 disabled students were registered at the University of Zagreb 10 years ago. In contrast, now (the academic year

---

46 Natječaj Studentskog centar u Zagrebu za smještaj studenata (n.d.), http://www.sczg.unizg.hr/smjestaj/smjestaj/kriteriji-za-raspodjelu-mjesta
47 Pravilnik o uvjetima i načinu ostvarivanja prava redovitih studenata na subvencionirano stanovanje (n.d.)
48 United Nations, Department for Economic and Social Affairs (2015)., https://sdgs.un.org/goals
49 Ured za studente s invaliditetom (n.d.), http://www.unizg.hr/studiji-i-studiranje/podrska-studentima/podrska-studentima-s-invaliditetom

2020/2021), over 400 disabled students are registered who use support. The latter data are indicative because they refer to students who have applied to the Office or faculties for the realization of rights. The assumption is, therefore, that the actual number of disabled students is slightly higher.

Disabled students express high expectations from the support system in higher education, as shown by the results of the IPA Project Multidimensional Analysis of Social Inclusion of Students with Disabilities in Higher Education – Quantitative Research conducted on a sample of 73 disabled students from the Croatian universities of Zagreb, Split, Rijeka, Osijek, Pula, and Zadar. The results of the same research showed that disabled students evaluate the existing support system as slightly positive, with a large dispersion of results indicating a large difference between student responses (Kiš-Glavaš 2014). However, disabled students from the University of Zagreb rate the support system more favorably than students from other Croatian universities. Likewise, university teachers from Zagreb assess their university's existing support system for disabled students as being significantly better than do university teachers from other Croatian universities (Kiš-Glavaš 2014).

Considering the strengths of the support model for disabled students at the University of Zagreb, it can be concluded that they are reflected in a combination of institutional (Office, Vice Rector, Commission for Students with Disabilities, coordinators) and individual (university teachers s and administrative and professional university staff) forms of support for disabled students.

Institutional forms of support must exist to define rules and procedures, enable participants in higher education to provide counseling, education, and supervision to disabled students, and have systematic evaluation, planning, correction, and expansion of activities to current needs.

Individual forms of support, in turn, reflect the idea of universal learning design with individual adjustment where it is needed. Empowered university teachers who always have someone to turn to for advice and get the necessary information and education (as well as administrative and professional university staff), if they express the need for it, understand that all students are their students, and are ready to prepare teaching materials, realize the teaching process, and conduct tests of acquired competencies for all (Kiš-Glavaš 2012a). The students understand and accept that the university teacher, and not some specialized person or service, is responsible for implementing adjustments following the individual student needs. This is exactly how quality, inclusive education open to and for all is created; it includes vulnerable students, but also promotes education and practice for "human rights, gender equality, promotion of a culture of peace and non-violence, global citizenship and appreciation of cultural diversity and of culture's contribution" (SDG 4.7),[50] and thus strongly approaches sustainable higher education.

However, although it is well thought out and has a procedural character through constant evaluation and improvement, there are some difficulties in this support system. The challenges certainly relate to the fact that there is no single law or regulation that clearly and precisely regulates the rights of disabled students in higher education or the rules of conduct and responsibility. All this remains at the level of recommendations, does not have to be consumed, and depends on the good will of each person because it is not binding.

The legal preconditions for ensuring equal opportunities, i.e. accessibility of higher education for disabled persons in the Republic of Croatia, exist and extend from the Constitution of the Republic of Croatia[51] through the Convention on the Rights of Persons with Disabilities

---

50 United Nations, Department for Economic and Social Affairs (2015), https://sdgs.un.org/goals
51 Ustav Republike Hrvatske (1990).

(United Nations 2006),[52] the Law on Scientific Work and Higher Education,[53] the Anti-discrimination Law,[54] the Law on the Single Body of Expertise,[55] the Act on Croatian Sign Language and Other Communication Systems of Deaf and Deafblind Persons in the Republic of Croatia,[56] and the National Strategy for Equalization of Opportunities for Persons with Disabilities from 2017 to 2020[57] to the University Statute, other documents, and tenders. What do not always follow these general regulations are the concrete and binding measures of the competent institutions to ensure that equal opportunities defined in the regulations are truly applied in higher education.

More specifically, when it comes to the rights of disabled students at the University of Zagreb, the Senate has made several recommendations, mentioned throughout this chapter, that are expected to be accepted by the faculties. Still, there are no mechanisms to ensure commitment to them, and faculty leaders generally follow the Senate's recommendations, at least at the declaratory level. Concrete support for students will depend largely on the sensitization and motivation of management, the skills and education of coordinators for students with disabilities, the involvement of disabled students and their representatives, the readiness of university teachers and administrative and professional university staff to additional education; it will also depend on additional engagement and investment of effort in implementing accommodation for disabled students.

The rights of disabled students depend on the good will of individuals including university management, which has a term of office and changes. Some university management teams are more sensitized, and some are less sensitized, to the needs of disabled students and are also more or less willing to cooperate with students and professionals. This does not guarantee the systematic implementation of support and, thus unfortunately, the sustainability of higher education for disabled students.

Resources exist but not mechanisms that would oblige participants in higher education of disabled students to use them. Disabled students themselves have a choice: they can register and ask for support at any time immediately before and during their studies, but they do not have to. The latter is certainly a good approach because disabled students must have the right to choose and, at the same time, bear responsibility for their own education. Moreover, the task for university teachers and administrative and professional university staff is to realize quality higher education for all students. In that sense, they must systematically educate and improve their teaching and communication skills to respond to the diverse educational needs of all students, thus providing everyone with quality, inclusive, and sustainable education. However,

---

52 Except for Strategy of the Rights of Persons with Disabilities (Union of Equality: Strategy of the Rights of People with Disabilities 2021–2030, 2021), the UN Convention on the Rights of Persons with Disabilities is the youngest human rights document in the new millennium, adopted in 2006. The Republic of Croatia signed the Convention on 30 March, 2007 as the third country in the world, and the Croatian Parliament ratified it on 1 June, 2007 (Pravobranitelj za osobe s invaliditetom, Pojmovnik: UN-ova Konvencija o pravima osoba s invaliditetom (n.d.), https://posi.hr/pojmovnik). The Convention is a powerful document in exercising and guaranteeing the human rights of persons with disabilities in the Republic of Croatia. At the same time, it is a strong incentive for the Government and society as a whole to use concrete measures to enable persons with disabilities to be educated and employed like other citizens of the country, to exercise the right to independent living in the community, and to be able to access health, cultural, and all other facilities (Pravobranitelj za osobe s invaliditetom, Pojmovnik: UN-ova Konvencija o pravima osoba s invaliditetom (n.d.), https://posi.hr/pojmovnik).
53 Zakon o znanstvenoj djelatnosti i visokom obrazovanju (2013).
54 Zakon o suzbijanju diskriminacije (2008).
55 Zakon o jedinstvenom tijelu vještačenja (2014).
56 Zakon o hrvatskom znakovnom jeziku i ostalim sustavima komunikacije gluhih i gluhoslijepih osoba u Republici Hrvatskoj (2015).
57 Nacionalna strategija izjednačavanja mogućnosti za osobe s invaliditetom od 2017. do 2020. godine (n.d.).

there is no mechanism to commit university teachers to such education: regular education and training exists, but participation is entirely voluntary.

Based on the premise that participation in this way of support is voluntary, it has been found that some university teachers and administrative and professional university staff, at the beginning of the process of developing forms of support at the University of Zagreb, were the biggest problem: some did not want to, while others often did not know if, when, and what adjustments should be made for disabled students, or how to execute these adjustments. Those university teachers, and some of them who are in the role of coordinators for students with disabilities, should be directed to understand that they must not reduce the criteria, that all students without exception must acquire defined learning outcomes of individual courses and the study program as a whole.

Unfortunately, difficulties in implementing the development-oriented support system are sometimes caused by the line ministry which adopts some positive discrimination measures. One such example is, as mentioned, the advantage of enrolling in a study program. This is an example of a measure that seeks to equate the disadvantaged position of candidates with disabilities to that of the typical population and is a privileged mode of treatment (Kiš-Glavaš and Nacionalna skupina za unapređenje socijalne dimenzije visokog obrazovanja/National Group for the Advancement of the Social Dimension of Higher Education 2016). This way of equalizing opportunities implies that disabled people are placed in a more favorable position than others because they are at a disadvantage due to their disability or the unsuitability of the environment for their abilities. Regrettably, very little is still being done in Croatia to raise the quality of education for disabled children in preparation for successful continuation of education at the higher education level, so this "temporary" measure has become permanent.

Ultimately, this approach to disabled people generally becomes counterproductive because it reduces the motivation of disabled people, increases the presence of negative attitudes of the community due to injustice in access, increases mistrust in the ability of disabled people, delays problem-solving (not permanently solving a problem that can escalate over the years), and is extremely expensive (Kiš-Glavaš 2012).

The approach also results in the fact that, due to the reduced enrollment criteria of candidates with disabilities, many disabled students are enrolled in many "attractive" study programs, which significantly increases the total number of students enrolled above the quota (Kiš-Glavaš and Nacionalna skupina za unapređenje socijalne dimenzije visokog obrazovanja/ National Group for the Advancement of the Social Dimension of Higher Education 2016). This can directly and negatively affect the quality of the implementation of the teaching process owing to difficulties with the organization and implementation of exercises, seminars, and practical classes caused by a large number of students.

In the research by Milić Babić and Dowling (2015), disabled student participants stated that positive discrimination should be stopped; this is manifested by the advantage of enrolling in the study with the criterion of disability or a certain percentage of physical impairment for disabled students.

Contrary to the Ministry's measures, the University of Zagreb decided to apply contemporary compensatory measures that include compensation for disadvantages, enabling disabled people to access all resources through reasonable accommodation, i.e. ensuring accessibility, aids, support, etc. In the context of higher education, this applies to ensuring the environmental accessibility and availability of customized information, adapting teaching materials and the manner of taking exams, providing aids in the teaching process, and the like. When implementing compensatory measures, care is taken to ensure that they lead to greater independence of disabled students and not to their greater dependence.

Ministry decisions are binding on universities and are often made unilaterally. Better and more open cooperation between the line ministry and the direct participants in higher education would greatly facilitate the daily implementation of inclusive higher education. Thus, the approach is uncoordinated, which may cause some practical problems as discussed in this chapter.

Another example is the imposed criterion of the percentage of physical impairment (60% and more) for exercising the rights of disabled students at the state level (which means at the university level, too), and excludes many groups of students who face barriers to higher education caused by their disabilities, diseases, or disorders, and do not have physical impairments (students with specific learning difficulties, mental health conditions, and some chronic diseases and disorders), thus discriminating against them (Kiš-Glavaš i Nacionalna skupina za unapređenje socijalne dimenzije visokog obrazovanja/National Group for the Advancement of the Social Dimension of Higher Education 2016).

It is similar to the role of the local community, especially the role and importance of NGOs, which are usually a strong support for successful higher education of disabled students. There are also examples of creating a parallel support system, sometimes of questionable quality. Lately, the so-called "educational assistance" coming from NGOs is one of the examples of alternatives to the course "Peer Support for Students with Disabilities." It serves as a primary solution for bringing opportunities closer to disabled students at some Croatian universities, including the University of Zagreb.

Unfortunately, this form of support has a number of disadvantages. First of all, unlike "Peer Support for Students with Disabilities," it is a paid support, so it is necessary to provide financial resources that can pose a problem for some faculties. The biggest complaint, however, is that there is no systematic preparation or education of student assistants or their systematic monitoring and evaluation of their work.

In light of these reasons, alternative forms of assistance could be the exception, but not the rule, or be followed by mandatory education, supervision, and evaluation of the work of assistants to disabled students. In addition, it should not be forgotten that the majority of disabled students realize the right to provide personal assistance through tenders of the Ministry of Labor, pension system, and family and social policy through the civil sector, so it should be introduced into the academic environment (Kiš-Glavaš i Nacionalna skupina za unapređenje socijalne dimenzije visokog obrazovanja/National Group for the Advancement of the Social Dimension of Higher Education 2016).

The absence or clear, consistent criteria and procedures can sometimes lead to a situation where some disabled students are not motivated to study, but use studying and realizing disabled student rights to try to solve some of their social problems (financial, housing, cultural) (Kiš-Glavaš and the National Group for the Advancement of the Social Dimension of Higher Education 2016). The research results by Urbanc et al. (2014) show that some disabled students are sometimes motivated by the uninventive environment in their place of residence to enroll in university regardless of personal preferences and motivation to study in general. A higher level of independence (leaving the family, more independent and free movement around the city, organized transport, less social control, the greater possibility of self-determination in general) is also a motivation; according to the interpretation of the group of participants in the qualitative research, which included a total of 20 students with profound disabilities from the universities of Zagreb, Osijek, Rijeka, and Zadar, going to study for some students is the only way to get away from parents and experience more independent life, given the unavailability of support in smaller places.

Although it has many social, cultural, and other goals, higher education should not be the way for young disabled adults to realize their various personal needs. For this purpose, systematically and at the state level, other measures and activities must be taken. Therefore, in addition to the rights they have, and the measures universities must take to enjoy them, decision-makers in higher education should certainly insist on fulfilling the student obligations of this group of students.

21.5 Guidelines for Progress and Sustainability

It is clear from the previous text that the University of Zagreb Support Model strives to be inclusive and sustainable. It has succeeded in part, but there is much room for progress that could bring it as close as possible to this goal.

Nevertheless, the model has been developed in full accordance with the current context and possibilities, strengths, and local specifics, and this is the only path to sustainability. There may not be perfect models that can be easily undertaken. Still, it is possible to learn – from successful, and even less successful, models – good solutions, activities and services, and difficulties and omissions. In doing so, there is a need to develop specific models of support for disabled students.

Such models should be based on the following settings:

- Individualization
- Cooperation
- Inclusion
- Accessibility
- Information/education
- Communication
- Supervision
- Quality
- Evaluation
- Development
- Sustainability

Individualization, the opposite of generalization, is the key to an inclusive approach. Individualization does not exclude the idea of the universal design but needs to be complemented by additional adjustment when necessary. All participants in the higher education of disabled students should be supported individually, i.e. respecting the characteristics and needs of each person.

Cooperation is imperative for successful higher education in general and higher education for disabled students in particular. It is joint work, joint action on the realization of the same goal. In the context of higher education of disabled students, cooperation starts in the student–university teacher relationship, and continues horizontally and vertically at department/faculty/university level, local communities, and the state and beyond, for example, in the European Union and the United Nations.

Inclusion (not only the physical, but also the active, the participatory) is participation in decision-making processes and activities in all areas of social life. This primarily refers to disabled students and all other direct, indirect, and even potential participants in higher education of disabled students.

Accessibility is, in general, availability. Accessibility of space, activities, and services enables the availability of all resources: material, social, educational, cultural, sport, etc. Without accessibility there is no realization of the human rights of disabled people, and thus no realization of the right to equal access to quality higher education for disabled students.

Information on rights, obligations, and opportunities should be prompt and clear when needed. Systematic education, according to the needs, should be mandatory for immediate participants (for example, teachers) and optional for other participants in the higher education system of disabled students.

Communication is a process by which we exchange information using words, signs, sounds, behaviors, and personal characteristics. We realize the educational process in verbal and non-verbal ways. In order for communication to be available to everyone, it is necessary to use different communication channels. Quality communication requires the availability of appropriate communication channels and mutual respect of participants in the communication process. This certainly applies to communication in tertiary education, including communication that involves disabled students and people in general.

Supervision is a reflection of the course of professional work, one of the forms of experiential and professional learning in the professional growth of participants in higher education of disabled students. It is professional intervention, essential in the professional development of all those who work directly with people. It is one of the key ways to ensure development and provide quality.

Developing quality culture means changing the attitudes and behavior of all individuals involved in higher education including disabled students, i.e. it implies both a bottom-up and a top-down approach. Quality culture implies proactive action of all members of the higher education community to improve all aspects of the institution and all its parts, essential for encouraging creativity and innovation.

Evaluation, as a systematic collection of data on activities, features, and outcomes of measures and procedures to judge them, improve their effectiveness, or make decisions on future measures and procedures in higher education for disabled students, is an indispensable procedure and an important aspect of development and quality culture.

Development is imperative for sustainable higher education, improving and adopting more appropriate, complete, and well-adapted measures and procedures.

Sustainable higher education means that education aims to acquire the necessary knowledge for critical thinking and develop the individual's ability to behave responsibly and make decisions. A prerequisite for this is respect for the integrity of every human being and encouraging their development in the cognitive, social, emotional, and physical realms. When we talk about disabled persons, here is a very important social model of disability that provides a way of explaining how society goes about disabling people with impairments. Sometimes referred to as a "barriers-approach," the social model provides a route map that identifies both the barriers that disable people with impairments face and how these barriers can be removed, minimized, or countered by various forms of support.[58]

It is also the responsibility of higher education to influence political, economic, and social changes to reduce poverty and global inequality, realize human rights, and accept differences with their complexity and dynamics in a wide range of globalization challenges (Magaš 2008). To achieve this, higher education has to follow UN's SDGs,[59] particularly SDG 4 (as given in Section 21.4 above: "Ensure inclusive and equitable quality education and promote lifelong learning opportunities for all"); but also SDG 8: "Promote inclusive and sustainable economic growth, employment, and decent work for all"; SDG 10: "Reduce inequality within and among countries"; SDG 16: "Promote just, peaceful and inclusive society"; and SDG 17: "Revitalize the global partnership for sustainable development."

---

58 Inclusion London: The Social Model of Disability (n.d.), www.inclusionlondon.org.uk/disability-in-london/social-model/the-social-model-of-disability-and-the-cultural-model-of-deafness
59 United Nations, Department for Economic and Social Affairs, 2015., https://sdgs.un.org/goals

Sustainability is certainly possible through quality and inclusive education, in which everyone is welcome, especially disabled students.

References

Aitken, J.E. and Palmer, R.D. (1988). Selecting a Q Sample: a Study of Communication Types among Students, Faculty, and Administrators in Higher Education. http://files.eric.ed.gov/fulltext/ED298590.pdf (accessed 8 August 2021).

Bačani, R., Čivrag, T., and Vukašinec, M. (2015). *Diskriminacija osoba s invaliditetom u visokom obrazovanju* (Discrimination against persons with disabilities in higher education). Unpublished work. Zagreb: Faculty of Education and Rehabilitation Sciences.

Barić, A., Đuričić, R., Jakir, A., et al. (2012). *Pristup informacijama i uslugama* (Access to information and services). Zagreb: University of Zagreb.

Brown, S. (1980). *Political Subjectivity: Applications of Q Methodology in Political Science*. New Haven: Yale University Press.

Brown, S.R. (1986). *Q technique and method*. In: *New Tools for Social Scientists* (ed. W.D. Berry and M.S. Lewis-Beck), 57–76. Beverly Hills: Sage.

Carter, C.J. (2004). *Providing services to students with disabilities in an academic library. Education Libraries* 27 (2): 13–18.

Centar za savjetovanje i podršku studentima (Centre for Counselling and Student Support) (n.d.). http://www.unizg.hr/studiji-i-studiranje/podrska-studentima/centar-za-savjetovanje-i-podrsku-studentima (accessed 22 April 2021).

Ćirić, J., Divjak, B., Doolan, K. et al. (2013). *Osiguravanje Minimalnih Standarda pristupačnosti Visokog Obrazovanja Za Studente S Invaliditetom U Republici Hrvatskoj, Analiza Stanja I Preporuke (Ensuring Minimum Standards of Accessibility of Higher Education for Students with Disabilities in the Republic of Croatia, Situation Analysis and Recommendations)*. Zagreb: Sveučilište u Zagrebu.

Dennis, K.E. and Goldberg, A.P. (1996). *Weight control self-efficacy types and transitions affect weight-loss outcomes in obese women. Addictive Behaviors* 21 (1): 103–116.

Disability Rights UK (n.d.). Social Model of Disability: Language. https://www.disabilityrightsuk.org/social-model-disability-language (accessed 6 August 2021).

Doolan, K., Košutić, I., and Barada, V. (2015). *Institucijski poticaji i prepreke za uspjeh u studiju: perspektiva studenata/ica (Izvješće o nalazima istraživanja) (Institutional Incentives and Barriers to Study Success: A Student Perspective (Research Findings Report))*. Zagreb: Institute for the Development of Education.

Državne stipendije – stipendije u sustavu visokog obrazovanja (State scholarships - scholarships in the higher education system) (n.d.). https://mzo.gov.hr/istaknute-teme/odgoj-i-obrazovanje/visoko-obrazovanje/drzavne-stipendije/162 (accessed 29 May 2021).

Fajdetić, A., Kiš-Glavaš, L., and Lisak, N. (2013). *Percepcija visokoškolske nastave pristupačne studentima s invaliditetom* (perception of higher education accessible to students with disabilities). *The Croatian Review of Rehabilitation Research* 49 (2): 28–41.

Ferić Šlehan, M., Kranželić, V., and Kiš-Glavaš, L. (2013). *Vršnjačka potpora studentima s invaliditetom u visokom obrazovanju: Iskustva studenata* (peer support to students with disabilities in higher education: Students' experience). In: *Summary Book, 7th International Academic Conference "Specijalna Edukacija I Rehabilitacija Danas" (Special Education and Rehabilitation Today)*, 149–150. Belgrade: University of Belgrade, Faculty of Special Education and Rehabilitation.

Fossey, E., Chaffey, L., Venville, A. et al. (2015). Supporting Tertiary Students with Disabilities: individualized and institution-level approaches in practice. Research Report. NCVER. Adelaide.

Franjkić, L., Kiš-Glavaš, L., and Novak Žižić, V. (2014). *Percepcija mogućnosti studenata s invaliditetom da udovolje zahtjevima studijskih programa* (Perception of the ability of students with disabilities to meet the requirements of study programs). *The Croatian Review of Rehabilitation Research* 50 (1): 70–80.

Inclusion London: The Social Model of Disability (n.d.). www.inclusionlondon.org.uk/disability-in-london/social-model/the-social-model-of-disability-and-the-cultural-model-of-deafness (accessed 11 August 2021).

Inclusive Education (n.d.). *Guide to Universal design for Learning.* https://www.inclusive.tki.org.nz/guides/universal-design-for-learning (accessed 15 May 2021).

Institut za razvoj obrazovanja (Institute for the Development of Education) (n.d.). https://iro.hr (accessed 29 April 2021).

Kiš-Glavaš, L. (2018). *Studenti S Invaliditetom I O Njima (Students with Disabilities and about them). Time 4 Science.* Varaždin: Faculty of Organization and Informatics.

Kiš-Glavaš, L. (2014). Multidimenzionalna analiza socijalne uključenosti studenata s invaliditetom u visokoškolskom obrazovanju – kvantitativno istraživanje (Multidimensional analysis of social inclusion of students with disabilities in higher education - quantitative research). In: T. Uzun, ed., *Multidimenzionalna analiza socijalne uključenosti djece s teškoćama u razvoju i studenata s invaliditetom u obrazovnom procesu* (Multidimensional analysis of social inclusion of children with developmental difficulties and students with disabilities in the educational process). Research report. Croatian Association of the Deaf-Blind "Dodir", ISBN: 078–953-7645-02-1.

Kiš-Glavaš, L. (2012). Studenti s invaliditetom u sustavu visokog obrazovanja u Republici Hrvatskoj (students with disabilities in the higher education system in the Republic of Croatia). In: *Opće Smjernice, priručnik Za Nastavno, Administrativno I stručno Osoblje sveučilišta (General Guidelines, Manual for Teaching, Administrative and Professional Staff of Universities)* (ed. L. Kiš-Glavaš), 35–69. Zagreb: University of Zagreb.

Kiš-Glavaš, L. (2012a). Univerzalni dizajn za učenje i akademski standardi (Universal design for learning and academic standards). In: *Izvođenje nastave i ishodi učenja, priručnik za nastavno, administrativno i stručno osoblje sveučilišta (Teaching and learning outcomes, manual for teaching, administrative and professional staff of universities)* (ed. A. Vulić-Prtorić, V. Kranželić and A. Fajdetić), 15–42. Zagreb: University of Zagreb.

Kiš-Glavaš, L. (2008). Predstavljanje Ureda za studente s invaliditetom Sveučilišta u Zagrebu (Presentation of the Office for Students with Disabilities of the University of Zagreb). *Zbornik radova simpozija "Obrazovanje i zapošljavanje osoba s invaliditetom: iskustva, novi smjerovi" Hrvatskog zavoda za zapošljavanje (Croatian Employment Service's "Education and employment of people with disabilities: experiences, new directions" Symposium Proceedings)*, Zagreb (25 September 2008), 47–50.

Kiš-Glavaš, L. and Nacionalna skupina za unapređenje socijalne dimenzije visokog obrazovanja (2016). *Smjernice za unapređenje sustava potpore studentima s invaliditetom u visokom obrazovanju u Republici Hrvatskoj* (Guidelines for improving the support system for students with disabilities in higher education in the Republic of Croatia). https://mzo.hr/sites/default/files/migrated/smjernice_za_unapredenje_sustava_potpore_studentima_s_invaliditetom_u_visokom_obrazovanju_u_rh.pdf, https://mzo.hr/hr/vlada-rh-usvojila-nacionalni-plan-za-unaprjedenje-socijalne-dimenzije-visokog-obrazovanja-uRH (accessed 30 April 2021).

Koordinatori za studente s invaliditetom (Coordinators for Students with disabilities) (n.d.). http://www.unizg.hr/fileadmin/rektorat/Studiji_studiranje/Podrska/SSI/koordinatori_ozujak_2021_2.pdf (accessed 13 May 2021).

Logsdon, A. (2020). *Using Person-First Language When Describing People with Disabilities.* https://www.verywellfamily.com/focus-on-the-person-first-is-good-eabiitiestiquette-2161897 (accessed 6 August 2021).

London Communiqué (2007). http://www.ehea.info/Upload/document/ministerial_declarations/2007_London_Communique_English_588697.pdf (accessed 25 May 2021).

Magaš, D. (2008). *Izvješća sa znanstvenih skupova* (Reports from scientific conferences). http://hrcak.srce.hr/file/48291 (accessed 11 June 2021).

McKeown, B.B. and Thomas, D. (1988). *Q Methodology-Quantitative Applications in the Social Sciences*. Beverly Hills: Sage.

Milić Babić, M. and Dowling, M. (2015). *Social support, the presence of barriers and ideas for the future from students with disabilities in higher education system in Croatia. Disability & Society* 30 (4): 614–629. http://www.tandfonline.com/doi/full/10.1080/09687599.2015.1037949 (accessed 17 May 2021).

Ministarstvo znanosti i obrazovanja (Ministry of Science and Education) (n.d.). https://mzo.gov.hr (accessed 29 May 2021).

Nacionalna strategija izjednačavanja mogućnosti za osobe s invaliditetom od 2017. do 2020. godine (National Strategy for Equalization of Opportunities for Persons with Disabilities from 2017 to 2020) (n.d.). *Narodne novine*, 42/2017.

Nacionalni centar za vanjsko vrednovanje obrazovanja (National Centre for External Evaluation of Education) (n.d.). https://www.ncvvo.hr/kategorija/drzavna-matura/provedeni-ispiti (accessed 29 May 2021).

Natječaj Studentskog centra u Zagrebu za smještaj studenata (Application of the Student Centre in Zagreb for student accommodation) (n.d.). http://www.sczg.unizg.hr/smjestaj/smjestaj/kriteriji-za-raspodjelu-mjesta (accessed 29 May 2021).

Novak Žižić, V. and Kiš-Glavaš, L. (2021). *Vršnjačka potpora studentima s invaliditetom – rezultati evaluacije* (Peer support for students with disabilities - evaluation results). Znanstveno-stručna konferencija "Odgojno-obrazovna, zdravstvena i socijalna infrastruktura za djecu s teškoćama u razvoju i osobe s invaliditetom" (Scientific and professional conference "Educational, health and social infrastructure for children with developmental difficulties and people with disabilities"), Croatian Association of Educational Rehabilitators, Faculty of Education and Rehabilitation Sciences of the University of Zagreb, Croatian Chamber of Educational Rehabilitators, Primošten, 6–8 April 2021.

Oblici potpore studentima s invaliditetom na Sveučilištu u Zagrebu (Forms of support for students with disabilities at the University of Zagreb) (n.d.). http://www.unizg.hr/studiji-i-studiranje/podrska-studentima/podrska-studentima-s-invaliditetom/oblici-potpore (accessed 29 May 2021).

Odluka Vlade Republike Hrvatske o programskom financiranju javnih visokih učilišta u Republici Hrvatskoj u akademskim godinama 2018./2019., 2019./2020., 2020./2021. i 2021./2022. (The decision of the Government of the Republic of Croatia on program financing of public higher education institutions in the Republic of Croatia in the academic years 2018/2019, 2019/2020, 2020/2021, and 2021/2022) (n.d.). *Narodne novine*, 87/2018.

Osiguravanje minimalnih standarda pristupačnosti visokog obrazovanja studentima s invaliditetom u Republici Hrvatskoj (Ensuring Minimum Standards of Accessibility of Higher Education to Students with Disabilities in the Republic of Croatia) (2012). http://www.unizg.hr/uredssi/index.php/lang-hr/dokumenti (accessed 16 May 2021).

People First Language (n.d.). Texas Council for Developmental Disabilities. https://tcdd.texas.gov/resources/people-first-language/#people (accessed 6 August 2021).

Portal Instituta za razvoj obrazovanja (Portal of the Institute for the Development of Education) (n.d.). www.stipendije.info (accessed 28 May 2021).

Pravilnik o izmjenama i dopunama Pravilnika o organizaciji i djelovanju Ureda za studente s invaliditetom Sveučilišta u Zagrebu (Regulation on Amendments to the Regulation on the Organization and Operation of the Office for Students with Disabilities of the University of

Zagreb) (2013). http://www.unizg.hr/fileadmin/rektorat/Studiji_studiranje/Podrska/SSI/Pravilnik_Izmjene_i_dopune.pdf (accessed 19 April 2021).

Pravilnik o obavljanju prijevoza osoba s invaliditetom (Regulation on the Transport of Persons with Disabilities) (n.d.). http://web1.zagreb.hr/default.aspx?id=21329 (accessed 28 May 2021).

Pravilnik o organizaciji i djelovanju Ureda za studente s invaliditetom Sveučilišta u Zagrebu (Regulation on the Organization and Operation of the Office for Students with Disabilities of the University of Zagreb) (2007). http://www.unizg.hr/fileadmin/rektorat/O_Sveucilistu/Dokumenti_javnost/Propisi/Pravilnici/Pravilnik_Ured_za_studente_s_invaliditetom.pdf (accessed 19 April 2021).

Pravilnik o ortopedskim i drugim pomagalima (Regulation on orthopaedic and other aids) (n.d.). *Narodne novine*, 7/2012, 14/2012, 23/2012, 25/2012, 43/2012.

Pravilnik o uvjetima i načinu ostvarivanja prava na novčanu potporu za podmirenje dijela troškova prijevoza za redovite studente s invaliditetom (Regulation on the conditions and manner of exercising the right to financial support to cover part of the transport costs for full-time students with disabilities) (n.d.). *Narodne novine*, 23/2015.

Pravilnik o uvjetima i načinu ostvarivanja prava redovitih studenata na subvencionirano stanovanje (Regulation on the conditions and manner of exercising the right of full-time students to subsidized housing in the Republic of Croatia) (n.d.). *Narodne novine*, 63/2019.

Pravobranitelj za osobe s invaliditetom (Ombudsman for Persons with Disabilities) (n.d.). https://posi.hr (accessed 6 August 2021).

Pravobranitelj za osobe s invaliditetom, Pojmovnik: UN Konvencija o pravima osoba s invaliditetom. (Ombudsman for Persons with Disabilities, Glossary: UN Convention on the Rights of Persons with Disabilities) (n.d.). https://posi.hr/pojmovnik (accessed 6 August 2021).

Pravobranitelj za osobe s invaliditetom, Pojmovnik: terminologija (Ombudsman for Persons with Disabilities, Glossary: terminology) (n.d.). https://posi.hr/pojmovnik (accessed 6 August 2021).

Prijedlog smjernica za razvoj sustava podrške studentima (Proposal of Guidelines for the Development of the Support System for Students) (n.d.). http://www.unizg.hr/fileadmin/rektorat/Studiji_studiranje/Podrska/Savjetovanje/Smjernice_za_razvoj_sustava_podrske.pdf (accessed 2 May 2021).

Salaj, I. and Kiš-Glavaš, L. (2018). *Perceptions of students with disabilities regarding their role in the implementation of the education policy: A Q method study. The Croatian Review of Rehabilitation Research* 53, Suppl.: 47–62.

Smjernice postupanja za studente sa psihičkim smetnjama i kroničnim bolestima u okviru akademskog okruženja (Guidelines for the treatment procedures for students with mental disorders and chronic diseases within the academic environment) (2015). Zagreb: University of Zagreb. http://www.unizg.hr/fileadmin/rektorat/Studiji_studiranje/Podrska/Savjetovanje/Smjernice_postupanja_psi_smetnje_i_krnicne_bolesti.pdf (accessed 13 May 2021).

SPECTRUM Centre for Independent Living (2018). Stick and Stones: The Language of Disability, Southampton, UK.

Stephenson, W. (1936). *The inverted factor technique. British Journal of Psychology* 26 (4): 344–361.

Stipendija Grada Zagreba za učenike i studente s invaliditetom (Scholarship of the City of Zagreb for pupils and students with disabilities) (n.d.). www.zagreb.hr (accessed 3 May 2021).

Strategija obrazovanja, znanosti i tehnologije (Strategy of Education, Science, and Technology) (n.d.). *Narodne novine*, 124/2014.

Strategija razvoja podrške studentima Sveučilišta u Zagrebu od 2013. do 2025. godine (Strategy for the Development of Support for the Students University of Zagreb from 2013 to 2025) (2014). http://www.unizg.hr/o-sveucilistu/dokumenti-i-javnost-informacija/dokumenti-sveucilista/strateski-dokumenti (accessed 17 April 2021).

Studentski centar Sveučilišta u Zagrebu (Student Centre of the University of Zagreb) (n.d.). www.sczg.hr (accessed 28 May 2021).

Sveučilište u Zagrebu (University of Zagreb) (n.d.). http://www.unizg.hr/homepage (accessed 16 April 2021).
Sveučilište u Zagrebu (University of Zagreb). Misija i vizija (Mission and Vision) (n.d.). http://www.unizg.hr/o-sveucilistu/sveuciliste-jucer-danas-sutra/misija-i-vizija-sveucilista (accessed 16 April 2021).
Tempus project Education for Equal Opportunities at Croatian Universities – EduQuality (n.d.). https://doktorski.unizg.hr/en/projects?@=5udk (accessed 18 April 2021).
United Nations, Department for Economic and Social Affairs (2015). *Sustainable development – 17 goals*. https://sdgs.un.org/goals (accessed 6 June 2021).
United Nations (2006). *Convention on the Rights of Persons with Disabilities*. https://www.un.org/development/desa/disabilities/convention-on-the-rights-of-persons-with-disabilities.html (accessed 13 April 2021).
Urbanc, K., Laklija, M., Milić Babić, M., and Branica, V. (2014). Multidimenzionalna analiza socijalne uključenosti studenata s invaliditetom u visokoškolskom obrazovanju – kvalitativno istraživanje (Multidimensional analysis of social inclusion of students with disabilities in higher education - qualitative research). In: *Multidimenzionalna analiza socijalne uključenosti djece s teškoćama u razvoju i studenata s invaliditetom u obrazovnom procesu, izvješće o istraživanju (Multidimensional analysis of social inclusion of children with developmental difficulties and students with disabilities in the educational process, Research report)* (ed. T. Uzun). Croatian Association of the Deaf-Blind "Dodir" https://www.dropbox.com/s/mqyuntrm4q0b9fu/Research%20report.pdf?dl=0 (accessed 15 April 2021).
Ured za studente s invaliditetom (Office for students with disabilities) (n.d.). http://www.unizg.hr/studiji-i-studiranje/podrska-studentima/podrska-studentima-s-invaliditetom (accessed 27 May 2021).
Ured za studente s invaliditetom Filozofskog fakulteta (Office for students with disabilities, Faculty of Humanities and Social Sciences) (n.d.). http://www.ffzg.unizg.hr/ssi (accessed 3 May 2021).
Ustav Republike Hrvatske (The Constitution of the Republic of Croatia) (1990). *Narodne novine*, 56/1990, 135/1997, 8/1998, 113/2000, 124/2000, 28/2001, 41/2001, 55/2001, 76/2010.
Vršnjačka potpora (Peer support) (n.d.). http://www.unizg.hr/studiji-i-studiranje/podrska-studentima/podrska-studentima-s-invaliditetom/vrsnjacka-potpora (accessed 1 May 2021).
Vučijević, D. and Luković, T. (2012). Etika vršnjačke potpore (Ethics of peer support). In: *Vršnjačka Potpora Studentima S Invaliditetom, priručnik Za Izvoditelje (Peer Support for Students with Disabilities, a Handbook for Implementers)* (ed. L. Kiš-Glavaš), 181–208. Zagreb: University of Zagreb.
Vulić-Prtorić, A., Fajdetić, A., Lončar-Vicković, S. et al. (2012). Oblici, metode i tehnike izvođenja nastave (Forms, methods and techniques of teaching). In: *Izvođenje nastave i ishodi učenja, priručnik za nastavno, administrativno i stručno osoblje sveučilišta (Teaching and learning outcomes, manual for teaching, administrative and professional staff of universities)* (ed. A. Vulić-Prtorić, V. Kranželić and A. Fajdetić), 77–157. Zagreb: University of Zagreb.
Zakon o hrvatskom znakovnom jeziku i ostalim sustavima komunikacije gluhih i gluhoslijepih osoba u Republici Hrvatskoj (Act on Croatian Sign Language and Other Communication Systems of Deaf and Deafblind Persons in the Republic of Croatia) (2015). *Narodne novine*, 82/2015.
Zakon o jedinstvenom tijelu vještačenja (Law on the Single Body of Expertise) (2014). *Narodne novine*, 85/2014, 95/2015.
Zakon o socijalnoj skrbi (Social Welfare Act) (n.d.). *Narodne novine*, 33/2012, 157/2013, 152/2014, 99/2015, 52/2016, 16/2017, 130/2017, 98/2019, 64/2020, 138/2020.
Zakon o suzbijanju diskriminacije (Anti-discrimination law) (2008). *Narodne novine*, 85/2008, 112/2012.
Zakon o znanstvenoj djelatnosti i visokom obrazovanju (Law on Scientific Work and Higher Education) (2013). *Narodne novine*, 123/2003, 198/2003, 105/2004, 174/2004, 46/2007, 63/2011, 94/2013, 139/2013, 101/2014, 60/2015, 131/17.

22

Barriers, New Developments, and Emerging Trends in Sustainability in HE

Kelum A. A. Gamage and Erandika K. de Silva

22.1 Barriers to Embedding Sustainability in Learning and Teaching

Scholarship on education for sustainability (ESD) presents economic, sociopolitical, technical, and policy-related challenges to sustainability. Apart from these, ESD also has disciplinary challenges. Since the onset of ESD, sustainability was embedded in obvious disciplines closely aligned with life sciences as sustainability education initially took the form of environment education (EE). Therefore, the early adopter disciplines were Geography, Landscape, Architecture, and Development Studies (Reid and Petocz 2006; Tilbury 2013), Life Sciences, Biology, and Environmental Sciences (Christie et al. 2014). One of the biggest challenges is the slow progress made in expanding the domain of sustainability beyond these early adopter disciplines. Traditionally, education for sustainability has been taught predominantly within the disciplines of Science, Engineering, Technology, Planning, Policy, Architecture, Business, Economics, and Law (PCE 2007; Stone and Baldoni 2006). What is noteworthy is that these programs have a single-disciplinary focus and that they are environmentally focused disciplines. Stakeholders who insist on the interdisciplinarity of ESD have found this single-disciplinary focus challenging.

As discussed throughout this book, integration of disciplines is crucial to promoting and sustaining ESD. The lack of integration still remains a significant challenge that needs to be addressed. Jones et al. (2010) maintain that this integrated approach to sustainability is the result of an investigation into many interconnected (political, social, economic, cultural, psychological, technological, and environmental) problems that were found to have characterized sustainability issues. Scholarship on ESD, therefore, stresses the importance of more interdisciplinary approaches within ESD to render holistic modes of understanding, inquiry, and knowledge to grapple with the complexities of sustainability issues (ibid., p. 19). Jones et al. also maintain that due to the complexities and multifaceted nature of many sustainability issues, single disciplines are not well-equipped to accommodate them. From an interdisciplinary perspective, ESD faces more challenges as many higher education programs do not use an integrative approach to education. However, Rusinko (2010) observes two forms of sustainability integration: a "narrow (discipline-specific)" form and a "broad (cross-disciplinary)" form. Citing Sammalisto and Lindhquist (2008), Rusinko maintains that in terms of implementation

The Wiley Handbook of Sustainability in Higher Education Learning and Teaching, First Edition.
Edited by Kelum A. A. Gamage and Nanda Gunawardhana.
© 2022 John Wiley & Sons, Inc. Published 2022 by John Wiley & Sons, Inc.

and delivery, sustainability can be introduced through already existing structures, or by creating new structures. For instance, sustainability can be integrated into higher education through an already existing course as a new topic, case, or module which gives it a narrow or discipline-specific focus. Similarly, sustainability can be integrated into higher education as a new structure, such as a new course, major, or program, which gives it a broad or cross-disciplinary focus.

With rigid compartmentalization of educational programs, cross-disciplinary and interdisciplinary programs are less common in higher education. This has resulted in an inhibition of sustainability education through collaborative approaches. Epistemological and paradigmatic differences between/among disciplines are barriers to integrating disciplines. For example, Villarraga-Flórez et al. (2016), in their study "Social Science in Forestry Curricula: A Case Study of Colombia Forestry Programs," discuss the pertinence of social sciences to forestry programs and sustainable forest management. Complex social interactions are at the core of tropical forest management. Understanding society is crucial to understanding the underlying anthropogenic causes of deforestation and to respond proactively. Hence, incorporating social sciences in the study of forest management is crucial. Although several studies examine the social dimension of forest management, information about the incorporation of social sciences in undergraduate forestry programs is scant. Villarraga-Flórez et al. (2016) note how foresters encounter challenges in the field despite their thorough knowledge in ecology, silviculture, forest measurements, and logging mechanics. They understand the cause for this as the lack of knowledge in the key elements of social sciences. In Colombia, a national law, with effect from 1999, requires all engineering programs to incorporate social sciences in their curricula (ibid.). In compliance, forestry education programs, too, include social science modules in their curricula under a category named sociohumanities (ibid.). However, due to the lack of research in this regard, the effiency of the law and the syllabi and their contribution to the sustainable management of the country's forest lands is questionable. Villarraga-Flórez et al. (2016) – quoting Dourojeanni (1985), Sample et al. (1999), Vonhof (2010), and Bullard (2015) – note that there is a persistent lack of training in the social aspects of forestry. According to the Food and Agriculture Organization of the United Nations, the term "sustainable forest management" encompasses the inclusion of social, economic, and ecological aspects of a forest (FOA 2014). However, forestry graduates in Columbia are challenged by the traditional boundaries of academic disciplines as they cannot transcend these boundaries to respond to associated complex forestry issues. Society undergoes rapid transformations but university curricula do not keep pace with such societal changes. Villarraga-Flórez et al. (2016) conclude on the note that the integration of biophysical and social sciences is essential for effective sustainable forest management and that social science knowledge, skills, and research techniques cannot be left as an option.

Inquiring into why embedding sustainability in higher education still remains a challenge, it is important to understand the attitudes of academics regarding embedding sustainability in education. Academics in certain countries sideline sustainability, and Reid and Petocz (2006, p. 120) note how Australian academics regard sustainability as a "bit of a nuisance, and possibly a sop toward political correctness that interrupts their real work." Dawe et al. identify five barriers to the successful embedding of ESD as recorded from subject center questionnaires: (i) curriculum too crowded already and lack of time to update courses; (ii) perceived irrelevance by staff (and) awkward fit with the subject area; (iii) lack of staff expertise and the need to acquire new knowledge; (iv) lack of institutional drive and commitment; (v) lack of staff awareness (Dawe et al. 2005). In this study, Dawe et al. further break down the barriers as perceived by subject centers for different disciplines. Moore's study (2005) identifies a number of barriers to ESD program design: (i) the disciplinary environment of most universities and internal competition, (ii) poor evaluation criteria and decision-making, and (iii) unclear priorities. Furthermore, Sherren et al. (2010) highlight the broad nature of sustainability issues and the financial and organizational constraints inherent in the process of curriculum design. Similarly, staff motivation and commitment also include the structural barriers to embedding sustainability in education. A common finding in all these studies is that academics view sustainability in a negative light. It is worth asking whether sustainability efforts get sidelined due to an (un)perceived antagonism between the International Development sector and academia. Since "sustainability" and related terminology is widely used in International Development, it seems to carry an extralinguistic value or baggage that alienates the term from other domains, eventually creating tension. On that note, an important question that needs to be addressed in moving forward is whether academia and the International Development sector do not view sustainability concerns in the same light, and if so, what needs to be done to reconcile these two domains in order to embed sustainability in education.

In addition, universities or faculty that are resistant to corporatization of education and curriculum revisions on market demand show reluctance to revise curricula based on the job market needs and the needs of external funding bodies. For instance, in the arts and humanities departments, curricula are relatively less oriented toward growing market demands partly because capitalistic economic interests do not align with the core humanistic values upheld in these disciplines. That is not to say these disciplines do not work toward sustainability: humanities and social sciences align with sustainability since, in a broad sense, their end-goal is to produce civic-conscious individuals who work toward creating an equitable world that upholds principles of justice, ethics, and human rights through their various disciplines. Also, humanities and social sciences align with sustainability principles in their approach to education. For instance, they promote interdisciplinary and cross-disciplinary approaches to higher education, research, and addressing social problems. Cross-listed courses and cross-disciplinary collaborations are understood as crucial to higher education. However, humanities and social sciences diverge from sustainability agendas on certain points. Thiruvarangan sees curriculum revisions stipulated by external funding bodies such as the World Bank and ADB as narrow, technocratic, and bureaucratic activities adopted uncritically by the University Grants Commission (UGC) (Thiruvarangan 2021). Inquiring into "the templatization of assessment," Thiruvarangan (ibid.) discusses the "outcome-based curriculum development model" and the challenges it entails. Likewise, although social sciences show congruence with sustainability concepts and concerns, and although most academics unanimously strive toward transformative curricula, oftentimes they observe major ideological issues with collaborating with external stakeholders and funding bodies in redesigning curricula. External stakeholders and/or funding bodies are perceived as threats to academic domains and external interventions in curricula revisions are perceived as a "neoliberal assault" on higher education (Thiruvarangan 2021). Therefore, sustainability efforts ought to acknowledge and address these potentially challenging structural barriers.

22.2 Emerging Good Practice in Promoting Sustainability in HE

Currently, there are no international guidelines and best practices on sustainability in higher education institutions (HEIs) and not many countries have national and institutional provisions for ESD. However, a considerable number of countries, from both the Global South and Global North, call for the integration of ESD and/or related educational concepts such as development education, peace education, global citizenship education, human rights education, and environmental education, in formal and non-formal learning (UNESCO 2017). ESD continues to grow as part of local, national, and global policies to address sustainable development issues such as environmental pollution, climate change, and waste mismanagement.

Costa Rica successfully embedded ESD into sustainable development policies in 2006 and Kenya, too, successfully embedded ESD into the national educational policy (UNESCO 2014a). Mauritius, Togo, Finland, and Manitoba, Canada have included ESD in different levels of the national education framework (UNESCO 2014b). In addition, the role of educators in facilitating ESD requires teacher education in this regard. UNESCO identifies that in order for teachers to be prepared to facilitate ESD, they must develop key competencies such as knowledge, skills, attitudes, values, motivation, and commitment toward sustainability. Jamaica and Greece are among the first countries to have successfully embedded ESD in teacher education (UNESCO 2014a).

Action-oriented transformative pedagogy is another good practice that contributes to the promotion of ESD. Pedagogical approaches such as learner-centred approaches, action-oriented learning, and transformative learning are employed to empower and motivate learners to become active sustainability citizens who are capable of critical thinking and proactive in shaping a sustainable future. The more traditional approach to ESD is sustainability in formal education in the form of curriculum design, interactive learner-centred teaching, and designing teaching and learning. Current curriculum mainstream practices are:

> Creating a standalone ESD-specific subject; Embedding ESD in existing subjects or across the curriculum; Adopting a thematic, issue or problem-based approach like climate change, air pollution, deforestation (etc.), based on the local realities; Incorporating the use of teaching and learning methodologies consistent with ESD principles of learner-centred and participatory approaches, such as field trips; Conducting ESD-based co-curricular or extra-curricular activities, such as the use of student clubs and associations and activities; Engaging with the local community, often through project-based learning opportunities. (UNESCO 2018).

This draws attention to the whole-institution approach to ESD. This approach understands ESD beyond teaching sustainable development and adding new content to courses and training. It translates ESD to an experiential level. Schools and universities themselves transform as places of learning and experience for sustainable spaces orienting toward principles of sustainability. A considerable number of universities globally have embarked on rethinking the curriculum, campus operations, organizational culture, student participation, leadership and management, community relationships, and research based on SDGs (UNESCO 2014a).

With the progressive development of ESD, there is a propensity to adopt a more informal curriculum in the form of outside the classroom initiatives. The University of Michigan, for instance, empowers its campus community to be agents of change through a number of initiatives: Planet Blue Student Innovation Fund, Student Sustainability Coalition, Planet Blue Ambassador Program, and U-M Sustainable Food Program. Furthermore, HEIs have now established research centers, study institutes, and offices for learning, teaching, and oversight purposes in ESD (University of Michigan 2021). UNESCO, too, provides a range of publications on ESD-related good practices with different focuses in various regions in the world. Some of them are: Education for Sustainable Development: Good Practices in Addressing Biodiversity (2005–2014); Education for Sustainable Development: Good Practices in Addressing Climate Change (2005–2014); and Good Practices in Education for Sustainable Development: Teacher Education Institutions (2007).

Among good practices of promoting sustainability are the efforts of HEIs in stretching out sustainability beyond formal university curricula, leading toward social responsibility, community practices, and institutional efforts. For instance, in Cornell University, apart from the formal university curriculum, the Strategic Plan for Sustainability focuses on a campus culture of sustainable and inclusive behavior, development of a dense, green and compact campus, and contributions to a just and sustainable future for the Finger Lakes region and New York State (Cornell University 2013). These goals and many other university and student initiatives have stemmed from the need to adopt informal university curricula, leading toward community practices and social responsibility as discussed throughout this book. These informal initiatives can be broadly classified into the following four key areas: (i) greening the campus, (ii) campus mobility, (iii) building energy efficiency in HEIs, and (iv) waste management in HEIs.

Salvioni et al. (2017) states that a socially responsible university adopts behaviors that involve needs assessments of its stakeholders and transfers these needs into strategic goals, monitoring and reviewing objectives, accountability, and enhancing community–university engagement (p. 2). HEIs also employ regular review processes and quality assurance processes in implementing their ESD goals. In addition to that, adopting problem-based approaches to learning and teaching is seen across many disciplines. One instance is cited in a study by Mohd-Yusof et al. (2015) titled "Inculcating Sustainability Among First-Year Engineering Students Using Cooperative Problem-Based Learning." It claims that engineering education for sustainable development (EESD) is crucial to developing and shaping future engineers. This claim is based on their analysis of the implementation of cooperative problem-based learning (CPBL) in a first-year Introduction to Engineering course for chemical engineering undergraduates in Universiti Teknologi Malaysia. Academics employ CPBL which integrates cooperative learning (CL) principles into the problem-based learning (PBL) cycle to create an effective learning environment. The findings of this study display how this CPBL learning environment proves to be effective in inculcating sustainable development in a typical engineering class. Pedagogical models unarguably play a major role in driving universities toward ESD. At the same time, universities are equally driven by sustainability assessment tools that enable more tailored development processes in higher education.

22.3 Conclusion

Embedding ESD in all levels of education, including primary schools, is significantly important, and similarly nurturing sustainability initiatives in the larger society for the active participation of the common masses is vital. ESD in HEIs takes both formal and informal curriculum design, and sustainability now transcends classroom learning. Among the informal ESD trends are campus greening initiatives, campus mobility initiatives, energy efficiency initiatives, and waste management initiatives on campus. Despite the diverse efforts of various stakeholders, there still remain unresolved barriers to embedding sustainability in higher education. It should be noted that sustainability in HEIs is structured on their disciplinary nature and this is manifest in the buildings, faculties, discipline-specific research programs, and funding availabilities. This in turn reflects the temporal, financial, and human resource limitations in the higher education sector and how they act as barriers to embedding sustainability in higher education. Promoting cross-disciplinary collaborations with a new generation of researchers and academic staff is also daunting. Collaborating with external stakeholders and funding bodies, and securing resources to support innovative programs and learning experiences may oftentimes be inorganic relationships in the higher education sector. This is where the strategic intervention of leadership is necessary. Introducing institutional provisions and policy frameworks can also mitigate these challenges as university communities will be more receptive to sustainability plans and policies generated within the university rather than policy frameworks imposed on them by external stakeholders. Cross-cutting program designs, interdisciplinary collaborations, and mobility between and across disciplines are efficient ways in raising awareness about the urgency of sustainability goals and sustainability concerns. Moreover, a global ranking system for ESD may become helpful in understanding sustainability indices across universities worldwide. Competition among universities can also help grow a healthy sustainability culture that is aligned toward the shared SDG goals. ESD, like sustainability, is not a destination: it is rather an ever-continuing experience of transformative learning that needs to be maintained at the pace of social transformation. If ESD is to contribute to sustainable communities, it needs to pay more attention to inclusive higher education wherein marginalized groups are provided equal access to ESD. For the successful implementation of ESD, barriers that impede this ever-continuing sustainability journey need to be addressed.

References

Christie, B.A., Miller, K.K., Cooke, R., and White, J.G. (2014). Environmental sustainability in higher education: what do academics think? *Environmental Education Research* 21 (5): 1–32. https://doi.org/10.1080/13504622.2013.879697.

Cornell University (2013). Cornell university sustainability: today and tomorrow. *Strategic Plan and Annual Report for the Ithaca Campus*. President's Sustainable Campus Committee. https://sustainablecampus.cornell.edu/sites/default/files/2018-12/201320Cornell%20Sustainability%20Plan.pdf (accessed 18 March 2021).

Dawe, G., Jucker, R., and Martin, S. (2005). Sustainable development in higher education: current practice and future developments. *The Site*. http://thesite.eu/sustdevinHEfinalreport.pdf (accessed on 18 March 2021).

FAO (2014). *State of the Word's Forests: Enhancing the Socioeconomic Benefits from Forests*. Rome, Italy: FAO.

Jones, P., Selby, D., and Sterling, S. (2010). More than the sum of their parts? Interdisciplinarity and sustainability. In: *Sustainability Education: Perspectives and Practice Across Higher Education* (ed. P. Jones, D. Selby and S. Sterling), 17–138. London: Earthscan.

Moore, J. (2005). Barriers and pathways to creating sustainability education programs: policy, rhetoric and reality. *Environmental Education Research* 11 (5): 537–555.

PCE (2007). *Outcome Evaluation: See Change: Learning and Education for Sustainability*. Wellington: Office of the Parliamentary Commissioner for the Environment.

Reid, A. and Petocz, P. (2006). University lecturers' understanding of sustainability. *Higher Education* 51 (1): 105–123. http://dx.doi.org/10.1007/s10734-004-6379-4.

Rusinko, C.A. (2010). Integrating sustainability in higher education: a generic matrix. *International Journal of Sustainability in Higher Education* 11 (3): 250–259.

Salvioni, D.M., Franzoni, S., and Cassano, R. (2017). Sustainability in the higher education system: an opportunity to improve quality and image. *Sustainability* MDPI AG 9 (6), S. 914, https://doi.org/10.3390/su9060914.

Sherren, K., Robin, L., Kanowski, P., and Dovers, S. (2010). Escaping the disciplinary straitjacket: curriculum design as university adaptation to sustainability. *Journal of Global Responsibility* 1 (2): 260–278.

Stone, L.J. and Baldoni, M.-J. (2006). *Progress and Pitfalls in the Provision of Tertiary Education for Sustainable Development in New Zealand*. Wellington: Parliamentary Commissioner for the Environment.

Thiruvarangan, M. (2021). The struggle for a democratic curriculum in neoliberal times. *The Island* (20 July). https://island.lk/the-struggle-for-a-democratic-curriculum-in-neoliberal-times (accessed 11 August 2021).

Tilbury, D. (2013). Another world is desirable: a global rebooting of higher education for sustainable development. In: *The Sustainable University: Progress and Prospects* (ed. S. Sterling, L. Maxey and H. Luna). Abingdon: Routledge.

UNESCO (2014a). Shaping the Future We Want. UN decade of education for sustainable development (2005–2014). Final Report. http://unesdoc.unesco.org/images/0023/002301/230171e.pdf (accessed 14 Feb 2021).

UNESCO (2014b). UNESCO roadmap for implementing the global action programme on education for sustainable development. http://unesdoc.unesco.org/images/0023/002305/230514e.pdf (accessed 14 February 2021).

UNESCO (2017). Education for sustainable development goals – learning objectives. http://unesdoc.unesco.org/images/0024/002474/247444e.pdf.

UNESCO. (2018). Integrating Education for Sustainable Development (ESD) in Teacher Education in South-East Asia: A Guide for Teacher Educators. p. 18. https://unesdoc.unesco.org/ark:/48223/pf0000265760 (accessed 10 February 2021).

University of Michigan (2021). Sustainability goals. Office Of Campus Sustainability, University Of Michigan. https://ocs.umich.edu/sustainability-goals (accessed 25 May 2021).

Villarraga-Flórez, L.F., Rodríguez-Piñeros, S., and Martínez-Cortés, O.G. (2016). Social science in forestry curricula: A case study of Colombia forestry programs. *Sustainability* 8 (1): 36.

Mohd-Yusof, K., Wan Alwi, S.R., Sadikin, A.N., and Abdul-Aziz, A. (2015). Inculcating sustainability among first-year engineering students using cooperative problem-based learning. In: *Sustainability in Higher Education* (ed. J.P. Davim), 67–95. Elsevier.

Sammalisto, K. and Lindhquist, T. (2008). Integration of sustainability in higher education: A study with international perspective. *Innovation in Higher Education* 32: 221–233.

Index

a

abstract conceptualization 40
access to education 1
access to the underprivileged 6
accessibility 386–387
action-oriented 3
action-oriented transformative pedagogy 3, 456
active experimentation 16
active learning 143–145, 265, 369
activist learning 13–35
activity theory 100–109
administrative and professional university staff 427–431, 441–443
affective learning approaches 14
anticipatory and strategic competence 48
apprenticeship-based 238–244
Aristotelian approach to virtue 61–64
assessment procedure 159, 163–170
assessment tools 154–157, 159–181
attitudinal barriers 385–388
audio technology 142–144
augmented reality 140

b

barriers to integration into the curriculum 214
barriers to ESD program 454
behaviorist movement in education 240
biodiversity 3, 283, 358, 368, 379, 456
blended learning (BL) 146–138
blueprinting 69–72
Brundtland report 1–2, 102, 189, 214
building energy efficiency in HEIs 8–9, 457
bureaucratic 312–313, 455
business administration 209, 214–216

c

campus mobility 7–8, 457
campus sustainability statement (CSS) 99, 114–124
capacity-building 57, 99–100, 104, 125–127, 154, 209, 298, 318–322, 327, 404
capacity building for research 5
capacity building mobilizing young people 5
capitalism 5, 209
capstone 269–270
challenges for humanity 1
change laboratory 99, 106–27
circular economy 280–292
climate action 3, 7, 51
climate change 44, 194, 243, 258–259, 283, 292, 354, 358, 362–374, 379, 455–456
clinical training 242–245
co-curricular 43–45, 456
cognitive learning 14, 17
cognitive and affective dimensions of learning 14
collaborative decision-making 3
collaborative learning 145, 243
commission for students with disabilities 434, 436, 441
communication barriers 397–417
community-based learning 245
community development 317
community organization and institutional framework 324
compartmentalized education 5

The Wiley Handbook of Sustainability in Higher Education Learning and Teaching, First Edition.
Edited by Kelum A. A. Gamage and Nanda Gunawardhana.
© 2022 John Wiley & Sons, Inc. Published 2022 by John Wiley & Sons, Inc.

competing priorities   24
computer-based technology   140–147
computer-mediated communication   145
concept of entrustable professional activities (EPAs)   240
concept of sustainability   2–4
consolidation and generalization   108, 112
constructivism   243
Convention on the Rights of Persons with Disabilities   403, 415, 423, 441
cooperation of university bodies   436
coordinators for students with disabilities   433–434
coronavirus SARS-CoV-2   187, 189, 195
cosmopolitanism   4
course educational objectives (CEOs)   42
course outcomes (COs)   41–50
COVID-19   7, 136, 187–216
creativity and agency   23, 29
critical and conceptual thinking   43
critical systemic thinking   62
cross-border higher education   344–349
cultivation technologies   359–364
cultural diversity   13, 188, 441
cultural heritage   324, 365
culture and learning   7
curricular adaptation and transversality   289
curriculum design   237–239, 455–457
curriculum development   237–241
curriculum evaluation   241
curriculum innovation   11
cyber-education market   139

d

decade for ESD   2
decarburization and energy   49
delivery modality   137, 338, 340, 345
demographic and geographical dimensions   317
developing nations   56
developing quality culture   446
digital revolution   49
digitization   196, 361, 424
direct and indirect assessment   43
disability awareness   389–392
disabled students   304, 383, 387, 389, 421–447
Disaster Risk Reduction (DRR)   3
discrimination based on disability   404
diseases and pests   359–360
disparities reduction   3
distance learning   192, 196, 340
double-stimulation   107, 109, 111

e

early childhood development   188
eco friendly homes   19
ecological balance   2
ecological literacy   4–5
ecological protection systems   359
economic challenges   1, 12
economic growth   51, 119
economic growth-oriented education   2
economic paradigm   60
economical restrictions   280
ecosystem services (ES)   359, 368
education for all (EFA)   301
education for sustainability (ES)   13–16, 59–61, 192–193, 214–216, 280–283, 300, 415, 453–459
educational materials (manuals)   430
educational paradigm   60, 312
educational policies   44, 281, 288
educational reforms   282
educational research network   319
educational theories   238–240
educational workshops   431
Egyptian education system   298–300
e-learning   139–141, 246–247, 340, 365
embodied *vs.* abstract Learning   25
emotional regulative function   66, 71
employability, 15, 18, 34, 41–42, 321, 390–391.
employment opportunities   1, 311, 379, 391, 433
energy accessibility   359
energy companies   69, 260–261
energy conservation   193
energy consumption   6–9, 193, 308
energy conversion   259, 265–269
energy economics   259
energy efficiency in HEIs   8
energy sector   258–262
energy supply   257–261, 270
energy transition   257, 261, 263, 272
engineering design   262, 268
English-speaking nations   321
entrepreneurial attitudes   208
entrepreneurship   15, 207–217, 287, 305
entrepreneurship education   207–217
environmental activist   22, 26, 374
environmental awareness   282
environmental communication   324

environmental degradation   10, 379
environmental education   61, 280–291, 455
environmental management plan (EMP)   8
environmental management systems (EMS)   153
environmental protection   1, 353, 363, 368, 371
equal access   55, 188, 259, 381
equal opportunities   55, 227, 385, 427–432, 441–442
EU eco-management and audit scheme (EMAS)   153
evolution quality education   188–191, 398
examination   44–49, 108, 112–114, 139, 333, 338, 380–389, 414
experiential learning   16–17, 214, 239–245
expressive Arts   398, 404–417
external leadership   5
extracurricular   43–45, 389

f
face-to-face learning   231–232, 340
360° feedback mechanism   54–56
Flexner model   238–242
fluid mechanics   262–270
for-profit providers   337–346
formal curriculum   14–34, 415–417
formative feedback and summative assessment   277–230
functional dimension   222–224
functional mix   222–225

g
gender equality   3, 13, 51, 188, 289, 303, 327–330
global action programme (GAP)   2
global agriculture   372–374
global citizenship education (GCED)   3
global emergencies   397–398
global knowledge economy   56, 334
global pandemic   329
global partnerships   2
global standards   333, 337–338
good practices   4, 279, 284–285, 353, 376, 456
government policies   380
government of the Republic of Croatia   422, 432, 438–439
graphical assessment of sustainability in universities tool (GASU)   154
Graz model for integrative development (GMI)   154
green economy   15, 279–384
green infrastructure   223, 365–366

greenhouse gas emission   12, 194, 243, 280–281, 373
greening the campus   5–7, 457
greening the curriculum   188, 192
greenwashing   192
guidelines and recommendations   428

h
harmonious entrepreneurship   209–217
HE flipped classroom   146–147
health professions education   237–252
healthcare and sanitation   1
hidden curriculum   15–18, 26–27, 33, 245
holistic approach to human learning   62
homogeneous educational environments   290
human capacity and demography   49
human capital investments   297
human rights   174, 188, 282, 381, 399, 421, 430

i
ICT integration in the curriculum   144
Incheon Declaration   2, 191, 403
individualization   15, 136, 241, 445
informal activism with staff involvement   34
informal environmental activist learning   19–28
innovations in health professions education   237–252
innovative ubiquitous learning tools   139
instructional technology   144–148
integrating blended learning in Higher Education (HE)   136
integration of disciplines   453
inter- and transdisciplinarity   3
interdisciplinarity   4, 453
interdisciplinary approaches   309, 408
international community   301, 333
international cooperation   189, 368, 435
internationalization   321
internet-based learning   139–140
intervention networks   2
intrapreneurship theory   215

j
judging (Integrative Function)   68

k
kindergarten   298
knowledge acquisition   62, 134, 141, 339, 342, 347–348
knowledge-building process   135
knowledge economy   56, 334, 347

l

land ownership   335
landscape and spatial planning   366–368
landscape architecture   222, 354, 357–374
laws and regulations   285, 313
learner-centered teaching and settings   3
learners with disabilities   397–417
learners with special needs   397–417
learning and capacity-building   154
liberal education   4
life cycle assessment (LCA)   258
literature review   101, 302
local community role   436–437
low-carbon economy   280

m

macro and micro reductionism   222
macro curriculum   238
malpractices in Higher Education   346–349
manifestations of globalization   334
mapping   44–67, 266–267, 325, 369
market mechanisms   60
market model   4
massification of higher education   334, 347
massive open online courses (MOOCs)   246, 291
mediator for communication   246, 291
medical education   238–247
meditation   70, 72
methodological approach   241
Millennium Development Goals (MDGs)   1, 188, 279
miller's pyramid   247–248
Minimal Standards of Accessibility of Higher Education for Students with Disabilities   431–433
ministry of education role   438
m-learning   141–142
mobile technology   141–142
mobility problem   7
moral agency   17
moral imagination   67–69
moralization   68
morphological dimension   222
mother language   298
multi- and interdisciplinary research   4
multidimensional analytical skills   262, 268
multidisciplinary educational teams   286
multidisciplinary research   215

n

national language   319
national workforce   307
needs of disabled students   382–392
neoliberal ideology   59
neoliberalism   62
new irrigation techniques   355, 363
new normal   187, 197, 198, 330
non-English speaking nations   321
non-formal and informal curricula   3, 14–18, 29, 33
non-governmental grants   371
non-technical skills   263
non-university education   298
nonverbal communication   397–417
non-violence   13, 188, 441

o

office for students with disabilities   423, 428–429, 433–436, 440
online course capabilities   139
online learning and teaching   197, 227–232
opportune advantages   317
optimal human growth   3, 60
outcome-based curriculum development model   455
outcome-based education (OBE)   41–57
overcrowded curricula   309

p

participatory teaching and learning methods   3
peace and justice   51
pedagogical measures   196
peer support for students with disabilities   428–430, 444
people first language   422–423
perceiving (constitutive function)   66–67
phronesis   65–73
physical and virtual learning environment   3
pillars of sustainability   102
pluralistic community   73
policies and procedures   12
policy initiatives   4, 382–283
political activism   17–18
pollution problems   360
positive psychology   317
post-pandemic world   324
poverty-stricken populations   2

power dynamics 32
practical (or psychomotor) domains of ESD 14
practical training 355–376
Pragmatic Mapping of Student Learning Outcomes 44
preparatory education 298
preschool to tertiary education 3
primary and secondary education 55
problem-/project-based learning approach 43
problem-based learning (PBL) 242–243
problem-based model 239
problem-orientation 3
problem-solving 48, 264, 146, 208, 240, 443
problem-solving and self-awareness competence 48
pro-environmental behavior 64, 288, 291
program educational objectives (PEOs) 41–44
program objectives (POBs) 46
program outcomes (POs) 41–53
public engagement cross-sectoral dialogue and action 5
public health and nutrition 324
public open space 223–226

q
quality service learning 17, 30
quality support 421
questioning 108–124, 135, 215, 310, 369

r
recycling 5, 7, 10, 25–26, 178, 192, 194, 212, 282, 287–292
reduced inequalities 51, 176, 322
reengineering educational programs 191
reflective observation 16
reflective practice 33, 242, 244–245, 252
regulatory systems 344, 349
Remote Higher Education Institutions 317
research and industry interaction 54
resource depletion and degradation 4, 7
reusable learning objects (RLOs) 246
rights of disabled students 425, 430–433, 441–444
rural development 324, 328

s
self-directed learning 3, 138, 242, 246, 264
self-initiative for learning and knowledge upgrades 43

service learning 17–30
skill assessment 48
skills acquisition process 133–134
smart cities 49
smart lockdowns 319
social distancing 197
social entrepreneurship 210–217, 305
social equality 280
social media and social platforms 143
social media networks 143
social movements 16, 22
societal transformation 3
society and the human condition 4
socioeconomic development 279, 304, 318, 327
sociospatial assemblage 229
sources of funding 12, 213
stakeholder engagement 103, 126
standardization of education 333
strategic-thinking 15
student-centered learning 145, 243
student learning outcomes (SLOs) 41–57
students' transience 23
students with disabilities (SWDs) 380–382
summative assessment 227–270
support services 4, 7, 424–425, 428, 431–432
Sustainability Assessment Questionnaire (SAQ) 154
sustainability in energy systems analysis 13
Sustainability of Innovations in Health Professions Education 237–252
sustainability-related terminology 101
Sustainability Tracking, Assessment & Rating System (STARS) 154
sustainable consumption and production (SCP) 3
sustainable growth in higher education 44, 54
sustaining place transformations 221–232
synchronous and asynchronous learning 140, 145, 227, 231
systems-thinking 15, 67

t
tech-enhanced classroom course in the science department 145
tech-enhanced classroom in the language course 144–145
tech-enhanced learning 137–139, 144–145
technology-enhanced education 133–147

technology-enhanced learning (TEL)   133–147
Tempus Project Education for Equal Opportunities at Croatian universities–EduQuality   424, 428
terminologies and concepts   337
three dimensional university ranking (TUR)   154, 162, 174
time higher education impact ranking system (THE)   154, 162
time management   24
tool structure   158–159
topic level mapping   50
tourism industry   281, 288, 326
traditional estates-based environmental management   13
traditional outcome-based education   240
traditional pedagogies   214
transformational education   3
transformational outcome-based education   240
transformative and emancipatory paradigm   61–62
transformative learning model   302
transformative pedagogy   3, 456
transitional outcome-based education   240
transmissive and instrumental approach of education   61
transversal skills   284–285
trends in sustainability in HE   453–459
triple bottom line (TBL)   102
typomorphology   224, 226

u
University of Zagreb Support Model   440–447
unsustainable consumption   1–2

urban design   221–227
urban design pedagogy   223, 230
urban morphology   222–229
urban movement network   225

v
values and norms   4, 62, 301
values-thinking   15
verbal and nonverbal communication   397–417
virtue   59–72
virtue in higher education for sustainability   59–61
virtue-oriented approaches to socioecological problems   62
vocational and technical education   55, 188, 329, 337, 383
vocational education and training (VET)   329
volatility   317

w
waste management in HEIs   9–15
water-holding capacity   355–357
water-related issues   355
work-based learning   244–245
world commission for environment and development (WCED)   1
World Summit on Sustainable Development   2, 188, 279

y
youth communicators   317–329
youth development at HEIs   319

Printed and bound by CPI Group (UK) Ltd, Croydon, CR0 4YY